A HISTORY OF

THE UNITED STATES

A HISTORY OF
THE UNITED STATES

Daniel J. Boorstin
Brooks Mather Kelley

with

Ruth Frankel Boorstin

GINN AND COMPANY

Cover:
Shaped canvas shield, anonymous, 1800s
Indianapolis Museum of Art
Gift of Nina and Gene Pulliam

Frontispiece:
Gilded pine eagle, anonymous, early 1900s
Museum of the City of New York

Design: Richard Bartlett
Production: Kirchoff/Wohlberg, Inc.
Photo Research: Judy Poe
Cartography: H. Shaw Borst
Cover Design: Kirchoff/Wohlberg, Inc.

GINN AND COMPANY

Home Office: Lexington, Massachusetts 02173

0-663-37421-9

To All Americans
present and future
Who explore the past
To rediscover the New World

"It may be said, That in a Sort,
they began the World a New."
Jared Eliot, 1748

"The Eagle has landed!"
Neil A. Armstrong and Edwin E. Aldrin, Jr.
July 20, 1969, from the Moon

About the authors

Daniel J. Boorstin, Pulitzer Prize-winning historian, educator, and author, was sworn in as the twelfth Librarian of Congress on November 12, 1975. He had previously been Director of the National Museum of History and Technology, and then Senior Historian of the Smithsonian Institution. Before that, he was the Preston and Sterling Morton Distinguished Service Professor of History at the University of Chicago, where he taught for twenty-five years.

Born in Atlanta, Georgia, and raised in Tulsa, Oklahoma, Dr. Boorstin received his undergraduate degree with highest honors from Harvard College and his doctorate from Yale. As a Rhodes Scholar at Balliol College, Oxford, he won a coveted "double first" in two degrees in law and was admitted as a barrister-at-law of the Inner Temple, London. He has served as a visiting professor at many leading universities throughout the world, and has lectured widely here and in many other countries.

Dr. Boorstin is an active author and editor whose books include the trilogy *The Americans.* The first volume of this work, *The Colonial Experience* (1959), won the Bancroft Prize. The second volume, *The National Experience* (1965), received the Parkman Prize, and the third, *The Democratic Experience* (1973), was honored with the Pulitzer Prize for History, and the Dexter Prize. In addition to writing many other books, Dr. Boorstin has served as editor of the 27-volume *Chicago History of American Civilization.*

Brooks Mather Kelley is currently Research Affiliate in History at Yale University, where he has held a variety of teaching and research posts since 1961. He was University Archivist and Curator of Historical Manuscripts at Yale from 1964 to 1967; he has also taught American History at the Illinois Institute of Technology and has been a visiting professor at Brown University.

Dr. Kelley was born in Lake Forest, Illinois, and attended school there and at Deerfield Academy. He received his B.A. from Yale University and his M.A. and Ph.D. from the University of Chicago. His publications include *Yale: A History* and *New Haven Heritage: An Area of Historic Houses on Hillhouse Avenue* in addition to numerous articles and book reviews. An active member of the New Haven Preservation Trust, Dr. Kelley served as that organization's president from 1975 to 1978.

EDITORIAL ASSOCIATE

Ruth Frankel Boorstin, a Phi Beta Kappa graduate of Wellesley College, went on to receive an M.A. in Social Science from the University of Chicago, where she ranked first in her class. She has worked at promoting the readability of technical literature in history and economics on the staff of the Cowles Commission, the Committee for Economic Development, and the National Opinion Research Center. Her publications include *The Peacetime Uses of Atomic Energy,* which she edited, and a weekly syndicated newspaper column for young people. Mrs. Boorstin has been an active collaborator on all her historian husband's books.

For her assistance as researcher, typist, and editor, we wish to express our deep appreciation to Suzanne Gray Burbank.

CONTENTS

Prologue

1 The making of Americans

2 Forming a new nation   1763-1800

3 E pluribus unum: One made from many   1800-1840

List of Maps

Prologue

American history is the story of a magic transformation. How did people from everywhere join the American family? How did men and women from a tired Old World, where people thought they knew what to expect, become wide-eyed explorers of a New World?

Our history is the story of these millions in search of what it means to be an American. In the Old World people knew quite definitely whether they were English, French, or Spanish. But here it took time for them to discover that they really were Americans.

What does it mean to be an American? To answer that question we must shake hands with our earlier selves and try to become acquainted. We must discover what puzzled and interested and troubled earlier Americans.

What has been especially American about our ways of living and earning a living? Our ways of making war and making peace? Our ways of thinking and hoping and fearing, of worshiping God and fighting the Devil? Our ways of traveling and politicking, of importing people, of building houses and cities? These are some of the questions we try to answer in this book.

Discovering America is a way of discovering ourselves. This is a book about us.

1

1

The making of Americans

The history of the United States begins in Europe before an America was known there, and in America before the Europeans came. In the Age of Columbus the peoples of Europe were on the move. They were discovering the world anew, reaching out to far and fabulous places.

Columbus's wonderful, puzzling find of unknown lands enticed others. From Spain and Portugal, from France and England and other nations of Europe, adventurers came. They risked their lives, their money, and their reputations to get rich and gain an empire.

The America they found already held millions of people, but these were spread thin across two continents. These Native Americans had not the ships or the science to reach out. Europeans first put them in touch with the world. What for Europe spelled empire and success, for most Native Americans spelled a rearguard fight to keep their land and preserve their way of life.

The hopes that people brought from the Old World to the New were as varied as their nations. Some came for gold or adventure, some for glory or the honor of their sovereign, some to flee a cruel government, some to worship in their own way, others to escape poverty or prison, and still others for a farm of their own. Some came without hope—to serve as slaves on plantations and in mines and mills. Gradually life in America made them all into Americans.

On this beautiful map, drawn in 1459 by Fra Mauro, an Italian monk, Europe, Africa, and Asia fill the whole planet. There is no room for America! Courtesy of Scala

3

CHAPTER 1

What Europeans found: the American surprise

The discovery of America was the world's greatest surprise. When the first Europeans came, their maps of the world left no place for America. They knew only three continents—Europe, Asia, and Africa. These seemed to be merged together into one huge "Island of the Earth." That big island was indented by lakes, and a few seas like the Mediterranean and the Western Ocean. The planet seemed covered mostly by land, and there was no room for another continent.

Columbus was not looking for a new continent. He thought he was on his way to China and India. Europeans were disappointed to find unexpected lands in their way. Still they insisted on calling the natives here the "Indians." So America was discovered by accident.

As more Europeans came and explored the unknown lands, their disappointment became surprise. They had found a world for new beginnings.

1. Christopher Columbus: Who he was and why he came

The adventure that Columbus had in mind was exciting enough. He aimed to sail westward from the shores of Europe until he reached the shores of Asia. Asia was then Europe's treasure-house. It supplied peppers and spices and tea for the table, silks and gold brocade for the dresses of noble ladies and for draperies in palaces, diamonds and rubies for rings and bracelets and necklaces. Until then the main way to the Orient had been the slow, long trek overland. From Venice it might take a year to reach Peking. You would not arrive at all unless you survived the attacks of bandits, the high-mountain snows, and torrid desert heats. Even after you arrived in Asia, it was hard to bring your treasure back overland. For there were no wagon highways and you had to pack your treasure in caravans on the backs of donkeys, horses, and camels.

A direct westward voyage by sea would make all the difference. You could avoid bandits and mountains and deserts. The spacious hold of your ship would safely carry back your treasure. This was a simple and appealing idea. The wonder is why more people before Columbus did not try it.

Earlier in the 1400s a few sailors had tried. But they were not prepared for so long a voyage, and they did not know the winds. Some reached out into the Atlantic Ocean as far as the Azores and beyond. But the winds were against them and the seas rough. They all soon turned back for home.

As a determined young man Christopher Columbus decided that he would sail into the Western

Ocean—to Asia and back. He had no doubt he could do it. He knew the sea, the winds, and the currents.

Early experiences. Columbus was born in 1451 in bustling Genoa, Italy, "that noble and powerful city by the sea." He was the son of a prosperous wool-weaver. For the first 22 years of his life he lived there. He saw ships bringing rich cargo from the eastern Mediterranean where the treasures of the Orient had been taken overland. When he went to sea, he sailed in all directions where ships went at the time. Once his cargo was wool and dried fish and wine carried from Iceland and northern Ireland to Lisbon and the islands of the Azores. Then he lived for a while in the Madeira Islands off the coast of Africa. He even sailed down the steaming African coast to distant Portuguese trading posts on the Gulf of Guinea.

When he left Genoa to settle in Lisbon, Portugal, that city was "the street corner of Europe." Its deep, sheltered harbor was the point of arrival and departure, a place of exchange, for the seaborne commerce of the whole western end of the continent. From there shipments went northward to the British Isles or the North Sea, southward for trade into Africa. And, why not westward—to Asia?

There in Lisbon the single-minded young Columbus laid his plans for his grand "Enterprise of the Indies." He called it an "enterprise" because he expected it to be not just a voyage of discovery but a money-making project. "The Indies" was the name for India and the other Asian lands of the Far East. Convinced that they had a great project to sell, Christopher and his brother Bartholomew made Lisbon their headquarters.

The "Enterprise of the Indies" would not be inexpensive. Ships would have to be bought or hired, crews found and paid. Food and other supplies had to be collected for the long voyage there and back. No ordinary merchant would have the wealth and the power needed. It would take a rich monarch. There was hope of great profit, but there was also great risk. Was there a ruler bold enough to take the big gamble?

No one knew exactly what the risks might be—or even how far it was from the coast of western Europe to the coasts of Asia. No one had ever made that trip before. The questions could not be answered from experience.

The learned men disagreed in their guesses. Some said it was about 2000 miles. Others said it was two or three times that long. The leading authority was the ancient Greek geographer Ptolemy. Columbus read the best geography books he could find. We still have some of them with his own marks. He underlined the passage that said, "this sea is navigable in a very few days if the wind be fair." He believed the writers who said the distance was short, and accordingly he made his plans.

Seeking support. Christopher and his brother traveled to the capitals of Europe trying to sell their project. The monarchs shunned Columbus's grand

Civico Museo Storico, G. Garibaldi, Como

No portraits of Christopher Columbus are known to have been painted during his lifetime. This picture by an unknown artist, painted some 30 years after Columbus died, is considered his earliest and best likeness.

Enterprise of the Indies. When in 1484 King John II of Portugal asked his committee of experts if Columbus could succeed, they said it was too far to Asia and told him not to take the risk. Instead King John sent daring sailors on the long way round Africa eastward to India. In 1488 Bartholomeu Dias succeeded in rounding the Cape of Good Hope. Now the eastern route to India was open. Why risk the uncertain way west when there was a sea-path to the east?

Columbus then went next door to Spain where Queen Isabella had a mind of her own. The bold mariner awakened her interest. To finance the trip she needed money from the royal treasury, but her committee of experts refused to approve the project. She kept the impatient Columbus waiting for six years. Finally, he gave up and prepared to take ship for France. At the last moment, the court treasurer convinced Isabella the gamble was worth the risk. She now became so enthusiastic she was even prepared to pawn her jewels to help Columbus. But that was not necessary. She was told the royal treasury could pay the cost. So Queen Isabella sent Columbus a promise of royal support. She also granted all his demands for noble titles and a 10 percent share of whatever wealth came from land he might discover.

Columbus formed his enterprise in the small port of Palos. It had a seafaring population and had done something illegal for which the queen could fine it two caravels. The caravels were the *Niña* and the *Pinta*. The third vessel of the expedition was the biggest, the *Santa Maria*, which Columbus chartered. The crew was mostly from Palos and nearby, and they were courageous and expert sailors.

The great voyage.

With his three ships Columbus set sail from the coast of Spain on August 3, 1492. In the next weeks he proved that he was the greatest mariner of the age.

Still, five weeks at sea is a long time when you are not sure what—if anything—is ahead. So Columbus's men grew rebellious and reached the verge of mutiny. But Columbus was a true leader. A man taller than most, blue eyed and red haired, he was respected by his followers. He altered the records of distances they had covered so the crew would not think they had gone too far from home. He convinced them to go on. Still, on October 9, Columbus agreed that if they did not find land in three days, he would turn back. But by then there were more and more signs of land—birds in the air, leaves and flowers floating in the water.

It was not enough to know the sea. The winds were the engine that took you there and back. Others had failed because they did not know how to use the winds. They had tried going straight west from Spain. That was their mistake. Instead Columbus first had sailed south to the Canary Islands off the coast of Africa, then sailed west from there. That was where the winds blowing from the east would carry his ships straight on to his destination. Also the Canaries were on the same latitude as Japan, so if he went due west he thought he would arrive where he wanted to be.

The winds blew just as Columbus expected. This, the most important sea voyage in history, had good weather and clear sailing. At 2 o'clock in the

National Maritime Museum, Greenwich, England

The astrolabe, first invented by the ancient Greeks, was used by mariners in the 15th, 16th, and even 17th centuries to try to find their latitude. This instrument was found off Ireland after the defeat of the Armada.

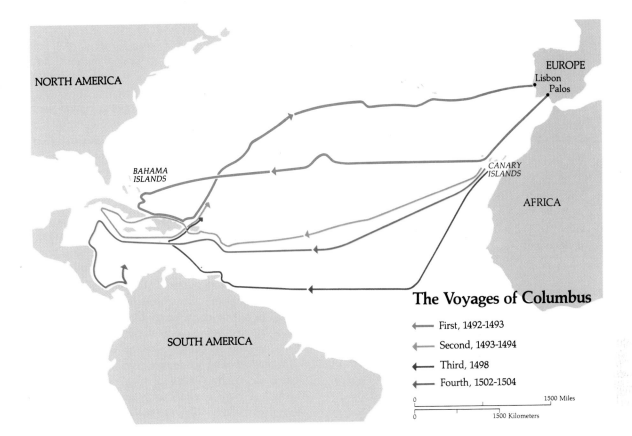

The Voyages of Columbus

←— First, 1492-1493

←— Second, 1493-1494

←— Third, 1498

←— Fourth, 1502-1504

0 ‹———————————————› 1500 Miles

0 ‹———————————————› 1500 Kilometers

morning on October 12, 1492, after thirty-three days at sea, a lookout sighted the white cliffs of an island in the Bahamas. The natives called it Guanahani, and Columbus named it San Salvador— Holy Savior. Columbus had discovered America— though he did not know it.

Columbus cruised about in the Caribbean Sea for several months. He landed on Cuba, which he thought and hoped might be Japan. After the *Santa Maria* was wrecked on a reef off Haiti, he built a fort on the island. They named the island Hispaniola (after Spain). He left about 40 men there when he headed for home January 4, 1493. Columbus had found little but the native people in his travels—no gems, spices, silks, porcelains, or precious metals. Still, he thought he had reached the outposts of the rich empire of Cathay (China).

By great luck Columbus did not try to sail back the way he had come. It would have been a mistake, for at that latitude the winds came from the east. Instead Columbus sailed north to about 35° north latitude. There the prevailing winds from the west blew him back to Spain.

When he arrived on March 15, 1493, he had accomplished much more then he knew. He had discovered a new world. The king and queen loaded him with honors and made his two sons pages at the court. Meanwhile he had shown sailors how to sail and where to sail so the winds would carry them to America *and back!* This made it possible for countless other ships to follow.

Columbus's other voyages. Three times on later voyages Columbus returned to the islands that he called the "Indies," or lands of the East. On these trips he established the first permanent settlement of Europeans in the Western Hemisphere, he skirted the shore of South America, and he explored the coast of Central America. He was always trying to prove that he had found the treasure lands of the East. But he finally reaped only misfortune and disgrace. When he returned to Spain in 1504 after his last voyage, he found Queen Isabella dying and his friends, his influence, and his reputation gone. Two years later Columbus died still believing that he had sailed to the coast of Asia.

1. Identify: Isabella, Enterprise of the Indies, Bartholomeu Dias, Cathay.

2. Locate: Peking, Genoa, Lisbon, Palos, San Salvador, Hispaniola.

3. Why did Columbus call the islands he found "The Indies"?

4. What important discovery did Columbus make about the winds?

5. Name some of the things Europeans wanted from the East.

6. Why did Columbus fail to receive the support of Portugal?

2. Before discovery

If it hadn't been for Columbus, years might have passed before the people of Europe "discovered" America. But it was only for the people of Europe that America had to be "discovered." Millions of Native Americans were already here! For them, Columbus, and all the sailors, explorers, and settlers who came later, provided their "discovery" of Europe!

For Europeans the "discovery" of America offered vast lands, treasures of gold and silver and timber, places to build cities and places of refuge. For them this was a happy discovery. In the long run it would be a great discovery for the world. But for the millions of Native Americans already here their "discovery" of Europeans was not quite so happy. For some it meant the end of their Native American civilization. For some it meant slavery. For nearly all of them Europeans brought shock, disease, and change.

The first people to come to America were the ancestors of those whom Columbus by mistake called Indians. They had arrived somewhere between 20,000 and 30,000 years ago during the last ice age. They were people on the move. For they themselves had come from an earlier homeland in Mongolia in central Asia.

So much of the sea had frozen into ice that it lowered the water in the Bering Strait. Then, as they tracked wild game that moved across the land, they could walk the 56 miles from Siberia to Alaska. There was no lack of game—huge long-horned bison, giant ground sloths, camels, and great mastodons and mammoths. In the thousands of years afterwards many other tribes followed.

These small bands slowly spread across North and South America. By about 9000 B.C. they had reached down as far as they could walk on the American continents. They stopped at the Strait of Magellan.

The high mountains and broad rivers separated the communities. There were hundreds of languages and many different styles of life. Some small bands of people had no fixed homes. They followed their quarry and lived the wandering life of hunters. Others settled down and after centuries built vast kingdoms with flourishing cities, temples and palaces, and lively commerce.

Mayas, Incas, and Aztecs. The grandest of these Native American cultures astonished the Europeans. South of the present United States—from central Mexico to Peru—they found the Aztecs, the Mayas, and the Incas.

In the mountains, deserts, and rain forests of Guatemala, Belize, Honduras, and Mexico the Mayas had built temples and pyramids clustered about broad plazas. We can still climb them. The Mayas invented their own writing. Although they had no telescope, they built their own kind of observatory and made accurate calendars. Their "Indian corn" (maize) had never been seen in Europe. It was originally a wild grass, but would become a staple food for the world.

In Peru the Incas had constructed palaces surrounded by high walls, and had connected their mountain-towns with a network of roads. To farm their steep land they had built terraces. Where water was scarce, they had cut canals and erected stone aqueducts to irrigate their crops. The Incas gave us the potato and the tomato.

When European explorers came to Peru, they were amazed by the Incan government. They never expected to find such powerful rulers so well organized in the mountain wilderness. The Incas had succeeded even without a system of writing. No Americans were richer. In Cuzco, the mountain capital of the Incan empire, even the buildings were covered with gold!

The Aztecs were a warlike people who lived in central Mexico. They were clever architects. Like the Mayas, they too built grand temples and high pyramids. Their capital, where Mexico City is

The great pyramid (above) at Chichen Itzá, Mexico, was part of a Mayan religious center. Machu Picchu (left) is located above the Urubamba River in Peru. This Incan center, with its terraces for farming, escaped destruction because of its inaccessible location. Pueblo Indians built these cliff dwellings (right) in Arizona.

FERDINAN:MAGAGLIANES

Scala/Editorial Photocolor Archives

Magellan's courage and toughness are shown
in this oil painting by an unknown artist.

tribes. On the shore of a Philippine island in a petty
skirmish over a cause he never understood, the great
Magellan was hacked to death. He was denied the
glory of completing that first trip around the world.

After his death in that trivial tribal fight, the
remaining crew pushed on. One ship, no longer
seaworthy, was left behind. Another was seized
by the Portuguese. A further year of danger—
completing three years at sea—at last brought one
ship, the *Vittoria,* with eighteen sailors and three
natives back home to Spain. Finally someone had
circumnavigated the globe!

No other voyage has equaled Magellan's contribution to our knowledge of the earth. Now the
notion that the world was round was no longer just
a theory. Magellan fulfilled Columbus's dream of
reaching the Indies by sailing west. The voyage
began to show how much of the earth is covered by
the sea. Even so, the extent of the Pacific would be

underestimated for many years to come. Most
important of all, Magellan's voyage—around
America—revealed that the new lands were not part
of Asia, not just a promontory of the Island of the
Earth. The Americas were continents by themselves. The American continents would be called
the Western Hemisphere—which filled a half of the
sphere that was the earth.

Spain and America. For more than 50 years after
Columbus, the Spaniards had the New World
mostly to themselves. Who dared challenge
Spain—the richest and most powerful nation in
Europe? In 1519 King Charles I of Spain was
elected Holy Roman Emperor and became Emperor Charles V. In theory the Holy Roman
Empire covered all of Christendom. The emperor
was supposed to rule it all. The armies of Charles V
defeated the French, then the only serious rival
power on the continent of Europe. His fleets
controlled the Mediterranean. And his Council of
the Indies at Seville was supposed to run the affairs
of the whole New World.

The Spanish court gave charters to one adventurer after another. Ferdinand and Isabella had
made Columbus the "Admiral of the Ocean Sea."
Some went without permission. Brave conquistadores led expeditions to the mainland of
America. There they set themselves up as viceroys,
or governors, of new provinces. Most spent their
lives searching for treasure that never existed.
Some actually conquered native empires and fulfilled their dreams with the New World's treasure.

Hernando Cortes and the Aztecs. Perhaps the
most courageous and successful conquistador was
Hernando Cortes. In 1519, the same year Magellan
set out on his voyage, the bold 34-year-old Cortes
landed on the coast of Mexico with 550 soldiers, 16
horses, and 10 brass cannon. Within a year he had
subdued the Aztec empire. He won by bravery,
ruthlessness, skill, luck, and the help of imported
European diseases which killed thousands of Indians. Cortes arrived in a ship larger than any seen
there before. Riding on horses, the Spaniards
seemed superhuman. Their guns killed at a distance with terrifying magic. No wonder the Aztecs
thought they had been invaded by the gods!

From Mexico Cortes brought to the king of Spain
the first rich cargoes from America. When the

Florida, a
others who
Narváez, the
find in Floric
America nort
Rocky Mour
that Cortes
landed with 4

Nothing w
years later.
Cabeza de
Dorantes, and
Spanish party
desert. The
Indian battles,
Mexico, of th
then the deat
party. For yea
they escaped
The Indians l
strangers. Stil
because they w
powers to hea

When at la
they reported
falo) that th
enticing rumc
walls.

Esteban and I
of exploring, tl
Vaca, Castillo,
Spain. Esteban
by Fray Marcos
cities with en
"Seven Cities
found the puel
still be seen in I
the Indians. Fa
the pueblos fro
located the fab

Coronado. O
Francisco de Co
pedition, set ou
treasures. Wit
1500 horses, mu
departed north
Cities. They als
Anian," the No

treasures of gold and silver reached the court of Charles V, Spaniards awoke to the fact that America was more than a mere obstacle to the Indies.

Pizarro and Peru. In Europe scores of other adventurers now hoped to find their fortune here. Early in 1531 another ambitious Spaniard, Francisco Pizarro, landed in Peru with a small force of 180 soldiers and 27 horses. In the splendid ancient city of Cajamarca he found the new Inca, or emperor, who had just won a civil war. The Inca greeted Pizarro as a friend. In return, Pizarro seized him. The Inca offered to fill a room with treasure to win his release, and Pizarro agreed. Soon the room was bulging with a glittering pile of gold, silver, and precious gems. When the gold was weighed, it totaled 13,265 pounds and the silver 26,000 pounds. Pizarro melted it down to divide between himself and his men. Each cavalryman received 90 pounds of gold and 180 of silver. Infantrymen received less, but everyone had enough to be rich for life.

The Spanish were afraid to release the Inca for fear he would lead an uprising against them. So they used treachery. They accused the Inca of crimes he had never committed and executed him. Then they took the Incan capital at Cuzco, which brought down the whole Incan empire.

When the treasure flowed back to Spain, countless adventurous young men laid plans for their own expeditions to America. To find another Mexico or Peru, was it not worth risking your life? Reckless, ruthless conquistadores crossed the ocean to face fever, starvation, shipwreck, and hostile Indians. They stumbled their way through pathless woods, swamps, jungles, and deserts—hoping to win their gamble for a fortune.

Exploration in the present-day United States. While some conquistadores explored southward from central Mexico, others were searching for gold—or something more precious—in North America. When Juan Ponce de León ventured to Florida in 1513, he was looking for an island named "Bimini." On that island there was said to be a fountain that would restore youth to all who bathed in it. Ponce de León named the mainland "Florida," either because of the flowers there or the fact that he arrived on or soon after Easter (Pascua Florida, or "Flowering Easter"). Unfortunately he never found the magic fountain.

American Museum of Natural History

This Incan llama and the Mayan eyes and mouth for a wooden figure are among the few pieces of the finely wrought Indian metalwork that escaped being melted down and sent to Spain.

Peabody Museum, Harvard University

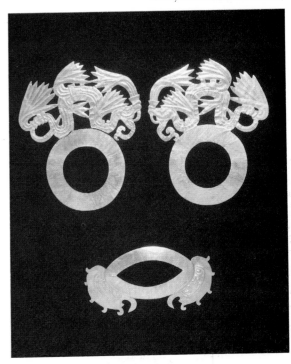

19

Since he did not find a suitable place that summer, he decided to go home and try again the following year. But on the trip back to England his ship sank in a storm, and he and all the crew were lost. Gilbert had failed, but he was the pathfinder of the British Empire.

Gilbert's dream did not die with him. Others agreed that England must plant overseas colonies. And they found the ideal advertiser. A patriotic and industrious geographer, Richard Hakluyt, collected accounts of *The Principall Navigations, Voiages and Discoveries of the English Nation.* These three volumes told exciting tales of English heroes overseas. They encouraged others to serve their country by building an empire across the world.

Gilbert's half brother Walter Raleigh wanted to pursue the dream of a colony in America. The dashing, brilliant Raleigh was one of the most remarkable men of a remarkable generation. Educated at Oxford, he wrote good poetry and lively history. He even turned out a *History of the World.* And he too was a man of action if there ever was one. It is no wonder that he was a favorite of Queen Elizabeth's. In 1584 she granted him the right to start a settlement in America.

When Raleigh's men discovered Roanoke Island in Pamlico Sound, North Carolina, they said it was blessed with friendly Indians and fertile soil. It seemed perfect for an English colony. Raleigh then persuaded Hakluyt to write a *Discourse on Western Planting* to convince Queen Elizabeth to "plant" a royal colony there. The thrifty Elizabeth refused to risk her own money on the project, but she found less costly ways to please Raleigh. She knighted him and allowed him to name the settlement "Virginia" after her, the Virgin Queen.

In 1585 Sir Walter sent out his own expedition of about 100 men and boys to found his colony on Roanoke Island. After suffering through a terrible winter, the settlers gladly left when Sir Francis Drake with a fleet of 29 ships came by in the spring. Drake was on the way home after raids in the Spanish West Indies and at St. Augustine.

Still Raleigh did not give up. Having spent so much of his own fortune, now he had to enlist other people's money. He did this by the novel device of a "joint stock" company. He persuaded many people to buy "shares" of stock. In this way the risks in the venture could be divided. People without much money could still invest and have a

This portrait of Sir Walter Raleigh and his son Wat is dated 1602. Just a year later, on the death of Queen Elizabeth, Raleigh was sent to the Tower of London.

and give jobs to the unemployed. Gilbert himself would lead the way, and he would pay for the expedition.

In 1578 the queen gave him England's first colonial charter. An expedition in 1578–1579 failed to establish a colony. In June 1583 Gilbert set forth with five ships to try his luck once again.

Early New

Spanish

◄••• Balboa 151
◄— Ponce de L
◄— Cortes 151
◄•— Pizarro 153
◄••• Narváez 15
◄•— De Vaca-Es
◄•— Coronado 1
◄— De Soto 15

ROCKY MOUNTAINS

Colorado R.

GRAND CANYON   Santa Fe

Coronado

Co

share of the profit. Investors divided the profits (or losses) according to the number of shares they had bought.

With Hakluyt's help in advertising, Raleigh raised enough money to send out in 1587 a group of men, women, and children. Again they settled on Roanoke Island. The next year Raleigh and his fellow "adventurers" (as the investors were called) had a fleet of seven ships ready to take supplies to the colony. But they were stopped by the threat of the Spanish Armada. No supply ships went out in 1588, and none sailed the next year. Not until 1590 did help reach Roanoke. There they found an empty island and only the word CROATOAN written on a post and CRO on a tree. No one was sure what it meant. But the rescuers thought it was the name of the island to which the settlers had fled. Because of bad weather the relief expedition could not reach the island of Croatan. No one ever saw any of the Roanoke settlers again. They came to be called the "Lost Colony." Their true fate remained a mystery. But the Croatan Indians have a legend that the settlers became members of their tribe. Family names of 41 of the colonists survived within the tribe.

SECTION REVIEW

1. Identify: the Tudors, Philip II, Humphrey Gilbert, Walter Raleigh, Richard Hakluyt, Croatoan, Lost Colony.
2. Locate: Cadiz, Newfoundland, English Channel, Roanoke Island.
3. What was the significance of the defeat of the Spanish Armada?
4. What was a joint stock company? Why was it used?

3. The planting of Virginia

Much had been learned from the failure of the Roanoke colony. Raleigh and Gilbert, helped by Hakluyt's advertising, had laid the groundwork for a British Empire in America.

At the end of Elizabeth's reign, England had the power and the will to found colonies in the New World. In a great burst of activity from 1606 to 1637, England planted Virginia, Maryland, and New England as well as colonies in Bermuda and the British West Indies.

Reasons for colonies. There were many reasons why England wanted to establish colonies. There was the lure of gold and silver. English sailors hoped at last to find a water passage through the North American continent to the rich trade of China and the Indies. And, of course, there was the chance to challenge Spain in North America!

The English hoped, too, that they would find in the New World the staple raw materials that they were spending their precious gold and silver to buy from other European countries. England was using up its own forests, and timber was needed for the navy. The settlers in America would be a market for British goods, especially for woolens. Commerce with the colonies would support a growing navy and merchant marine.

In England the rise in sheep farming had forced many men and women off the land. These jobless displaced people were flocking to the cities and increasing the crime there. If they were sent overseas, they could make their own way. And they could help convert the Indians to Protestant Christianity.

The unknown land. Even with all these motives, most people still did not want to emigrate. Why should they leave their familiar homeland for the dangers of an unknown America? Most of the facts they were told about the new country were wrong. Some of these imagined facts were printed because honest promoters did not know the truth. But much of what was printed was a sales pitch. The fantastic advertising brochures invented "facts" to help sell land in America. People who had invested in the American land knew that if nobody went out there it would remain a wilderness. And their land would be worthless.

So the promoters drew imaginary pictures, using ancient legends mixed with their wildest hopes and fondest dreams. The weather in America, they said, was always sunny. The oranges, lemons, apples, pears, peaches, and apricots were "so delicious that whoever tastes them will despise the insipid watery taste of those we have in England." The American venison was so juicy that English people would barely recognize it. The fish were large and easy to catch. In America there were no diseases—and no crowds. Everybody stayed young and everybody could live like a king. Come to this American paradise!

John Visscher's 1616 engraving of London Bridge shows a crowded city with no grass or trees. Promoters of the colonies emphasized the healthy life and open space to be found in America.

The real America was very different. Of course the Europeans heard rumors about the Indians, and what they heard was not encouraging. The "savages" of America, it was said, were not content merely to kill their victims. There were stories that they liked to torture their captives and even to eat them. Some Indian cruelties were supposed to be too horrible to tell.

It is surprising that English men and women dared to come to America at all. For in addition to all the real threats of a "hideous and desolate wilderness," they were haunted by horror stories and nightmares. Out there in Virginia the cheery advertising boasts were not much help. And it is still more surprising that, in spite of all their wrong "facts," the settlers in Virginia and elsewhere along the Atlantic Coast not only survived but managed to build lasting colonies.

Settling Jamestown. The first successful colony that these English people founded was in Virginia. A joint stock company named the Virginia Company of London (often called the London Company) was granted all the westward-stretching land between what is now the northern end of New Jersey and the middle of South Carolina.

In 1603 King James I succeeded Queen Elizabeth on the throne. He was the son of Mary Queen of Scots, who had been executed by Queen Elizabeth. With his passion for theories, he was as different as possible from the practical Virgin Queen. He could not get along with Parliament and was known as "the most learned fool in Christendom."

James I gave the Virginia Company its grant in 1606. The company quickly sent out three ships. This time the settlers avoided Roanoke Island and shallow Pamlico Sound and sailed instead into the broad, deep Chesapeake Bay. The settlers went up a river about 32 miles, landed on a peninsula, and began to build a town. Both the river and the town they named after their king.

In selecting the spot for Jamestown these settlers showed poor judgment. The site was low and swampy—just what the company had warned against. But the 104 men and boys who landed in this wilderness on May 23, 1607, somehow thought the site would be easy to defend against the Indians and the Spanish. From the swampy ground came mosquitoes carrying malaria, and from their well water came dysentery. They would have been better off if they had faced their enemies on dry and solid ground.

The council that governed the colony had no head. Members wasted time arguing, while no one had the power to make decisions. Disrupted by its squabbling council and weakened by disease, Jamestown was also menaced by Indian raids. These raids were brought on by rash acts of the colonists themselves.

Still, the colony was blessed with a remarkable leader, Captain John Smith. He had been a merchant's poor apprentice in England. But adventure was his middle name, so he had joined armies and fought in distant Hungary and Turkey. He had the bad luck to be made a slave in Turkey. But he escaped, returned to England, and joined the new Virginia Company.

Smith saved the settlers from themselves. With his courage and his wide experience he knew how to stop the settlers' quarreling. He worked to keep peace with the Indians. The Indians traded him the corn needed to feed the settlers till they could raise their own crops. Even then, more than half the colonists died of fever, starvation, or the arrows of Indians before the winter was over.

Fortunately, the company back in London was committed to make the colony succeed. In 1608 they sent out new recruits—men, women, and children—and supplies. In 1609 alone about 400 colonists arrived. Unfortunately, some of them were carrying a terrible disease known as the plague. Then the colony lost its leader when John Smith was injured by a gunpowder explosion and was forced to return home. The bitter winter of 1609–1610 was called "the Starving Time." There were ghastly tales of cannibalism. About 440 settlers died of starvation or disease. Only 60 were left when spring arrived.

Over the next years the company still poured in settlers and supplies. But the colony could not be self-supporting unless they could produce something they could sell. What they found was quite a surprise. The Spanish had brought tobacco to Europe some years before, and the English had quickly taken to smoking. They smoked not only because they enjoyed it. Doctors at the time said it would cure almost any disease. In 1612 John Rolfe, who later married the Indian princess Pocahontas, learned how to grow a kind of tobacco in Virginia that English people especially liked. Because the English were eager to buy this crop, the colony now finally had found a solid economic base.

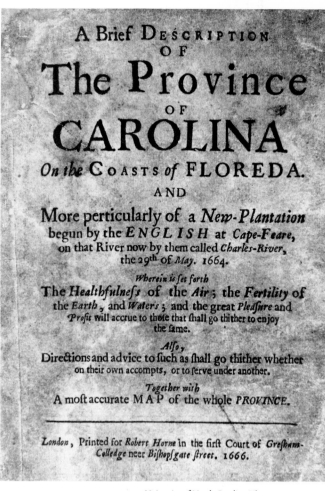

Advertisements glowed with the wonders— real and imaginary—of the New World. Printers at this time often used a letter something like an "f" where we use an "s."

A colony established. By 1619 the Virginia colony was well on its way to success. The company was sending out hundreds of craftsmen and laborers. New directors in London then decided to give the settlers more freedom. Up to then the colonists had lived under strict martial law. For example, every man and woman had to attend church twice daily and could be fined a full day's pay for one absence, whipped for a second, and put in jail six months for a third. Strict discipline helped the colony survive the early years. But it would scare away new settlers. The company sent out a new governor with orders to let the people work for themselves as

THE INCONVENIENCIES
THAT HAVE HAPPENED TO SOME PERSONS WHICH HAVE TRANSPORTED THEMSELVES

from *England* to *Virginia*, vvithout prouisions necessary to sustaine themselues, hath
greatly hindred the *Progresse of that noble Plantation: For preuention of the like disorders*
heereafter, that no man suffer, either through ignorance or misinformation; it is thought requisite to publish this short declaration: wherein is contained a particular of such necessaries, as either priuate families or single persons shall haue cause to furnish themselues with, for their better
support at their first landing in Virginia; whereby also greater numbers may receiue in part,
directions how to prouide themselues.

Apparrell.	li.	s.	d.
One Monmouth Cap	00	01	10
Three falling bands		01	03
Three shirts		07	06
One waste-coate		02	02
One suite of Canuase		07	06
One suite of Frize		10	00
One suite of Cloth		15	00
Three paire of Irish stockins		04	
Foure paire of shooes		08	08
One paire of garters		00	10
One doozen of points		00	03
One paire of Canuase sheets		08	00
Seuen ells of Canuase, to make a bed and boulster, to be filled in *Virginia* 8.s.			
One Rug for a bed 8.s. which with the bed seruing for two men, halfe is		08	00
Fiue ells coorse Canuase, to make a bed at Sea for two men, to be filled with straw, iiij.s.			
One coorse Rug at Sea for two men, will cost vj.s. is for one		05	00
	04	00	00

Apparrell for one man, and so after the rate for more.

Victuall.			
Eight bushels of Meale	02	00	00
Two bushels of pease at 3.s.		06	00
Two bushels of Oatemeale 4.s. 6.d.		09	00
One gallon of *Aquauita*		02	06
One gallon of Oyle		03	06
Two gallons of Vineger 1.s.		02	00
	03	03	00

For a whole yeere for one man, and so for more after the rate.

Armes.			
One Armour compleat, light		17	00
One long Peece, fiue foot or fiue and a halfe, neere Musket bore	01	02	
One sword		05	
One belt		01	
One bandaleere		01	06
Twenty pound of powder		18	00
Sixty pound of shot or lead, Pistoll and Goose shot		05	00
	03	09	06

For one man, but if halfe of your men haue armour it is sufficient so that all haue Peeces and swords.

Tooles.	li.	s.	d.
Fiue broad howes at 2.s. a piece		10	
Fiue narrow howes at 16.d. a piece		06	08
Two broad Axes at 3.s. 8.d. a piece		07	04
Fiue felling Axes at 18.d. a piece		07	06
Two steele hand sawes at 16.d. a piece		02	08
Two two-hand sawes at 5.s. a piece		10	
One whip-saw, set and filed with box, file, and wrest		10	
Two hammers 12.d. a piece		02	00
Three shouels 18.d. a piece		04	06
Two spades at 18.d. a piece		03	
Two augers 6.d. a piece		01	00
Sixe chissels 6.d. a piece		03	00
Two percers stocked 4.d. a piece		00	08
Three gimlets 2.d. a piece		00	06
Two hatchets 21.d. a piece		03	06
Two froues to cleaue pale 18.d.		03	00
Two hand-bills 20. a piece		03	04
One grindlestone 4.s.		04	00
Nailes of all sorts to the value of	02	00	
Two Pickaxes		03	
	06	02	08

For a family of 6. persons and so after the rate for more.

Houshold Implements.			
One Iron Pot		07	
One kettle		06	
One large frying-pan		02	06
One gridiron		01	06
Two skillets		05	
One spit		02	
Platters, dishes, spoones of wood		04	
	01	08	00

For a family of 6. persons, and so for more or lesse after the rate.

For Suger, Spice, and fruit, and at Sea for 6. men — 00 | 12 | 06

So the full charge of Apparrell, Victuall, Armes, Tooles,
and houshold stuffe, and after this rate for each person,
will amount vnto about the summe of — 12 | 10 |

The passage of each man is — 06 | 00 |

The fraight of these prouisions for a man, will bee about
halfe a Tun, which is — 01 | 10 |

So the whole charge will amount to about — 20 | 00 | 00

Nets, hookes, lines, and a tent must be added, if the number of people be grea-
ter, as also some kine.
And this is the vsuall proportion that the Virginia *Company doe*
bestow vpon their Tenants which they send.

Whosoeuer transports himselfe or any other at his owne charge vnto *Virginia*, shall for each person so transported before Midsummer 1625,
haue to him and his heires for euer fifty Acres of Land vpon a first, and fifty Acres vpon a second diuision.

Imprinted at London by FELIX KYNGSTON. 1622.

well as for the company. The governor allowed the colonists to elect an assembly to help make their own laws. The House of Burgesses, as Virginians called it, met at Jamestown on July 30, 1619. It was the first elected legislative assembly in America.

That same year saw the arrival of two groups who played a leading role in the colony's future. Jamestown was changed from a military outpost into a full community when the Virginia Company sent out from London a group of "respectable maidens" who soon married men of their choice. About the same time a Dutch ship arrived carrying twenty blacks. These were probably not slaves but indentured servants (like many of the white settlers). An indentured servant was a person who had signed an "indenture," an agreement to serve a master for a certain number of years. (It was called an "indenture" because the two parts of each agreement—one for master, one for servant—were indented to fit together.) Outright slavery probably did not appear in the English colonies until later.

In the next few years the company sent many more settlers to Virginia—often without the needed supplies. Some 5000 arrived between 1619 and 1624. And yet by 1624 the total population in the colony had increased by only 200. Sickness killed most of the newcomers, starvation took some, and others fell to the tomahawk. In 1622 the Indians attacked in an all-out try to drive the European invaders from their land. The colony lost 350 lives (including John Rolfe), and the settlers were pushed back close to Jamestown.

The men running the Virginia Company included some of King James's opponents in Parliament. He used the problems of the company to persuade his judges to annul the company charter. The settlement now became a *royal colony* with its governor appointed by the king. But after a brief pause the legislative assembly was allowed to continue.

The London Company had founded the first permanent English settlement in America. Tobacco—its staple crop—gave the colony a firm

This 1622 English handbill advises families leaving for America to take the necessary tools and supplies to avoid "inconveniencies."

This painting shows Pocahontas, also known as Matoaka, in English clothes. She married John Rolfe and died in England in 1617 just as she was about to return to America.

economic base. And the settlers in Virginia had set the pattern of representative government for future English colonies. All this had been done at fearful cost in money and lives. But the Virginia experience—the successes and the failures—would save lives and light the way for later settlers.

SECTION REVIEW

1. Identify or explain: John Smith, John Rolfe, Virginia Company of London, the Starving Time, indentured servant.
2. Locate: Jamestown, Chesapeake Bay, James River.
3. Why did England want colonies?
4. What major problems faced the Jamestown settlers in the early years?
5. What significant events happened in Virginia in 1619? Why was each important?

4. The Puritans come to New England

The settlement of Virginia was mostly a business enterprise. Settlers of New England also hoped to make money. But their lives and their hopes were ruled by religion. The people who went there were called "Puritans" because they wanted to purify the Church of England. They wanted to do away with the colorful robes of priests, with prayer books, and even with altars. Some Puritans remained inside the Church of England and worked for reform there. Others were known as "Independents" or "Separatists." They went out of the church—separated from it.

The Pilgrims. Three centuries ago kings and queens believed that the religion of their people helped keep them loyal and obedient. Subjects who were allowed to make up their own minds about religion might also make up their own minds about politics—and even about whether to obey the king! James I began his reign by declaring that his subjects had to "conform" in religion or he would "harry them out of the land."

The Separatist congregations of some little villages in the east of England were harried until in 1608 they took refuge in Holland. That was the only country in Europe where complete religious freedom was allowed. But after they had lived there for a few years, they began to fear that their children would forget the customs and speech of England. These Separatists decided to move on to the new land of America. They were given permission by the London Company to settle in Virginia.

They went back to England, where they set out from Plymouth in the *Mayflower* on September 16, 1620, with 102 passengers. After a seven-week voyage in cramped quarters, they first sighted land in early November. They looked for a suitable place and finally landed on December 21, 1620. The winter was harsher than anything they had known in England.

Their pilot brought them by mistake to Cape Cod. They had no right to own the land there, for that required a *patent,* or land grant. They had no power either to establish a government, for that required a charter.

But they had something far better. They had a plan to build a purified society, and they had a guide in the Bible. This was important, for in the mysterious New World you would surely be lost unless you had some plans of your own. If you had goals, they would guide and encourage you while you were discovering what America was really like. Your plans had to be definite, but not too definite. You had to be willing to change your plans when you ran into trouble, or when the New World did not offer what you expected. You had to be prepared for disappointment. Yet you had to have self-confidence, faith in your mission and in yourself. The Pilgrims and other Puritans had all this. They were equipped, too, with just the right combination of hopes and fears, optimism and pessimism, self-confidence and humility to be successful settlers. And this was one of the most fortunate coincidences in our history.

The Mayflower Compact. When the Pilgrims reached Cape Cod, they were outside the boundaries where they had permission to settle. Some unruly passengers noticed this. They threatened "that when they came ashore they would use their own liberty, for none had power to command them, the patent they had being for Virginia." But the *Mayflower* leaders, anxious to land and begin their colony, could not tolerate a community without government. Why should their plans be spoiled by a few roughnecks?

So they decided on shipboard, then and there, to create a new government to serve their very special purposes. Their leaders included the steady William Bradford, who would be governor of Plymouth Colony for 31 years, and Captain Miles Standish, whom they had hired to head their militia. Like people making up rules for a club that already existed, they wrote out and signed an agreement. This was the famous Mayflower Compact. In it they pledged allegiance to the king, combined themselves "into a civil body politic," and bound themselves to obey all the laws this new government might enact. They created an instant government. It worked surprisingly well for the infant colony, and later became the foundation for the state of Massachusetts.

Squanto to the rescue. The Pilgrims and other Puritans thought God was on their side when they settled in the wilderness. And often it seemed that He was. The Pilgrims might all have died if a remarkable Indian had not come to help them.

Squanto was an Indian kidnapped a few years before by an English sea captain, who had sold him into slavery in Spain. He escaped to England, where he learned some English, and then returned to New England in 1619. There he found that his whole village had died of the plague. Now, in March 1621, it was Squanto—of all the thousands of Indians in America—who happened to turn up in Plymouth! He knew enough English to act as an interpreter. And he showed the Pilgrims how to plant corn (which was not known in England), how to fertilize the soil, where to catch fish, and how to trap beaver. No wonder the Pilgrims called him a "special instrument sent of God for their good beyond their expectation."

The Plymouth Colony never grew very large, and in 1691 it was absorbed into the Massachusetts Bay Colony. But we still revere the Pilgrim Fathers as the first successful settlers of the New England shore, who began an American custom—finding a way of self-government for every occasion.

The Massachusetts Bay Colony. Charles I's archbishop, William Laud, and other high officials within the established Church of England tried to force the Puritans to conform to the rules of the church. Many Puritans then made up their minds to leave England, and fortunately they had a place to go to. Some of them had received a charter from King James for a company that was allowed to create settlements in the Massachusetts Bay area in New England.

The most significant point about this charter was that it did not say where the company headquarters had to be. It did not say where the company should hold its meetings to admit new members, to select officers, or to make laws. This meant that if the company headquarters was transferred from England to Massachusetts, the stockholders in Massachusetts would be able to run the company. Since they were settlers, it also meant that settlers would be governing themselves.

In 1629 the company members voted to transfer the company to Massachusetts Bay. Certain strong Puritans, leaders like John Winthrop, were now willing to go there. From the start, Massachusetts Bay was a self-governing colony.

One thousand settlers went out in the summer of 1630 and planted settlements around Massachusetts Bay. By the end of the first decade, 20,000 settlers

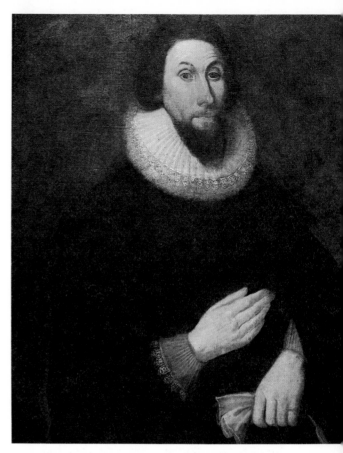

American Antiquarian Society

John Winthrop, whose portrait was painted by an unknown artist in England, provided strong leadership as governor of the Massachusetts Bay Colony.

had arrived. Among these, right from the start, were more people of means and influence than in any other group of colonists. When the settlers arrived, they soon founded settlements at Boston, Charlestown, Watertown, Lynn, Medford, Dorchester, and Roxbury.

The Puritan religion was admirably suited for settling the wilderness. A church (by which the Puritans meant the members of a congregation) would receive a grant of land from the Great and General Court (a meeting of the company). Then it would move as a group to a spot already selected and surveyed. There a village would be built around a meetinghouse with the fields scattered outside the village.

The Newport Historical Society

Beautiful Touro Synagogue in Newport, Rhode Island, was designed by Peter Harrison, a merchant and amateur architect. He based the interior on the design of Whitehall Palace in London.

A City upon a hill. The Puritans had a grand purpose in America. John Winthrop, who was to be their governor for many years, spoke to them on the boat coming over:

> We shall be as a City upon a hill, the eyes of all people are upon us; so that if we shall deal falsely with our god in this work we have undertaken and so cause him to withdraw his present help from us, we shall be made a story and a by-word through the world.

Winthrop was saying what many Americans then and since have felt. The American example could help shape the lives of people everywhere.

With their beliefs, it would have been difficult for the Puritans to fail. Even the Devil, who was a lively presence for them, could not really defeat them. Sooner or later, they knew, God always won. He would see that His own people were not destroyed. The troubles of this world—New England blizzards, Indian arrows, the plottings of enemies in England, or the crimes of their own people—never overwhelmed them. The Puritans were ready for what wilderness America demanded.

Rhode Island. The Puritans who settled Massachusetts Bay did not believe in religious freedom. They thought that they knew God's truth and that all reasonable men and women should be able to see that truth. If you disagreed with them, you had the right to go away but not to stay in Massachusetts.

Roger Williams, the young pastor of the church in Salem, would not agree to the Puritan version of the truth, so he was banished from Massachusetts Bay. He made his way, in 1636, to Narragansett Bay. There he purchased a tract of land from the Indians and began the settlement we know as Rhode Island.

Rhode Island was a haven for independent thinkers. One who went there was the bright, brave, freethinking Anne Hutchinson. She had held meetings at her house in Boston to discuss the preacher's Sunday sermons. Then she had begun to put forth her own ideas. Soon she was disagreeing with some of the accepted doctrines of the churches of the Bay Colony and criticizing many of its ministers. So Mrs. Hutchinson was banished. She moved to Rhode Island. Later she settled in New York where, in 1643, she and all but one of her household were massacred by Indians.

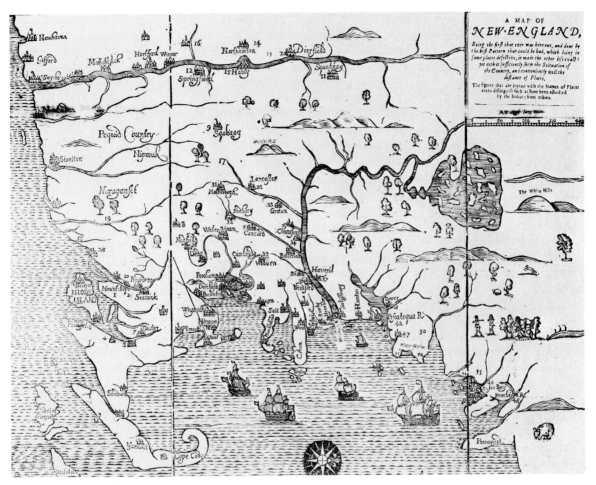

This 1677 woodcut by John Foster is the first such map made in the colonies. West is at the top. The map shows Puritan settlements stretching from Maine to Connecticut. The Charles River (center) and Connecticut River (top) are featured.

The scornful Puritans in Massachusetts called the Rhode Island people "the Lord's debris." They sneered that if any man had lost his religion he would be sure to find it in some Rhode Island village. Still, Rhode Island grew and prospered as a refuge for liberty.

In the 1650s, Quakers (considered in Massachusetts the most dangerous of all Separatists) and Jews began to appear in the colony. The Jews formed their first congregation there in 1658. In 1763 they built the beautiful Touro Synagogue, which still stands in Newport. But Catholics were not welcomed even in Rhode Island. They were allowed to settle there but were not allowed to vote.

Other New England settlements. In 1636, men and women from several Massachusetts towns were granted permission to "transport themselves and their estates" westward to the Connecticut Valley, noted for its rich farmland. They were the first wave of the mighty overland movement to the West that marked American history for 200 years. In Connecticut the first settlers founded Hartford, Windsor, and Wethersfield.

In 1639 the Connecticut settlers adopted their own "Fundamental Orders." This was a frame of self-government with a governor, a legislative assembly, and courts. Voting was restricted to male property owners, as was customary at that time. To vote in Massachusetts Bay, you still had to be a member of the church, but not here. Features of the Fundamental Orders remained the basis of Connecticut's government long after it became a state.

Another group of settlers who left Massachusetts Bay founded the New Haven Colony. They had no real quarrel with the Bay Colony—except that it was not quite strict enough! They had come from England to start commerce here, and they could find no harbor to their taste in Massachusetts Bay. At New Haven they had the harbor they needed. They settled there in 1638. This colony attracted many of the wealthiest settlers who had yet come to America. But the location they had chosen was not as good as they had thought. The harbor was too shallow. And hemmed in by Connecticut, they lacked lands to produce goods to export. The New Haven Colony was absorbed by Connecticut in 1664.

Settlers also went north from the Massachusetts Bay Colony. Some moved into New Hampshire, which became a royal province in 1679. Others traveled to Maine where Sir Ferdinando Gorges had tried in vain to plant a colony. He wanted one, unlike Massachusetts Bay, that would be faithful to the king and the Anglican church. But Maine remained a province of Massachusetts until 1820.

SECTION REVIEW

1. Identify or explain: Separatists, Puritans, Pilgrims, James I, Squanto, John Winthrop, Roger Williams, Anne Hutchinson, Fundamental Orders of Connecticut.
2. Locate: Cape Cod, Plymouth, Massachusetts Bay, Narragansett Bay, Connecticut Valley, Hartford, New Haven.
3. What was the Mayflower Compact? Why was it important?
4. Why did the Puritans make successful settlers?
5. Why was the Rhode Island Colony founded?
6. What other colonies were offshoots from Massachusetts Bay?

5. Other Europeans in North America

Three centuries ago the kings and queens of Europe regarded as their own private property any lands that ships flying their flag discovered. They granted these lands as they pleased to settlers or trading companies. Vast tracts of land in America were sold for cash or given away to favorites by the States-General (parliament) of the Netherlands and by the English, French, and Swedish kings.

New France. Samuel de Champlain—expert navigator, student of science, brave explorer, earnest missionary—became the founder of New France in America. At Quebec in 1608 he planted the first permanent French settlement in the New World.

For the French that was only a foothold. From Quebec, their explorers, missionaries, fur trappers, and settlers moved up the St. Lawrence River, through the Great Lakes, and down the Mississippi. In time, they claimed an empire that stretched over a great arc—behind the English. The French Empire reached from New Orleans on the Gulf of Mexico to the powerful Canadian fortress, Louisbourg, on the Atlantic Ocean.

But while New France was vast in area, it remained small in population. The reasons are not hard to find. Only French Roman Catholics were allowed in the colony. The large tracts were granted to a few proprietors. The French overlords rented out small strips, usually along the riverbanks, in exchange for produce or for labor on their big estates. Colonial officers, chosen in France, ruled without the advice of any representative assembly. In the courts there was no trial by jury.

All of this still might not have stopped settlers from coming. But the French crown, unlike the English, did not allow those who were discontented at home to go abroad. The English monarchs wisely let their dissenters leave. The French rulers insisted on keeping the Huguenots at home where they could be watched and punished. As a result, by 1700 the English population along the Atlantic seaboard had grown to a quarter of a million. Meanwhile, the French population in Canada had barely reached 18,000.

The Dutch colony on the Hudson. The best place on the Atlantic Coast for a trading colony was at the present site of New York City. Its grand natural harbor invited commerce from the whole world. At the same time a broad river provided a superhighway for furs from the interior. Not the English but the Dutch took possession of this choice region. In September 1609 Henry Hudson, an English captain in the service of the Dutch, sailed up the river that now bears his name. Like countless other mariners in those days, Hudson was searching for the Northwest Passage from Europe to Cathay.

After Hudson's voyage, the Dutch set up a trading post on the river near the present site of Albany. Later, in 1623, they settled at Manhattan for their marketplace. They bought the island with trading goods valued at 60 Dutch guilders (about $24) from several Indian chiefs. Of course, in those days $24 was worth what several thousand dollars would be worth now. The Dutch called their colony New Netherland. But unlike the Puritans, the Dutch settlers were less interested in building "a City upon a hill," a model community as an example to the world, than in making money.

The Dutch were the merchants of the world. There on Manhattan Island they began the great American democracy of cash. If you had money or goods, the Dutch would trade with you. It didn't matter who you were or what you believed. The Dutch let in nearly everyone to New York—not so much because they believed in toleration, but simply because it meant profit.

The Dutch colony was a wedge between New England and the southern colonies. So in 1664, when England was on the verge of war with Holland, Charles II granted his brother James, Duke of York, all the land between the Connecticut and Delaware rivers, including New Netherland.

When a fleet sent out by the Duke of York arrived at the fort at the foot of Manhattan Island and called for the surrender of the colony, the stubborn Dutch Governor Peter Stuyvesant refused. But the leading citizens, hardheaded merchants, knew that resistance was hopeless. They finally persuaded Stuyvesant to yield, and New Netherland fell without a blow. The English flag now waved over an unbroken coast from Canada to the Carolinas.

New Sweden. When New Netherland fell to England, so did the land that had once been New Sweden. This was a colony first settled by Swedes and Finns in 1638 on the New Jersey shore of the Delaware River near what is now Wilmington. But since the settlement was small and weak, it was easily seized by the Dutch in 1655.

New Sweden gave America the log cabin. In the cold Swedish forests farmers had learned to use rough logs to build a cozy weather-tight house. Clever Swedish builders brought here their skill with logs. And the log cabin became standard housing on the western frontier.

SECTION REVIEW

1. Identify: Samuel de Champlain, Peter Stuyvesant, Duke of York.
2. Locate: Louisbourg, New Orleans, Albany, Hudson River, Delaware River, New Sweden.
3. Why did the English colonies grow while the French colonies stayed small?
4. What was distinctive about New Netherland in American history?

6. The proprietary colonies

Of the thirteen colonies that later united to form the American nation, all except Virginia and the New England settlements had been founded as *proprietorships*. This was halfway between a royal province and a self-governing colony. The king let control out of his hands, but he did not give it to a company or to the colonists. Instead it went to a man or a group of men, usually the king's personal friends. The "proprietors" then appointed the governor, set up law courts, and collected land tax ("quitrent") from the settlers. They also offered bonuses to lure settlers to their lands. They managed their provinces as business ventures, under whatever rules the king had put in their charters.

The proprietors were also limited by elected assemblies. All the proprietors except the Duke of York (who finally agreed in 1683) allowed the people some form of self-government. They could not attract settlers on any other terms. Even the royal provinces had to allow assemblies.

Starting with Maryland in 1634 a series of proprietary colonies was founded: the Carolinas in 1663, the Jerseys in 1664, Pennsylvania in 1681, Delaware in 1702 (with the Penns as governors), and finally Georgia, first settled in 1733. Each colony faced its own problems, enjoyed its own successes, suffered its own failures.

Maryland, a colony founded for Catholics, like Rhode Island allowed religious freedom from the first. It passed an Act of Toleration in 1649. This permitted religious freedom only for all who believed in the Trinity—God, Jesus Christ, and the

Holy Ghost. It was the first legislative act of religious toleration in the colonies.

The Carolina proprietors tried to rule their colony by an elaborate constitution called the "Grand Model" drawn up by English philosopher John Locke. But the philosopher's theories proved unfit for the problems of government in the wilderness.

Pennsylvania. Pennsylvania was founded by Quakers. They were a special kind of Puritan. They rejected all ceremonies of religious worship and all authority of priests, bishops, or ministers. They obeyed only the "inner light" of conscience. In their meetinghouses there were no ministers. Anyone could stand up and say what God had told him or her to say, on any subject. The Quakers really believed in equality. They refused to bow or to remove their hats in the presence of officials. It is not surprising, then, that royal officials became impatient with them and persecuted the Quakers for any reason they could think up. The Quakers were not welcome in England.

So William Penn, who had been in jail for his religious beliefs, decided to found a colony for his fellow Quakers. Penn was the son of a rich British admiral who was not a Quaker and who had loaned money to King Charles II. No doubt this helped young Penn, who was shrewd and persuasive, to secure a vast colonial grant from Charles. At the king's demand, the new land was named in honor of Penn's father.

Back in England the Quakers had been strict pacifists. They opposed war and refused to fight in any way for any reason, even in self-defense. Back in England they were nothing but a small group of peculiar people. If they refused to fight, the country could still be defended. It was quite another matter in Pennsylvania. Here at first they were the majority, but they ran the government until 1756, long after they had stopped being a majority. In Pennsylvania, if the Quakers refused to raise an army, the countryside was left defenseless. This is precisely what happened.

For some time, by various dodges, the Quakers did try to help defend the colony without violating their consciences. In one case they voted money "to feed and clothe the Indians" that they knew would go to defense instead. In another they voted "other grain" for a military garrison, even though they knew "other grain" really meant a not-very-nourishing grain called gunpowder.

But in 1755, dodges ceased to be enough. Total war broke out in western Pennsylvania. The Indians burned homes, ruined crops, and killed or captured women and children. Panic gripped the land, and eastern towns were filled with refugees. The Quakers insisted on remaining pacifists even as western Pennsylvania ran red with the blood of the settlers.

At that time the Quakers, although numbering only one-quarter of the colony's population, still held over three-fourths of the seats in the legislature. And they would not vote funds for defense. They insisted they could not violate their consciences by helping to fight a war against anybody. Now, however, the non-Quakers had had enough.

That William Penn was more than just a visionary Quaker is apparent in this early portrait. The toughness, practicality, and pertinacity needed to found a successful colony all shine through.

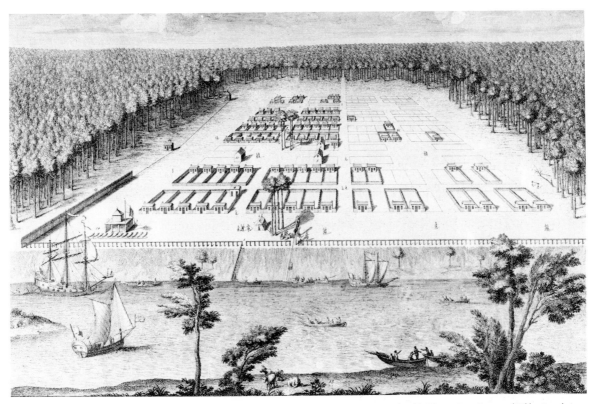

Here is the neat checkerboard scheme that the London planners imagined for the city of Savannah in Georgia. This 1734 engraving by Pierre Fourdrinier was designed to attract settlers. But the real Savannah had another look.

They forced the Quakers to resign their control of the government. The Quakers never ruled the colony again.

After that the Quakers became the gadflies and prophets of America. They remained pacifists, spoke out against slavery, and opposed alcoholic drinks. They were the voices of everybody's conscience. That was their strength and their weakness. They were not meant for governing a colony.

Georgia.

Georgia. If Pennsylvania faced problems because of the beliefs of its settlers, Georgia suffered because of its English founders' ignorance and idealism. The 21 men in England who secured a charter for Georgia in 1732 thought they were very practical. The best known of them was James Oglethorpe. He was a tough-minded soldier who combined a passion for building the British Empire with a passion for reform. Oglethorpe and his friends had their eyes not so much on the Bible or on their own consciences as on the practical problems of their day. In London they worried over the growing unemployment and the increasing crime.

The land south of the Carolinas was rumored to be a new paradise. There they would settle some of London's criminals and the drunken, idle poor. That also happened to be right where the empire needed to block the Spaniards, who were trying to push their settlements northward. In Georgia, named after King George II, these unlucky people could serve as a human barricade. At the same time in that tropical climate they could provide the exotic products needed at home in England.

The founders even knew what the colony ought to produce—silk. At that time Britain was spending a fortune in gold and silver to buy silk. If the English could grow silk themselves, they would save their gold and silver and also provide work for the unemployed. The London promoters therefore ordered every settler in Georgia to grow mulberry trees so the leaves would be food for silkworms. Unfortunately, the black mulberry trees that grew in Georgia were not the kind the silkworms liked. This was a little fact that the London promoters had not bothered to notice.

Plans bred more plans. The ill-informed trustees of Georgia, sitting in their easy chairs in London, went on drawing their plans. Not only did they require mulberry trees to be planted, but they laid down rules on just where the people could live. They prohibited "Rum, Brandies, Spirits, or Strong Waters." They would not let the settlers own or sell the land they worked. The settlers could use the land only according to company rules. No black slaves were to be allowed.

Georgia was intended to be a charity colony. It was the only English colony whose founders did not expect to make a profit. Because the people who were sent out were charity cases, they were not allowed to govern themselves. Almost as if they were in a Spanish colony, the inhabitants of Georgia had everything decided for them.

It is not surprising that colonial Georgia did not flourish. An empire builder's dream turned out to be a nightmare. The settlers rebelled, and the trustees who had founded the colony gave up. By the time of the American Revolution, Georgia—the spoiled child of charitable London—was the least prosperous and least populous of all the English colonies.

"The poor inhabitants of Georgia," a settler lamented, "are scattered over the face of the earth; her plantations a wild; her towns a desert; her villages in rubbish, her improvements a by-word, and her liberties a jest; an object of pity to friends, and of insult, contempt and ridicule to enemies."

SECTION REVIEW

1. Identify: William Penn, John Locke, James Oglethorpe, Quakers.
2. Define a "proprietary" colony.
3. Why did both the Quakers and the proprietors of Georgia find it difficult to rule their colonies? How were they different? How were they alike?

CHAPTER REVIEW

MEETING OUR EARLIER SELVES

1. Compare the Spanish and the English colonies in North America. Mention such things as (a) the number and treatment of Indians, (b) slavery, (c) population characteristics, and (d) control by the parent country.
2. What developments in the 1500s enabled England to challenge Spain in North America?
3. How did false advertising and rumors affect the settlement of the English colonies?
4. The final sentences of the chapter introduction (p. 26) point out that both planning and luck had much to do with the success of the European settlements in America. Find examples of good or bad planning and good or bad luck.
5. In which colonies were the religious beliefs of the founders or early settlers a powerful force in shaping the character of the colony? For each colony, point out some distinctive institution that was shaped by religious belief.

QUESTIONS FOR TODAY

1. The Puritans, Separatists, and Quakers were religious dissenters. Are there religious groups in the United States today who might be labeled "dissenters"? If so, how are they treated?
2. Planting colonies was a chief way for a nation to grow in power in the 1500s. What opportunities exist today for a nation to become more powerful? What arrangements in the world today are designed to keep nations from gaining power at the expense of others?

YOUR REGION IN HISTORY

What European country, if any, about 1650 claimed the land where you live? What European exploration or settlement had taken place in your state or region by that time? What evidence of that country's claim exists in nearby place names or old structures or historical markers?

SKILLS TO MAKE OUR PAST VIVID

Draw a contemporary poster for a colonial proprietor to use in recruiting colonists for his English colony in America.

CHAPTER 3

New ways in a New World

During these early colonial years, American ways of life began to appear. They emerged from how Americans defended themselves in war and governed themselves in peace. Challenged by a New World, they developed their own ideas about government, law, and politics. Still, the British colonists in America considered themselves loyal Britons. In 1763, at the end of the French and Indian War, few people anywhere would have predicted the break that was to come. The next twenty years were a time of surprising change. Before the colonists could realize it, they had made themselves into a new, self-governing nation.

How did that happen? To understand how this New World novelty was created, we must look at the relations of Americans to each other, to England, and to the wars that France and England exported to America.

1. Many kinds of Americans

During the seventeenth century the English settlements in America grew slowly. One hundred years after the landing at Jamestown the colonies still held only 250,000 people. Then the 1700s saw immigration and a high birthrate create the first American population explosion. The number of people more than doubled every 25 years. By 1765 they counted two and a quarter million. These were no longer just European emigrants, but a new breed of people, shaped by a New World.

A land of many peoples. The people who lived in the thirteen colonies at the end of the French and Indian War came from many lands. But the population was more English than it would ever be again. Since about 60 percent of all the white settlers had come from England, it is not surprising that the English language, English customs, English law, and English ways of government dominated the land. Pennsylvania had the most mixed population of all, but even there the English stock made up at least half of the population.

What transformed Britons into Americans was that here they had the challenges of living with Africans, Scots, Scotch-Irish, Irish, Portuguese Jews, Swedes, Finns, Swiss, and even a few Austrians and Italians. This made life here much more interesting than life back home. Of course it made some new problems, but it created new opportunities.

These many peoples had come for many different reasons. Most came because they wanted to, some because they were forced. Some, like the Swedes, learned English and became Americans quickly. Others, like the Germans, tried to hold on to their own language and their own customs, even in this New World. Still others, like the indentured servants and many of the blacks from Africa, might

Henrietta Johnson, an English artist, made this portrait in Charlestown in 1720.

have wanted to become full-fledged Americans but were not yet allowed that chance.

Black Americans had been brought here against their will. Most were slaves, but at an early date there were a few who were free. In 1765 the colonies held 400,000 blacks scattered from Massachusetts Bay to Georgia. Over half worked on the tobacco plantations in Virginia and Maryland. Only 40,000 were found farther north.

Besides colonists of English or of African descent, the largest group consisted of the Scots, the Irish, and the Scotch-Irish (the Scots who had tried to settle in Ireland). These hard-bitten, intelligent people took naturally to the frontier. They could usually be found in the "back country." This was a new American expression for the unsettled lands that stretched from Pennsylvania down through the mountains into the Carolinas.

A smaller number were the Germans, industrious and thrifty, who settled mainly in Pennsylvania. So many came in the mid-eighteenth century that the English settlers there feared that the whole colony would become German.

The Germans worked large farms on the rich limestone soil. Some of their descendants are still

working the same lands today. They are often mistakenly referred to as Pennsylvania Dutch (from *Deutsch,* meaning German). They were ingenious and willing to try new ways. For hunting they replaced the old-fashioned musket with the accurate long rifle of frontier fame. For travel they built the sturdy Conestoga wagon, which took many pioneers west. And to warm their houses in the winters, which were much colder than those in Europe, they developed and improved the iron stove.

The French Protestants, a small group, had an influence all out of proportion to their numbers. These Huguenots came to America after 1685 when the French government deprived them of their religious freedom and their right to take part in government. An older French law, the Edict of Nantes, which had once given them religious liberty, was repealed. Now they joined the stream of refugees who, over the centuries, came here to escape persecution. It was against the law for them to leave France, but they came anyway. Their intelligence and their skills enriched the colonies.

One famous descendant of the French Huguenots was Paul Revere, who made the celebrated ride in

Paul Revere's likeness was painted in 1765 by John Singleton Copley. It shows him in his silversmith's work clothes holding an elegant example of his craft.

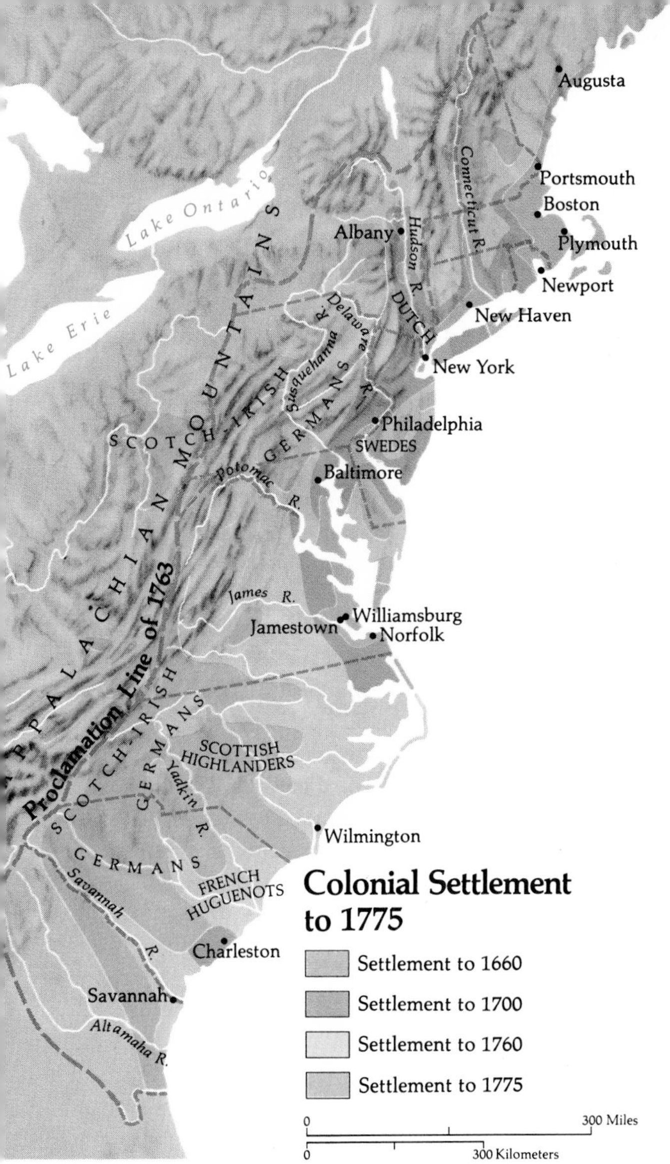
Colonial Settlement to 1775
Settlement to 1660
Settlement to 1700
Settlement to 1760
Settlement to 1775
0
300 Miles
0
300 Kilometers
Augusta
Portsmouth
Boston
Plymouth
Newport
New Haven
New York
Albany
Philadelphia
Baltimore
Williamsburg
Jamestown
Norfolk
Wilmington
Charleston
Savannah
Lake Ontario
Lake Erie
Connecticut R.
Hudson R.
Delaware R.
Susquehanna R.
Potomac R.
James R.
Yadkin R.
Savannah R.
Altamaha R.
DUTCH
SWEDES
GERMANS
SCOTCH-IRISH
SCOTTISH HIGHLANDERS
FRENCH HUGUENOTS
APPALACHIAN MOUNTAINS
Proclamation Line of 1763

1775 to tell the people that British troops were on their way to Concord and Lexington. Revere made his living as a silversmith, and his elegant work can be seen in many museums today.

Empty land creates opportunity. Most colonists found here a greater dignity and a better life than they had had before. At long last they could buy their own tract of land and run their own farm. The vote in all colonies was restricted to male landowners, but most adult white males did own land and thus could vote.

Even poor people could eventually own land in America. Many immigrants, either before or after they arrived in the colonies, hired themselves out as indentured servants—sometimes for as long as seven years—to someone already here. In a few cases indentured servants were treated no better than slaves. Some of them ran away. But if they worked out their full term, they usually received clothes and tools, and sometimes a little cash or even a piece of land to give them a new start in life. In America the shortage of labor and the abundance of land spelled opportunity—the chance to become a landowner.

Empty land creates slavery. To grow tobacco economically a planter needed a large estate and a sizable work force. It was easy to find the land, but hard to find the workers. Many indentured servants, once free, would go off and start their own farms. Why should they work for someone else?

Since the planters could not fill their labor needs with Europeans, they turned to slaves from Africa or the West Indies. The institution of slavery was ancient and familiar in western Europe and throughout Africa. People defeated in war, instead of being killed, were often enslaved. In Europe, with the passing centuries, slavery became reserved for people who were not Christians. They were called pagans. To justify the institution, slaveholders argued that they were helping pagans by making them into slaves so in time they could become Christians. When Jamestown was settled, slavery hardly existed in England. But English ships plied the slave trade between Africa and the Spanish colonies. And when the planters in the English colonies needed workers, they were supplied with African slaves.

Africans were not the only people who were brought to America by force. In England kidnappers seized unsuspecting poor people—children and adults—and then made a profit by selling them as indentured servants in the colonies. Political radicals, religious nonconformists—along with thieves and murderers—were "transported" to America as a punishment or simply to get them out of the way. When the term of their indenture was over, they were freed. But blacks, and sometimes Indians, were kept in slavery for life. Since Indians knew how to survive in the American wilderness, they could more easily run away. So southern planters turned more and more to using black slaves as their workers.

Worcester Art Museum

Isaiah Thomas's indenture papers apprenticed
him to a printer. During the Revolution
Thomas was the official printer for the
Massachusetts patriots. Later he became a
leading American publisher and founded the
American Antiquarian Society.

How the ocean tied some to England. The
southern colonies, stretching from Maryland and
Virginia down the seacoast to Georgia, were covered with plantations. In Maryland and Virginia
the planters grew tobacco, and in the Carolinas and
Georgia they grew rice and indigo (a blue dye used
by English textile manufacturers). In all these
colonies there were some small farmers growing
whatever they could.

The great plantations set the tone for these
southern colonies. To understand the plantation
South, we must understand Virginia.

Virginia was a land of riverways. Viewed from
Chesapeake Bay, Virginia had no solid seacoast but
was a half-dozen outreaching fingers of land separated by inreaching fingers of water. These were
the rich lowlands of "tidewater" Virginia, so called
because the ocean tides reach there. The land and
the sea seemed perfectly married. Deep navigable
rivers—the Potomac, the Rappahannock, the York,
and the James—divided Virginia into strips stretching southeastward. Each of these strips was nearly
an island. Each in turn was veined by smaller rivers,
many large enough to carry traffic to the ocean.

These riverways brought the whole world to the
door of every great plantation. From the ocean
came ships carrying slaves from Africa and the West
Indies, and carrying muskets, hoes, clothing, furniture, and books from London. Down to the ocean
went ships carrying large barrels (called hogsheads)
of tobacco from the broad plantations of the Lees,
the Carters, and the Byrds.

Every large plantation had its own dock. Goods
arrived there direct from London. Virginians felt
little need to have their own cities, for London was
their shopping center.

Planters with riverways running direct to London from their door felt close to Old England. In
those days before railroads, it was slow and expensive to carry anything across the land. It was easier
at that time for a Virginia family to get all the
way from London the products it needed than it was
for someone living five miles outside of London.
The ships that carried the large barrels of tobacco
back to England were happy to have a cargo to carry
to America. For very little cost they would bring
furniture and carriages from London to the wealthy
families of Virginia.

Planters could order from England almost everything they needed. Most purchases were made

Godfrey Meynall, an eyewitness, painted this watercolor of the hold of the slave ship *Albatross* in 1846. Similar conditions were the rule throughout the existence of the slave trade.

through an agent in London, generally the same man who helped sell the planter's tobacco there. The London agent ran a kind of mail-order shopping service. He supplied all sorts of things—a set of law books, a fancy bonnet, a case of wine, shoes for slaves. He arranged the English education of a planter's son or daughter. He reported this season's London styles and sent the latest market news. The London agent advised which recent books were worth reading, and he recounted court scandal or the latest trends in English politics. Sometimes he even helped a lonely bachelor-planter find a wife.

Virginia planters thought of themselves not so much as Americans, but as English country gentlemen who happened to live in America. They still relied on England for almost everything. The easiest way for them to send goods to Boston was to send the goods to London first, where they would be shipped out to Boston on an English vessel. Virginia Englishmen—including leaders of the American Revolution like George Washington and Thomas Jefferson—owed most of the furniture of their houses and of their minds to England.

The ocean that tied them to the English homeland helped them keep the habits and ideas of English gentry. With few exceptions they were moderate, sensible men and women. They would make no trouble and would stay loyal so long as they could prosper.

The colonies south of Chesapeake Bay also lived a tidewater life. This was true even though the Carolina and Georgia coast had shallow waterways which were harder to reach by ocean-going boat than the rivers in Virginia and Maryland. South Carolina's crops of rice and indigo were shipped to London from the deep harbor of the city of Charleston. Here many planters and their families would come to spend the summers away from the heat and malaria of their plantations. Charleston, one of the largest cities in America, had an active business life and more rich people for its size than any other city in the colonies. It was well known for its bustling, bubbling ways. It was a town full of people trying to rise, people trying to grow rich or richer. Most of Charleston's active trade was with England, so here too the ocean tied the people to the homeland.

Joshua Winsor was active in the mackerel and cod fishing industry. His house, built about 1768 in Duxbury, Massachusetts, was typical of seaside architecture. In the late 1700s Winsor's son-in-law, Dr. Rufus Hathaway, painted this picture showing the wharves, countinghouse, and fishing fleet. Winsor is in the foreground, holding his keys.

How the ocean led others out to the world. The same ocean that tied southern plantation owners to Mother England led the New Englanders elsewhere. The rough and rocky coast of New England offered few gateways to the interior. There were sheltered bays and deep harbors—Salem, Boston, Plymouth, and many others. But New England rivers, with few exceptions, ran steeply downhill. Although they were good for turning a millwheel, most of them were one-way streets tumbling to the ocean. In New England you could not take an ocean vessel very far inland.

New England bays became havens for big ships that traveled the oceans of the world. On the rocky New England soil, covered by snowy winters far colder than those of Old England, there grew no single staple crop. There was little tobacco, no sugar or indigo or rice. New England found its wealth in the sea.

"The abundance of sea-fish are almost beyond believing," Francis Higginson wrote in 1630, "and sure I would scarce have believed it with mine own eyes." There was seafood for every taste: mackerel, bass, salmon, lobster, herring, turbot, sturgeon, haddock, mullets, eels, crabs, mussels, clams, and oysters. A small quantity the New Englanders themselves ate. Most they dried, salted, and carried to far parts of the world. Some they sold to the Catholics of Europe, who ate much fish on Fridays. The scraps and leavings went to the Caribbean plantation owners as cheap food for their slaves.

Fishing became the main industry of Massachusetts Bay. In 1784 the Massachusetts House of Representatives voted "to hang up a representation

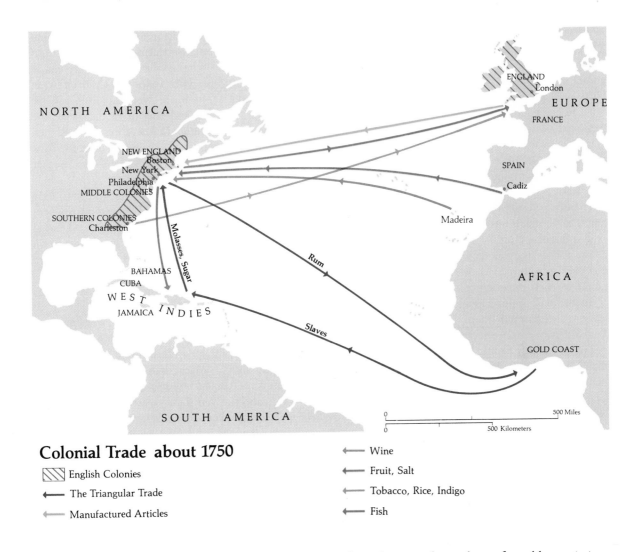

Colonial Trade about 1750

- ▨ English Colonies
- ← The Triangular Trade
- ← Manufactured Articles
- ← Wine
- ← Fruit, Salt
- ← Tobacco, Rice, Indigo
- ← Fish

Map labels: NORTH AMERICA, EUROPE, ENGLAND, London, FRANCE, SPAIN, Cadiz, NEW ENGLAND, Boston, New York, Philadelphia, MIDDLE COLONIES, SOUTHERN COLONIES, Charleston, Madeira, AFRICA, BAHAMAS, CUBA, WEST INDIES, JAMAICA, Molasses, Sugar, Rum, Slaves, GOLD COAST, SOUTH AMERICA, 500 Miles, 500 Kilometers

of a codfish in the room where the House sit, as a memorial of the importance of the codfishery to the welfare of the Commonwealth." The codfish became the totem of the state. It hung over the Speaker's desk until the middle of the twentieth century.

The New England fisheries actually helped bring on the Revolution. Deep-sea fishermen need ships, and the New Englanders began building their own fishing ships in large numbers. This worried the English. They wanted to be sure the trade of the New Englanders benefited the mother country. And this was one of the reasons why the English clamped the Navigation Acts on the colonies, telling them where they could sail their ships and limiting where they could carry some of the produce of the colonies. Over the years the English went on to

tighten their senseless and unenforceable restrictions against colonial trading (p. 58). Faneuil Hall (which still stands in Boston), the meeting place of the Massachusetts rebels, was given to the city by Peter Faneuil, son of a French Huguenot immigrant and one of the many merchants who had become rich by shipping New England codfish to forbidden distant markets.

Why should bold and adventurous New England sailors obey boundaries marked off by a few English politicians? Even before the new United States was launched as a nation, New England sailors were showing their independence. They were shipping whatever they could find or make—and to wherever they were attracted by whim or profit.

New England ships roamed the world. Their sailors went to Portugal, Spain, France, Syria, the

West Indies, Brazil, Guinea, and Madagascar. They carried fish to trade for salt from Cadiz, wine from the Azores and Madeira, iron from Bilbao, grapes from Málaga, and oranges from Valencia to ports in England and the colonies. To get oil to burn in their lamps for light, whaling expeditions went out on long voyages from New Bedford and Nantucket south to the coast of Brazil and north to the Arctic Ocean. They took rum from New England ports to the west coast of Africa, where they traded it for slaves whom they then took to the Caribbean and sold for sugar, which was then taken north to be made into more rum. This was called "the triangular trade." They were willing to "trye all ports," as they said, with all kinds of freight. Nothing was too small or too big for their commerce or their imaginations.

In the days before independence when English laws still hemmed them in, enterprising New Englanders had to be smugglers. For them, American independence would be a great relief. It would make them honest, law-abiding traders. But long before the American Revolution, the minds and hearts and pocketbooks of bold New Englanders were attached to the whole world.

The Dutch, Germans, Swedes, and Finns who had settled in the Middle Colonies (New York, New Jersey, Pennsylvania, and Delaware) had no special ties with England. Their relatives were in their own homelands. For them the ocean was a highway to everywhere.

These Middle Colonies had the best-balanced economies of any of the English colonies. A wide variety of products came from the rich soil of their farms. Unlike the southern planters they did not depend on a single staple crop sold in England. They sold their produce to merchants in the thriving cities of Philadelphia and New York. The city merchants in turn sent the produce overseas wherever they could find the best market—no matter what the Navigation Acts said.

Family life. Life in colonial America put heavy demands on the family. On the farm, where most Americans lived, labor was in short supply. Every member of the farm family had work to do. Women took care of the cows, hogs, and chickens, and made the butter and cheese. In the fields they were expected to sow, hoe, and reap the corn. They also sewed the clothes, cooked the food, and kept the simple houses clean and neat. A woman had to be a combination farmer, chef, and tailor!

In addition to all this the women bore many children. Families with 10 or 12 children were common, and 22 or more were not unheard of. From poor nutrition and lack of medical care the mortality rate was high. Many of the children died young. For the children who survived, in the back country where there were no schools the mother was their only teacher.

What doctors prescribed was less likely to cure than to kill the patient. A sensible person would try to stay out of the hands of a doctor. George Washington died in 1799 after he was bled of two quarts of blood by leeches and then "dosed to nausea and blistered to rawness." Even Washington's sturdy constitution could not survive that sort of treatment.

There were few things women were not expected to do in America. Most women married, and usually they helped their husbands on the farm or in the shop. After their husbands died, the women kept the farms and plantations running. Women also showed their versatile talents as shopkeepers, shoemakers, printers, newspaper publishers, teachers, lawyers, and even as blacksmiths, gunsmiths, and shipwrights. Although women could not hold office and usually could not vote, they took an active interest in politics.

One of the most remarkable colonial women was Margaret Brent. A large landholder in Maryland, she ran her own plantation and actually led a force of men to put down a rebellion against Lord Calvert in 1646. When Lord Calvert died, she was made the executor of his will. She ran his estates and collected his rents. She was also attorney for Lord Baltimore to take care of his affairs in Maryland. Naturally, she thought all this ought to give her the right to vote in the colonial assembly. When the new governor refused to let her have her rightful place in the colonial government, she moved to Virginia, where she made a new home and ran great estates until her death in 1671.

Few women were rich enough and willful enough to be as successful as Margaret Brent was in a man's world. The English common law which governed the colonies gave few legal rights to women. Husbands controlled the family property.

In those days, unlike ours, children were not allowed to make up their own minds. Parents decided whether a boy would be apprenticed to a shoemaker or a blacksmith, or be educated to become a minister or a lawyer. If not bound out as an indentured servant, the child worked for his parents, on the farm or in the shop.

Usually parents arranged marriages for their children. But in the New World things began to change. In New England more young people were beginning to be allowed to select their own mates.

The colonial family, of course, had no cars, no electric lights, no radios or television sets, no running water, no heat in winter except from the fireplace or, after around 1740, the iron stove. They had to take care of themselves and one another. They looked to other family members not only for love and advice, for food, shelter, and clothing, but they also needed them for their education and entertainment.

Education in the colonies. Compared to Europeans in their time, the American colonists were a well-educated people. Most were Protestants who believed that all Christians should be able to read the Bible. Massachusetts Bay Colony passed a law requiring every town of 50 families or more to maintain a school to teach the boys reading, writing, and arithmetic. Every town of 100 families or more was to have a "grammar school" where boys could

These portraits of Boston merchant and lawyer John Freake and of his wife, Elizabeth, with their child Mary are the work of an unknown artist in the 1670s. As the photograph of the tombstones of the six Langley children shows, many children died young.

The Pilgrim Society

The Metropolitan Museum of Art, Samuel D. Lee Fund, 1938

prepare for college. Girls had little formal education. Instead they were expected to learn the household arts of sewing, cooking, housekeeping, and childrearing. Books were not for them.

In 1636, only six years after the first settlers of Massachusetts Bay arrived in the New England wilderness, the people founded Harvard College. In the Old World, colleges and universities were ancient and honored institutions. Would it be possible to establish such an institution in the wilderness? The colonists said they needed Harvard College "to advance *Learning* and perpetuate it to Posterity; dreading to leave an illiterate Ministry to the Churches." Many farmers' sons went to Harvard to learn to serve as ministers or lawyers, judges or governors—or simply to be well-educated citizens.

Outside New England the colonies were not so quick to establish schools. Teachers lived with families while they taught the boys living nearby to read and write. Women opened "dame schools" to teach reading to young boys and sometimes even to girls. Where there were no schools, parents had to teach their children at home. On large southern plantations, private teachers were hired to live on the estate and instruct the children. Then the boys sometimes went back to England to attend college at Oxford or Cambridge. A few went to London or Edinburgh to study law or medicine.

By the time Yale was founded in Connecticut in 1701, there were only two other colleges: Harvard (1636) and William and Mary (1693) in Virginia.

But William and Mary remained little more than a grammar school for its first 35 years. Not until the 1740s were more colleges founded. Before that the colonies were too poor and the hardships and dangers of transportation too great. As the colonies flourished, new colleges appeared. Between 1746 and 1769, we see the founding of the College of New Jersey (Princeton), the University of Pennsylvania, King's College (Columbia) in New York, Rhode Island University (Brown), Queen's College (Rutgers) in New Jersey, and Dartmouth in New Hampshire. In 1784 Yale College, with its 270 students, had the largest student body. By the time of the American Revolution the colonies actually had a surprising number of institutions of higher learning. Of course they were not as well equipped—with libraries or scientific instruments—as their English counterparts. But for the remote New World colonies these colleges were a wondrous beginning.

Journalism and the arts and sciences. Outside the cities, life in the colonies was simple. "Some few towns excepted," wrote John Dickinson on the eve of the Revolution, "we are all tillers of the soil from Nova Scotia to West Florida." The settlers, busy creating a new life in a New World, did not have much time for the arts or sciences.

The first successful newspaper did not appear until 1704, and as late as 1754 three of the colonies still had no newspaper. Despite their small numbers, American journalists pioneered in free-

© Sotheby Parke-Bernet; Agent: Editorial Photocolor Archives

Colonial goods ranged from heavy carved and painted chests like this one made by the Pilgrims (right) to homemade items like this needlepoint card table cover stitched by Mercy Otis Warren (left) to luxurious silver objects like this bowl made by Cornelius Kierstede of New York.

dom. In 1733 a bold printer, John Peter Zenger, was arrested and tried for libel for printing articles critical of the governor of New York. But he went to court and won the right to print unpleasant political facts in his newspaper. This was a momentous step in establishing the freedom of the press in America. Gouverneur Morris later called the Zenger case "the morning star of that liberty which subsequently revolutionized America."

Colonial America, far from the Old World treasures of learning, produced a surprising number of original thinkers. Jonathan Edwards, though his writings are hard to understand, was a profound theologian who still has much to teach us. Benjamin Franklin won worldwide fame for his researches in electricity (he first suggested the lightning rod!) and his many practical inventions (he invented the Franklin stove). There were some others, too—other scientists, political philosophers, theologians, and historians.

Some colonists made their living as cabinetmakers and silversmiths. The desks designed by John Goddard of Newport, Rhode Island, were equal to the best made in Europe. Handsome silver bowls, beakers, and candlesticks by Paul Revere in Boston, Myer Myers in New York, and others in Newport, Philadelphia, and Charleston, adorned colonial tables and churches.

In those days before the camera, colonial painters traveled the countryside. They painted lifelike portraits for the family living room and for town halls. John Smibert, the Englishman who designed Faneuil Hall in Boston, preserved the faces of sturdy New England families. John Greenwood went to Surinam, where he portrayed the lonely sea captains away from home.

Most colonists, of course, could not afford fine furniture and silver or the price of a family portrait. At home they made what they needed. Their quilting, weaving, and needlework had a special simple charm. German gunsmiths in Pennsylvania turned out long rifles, which also were works of art.

American art reflected American lives. These were a practical people in search of a better life.

SECTION REVIEW

1. Suppose Margaret Brent wanted to employ the following people: Paul Revere, John Smibert, John Peter Zenger, John Goddard, and Myer Myers. What products or services would each provide?

2. If you were to visit Salem and Charleston in colonial times, what kinds of products would you expect to see on the ships that sailed from these two ports?

3. How did the large amounts of open land affect those who came to America?

4. How did the ocean tie some colonies to England and others to the rest of the world?

5. In what ways would your life be different from today if you were a colonial child? if you were a colonial woman?

2. The colonists govern themselves

For 150 years after the founding of the first English colony, new colonies were settled, and the English empire grew, with little attention from England. In the seventeenth century the English people had problems enough at home. They were moving from the medieval world of monarchy into a modern world of representative government. In England Parliament was demanding the power to govern the nation.

England from civil war to Glorious Revolution.
In the 1640s the English suffered through wars between the king and Parliament. After King Charles I was beheaded in January 1649, for a decade England was ruled by the obstinate and courageous Oliver Cromwell, who had led Parliament's army against the king. When Oliver Cromwell died, his son tried to rule, but failed dismally. Parliament called Charles II to the throne. Then Charles's brother, the foolish James II, who inherited the throne in 1685, soon alienated everyone.

The next explosion came with the "Glorious Revolution" in 1688. Then the king's opponents summoned William and Mary (daughter of James II) from Holland to take the throne as joint monarchs and preserve the power of Parliament. James II fled to France. When William and Mary came to the throne in 1689, they opened a new era of representative government. Parliament had shown that it was supreme. The monarch owed power to the people's representatives in the House of Commons. Never again would there be an absolute ruler in England.

William of Orange, who came to the throne with Mary, was also the leader of the Dutch. They had been fighting against France for their independence. The French under Louis XIV had replaced Spain as the dominant power on the continent. So in 1689, William brought England into the battle against France. From then until 1763, England fought four wars against the French on battlefields that stretched across the world—from Europe to India to Egypt to the West Indies to Canada. Meanwhile—when the government in London was too busy to notice—the American colonies were prospering. In 1763 England made peace with France. Then the government of England could turn its attention again to its colonies.

During these years of salutary neglect, the colonies developed their own institutions. These would make it difficult for England ever again to rule them. But now that peace had come, England intended to enforce the policy of mercantilism. This was the same policy that Spain had so long followed in its colonies (p. 28). Colonies were only servants of the mother country. It was the prosperity back home in England that was important. Colonists were not to be allowed to manufacture anything that competed with products at home. They must be encouraged to grow what England needed. They must not buy from anybody but the English; they must not ship their products to any country but England. To help the English shipbuilders, the colonists must use only English ships built in England or the colonies.

This was the theory. In fact, the policy was not enforced until after Cromwell took over. The Dutch had begun to trade with the colonists while England was embroiled in civil war. In this way the Dutch reaped profits that England wanted for itself. To bar the Dutch traders from America, Parliament passed a series of Navigation Acts. These laws, from the 1650s down to the 1770s, gave bounties to the colonists for growing certain crops and dictated what goods they could manufacture, in what ships they could transport their goods, where they could buy and sell.

Earlier laws listed only a few items that had to be bought directly from England. This list gradually grew longer. At first goods could be carried in any ships, provided these were *owned* by Englishmen, but by 1696, *all* trade between the colonies and England had to be carried in English-*built* (which included colonial-built) ships. *All* European goods for the colonies had to come from or through England. The principal colonial products could be exported only to England or to another British colony. Trade with the English or not at all!

It is not surprising that energetic people, who had crossed the ocean and were just beginning to explore the resources of a vast new world, would not let themselves be fenced in. They wanted to ship everywhere and buy everywhere.

Smugglers and pirates.
But the Navigation Acts were not regularly enforced. In fact they couldn't be. The British navy, busy fighting France, had no time left for trying to catch smugglers.

This painting from the 1750s shows British privateers and captured French ships in New York Harbor.

Smuggling then became a wonderfully profitable business in the colonial period. Many famous old New England and New York families like the Cabots, the Hancocks, and the Livingstons built their fortunes on colonial smuggling. It was descendants of these same families who looked down their noses at later immigrants in the nineteenth century. They said that these new arrivals might not have enough respect for law and order.

A "privateer" was a legally licensed pirate. After the first Navigation Acts, the word came into use about 1664 to describe someone who had a "private" ship that he used for government purposes. The owner of a private vessel in time of war could get a license from his government (called a "letter of marque," after the old French word meaning *to seize*) allowing him to seize enemy ships. Since he helped the war effort by crippling the enemy, he was allowed by his own king to keep a share of the loot. But when a privateer with a letter of marque happened to find any ship carrying a rich cargo, he was tempted not to take too much trouble to find out its exact nationality.

Once a privateer (or "pirate," to use the less respectable name) had loaded his ship with treasure, he would hurry to an American port, such as New York. In port, he simply showed his letter of marque and explained that he had seized his rich cargo as a patriotic duty to help the war effort. New York merchants, who themselves found this trade profitable, did not want to know whether the goods were from enemy ships or whether they were actually stolen goods. They were only too glad to have the privateers deliver merchandise to them that they could not buy from England, and which they were forbidden to buy elsewhere.

The pirates found New York especially to their taste. His Majesty's governor and officers were pleased to have them around. The pirates paid handsome "protection money" to the governor. He issued their letters of marque, and he protected them while they sold their booty. There were few other places in the world where the market for pirates' booty was so good. Prosperous New Yorkers were ready to pay high prices for all the glittering items—heavily carved and inlaid tables and chairs, filigreed daggers, feathered fans, ornate porcelain, and gold-embroidered cloth—that the pirates had captured from "enemy" ships trading with the Orient. In this way the unenforceable laws and the continuous wars of the British Empire transformed reckless pirates into respectable merchants.

The problems of governing.

Even if the American colonists had not already been independent minded and determined to govern themselves, the vast ocean would have made them so. In the days before the steamship or the transatlantic cable, the colonial office in London could not govern across three thousand miles of water. The ocean was the father of self-government.

When Charles II finally created the Lords of Trade in London in 1675 to manage colonial affairs, they had to do their business by mail. But in those days there was no regular mail service. Letters from London to Boston went by ships that depended on wind and weather and often took many weeks. If the mail-ship was captured by the French or Spanish, the letters were delivered to the bottom of the ocean.

Although each colony had its own representative assembly, the person who had the greatest power and the highest social prestige was the governor. In most colonies he came from England, but wherever he came from he received his orders from London. The Lords of Trade depended on him for information about his colony. But it was hard for him to get his messages across the ocean. If no ship was sailing, no message could go. The governor of North Carolina, for example, normally received his communciations by way of Virginia. In June 1745 the Board of Trade in London (successor to the Lords of Trade) wrote Governor Johnson of North Carolina complaining that it had had no letter from him in the past three years. A full year later he replied from North Carolina that their letter had only just reached him.

During the long New England winter when Boston Harbor was frozen or impassable, the whole colony received no word from the outside world. A letter that the governor of Massachusetts Bay wrote in late November was not likely to reach London before the following April or May. By that time the information it carried would be ancient history. Even if the mail actually reached an English port, there were more delays. It might take weeks or months for mail arriving at Bristol or Falmouth to be carried overland to London. Papers addressed to the Board of Trade were sometimes lost in the customshouse, or they might lie there for a year before anyone bothered to deliver them.

Still, the king did try, from time to time, to control the situation so he might rule his distant subjects. Of all his domains, New England was one of the most troublesome. With its rocky soil, it could grow few crops that England needed, and so it did not fit well into the mercantile system. Its adventurous seamen were always daring to trade in prohibited areas.

The people of Massachusetts Bay, the richest and most populous of the New England colonies, found countless ways to irritate their king and express their rebellious spirit. Determined to "obey God rather than man," they went their own way. They coined their own money. They left the king's name off their legal forms. They ignored the Navigation Acts. They banned the Anglican church. They gave the vote only to their own church members. They even hanged Mary Dyer and three other Quakers on Boston Common.

Charles II had no love for these Puritan relatives of the fanatics who had beheaded his father. When Charles II sent commissioners to find out what was going on in the colony, they were insulted and ignored. Finally, in 1684, the king accused his unruly subjects of disobeying English laws. He managed to have his judges nullify the Massachusetts Bay Colony charter. The colony then became, like Virginia, a royal colony with a governor and council appointed by the king.

The Dominion of New England.

In 1685 James II succeeded his brother Charles II on the throne. James had been the proprietor of New York and New Jersey, so when he became king they automatically became royal provinces. From that start, on the advice of the Board of Trade, James decided to unite New York and New Jersey with all the New England colonies into one large Dominion of New England. It would be ruled by a single royal governor assisted by a council also appointed by the crown. Representative assemblies would be abolished. At last the king himself would really rule.

All of these changes were bad enough for the independent colonists. James II made matters worse by appointing as governor Edmund Andros, a faithful servant and honest man, who happened also to be harsh, narrow, and unbending. He quickly antagonized everyone. At first non-Puritans and some wealthy merchants who were tired of the "rule of the Saints" in Massachusetts welcomed Andros. But he soon lost their support, too, when he tried to stop their smuggling along with the privateering and the piracy that made them rich.

The colonists were saved from Andros and the Dominion of New England by the Glorious Revolution of 1688. Without even waiting to hear if it was a success, the people of Boston seized Governor Andros and threw him in jail. Then the separate colonies went back to running their own affairs.

England would not again try to combine colonies. It was just as well, because communication was too slow for the effective government of large areas from a single center. Anyway, each colony had become accustomed to governing itself.

William and Mary revise the colonial governments. At first, William and Mary had too many problems in England and Holland to worry about the colonies. But by 1696 the English merchants saw that they were losing large profits because the colonial merchants were flouting the mercantile laws. They complained to the king and demanded that he turn his attention to America. He then formed a new Board of Trade (its full title was "the Lords Commissioners of Trade and Plantations") to oversee colonial affairs. For each colony he provided a regular customs service and special Admiralty Courts (which had no juries) to catch and punish New England smugglers.

He imposed "royal" government on one colony after another. This meant rule by governors appointed by the king. In 1682 there were only two royal provinces, Virginia and New Hampshire. By 1729 all the colonies except Connecticut, Rhode Island, and Georgia had governors either named by the crown or appointed by proprietors subject to the king's approval (Pennsylvania, Delaware, and Maryland). Georgia became a royal colony in 1752.

The colonists did not really suffer much from these new efforts to enforce the Navigation Acts. Customs officers were glad to be bribed. The Admiralty Courts became tangled in all sorts of legal technicalities. The royal governors found that they could not govern without the agreement of the colonial assemblies.

This "Old Colonial System," as the years of salutary neglect were called, turned out to be a "system" for not enforcing the Navigation Acts. It seemed to work as long as everybody agreed to leave well enough alone. And so during the many years while England's wars kept the government busy, the population of the colonies grew and their wealth accumulated. Between 1700 and 1760 the foreign trade of the thirteen mainland colonies increased fivefold.

SECTION REVIEW

1. Identify or explain: letter of marque, Charles I, Oliver Cromwell, Charles II, James II, William and Mary, Edmund Andros.
2. What was the meaning of the Glorious Revolution for the British colonies in America?
3. What was the Dominion of New England and why was it important?
4. Summarize the provisions of the Navigation Acts. Why were these laws not strictly enforced?
5. Why was it difficult for England to govern America?
6. What was the Old Colonial System?

3. Britain against France

The growth of the English colonies made a clash with France inevitable. From Louisbourg through Quebec, Montreal, Detroit, Sault Ste. Marie, Vincennes, and Natchez to New Orleans and Mobile a string of French forts tied together an immense, thinly settled empire.

For some time the French and English stayed far enough apart so that they did not bother each other. But the English were ever pushing westward. And after the Glorious Revolution when the energetic Dutch leader William of Orange and his popular wife, Mary, came to the English throne, it was not long before the two leading colonial powers of North America were at war.

America was a battlefield for European rivalries. A series of conflicts began as attacks by French soldiers and by their Indian allies upon outlying English settlements. King William's War (1689–1697), Queen Anne's War (1702–1713), and King George's War (1744–1748) climaxed in the French and Indian War proper (1754–1763). Life on the frontier became a nightmare. Unpredicted attacks by French regular troops and Indians were followed by massacres. Scalps were taken. Men, women, and children were kidnapped.

The Deerfield Massacre.

One cold night in February 1704 the 300 inhabitants of the frontier village of Deerfield, Massachusetts, were sound asleep. Suddenly the silence was broken by French and Indian war cries. Within a few hours 50 settlers were dead and 17 of their houses burnt to the ground. One hundred and eleven settlers (including the town's minister, John Williams, his wife, Eunice, and one of his children) were taken prisoner. Eunice Williams, weakened by recent childbirth, could not keep up with the group as they were hastened north through the winter snow. She and others who fell behind were tomahawked and left to die.

Most of the tough New England settlers were more lucky. All but 17 of the 111 captives lived through the march to Canada. Finally, 60 of the Deerfield villagers, including John Williams himself, returned to the English colonies. Of those who did not go home, some died, some married Canadians, some converted to Catholicism, and a few, including Williams's own daughter, married Indians and made a new life with their captors.

The colonial reaction.

English colonists reacted to these raids by attacking Quebec or some other stronghold in New France. Once, in 1745, they captured Louisbourg, France's Gibraltar in the New World. When the English government returned Louisbourg in exchange for Madras in India, New Englanders were outraged. Their interests seemed to count for nothing when the government back home saw a chance to add a distant piece to the empire.

By 1750, English colonists were beginning to make their way through the Allegheny barrier into the valleys that led down to the Ohio and the Mississippi rivers. The governors of the English colonies called for forts to protect them against the French. The French, at the same time, moved vigorously to bolster their defenses. In one of the backwoods clashes, at Great Meadows near the forks of the Ohio where Pittsburgh now stands, a Virginia militia force was commanded by 22-year-old George Washington. There he won his first skirmish, but was soon forced to retreat to Virginia.

The Albany Plan of Union.

The war that began at Great Meadows in 1754 was to continue until 1763. During these years battles were fought not only in America and in Europe, but even in India. This was truly a world war. Even before it had begun, American leaders had been calling for some union of the colonies. Now it seemed urgent against the bloody French and Indian menace.

In June 1754, just two weeks before Washington had to retreat from the French force, a colonial congress met at Albany, New York. Albany was then a small town on the Hudson River, sheltered from attack by a wooden stockade. The Iroquois in that area had long helped to protect the English from attacks down the Mohawk Valley because their traditional enemies, the Hurons, were allied with the French. The Albany meeting had been ordered by the British government to try to keep the Iroquois happy and firmly allied with the British.

The Albany Congress, attended by 150 Indians and representatives of seven colonies, renewed the alliance with the Iroquois. At the same time the colonial delegates voted to adopt a plan suggested by Benjamin Franklin for a new union of the colonies.

A Grand Council of 48 members (similar to that which the Iroquois used to govern their tribe) was to be chosen by the colonial legislatures. Meeting annually, this council would regulate Indian affairs, control a colonial army, manage the public lands, pass laws for the general good, and levy taxes for the common defense. A president-general appointed by the king would name the other high officials and could veto laws passed by the council.

But even the threats of war on their borders could not unite the colonies in this sensible common plan. The colonial legislatures turned it down. Each colony feared it would lose its power to govern itself. The king also rejected the plan because he feared that the union might give all the colonies together too much self-government.

The French and Indian War.

At first the war that opened with Washington's skirmish at Great Meadows went badly for the English. To strengthen the defense of the colonies, in the summer of 1755 the British General Edward Braddock set out with 1400 British regular troops and 450 colonials to try to take Fort Duquesne. The French had built this fort at the point called "the

HUDSON'S BAY COMPANY

NEW FRANCE

BRITISH COLONIES

LOUISIANA

NEW SPAIN

FLORIDA

ATLANTIC OCEAN

GULF OF MEXICO

Ft. Louisbourg
Ft. Cumberland (British)
Port Royal
Quebec
Three Rivers
Montreal
Ft. La Pointe
Sault Ste. Marie
Ft. St. Croix
Ft. Michilimackinac
Ft. Frontenac
Ft. Oswego
Boston
Albany
Deerfield
Ft. Niagara
Ft. La Baye
New York
Ft. Trempealeau
Ft. Detroit
Ft. Presque Isle
Ft. St. Nicolas
Ft. Le Bouef
Philadelphia
Ft. St. Joseph
Ft. Venango
Ft. St. Louis
Ft. Duquesne
Ft. Miami
Great Meadows
Ft. Crevecoeur
Ft. Ouiatenon
Ft. Orleans
Vincennes
Jamestown
Kaskaskia
Ste. Genevieve
Ft. Prudhomme
Charleston
Arkansas Post
Savannah
Ft. Toulouse
Ft. Tombeche
Ft. St. Pierre
Mobile
St. Augustine
Natchez
Biloxi
New Orleans

Mississippi R.
Wisconsin R.
Lake Superior
Lake Michigan
Lake Huron
Lake Ontario
St. Lawrence R.
Lake Erie
Allegheny R.
Des Moines R.
Fox R.
Illinois R.
Wabash R.
Ohio R.
Platte R.
Missouri R.
Tennessee R.
Arkansas R.
Red R.
Mississippi R.
Tombigbee R.

New France and Louisiana before 1763

- French
- English
- Spanish

400 Miles

400 Kilometers

forks of the Ohio," where the Allegheny and Monongahela rivers meet.

Braddock had been warned by Benjamin Franklin, who was shrewd also in military matters, to watch out for surprise attacks by the Indians. But Braddock did not listen. He expected the Indians to behave like troops in the orderly wars in Europe. Over there, battles were usually fought only in good weather, when small professional armies faced each other on open fields. But the French and Indians did not follow the etiquette of Old World warfare. They caught Braddock off guard when they attacked his army from behind rocks and trees. The general was killed, and 976 of his men were killed or wounded.

In 1757, when the brilliant and self-confident William Pitt came to power as prime minister of England, he declared, "I am sure that I can save the country, and that no one else can." He put new life into the nation's armies and its fleets spread over the globe. He was the architect of the first British Empire. He removed weak commanders, jumped young men over older ones into positions of command, and gave colonial officers their due rank. Pitt realized that the British troops in America were fighting for a worldwide empire and not just defending American colonists. When he assured the colonies that England would pay the costs of raising and supporting their armies, the colonists offered the British their manpower and their cooperation.

In the campaigns of 1758, the British and Americans working together were victorious against the French all along the line. The cold and capable 41-year-old General Jeffrey Amherst and General James Wolfe, a bad-tempered upstart of 30, both of whom Pitt had promoted to command, recaptured the stronghold at Louisbourg. Another Pitt appointee, Lt. Col. John Bradstreet, led an expedition of 3000 men through miles of wilderness waterways to take Fort Frontenac on Lake Ontario. Since this cut the French line of communication between Canada and Fort Duquesne, the French troops there soon had to be withdrawn. The English occupied the fort and renamed it Fort Pitt (later Pittsburgh) in honor of England's great leader.

The fall of Quebec.

Pitt was now ready to carry out his grand strategy for the invasion of Canada. One army under General Amherst would go by the natural valley through the mountains up the Hudson River-Lake George-Lake Champlain route to attack Montreal in the heart of French Canada. At the same time another force under General Wolfe would come by sea up the St. Lawrence to attack Quebec in the east. Wolfe's expedition reached Quebec in June 1759. But from then until September, while the British fleet lay in the river before the great rock of Quebec, Wolfe vainly sought an undefended landing place.

After a summer during which he was painfully weakened and often forced to keep to his bed by a mysterious disease, it seemed that Wolfe had failed. But he did not give up. Instead he devised an ingenious surprise tactic. He shifted his forces one way to fool the French and then under cover of darkness slipped his men ashore at a point upriver where they were not expected. When daylight came, the French commander, the Marquis de Montcalm, was astonished to see the redcoats forming their lines of battle on the high Plains of Abraham west of the city.

In a battle in the classic European style the two sides drew up ranks and faced each other on an open field. Since Wolfe had trained his men in marksmanship (which was unusual at a time when muskets could be aimed only crudely), the powerful volleys of the English soon broke the French and gave Britain the victory. Both opposing generals—Wolfe and Montcalm—were mortally wounded.

The French tried but failed to retake Quebec that winter. The next summer when British General Amherst marched into Montreal, the French and Indian War in America was brought to an end. Elsewhere, war continued for two more years. Spain made the mistake of joining the conflict and lost Havana in Cuba and Manila in the Philippines. The French and Spanish empires in North America had begun to dissolve. Britain's navy now controlled the seas, and the British Empire reached from India west to the Mississippi River.

The Peace of Paris.

A peace treaty between Britain and France was signed in Paris in 1763. In the part of the treaty dealing with America, France ceded to England all of Canada and all French lands between the Mississippi and the Appalachian Mountains. France retained only two small islands south of Newfoundland—St. Pierre and Miquelon. These were not to be fortified and were only to be used for drying fish. England gave back to France the sugar islands—Guadeloupe and Martinique—it had seized in the West Indies. To its ally Spain, France ceded New Orleans and all its country west of the Mississippi, the land called Louisiana (after the French King Louis XIV). England kept Florida, but gave Havana and Manila back to Spain.

Before they sat down at the peace table, the English leaders saw that if they really wanted France to stop fighting they could not keep all the French lands taken during the war. They had to choose. Canada was vast. But its cold climate resembled that of New England, and the land produced little that the homeland needed. At the same time, the tiny Caribbean tropical island of Guadeloupe was rich in sugar, which England desperately wanted. Some argued, too, that if the French menace was removed from the colonial frontiers, it would be harder to keep the American colonies in line. According to the mercantile theory, Guadeloupe was clearly more valuable than Canada. But William Pitt had a wider vision. He saw that Canada might be the bulwark of a grand new empire.

Benjamin Franklin, who was in London at the time as a colonial agent, wrote a persuasive pamphlet on the subject in his usual simple style. He predicted that Canada would become a populous and prosperous agricultural community. Then Canadians would buy English goods and enrich the merchants of the homeland. American colonists who saw the English flag flying from the arctic seas to the Gulf of Mexico would be proud of their Englishness and doubly loyal to the homeland. The English, he said, need not fear that the colonists would ever unite against their own nation. If they had not been able to unite against the French and Indians, surely they would never combine against the land of their beloved ancestors.

Franklin won his point. England took Canada from France and gave back Guadeloupe. Thirteen years later the colonies declared their independence.

SECTION REVIEW

1. Identify: Edward Braddock, James Wolfe, Montcalm, William Pitt, Jeffrey Amherst.
2. Locate: Sault Ste. Marie, Vincennes, Natchez, Great Meadows, Fort Pitt, Lake Champlain, Plains of Abraham, Guadeloupe.
3. Describe the Albany Plan of Union.
4. Why did some people believe that England should give Canada back to France and take Guadeloupe instead?
5. Summarize the terms of the Peace of Paris.

CHAPTER REVIEW

MEETING OUR EARLIER SELVES

1. By 1765 about 40 percent of the settlers in the English colonies were of non-English stock. What were some effects of this mixture?
2. Why did plantation owners turn to using slaves to grow and harvest their crops? What effect do you think this may have had on where immigrants chose to settle? Why?
3. Why did colonial artists specialize in painting portraits?

4. How did American colonial crafts reflect American lives?
5. What evidence can you find to show that there was an "American Revolution" under way long before fighting broke out? What was the nature of that revolution?
6. Britain's "old colonial system" worked best when it worked least. Why?
7. To what extent was America involved in a "world war" from 1689 to 1763? How did this involvement shape the future of the colonies?

QUESTIONS FOR TODAY

1. A recent Census Bureau report estimated that about 12 percent of our country's population was of English, Scottish, and Welsh origin. Have English influences on American culture declined in proportion to the drop in "English" population? Explain.
2. How did the training of children for adult responsibilities differ in colonial times from today?
3. In what ways is mercantilism like our modern ideas of trade? How is it different?

YOUR REGION IN HISTORY

1. How, if at all, did the Peace of Paris (1763) affect the region where you live?
2. What settlements (Indian or colonial) existed within 50 miles of your home by 1763? What was life like there?

SKILLS TO MAKE OUR PAST VIVID

1. How would each of the following kinds of evidence help explain the development of the "new American"? Why? (a) The letters between the Board of Trade in London and the governor of North Carolina between 1740 and 1760. (b) The diary of a New England merchant and sea captain who traded along America's coast between 1740 and 1760. (c) An eyewitness account of the proceedings of the Albany Congress in 1754.
2. As an unhappy Quaker living in the Massachusetts Bay Colony in 1670, you decide to travel overland to the "Quaker colony." List the colonies and major towns you will travel through before you reach your destination.

2

Forming a new nation
1763–1800

The American Revolution began on April 19, 1775, with the battles at Lexington and Concord. This engraving of the battle at the North Bridge in Concord, from the Print Division, The New York Public Library, was made by Amos Doolittle in 1775.

Winning the American Revolution, John Adams once said, was like trying to make thirteen clocks strike at once. The colonies were so different that it would have been an astonishing coincidence if they had come to the same idea at the same time. Starting as colonies at different times and with different goals, they moved to independence in thirteen different ways. To bring the people of any one colony—of Massachusetts or Pennsylvania or New York—to agree was difficult enough. To lead thirteen different colonies to take common action seemed next to impossible. This was the main American problem in the War of Independence.

But the variety of the colonies turned out to be a secret weapon in the war. If the Americans were dispersed, if they lacked any single headquarters, this made trouble for the enemy. The colonies were like a monster with many heads. They could survive the loss of several of them. Nothing was more baffling to the British generals. Nothing did more to make it impossible for the British to win the war.

In peacetime, when the new nation was being born, this peculiarly American variety again became a problem. Each new state wanted to act like an independent nation. It was hard for the new states to see that they ought to work together. During the early years under a new constitution, the Americans were still trying to find out what it meant to be the people of one nation.

CHAPTER 4

The road to revolution and victory

In 1763 few people in Great Britain's American colonies would have foreseen that in little more than a decade the colonists would declare their independence. Fewer people, still, would have predicted that in a revolutionary war the thirteen former colonies, which had never been able to cooperate on anything, would be able to defeat the most powerful nation in the world. Yet strangely enough, against all belief, that is exactly what happened.

1. The British take a collision course

After their victory over the French in 1763 the British Empire was bigger than ever, which made the thirteen American colonies only a small part of the empire. To the north of the thirteen colonies the British had now added all of Canada, and to the west and south all the regions east of the Mississippi River, including Florida. The people living in these vast lands became new members of the British Empire.

The British situation in 1763. Between the Appalachian Mountains and the Mississippi River there lived 200,000 Indians who were now part of Britain's new empire. They had heard stories from the French that their new English masters were going to rob them of their hunting grounds. Indeed, in the spring of 1763 the Shawnee, Delaware, Seneca, and Ottawa were in the forefront leading the Indians of the West on the warpath.

By June the tribes had captured eight of the eleven British forts west of the mountains, and many settlers had died. Only Niagara, Fort Pitt, and Detroit remained, and Detroit was under siege by the Ottawa led by their able chieftain, Pontiac. This garrison was of such strategic importance that

the British came to call the whole war "Pontiac's Conspiracy."

The British were so desperate that they even resorted to sending blankets infected with smallpox to the tribes. Many Indians died of the disease. Illness and British troops broke most Indian resistance by 1764, but not until the following year were Pontiac and his followers put down.

The English government came to the conclusion that it would take a standing army of 10,000 men to control the western Indians and to protect all the American colonies. This task they could not entrust to the colonists. The French in Canada did not like their conquerors. The Americans could not even unite to defend themselves. In fact, some of them had even aided the enemy by carrying on forbidden trade with the French and Spanish West Indies. So the government would have to send over an army to America. And it was decided the colonists ought to be made to pay part of the costs of this army sent to protect them.

The Proclamation Line of 1763. The trouble really began when the well-meaning men running the government in London decided in 1763 to set this far-flung empire in order. Their plans were much too simple and old-fashioned to work on a continent that was nearly all wilderness. To prevent fighting among the colonies, and to avoid war with the Indians, the officials in London decided to try to keep the colonists confined where they already were. Settlement of the new lands would have to wait until Indian relations and a land policy were worked out.

The British thought that the Appalachian Mountains, which ran roughly parallel to the Atlantic coastline a few hundred miles inland, would be a useful barrier to keep the colonists separated from the Indians in the west. They proclaimed that for the time being the colonists should not settle on the western side of those mountains, and that the Indians should not go eastward.

This Proclamation Line of 1763 was a neat enough idea, but hardly designed to please Virginians. They were always looking for new tobacco land and were hoping also to make money from wilderness real estate. Virginians and other colo-

nists wanted to go west now. Was not the continent theirs every bit as much as it was the Indians'?

The Sugar Act of 1764. At the same time George Grenville, who was in charge of the British treasury (his title was "Chancellor of the Exchequer"), was desperately looking for ways to pay the bills left over from a century of wars. He was aware of how much the American colonists had eventually benefited from the successful outcome of the British wars against the enemies of the empire. In the backwoods, colonists had seen their homes burned and their families killed by the French and Indians. On the sea, colonial merchants had lost ships and goods to marauding French and Spanish and Dutch privateers. The empire had come to their aid and ended all that. Why should not Americans now at last pay a fair share of the bills for keeping peace and defending the empire?

Grenville therefore persuaded Parliament to pass the Sugar Act in 1764. This act replaced the old

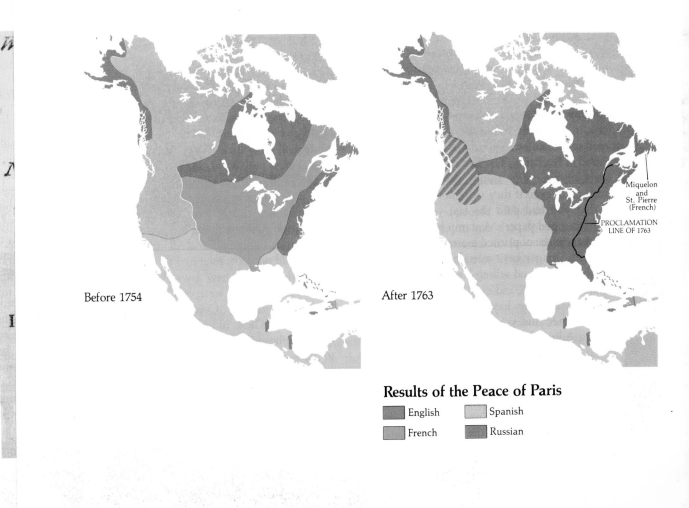

Before 1754

After 1763

Miquelon
and
St. Pierre
(French)

PROCLAMATION
LINE OF 1763

Results of the Peace of Paris

English   Spanish
French   Russian

gave British troops in America the power to take over taverns, and even to live free of charge in private homes.

To these measures Parliament foolishly added the Quebec Act, which seemed one more attack on the colonists' freedom. From the British point of view the Quebec Act was only an innocent attempt to organize into the empire the area taken from France in the French and Indian War. But when the act extended the province of Quebec southward to the Ohio River, it cut off the claims of Massachusetts, Connecticut, Virginia, and New York to their western lands. For that area the act set up a government without a representative assembly and gave special privileges to the Catholic church. The irritated and suspicious colonists saw the Quebec Act as a signal of what might happen to the thirteen colonies.

SECTION REVIEW

1. Identify or explain: Pontiac, George Grenville, Molasses Act of 1733, Sugar Act of 1764, Sons of Liberty, Declaratory Act, Townshend Acts, Sam Adams, Boston Massacre, Committees of Correspondence.

2. What was the Proclamation Line of 1763?

3. Why did the Americans oppose the Stamp Act?

4. What were the Intolerable Acts? Why were they passed?

5. Why did the colonists view the Quebec Act as a threat?

2. Declaring independence

Until the conflicts with the British government, the colonies had gone their separate ways. There had not been any congress or any central government where all thirteen colonies could meet and talk about their problems. Franklin and others had tried to persuade the colonies to join hands, but with very little success. Now within only a few years, the bungling politicians in London did more to push the colonies together than colonial statesmen had accomplished in over a century.

The First Continental Congress. In response to a call from Massachusetts to stop all trade with Great Britain, twelve of the colonies—all except Geor-

gia—sent delegates (56 altogether) to Carpenters' Hall in Philadelphia on September 5, 1774. The meeting called itself the Continental Congress. It was not really the congress of any government, for there was no *American* government. It could be nothing more than a *continental* congress—a collection of delegates from the colonies that happened to be neighbors on the same continent.

At first each colony believed it had all the powers of a nation. Yet, because each had been part of the British Empire, many of the usual tasks of a national government—for example, building an army or navy, or conducting diplomacy—had been left to London. When the First Continental Congress met, then, it had to start from scratch.

The delegates to the Congress were men of widely varying views. Joseph Galloway, a conservative lawyer from Philadelphia, revived the Albany Plan that Benjamin Franklin had proposed twenty years before. Sam Adams and Patrick Henry desired outright independence. No one got his way entirely, but Sam Adams cleverly led the delegates along the radical path.

The Congress agreed to form a Non-Importation Association and cease all trade with Great Britain. Committees chosen in every county and town were to see that the boycott was obeyed.

The delegates also dealt with the difficult problem of the relationship of the colonies to Parliament. In a Declaration of Rights and Grievances written by John Adams, the Congress appealed to both the unchangeable "Laws of Nature" and the British constitution to deny any right of Parliament to tax the colonies. The colonists, they told the British government, could only be taxed by their own assemblies. To show that they were not unreasonable, however, they agreed to *allow* Parliament to regulate trade as it had in the Navigation Acts before 1763.

The battles of Lexington and Concord. Some Americans still hoped somehow to find their way back into the empire. But, in April 1775, within a few months after the First Continental Congress, dramatic events would put an end to their hopes. Massachusetts had been hardest hit by the British acts of force. And, without waiting for others, Massachusetts began to prepare for war by collecting military supplies in the little town of Concord, about twenty miles inland from Boston.

When the British Secretary of State for Colonies heard of this, he decided to act quickly to destroy that first supply base before the Americans were any better organized. Bostonians learned of the plan and on the night of April 18, 1775, sent Paul Revere and William Dawes on their celebrated ride to Lexington, which was on the road to Concord. They warned Americans to form ranks to stop the king's troops before they could reach and destroy the colony's Concord supply base.

Early the next morning when the 700 British troops reached Lexington, they found 70 American minutemen—militia who had agreed to be ready at a minute's warning—arrayed against them on the town common. The British killed eight and wounded ten Americans before hastening to Concord. As if by magic, the countryside sprang to arms. From nowhere appeared thousands of American militiamen. They harassed the British troops, who, before returning to their ships in Charlestown Harbor, suffered nearly 300 dead and wounded while the American losses were fewer than 100.

Now talk was at an end. War had begun. There was no turning back.

The Second Continental Congress.

When delegates from twelve colonies (all but Georgia's, who arrived late) met again in their Second Continental Congress in the Philadelphia State House in May 1775, they were no longer American children pleading for better treatment from their British parent country. Instead they were armed colonists demanding their rights. George Washington was chosen commander in chief of the "Continental Army," which was drawn up around Boston. It could not be called the Army of the United States, for there was yet no United States.

The Continental Congress quickly realized that they would need a navy. Following the old British example, the Congress, with their own letters of marque, began creating privateers. But now they were *American* privateers in hot pursuit of all British ships.

The Battle of Bunker Hill.

Sixteen thousand militiamen from New Hampshire, Connecticut, Rhode Island, and Massachusetts gathered around Boston after the battles of Lexington and Concord. Even before Washington could join his troops, these

Broadsides or posters were used to recruit volunteers for privateers to attack British ships.

colonial militia met the English regulars in the bloodiest conflict that had ever taken place on the soil of British North America.

During the night of June 16, colonial militia under Colonel William Prescott were sent to fortify Bunker Hill across the water from Boston. By mistake, he and his men fortified Breed's Hill, and that was where a great battle was fought. But it was given the name of Bunker Hill—the hill where they should have been!

The next day the British decided to drive the Americans away from Breed's Hill. Twice the redcoats charged up the hill against Americans who were behind a rail fence stuffed with hay. Twice they were met with deadly fire and driven back with terrible losses. On the third attack the colonials, with powder gone, were forced from their position with bayonets.

But the American defeat in the Battle of Bunker Hill was a moral victory. It showed that the raw colonial troops could face regulars without flinching. When Washington heard of the battle, he said, "The country is safe." The British General Howe's loss of 1000 men was more than double that of the Americans. One-eighth of all the British officers killed in the Revolutionary War fell at Bunker Hill. "I wish we could sell them another hill at the same price," said one American officer.

The Americans offer peace and go to war. After Bunker Hill the Continental Congress sent a petition, called the Olive Branch Petition, to King George. It asked the king to stop the efforts of Parliament to enslave them and said that they wanted peace and harmony with England. The king refused to receive the petition. But even before that, on July 6, 1775, Congress issued a spirited declaration of war:

> We are reduced to the alternative of choosing an unconditional submission to the tyranny of irritated ministers, or resistance by force. The latter is our choice. We have counted the cost of this contest, and find nothing so dreadful as voluntary slavery. . . . Our cause is just. Our union is perfect. . . . In defense of the freedom that is our birthright . . . we have taken up arms. We shall lay them down when hostility shall cease on the part of the aggressors.

Though Congress still said that it did not want to separate from Great Britain, the breach between the two sides deepened. The king hired 30,000 mercenary troops from the German princes of Brunswick, Hesse, and Anhalt to help put down the rebels. In America, royal governors took refuge on warships. Their legislatures were refusing to obey them and were converting themselves into popular conventions controlled by the radical leaders. Congress was laboring to increase Washington's army and provide it with food, clothing, and money.

Brave captains of speedy privateers were attacking British supply ships and seizing barrels of flour and gunpowder. Eighty yoke of oxen were dragging cannons, captured in May at Fort Ticonderoga by Ethan Allen and the Green Mountain Boys, over the December snow to Boston. Richard Montgomery and Benedict Arnold were leading American troops to invade Canada. On the last day of 1775, in the midst of a blinding snowstorm, Montgomery was killed and Arnold severely wounded in a vain attempt to capture the town of Quebec. So ended the patriot effort to conquer Canada.

Common Sense *stirs the colonies.* On January 15, 1776, the most influential pamphlet ever to be published in America appeared. *Common Sense* was written by Thomas Paine, an Englishman who had come to America on Franklin's advice to help the cause of freedom. Paine urged that it was simply

This engraving of the Battle of Bunker Hill was made by Bernard Romans, an eyewitness, who was captain of a Pennsylvania artillery company. Later captured, he was taken to England.

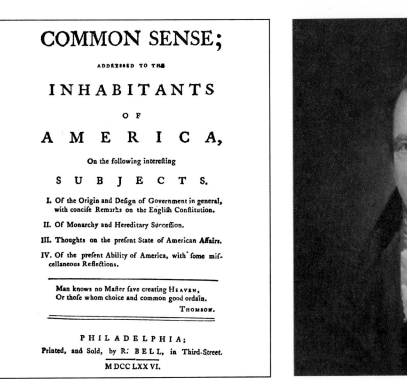

COMMON SENSE;

ADDRESSED TO THE

INHABITANTS

OF

AMERICA,

On the following interesting

SUBJECTS.

I. Of the Origin and Design of Government in general,
with concise Remarks on the English Constitution.

II. Of Monarchy and Hereditary Succession.

III. Thoughts on the present State of American Affairs.

IV. Of the present Ability of America, with some miscellaneous Reflections.

Man knows no Master save creating HEAVEN,
Or those whom choice and common good ordain.
THOMSON.

PHILADELPHIA;
Printed, and Sold, by R. BELL, in Third-Street.
MDCCLXXVI.

Thomas Paine's 47-page pamphlet *Common Sense* roused the colonies against British rule. The painting of Paine is by John Wesley Jarvis, one of the leading portraitists of the time.

"common sense" to stop recognizing the "royal brute," King George III. America should break all connection with Great Britain. This nation, he wrote, was destined to show the whole world how a people could rule themselves and be free of the tyranny of kings and nobles.

Common Sense swept the colonies. More than 100,000 copies were quickly sold. Many colonists agreed with George Washington that Paine's reasoning left no room for rebuttal. Edmund Randolph, a Virginia statesman, believed that, next to King George, Thomas Paine was the man most responsible for the declaration of our independence.

The British leave Boston.

Washington brought the long siege of Boston to an end in March 1776 by seizing Dorchester Heights. There the cannon brought from Fort Ticonderoga over the snow looked down upon the town and the British fleet in the harbor. This forced the British general, William Howe, to sail away with his troops to Halifax, Nova Scotia. With Howe went 1100 Tory refugees (Loyalists, the British called them) representing many of the "best families" of the colony.

Secret aid from France.

What the Americans most needed was the aid of France with its great navy and, if possible, also the aid of Spain. So in March 1776 Silas Deane of Connecticut was sent to France to ask for help in men and money. To encourage this aid, the Continental Congress on April 6, 1776, at one stroke abolished a whole century's accumulation of Navigation Acts. They opened all American ports to all nations of the world, except Britain.

Meanwhile, fortunately for the Americans, the French were already conspiring with the Spanish to use this opportunity to tear apart the British Empire. The French King Louis XVI secretly arranged to supply gunpowder to the American rebels. From the French the American armies received nearly all the gunpowder they used during the first two years of war. But this was only the start of French aid.

The Declaration of Independence. In May the Congress advised all the colonies to form their own governments. American independence was rapidly becoming a fact. The Americans had set up their own Congress, they had organized their own army, they were beginning to organize a navy. They had already plainly declared commercial independence by abolishing all the British laws of navigation. Then, on July 2, 1776, the Continental Congress adopted a short resolution "that these United Colonies are, and of right ought to be, free and independent states," and that all political connection with Great Britain was now broken.

With the resolution on July 2, Americans *announced* their independence. They gave out the news that a new nation was born, but they had not yet given out the reasons. Strictly speaking, American independence was not yet *declared*. ("Declare" comes from the Latin word meaning *to make clear.*) It was not the mere announcement, but the "declaration"—the explanation—of independence that Americans would always celebrate. For Americans were proud of the reasons for the birth of their nation. These reasons gave the new nation a purpose that it would not forget.

One of the remarkable things about the United States, which made it different from the older nations of Europe, was that it could actually point to the reasons why it had become a separate nation. These reasons were listed in a Declaration of Independence prepared and approved by the very men who made the nation independent.

Three weeks before the Continental Congress adopted its brief resolution announcing independence, it had named a committee to prepare a longer Declaration of Independence. Virginia's brilliant Thomas Jefferson, then only 33 years of age, was appointed chairman. Also on the committee were John Adams and Benjamin Franklin, but Jefferson did the writing and the others only changed a word here and there.

Jefferson did not try to be original in the Declaration; he only tried to state clearly what everybody already believed. He tried to write the common sense of the subject. He was speaking to the whole world. It was no good trying to persuade the world unless you started from what lots of people everywhere already believed. That is precisely what Jefferson did.

The opening part of the Declaration, usually called the "preamble," was cribbed from various books and declarations that Englishmen had written a hundred years before when, at the time of the Glorious Revolution, they removed James II and replaced him with William and Mary. The British then could not possibly deny Jefferson's words in his Declaration—that governments derive "their just powers from the consent of the governed." Nor "that whenever any form of government shall become destructive of these ends"—life, liberty, and the pursuit of happiness—"it is the right of the people to alter or to abolish it, and to institute new government . . . in such form as to them shall seem most likely to effect their safety and happiness." Their own British government, as they were repeatedly saying after 1688, was made by precisely that formula. You could hardly call an idea radical if it was the basis of the very respectable government of England.

After the common sense in the preamble there came a long list—"a long train of abuses and usurpations." Every item showed how the British king, George III, had disobeyed his own laws. The king aimed to reduce the colonists to "absolute despotism," to establish "an absolute tyranny over these states." His many crimes included "cutting off our trade with all parts of the world," "imposing taxes on us without our consent," and "quartering large bodies of armed troops among us." They also included the king's crimes against the very special rights of Englishmen—for example, taking away the right of trial by jury and violating the legal charters given to the colonies.

The colonists, Jefferson explained, had shown great respect for their king and great love for their "British brethren." "In every stage of these oppressions we have petitioned for redress in the most humble terms: Our repeated petitions have been answered only by repeated injury." The king had proved himself a tyrant, "unfit to be the ruler of a free people." If the king would not respect the colonists' rights, the Americans had no choice. They had to set up their own government.

Jefferson's Declaration simply ignored the British Parliament. For, according to Jefferson, Parliament had no rights over the colonies. It was the king's duty to hold the empire together and to protect all his subjects. The Americans demanded nothing but

The Second Continental Congress approves the Declaration of Independence. Benjamin Franklin is seated in the center.

their simple rights as British subjects. The king had denied those traditional rights. The law was on the side of the Americans. If Americans wondered why they were fighting, here was their simple answer.

On July 4, 1776, Jefferson's Declaration of Independence was approved by the Second Continental Congress, signed by John Hancock, the president of the Congress, and certified by the secretary. Then copies were sent out to all the states. As new members arrived to represent colonies in Congress, they too signed the Declaration, even though they had not been there when Jefferson first presented it. As late as November some representatives were still signing (there were finally 56 signatures altogether). In this way, they showed that they believed in the Revolution.

Jefferson had written an eloquent birth certificate of the new United States, which would inspire people all over the world. A few years after the American Revolution was won, when the French people decided to defend their own rights against their king, they found inspiration in Jefferson's words. In the 1820s, when colonists in South America separated from Spain, they turned to the same source. Jefferson's Declaration of Independence, like other documents that live and shape history, has had the magical power to be filled with new ideas. In the twentieth century, when colonists in Asia and Africa tried to explain to the world why they were fighting for their independence, they still recalled the Declaration of Independence of the thirteen American colonies.

SECTION REVIEW

1. Match each of the following with another in the list: Joseph Galloway, Paul Revere, *Common Sense,* William Howe, William Dawes, Tories, First Continental Congress, Thomas Paine. Explain why each pair should go together.

2. Could one soldier have fought at Lexington, Bunker Hill, and Ticonderoga? Why?

3. Name three tasks the First Continental Congress accomplished.

4. The first shot fired at Lexington has sometimes been called "the shot heard 'round the world." Why?

5. Although losing at Bunker Hill, the patriots considered the battle a victory. Why?

6. Why did America need French aid? Why was France willing to help?

7. Why did the Second Continental Congress adopt a Declaration of Independence? Explain what it contained.

3. How British power was overthrown

America produced a new style of warfare. Here the skirmish, not the battle, was important. Communications did not exist, the land was vast. There was no way of directing operations from a center. Every man for himself! Colonists had learned to hide behind rocks and tree trunks.

"In our first war with the Indians," the Puritan missionary John Eliot noted back in 1677, "God pleased to show us the vanity of our military skill, in managing our arms, after the European mode. Now we are glad to learn the skulking way of war."

War in Europe in the 1700s. In Europe it was the Age of Limited Warfare. Armies fought according to certain definite rules, which made a battle in many ways like a football match. Battles took place on open fields, in good weather. Each side set up its men in neat array. Each side knew what forces the other possessed, and each part of an army was expected to perform only certain maneuvers. To begin a battle before the heralds had sounded their fanfares, to use sneak tactics or unusual weapons, were generally frowned upon.

The only people who fought were the professionals out there on the battlefield. Officers came from the aristocracy. They knew the rules and were willing to abide by them. At nightfall, or when the weather was bad, officers from opposing armies would actually entertain one another at dinner parties, concerts, and balls. Then the next day they would take their places on the battlefield. The privates were human dregs who had been dragged out of jails and bars. The best-trained and most reliable soldiers often were mercenaries—like the Swiss or the Hessians—who made a living from hiring themselves out to the highest bidder.

Patriotism had very little to do with those battles. Armies were small. The men were seldom fighting to preserve their country, but more often for some secret purpose known only to the monarch and his few advisers. By modern standards, the casualties were few. Weapons were crude. The old-fashioned musket had a poor aim, was hard to reload, and would not fire at all in wet weather—so armies had the pleasant custom of going into winter quarters. Kings could have their battles, and yet interfere very little with the peaceful round of daily life. The people could leave the fighting to the professional soldiers.

The American soldier. In America, the Indian had never heard of the polite tradition of war-by-the-rules. The Indian conducted a primitive form of total war. And the colonists' only good protection was a primitive form of total defense. Colonists could not leave their defense to professional soldiers far away on some neat battlefield. Where everybody was a target, every man, woman, and child had to be a soldier. Here, then, grew a new and American kind of army. The colonists called it their "militia." The militia was not really an army at all, but only a name for all the men who bore arms. Regular membership in the militia usually began at about 16 years of age, and might last till a man was 60. There was no uniform, not much discipline, and little of the colorful ritual of the European battlefields.

Still, against a professional army like that of the British Empire, the militia had some grave disadvantages. American militiamen often ran away or just stopped fighting if they felt like it. The very idea of enlistment—which kept men in the army even when it was personally inconvenient—did not suit the militia. These were vexing problems for George Washington. His forces consisted largely of militiamen, but he could never be sure how many he could count on.

Militia were a home guard and not an imperial army. They did not like to travel far from home. But the American Revolution had to be fought wherever the battle required and against a large regular army. George Washington's first, and probably his greatest, achievement was somehow to create a Continental Army.

This Continental Army was made up of men who were enlisted and paid by the Continental Congress. It was a small regular army of the European sort, but it could always be helped by the militia. If it was hard to bring the militia together, that was because they were spread all over the continent. In vast and trackless America, that itself could be helpful. You did not have to transport all your soldiers. Wherever you were, or wherever the enemy was, the militia was always there.

The major problem with the militia was that you could not depend on them. Forces of militia melted away whenever the men decided to go home to help bring in the harvest, or to be present at the birth of a child, or sometimes simply because they were tired of fighting. When General Washington begged

I. N. Phelps Stokes Collection, Prints Division, New York Public Library. Astor, Lenox and Tilden Foundations

This engraving by Amos Doolittle shows how British soldiers fought out in the open in neat rows and bright uniforms. From the Indians Americans had learned a different way of fighting. Here minutemen hiding behind a stone wall harass the British retreating from Concord in 1775.

Congress for a regular army organized in the European way, he complained that he had never seen a single instance of militia "being fit for the real business of fighting. I have found them useful as light parties to skirmish in the woods, but incapable of making or sustaining a serious attack."

So the militia were useful and useless. They were everywhere and nowhere. They might by their very presence keep an enemy from winning, but could a militia ever *win*?

Washington creates, and saves, an army.
After the evacuation of Boston by the British troops, the military history of the American Revolution falls into two stages. The first part was the critical period from 1776 to 1778, when fighting took place in the North. During this time Washington's greatest tasks were to organize an army and then keep it in the field and prevent it from being destroyed by the British. The second stage of the war came in the years 1779 to 1781. Washington had proved in the first phase that he could not be easily defeated, so fighting moved to the South, where the British hoped the Loyalists would rise to help them. If the southern colonies surrendered, the British expected that it would be easier to reconquer the North.

In the beginning of the first phase, Washington had to create a Continental Army and also fight the British. After the British left Boston, Washington moved to New York City and Long Island, where he expected the next attack. The British did not

83

disappoint him. In July and August 1776, they poured men and equipment onto Staten Island until they had a force there of 32,000 soldiers. New York City in normal times contained only 25,000 people! Washington faced this great force with 23,000 men, most of whom were militia.

The British general, William Howe, crossed from Staten Island and landed 20,000 well-trained soldiers on Long Island during August 22–25, 1776. They attacked Washington's untrained troops on the 27th, inflicting heavy casualties. The American army retreated, and Colonel John Glover and his Massachusetts regiment of Marblehead fishermen ferried the army together with its horses, cannons, food, and equipment across the East River to Manhattan Island under the cover of fog. In this retreat, and again in the retreat from Manhattan Island that followed when Howe's redcoats crossed the river on September 15, the most important thing was for Washington to get his army away. Had Washington's army been trapped at that time, the rebellion might have been over. Cities the British could have, for there was no center in America whose loss would really matter. But if the American army was lost, all might be lost.

The British followed Washington out of New York and across the Hudson River. As he retreated through New Jersey in November 1776, the redcoats were close behind. This was the low point of the war for Washington and for the American cause. The militia drifted off to their homes. The regular troops were on one-year enlistments that would end on December 31. With the military situation looking so bleak, they would not re-enlist, and new men were unlikely to take their places. Washington's army would just fade away.

On December 7, 1776, Washington crossed the Delaware River into Pennsylvania. The last boat-loads were just crossing from Trenton when the British entered that town. On December 18, Washington informed his brother, "If every nerve is not strained to recruit the new army, . . . I think the game is pretty near up." Thomas Paine called this *The Crisis* and wrote:

These are the times that try men's souls. The summer soldier and the sunshine patriot will, in this crisis, shrink from the service of their country; but he that stands it *now*, deserves the love and thanks of man and woman.

Even after receiving reinforcements from other units, and 2000 militia from Pennsylvania, Washington had fewer than 8000 men. Nevertheless, he decided he must attack while he still had some soldiers. So on the night of December 24, John Glover and the Marblehead men ferried Washington and 2400 of his troops across the ice-filled Delaware River in a driving sleet storm. On Christmas Day they struck Trenton, where Hessian mercenaries were sleeping off their holiday celebration. The surprise was complete. With a loss of only four men, the Americans took 900 prisoners.

The victory at Trenton, and Washington's persuasive powers, encouraged many of his soldiers to re-enlist for a little longer. Then he moved on the British again. He fooled General Charles Cornwallis and the main British army by marching away in the night from his burning campfires. Before Cornwallis had time to react, Washington had routed the British rear guard at Princeton.

After the battle at Princeton, the British evacuated New Jersey and returned to New York. Then both armies went into winter quarters. In a brilliant campaign of ten days Washington had saved the cause of independence. American morale shot up, enlistments increased, the war would go on. Lord George Germain, the new British Minister of War, sadly confessed that all his hopes "were blasted by the unhappy affair at Trenton."

Victory at Saratoga brings help from France.

The British drew up an elaborate plan for the military campaigns of the summer of 1777. Three armies were to invade New York and unite at Albany. By controlling the Hudson River they would shut off New England from the other colonies. Pleasure-loving "Gentleman Johnny" Burgoyne was to come down from Montreal by way of Lake Champlain and the upper Hudson. General St. Leger was to move eastward from Lake Ontario through the Mohawk Valley, and General Howe was to come up the Hudson. So the plan said.

This scheme showed how little the British had learned from Braddock's defeat of twenty years earlier. For it totally disregarded the conditions of travel in northern and western New York. Had the forces succeeded in meeting at Albany, it is doubtful they could have held the land they had marched through. In addition the British had come up with

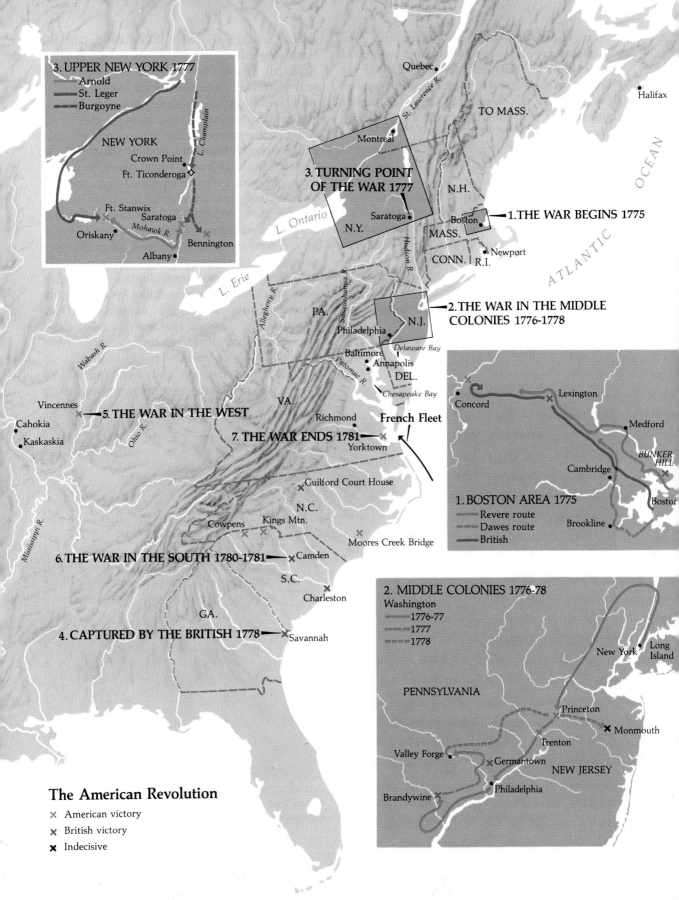

3. UPPER NEW YORK 1777
— Arnold
— St. Leger
--- Burgoyne

NEW YORK

Crown Point
Ft. Ticonderoga
Ft. Stanwix
Saratoga
Oriskany
Mohawk R.
Albany
Bennington
L. Champlain

Quebec

Halifax

St. Lawrence R.

TO MASS.

Montreal

**3. TURNING POINT
OF THE WAR 1777**

Saratoga

N.H.

Boston ← **1. THE WAR BEGINS 1775**

N.Y.

MASS.

L. Ontario

Hudson R.

CONN. R.I. Newport

ATLANTIC

OCEAN

L. Erie

Allegheny R.

Susquehanna R.

PA.

Philadelphia

N.J.

→ **2. THE WAR IN THE MIDDLE
COLONIES 1776-1778**

Baltimore
Annapolis

Delaware Bay

DEL.

Chesapeake Bay

Wabash R.

Vincennes ×— **5. THE WAR IN THE WEST**

Cahokia

Kaskaskia

Ohio R.

VA.

Richmond

French Fleet

7. THE WAR ENDS 1781

× Yorktown

Mississippi R.

Guilford Court House

N.C.

Cowpens Kings Mtn.

Moores Creek Bridge

6. THE WAR IN THE SOUTH 1780-1781 — × Camden

S.C.

Charleston

GA.

4. CAPTURED BY THE BRITISH 1778 — × Savannah

1. BOSTON AREA 1775

Concord
Lexington
Medford
Cambridge
*BUNKER
HILL*
Brookline
Boston

Revere route
--- Dawes route
— British

The American Revolution

× American victory

× British victory

× Indecisive

2. MIDDLE COLONIES 1776-78

Washington
— 1776-77
--- 1777
--- 1778

PENNSYLVANIA

New York
Long Island

Princeton
× Monmouth

Trenton

Valley Forge

Germantown
NEW JERSEY

Brandywine
Philadelphia

learned that a French fleet under Admiral de Grasse was on its way there. Moving swiftly, Washington marched his troops strengthened by a French force under General Rochambeau to the head of Chesapeake Bay, where de Grasse ferried them to the Yorktown peninsula.

Cut off from the British fleet by the French ships, surrounded on the land side by Washington and Rochambeau whose troops outnumbered his two to one, Cornwallis was caught. As the siege lines drew closer, the British army could find no way out. On October 19, 1781, Cornwallis surrendered his entire army of 7750 regulars, together with 850 sailors, 244 cannon, and all his military stores. When news of Yorktown reached England, Prime Minister Lord North exclaimed, "My God! it is all over."

Wartime in America. The war affected every American in the thirteen colonies—patriot, loyalist, or indifferent; man, woman, or child; black, red, or white; slave, indentured, or free. Even in areas that never saw a redcoat, the war was felt, if in no other

Abigail Adams was a woman of many talents. Her vivid letters to her husband are some of the best sources for life in the age of the Revolution. This painting was made in 1800.

way than by inflation. To finance the war the Continental Congress and the state governments printed money as fast as they could. The phrase "not worth a continental" soon showed what people thought of this money.

The war brought prosperity to many. Farmers included 90 percent of all Americans, and many of them prospered by selling their crops to both the British and the American armies. They sold to whichever side paid more. Washington's men were starving at Valley Forge in the winter of 1777–1778, while the British, only a few miles away, were being well fed from the rich farms of Pennsylvania and New Jersey. Washington could never forget the irony of his army lacking food in a country filled with farms. One army officer, bitter about profiteering, wrote, "I despise my countrymen. I wish I could say I was not born in America."

Women at war. The departure of men for war forced women to take up many jobs. Like women who were widowed, they operated the farms, ran the printing presses, served as artisans and shopkeepers—doing whatever needed to be done. Some women gathered their children and followed their husbands to the army. They went with the army wherever it moved, and they helped to nurse the wounded, make camp, cook, do the laundry, carry out clerical tasks, and, in battle, carry water and bullets to the soldiers, even load and fire muskets and cannons.

Margaret Corbin followed her husband to war from their home in Pennsylvania. When he was killed while commanding a cannon at the Battle of Fort Washington, New York (November 16, 1776), she filled his place until she was severely wounded. More famous, though no more courageous, was Mary (Molly) McCauley, known as Molly Pitcher for the pitcher of water she carried back and forth during the hot weather and hot fighting of the Battle of Monmouth, June 28, 1778. When her husband fell in the battle, she too took his place at a cannon till the battle was over.

We know of at least one woman, and there were probably more, who passed as a man and fought as a soldier. Deborah Sampson enlisted in the 4th Massachusetts Regiment in 1782 and served for more than a year.

Abigail Adams, brilliant wife of John Adams, played another kind of role. She ran the farm and

THE SENTIMENTS of an
AMERICAN WOMAN.

ON the commencement of actual war, the Women of America manifested a firm resolution to contribute as much as could depend on them, to the deliverance of their country. Animated by the purest patriotism, they are sensible of sorrow at this day, in not offering more than barren wishes for the success of so glorious a Revolution. They aspire to render themselves more really useful; and this sentiment is universal from the north to the south of the Thirteen United States. Our ambition is kindled by the fame of those heroines of antiquity, who have rendered their sex illustrious, and have proved to the universe, that, if the weakness of our Constitution, if opinion and manners did not forbid us to march to glory by the same paths as the Men, we should at least equal, and sometimes surpass them in our love for the public good. I glory in all that which my sex has done great and commendable. I call to mind with enthusiasm and with admiration, all those acts of courage, of constancy and patriotism, which history has transmitted to us: The people favoured by Heaven, preserved from destruction by the virtues, the zeal and the resolution of Deborah, of Judith, of Esther! The fortitude of the mother of the Macchabees, in giving up her sons to die before her eyes: Rome saved from the fury of a victorious enemy by the efforts of Volumnia, and other Roman Ladies: So many famous sieges where the Women have been seen forgetting the weakness of their sex, building new walls, digging trenches with their feeble hands, furnishing arms to their defenders, they themselves darting the missile weapons on the enemy, resigning the ornaments of their apparel, and their fortune, to fill the public treasury, and to hasten the deliverance of their country; burying themselves under its ruins; throwing themselves into the flames rather than submit to the disgrace of humiliation before a proud enemy.

Born for liberty, disdaining to bear the irons of a tyrannic Government, we associate ourselves to the grandeur of those Sovereigns, cherished and revered, who have held with so much splendour the scepter of the greatest States, The Batildas, the Elizabeths, the Maries, the Catharines, who have extended the empire of liberty, and contented to reign by sweetness and justice, have broken the chains of slavery, forged by tyrants in the times of ignorance and barbarity. The Spanish Women, do they not make, at this moment, the most patriotic sacrifices, to encrease the means of victory in the hands of their Sovereign. He is a friend to the French Nation. They are our allies. We call to mind, doubly interested, that it was a French Maid who kindled up amongst her fellow-citizens, the flame of patriotism buried under long misfortunes: It was the Maid of Orleans who drove from the kingdom of France the ancestors of those same British, whose odious yoke we have just shaken off; and whom it is necessary that we drive from this Continent.

But I must limit myself to the recollection of this small number of atchievements. Who knows if persons disposed to censure, and sometimes too severely with regard to us, may not disapprove our appearing acquainted even with the actions of which our sex boasts? We are at least certain, that he cannot be a good citizen who will not applaud our efforts for the relief of the armies which defend our lives, our possessions, our liberty? The situation of our soldiery has been represented to me; the evils inseparable from war, and the firm and generous spirit which has enabled them to support these. But it has been said, that they may apprehend, that, in the course of a long war, the view of their distresses may be lost, and their services be forgotten. Forgotten! never; I can answer it in the name of all my sex. Brave Americans, your disinterestedness, your courage, and your constancy will always be dear to America, as long as she shall preserve her virtue.

We know that at a distance from the theatre of war, if we enjoy any tranquility; it is the fruit of your watchings, your labours, your dangers. If I live happy in the midst of my family; if my husband cultivates his field, and reaps his harvest in peace; if, surrounded with my children, I myself nourish the youngest, and press it to my bosom, without being affraid of seeing myself separated from it, by a ferocious enemy; if the house in which we dwell; if our barns, our orchards are safe at the present time from the hands of those incendiaries, it is to you that we owe it. And shall we hesitate to evidence to you our gratitude? Shall we hesitate to wear a cloathing more simple; hair dressed less elegant, while at the price of this small privation, we shall deserve your benedictions. Who, amongst us, will not renounce with the highest pleasure, those vain ornaments, when she shall consider that the valiant defenders of America will be able to draw some advantage from the money which she may have laid out in these, that they will be better defended from the rigours of the seasons, that after their painful toils, they will receive some extraordinary and unexpected relief; that these presents will perhaps be valued by them at a greater price, when they will have it in their power to say: *This is the offering of the Ladies.* The time is arrived to display the same sentiments which animated us at the beginning of the Revolution, when we renounced the use of teas, however agreeable to our taste, rather than receive them from our persecutors; when we made it appear to them that we placed former necessaries in the rank of superfluities, when our liberty was interested; when our republican and laborious hands spun the flax, prepared the linen intended for the use of our soldiers; when exiles and fugitives we supported with courage all the evils which are the concomitants of war. Let us not lose a moment; let us be engaged to offer the homage of our gratitude at the altar of military valour, and you, our brave deliverers, while mercenary slaves combat to cause you to share with them, the irons with which they are loaded, receive with a free hand our offering, the purest which can be presented to your virtue,

By An AMERICAN WOMAN.

American Antiquarian Society

The author of this article, recalling notable achievements of women in wartime, urges women to work and sacrifice for the Revolution.

business while her husband was away at the Continental Congress. She kept him aware of what was going on at home. She told him of the profiteering, of how the people felt, and she discussed ways to recruit soldiers and finance the war. Abigail tried to improve the lot of women in the new country, but John was not impressed: "Depend on it," he wrote, "we know better than to repeal our masculine systems."

Blacks in the Revolution.
Many blacks were involved in the war right from the start. They were present at the battles of Lexington and Concord. At the Battle of Bunker Hill, Peter Salem and Salem Poor stood out for their bravery.

After George Washington took over the army, however, it was decided not to have blacks in the service any more. But this policy did not last long because the British promised freedom to all blacks who came to them. Whenever British armies appeared in the South, large numbers of slaves, seeking to be as free as white Americans, joined them. At war's end 14,000 sailed away with the British.

As blacks flocked to the British, George Washington, Congress, and all the states except South Carolina and Georgia changed their minds. They enlisted blacks and promised slaves that they would receive their freedom after the war. Of course, slaves could not join without their masters' permission, so of the 5000 blacks who fought in the war, most were from the North. In general, they served in mixed units and were present at almost all the military actions of the war.

The Loyalists.
A substantial number of Americans opposed the war and wanted to stay with Great Britain. The Loyalists came from every occupation and were of every degree of wealth. Many kept quiet about how they felt and were not bothered by the patriots. Some went to Canada or England. A few, like Jedediah Smith and Phineas Lyman of New England, took their families from comfortable homes and headed west to try to establish a new life in the wilderness—far from the problems of empire and freedom. About 60,000 became soldiers and fought on the British side.

Loyalists who did not leave their homes, but whose sentiments were known, often found themselves shunned by their neighbors. Some were tarred and feathered, and many lost their property by state confiscation or patriot plundering. Others were treated as traitors and were imprisoned or exiled to towns far from home.

During the course of the war, and at its end, thousands of Loyalists left America never to return. Most went to Canada. There they added a strongly British element to the largely French population. They became useful citizens, serving in the assemblies and as judges and governors.

The United States in 1783

■ United States

■ English

■ Spanish

▤ Claimed by U.S. and England

▨ Claimed by U.S. and Spain

The Treaty of Paris. Even after the Battle of Yorktown, King George III showed his usual misunderstanding of the American situation when he wanted to keep fighting. But from the British point of view conditions were hopeless. The American phase of the war was over. In March 1782 a new government came to power in England with the sole condition that there would be "no veto to the independence of America." Peace negotiations began in Paris the next month.

The American delegates—Benjamin Franklin, John Adams, and John Jay—had been instructed by Congress to take no step "without the knowledge and agreements" of the French government. In spite of these instructions, thinking it more advantageous to act independently, they went ahead and concluded an agreement with the British without consulting Vergennes, the French minister of state.

In fact, Vergennes did not protest too much over American activities. After all, the treaty was only preliminary and would not go into effect until

France had signed a treaty with England. This finally occurred on September 3, 1783, when peace treaties were signed between Great Britain and its enemies France, Spain, and the United States.

For America, the Treaty of Paris had the following provisions: England acknowledged the independence of the United States with approximately the present northern boundary, a western boundary set at the Mississippi River, and a southern border at Florida. The commissioners had tried to have Canada made part of the United States, but in this they failed. If Spain had had its way, however, America's western boundary would have been the Appalachian Mountains. The Mississippi River was to be open to the shipping of both America and Britain, and Americans were to be able to fish in England's Newfoundland fisheries. No legal obstacles were to be placed in the way of British businessmen collecting debts owed them by American merchants.

Finally, there was the difficult problem of what to do about the Loyalists whose estates had been confiscated during the war. Feelings still ran too high for Congress to vote that their property should be returned to them. The treaty merely promised that Congress would "recommend" to the states to restore their property. Everybody took it for granted, however, that neither the nation nor the states, both burdened with a nearly worthless currency and heavy war debts, would do much about the Loyalists. Eventually Britain helped many of them with money and land in Canada.

French foreign minister Vergennes was astounded at England's generosity! "The English buy the peace rather than make it; their concessions as to boundaries, the fisheries, the Loyalists, exceed everything I had thought possible."

Why the British lost. At the end of the war, George Washington wrote that people in future years would hardly believe that the Americans could have won. "It will not be believed that such a force as Great Britain has employed for eight years in this country could be baffled in their plan of subjugating it by numbers infinitely less—composed of men sometimes half-starved, always in rags, without pay, and experiencing at times every species of distress which human nature is capable of undergoing." Even today it is not easy to understand how the Americans managed to win.

Benjamin West began this painting of the negotiations for the Treaty of Paris in 1783. The Americans are (from left to right) John Jay, John Adams, Benjamin Franklin, Henry Laurens, and William Temple Franklin. West did not finish the painting because the British negotiators refused to pose.

It is easier to explain why the British lost. The British were separated from their headquarters by a vast ocean. Their lines of communication were long. The British government was badly informed. They thought the Americans were much weaker than they really were. And they expected help from uprisings of thousands of Loyalists. But these uprisings never happened.

The most important explanation was that the British had set themselves an impossible task. Though they had an army that was large for that day, how could it ever be large enough to occupy and subjugate a continent? The British knew so little of America that they thought their capture of New York City would end the war. After the Battle of Long Island in August 1776, General Howe actually asked the Americans to send him a peace commission, and cheerfully expected to receive the American surrender. But he was badly disappointed. For the colonies had no single capital that the British could capture to win the war.

American success was largely due to perseverance in keeping an army in the field throughout the long, hard years. George Washington was a man of great courage and good judgment. And Americans had the strengths of a New World—with a new kind of army fighting in new ways. Still, it is doubtful the Americans could have won without the aid of France.

Although many Americans opposed the Revolution, and some were lukewarm, it was a people's war. As many as half of all men of military age were in the army at one time or another. Each had the special power and the special courage that came from fighting for himself, for his family, and for his home.

American Antiquarian Society

This 1789 magazine frontispiece reflects the American desire to copy the glories of ancient Greece and Rome. It also shows new symbols like the liberty cap and eagle.

there were supposed to be no governments) that John Locke and other political writers had imagined once existed. In fact, the new states already had governments operating, since the provincial assemblies continued to meet after the Revolution broke out and the royal governors fled.

The colonists really had no desire or intention to form brand-new governments. They had been practicing a form of self-government for 150 years. They had nothing in particular against their colonial governments. Their main desire now was to change certain features so that government could never again become tyrannical.

How were they to go about forming—or "reforming"—these colonial governments? The Declaration of Independence said, and English and American experience agreed, that governments derive "their just powers from the consent of the governed." Plainly, "the consent of the governed" had to be secured in each colony and in the whole new nation.

Ways of constitution making. Beginning in 1776 the thirteen states (formerly the colonies) began creating new governments. In most states the existing assemblies drew up the new constitutions. In some, special elections were held for the assembly that was to draw up the constitution. But whether a special election was held or not, the legislators assumed that, because they had been elected, they had the "consent" of the people. So they drew up new constitutions and put them into operation.

In Massachusetts, the provisional assembly asked the local town meetings to consent to its drawing up a new government. Most towns agreed, and the assembly went to work. But then Concord objected. The Concord town meeting, in a series of resolutions that were circulated throughout the colony, challenged this procedure. The people of Concord pointed out that if the regular legislature wrote the constitution, it would be able to change it just as easily later on. To the people of Concord, that did not seem much protection for their liberties. Instead, Concord suggested that a special assembly should be elected that would have no other purpose than to draw up a new constitution. When it had finished its job, it would go out of existence.

The Massachusetts assembly paid no attention to Concord. But the independent-thinking townspeople of the state were listening. The assembly's new constitution was quickly rejected by the voters of the state when it was presented for their approval in 1778. The main reason was that they disapproved of the way it was drawn up.

The Massachusetts assembly finally followed the procedure demanded by the citizens of Concord. In 1779 a constitutional convention was called. The elected members drew up a new constitution, which was submitted to the people in March 1780 and approved by them in June.

A similar procedure was followed by other states when they revised their constitutions and, a few years later, when the whole new nation made a new frame of government.

Americans had found a way to make government by the consent of the governed into a living reality.

Written constitutions. These new frames of government, no matter who drew them up, were all *written constitutions.* Like the constitutional convention, the written frame of government was an American institution that would be admired and imitated all over the world for centuries to come. Colonial charters themselves provided a handy framework for new written constitutions. In Connecticut and Rhode Island, for example, the colonial charters had been so liberal that all that was needed was to strike out mention of the king. Then these charters could become the new constitutions.

The British constitution was a plan of government that could not be picked up and read. It consisted of some basic documents like the Magna Carta and the English Bill of Rights. But much of it was a concoction of tradition, habit, and belief. Many Americans thought their rights to govern themselves would be safer if these were stated in plain language so that government officials could see them and citizens would never forget them.

The new state constitutions. The new state constitutions followed a pattern. Generally they began with a brief declaration of independence. Then came a section declaring the rights that the citizens reserved for themselves against any government. These included freedom of the press, the right to petition the government against abuses, freedom from unreasonable search of their homes, freedom from the burden of standing armies, and the right to trial by jury and other proper legal procedures.

Most state constitutions provided a framework similar to that of the old colonial governments. All but one state had a governor, an upper house, and a lower house of the legislature. But now all were elected directly by the people or by their elected representatives. Only in Pennsylvania did the constitution create a one-house legislature.

In all colonies there was an attempt to weaken the powers of the governor. He had represented the king in colonial days and had become a symbol of government from afar. Now most states deprived the governor of his power to veto legislation or to dismiss the legislature or suspend its meetings. In many states the governor was now elected by the legislature for a short term. The legislature could impeach the governor. The people of Pennsylvania were so fearful of the governor's powers that they abolished that position entirely.

Other posts that had been appointive in colonial times were made elective. Members of the upper houses and the judges—all formerly appointed by the crown—were selected by the voters.

Equality in the states. Although Jefferson, in the Declaration of Independence, asserted that "all men are created equal," there were many ways in which the colonial governments treated people as if they were unequal. Most Americans probably thought Jefferson's phrase meant that Americans were the equals of the English. But the statement itself, and the Revolution, led people to think more about the meaning of equality. In every colony in order to vote, a man had to own property or have a certain income. In no colony were women allowed to vote or hold public office. And then, of course, there were the slaves, who did not even have civil rights, much less political rights like the right to vote or hold office.

In most colonies from Pennsylvania south, settlers in the West had not been as well represented in their assemblies as were settlers in the East. The new state constitutions did give Westerners in those states somewhat better representation in the legislatures, but Easterners still continued to hold more than their share of the power. The amount of property needed to vote or to hold office was generally reduced. Most white American males did hold property and could vote.

The war helped to redistribute wealth. Loyalist estates were broken up and sold to other Americans. Wartime prosperity, especially on the farms, assisted more people to buy farms or enlarge their existing acreage.

First moves against slavery. As early as 1774, Rhode Island passed a law providing that "those who are desirous of enjoying all the advantages of liberty themselves should be willing to extend personal liberty to others." Any slave brought into the colony from that time on would be free.

Abigail Adams wrote to her husband, John, who was away attending the Congress, "It always appeared a most evil scheme to me to fight ourselves for what we are daily robbing and plundering from those who have as good a right to freedom as we have." That same year the Continental Congress passed a law that no slaves were to be imported after December 1, 1775.

When Jefferson tried to include the slave trade in the Declaration of Independence as one of the king's abuses, the southern colonies objected. Still, the War of Independence did lead to freedom for many blacks. Some, as we have seen, received their liberty for fighting in the American cause. When a slave in Massachusetts sued for his freedom because the new state constitution declared, "all men are created free and equal," the court agreed with him. With that decision in 1783, slavery ended in Massachusetts.

Pennsylvania began the gradual abolition of slavery in 1780. Connecticut and Rhode Island followed with their own gradual abolition plans in 1784. Virginia and North Carolina, which had long prohibited the practice, now passed laws that allowed owners to free their slaves.

SECTION REVIEW

1. Why did the townspeople of Concord object to having the state legislature draw up a new constitution for Massachusetts?
2. Why did Americans want *written* constitutions?
3. Why did the new state constitutions reduce the power of the governor's office?
4. In what ways did the new state constitutions help to promote equality?
5. What efforts did some states make to end slavery?

2. The Continental Congress

When, on June 7, 1776, Congress declared war on Great Britain, it also called for a plan of confederation to help the states cooperate in the war effort. A committee of thirteen, with John Dickinson of Pennsylvania as chairman, prepared Articles of Confederation. These Articles, adopted by Congress in November 1777, were not ratified by the last of the thirteen states until March 1, 1781.

An illegal assembly.
Because the Articles of Confederation were not ratified for so long, the Second Continental Congress, though still an "illegal" assembly, assumed the powers of government. The central governing was done for six years by the Continental Congress, which took the place of the British government. This Congress issued the Declaration of Independence, advised the states to form governments, and conducted the war against Great Britain nearly to its successful conclusion at Yorktown.

Young congressmen.
At the beginning of the war, the Continental Congress was an assembly of talented men which included almost every leader of the Revolution. Jefferson, his teacher George Wythe, and Richard Henry Lee were there from Virginia. So was Washington, until he was sent off to lead the army. Sam and John Adams, Elbridge Gerry, and John Hancock came from Massachusetts. Ben Franklin and Robert Morris were delegates from Pennsylvania. Roger Sherman and Oliver Wolcott were there from Connecticut. These men were young—most were just over 40, and Jefferson was only 33 in 1776. They generally stood to lose a good deal of property—and possibly their heads as well—if the Revolution was lost. Of the 56 men who signed the Declaration of Independence, 25 were lawyers, 8 were merchants, 6 were physicians, and 5 were farmers. The rest came from a variety of occupations. They were clearly not a rabble in arms.

During the war, the quality of the members of Congress declined. Many of the most talented men went back to their states as the state governments became more powerful. For the states kept their independence. They had their own armies and navies, competed with Congress for supplies, and some sent out their own "ambassadors." At the same time, Congress had to face the difficulties of wartime. It had to avoid being captured by the British army. Sometimes it had too few members present to pass laws. Often its members were late arriving for meetings of Congress. Sometimes members went home when they were tired, when they did not like the weather, or just when they had something else to do. In these ways Congress was not unlike the militia.

Congress's successes and failures.
Despite the difficulties of wartime, the lack of any legal grant of power, and the jealousy of the states, the achievements of the Second Continental Congress were substantial. It established the army, navy, and marines. It had the wisdom to appoint George Washington to lead the army—and to keep him there through bad times. It kept the army supplied

John Hancock served as president of the
Second Continental Congress. His portrait
(below) was painted by John Singleton
Copley.

Ralph Earl painted this portrait of Roger
Sherman—the only man to sign the
Declaration, the Articles, and the
Constitution.

Robert Morris, shown below in a Robert Pine
painting, served as a delegate to Congress and
was the new nation's financial director.

Richard Henry Lee, shown in the portrait
below by Charles Willson Peale, introduced
the resolution for a declaration of independence.

American Antiquarian Society

Congress could not keep its promise to redeem "continental currency" in gold or silver.

with ammunition. No battle after Bunker Hill was ever lost because of lack of gunpowder. Congress had more of a problem keeping Washington's troops fed, clothed, and paid.

Congress's greatest failure was in financing the war, and that was largely due to the states. They would not give Congress the right to tax, and when Congress asked for money, the states often failed to contribute. As a result, to obtain money Congress simply used the printing press. By the time the government under the Continental Congress was replaced by the new government under the Articles of Confederation, it was costing more to print the paper bills than they were worth as money.

The Continental Congress created a diplomatic corps, and won a great diplomatic victory when France recognized the United States as an independent nation and entered the war. In addition, it created a postal service and drew up the Articles of Confederation. For any assembly—legal or illegal—this was an impressive record.

SECTION REVIEW

1. Characterize the members of the Continental Congress.
2. Why did the quality of the members of Congress decline during the war?
3. Describe the successes and the failures of the Continental Congress.

3. A weak confederation

When the Continental Congress turned to the problem of setting up an effective central government, they found it was easier to get rid of a government than to create a new and better one. Their new government would have to handle all the problems the empire had dealt with—regulating trade, making war and peace, and imposing taxes—yet none of the members of Congress had any experience in imperial administration.

The states and Congress. Congress also had to cope with the jealousy of the states. The states, having disposed of one tyranny, were wary not to put themselves under another. They had rid themselves of royal officials—governors, judges, and hated customs collectors. They had no desire to create a whole new set of officials to interfere in their affairs. They were happy to be able to levy their own taxes, to set up their own courts, and to regulate their own commerce, currency, and the right to vote.

The states wanted a new government strong enough to serve them but not so potent that it might dominate them. They feared the powers of a central government so far away that it would be beyond the people's control. Therefore the Articles of Confederation, which the Continental Congress now drew up, announced a "perpetual union" of the states and "firm league of friendship." But it preserved for each state "its sovereignty, freedom and independence, and every power and jurisdiction and right" that was not expressly delegated to the new Congress under the Articles of Confederation.

There was an argument over how the states were to vote in the Congress of the Confederation. It was finally decided—though the more populous states did not like it—to give each state just one vote. That would show that this was only a confederation of the thirteen sovereign states, and not a new government representing the people themselves. The agreement of nine states was required for important matters, and any change in the Articles had to receive the vote of every state. There was no provision for a President or other executive officers or for judges or courts.

The powers of Congress. Congress was given the sole power to deal with foreign countries, to settle disputes between the states, to decide admiralty cases (those involving ships at sea), to declare war, and to make peace. It could coin money, run the postal service, establish weights and measures, and trade with the Indians outside the states. It could borrow money, and it could request each state to contribute money in proportion to the value of the property in the state. Under this arrangement a large state, which had only one vote, was still supposed to donate more money than its less wealthy neighbors. Congress could only request financial support from the states. But if a state refused to help, there was nothing the Congress could do.

In fact, the Articles only outlined what the Continental Congress was already doing. But many people feared the powers of the new Congress and imagined that it might "swallow up the states." Despite these fears the Congress actually had no way to enforce its decisions. The Articles of Confederation provided, in the words of Gouverneur Morris of Pennsylvania, nothing but a "government by supplication"—a government by begging and pleading.

When the Articles of Confederation were sent to the states, the same questions that the Continental Congress had debated were now discussed all over again in town meetings and in the state legislatures. Most of the amendments suggested by the states would further limit the powers of Congress. Americans did not want to rush into a new government.

Western lands. Some of the smaller states were especially worried about the large areas of land that other states claimed in the West. Massachusetts, Connecticut, Virginia, North and South Carolina, and Georgia had claims from "sea to sea" based on their colonial charters. Virginia's claim was strengthened by George Rogers Clark's conquest of the Northwest, which had been carried out in the service of Virginia. New York claimed western lands, on the basis of treaties made with the Indians, but in 1780 voted to cede them to Congress.

The small states that had no western land claims were led by Maryland. They refused to agree to a general government until the other states gave up their claims to the land west of the Appalachians. The land-poor states thought that the land-rich states like Virginia and Massachusetts would be able to pay their war debts and the day-to-day costs of

state government with the income from the sale of their western lands. This would let those states keep their taxes low compared to the land-poor states. The small states feared their citizens would leave to go to the big land-rich states where taxes were lower.

Here an interesting, enterprising, and especially American kind of businessman came on the stage of history—the speculator. He would play a lively and leading role in developing the American continent. Land speculators had formed their companies and bought land from the Indians out west. The officials of Virginia had refused to recognize their claims. But the speculators thought the Congress might support their interests.

The small states and the speculators, both protecting their own self-interests, worked to have the Articles revised to give Congress control over the western lands. Most states, under wartime pressure, were willing to sign the Articles simply to get some kind of government going to conduct a successful struggle for independence. They planned to amend the Articles later. But land-poor Maryland refused to take the risk. The Articles could not go into effect until all the states—including Maryland—accepted them.

Virginia gives in. Finally the stalemate was broken when Virginia gave in. It was the largest state and the one with the best claim to the western lands. When the British army under Lord Cornwallis headed their way, Virginians needed little persuading that a strong, well-supported union of the states was required to help them win independence. On January 2, 1781, the state offered to cede its land to the central government. At the same time, Virginia insisted that as the land filled with people new states should be admitted with the same "rights of sovereignty, freedom, and independence as other States."

But Maryland—continuing to cooperate with the speculators—still refused to sign the Articles. As Marylanders felt British troops breathing down their necks, they asked the French naval forces to protect them. Then the French again aided the American cause. They refused to do anything to help Maryland until the state agreed to the Articles. In February 1781, Maryland finally signed, and on March 1 the Articles of Confederation became the law of the land.

Western Land Claims Ceded, 1784-1802

- States in 1792
- Lands Ceded to Congress

0 _____ 500 Miles

0 _____ 500 Kilometers

The treasury of the nation. This new government had no power to enforce its will on the states, yet it had to finish the war and guide the country into peace. Despite its weakness, the new government would accomplish a great deal.

The western lands became the treasury of the new government. Since the Confederation had no power to tax and could only beg the states to donate money, lands took the place of taxes. These unsettled tracts (called the "public domain") were larger than all the settled states put together. By selling the land, the weak new government obtained the money that it could find in no other way.

The vast unsettled West would give the new government an important peacetime job. No nation, new or old, had been blessed with such a land-treasure in its own backyard. What should be done with it? This public domain, which belonged to all the states together, was far larger than France or England or Spain.

Unlike the sparsely settled lands controlled by those European nations, these lands would not become colonies. They would not be used by the thirteen original states to make themselves rich and strong.

Instead they would become (in Jefferson's phrase) an "Empire for Liberty." This Empire would be built by adding new states. Each new state would be the equal of all the older states. Nowadays this seems an obvious and sensible way for a nation to grow. But in those days it was quite a new idea.

Congress took the first step by passing the Land Ordinance of 1785. It provided that the land be carefully surveyed into townships—areas of land 6 miles square made up of 36 sections, each containing 640 acres. One section in each township was reserved for the support of public schools; four more were reserved for the central government. The rest were to be sold.

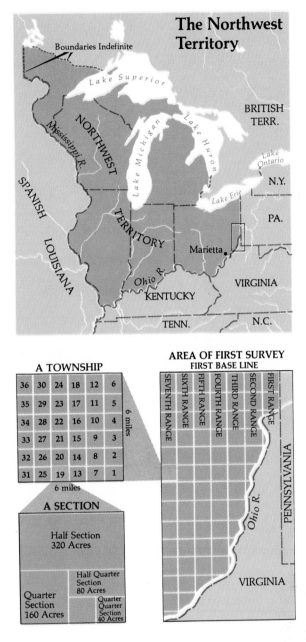

The Northwest Ordinance of 1787: an Add-a-State Plan.

For many years Thomas Jefferson, with his usual uncanny foresight, had been working on a plan for settlements in the western wilderness. The Northwest Ordinance of 1787 put his scheme into law. This American way of growing gave instructions for what we can call an Add-a-State Plan.

The plan was simple. Every part of the public domain would in time become a full-fledged state of the Union "on an equal footing with the original states in all respects whatsoever." This goal was reached by three simple stages described in the Northwest Ordinance. First, when there were still almost no people in a territory, it would have a governor, a secretary, and three judges named by Congress. Then, as soon as there were 5000 adult free men, there would be a legislature where the people of the territory could make laws for themselves. And finally, when the free population numbered 60,000, the people could apply for admission to the Union as a state.

How many new states should there be? It was anybody's guess. Congress had heard that the land out there was not good for much. It was said, for example, that there were vast areas that did not have even a single bush on them. Members of Congress did not realize that the treeless plains were some of the richest farmland in the world—and were all the better for farming because they were not cluttered by trees. Since the rumors made western land seem so poor, it was decided that the new states would have to be big. The Northwest Ordinance of 1787 therefore said that in the whole area northwest of the Ohio River there should eventually be "not less than three nor more than five states."

The Ordinance also provided for religious freedom. And in a section probably inserted to attract

101

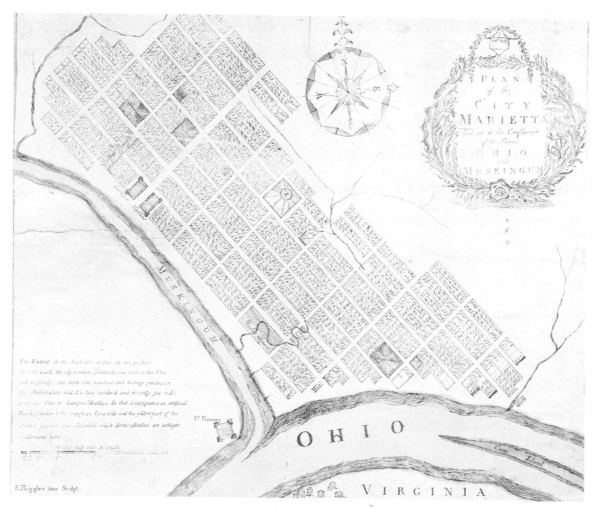

Town-building in the Northwest Territory began at Marietta and spread westward along the Ohio.

New Englanders to the Northwest Territory, slavery was prohibited there.

New Englanders settle along the Ohio.

The year after the Congress of the Confederation passed the Land Ordinance of 1785, a group of New Englanders formed the Ohio Company of Associates to promote the settlement of land along the north bank of the Ohio River. The first Ohio Company had been founded by Virginians in 1748 to explore the Ohio territory. But it was the company formed in 1786 that made the first organized settlements in Ohio—indeed in the Northwest Territory.

One of the leaders was General Rufus Putnam, who like his cousin General Israel Putnam served with distinction in the Revolution. Another leader was the Reverend Manassah Cutler of Ipswich, Massachusetts. Cutler was a talented man with wide interests. He had practiced law and medicine, measured the distances of the stars, surveyed the altitude of Mt. Washington in New Hampshire, and made the first systematic account of the plant life of New England.

As soon as the Ohio Company was organized, Cutler went to New York City to persuade the Congress to give the company the right to buy up to 1.5 million Ohio acres at about 8 cents an acre. A government contract was signed on October 27, 1787. While in New York Cutler helped to draft the Northwest Ordinance.

Before the year's end, General Putnam was on his way west with an advance party. The 48 pioneers had set out in two units—one from Danvers, Massachusetts, and the other from Hartford, Connecticut. On April 2, 1788, they all embarked together from Sumrill's Ferry in western Pennsylvania for the trip down the Monongahela and then down the Ohio River. On April 7 the party landed on the east bank of the Muskingum where it joined the Ohio, just opposite Fort Harmar.

Under Putnam's direction the men quickly laid out their town on the compact New England model. Each settler was given a small "in-lot" within the town for a residence and an "out-lot" of eight acres for crops. On July 2, 1788, the agents and directors of the Ohio Company held their first meeting on the spot and named the town Marietta. Again following the New England example, they promptly provided a church and a school, both of which were operating before the end of July. Within a few months fifteen more families and many single men joined the town.

The Indians raided small parties that were tempted to go off and settle by themselves. This soon taught the Ohio pioneers to build garrison settlements of fifty or more people. One such raid in 1791 induced some settlers to build Fort Frye. It was a triangular palisade enclosing twenty families, ten single men, and eight or ten soldiers from Fort Harmar. Soon there was a string of such groups along the Ohio—at Farmers Castle, Belpre, Columbia, Losantiville, Ft. Washington (later called Cincinnati), North Bend, Gallipolis, Manchester, and many other places.

The heroic individual—like Daniel Boone, Meriwether Lewis and William Clark, Zebulon Pike—has held the spotlight of history. But in the settlement of the American continent the lone adventurer was rare. Early settlers, those who took one-way passage and became the backbone of new western communities, generally went together. People moving these great distances into an unknown landscape, threatened by numerous nameless dangers, banded together. They did so not because they especially loved their neighbors or had any ties to them, but because they needed one another.

Successes and failures of the Confederation.
Planning an Empire for Liberty—charting the settlement of the vast western public domain—was the greatest single achievement in domestic policy for the Confederation. In military matters, the Confederation brought the War of Independence to a successful end.

In foreign policy the Confederation's greatest achievement—really its only one—was the peace treaty with England. In other foreign affairs the Confederation was a failure. England did not even bother to send a minister to the United States until 1792. Though King George III graciously received John Adams as our first minister to England in 1785, Adams could not get the commercial treaty we badly needed. Even France did not take the United States seriously. Jefferson, our minister to France from 1785 to 1789, wrote home, "We are the lowest and most obscure of the whole diplomatic tribe."

Out beyond the mountains there were diplomatic problems, too. Great Britain held onto its fur trading posts on United States territory in the Northwest. Spain hoped to coop up the United States behind the Appalachians and even to make the settlers in Kentucky and Tennessee become part of the Spanish Empire. To encourage this move, Spain closed the mouth of the Mississippi to citizens of the young nation. Since that was the easiest way for western settlers to ship goods out, Spain hoped the settlers there would join the Spanish Empire in order to use the Mississippi.

When Spain closed the mouth of the Mississippi, it was bad enough for the Westerners. Then Congress was about to make a treaty with Spain giving up the right to use the Mississippi for 25 years in return for the right to use Spanish ports to sell American goods. This would have favored eastern merchants and hurt western settlers. Such an agreement would have permanently alienated the Westerners, but luckily the treaty was defeated in Congress.

Each state could keep out the farm produce and manufactured goods of its neighbors, much as the British Empire had kept out the products of the French. Instead of facing one large power across the ocean, each of the new states now found itself surrounded here in America by a lot of other annoying little states.

The great depression.
These problems were all bad enough, but with the end of the war there soon came a financial depression. As long as the war lasted there had been a business boom. When goods were scarce, anybody with something to sell found lots of buyers. After the peace in 1783,

Americans were still hungry for the things they could not buy during the war. Once again they began importing from Great Britain. But they bought a good deal more than they could pay for.

Each state issued its own paper money. Nobody knew just how much a New York dollar was worth compared to one from Pennsylvania or Rhode Island. The more money there was in circulation, the less a dollar bought. Then came the financial collapse. Paper money was refused as worthless. Gold and silver were hoarded by people who feared the future. For five long years after 1784 there was the worst business depression the colonies had ever suffered.

Shays's Rebellion. The depression hit people in debt especially hard. Their paper dollars were refused as payment. They had no gold or silver.

In the prosperous days of the war and its aftermath, many farmers had gone into debt to improve their farms, buy more land, or just to purchase luxuries they wanted. But the depression meant they could sell their crops only at very low prices. Thus it took many more bushels of corn or wheat than it once had to pay their debts and the taxes on their land. Farmers and debtors wanted their states to issue paper money with which they could pay their bills. Rhode Island passed a law that made it illegal for a person to refuse to accept that state's worthless dollars. Other states also tried to help the debtors by issuing paper money. But some states, including Massachusetts, refused to injure those who had loaned money just to help those who had borrowed it.

Debtors were often hauled into court where they had to pay high fees to lawyers and judges. And if they still failed to pay their bills, they could go to jail and be kept there until they finally did pay. The farmers of western Massachusetts were particularly upset about all this. In one year alone, 1784, there were more than 2000 suits for debt in Worcester County. Farmers there—and elsewhere—rioted to protest against the failure of the states to help them.

In western Massachusetts the popular Daniel Shays, a former captain in the Continental Army, led a rebellion. He demanded more paper money, tax relief, relief for debtors, and an end to imprisonment for debt. During the summer of 1786, these Shaysites traveled around the state preventing the collection of debts or the sale of property for debt. In January 1787, when Shays and his mob of farmers went to the Springfield armory to get more guns and ammunition, they were met by the state militia, which had been paid by wealthy merchants. Shays and his men were driven off, then pursued and captured in February 1787.

The effect of this rebellion was to swing many people over to demanding a change in the national government. In fact, things were not nearly as bad as they seemed. The depression was now coming to an end. The country was growing stronger.

Still, the central government lacked the power to deal with the states. As James Wilson pointed out in the summer of 1787, the states by their "jealousy and ambition" had reduced the Confederation to an "impotent condition." Men of property saw Shays's Rebellion as an attack on them. They considered cheap paper money as bad as taxation without representation.

SECTION REVIEW

1. Name some powers of Congress under the Articles of Confederation. What important power did it lack?
2. Why did the land-poor states want the states with western lands to cede those lands to the central government?
3. Describe the provisions of the Northwest Ordinance of 1787.
4. What were the major achievements under the Articles of Confederation?
5. What were some demands of Shays and his followers? How did these lead to change in the national government?

---

4. Writing a nation's constitution

The thirteen new American governments had found it impossible to live with a strong London government. They now found it impossible to live without it. Yet nobody wanted to risk replacing the old British tyranny by a new American tyranny.

This was a decisive moment in history. Would America become another Europe? Would the New World become only a new battlefield for thirteen new little nations? Had they risked their "lives, their fortunes, and their sacred honor" only to turn the continent into a sea of anarchy?

Historical Society of Pennsylvania

The Constitutional Convention met in Philadelphia at the State House, later renamed Independence Hall. This 1790 engraving by William Birch shows a rear view of the hall.

Wise Americans dared not let this happen. Their children and their grandchildren, they said, would curse them if they threw away this opportunity to explore together and in peace the vast, mysterious, rich New World.

The Annapolis meeting. In January 1786, Virginia sent an invitation to all the states to meet and discuss one of their major problems—the regulation of commerce. Nine states accepted the invitation, but only twelve men (representing five states) actually came to the meeting at Annapolis, Maryland, that September. By then farm workers could barely support themselves on their declining wages. Money lenders were seizing farms, and the Shaysites were rampaging through Massachusetts.

With fewer than half the states represented at Annapolis, there was not much they could do. Luckily, one of the twelve men there was the bold, young Alexander Hamilton. Born in the Virgin Islands of a good family that had fallen on hard times, he had attended King's College (later Columbia University) in New York City. During the war General George Washington, recognizing Hamilton's brilliance, made him his close adviser and gave him the job of organizing military headquarters.

In 1786 when Hamilton was only 29 years of age, he saw that the thirteen states would never prosper until they formed a strong union. He demanded that the states send delegates at once to a larger meeting to see what could be done. The Congress of the Confederation issued the invitations. If Hamilton had never lived another day, his courage and vision at the Annapolis convention would entitle him to a place in American history.

The Philadelphia Convention. The states responded to the call. Within a year 55 delegates from twelve states met in Independence Hall in for twenty years and that Congress could regulate commerce but could never levy duties on exports.

A government "partly national and partly federal." To satisfy those who wanted a union truly "national," the new government was given the power to tax, to control commerce, to make war, to raise an army and a navy, and to conduct foreign relations. To satisfy those who wanted a union merely "federal," the Constitution gave each state the power to make the laws controlling its daily life and all the powers not expressly given to the new central government.

This new government, as one member put it, was "partly national, partly federal." In the Constitution you will not find either the word "federal" or the word "national." The members of the convention knew that each of these words would be a

Oliver Ellsworth, who helped to work out the Great Compromise, and Abigail Wolcott Ellsworth are seen in their library. Painter Ralph Earl cleverly showed their house and yard in the window.

red flag to some members. They purposely left everybody to guess to what extent the new government was either federal or national. That way each side could think it had won a little more than the other.

If they did not call the new arrangement either "federal" or "national," what would they call it? Their answer was very wise and very simple. Every time they themselves mentioned the new government in the Constitution, they just called it "the United States."

The members of the convention were also wise enough to include in the Constitution itself instructions for changing it. Then, if the people in the future found they needed changes, they would not have to junk the whole Constitution and start all over again. They could keep the Constitution as a whole, while following the rules for making the few amendments they needed. This was a masterstroke, and was as new as anything else the convention did.

The final document repaired many of the weaknesses of the Articles of Confederation. The government under the Articles had no President and lacked the power to tax or to raise and maintain an army and a navy. The new government would have a strong President. It would have the power to tax, to borrow, to maintain an army and navy, to declare war, to put down rebellions, to regulate commerce, to coin money, and to spend money for the general welfare.

SECTION REVIEW

1. Identify or explain: Annapolis meeting, Alexander Hamilton, James Madison, Edmund Randolph, Virginia Plan, William Paterson, New Jersey Plan, Connecticut Compromise, direct taxes, export duties.
2. What did "federal" mean in the 1700s? What would be the difference between a federal union and a national union?
3. Describe the Great Compromise. Why was it important?
4. What was the three-fifths compromise?
5. What powers that the Confederation lacked did the new government have under the Constitution?

5. The states ratify

It was not enough for the delegates to the Constitutional Convention to draft the document. It had to be ratified too. Here again the convention showed its wisdom—and its ability to go beyond the letter of the law.

Bypassing the states. The convention submitted the Constitution to Congress and asked that it be sent to state constitutional conventions for approval. This procedure would assure that it was ratified by the people themselves and not only by the state governments. Many believed that this would make it clear that the Constitution was superior to state laws. The state legislatures might not have made an impartial decision, because they were destined to lose powers under the new government. To go into effect the Constitution required the approval not of all thirteen but of only nine states. This would keep an obstinate few from sabotaging the work of the cooperative many.

The fight for approval. Since the convention had done its work in secret, there was great public interest both in what the new Constitution said—and in what it really meant. Those who supported the new Constitution were called *Federalists,* and their opponents were called *Anti-Federalists.* The Anti-Federalists feared that the new Constitution would create a super-government that might destroy the very liberty that the Revolution was fought to win. The Constitution contained no bill of rights like that found in the state constitutions. And what would prevent the President from becoming a king?

The bitter struggle for ratification had intelligent, well-meaning people on both sides. The outcome was not certain until the very end. Only hard work and a number of political tricks by the Federalists brought about ratification of the document by the required number of states.

The process began easily enough. On December 7, 1787, Delaware by unanimous vote became the first state to give the new Constitution its approval. The Pennsylvania Federalists planned to rush through approval before the Anti-Federalists could muster their forces and reach the voters. They bought up newspapers to keep Anti-Federalist speeches from being printed. And their undemocratic strategy succeeded on December 12, when the this federal Constitution had such a long and successful life? How has a short document written nearly two centuries ago for thirteen struggling seaboard colonies been able to give strength and liberty to a vast, two-ocean nation of more than 200 million people?

Oddly enough, the shortness of the document itself is one explanation. The Constitution did not go into details. It left to future generations the right and the opportunity to apply the scheme, and so to grow in unpredictable ways. It is not surprising then that one of the shortest constitutions ever adopted by a nation was to become in time the oldest living written constitution.

SECTION REVIEW

1. Why was it significant that the Constitution was ratified by the people of the states and not simply by their legislatures?
2. Why did the Anti-Federalists oppose the Constitution?
3. What did Massachusetts do that assisted in getting other states to ratify the Constitution?
4. What factors helped to win ratification in Virginia and New York?
5. How did the brevity of the Constitution contribute to its long life?

An express rider took eight days to carry the news to the New York ratifying convention in Poughkeepsie that Virginia had ratified the Constitution. This news helped sway the delegates at the New York State convention to ratify. Virginia's resolution, as we see, expressed hope for early amendments to correct the Constitution's imperfections.

New York Public Library, Rare Book Division, Astor, Lenox and Tilden Foundations

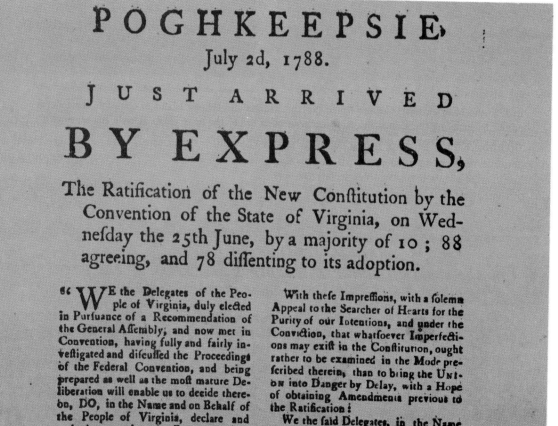

POGHKEEPSIE,
July 2d, 1788.

JUST ARRIVED

BY EXPRESS,

The Ratification of the New Conſtitution by the Convention of the State of Virginia, on Wedneſday the 25th June, by a majority of 10 ; 88 agreeing, and 78 diſſenting to its adoption.

"WE the Delegates of the People of Virginia, duly elected in Purſuance of a Recommendation of the General Aſſembly; and now met in Convention, having fully and fairly inveſtigated and diſcuſſed the Proceedings of the Federal Convention, and being prepared as well as the moſt mature Deliberation will enable us to decide thereon, DO, in the Name and on Behalf of the People of Virginia, declare and make known, that the Powers granted under the Conſtitution being derived

With theſe Impreſſions, with a ſolemn Appeal to the Searcher of Hearts for the Purity of our Intentions, and under the Conviction, that whatſoever Imperfections may exiſt in the Conſtitution, ought rather to be examined in the Mode preſcribed therein, than to bring the Union into Danger by Delay, with a Hope of obtaining Amendments previous to the Ratification:

We the ſaid Delegates, in the Name and in Behalf of the People of Virginia, do by theſe preſents aſſent to and ratify

CHAPTER REVIEW

MEETING OUR EARLIER SELVES

1. The state constitutions were (and still are) longer and more detailed than the United States Constitution. Why might you expect this? What advantage, if any, do you see in a relatively short constitution?

2. In writing their constitutions the states tended to base them on their old charters. What advantages do you see in using an existing framework as a base for a new constitution?

3. How does the Constitution reflect the ideas contained in the Declaration of Independence?

4. Certain situations in the 1780s promoted separatism among the states, while others promoted the desire for closer unity. Give examples of these situations (or forces) and explain them.

QUESTIONS FOR TODAY

1. From time to time various states have petitioned Congress to convene a constitutional convention to propose a specific amendment. Is any such move under way today? What are the arguments for and against the convention method of proposing amendments to the Constitution of the United States?

2. Investigate a major public policy bill recently passed by Congress. What were the main conflicting issues involved? What compromises were made to get the bill passed?

YOUR REGION IN HISTORY

1. In what major ways does your state's present constitution differ from its first constitution?

2. If you live in one of the original thirteen states, investigate and report on the struggle for ratification of the federal Constitution in your state.

3. When was your state's constitution adopted? How was it drafted? How was it approved by the people?

SKILLS TO MAKE OUR PAST VIVID

1. What cities, towns, or counties in your state have the same name as that of one of the signers of the federal Constitution? Describe a simple way to obtain this information.

2. By listing the number of the Article or Amendment (and the section number if one is given), indicate where the federal Constitution provides for (a) the powers of Congress; (b) the qualifications to be President; (c) the power of the Senate to ratify treaties; (d) the admission of new states; (e) voting rights for 18-year-olds; (f) freedom of speech; (g) filling a vacancy in the Vice-Presidency; (h) the right of an accused person to have a lawyer's help; (i) the present meeting time of Congress; (j) the use of search and arrest warrants.

Yale University Art Gallery, Gift of the Associates in Fine Arts and Mrs. Henry F. Loomis in Memory of Henry Bradford Loomis, BA 1875

This portrait of Washington at the Battle of Princeton was painted three or four years after the fight by Charles Willson Peale, who served as an officer in the American army there. Although not a realistic battle scene, the painting shows Washington's self-confidence and poise. Peale set up one of the first museums in America.

2. George Washington sets the course

George Washington took office with a firm faith. The "sacred fire of liberty" as well as "the destiny of the republican model of government" depended on the outcome of the "experiment" the Americans had undertaken. No country in the world had ever tried this form of government. Washington knew that it was up to the first President and the first Congress to see that the experiment did not fail.

A strong executive. Washington believed that if the young nation was to survive in an envious, hostile world, the Chief Executive of the new government must lead. By showing the courage to be strong at a time when people accused him of trying to become a king, he earned a place too as an American peacetime hero. He had done more than anyone else to help the nation win independence. He now led the nation along the path to survival.

Washington's personal prestige gave the Presidency the dignity it needed. His physique and his stature helped. He was six feet, two inches tall, and his face appeared chiseled from granite. He looked every inch the national leader. But his commanding manner and his elegant way of life seemed to justify the suspicions of those who feared he wanted to seduce the nation to monarchy. He rented one of the finest houses in New York City, the nation's first capital, and staffed it with servants in uniform. He traveled in a canary-colored coach (drawn by six horses) on which was painted the Washington coat-of-arms. He held formal parties where he appeared in black velvet and silk stockings.

Washington wanted his office to seem dignified and important to all the world. He well knew, as he wrote, that "there is scarcely any part of my conduct that may not hereafter be drawn into precedent."

Creating a new government. The federal government, with no money, inherited numerous war debts to the French government, to Dutch bankers, and to its own citizens. To make the new nation respectable and trusted, Congress would have to raise money and begin to pay off those debts. Congress also had to provide for the national defense and deal with the Indian tribes. To fix the number of seats for each state in the House of Representatives, the Constitution said the federal government must take a national census each ten

Federal Hall, in the center of this engraving, was located in New York City on Wall Street at the head of Broad Street. Here George Washington took the oath of office as the first President.

years. Congress also needed to organize territories, establish federal courts, and regulate trade. Then there were diplomatic and commercial problems with England, France, and Spain. There were the executive departments to be set up—and a host of other tasks to accomplish.

The new House of Representatives, advised by Representative James Madison of Virginia, at once turned its attention to the first ten amendments—the Bill of Rights. These were drawn up by Madison based on the objections to the Constitution that had been raised by some of the states. The House also quickly passed a modest tariff bill to bring in some badly needed money.

Meanwhile, the Senate turned to creating the federal courts. The Judiciary Act of 1789 set up the Supreme Court, three circuit courts, and thirteen district courts (one in each state). To each district court it attached a United States Attorney to serve as a federal prosecutor and a United States Marshal to serve as the federal police. The act also set procedures for the federal courts. Disputes over the meaning of federal laws and treaties would, in the end, be settled by the United States Supreme Court as would conflicts between state law and federal law.

The Congress also set up the departments of Treasury, State, and War. These, with the Attorney General and the Postmaster General, were the only executive departments at the start.

For the important post of Secretary of the Treasury, Washington chose his brilliant young friend and onetime aide, Alexander Hamilton. Edmund Randolph of Virginia became Attorney General. The War Department was entrusted to General Henry Knox of Massachusetts. Thomas Jefferson was called home from Paris, where he had been minister since 1785, to become the first Secretary of State.

Roles are clarified. The relationship of the new departments and their Secretaries to the Congress or even to the President was not at all clear. Some people thought that the new departments should just carry out the laws and keep out of politics. The

Secretaries, then, would stay in office under successive Presidents. Hamilton saw the department heads as having a share in making policy. He thought that Secretaries, like English cabinet members, would go to Congress to speak in favor of bills that they wanted passed. But Congress refused to hear Hamilton when he tried to report, so the executive departments did not form close ties with Congress.

Some thought that the Senate, because it was to "advise and consent" on treaties, might become like the English Privy Council, which advised the king. One day Washington arrived at the Senate, sat down in the Vice-President's chair, and told the Senate that he and the Secretary of War had come to get their advice on an Indian treaty. But the Senate refused to debate the question in his presence. The Senate wanted to discuss the treaty without being overawed by the President. So Washington left without any advice and soon gave up trying to get the counsel of the Senate.

In domestic affairs, Washington believed it was the President's job to enforce the laws Congress made, not to lead the Congress in making laws. He allowed Hamilton to go his own way in handling the financial affairs of the country. But diplomatic problems were different. Washington often consulted with Jefferson, and he soon began to call in the Attorney General, and the Secretaries of State, War, and the Treasury for advice on complex problems in foreign affairs. Acting as an advisory group, the department heads slowly became the President's Cabinet.

Alexander Hamilton prepares financial plans.
During Washington's first term the great questions concerned finances. The disputes that arose produced the first significant arguments over the nature of the Constitution and drew the issues for our first political parties. Alexander Hamilton put the issues into focus. Though not tall (he was 5'6"), he was handsome and debonair. Intelligent and hard working, he had earned the full confidence of President Washington. But Hamilton's personal ambition and his lack of faith in the people sometimes tempted him to grand and clever schemes.

The House of Representatives, under Madison's leadership, directed the Secretary of the Treasury to prepare proposals for collecting the revenue and dealing with the public credit. Hamilton was told to present these plans to the House of Representatives—where, according to the Constitution, money bills had to originate.

In response to these directions Hamilton put together a design of breathtaking scope. He presented that program in three major reports: on the Public Credit (January 1790), on a National Bank (December 1790), and on Manufactures (December 1791). These reports were to help shape the future history of the United States.

The Report on the Public Credit.
Upon taking office, Hamilton found that the United States had debts amounting to $54 million. Of this sum, $10 million was owed to our wartime ally, France, and to Dutch bankers. The remainder was owed to United States citizens. In addition, many of the states had unpaid war debts amounting to $20 million.

Hamilton saw an ingenious way to use this heavy debt to strengthen the central government. His plan would provide capital for a national bank and even create wealth that could be invested in new private enterprises. He proposed that the United States should pay all these debts in full. But they would be paid in a way that would both stimulate business and give the wealthy classes good reason to support the new government.

Now everyone agreed that the United States must repay the French and the Dutch if the credit of the United States was to be any good in the outside world. Who would lend us money in the future if we failed to pay these debts?

There was opposition, however, to paying back American holders of the nation's debt. The reason for this dispute had to do with the history of the debt.

During the war Congress had issued paper certificates, or bonds, which promised to pay the holder at some point in the future the amount printed on the face of the paper plus interest at a certain rate. These bonds had been sold to people at their face value or given to soldiers to induce them to enlist. During the years of war and depression many of these original holders had been forced to sell their bonds for whatever they could. Speculators willing to gamble on the future bought up the bonds for as little as 15 or 20 cents on the dollar. Even as Secretary of the Treasury Hamilton made

The cartoonist here accuses Robert Morris, a prominent Federalist from Philadelphia, of some trickery in the moving of the capital from New York City to Philadelphia. Morris carries the Capitol (Federal Hall) on his shoulder, while the devil leads him on.

his proposal, some members of Congress, joining the other speculators, bought all the bonds they could find.

Madison tried to persuade Congress to accept a complicated proposal to pay bondholders differing amounts based upon when they had bought their bonds. Congress rejected this plan and followed Hamilton. And Congress was right—even if some of its members stood to make money by their votes. The whole point of Hamilton's bill was to restore national credit. That could only be done if all those who had bought the bonds, at any time and for whatever reason, were paid in full.

Before the vote was taken on the payment of the debt of the United States, the question of having the national government pay the debts of the states had to be settled. This was even more difficult than the problem of the national debt. Some states, such as Virginia and Maryland, had already paid their debts. Why should they have to help pay the debts of states like Massachusetts and South Carolina? Hamilton replied that since the war had been fought for the benefit of *all* the states, the government which now represented all the states should pay the whole debt.

Madison had enough votes to defeat Hamilton's proposal to assume the state debts. But Madison believed that the United States should pay its own debts. The speculators warned him, however, that if he defeated *assumption* of the state debts by the national government, they would defeat the payment of the national debt.

At this point there was struck the most famous "deal" in American political history. The permanent site of the nation's capital had not yet been decided. Hamilton had a suggestion for Thomas Jefferson, who had just arrived from France to become Secretary of State. Hamilton would have his supporters in Congress vote to locate the capital at Philadelphia for the years 1790–1800, and then move it to a spot on the Potomac River favored by Virginia. In return, Madison and his friends should allow the federal government to assume the state debt. Madison and Jefferson accepted Hamilton's bargain, so the bill dealing with the debt was passed in July 1790.

The total debt of $75 million was then "funded." This meant exchanging the old bonds for new ones bearing interest, some at 6 percent, some at 3 percent. The new bonds went mainly to bankers, merchants, and wealthy speculators who owned most of the old bonds. As Hamilton had predicted, these influential people then became firm supporters of the national government. It had to survive in order to preserve the value of the new bonds. When the federal government assumed the state debts, it undercut the importance of the state governments to those who had once held the state bonds. And the national credit was now secure.

Hamilton's opponents accused him of creating a new wealthy class—those people who had bought the national and state bonds at low prices. But that was just what Hamilton intended. If the nation was to develop from a land of farms into a dynamic country of mines, factories, ships, and shops, it needed persons of wealth who were willing and able to invest large sums of money in new projects.

Hamilton's plan was both farsighted and daring. The opposition to it, however, disclosed a sectional split between the agrarian South and the mercantile North. That split, reinforced by the great moral issue of slavery, would endanger the future of the nation.

The Report on a National Bank. Hamilton revealed the next phase of his plan in December 1790. He proposed that the United States create a new bank. The federal government would put in $2 million (one-fifth ownership) of the bank's $10 million capital and appoint one-fifth of the bank's directors. Private investors would supply the rest of the capital and elect the other directors. And they were even to be allowed to use their government bonds for part of their share.

What would the United States get for its money? Far more than just another commercial bank. This bank would serve as the government's financial agent—collecting taxes, providing a safe place to deposit the government's cash, and lending the government money when needed.

The bank could also provide a much-needed paper currency. Based on its capital, the bank would issue bank notes to supplement the specie (gold and silver coin) which was in short supply.

These bank notes could be used to pay taxes and import duties. They would keep the currents of commerce flowing.

The Bank of the United States, by loaning its funds, would also help develop new businesses. This goal, too, was very much in Hamilton's view. For at that time, when the nation had only three banks, business leaders were in desperate need of capital.

"Broad" versus "strict" construction of the new Constitution. The bank proposal at once ran into heated opposition. Thomas Jefferson voiced the belief of many Americans that farmers were "the chosen people of God." They did not want to see America become a land of cities, mills, mines, and factories. Instead they wanted a pastoral land where people tilled the soil and put their faith in the rewards of hard work and the produce of sun and rainfall. Only reluctantly had they gone along with Hamilton on paying the national and state debts. The new bank proposal was too much.

Jefferson, joined by Madison, told President Washington that since the Constitution did not give Congress the power to establish a bank, the bank should not be allowed. This kind of argument became known as a "strict construction" of the Constitution. They argued that the Congress or the President had no power to do anything unless the Constitution gave the federal government that power in so many words.

On the other side, Hamilton defended his bank by arguing that the government had the right to do everything necessary and proper to carry out any of the powers granted in the Constitution. The bank, he argued, was a necessary and proper way to borrow money and to regulate the currency, both of which powers the Constitution had plainly assigned to the Congress. This became known as a "broad" construction of the Constitution. Washington was never entirely convinced by Hamilton's theory. But seeing the nation's need for banks, he signed the bill into law on February 25, 1791.

The dispute that began over the first Bank of the United States between the "strict" and the "broad" interpretation of the Constitution still continues. But who takes which side never stays the same. In general, strict interpretation has been used by those out of power against those who hold the Presidency. As political parties began to emerge behind

Hamilton hoped that his financial plans would help manufacturers and merchants like those named here on trade cards (top and right) and on a customer's bill.

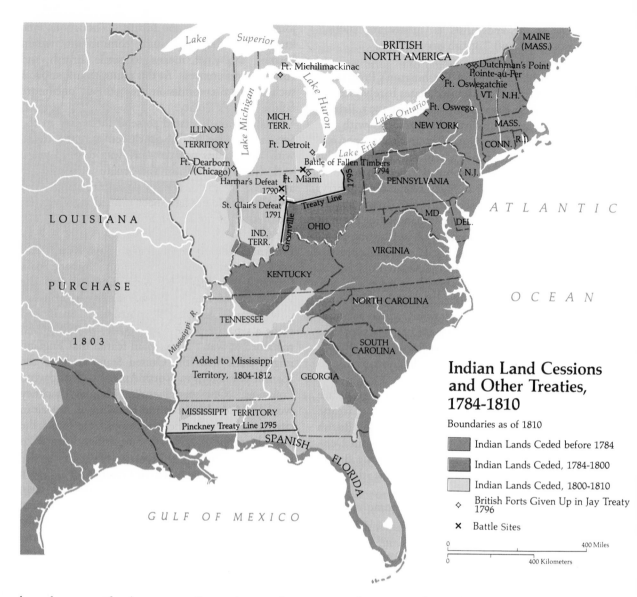

Indian Land Cessions and Other Treaties, 1784-1810

Boundaries as of 1810

- ▨ Indian Lands Ceded before 1784
- ▨ Indian Lands Ceded, 1784-1800
- ▨ Indian Lands Ceded, 1800-1810
- ◇ British Forts Given Up in Jay Treaty 1796
- ✕ Battle Sites

brought peace, if only temporarily, to the Northwest. They gained recognition of the borders won from England in the Revolution. They enabled the United States for a few more years to stay out of the war that was raging in Europe. They allowed Washington to end his term with the nation at peace with the world.

The Whiskey Rebellion. This busy—and successful—diplomacy strengthened the struggling young nation, and especially increased the influence of the Federalist party. So, too, had an event that occurred the previous year. In 1794 the farmers of western Pennsylvania protested against the whiskey tax. This was an "excise" tax—an internal tax—passed a few years before to raise additional funds for the national government.

The whiskey tax angered farmers in the West because it was usual there to make grain (corn or wheat) into whiskey in order to carry it more easily across the mountains to market. Also, where specie and bank notes were in short supply, whiskey was used as a form of money. To the farmers Hamilton's excise tax on whiskey seemed to be a tax directed against them and their crops. They refused to pay the tax when the United States marshal tried to collect it, and in 1794 they staged a "rebellion." The governor of Pennsylvania thought the courts

After the Battle of Fallen Timbers, General Anthony Wayne negotiated the Treaty of Greenville, by which Indian tribes of the Northwest Territory ceded their lands to the United States. A member of Wayne's staff painted this picture, showing Wayne meeting with a group of Indians.

could handle the matter. But Washington, urged on by Hamilton, saw the "rebellion" as a direct attack on the authority of the government. Just as in the days of Daniel Shays, it seemed the state had become a victim of mob rule.

Fulfilling his duty under the Constitution to maintain a "republican form of government," Washington called out the militia. Fifteen thousand strong, it marched west to put down the farmers. In no mood to fight the militia, they returned to their homes. But the ringleaders were seized. Two of them were convicted of treason but were pardoned by the President, who wanted only to prove the strength of the new government. His decisive handling of this affair attracted supporters to the Federalist cause.

The Farewell Address. In September 1796, in his "Farewell Address," Washington announced that he would not serve again. One of the most important statements ever made by an American President, it was largely written by Alexander Hamilton. Al-

though Washington never delivered it as a speech, it was published in the newspapers. Washington still called the United States an experiment. He urged his fellow citizens to remain loyal to the Union and to a republican form of government. He warned against sectionalism, foresaw the danger of secession, and cautioned against political partisanship. His most memorable warning was against "entangling alliances"—playing favorites in the community of nations.

The election of 1796. The Federalist candidate for President in the election of 1796 was John Adams. His services to his country had put him far ahead of any other member of his party. The Republicans nominated Thomas Jefferson. In the electoral college, Adams won by a narrow margin—71 to 68.

Since he had the second largest number of votes, according to the Constitution Jefferson became Vice-President. Hamilton, who did not like the independent-minded Adams, had wanted someone in office who shared his belief in the virtues of the rich. That was not Adams. So Hamilton had tried to persuade the Federalist electors to leave Adams's name off their ballots and instead elect Adams's vice-presidential running mate, Thomas Pinckney, to the Presidency. But Adams's New England friends also knew how to use the electoral college. They simply left Pinckney's name off their ballots. The result was that the votes for Pinckney were fewer than those for Jefferson, so Jefferson became Vice-President.

Washington goes home. George Washington had led his country through its first difficult years. He had led the nation to victory in its battle for independence. A major influence in shaping the new Constitution, he had been the chief force in starting the new government. Now he had given the country time to grow by avoiding a needless war with England. Cold, practical, lacking the brilliance of Jefferson or Hamilton, he made up for his shortcomings by his unswerving devotion to his country. He deserved the country's gratitude. Still, some envious partisans accused him of kingly ambitions and rejoiced when he left public life.

SECTION REVIEW

1. Identify or explain: Edmond Genêt, Jay's Treaty, Pinckney's Treaty, Treaty of Greenville, Battle of Fallen Timbers.
2. As Washington's second term opened, what problems did he face: (a) with England, (b) with Spain, (c) with France?
3. Why were some Americans, who had fought their own revolution, upset by the French Revolution?
4. What was the significance of the Whiskey Rebellion?
5. What dangers did Washington warn against in his Farewell Address?

4. John Adams and the rise of parties

To John Adams now fell the difficult task of guiding a young nation divided by party strife at home and endangered by war in Europe. But Adams was no military hero. Short of stature, with an acid personality, he lacked Washington's enormous prestige.

Adams National Historic Site: photo by George Dow

John Adams was born in the house on the right. He and his wife, Abigail, later lived in the house on the left, and there John Quincy Adams was born. The two houses still stand in Quincy, Massachusetts, where the much larger family home may also be visited.

Sixty years of age when he became President, Adams was the descendant of a line of solid Massachusetts small farmers. He trusted neither the rich nor the poor, but only the wise and the able. And he had served his country well in the trying years of revolution. He had been in both the First and the Second Continental Congress. There he had helped write the petition to the king and the Declaration of Rights and Grievances, and had recommended Washington for commander of the army. Having served on the committee that wrote the Declaration of Independence, he then defended that document vigorously. His 80 committee assignments during the war (he chaired 25 of these committees!) included the crucial Board of War and Ordnance. Then he represented the new nation abroad—in England, France, and Holland. In his home state of Massachusetts, he was principal author of its new constitution of 1780. Working with Franklin and John Jay, he negotiated the peace treaty with Great Britain in 1783. Most recently he had filled the thankless position of Vice-President for eight years. There was no doubt of his patriotism, honesty, and courage.

Adams was, in fact, a great man. But he was also vain, willful, stubborn, prickly, and lacking in tact. Benjamin Franklin described him as "always an honest man, often a wise one, but sometimes and in some things, absolutely out of his senses." Confident of the rightness of his opinions, he made little attempt to harmonize conflicting views in his Cabinet, in the Congress, or in his party. He followed Washington in refusing to take account of political parties. But by his time party politics had already become fierce, and party demands could not be ignored.

The Cabinet.

Adams made his first, and one of his worst, mistakes when he retained the chief Cabinet officers of Washington's second term. These men, Secretary of State Timothy Pickering, Secretary of the Treasury Oliver Wolcott (Hamilton had resigned in 1795), Secretary of War James McHenry, and Attorney General Charles Lee were second-raters. Even worse, they were devoted friends of Adams's personal enemy, Alexander Hamilton, from whom they continued to take their orders. In Adams's defense, it might be said that, of course, there was still no tradition for Cabinet members to be replaced at the end of a President's term. This

was the first time the Presidency had changed. But even after he learned that these men were not really working for him, Adams waited too long to change his top command.

Renewed troubles with France.

Adams's administration was dominated by the problem of France. A new government of five men, called the Directory, had come into power in France in 1795. They had been angered by Jay's Treaty and by the recall of our minister, James Monroe. As a Republican, Monroe had been too friendly to the French for Federalist tastes. The French Directory began seizing our ships in their harbors, refused to receive C. C. Pinckney, Thomas Pinckney's brother, whom President Washington had sent to replace Monroe, and actually ordered Pinckney to leave France.

Angered by the treatment of our minister, Adams declared in a speech to Congress that we must convince France and the world that we were "not a degraded people, humiliated under a colonial spirit of fear." But since he was still determined to keep the nation at peace, he sent John Marshall and Elbridge Gerry to join Pinckney as a commission to deal with the French.

The XYZ Affair.

These envoys immediately ran into problems. The French foreign minister, Talleyrand, would not see them personally, but instead sent secret agents to meet them. The French agents told them that there could be no talks unless the United States apologized for President Adams's speech, promised to loan France $10 million, and paid a bribe of $250,000 to Talleyrand.

When they heard these insulting demands, the envoys answered, "No! no, not a sixpence." Marshall and Pinckney returned home at once. There they stirred the nation's patriotism and fervor against France by the story of their treatment. The whole incident was known as the "XYZ Affair," because the Secretary of State had substituted the letters X, Y, and Z for the names of the agents whom Talleyrand had sent to ask our commissioners for bribes.

Naval war with France.

Republicans and Federalists alike rallied to support Adams in his measures to compel respect for our envoys as "representatives of a great, free, powerful, and independent nation." For a rare moment in his life, the peppery

"Preparations for a War to Defend Commerce," William Birch entitled his 1800 engraving. It shows work on the frigate *Philadelphia*, which was not completed in time for the undeclared naval war with France.

John Adams was popular everywhere. Fellow citizens applauded his language of defiance. They bellowed the new national song, "Hail, Columbia." They adopted as a slogan (to serve again and again later in our history) the toast proposed at a banquet for the returning hero John Marshall: "Millions for defense, but not one cent for tribute!" Preparations for war were begun. Again Washington was called to lead the army, though it was agreed that he would not be expected to leave his home at Mt. Vernon unless there was open battle. Hamilton was to be second in command. A new Navy Department was created by Congress.

War was not formally declared, but Congress renounced the treaty with France that had been signed in 1778 and authorized our ships to prey upon French commerce. Actually, during the two years 1798–1800 a state of war at sea existed with France. More than 80 French ships were captured.

Talleyrand now saw that he could not threaten or bribe the United States. Not wanting war, he hastened to assure our minister to Holland that a new American commission would be received with due respect. At that moment President Adams, to his everlasting credit, resisted the demands of Hamilton and many other Americans (including his own Cabinet) that the nation should fight. That might have been a popular decision, but it would not have served the weak new nation. To the surprise of Federalist Hamiltonians, Adams sent a message to Congress simply nominating a new minister to France. He would send envoys to deal with this sly Talleyrand. Four days after the new envoys sailed, the upstart Napoleon Bonaparte overthrew the corrupt Directory.

Napoleon, intent on establishing his power in France and Europe, wanted no trouble with the United States. In September 1800, therefore, he signed an agreement that ended the treaty of alliance of 1778, thus freeing the United States from any obligation to help France in war. In return the United States gave up all claims against France for damages done to our shipping by French cruisers since 1793. This fair bargain enabled the United States to enter the 1800s at peace.

The Alien and Sedition Acts, 1798.

In 1798 when anger against the French had become the most violent, the Federalists took advantage of the situation. They passed a series of laws to suppress Republican opposition and insure power for their own party. But, in fact, they misjudged the temper of the nation. Their oppressive measures outraged many Americans and helped lead to the downfall of the Federalist party.

Leading Federalists believed—or pretended to believe—that most foreigners who came to the United States joined the Republicans. In the Naturalization Act, then, they extended the time it took to become a citizen from 5 to 14 years. In the Alien Act they gave the President at once the power to deport any alien he thought dangerous to the nation's security and then, in time of war, the power to deport or arrest all aliens who came from an enemy nation.

The Sedition Act was especially harsh. It provided a heavy fine and a jail term for any person found guilty of "combining and conspiring to oppose the execution of the laws, or publishing false, scandalous, or malicious writings against the President, Congress, or the government of the United States." These words were so vague and general that the Federalists could use the law to stop public criticism of the government by their opponents. This would spell the end of free representative government.

Some Federalist leaders, including Hamilton, actually disapproved of these laws that were pushed through Congress by extremist members of their party. John Adams had not promoted the mea-

sures, but on the other hand he did not veto them or prevent their use against the Republicans.

The Virginia and Kentucky Resolutions.

The Sedition Act was used to silence Republican writers and newspaper editors who criticized President Adams. For example, Thomas Cooper, who later became president of South Carolina College, wrote a pamphlet in which he said Adams "was hardly in the infancy of political mistake" when he took office. Cooper admitted Adams had not yet interfered with a court of justice, though he implied Adams might still do so. For his writings, Cooper was fined $400 and spent six months in jail.

Only ten Republicans were convicted under the Sedition Act. Many other members of that party— but no Federalists—were tried. This attack on freedom of speech and the press outraged Republicans. Even some Federalists, most notably John Marshall, who was later to become Chief Justice, spoke out against it.

If the courts would not defend the people against the Alien and Sedition Acts or other tyrannical measures, who could do so? Madison and Jefferson believed that in this situation the only power able to oppose the federal government was the states. Resolutions passed by the Virginia legislature (and drafted by Madison) declared that each state had the right to judge the constitutionality of measures passed by Congress. The Kentucky Resolutions, which Jefferson wrote, went even further. He said that a state could declare acts of Congress "null and void" and that the rightful response to an unconstitutional act of Congress was *"nullification"* by the states.

The Constitution did not say who was to judge if Congress went beyond the powers granted in the Constitution. Madison and Jefferson believed the states had that right. The states' rights doctrine they championed would at last be carried so far that it would lead to civil war. Then it would be clear that the federal government, through its courts, had to be the judge of its own powers.

The election of 1800.

John Adams was proud of what he had accomplished as President. He had a right to be, even though his main achievement was to keep the nation out of war. He hoped, however, that in a second term he could make a more positive record.

A supporter celebrated Thomas Jefferson's election in 1800 by making this flag. Items like banners, posters, and buttons are still an integral part of American elections. They reflect changes in styles as well as politics.

But Adams was not reelected, in part because of the Alien and Sedition Acts, but mostly due to the enmity of Alexander Hamilton, who was a member of his own party. Republicans stumbled across Hamilton's bitter criticism of Adams and published it in their newspapers. At the same time Hamilton worked to defeat Adams in the electoral college in order to elect Adams's running mate, C. C. Pinckney. Hamilton's opposition took its toll. Meanwhile, of course, the Republicans had taken their own more careful steps to defeat Adams.

When all the electoral votes were counted, Adams had 65 votes, and Pinckney had 64. Then came the surprise. The Republicans had won a very close election, but their two candidates for President and Vice-President, Jefferson and Aaron Burr, each had 73 votes. The Republicans had made a serious mistake. Since the electors in the electoral college had to vote for two persons on their ballots without distinguishing between President and Vice-President, one Republican elector was supposed not to vote for Burr. That would have made Jefferson President and Burr Vice-President. Instead, they all voted for Burr. Since there was then a tie, according to the Constitution the election had to be decided in the House of Representatives.

As the country eagerly awaited the name of its next President, Congress gathered on Wednesday, February 11, 1801, in a partly completed Capitol in the raw new capital city of Washington. The House then voted on and off for several days. Some Federalists hoped to make Aaron Burr President. But Hamilton, despite his personal dislike for Jefferson, showed his patriotism and good judgment by opposing Burr. "Jefferson is to be preferred," he wrote his friends. "He is by far not so dangerous a man; and he has pretensions to character." Finally, on Monday, February 16, after receiving assurances that the public credit and the navy would be maintained, and that there would be no mass eviction of their fellow party members from office, the Federalists allowed Jefferson to be elected President.

After this election, the Twelfth Amendment to the Constitution was enacted in 1804. It provided for the naming of the President and the Vice-President separately on each elector's ballot.

The election of 1800 was the last time the Federalists came close to winning an election. But their Presidents—Washington and Adams—had served their country well. They put the nation on its way and set many useful precedents. They laid the foundation for a government based on broad construction of its powers. True enough, they failed to resolve the hard questions of the links between the executive and the legislature or between the central government and the states. That would take time—and in the end would cost the bloodshed of a civil war. Meanwhile they helped the nation grow strong by keeping the nation at peace during its critical early years.

John Adams, the last Federalist President, was a better man than history has often credited him with being. He sadly left the city of Washington early on the morning of Jefferson's inauguration and returned to Massachusetts. During the years that followed, he made up his differences with his former friend, Thomas Jefferson. They began a lively correspondence full of wit and wisdom that lasted the many years till their death. By an uncanny coincidence John Adams, then 90 years old, died in Massachusetts on the very same day that Jefferson died at Monticello in Virginia. That day was July 4, 1826, the fiftieth anniversary of the Declaration of Independence.

SECTION REVIEW

1. How did it happen that Jefferson became Adams's Vice-President?

2. What was the XYZ Affair?

3. What were the Alien and Sedition Acts? Why were they passed?

4. What were the Virginia and Kentucky Resolutions? How did they differ? Who wrote them and why?

5. What is the Twelfth Amendment? Why was it passed?

CHAPTER REVIEW

MEETING OUR EARLIER SELVES

1. Considering the "state of the Union" in 1790, as described in section 1 of this chapter, what kinds of measures might a Federalist propose to strengthen the nation?

2. List in order of importance some major accomplishments of Washington or his administration in his two terms of office. Justify your ranking of items 1 and 2 in your list.

3. How did it happen that the new government started out with a big national debt? How did paying the debt in full benefit the country? How was "payment in full" unfair?

4. The Constitution failed to provide numerous specific directions on how the new government was to operate. Point out some of these omissions and show how officials in 1789–1800 responded to them.

5. How did Hamilton and Jefferson differ in their views of the ideal America? In which sections of the country were Hamilton's views most popular? Jefferson's? Why?

6. Why did the Indians of the Northwest and Southeast side with the British and Spanish against the United States?

7. What situation gave rise to the claim that the states could nullify an act of Congress? Why was such a view dangerous?

QUESTIONS FOR TODAY

1. Find examples of recent laws that would not have passed if Congress followed a strict interpretation of the Constitution.

2. The Whiskey Rebellion was a tax revolt. How would you expect contemporary Americans to respond to what they considered unfair taxation?

3. What symbols and ceremonies have grown up around the Presidency to give the office dignity? Of recent Presidents, which have adopted the most ceremony? the least?

4. Was it wise for Washington to keep both Hamilton and Jefferson in the Cabinet, considering their widely different views on public policy? How would a modern President avoid or handle such a situation?

YOUR REGION IN HISTORY

1. What events described in this chapter had some special significance for your region? Explain.

2. If you live in one of the original thirteen states, how many United States Representatives did it have in the First Congress? If your state joined the Union later, what was the number of the Congress to which your state first sent senators and representatives? (The years of the First Congress are 1789–91; the Second, 1791–93; the Third, 1793–95; etc.)

SKILLS TO MAKE OUR PAST VIVID

1. If you lived in western Kentucky in the 1790s, you could have traveled to Philadelphia by water or land. Trace both routes on the map on page 115. About how many miles would you have to travel by water? by land? Which route would you probably have taken? Why?

2. Construct a timeline of important events mentioned in this chapter. Underline the items that would have pleased the Federalists more than the Republicans.

3

E pluribus unum: One made from many 1800–1840

The Americans had won their independence and established a government. They had held elections and peacefully transferred power from one political party to another. But they had not yet created a strong nation. Many observers wondered whether they possibly could.

The people occupied a land four times as large as France, but with less than one-fifth of that nation's population. They were scattered over hundreds of thousands of square miles of wilderness. They had few roads and even fewer cities. The very vastness of the land—a source of pride and future power—was also a weakness. For the people tended to be more closely tied to their state governments and their regions—New England, the Middle States, or the South—than to the weak central government in its swampy forest clearing on the banks of the Potomac.

But the nation discovered new ways to grow. It fought a "second war of independence" with England. Its politics and political parties became ever more democratic. This created new traditions and fed national pride, which would tie all the states and all the regions together. Americans were shaping a new kind of government. Strong leaders would respond to the people.

CHAPTER 7

Jefferson in power

Four of the first five Presidents of the United States were Virginia men. These were Washington, Jefferson, Madison, and Monroe. We usually call them the "Virginia dynasty." They had faith in the people.

Why did so many of our nation's first leaders come from a single state? An explanation lies in the special features of colonial Virginia. Young aristocrats like Washington and Jefferson and Madison and Monroe led a cozy life. A few families owned the largest tobacco plantations and most of the slaves. They not only ran the government, but members of these lucky families might hold more than one office. George Washington, for example, was at the same time a church vestryman, a justice of the peace, a commander of the militia, and a delegate to the House of Burgesses. This was aristocracy American-style.

For Virginia's representative government there had to be elections. But these were very different from the rough-and-tumble contests in modern cities. In our day, anybody can run for office and nearly every adult can vote. But not in colonial Virginia! There only substantial property owners could vote, and only the well-to-do were eligible for high office. Slaves, of course, had no vote. And Virginia had no cities where unruly immigrants or discontented working people could secure a share in government. Is it any wonder that Virginia's aristocrats had great faith in what *they* called representative government? The only kind of representative government they knew was safe and sane. Even the ownership of slaves helped to reinforce their belief in "representative" government. It meant that their poor workers had no hope of voting or sharing in the government.

When these Virginia aristocrats talked of "the people," they meant substantial property owners like themselves and other smaller property owners who respected their "betters." We can understand why they had a great deal less fear of "the people" and a great deal more confidence that "the people" would choose good representatives than did other thoughtful Americans of that age. John Adams of Massachusetts, Alexander Hamilton of New York, and Gouverneur Morris of Pennsylvania and New York—who all lived in or near big cities—knew the fickle city mobs. They put their faith elsewhere.

138

1. The man and his policies

Thomas Jefferson became the President of a sharply divided country. The Federalists called him "godless" because he was no orthodox churchman, because he was so tolerant, and especially because he had supported the bloody French Revolution. They feared that this country too might soon be swept by a "reign of terror." But Thomas Jefferson's first term was to be one of the most successful presidencies in American history. A surprising number of Americans in all sections of the country were drawn into a united nation.

The new capital city. Jefferson was the first President of the United States to be inaugurated in the new capital, which his deal with Hamilton in 1790 had located on the Potomac River. The city had been laid out and surveyed in the following years. One of those who did this important job was Benjamin Banneker, a free black mathematician and scientist. Banneker was probably the first black civilian to work for the federal government.

The architect for the city had been a Frenchman, Major Pierre-Charles L'Enfant, who had served with the American army during the Revolutionary War. In 1801 the long vistas, grand avenues, and noble buildings he had envisioned for the wilderness were far from complete. Washington was only in its first stages of construction. The two wings of the new Capitol building, on a height overlooking the future city, were nearly finished, but the rotunda in the middle was still open to the skies. Since there were no hotels, the members of Congress stayed in nearby boardinghouses.

Between the Capitol and the President's house, one and a half miles away, lay swamp and woodland crossed only by a muddy track which was grandly named Pennsylvania Avenue.

L'Enfant's 1792 plan of Washington showed broad avenues meeting at the Capitol circle.

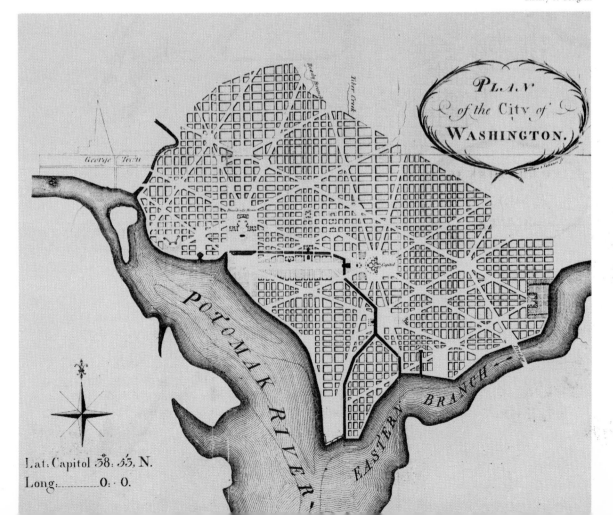

This portrait of Thomas Jefferson shows the Natural Bridge in Virginia, a spectacle which he much admired. His *Notes on Virginia* describes these natural wonders.

The President's "palace" was not yet known as the White House. It only got that name after it was burned by the British in the War of 1812. Then the Acquia Creek sandstone of which it was built was painted white to cover the scorch marks from the fire. The house was still unfinished in March 1801, but it had been lived in during the previous fall and winter by President Adams and his family. When the sharp-tongued Abigail Adams saw the new capital city for the first time, she described it as having "houses scattered over a space of ten miles, and trees and stumps in plenty." Mrs. Adams estimated it would take 30 servants to run the "castle of a house" when it would be completed. Meanwhile, she dried the family wash in the unplastered East Room during stormy weather.

"We need nothing here," one senator reported, "but men, women, and other little trifles of the kind to make our city perfect." In sober fact this new federal city had no shops, no theaters, no libraries— and few people. The legislators suffered the discomforts of monks living in a monastery, but they had taken no monastic vows.

Thomas Jefferson. On March 4, 1801, the day of his inauguration, Thomas Jefferson stepped out the door of the boardinghouse where he was staying and walked the short distance to the Capitol. He was escorted by a crowd of congressmen and other citizens.

Looking like a "tall, raw-boned farmer," he avoided the pomp that Washington and Adams had thought necessary for the President. Six feet tall, thin and angular, with light-colored hair tinged with red, Jefferson, unlike his predecessors, did not wear a wig. His clothing was—depending upon your point of view—either casual or just plain sloppy.

In place of the formal weekly receptions begun by Washington there were now informal gatherings. Citizens, with or without invitations, thronged to shake the President's hand. But life in the White House was far from simple, for Jefferson was still a southern aristocrat. He liked to live well, and during his years in Paris he had developed a taste for elegant French cooking. At his gracious dinner parties in the President's mansion, his lucky guests enjoyed a French chef's masterpieces. These were washed down by French wines of choice vintages. In a single year Jefferson's wine bill came to $2800.

Relaxed and easygoing in a small company, Jefferson was a charming conversationalist. But he disliked crowds. He was a halting public speaker, and he generally avoided formal public speeches. He did not follow the practice—begun by Washington and Adams—of addressing Congress in person. Jefferson said that he did not want to act like a king speaking to Parliament from a throne. But

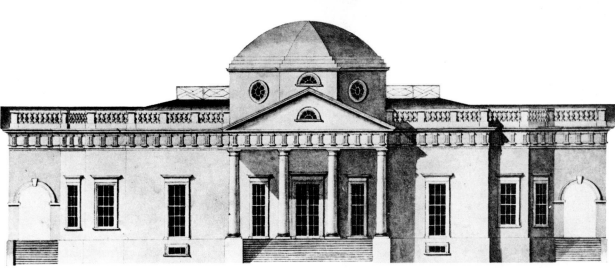

Thomas Jefferson modeled his home Monticello (near Charlottesville, Virginia) after an ancient
Roman building that he saw in the south of France. The plan of the front shown here was drawn
by Robert Mills, who studied architecture under Jefferson. Below, Jefferson used pencil and ink
on graph paper to make a drawing of the first floor. In the front hall, under the dome, Jefferson
displayed sculpture and curiosities of natural history.

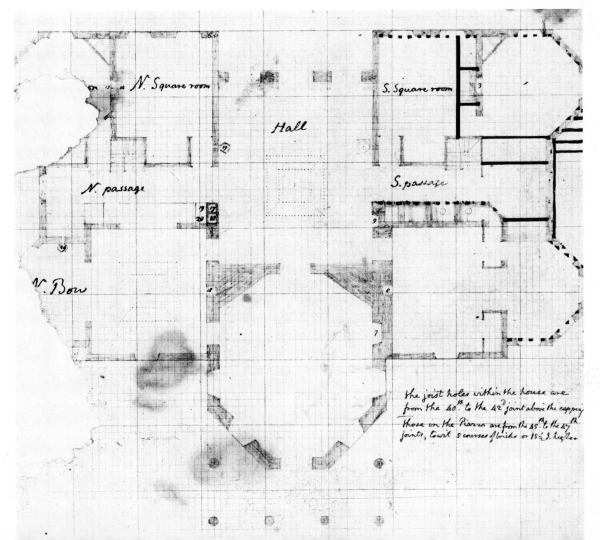

Jefferson's entry in his "Garden Book" notes
an untimely killing frost on May 5 in 1774.
Luckily some fruits and vegetables survived.

perhaps this was just an excuse to save himself from
the public appearances which he never enjoyed.

Jefferson believed that slavery was a great moral
evil. Still, he saw no easy way to abolish the
institution that supported the southern plantation
system. "We have the wolf by the ears," he once
wrote, "and we can neither hold him, nor safely let
him go. Justice is in one scale, and self-preservation
in the other." He was himself the owner of large
plantations and about 150 slaves. But unlike
George Washington, he did not free his slaves upon
his death.

A remarkably versatile man, Jefferson was also
one of the best American architects of his age. He
designed his own home in Virginia, and throughout
his life he worked to improve it. We can still visit
the delightful Monticello and can enjoy the gardens
he planned and planted. We can admire his ingenious contraptions including a clock two stories
high, designed to alert the household to the hours of
their duties. To this house he brought his beloved
wife, Martha Wayles Skelton, in 1772. She bore six
children—four of whom died in childhood. When
she herself died only ten years after her marriage,

Jefferson was plunged in grief. Partly to recover
from this tragedy, he threw himself into an active
public life.

Jefferson was also a surveyor, a philosopher, a
scientist, and an inventor. At ease in French,
Italian, and Spanish, as well as Latin and Greek, he
corresponded with the eminent thinkers of his day
wherever they were. He declared that they were
all citizens of a worldwide "Republic of Letters."

The inaugural address. In his inaugural address
Jefferson tried to play down the differences between
himself and his opponents. He said they were "all
Republicans, all Federalists" in their devotion to the
Union. He promised (1) "equal and exact justice
to all men" of every shade of political and religious
opinion; (2) friendship with all nations but no
alliances; (3) respect for the rights of the states while
still preserving the "constitutional vigor" of the
national government; (4) encouragement of agriculture and commerce; (5) freedom of speech, press,
and elections; (6) economy and honesty in the
management of the country's finances.

This was hardly a program to frighten the
Federalists. Jefferson saw that many Federalists
were unhappy with their leaders and were ready to
become Republicans if he followed a moderate
course. Elected by only a narrow margin, he had to
widen the base of his public support if he was to
govern successfully.

In later years Jefferson called his election "the
revolution of 1800." He believed that election had
turned the country away from militarism and
monarchy. But he probably exaggerated those
dangers. John Adams had already saved the nation
from militarism by avoiding war with France, and
there was never a real threat of monarchy.

Jefferson, unlike Hamilton, did not want to see
an industrialized nation of cities. He hoped the
country could remain a community of farmers who
governed themselves in local assemblies. The government in Washington should confine itself, he
thought, to managing the nation's dealings with
foreign powers. Such a task could be performed by
only a few public servants. Pursuing this policy,
Jefferson aimed to reduce the army and navy and to
apply the public revenue to paying off the public
debt. No longer, Jefferson said, would the government "waste the labors of the people under the
pretense of taking care of them."

The Barbary States

0   500 Miles

0   500 Kilometers

For his Cabinet Jefferson selected the ablest men, including the architect of the Constitution, James Madison of Virginia, to be Secretary of State and Albert Gallatin, a brilliant Swiss-born financier from Pennsylvania, to be Secretary of the Treasury.

Following Jefferson's ideas Gallatin insisted on strict economy in government. He introduced a modern budget with specific sums for each item of national expense. The amount of money spent on the army and navy was reduced by half, and about 70 percent of the nation's revenue, more than $7 million a year, was used to pay off the national debt.

The Alien and Sedition Acts, which had expired at the end of the Adams administration, were not renewed. A new naturalization act was passed, restoring the short five-year waiting period for those who wanted to become citizens. The Bank of the United States was allowed to continue, as was the tariff. But the excise tax that had started the Whiskey Rebellion was repealed. There was not a great deal to distinguish Jefferson's policies from those of the Federalists.

The Barbary pirates.

We remained at peace with the nations of Europe during Jefferson's first term. Our commerce and wealth increased rapidly. But one foreign problem grew more serious as our commerce expanded. For many years the Arab rulers of the Barbary States on the north coast of Africa (Morocco, Algiers, Tunis, and Tripoli) had sent out pirates to seize ships on the ocean, especially in the Mediterranean Sea, and hold their crews for ransom. The European nations paid tribute to these pirates and kidnappers as a cheap substitute for war. And we had done the same. In the decade 1790–1800 we gave them "presents" amounting to $2 million.

Jefferson was determined to put an end to the payments to these racketeers. So in spite of his devotion to peace and economy, he sent naval squadrons to punish the pirates. This was a costly business, and Congress had to impose an extra 2.5 percent tax on imports as a "Mediterranean Fund." But the results justified the sacrifice. The peace concluded with Tripoli in January 1805 discouraged the piratical raids.

The other Barbary States continued to ask for payments, though at a lower rate, and after the War of 1812 this problem had to be faced again. In 1815 Stephen Decatur, who had been a hero in the earlier because Haiti had not yet been reconquered. Toussaint was captured by treachery, but still the war went on. By January 1803 the French General LeClerc was dead of fever, Haiti was a ruin, and the French army had been destroyed by its black opponents and by yellow fever. Tons of expensive supplies had been lost. General Rochambeau, who succeeded LeClerc, wrote home that he must have 35,000 new troops to put down the blacks.

Napoleon decides to sell Louisiana. Napoleon was a man who could make up his mind quickly. He could change his mind just as quickly. Since he could not control Haiti, he wondered how he could hold huge Louisiana. Without telling anyone, he suddenly decided to get what he could for his American empire. When the Americans in Paris offered to buy the small piece of land around the entrance to the Mississippi River, there was an amazing reply. Napoleon would *not* sell or even rent them that little piece. But he *would* sell them the whole of Louisiana!

Napoleon's offer to sell all of Louisiana was the last answer Monroe and Livingston had expected. They were not prepared for it. What should they do? Should they simply tell Napoleon they could give no answer till they had word from the President and Congress back in Washington? That would take weeks—or maybe even months—and by then the changeable Napoleon might very well say the deal was all off. Or should they, for the sake of their country, do what they really had no power to do? Should they snatch up this unexpected bargain and then pray that the people back home would support them?

This was one of the fateful moments of American history. It was not surprising that the French dictator had made a bold decision. But the young United States was a representative government under a Constitution that carefully described and limited the powers of the Congress. Could this self-governing nation match Napoleon's boldness? Or were the people of the Republic doomed to be slow and timid?

The American ministers in Paris, Livingston and Monroe, took the bold and dangerous way. They decided to take up Napoleon's offer. On their own judgment they offered $15 million for all Louisiana. And Napoleon accepted. As soon as the deal was closed, they began wondering whether what

they would have to share was praise or blame. It was some years before either of them dared claim any credit for this move.

Jefferson makes a hard decision. When the news finally reached the United States, it was greeted by shock, delight, and dismay. These two Americans, some complained, had been sent to Paris simply to buy a small piece of land in order to keep the riverways open in the West. Instead, they had allowed a whimsical dictator to trap them into buying half a billion acres of worthless wilderness!

This was perhaps the greatest test of statesmanship that Jefferson ever had to face. He was on the spot. The Constitution said nothing at all about whether or how Congress could buy land from a foreign country. Again and again, in many other cases, Jefferson had argued that Congress had only those powers that the Constitution had assigned in so many words. Maybe the power to buy land from foreign countries had been left out of the Constitution *on purpose*—to prevent the United States from playing the dangerous, old-fashioned game of empire. The people of the new United States had tried to escape from the ways of the Old World, where the rulers were in the habit of buying and selling, bartering and gambling faraway lands and unknown peoples.

Now would Jefferson go against everything he had been saying for years? If he had been weak, he would have been afraid to change his mind. But he decided to show the same courage that Livingston and Monroe had shown in Paris. It was harder for him, because he had to stand up and change his mind in public. All his enemies were there to hoot at him. Still, Jefferson decided to ask the members of Congress to vote the money to buy Louisiana. He asked them to forget technicalities—"metaphysical subtleties" is what he called them—and instead to think of the future of the nation. He asked the Congress to approve afterwards what it had not been foresighted enough to authorize in advance.

After long and bitter debate, the Congress agreed. In October 1803, when the Senate ratified the treaty with Napoleon, Louisiana became the property of the United States. Within a year, an American governor was sitting in New Orleans, where he could see that the Mississippi River would stay open. Western Americans would have their highway to the world.

3. Jefferson, Marshall, and the courts

During his first term Jefferson had tried to keep the Federalists happy. He had been moderate in his approach to most problems. He had even managed to help New England merchants (mainstay of the Federalist party) by his attack on the Barbary pirates who were menacing their commerce. New England fishermen were pleased that he supported a bounty on codfish.

The "midnight judges" and the patronage. At one point, however, Jefferson directly attacked the Federalists. After their loss of the Presidency and of Congress in the 1800 elections, the Federalists tried to keep control of the federal courts and of as many other offices as possible. In the Judiciary Act of 1801, passed just before they went out of power, they had actually increased the number of judges and added some minor judicial offices. They intended, of course, to fill these places with appointees from their own party before Jefferson and his Republicans took office on March 4. President Adams hastily nominated Federalists for the new positions, and they were quickly confirmed by the Senate. In order to put a small army of Federalists into these important permanent jobs, Adams signed some of their commissions on his final night in office. The last-minute appointees were sneeringly called "the midnight judges."

Adams had spent his last days seizing every chance to maintain Federalist influence by appointing many lesser officers: collectors of customs, consuls, postmasters, and clerks.

Jefferson was angered by this attempt of the defeated Federalists to keep "a dead clutch on the patronage." Once in office, he sent word to all those whose commissions had not yet been delivered to consider the appointments as never having been made. His first Congress then quickly repealed the Judiciary Act of 1801.

In this way began the first struggle between the political parties over the right to fill the offices of government with members of their own party. The struggle would never cease. The party going out of power always wanted to keep its supporters in office. Yet the victors in the election assumed that they had a right to appoint officials who supported their party. Jefferson naturally believed that he should have Republicans helping him in govern-

National Portrait Gallery, Smithsonian Institution

Keen-witted and persuasive, John Marshall was Chief Justice of the United States for 34 years.

ment offices if he was to do his best. Also this would help build a strong political party. After refusing to honor the commissions that Adams had signed at the end of his term, Jefferson picked Republicans for these posts. Whenever a job opened up due to a death or retirement, a Republican was appointed. In this way, by the end of his first term, Jefferson had named members of his own party to about half the highest positions in the government.

There was one position, however, that he had not been able to do anything about. The high office of

Chief Justice of the Supreme Court was held by his cousin and fellow Virginian, John Marshall. In his personality and his manners Marshall was much like Jefferson. He was sloppy in his dress and easygoing. Like Jefferson he had a brilliant and vigorous mind. And like Jefferson he insisted on seeing things his own way. But there were hardly any issues on which the two great men agreed. Before Marshall's appointment, it did not seem that the Supreme Court would play a major role in shaping the new nation. But under Marshall's leadership the Court became an active force protecting private property from state interference and building a strong central government.

Marbury v. Madison. When Jefferson refused to deliver the commissions signed by Adams, he gave Chief Justice Marshall the chance he had been looking for. One of Adams's "midnight" appointees, William Marbury, sued Jefferson's Secretary of State, James Madison, to compel him to deliver his commission (already signed and sealed by President Adams) as justice of the peace. Marshall decided to use the case to assert—even to create—crucial powers for the Supreme Court. The case of *Marbury* v. *Madison,* heard by the Supreme Court in February 1803, would become a landmark in American history.

Chief Justice Marshall said that Marbury had a right to his commission as a justice of the peace. But he did not let the matter rest there. If he had, Marbury's name would be unknown in American history. Instead, he went on to declare that the section of the Judiciary Act of 1789 that gave Marbury the right to demand the delivery of his commission was unconstitutional, since no such right was granted in the Constitution. As a result, Marshall concluded, there was no way for Marbury to get his commission from Madison.

The important question, of course, was not whether the unknown William Marbury should hold the lowly office of justice of the peace. Of the greatest significance to the nation was whether the Supreme Court had the power to declare a law of the land unconstitutional. In his brilliant, if devious, decision the strong-willed Chief Justice answered that question with a resounding, epoch-making Yes!

The Founding Fathers had, in fact, assumed that the Supreme Court would have the power to declare acts of Congress unconstitutional. But they had not put that power in so many words in the Constitution. So by a strict reading of the Constitution the Court had no such right. Nor had it ever used the right since the Supreme Court was created in 1789. Now in 1803 the Court suddenly assumed the right of *judicial review* in its role as guardian of the Constitution. The leading role ever since of the Supreme Court in American history has followed from this bold decision of Chief Justice Marshall.

The Supreme Court makes its decisions by a majority vote. In Marshall's day, when there were only six justices on the Supreme Court, any four of the justices had the power to overrule the President and the Congress on the meaning of the Constitution. Today, when there are nine justices on the Court, this power rests in the hands of five justices. In few other nations have the courts held such powers.

An attempt to change the courts by impeachment. Jefferson and the Republicans feared the power of judges. They were appointed for life, and there was no way for the Jeffersonians—or anybody else—to remove them except by the long impeachment process. What guarantee was there that these judges (who did not owe their positions to the voters) would show a proper respect for the will of the majority? Of course the Republicans feared the judges more because so many happened to be Federalists.

The Republicans started impeachment proceedings against several judges. Most important was their trial of Samuel Chase of the Supreme Court. Though a signer of the Declaration of Independence, Chase was open to attack. In his charges to juries in cases brought under the Sedition Act, he had gone out of his way to denounce Republicans. He called them "Jacobins" and "revolutionaries." The trial of Justice Chase before the Senate in January 1805 was especially dramatic. It was presided over by the flamboyant Vice-President Aaron Burr, who had only recently killed the famous patriot Alexander Hamilton. Burr took his role as judge seriously and conducted the trial with an even hand. All the while Jefferson, who felt his political prestige and power were at stake, was putting pressure on members of the Senate to convict Chase. Though the Republicans held a majority of seats in the Senate, Chase was acquitted.

The problem faced by the Senate was that the Constitution said (Art. III, sec. 1) that judges "shall hold their office during good behavior." But what did "good behavior" mean? Another section of the Constitution (Art. II, sec. 4) gave a clue. It declared that civil officers, meaning all government officers except those in the military, might not be impeached except for "treason, bribery, or other high crimes and misdemeanors." Fortunately, the Senate decided that Chase's behavior did not amount to an impeachable offense.

If Chase had been convicted, the next candidate for impeachment would probably have been Chief Justice John Marshall. And if Marshall had been impeached—simply because of an honest difference between him and the President over the meaning of the Constitution—the government of the United States might have been very unlike what it has become. Again and again, every party in power would have been tempted to use the tool of impeachment to destroy its political enemies. A system of two strong and freely disagreeing political parties might never have survived.

The election of 1804. Few administrations in our history have been as successful as Jefferson's first term. Our foreign trade had doubled. The customs' receipts far outran Gallatin's estimates. In fact, the national debt was reduced by $25 million, even after paying for the Louisiana Territory. The country between the Alleghenies and the Mississippi was filling rapidly. Mississippi had become a territory in 1798. Indiana had followed in 1800. Ohio had enough people to become a state in February 1803.

Except for what Jefferson called "bickerings" with Spain over West Florida, an area Jefferson still wanted to make part of the United States, our relations with European nations were friendly. Our commissioners under Jay's Treaty had satisfied the British merchants by awarding them more than $2.5 million in payment of long-standing debts from American citizens. We had compelled respect for the American flag by the Barbary pirates. We had acquired a vast domain west of the Mississippi.

The quarrelsome opposition of a few Federalists was drowned in the general chorus of approval. It was no wonder that in the next election Jefferson carried all but one state. Of the 176 electoral votes cast, Jefferson received 162. He won in a landslide

Office of the Architect of the Capitol

This photograph shows the recently restored old Supreme Court chamber. John Marshall presided in this ornate chamber for 25 of his 34 years as Chief Justice.

over South Carolina's C. C. Pinckney, the Federalist candidate.

Here was a President whose election four years before had brought predictions of the ruin of our commerce, the end of efficient government, and the destruction of the social order. The happy result of Jefferson's first term had been quite the opposite. When Jefferson took the oath of office a second time, on March 4, 1805, he congratulated his fellow countrymen that "not a cloud appeared on the horizon."

SECTION REVIEW

1. Identify or explain: "midnight judges," Judiciary Act of 1789, John Marshall, impeachment process, C. C. Pinckney.

2. How did the Federalists seek to retain influence in the federal government after their defeat in 1800?

3. Why is *Marbury* v. *Madison* a landmark case?

4. Why was Samuel Chase's impeachment trial important?

4. Trouble on the seas

In the spring of 1803 war between England and France was renewed. In October 1805 Lord Nelson destroyed the combined French and Spanish fleets off Cape Trafalgar near the Strait of Gibraltar. A few weeks later Napoleon defeated the Russian and Austrian armies at Austerlitz. So, like the tiger and the shark, Napoleon was master of the continent of Europe, and England ruled the seas. What would this division of empires mean for the young United States?

British Orders and French decrees. Each of the two great powers now tried to damage the other by shutting off its commerce. The British issued *Orders in Council,* forbidding neutral ships to trade with ports under Napoleon's control on the continent. Napoleon replied with *imperial decrees* that authorized French seizure of all ships that traded with the British Isles or that allowed themselves to be searched by a British cruiser. Naturally, the British Orders were more damaging to America since Britain controlled the seas, but both orders and decrees cost Americans ships and cargoes.

The commerce of the United States was threatened with ruin. As a neutral nation willing to trade with all nations, we had profited from the wars in Europe by building up a prosperous foreign trade throughout the world. The sturdy American sailing ships were the favorite carriers for the merchandise of South America, the West Indies, and the Far East to all the ports of Europe. Our own exports too—the fish and lumber of New England, the cotton and rice of the South, the wheat and livestock of the trans-Allegheny country—had increased threefold since Washington took office.

Beginning in 1785, ships from the United States began to trade with China. Here the American flag flies with other flags over Canton, the only Chinese city open for foreign trade until 1842.

The Peabody Museum, Salem: photo by Mark Sexton

Napoleonic Europe

- French Empire
- Dependent on Napoleon
- Allied with Napoleon
- ✕ Battle Sites

Our merchant marine was growing at a rapid rate. So many new ships were added in 1805 that 4200 more sailors had to be hired. Sailors' wages rose from $8 to $24 a month. To share this prosperity, hundreds of foreign seamen, mostly British, became naturalized citizens of the United States. They wanted to escape the brutal discipline of the British navy. They wished to enjoy the higher pay, better food, and more humane treatment found on American vessels. But this brought some unexpected new problems.

The Chesapeake affair.

The United States frigate *Chesapeake*, Captain Barron commanding, weighed anchor from Norfolk, Virginia, on June 22, 1807. She was bound on the long voyage to the Mediterranean, so her guns were still unmounted and her decks littered with tackle. Shortly after the *Chesapeake* reached the sea, the British warship *Leopard* overtook her. *Leopard* tricked *Chesapeake* into stopping by saying that they had dispatches for her. After the *Chesapeake* had heaved to, the *Leopard* demanded to be able to search the American ship for deserters from the British navy. Captain Barron refused and the British vessel thereupon poured three full broadsides into the *Chesapeake*, killing three men and wounding eighteen, before Captain Barron could reply. Unprepared to resist, Captain Barron struck his colors after firing a single gun. Then the British officers took four alleged deserters from the American frigate. They left her to limp back into Norfolk with her dead and wounded.

The impressment of American seamen. Napoleon showed no more respect than England had shown for American rights on the sea. But he did not have the cruisers to capture our ships on the high seas, to force them to France to pay duties, or to search them for departing sailors. All he could do was to seize our ships in his continental ports and sell their cargoes for the benefit of his treasury. Compared to the British, the French could do the American merchant marine very little damage.

In its desperate struggle with Napoleon, Great Britain needed every man who could be found to serve in the navy. It mattered little that the sailor had American naturalization papers. British law did not allow a British subject to switch his loyalty to another country. Furthermore, many of the naturalization papers were forged.

No one knows just how many legitimate American citizens were taken off United States ships by the British impressment officers. Shortly before the United States went to war with Great Britain in 1812, President Madison told Congress that more than 6000 American seamen had been "impressed and held in bondage" during the preceding years. And this was probably a good estimate.

Jefferson's difficulty. The British firing on the *Chesapeake* in June 1807 caused a storm of fury in the United States. Had he wished it, Jefferson could have had war in a minute. But Jefferson did not want war. Instead, he at once ordered British warships to stay out of our waters. He also sent orders to James Monroe, our minister in London, to demand an apology for the attack on the *Chesapeake* and an end to impressment.

The British were in no mood for the complete surrender that Jefferson demanded. Their government was determined to let nothing stand in the way of crushing Napoleon. "An insignificant and puny power," as one newspaper called the United States, certainly could not be allowed to interfere with Britain's control of the seas.

The reply of the British foreign secretary, George Canning, came in December 1807. Canning wished to avoid war and was eager to right the wrong done by the attack on the *Chesapeake*. Indeed, the admiral whose orders led to that attack had already been dismissed from his command. But on the crucial question of the right of search and impressment, the British ministry would not yield.

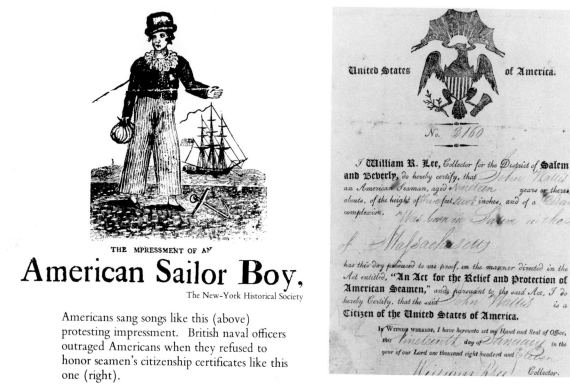

THE IMPRESSMENT OF AN

American Sailor Boy,

The New-York Historical Society

United States of America.

No. 3160

I William R. Lee, Collector for the District of Salem and Beverly, do hereby certify, that John Wallis an American Seaman, aged Nineteen years or thereabouts, of the height of five feet two inches, and of a Dark complexion, was born in Salem in the State of Massachusetts

has this day produced to me proof, in the manner directed in the Act entitled, "An Act for the Relief and Protection of American Seamen," and, pursuant to the said Act, I do hereby Certify, that the said John Wallis is a Citizen of the United States of America.

In Witness Whereof, I have hereunto set my Hand and Seal of Office, this Nineteenth day of January in the year of our Lord one thousand eight hundred and October

William Lee, Collector.

The Essex Institute

Americans sang songs like this (above) protesting impressment. British naval officers outraged Americans when they refused to honor seamen's citizenship certificates like this one (right).

The embargo. Cutbacks in the army and navy under Jefferson left them too weak to fight a war. Jefferson figured that our trade was so important to the nations of Europe that we would not need to fight for what we wanted. If we cut off our trade, they would be sure to do as we wished. Now he decided to try this form of "peaceful coercion" to bring both Britain and Napoleon to terms.

On December 17, 1807, Jefferson asked Congress for a law prohibiting any American vessel from sailing for any foreign port. Congress quickly passed the Embargo Act by large majorities.

The Embargo Act failed to scare Britain and France into a change of policy. It would take time for the British and the French merchants and workers to be hurt by the loss of our trade. But by that time, the embargo might then have destroyed the very American commerce it was designed to protect.

Soon there were signs that the merchants' worst fears were well founded. Ships were tied up at the wharves. Merchandise spoiled in warehouses. Thousands of people in the shipping ports were thrown out of work. Planters and farmers saw their exports of cotton, tobacco, rice, wheat, corn, and livestock fall off sharply. Our foreign trade during the "embargo year" of 1808 shrank to one-third of its value in 1807.

The farmers and the laborers, who had formed the chief support of the Republicans in the northern states, now began to desert the party. Shipowners disobeyed the embargo. Town meetings in New England passed resolutions of protest. Once again there was serious talk of New England leaving the Union.

But the increasing numbers of people on the frontier across the Appalachians had a different point of view. They thought the British were arming the Indians against them. Frightened and angry, they had little use for such soft measures as an embargo. They wanted war. They even talked of capturing Canada.

The embargo repealed. The year 1808 was an election year. Jefferson wanted his Secretary of State, James Madison, to succeed him. He persuaded the Republican members of Congress to pick Madison as the party's candidate. A congressional caucus (party meeting) was the usual nominating method at that time. But the election looked very

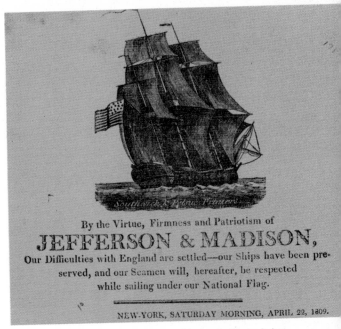

By the Virtue, Firmness and Patriotism of
JEFFERSON & MADISON,
Our Difficulties with England are settled—our Ships have been preserved, and our Seamen will, hereafter, be respected while sailing under our National Flag.

NEW-YORK, SATURDAY MORNING, APRIL 22, 1809.

American Antiquarian Society

Later events proved that the claims in this Republican broadside were too optimistic.

doubtful. "The Federalists will turn us out by the 4th of March next," Albert Gallatin wrote in June. Yet these fears proved unfounded. True enough, as expected, Madison lost every New England state except Vermont. But the South and the West stood by him, and Madison defeated his Federalist opponent, again General C. C. Pinckney, by 122 electoral votes to 47.

In spite of their impressive victory, the Republicans could see that the embargo was destroying their broad support in the nation and was wrecking their party. On March 1, 1809, three days before Jefferson left office, the Republican Congress repealed the embargo. In its place they passed a Nonintercourse Act that forbade trade only with Great Britain and France. Furthermore, they authorized the President to reopen trade with either country should it cease to violate our neutral rights.

Jefferson continued to believe that, if the embargo had been kept in force, Great Britain and France would have come to respect American rights. He thought that the embargo had not been given a fair test. He hated war, for he thought that commerce was the proper weapon of civilized people.

SECTION REVIEW

1. Identify or explain: Orders in Council, imperial decrees, *Chesapeake* affair, impressment, George Canning, embargo.
2. How did the war between England and France threaten American commerce?
3. What British actions at sea angered Americans?
4. What was the Embargo Act? Describe its results. What law replaced it?

CHAPTER REVIEW

MEETING OUR EARLIER SELVES

1. American Presidents have often shifted from the views they expressed before taking office. How would you account for such shifts? What turnabouts did Jefferson make?
2. The conflict with Great Britain that began in Jefferson's term finally led to the War of 1812. After that time the United States was able to resolve differences with Great Britain and Canada peaceably. If the United States had not bought the Louisiana Territory, would it have been any more difficult for the United States to maintain good relations with a French neighbor on the western side of the Mississippi? Explain.
3. Find instances in this chapter where political leaders put their personal or party interests ahead of what seems to have been the national interest. Can you find an instance where someone put the national interest above personal or party advantage?
4. Would we have an effective check-and-balance system (a) if the Supreme Court had never asserted its right to declare acts of Congress unconstitutional? (b) if the Senate had convicted Justice Chase in the impeachment trial? Explain.
5. A panel of 75 historians in 1962 ranked Thomas Jefferson as one of five "great" Presidents of the United States. What achievements, in order of their importance, would merit such a rating? What failures or mistakes of Jefferson's would you expect such a panel to consider in arriving at a fair judgment?

QUESTIONS FOR TODAY

1. Each year the Supreme Court accepts cases in which one of the parties claims that some law or regulation violates the Constitution. Try to find such a case currently or recently in the Court and explain the constitutional issue involved.
2. For five months in 1973–1974 the Arab oil-producing nations put a total embargo on petroleum to the United States and certain other countries friendly to Israel. Compare that embargo with Jefferson's embargo of 1807 with respect to (a) length, (b) products involved, (c) effect on the nations involved. What conclusions, if any, can you draw about the effectiveness of an embargo as a tool in international relations?

YOUR REGION IN HISTORY

1. If your state or any part of it was once in the Louisiana Territory, name some features of the land and native population that would have been noteworthy in a report by an exploring party sent out by the central government in Washington.
2. If your state is east of the Mississippi, how and to what extent was it probably affected by Jefferson's embargo?

SKILLS TO MAKE OUR PAST VIVID

1. Flatboats loaded with western farm products and headed for New Orleans could begin their trip on any one of many rivers of the Mississippi River system. Using an atlas, find the name of the river where a boat might be loaded with products grown near (a) Dayton, Ohio; (b) Indianapolis, Indiana; (c) Nashville, Tennessee; (d) Greenwood, Mississippi. On an outline map trace the route of each of these boats to New Orleans.
2. Using modern highway maps, prepare an itinerary from St. Louis to Astoria, Washington, for an auto camper trip that follows as closely as possible the route west taken by Lewis and Clark.

CHAPTER 8

Struggles of a young nation

The presidencies of Madison and Monroe were marked by the growth in American minds of two opposite sentiments. The first was *nationalism*, the sentiment that binds people to their country and makes them feel that from it all their blessings flow. But growing along with nationalism was the spirit of *sectionalism*. This was the belief that your section of the country, be it the North, the South, or the West, was where you actually owed your loyalty and your love. During the last years of the Virginia dynasty of Presidents, national enthusiasm—fed by war, foreign affairs, and visions of a great future for the United States—was growing rapidly. But lurking in the background, ready to leap out at any moment over everyday issues like roads and canals and banks and tariffs, were the forces of sectional interest.

1. The War of 1812

The War of 1812 was the most peculiar conflict in our history. It began after the cause for it had ceased to exist. It was not fought for the reason declared. The nation's main military victory came after the peace treaty had been signed. The peace itself gave Americans none of the things they had fought for. But despite all these failings, the United States emerged from the war a prouder, stronger, and more unified nation. It was ready at last to turn its back on the affairs of Europe and to build an American Empire for Liberty.

James Madison. The man who succeeded Thomas Jefferson came from a wealthy Virginia family and lived on a grand 2500-acre estate called Montpelier. James Madison was admirably trained to be a President. A leader in the Constitutional Convention, he kept the most complete records of

what everybody said. His skillful arguments helped secure ratification. Then he served President Washington as adviser, and he did as much as anyone else to shape the new government. A disciple of Jefferson, he helped found the old Republican party and served loyally as Jefferson's Secretary of State.

The wrinkled little Madison was 58 years old when he became President. With friends he could be charming, brilliant, and entertaining, but he lacked the great leader's power to dominate. He was a man of ideas.

Macon's Bill #2. When Jefferson's embargo was lifted, it was replaced by a Nonintercourse Act that forbade trade only with Great Britain and France. This act was due to expire in 1810. As the deadline approached, Madison was hesitant and indecisive. The Congress, without guidance from the President,

This painting of James Madison by Gilbert Stuart was one of hundreds from his studio.

had to grope for its own policy. The result was a law that would cause trouble, Macon's Bill #2. Named for the chairman of the Senate foreign relations committee, it threw our commerce open to all the world. But it authorized the President, in case either Great Britain or France should withdraw its restrictions on our commerce, to cut off trade with the other power.

Now the wily Napoleon saw his chance. The French dictator quickly promised to lift his decrees if we would then stop trading with Great Britain. Madison fell into the trap. Though France in fact continued to seize our ships—and in spite of warnings from our ambassadors abroad that it was a trick—Madison agreed to Napoleon's terms. The President really wanted to believe that our diplomacy was working—that at last the French decrees would be repealed and that a renewed threat of nonintercourse with Britain would bring about a change in the British Orders. So he accepted Napoleon's word and in February 1811 issued orders that forbade all trade with Great Britain and its colonies.

The rise of the War Hawks.

When Congress met in November 1811, there were many new faces. These representatives championed a new spirit of expansive nationalism that had swept through the South and West. Tired of cautious diplomacy, they demanded a firm defense of our national rights. The leaders of this movement had little or no experience in public affairs, but they were bright, energetic, and young. Among them were men like Henry Clay of Kentucky and John C. Calhoun of the South Carolina hill country. They soon became known as the "War Hawks." Though not in a majority, they were so shrewd politically that they were able to elect Clay as Speaker of the House. Then these few young men pushed the nation into war.

Clay and his friends were not merchants or shippers. The frontier they cared about was not on the sea but in the American West. They wanted more land. In our day it seems strange that in a nation with millions of empty acres some people still called for more. The reason lay in the very abundance of the land and in the scarcity of people. The virgin western lands produced well enough for the first men, women, and children who farmed them. But after a few years the land could produce plentifully only with fertilizer, crop rotation, and careful cultivation. This meant lots of labor, which America had very little of. Here land was cheap, but labor was scarce. Instead of nursing the land, it was easier on the frontier to abandon old farms and make new farms in the wilderness.

But the way west was now blocked by Indians who would not let themselves be pushed around. The frontier people imagined that the Indians opposed their advancing settlements only because they were stirred up by outsiders—the British in Canada and the Spanish in Florida. Therefore, they argued, Great Britain and Spain must be driven out of America.

The Battle of Tippecanoe.

Over the years, the most common way for the advancing settlers to acquire land from the Indians was for the government to purchase it. In this way, between 1795 and 1809, the Indians of the old Northwest gave up 48 million acres of land, and in general they obeyed their treaties. But white settlers squatted on the Indian lands, and then attacked the people they had dispossessed.

Finally some Indians, led by two able and intelligent Shawnee brothers, said they had had enough. Tecumseh, the politician and warrior, and Tenskwatawa, the religious leader known as the Prophet, decided to form all the Indian tribes from Canada to Florida into one large confederacy. They would sell no more land and would fight to keep the white people out. Settlers on the frontier were frightened.

Governor William Henry Harrison of Indiana Territory took action. He persuaded some other Indians to make a treaty that took away from Tecumseh and his people 3 million acres of their hunting grounds. This brought the frontier of settlement to within 50 miles of Tecumseh's village. Tecumseh went to the capital at Vincennes. There in a moving speech before armed white men and Indians and the governor himself, he demanded the lands back. He told the governor that if the United States agreed and also promised not to buy any more land except with the consent of all the Indian tribes, he would join them against the British.

Harrison did not accept this offer. Instead he waited until Tecumseh had gone south to persuade the Creeks, Cherokees, and Choctaws to join his confederacy. Then Harrison gathered a force of 900 men and marched to the Tippecanoe River, close to Tecumseh's village. Tecumseh had left strict orders to avoid war, but the Indians feared they were about to be attacked, so they struck first. In a brief encounter on November 7, 1811, Harrison's men defeated the Indians and then burned their village.

Most frontier people believed that British officials had been inciting the Indians. Harrison lent substance to their fears when he reported the capture at Tippecanoe of new guns and "ample supplies of the best British glazed powder." The British had, in fact, helped the Indians resist the invasion of their lands and had encouraged the formation of an Indian confederacy. But they had also opposed war. The Indians were happy to

Area of the Tecumseh Confederation

0   300 Miles

0   300 Kilometers

accept British help, though they needed no encouragement to defend their homelands.

After Harrison's attack, the Indians of the old Northwest went on the warpath. They killed settlers or drove them back to the few scattered towns and forts. The Battle of Tippecanoe became the first battle of the War of 1812, for it inflamed the West and stirred the War Hawks to cry for war. They could easily take Canada, they said, and that would end the Indian menace for good. John Randolph of Virginia complained that all he heard in Congress was "one eternal monotonous tone—Canada, Canada, Canada."

The declaration of war. During the winter of 1811–1812, the war spirit rose steadily in the West and South. Only those occupied with commerce in the East resisted it as a threat to their trade and prosperity. They also feared that an American victory in the war would strengthen the political power of the South and the West.

The War Hawks made fiery speeches. They predicted that a thousand Kentucky riflemen could easily take Canada. So they swept the nation toward a war for which it was unprepared. In April 1812, Congress imposed a 60-day embargo on American shipping in order to give our ships time to reach home before war was declared. In May, news arrived from England that the British ministry refused to change its Orders in Council until it was convinced that Napoleon had really repealed his decrees. This dispatch, Madison wrote many years later, was "the more immediate impulse to war." We had to choose, he said, between war and submission to shameful treatment.

On June 1, 1812, President Madison sent a message to Congress in which he reviewed "the injuries and indignities which had been heaped upon our country" by Great Britain: impressment, blockades, incitement of the Indians. A divided Congress, representing a divided country, responded to Madison's message by voting 79 to 49 in the House and 19 to 13 in the Senate to go to war. The states of the South and West, joined by Pennsylvania and Vermont, favored war. New York, New Jersey, and the seaside New England states were for peace.

This was expected to be a short war. Canada would fall quickly and then it would all be over. After declaring war, therefore, Congress adjourned without even voting the higher taxes needed to arm the nation.

The avoidable war. As the United States moved toward a declaration of war, its ban on trade with England was at last beginning to work. At the same time Napoleon, who was at the height of his power, prevented Great Britain from trading with western Europe. British factories closed, and British workers were thrown out of work because the warehouses were already full of goods that could not be sold. On top of that, a crop failure in 1811 led to a food shortage and high food prices in the following winter.

The British Prime Minister Spencer Perceval was seriously considering the repeal of the Orders in Council when he was assassinated by a madman on May 1, 1812. By the time his successor, Lord Castlereagh, acted and lifted the Orders, the United States had declared war. Jefferson's policy of peaceful persuasion had succeeded—but too late. A President who could not lead and a foolhardy Congress had already shoved the nation into a war it did not need and for which it was not ready.

False hopes of readiness to fight. The United States thought it could win easily. In the first place, we were now the unwitting ally of Napoleon, who invaded Russia just six days after our declaration of war. Our population was now more than 7 million. Canada had only 500,000 people, many of them French-Canadians who were less than eager to help the British.

The fighting forces of the two nations, however, were not so lopsided. Canada had 8500 regular troops—four British and four Canadian regiments. These would be helped by some 4000 militia and more than 3000 of Tecumseh's warriors. Against them the United States had fewer than 7000 men in its regular army. Congress had voted to increase this number to 15,000, but enlistments came in slowly. More than 400,000 militia, the home guard of all men who bore arms, were called up during the war. The militia still showed all the weaknesses they had revealed during the Revolution.

The United States Navy had only 16 sea-going vessels to face Britain's 97 vessels on this side of the ocean. The fast new American frigates were superior to the British ships, but they were greatly outnumbered.

The war in 1812–1813. The first summer of action saw a series of defeats on land. The grandiose plans to invade Canada ended in the loss of Fort Dearborn (Chicago) on August 15, 1812, and Detroit the following day. This left the British in control of a large part of the old Northwest.

The navy, however, helped relieve the gloomy picture. The *Constitution* ("Old Ironsides") defeated the *Guerrière* and the *Java* in 1812, while the *Wasp* was whipping the *Frolic*. The frigate *United States,* commanded by Stephen Decatur, even seized the British frigate *Macedonia* and brought her home as a prize. The British were stunned—just as the Americans were elated—by these naval victories. But their main result was to lift American morale. For soon most United States warships were blockaded in home ports.

Madison won a second term in the fall of 1812. Yet DeWitt Clinton of New York, supported by Federalists and Republicans who wanted peace, carried every eastern state north of the Potomac except Pennsylvania and Vermont.

The war might have ended in 1812 if the British had been willing to stop taking British sailors from

American ships and impressing them into their navy. They would not concede this point, so the war went on.

In 1813, United States military actions did not fare much better. In June the unlucky frigate *Chesapeake* accepted a challenge for a fight from Britain's *Shannon*. Outside Boston Harbor, Captain James Lawrence was killed and the *Chesapeake* was captured. Before he died, however, Lawrence spoke his memorable words, "Don't give up the ship."

Hundreds of miles away, those words were to fly on Commodore Oliver Hazard Perry's blue battle flag when he fought the British at Put-in-Bay on Lake Erie in September. Perry had built his fleet of small vessels during the winter of 1812–1813. Overcoming many difficulties, he was able to get his ships into Lake Erie and face the British fleet in September. There was a hot battle, during which the fleets fired away at each other at point blank range. Perry was able to report, "We have met the enemy and they are ours." He had worried about

Along with the *Wasp*, the American ship *Hornet* stung Britain (John Bull) in 1812. The cartoon makes puns on the names of naval heroes Isaac Hull and William Bainbridge.

This painting, done during the War of 1812, shows the *Chesapeake* (left) with a banner for "Free Trade and Sailors' Rights" surrendering to the British ship *Shannon* (right) after a fierce battle.

his new sailors, "blacks, soldiers, and boys," but they had fought bravely. Of the 50 blacks in his crew, he said, "they seemed absolutely insensible to danger."

Perry's success meant that the British at Detroit could be cut off from Canada. So they were forced to retreat. William Henry Harrison, now a general, led 10,000 Kentucky volunteers in pursuit. The Americans overtook the British at the Thames River on the Ontario peninsula and routed them. The British commander was almost captured, and the brave and visionary warrior Tecumseh—now a brigadier general in the British army—was killed.

Other American generals had less success in 1813. So, as winter closed in, the conquest of Canada was little nearer than it had been the year before. In the meantime, the British blockade grew tighter. Few ships were able to enter or leave our ports. Trade dropped to almost nothing.

Our swift-sailing privateers stayed abroad and successfully attacked the British merchant marine on all its worldwide lines of commerce. Even in the English Channel they were not safe from our raiders which, during the course of the war, captured some 1300 British ships and cargoes valued at $40 million.

Great Britain takes the offensive. During 1812 and 1813 the British were more concerned about fighting Napoleon in Europe than the United States in America. But the Russian winter would bring Napoleon's downfall. With his exile to Elba in April 1814, England was free to turn its full attention to the war with the United States. Some 14,000 of the Duke of Wellington's battle-seasoned regulars were now sent to America to bring about a quick British victory.

Offensive operations by the British began in August 1814 when a large fleet sailed into Chesapeake Bay and 4000 regulars landed on the banks of the Patuxent River. They brushed aside a militia force outside Washington and entered the capital on August 24. President Madison and his intelligent and attractive wife, Dolley, gathered a few valuables and fled to Virginia. Since an American force had burned York (Toronto) in 1813, the British now retaliated. After capturing the city, they set fire to the Capitol (with the Library of Congress), the White House, and some other public buildings.

The triumphant redcoats then sailed to Baltimore, where the citizens had been strengthening their defenses during the attack on Washington.

There the British troops were repulsed, and their commanding general was killed. But before they gave up and headed out of Chesapeake Bay, their fleet undertook an all-night bombardment of Fort McHenry, the American stronghold.

It was during that "perilous night" of shelling that a young Washington lawyer, Francis Scott Key, watched from an American ship "until dawn's early light" revealed to his relief that "our flag was still there." "The Star-Spangled Banner" was written under these painful circumstances.

In early September 1814 another large, well-trained British army containing some of Wellington's tough regulars was following Burgoyne's route along the shore of Lake Champlain. They were opposed by a much smaller force of American militia stationed behind strong fortifications at Plattsburg in upstate New York. The British put a strong fleet on the lake to support their attack. An American naval force on the lake was commanded by Commodore Thomas Macdonough. Although only 30 years old, he was already an experienced naval officer. His fleet was outgunned by the British vessels, but he handled his weaker force so skillfully that he gained a decisive victory. With the Americans in control of the lake, the British army turned back on September 12, 1814.

Macdonough's victory and the British departure from Baltimore at last lifted American spirits. Until then the nation's future had seemed dark. Our war vessels had been driven from the ocean, our coasts blockaded, and our commerce ruined. The Treasury was empty. The Capitol and the President's house lay in scorched ruins.

Andrew Jackson wins fame. There were other heartening events in 1814 that brightened the nation's future and created a new national hero. These were the deeds of the tall, rough-hewn Tennessean, General Andrew Jackson. Westerners were delighted when he invaded the lands of the Creek Indians and defeated them in the Battle of Horseshoe Bend. Then by the Treaty of Fort Jackson he forced them to give up two-thirds of their Alabama lands.

For his successes Jackson was promoted from the position of general of volunteers to the post of major general in the regular army. He invaded Spanish East Florida in November 1814 and captured a British force at Pensacola. Hastening to New

The War of 1812

Legend:
- Spanish
- British
- United States

0 — 300 Miles

0 — 300 Kilometers

CANADA

Lake Superior

Lake Michigan

Lake Huron

St. Lawrence R.

Montreal

MAINE
(MASS.)

**7. MACDONOUGH
DEFEATS BRITISH 1814** ✕ Plattsburg

VT.

N.H.

**2. BRITISH CAPTURE
THE CHESAPEAKE 1813** ✕

NEW YORK

MASS.

CONN.

R.I.

MICHIGAN TERRITORY

Detroit

Lake Erie

**1. BRITISH SEIZE DETROIT
AND FT. DEARBORN**

Ft. Dearborn ◇
(Chicago)

PENNSYLVANIA

N.J.

Baltimore

OHIO

Washington   MD.   DEL.

✕ Battle of Tippecanoe 1811

INDIANA
TERR.

ILLINOIS TERRITORY

VIRGINIA

Wabash R.

Ohio R.

KENTUCKY

NORTH CAROLINA

TENNESSEE

Mississippi R.

SOUTH CAROLINA

GEORGIA

**8. JACKSON DEFEATS
CREEK INDIANS 1814**

MISSISSIPPI TERRITORY

ATLANTIC OCEAN

✕ Horseshoe Bend

LOUISIANA

Mobile

WEST FLORIDA   Pensacola

• New Orleans

EAST FLORIDA

GULF OF MEXICO

Inset (upper right):

Lake Huron

**4. HARRISON
DEFEATS
BRITISH 1813**

CANADA

MICHIGAN
TERRITORY

Thames R.

✕ Battle of
the Thames

Detroit •

Lake Erie

**3. PERRY DEFEATS
BRITISH 1813**

Put-in-Bay ✕

OHIO

Inset (middle right):

PENNSYLVANIA

Philadelphia •

MARYLAND

N.J.

Baltimore • ◇ **6. DEFENSE
OF FT. McHENRY
1814**

**5. BRITISH BURN
WASHINGTON 1814**

Washington •

Patuxent R.

Chesapeake Bay

DEL.

Potomac R.

VIRGINIA

Richmond •

← British Fleet

Inset (lower right):

Mississippi R.

MISSISSIPPI TERRITORY

Alabama R.

WEST FLORIDA
Mobile •

FLORIDA

LOUISIANA

Pensacola •

**9. JACKSON CAPTURES
BRITISH FORCE 1814**

New Orleans • ✕ — Lake Borgne

10. AMERICAN VICTORY 1815

GULF OF MEXICO

← British Fleet

← Jackson

"The Battle of New Orleans" was painted from sketches that the artist, an engineer with the American army, had made on the battlefield. The battle was fought on plantations five miles south of the city. Note the strong American defensive positions.

Orleans in case the British should arrive there, he reached the city just in time.

A force of 7500 redcoats—Scots Highlanders, West Indian black regiments, and English regulars—under the command of the Duke of Wellington's brother-in-law, Sir Edward Pakenham, had secretly landed 15 miles from New Orleans. If the British had attacked Jackson's forces right then, they probably would have defeated him. But by delaying, they gave his motley band of militia, blacks, and pirates the time to throw up earthworks and bring in their artillery.

When the inept British general finally ordered a frontal attack, it was a disaster. In a battle of less than half an hour on the morning of January 8, 1815, the British suffered more than 2000 killed or injured, including the death of Pakenham himself

and two other generals. Only 13 Americans were killed and 58 missing or wounded. The redcoats then boarded their vessels and sailed away. Jackson became "the hero of New Orleans," and a future President—one of the nation's strongest leaders—had been created. Among the many oddities of the War of 1812 none was odder than the fact that its greatest victory, the Battle of New Orleans, was won after peace had already been negotiated in a distant European town. And a great military hero was made in a battle that really decided nothing.

The Treaty of Ghent. Peace discussions between American and British envoys had begun in Ghent, Belgium, in August 1814. The British demanded large tracts of land in their first proposals, but then Macdonough's victory on Lake Champlain made them realize that Britain could not win the war. The depletion of their treasury by the long Napoleonic Wars, together with many new problems in Europe, forced the English envoys to lower their demands. On December 24, 1814, a peace treaty was signed. If telegraph, telephone, or radio had existed, the Battle of New Orleans would probably not have been fought two weeks later. But, in fact, America did not learn of the treaty until the middle of February 1815.

The terms of the treaty made at Ghent simply provided for a return to the conditions that existed before the war. Lawyers called that the *status quo ante bellum.* It was agreed that certain issues would be settled later. Since neither side gained or lost anything, the treaty became the basis for a reconciliation between the parent country and its former thirteen colonies. Unlike most peace treaties, this one did not bear the seeds of future war. The peace was ratified unanimously by the Senate on February 14, 1815.

There is good reason to call the War of 1812 the Second War of Independence, for now at last the new American nation had stood up with its own army and navy in full-scale war against a major European power. And this was in spite of some dangerous quarrels at home.

Opposition in New England to the war.

As the war was drawing to a close, opposition in the North was rising rapidly. Every seaside state north of Maryland had voted against Madison (which meant against the war) in the election of 1812. New England, the richest section of the country, subscribed for less than $1 million of an $11 million loan authorized by Congress in 1812. "Organize a peace party," the Massachusetts legislature recommended a week after the war was declared. "Express your sentiments without fear and let the sound of your disapproval of this war be loud and deep. . . . Let there be no volunteering except for a defensive war." Some New Englanders were so disgusted with the war that they sold beef to the British army in Canada. The New England states and New York were unwilling to let their militias serve outside their home states.

The British blockade closed off the seaborne commerce of the United States. Exports and imports in 1814 were a mere 10 percent of what they had been in the peak year of 1807. One observer later reported, "Our ships were rotting in every creek and cove where they could find a place of security; our immense annual products were mouldering in our warehouses." Impoverished towns petitioned the Massachusetts legislature to take steps toward amending the Constitution of the United States to "secure them from further evils." Pessimists began to fear that the Union itself was in danger.

The Hartford Convention.

At the suggestion of the Massachusetts legislature, delegates from the five New England states met in a convention at Hartford, Connecticut, on December 15, 1814. These delegates, remnants of the old Federalist party, denounced the "ruinous war." They adopted resolutions, like those of Virginia and Kentucky in 1798, in which they proclaimed that when the Constitution was violated it was the duty of the states to "interpose their authority for the preservation of their liberties." They also proposed a number of amendments to the Constitution that were designed to lessen the power of the South and West, to secure the interests of commerce, and to check the seemingly endless succession of Presidents from Virginia.

By a lucky coincidence the messengers carrying these disruptive demands arrived in Washington just at the moment when events made their demands seem absurd. For the city was rejoicing over the news of Jackson's victory at New Orleans and

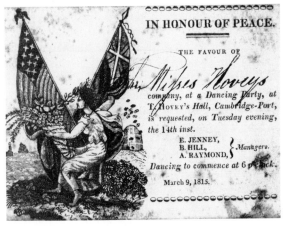

The Huntington Library, San Marino, California

The American and British flags both appear on this Cambridge, Massachusetts, invitation to a dance celebrating the end of the war.

The Huntington Library, San Marino, California

The cartoonist accuses four of the New England states present at the Hartford Convention of planning to rejoin England. George III seems eager to welcome back his "Yankey boys."

the tidings of the peace from Ghent, which reached Washington on the same day. The Republican triumph was complete, and the Federalist party was doomed.

There was nothing "treasonable" in the propositions of the Federalists at Hartford, for they were trying to amend the Constitution. But they made a bad mistake in their timing. As a party measure they were opposing a war at a time when it had become a struggle for the nation's very existence. Therefore there was reason enough for many Americans to call the Hartford Convention unpatriotic. The Federalists as a party put partisan or sectional interests above those of the whole country. For the last time, in the presidential election of 1816, the Federalists named a candidate. Rufus King of New York was easily defeated by the Republican James Monroe, Madison's Secretary of State. The Virginia dynasty would govern the nation for another eight years.

SECTION REVIEW

1. Identify or explain: Macon's Bill #2, Henry Clay, John C. Calhoun, Tecumseh, the Prophet, Stephen Decatur, DeWitt Clinton, James Lawrence, Oliver Hazard Perry, Francis Scott Key, Thomas Macdonough.

2. Locate: Tippecanoe, Fort Dearborn, Thames River, Put-in-Bay, York, Fort McHenry, Plattsburg, Horseshoe Bend, Hartford.

3. Why was the War of 1812 the "most peculiar conflict in our history"? Was it avoidable?

4. Who were the War Hawks? Why did they argue for war?

5. List some major land and sea battles in the War of 1812 and give their results.

6. Summarize the terms of the Treaty of Ghent.

7. Describe the opposition to the war.

2. Madison and Monroe

The War of 1812 had hardly been a great American success story. It had revealed grave weaknesses in our government—especially in the nation's finances and in defense. At times during the conflict, the fate of the nation had hung in the balance.

Yet the war finally produced solid benefits. Never again would Great Britain believe that the United States could easily be defeated on the battlefield. Americans would no longer assume that Canada could be conquered by a thousand Kentucky riflemen. Both nations—the former homeland and the nation of former colonies—would be more willing to settle their differences at a conference table.

The other result was stranger. Out of a war in which the nation had attained none of its declared goals, the people emerged more united, more patriotic, and more filled with national pride than ever before.

"We have met the enemy and they are ours," "Don't give up the ship," and other fighting slogans became popular. "The Star-Spangled Banner" would become our national anthem. An energetic Jackson and his frontiersmen, blacks, and pirates were remembered trouncing the British at New Orleans. The near loss of much of the Northwest and the burning of Washington were almost forgotten.

The annual message of 1815.

The new national spirit was revealed in President Madison's annual message to Congress in December 1815. This Republican President's program included: (1) funds for national defense, (2) frigates for the navy, (3) a standing army and federal control of the militia, (4) federal aid for building roads and canals, (5) a protective tariff to encourage manufactures, (6) re-establishing the national bank, and (7) federal assumption of some state debts. It seemed that Hamilton had replaced Jefferson as the idol of the old Republican party.

Henry Clay later referred to this program as the "American System," which would benefit every section of the country. The protective tariff would aid the manufacturers of the Northeast and create a large market for their products in the South and West. Internal improvements—roads and canals—would tie the country together and make it easier for Westerners and Southerners to get their crops to eastern markets. The national bank would provide the currency and the capital for the entire nation's economic growth. But each section found something in the package that it did not like.

The Tariff of 1816.

American manufacturers wanted a protective tariff. After the British blockade had cut off our foreign commerce, large sums of capital were switched to manufacturing, in New England especially, so that we might make the items we had once imported. By the end of 1815 the cotton mills in New England had multiplied. Iron manufacturing was booming in Pennsylvania. Pioneer industries—in iron, wool, and cotton—had even appeared in the Ohio Valley between Pittsburgh and Cincinnati.

WEST POINT FOUNDERY
and
BORING MILL.

The tariff of 1816 was designed to protect small industries like this one in West Point, New York.

The British manufacturers who had supplied the rapidly growing American demand ever since colonial days did not wish to lose their market. Even before the Senate ratified the Treaty of Ghent, British ships were waiting off New York Harbor, loaded with goods that had been dammed up in English warehouses during the wars in Europe and America. These goods were to be sold even below cost in order to bankrupt America's new manufacturing plants.

To protect America's "infant industries" Congress enacted a tariff (April 1816) that continued the high duties that had been imposed as a war measure in 1812. South Carolina—later to lead the opposition—now strongly favored the tariff. Representative John C. Calhoun of South Carolina supported the measure because he believed the United States needed to build up its army, pay its national debt, and develop its new industries. Only in that way, he argued, could the United States be truly independent. The South as a whole, however, was not convinced. Southern members of Congress voted heavily against the tariff.

The second Bank of the United States.

The Bank of the United States, which had not been rechartered in 1811, had closed its doors. Without a national bank it was doubly difficult for the nation to pay for the war. Instead of being able to borrow from one central bank, the government had to deal with many. Without any Bank of the United States, state banks (private banks chartered by the states) had multiplied rapidly, each issuing its own paper money. There was no one national currency. In the dark days of the war, after the British burned Washington, many holders of these state bank notes tried to convert them to gold and silver (specie) as the banks had promised. But, lacking specie, the banks refused. As a result the value of the state bank notes declined. The bonds of the federal government sold below their face value, and the national debt soared.

To deal with these hard economic problems, the federal government decided to charter a bank similar to Hamilton's bank of 1791, but with a larger capital. Again the government would hold one-fifth of the stock and would name one-fifth of the directors. Southern statesmen who had argued against the constitutionality of the old bank now suddenly changed their tune. They favored the second Bank of the United States. Madison, who had called Hamilton's bank unconstitutional, signed the new bank bill on April 10, 1816.

Calhoun's Bonus Bill.

One of the lessons of the war was the need for better means of transporting goods and troops. All the sails, cannon, and cordage for Perry's fleet on Lake Erie and for Macdonough's on Lake Champlain had been laboriously carried overland. Supplies for the army were dragged over rough trails in the wilderness. Western farmers found it difficult and expensive to bring their crops and livestock to market.

John C. Calhoun, eloquent spokesman for the South, warned Congress that unless it found ways to tie the rapidly growing nation together there was a strong chance of "disunion." In December 1816, Calhoun introduced a bill to pay for roads and canals—what were called "internal improvements." The $1.5 million that the new Bank of the United States would pay for its charter (the so-called bonus) would support these new projects. In addition, the dividends that the United States would receive on its fifth of the bank's stock would help build roads and canals. The bill passed Congress in February 1817.

President Madison now suddenly returned to his old Republican beliefs. He had called for building roads and canals in his 1815 message. But now he decided that Congress had no such powers because they were not expressly given in the Constitution. So Madison vetoed the Bonus Bill.

It was unfortunate for his place in history that Madison chose to show constitutional scruples so near the close of his Presidency. The "American System" of the tariff, bank, and internal improvements was a package. Few liked all three items. Some Westerners were against the bank because they liked the easy money of the state banks. The South opposed the tariff. And New England disliked both the bank (now that it was a Republican measure) and internal improvements at government expense. Only the Middle States—New York, New Jersey, and Pennsylvania—voted for all three. When Madison vetoed the Bonus Bill, the "system" ceased to exist. Now the West, which most wanted roads and canals, felt left out.

A further problem with the veto was that the northern states had the money to spend for internal improvements while the South did not. When the North built roads and canals and, later, railroads to the West, the trade of the West naturally was drawn to the northern states. As a result the South remained agricultural, raising the staple crops of rice, tobacco, cotton, and sugar. With internal improvements at national expense, the economy of all the sections might have been different. And the South might have developed a mixed economy of farm and factory instead of becoming enslaved to slavery.

"First Harvest in the Wilderness," painted by Asher Durand in 1855, suggests the grueling effort needed to carve a farm out of forested highland. Durand was one of the painters known as the Hudson River School. They painted the wild and wonderful beauties of the American landscape.

The "Era of Good Feelings." Madison's veto of the Bonus Bill was his last official act. The next day he saw his hand-picked successor, James Monroe, the last of the Virginia dynasty, take the oath of office.

The inauguration of President James Monroe began a curious period in American party politics. When the new President toured the North and the West, he was so well received that even a staunchly Federalist Boston newspaper called him the herald of an "era of good feelings."

President Monroe's term in office proved to be an era without political parties. The Federalist party died in 1816. The Jeffersonian Republicans had taken over their issues—banks, tariffs, and an active central government. When only New Englanders were found in the Federalist party, it had ceased to be national.

As the Federalists disappeared, so too did the Republicans. Without opposition there was no reason for them to stay together, and they fell apart into squabbling factions. With astonishing swiftness, the Era of Good Feelings became an era of bad feelings marked by the hot pursuit of the Presidency by several self-seeking so-called Republicans. Sectional bitterness boiled up, and a coherent national policy disappeared. Meanwhile, James Monroe avoided making domestic policy and drifted with the times.

Economic sectionalism. In Monroe's day the United States was divided into geographic sections each as large as a European nation, each with its own economic interests. The East depended on commerce and industry. The South lived on an economy of large plantations. The West was a land of small farms. The differing economic interests of the sections produced conflicting ideas about the tariff, banks, internal improvements, slavery, the right to vote, and almost everything else.

For a time after the War of 1812 these sectional differences remained hidden. While the whole country prospered, national feelings overshadowed all others. But with the onset of a severe depression in 1819, people in each section looked for someone—elsewhere in the nation—to blame. Each section demanded new laws in its own special interest.

Adjustments with Great Britain.

Monroe's term of office began well, however, and a national spirit filled the air—a pride promoted by American diplomatic successes.

John Quincy Adams, Monroe's Secretary of State and the son of former President John Adams, was one of the ablest and most farsighted statesmen in our country's history. The agreement with Great Britain that he negotiated in 1817 (and which survives to this day) pledged each country not to keep warships on the Great Lakes. This policy was later expanded to a pledge not to arm the land borders between the United States and Canada. As a result, the northern border of the United States remains the longest unfortified international border in the world. The pact came to be known as the Rush-Bagot Agreement because it was contained in an exchange of notes between the acting Secretary of State, Richard Rush, and the British minister to the United States, Charles Bagot.

In the following year it was agreed that the 49th parallel would mark the boundary between Canada and the United States from Lake of the Woods in Minnesota to the Rocky Mountains. Also, for ten years Britain and the United States would jointly occupy the Oregon territory between the Rockies and the Pacific.

Spain cedes Florida.

The United States had long wanted all of Florida. Then in 1818, the federal government ordered General Jackson to protect southern and western settlers against Indian attacks from eastern Florida. He was told that he could follow Indian raiding parties back into Spanish Florida. Jackson—who was no Indian lover—responded to this assignment with enthusiasm. Supposedly chasing Indians, he swept across East Florida, capturing the Spanish strongholds of Pensacola and St. Marks on the way. During this campaign he executed two Englishmen who were suspected of supplying arms to the Indians. When Jackson went back to Tennessee in May 1818, he had turned Florida into a conquered province.

Jackson's deeds made him a hero in the West but seriously embarrassed the government. He might easily have caused a war with both Spain and England. The President's Cabinet was divided. Secretary of State John Quincy Adams supported the rash Jackson. But all the other Cabinet members wanted him to be censured and his acts disavowed.

Adams and Jackson prevailed, and the President sent Spain an ultimatum: either control the Indians or sell Florida to the United States.

The weak Spanish government, plagued by revolts in its other American colonies, had no way to control the Indians. So rather than have the United States take Florida for nothing, Spain decided to sell the land for what it could get. In the Adams-Onís Treaty of 1819, the United States received Florida. In return the United States government agreed to pay to its own citizens about $5 million—the damages American shippers claimed against Spain for Spanish interference with American commerce during the Napoleonic Wars.

The same treaty finally fixed the boundary between the Louisiana Territory and Spanish holdings to the west. This line had been in dispute ever since 1803. The United States gave up its claim to part of Texas, but in return Spain gave up its claim to the Pacific Northwest. The border of the United States now was drawn all the way to the Pacific!

John Marshall's decisions.

The rise of nationalism during these years was encouraged by a series of decisions of the Supreme Court under its strong Federalist Chief Justice John Marshall. When the Supreme Court decides a case, the justices write opinions giving the reasons for their decisions. Usually one justice will write an opinion for the majority. Marshall was noted both for the masterful opinions that he wrote and for his skill in winning other members of the Court to his views.

In *Martin* v. *Hunter's Lessee* (1816) and *Cohens* v. *Virginia* (1821) the Supreme Court insisted on its right to review decisions of state courts that dealt with matters arising under the federal Constitution.

In 1819 in the *Dartmouth College Case,* the Court protected private property from state interference. It annulled an act of the New Hampshire legislature that would have altered the college charter. States were forbidden by the Constitution to "pass any law impairing the obligation of contracts." A charter passed by a state legislature, Marshall said, was a "contract." Marshall was always willing to interpret the Constitution broadly when it increased the powers of the national government—or the Supreme Court. The decision in this case also encouraged business firms to invest their capital and to rely on the charters of their corporations without fearing the whimsies of state legislatures.

Marshall's most famous opinion came in *McCulloch* v. *Maryland* (1819). That decision became a bulwark of a strong central government in the United States. The state of Maryland had tried to force the Bank of the United States out of the state by taxing it. Marshall asserted that no state had the right to hinder or control any national institution established within its borders. "The power to tax," he said, "is the power to destroy."

Marshall seized the occasion to deal once again with the question whether the Constitution gave Congress the power to set up a national bank. Before signing the bill that had created the first Bank of the United States, President Washington had received conflicting advice on the issue from Thomas Jefferson and Alexander Hamilton (p. 122). But the power of Congress to create the bank had not been tested in the courts. Now Marshall had a chance to deal with the clause that gave Congress the right "to make all laws necessary and proper" for carrying out the powers granted it under the Constitution (Art. I, sec. 8).

Did these words mean "absolutely necessary and therefore proper"? Marshall said No! To carry out any of its direct powers, Congress could choose the appropriate means. Congress could create a bank as a convenient or useful means to carry out its direct powers to collect taxes and borrow money. It was only necessary that the means be within "the letter and spirit of the Constitution" and not prohibited by it. The decision therefore had the effect of broadening the powers of Congress and thereby the national government. The laws of the United States were "the supreme law of the land," and the states had no power to prevent the growth of a national government.

In *Gibbons* v. *Ogden* (1824), the famous "Steamboat Case," the Marshall Court drew some powerful conclusions from the clause in the Constitution that gives to Congress the power to regulate commerce with foreign nations, between the states, and with the Indian tribes (Art. 1, sec. 8). A monopoly of steamboat passenger service on the Hudson River that New York had granted to Robert Livingston and Robert Fulton could not be allowed to stand. Marshall now defined "commerce" so broadly that the champions of "states rights" accused him of trying to abolish the state governments altogether. Ultimately, Congress, by overseeing "interstate commerce," would regulate telephones, telegraphs,

After Fulton and Livingston's steamboat monopoly was broken, competition flourished.

and oil pipelines. Even manufacturing *within* a state would be regulated when the workers, the raw materials, or the products came from or went to other states. Henry Clay and other promoters of the "American System," advocates of a strong, unified nation, welcomed Marshall's words.

SECTION REVIEW

1. Identify or explain: "American System," "infant industries," Bonus Bill, "Era of Good Feelings," Rush-Bagot Agreement, Adams-Onís Treaty.

2. How did Madison's annual message to Congress in 1815 express a spirit of nationalism?

3. What did the North, South, and West each like or dislike about (a) a protective tariff, (b) internal improvements, (c) the national bank?

4. Why did Madison veto the Bonus Bill? Why was the veto significant?

5. What important agreements were made with Great Britain in 1817–1818?

6. What events led to the treaty with Spain in 1819? What were its chief provisions?

7. Name some important cases decided by the Supreme Court under John Marshall and tell how each strengthened the power of the national government.

Missouri Compromise 1820

- Free States and Territories
- Slave States and Territories
- Maine. Admitted as a Free State, 1820
- Missouri. Admitted as a Slave State, 1821

3. The Missouri Compromise

One sectional interest in America was more sensitive and more explosive than all others—slavery. Unlike other economic issues, slavery was a great moral problem. In the early days of the Republic, it had appeared that slavery might die out. The price of tobacco was so low that many plantation owners were finding the use and care of slaves unprofitable. But then a single invention suddenly changed the picture.

Eli Whitney was a recent Yale College graduate who had gone south to be a tutor to the children of a plantation family. In those days there were few public schools in the South. The children of slaves were not sent to school, and the children of plantation owners were usually taught by a private tutor who came and lived in the mansion. The position of tutor was no longer vacant when Whitney reached Savannah in the fall of 1792, but he was invited to remain in Georgia for a time as the guest of Catherine Littlefield Greene, the widow of the Revolutionary War General Nathanael Greene.

While on Mrs. Greene's plantation, Whitney saw how well short-staple cotton grew in the southern uplands. He also saw that a slave had to labor a whole day to pick the seeds out of a pound of cotton in order to make the cotton usable for thread or for cloth. Whitney, who was handy with tools, was urged by Catherine Greene to try to find a better way to remove the seeds. He was a clever young

man with a wonderful power of concentration. Within ten days he had solved the problem. By April 1793 he had a working machine that made it possible for one slave to clean 50 pounds of cotton in a single day.

Whitney's cotton "gin" (for "engine") suddenly made the production of short-staple cotton highly profitable. Plantations would prosper if only they could find the workers to plant, to cultivate, to pick, and to "gin" the cotton. Black slaves seemed the obvious labor supply, and slavery began to seem "necessary" for southern prosperity. At the same time planters wanting more land to grow more cotton were moving rapidly westward.

The slavery question rises in the West. By 1818 some 60,000 settlers had crossed the Mississippi and were pushing up the valley of the Missouri River. St. Louis was a bustling city and the center of the western fur trade. Although most of the settlers in Missouri were from the states north of the Ohio, where the Northwest Ordinance prohibited slavery, there were some from slaveholding states like Kentucky and Tennessee. They had brought with them about 10,000 slaves.

Missouri's request for admission to the Union as a slave state opened up a heated argument over the expansion of slavery. The question began as a matter of power. Up to this time when new states were brought into the Union, there had been an effort to keep an even balance between free and slave states. Slaveholding Alabama and Mississippi had been balanced by Indiana and Illinois. When Missouri applied for admission, there were 11 free states and 11 slave. There seemed to be no free state at that time that could be paired with Missouri to keep the balance even. And if Missouri was brought in alone, the slave states could outvote the free states in the Senate.

In 1819, the year when the issue came to a head, a deep economic depression split the country. The Bank of the United States was under attack as the villain that had created the depression to enrich a few greedy Northerners. Manufacturers in the Northeast called for higher protective tariffs, which would have raised the price of nearly everything Southerners bought. Whoever controlled the Senate, it was argued, would then be able to control government policy on the Bank, on tariffs, on federal outlays for roads and canals, and especially

This scene of the steamboat *Yellowstone* on its way down the Mississippi was painted by George Catlin, the Pennsylvania painter who portrayed the American West. Besides being a bustling river port, St. Louis in the background was a stagecoach center for those heading east or west.

on slavery. Slave-owning Southerners began to see a life-and-death struggle. How long could it be before Northerners would insist on abolishing slavery? And how could the South survive without the labor force that produced its cotton? A new bitterness entered the halls of Congress.

Achieving a compromise. The "Missouri Compromise," which Congress passed in 1820 after a whole year of debate, was not so much a compromise as a stalemate. Following the rules of the North-South tug-of-war, which had already been going on for at least twenty years, each side added one new state to its team. Missouri was added as a slave state, while Maine came in as a free state. At the same time the law drew a line through all the rest of the lands of the Louisiana Purchase excluding slavery "forever" from north of the parallel of

36°30′ (the southern boundary of Missouri) except for the state of Missouri itself.

Although people at the time called it a compromise, it was not really like the compromises made by the framers of the Constitution in 1787. Those earlier compromises—for example, the one between the large and small states—were designed to give each side on every question part of what it wanted. Then everybody could consider the question settled and move on to other things. But slavery was a different kind of question. Both sides saw it as all-or-nothing. Both sides were simply biding their time.

Farsighted leaders realized that the Missouri Compromise was nothing more than a truce that announced the opening of a fight to the finish. The aged Thomas Jefferson, retired at Monticello on his Virginia mountaintop, was saddened. This was, he said, "a fire-bell in the night . . . the [death] knell of the Union." John Quincy Adams saw it as "a title page to a great tragic volume."

SECTION REVIEW

1. How did Eli Whitney influence (a) the growth of slavery and (b) its westward expansion?

2. Why did the westward expansion of slavery become a serious political issue?

3. What was the Missouri Compromise designed to settle? How was it supposed to do so?

4. The Monroe Doctrine

President Monroe played only a minor role in the crisis that finally produced the Missouri Compromise. In domestic affairs, he believed, it was the job of Congress to make the laws, and the President should only carry them out. But in foreign affairs, it was plainly the President's duty to lead the way in defining the nation's role. Monroe was assisted by his strong-minded Secretary of State, John Quincy Adams. Behind their determination to make the United States a leader in world affairs they had the support of the American people. Despite growing sectional differences, Americans of all regions shared a new national pride. The young nation's Second War of Independence, the War of 1812, had given them all a lift. The nation's growing self-confidence was revealed in the Monroe Doctrine.

Europe and America. During the Napoleonic Wars the Spanish-American colonies had begun to break away from Spain and to follow the example of the United States by declaring their independence. For those colonies it was a time of struggle—and an hour of decision. The United States feared that the continental European powers—Austria, Russia, Prussia, and France—would help Spain to reconquer its colonies.

At this point the British foreign secretary, George Canning, proposed that the United States and Great Britain make a public declaration against the attempt of European nations to use force to keep their former colonies in subjection. Monroe thought that we should accept Canning's offer. Madison and Jefferson agreed. But Secretary of State John Quincy Adams had misgivings. He knew the ins and outs of European diplomacy from his fourteen

years as minister to the Netherlands, Prussia, Russia, and Great Britain, and he had helped negotiate the treaty with Britain that ended the War of 1812. Adams distrusted the British government and thought the United States should make its own foreign policy. The United States, he told the Cabinet, should not "come in as a cockboat in the wake of the British man-of-war."

Monroe's message to Congress. Following Adams's advice, President Monroe announced a new policy to the world in his annual message to Congress on December 2, 1823. Though containing the ideas of John Quincy Adams, it came to be called the Monroe Doctrine: (1) The Western Hemisphere was no longer open to further colonization by European powers. (2) Any attempt of those powers to extend their political system (government by kings and not by elected representatives) to any portion of the American continents would be taken as a sign of unfriendliness toward the United States. (3) The United States would not meddle with European politics. (4) In return, Europe must not disturb the political status of the republics on this side of the ocean. In 1822 the United States had already recognized the independence of the new republics created from the old Spanish Empire. Now we proceeded to guarantee their independence against European interference.

The Monroe Doctrine was a defiant warning to strong and belligerent European powers. But like some later ringing American declarations it was a warning that the United States did not have the power to enforce. Then, as later, there were dangers in making threats if there was no strong army or navy behind them. At that time the only hope for enforcing the Monroe Doctrine was that it coincided with British foreign policy and that therefore it would be supported by the large British fleet. Whether European governments would pay attention to it in the future if it did not coincide with British policy would depend on the power of the young nation itself.

SECTION REVIEW

1. How was the Monroe Doctrine an outcome of revolutions in Latin America?

2. What did the Monroe Doctrine proclaim?

3. How was Great Britain involved?

The Americas in 1823

- British Territory
- United Provinces of Central America
- Spanish Territory
- Territory Claimed by England and United States
- ▷ Protected by Monroe Doctrine

0   1500 Miles

0   1500 Kilometers

CANADA

OREGON

NEWFOUNDLAND

42°

EMPIRE OF MEXICO

UNITED STATES

CUBA

JAMAICA

REPUBLIC OF HAITI

PUERTO RICO

BRITISH HONDURAS

GUATEMALA

HONDURAS

EL SALVADOR

NICARAGUA

COSTA RICA

VENEZUELA

BRITISH GUIANA

DUTCH GUIANA

FRENCH GUIANA

GREATER COLOMBIA

ECUADOR

EMPIRE OF BRAZIL

PERU

UPPER PERU (BOLIVIA) Independent, 1825

PARAGUAY

CHILE

UNITED PROVINCES OF RIO DE LA PLATA

URUGUAY (Independent, 1828)

Patriotic designs, like the ones woven into this 1825 coverlet, were popular decorations.

5. A national spirit

In 1824 President Monroe invited the French hero of the American Revolution, the aged Marquis de Lafayette, then nearing 70, to visit the United States again. He arrived in August, and his triumphal tour through all parts of the country lasted a full year. The wild enthusiasm that greeted Lafayette everywhere showed that despite sectional differences a national spirit flourished.

Words, slogans, and symbols. Perhaps the chief symbol of the new American nationalism was the flag. On June 14, 1777, Congress had adopted the first flag, which had 13 alternate stripes of white and red, and a circle of 13 white stars on a blue field in the upper left-hand corner. Later the small stars were arranged in the form of a large star, but finally they were set in horizontal lines on the field of blue. An act of Congress of April 4, 1818, provided that a new star should be added for each new state.

Another symbol was the American bald eagle. Benjamin Franklin had jokingly suggested that the turkey should be our symbol. But instead the fierce eagle was chosen. It appeared on the official seal of the United States and on coins. It was a popular decorative device on walls, in pictures, on signs—wherever people could think to use it.

The Constitution itself, the nation's instrument of government, also became a revered symbol. After the Constitution was ratified, it was the custom to refer to the Constitution as if it had always existed. The Constitution became the nation's sacred document, the final arbiter of any discussion. Of course, people might differ over what the Constitution *meant,* but who dared question its authority?

"Liberty," "freedom," and "union" became national slogans. Although the nation was still young, it already had a history, with heroes and stirring mottoes. At the Battle of Bunker Hill, General Putnam ordered: "Don't fire until you see the whites of their eyes." When the British commanded John Paul Jones to surrender his ship, he retorted, "I have not yet begun to fight." With the War of 1812, "Don't give up the ship" entered the vocabulary of American patriotism. The sharpshooting Kentucky rifleman in his buckskins—who had fought at the Thames and New Orleans—now was hailed as a new, and peculiarly western, national hero.

Heroes of the Revolution. The American people were long reminded of their fight for independence by the inspiring presence of men who had actually fought in the Revolution. No Fourth of July parade was complete without a veteran of the war. Some of the best American artists like Gilbert Stuart and Charles Willson Peale made their reputations (in those days before photography) painting portraits of heroes of the Revolution. John Trumbull told the whole history of the Revolution in a series of panoramic paintings. The nation's leading museum, in Philadelphia, featured Peale's portraits of the leaders in the fight for freedom.

The grand hero of the Revolution, of course, was George Washington. Painting his portrait became an industry in itself. Gilbert Stuart copied his own first portrait of Washington 39 times. He painted the President twice thereafter and made more copies. Washington's birthday began to be celebrated by the nation even before his death. His Farewell Address became a classic of schoolroom oratory. It is still read in the Congress every February 22.

The cult of George Washington was further promoted by solemn biographies like that by John Marshall (in five large volumes!) and popular lives like that by Parson Weems, who invented the famous story about Washington cutting down the cherry tree.

A national education. After the Revolution numerous plans were proposed for a national system of education. Democracy surely could not succeed without an educated citizenry. This meant, of course, that everyone should go to school and learn to read. Elementary schools and high schools were left to the local communities. But there were many proposals for a national university. Every President from Washington through John Quincy Adams favored some kind of national university that would instill patriotism and prepare citizens to govern.

In the United States, unlike most other countries of the world, the public schools would not be run by the national government. But a national spirit would still stir the American schools through textbooks—like those of Noah Webster and Jedidiah Morse. Webster, beginning in 1782, wrote spelling and other books which he hoped would create a uniform and pure *American* (as opposed to English) language. With the same hope in 1828 he produced the first important *American* dictionary. It was so respected that in the United States the name "Webster" has become a synonym for our dictionary. Just as Webster bred pride in our language, Jedidiah Morse helped spread knowledge of our

The Reverend Jedidiah Morse, author of the first textbook on American geography, uses a globe for a family geography lesson. Samuel F. B. Morse, inventor of the telegraph, painted this watercolor of his parents' household in 1811 when he was only 20 years old.

This wooden figure of Andrew Jackson was carved for the *Constitution* in 1834.

wealthy member of the Tennessee frontier upper class.

Still, Jackson transformed American politics. Unlike Jefferson, who was a man of learning and who liked to speak of the international Republic of Letters, Jackson was proud of not being literary. He was not good at spelling, and once even said that he had no respect for a man who could think of only *one* way to spell a word!

Democracy in office-holding. Although he was a wealthy plantation owner and slaveholder when he became President, Andrew Jackson thought of himself as one of the common people. After all, he had not inherited his wealth but had earned it by his own efforts. And couldn't other industrious Americans do the same? Although the people thought they had been robbed of their choice by the "Corrupt Bargain" between Adams and Clay in the election of 1824, now in 1828 they finally had their man.

It was not enough, Jackson argued, for the common people to have their own President. They had the right to hold all the offices in their government. According to Jackson this meant that anybody would be about as well qualified as anybody else—provided, of course, that they had supported Jackson.

"The duties of all public officers are . . . so plain and simple," he said, "that men of intelligence may readily qualify themselves for their performance." Instead of there being an office-holding class, the government offices should be "passed around." President Jackson was happy to use this persuasive democratic argument to throw out of office the followers of the hated Adams and Clay and make way for his own henchmen.

This "spoils system" of rewarding political supporters with jobs was an old story in many states, especially in New York. Jackson's bark was worse than his bite, however, for in the eight years of his Presidency only about one government employee in six was removed from office. That was not much different from what earlier Presidents had done. But Jackson and his political friends actually boasted of these removals as if they were a new kind of public service. The Jacksonian motto (borrowed from the battlefield)—"to the victors belong the spoils"—became the guiding principle of the national political parties.

1. How did voter qualifications change between 1800 and the mid-1820s? What groups still could not vote in 1828?

2. How did the early printed paper ballots affect voter turnout? corruption at the ballot box?

3. How did the method of nominating political candidates change? How did the American hotel help to promote the change?

4. What was Andrew Jackson's special voter appeal?

5. What was the "spoils system"? Why is Jackson associated with it?

3. Jackson takes command

Andrew Jackson believed in the southern code of honor, which required a gentleman to fight a duel against another gentleman who insulted him or his family. In 1806 Jackson faced a man who had insulted Mrs. Jackson. His opponent, Charles Dickinson, was a successful young lawyer who had learned his profession from Chief Justice John Marshall. He was a fine young southern gentleman—and a crack shot, too. When the two men aimed pistols at each other on the dueling grounds, Dickinson fired first, swiftly and surely. His shot hit Jackson near his heart but missed the fatal spot because Jackson's coat hung so loosely on his tall, thin frame. For a moment, Jackson believed he had been killed. But by force of his powerful will he held himself upright, waited for his eyes to clear, and then shot the man opposite him. His rival died the following day.

The incident clearly revealed several traits that marked Jackson as President—his fierce pride, his deep sense of honor, his unbending will.

The problem of Peggy Eaton. Andrew Jackson, at age 61 when he took office, felt sick and tired. His beloved wife, Rachel, had died only two months before. But, despite his grief, the gaunt, gray-haired old general radiated power.

It was his good luck, however, that in those days, although the President took office on March 4, the Congress did not assemble until the first Monday in December. So Jackson was able to spend his first nine months in office regaining his health, coping with the hordes of office seekers, and surveying the tasks of a President. One item that took much of his energy was nowhere listed in the laws or the Constitution. It was the troublesome problem of pretty Peggy O'Neale.

The daughter of a Washington tavernkeeper, Peggy was married to John Eaton, whom Jackson appointed Secretary of War. But she was not thought to be socially acceptable by Vice-President John C. Calhoun's wife, Floride, or by the wives of the other Cabinet members. This minor social problem would not be worth a line in a history book except that Andrew Jackson sided with the Eatons. He stopped meeting with his Cabinet and started taking advice from a group of friends, whom his enemies referred to as the "Kitchen Cabinet." Even more important, Secretary of State Martin Van Buren of New York used the problem to win the special favor of Andrew Jackson.

A blond, dapper little man, Van Buren liked to wear white trousers, a tan coat, a lace tie, and yellow gloves. He was a member of the new class of professional politicians, and he knew how to deal with people. He was always friendly, never angry, and never bothered to justify his actions with elaborate explanations. As an experienced New York politician he knew the spoils system and how to use it.

Van Buren, like Jackson, was a widower. So he could join Jackson without creating problems at home. His kindness to Peggy Eaton made Jackson grateful to him.

At last, the clever Martin Van Buren found a way to solve the problem of Peggy Eaton. He resigned as Secretary of State and engineered the resignations of Eaton and all but one of the other Cabinet members. For ridding him of the Eatons and the Cabinet members he could not work with, Jackson thought so highly of Martin Van Buren that Van Buren became his candidate for the next President of the United States.

At the same time, Calhoun had lost the President's confidence because his wife had been a leader in snubbing Peggy Eaton. This trivial incident checked, at least temporarily, Calhoun's march to the Presidency. Instead of Calhoun's rising as he had hoped from Vice-President to President with Jackson's support, Jackson now favored someone else. The South's most able spokesman would not

Speech/label text within cartoon:
"Major! Major! What shall I do." "It seems to me Major that no man is placed so often in such real. TROUBLE as I am. Matty has made too hot a fire and burnt our Bank Beef all to a cinder— Barry is in for it—Amos has seasoned everything and Taney has stumbled over the TREASUREY Pot and spilt all the gravy.

"General there is one Major in this Kitchen that makes pretty mi[...]"

"I keep an eye on some on 'em, and an ear on pretty much all on'em."

"My tools work well!"

Jackson and his "Kitchen Cabinet" feel the heat in this cartoon criticizing their money and banking policies (pp. 196–198). They have spilt the Treasury gravy and burnt the bank beef. The "Major" is Jack Downing, a humorous figure created by Maine writer Seba Smith.

be President during the coming struggle between the sections for national power.

South Carolina and the tariff.
Southerners opposed the protective tariff because it raised the prices of the manufactured goods they purchased. Since the higher prices went to northern manufacturers, they felt that they were being impoverished to enrich the businessmen in another section of the country. In South Carolina, a state that had been

especially hard hit by the depression of 1819, the opposition was violent. Overproduction had made cotton prices plummet. The price of cotton fell from almost 31 cents a pound in 1818 to less than 10 cents in 1828. This caused great distress in South Carolina. There the worn-out fields produced fewer pounds per acre than did the new fields west of the mountains.

The slaveholding South Carolinians had other reasons, too, to be worried. In 1822 they had discovered what appeared to be a widespread slave conspiracy. It was headed by Denmark Vesey, a free black who lived in Charleston. Thirty-six blacks were executed, and many others were exiled. But since none of the plotters would talk, their exact plans were never discovered. Still, South Carolinians were terrified. They put the blame for the Vesey rebellion on the northern critics of slavery who had spoken out during the debates over the Missouri Compromise. They began to feel that slavery—the South's "peculiar institution"—must be treated as if it were a sacred institution. They would not consider any change, and they dreaded to discuss the issue. They also began to imagine that enemies of the South lurked everywhere.

So they became strong opponents of tariffs and internal improvements by the federal government. If a strong federal government could take money away from the South with a protective tariff to benefit the businessmen of another section (the North), if it could enter a state to build a road or canal, what would prevent it from entering a state to meddle with, or even abolish, slavery?

When the Tariff of Abominations was passed in 1828, flags were flown at half-mast in Charleston. South Carolina orators urged a boycott against the states that profited from the tariff. One excited journalist even announced that it was high time "to prepare for a secession from the Union."

The most influential protest came from the pen of Vice-President Calhoun. He continued to think of himself as a nationalist, but he felt the Union could not be preserved if the rights of the states could be so infringed. In an unsigned essay, "The Exposition and Protest of South Carolina," he argued that a protective tariff was unconstitutional because it unfairly taxed one section of the country for the benefit of another. He reviewed the ideas of the Virginia and Kentucky Resolutions of 1798 that the Union was a compact of states. Each state, then, had the right to judge whether Congress was exceeding its powers. Within its borders, Calhoun argued, any state could nullify an act of Congress that it considered unconstitutional. For Congress to override that "nullification," it would then be necessary to use the long and clumsy amending process described in the Constitution. For that purpose the power asserted by the Congress, even if questioned by only one state, would have to be approved by three-fourths of the states.

The Webster-Hayne debate.

Soon this very question (and Calhoun's theory of "nullification") would be debated in Congress. The issue arose over the public lands. Many Easterners believed that the price of western land still owned by the government should be kept high. In that way the settlement of the West would proceed only slowly. Money and workers would not be drained away from the industrial East. But naturally enough, Westerners wanted all the land they could get. They wanted it fast, and they wanted it cheap!

At this point, southern planters saw their chance to create an alliance with the West. If they could join forces in Congress, the Westerners could get cheap land in return for their promise to help block any laws that touched slavery. On January 21, 1830, Senator Robert Y. Hayne of South Carolina moved in that direction. In his long speech that demanded the opening up of the public lands, he preached Calhoun's doctrine of nullification.

The reply to Hayne was delivered on January 26–27 by Senator Daniel Webster of Massachusetts. Someone said that no one could really be as great a man as Webster seemed to be. He was not only one of the nation's most skillful lawyers, but in the style of his time he was a tireless orator. He had a rich, deep voice and held his audience spellbound. His high forehead, thick eyebrows, burning eyes, and powerful form made him overwhelming and impressive in debate—a "great cannon loaded to the lips," Ralph Waldo Emerson called him. This particular speech, according to some listeners, was the most powerful ever given in Congress.

Over the course of some six hours of oratory in two days, Webster made his case. He rejected the idea that the Union was only a league of sovereign states. According to Webster, not the states but the people had made the Union. "It is, sir, the people's Constitution, the people's government made for the people, made by the people, answerable to the people." Only the Supreme Court had the power to declare a law void. If Pennsylvania could annul one law, Alabama another, and Virginia a third, then Congress would soon become a mockery. The Constitution would be a mere "rope of sand." The Union would fall apart, and the states would return to anarchy. In his emotional ending, Webster prayed to God that he would never live to see the Union destroyed. He rejected the idea of "Liberty first and Union afterwards." Instead he called for

Webster replies to Robert Hayne (front, hands folded) in the chamber used by the Senate until 1860. Visitors crowd the galleries and pages sit at the front in this painting by G. P. A. Healy.

"Liberty *and* Union, now and forever, one and inseparable."

Webster's speech swept the nation. For generations schoolchildren memorized its famous passages. He had caught the spirit of the United States in 1830 as Hayne and Calhoun had not. Few Americans were fearful any longer that a strong federal government would follow the example of King George III. The colonial experience was two generations in the past. Since the War of 1812 they had come to realize that their liberties could be preserved only by a strong Union. But John C. Calhoun, Robert Y. Hayne, and other Southerners believed that slavery was a sacred institution on which the prosperity of their region depended. They were not compromisers, and they had already set out on a collision course that could only lead to bloody civil war.

The Jefferson Day dinner.

President Jackson had not, of course, played any part in the great debate in the Senate. Some of Calhoun's supporters, however, hoped that the President from Tennessee could be enlisted on the southern side. In that same year of 1830 they arranged a banquet at Brown's Indian Queen Hotel in Washington to celebrate Jefferson's birthday (April 13). In that way they could call attention to the late Thomas Jefferson's Kentucky Resolutions, which they thought supported Calhoun's theory of "nullification."

When Jackson was invited to the celebration he realized that if the evening went off as Calhoun and his friends had planned, it might menace the stability of the Union. So he carefully prepared a toast to deliver at the dinner. When he was called on, he lifted his glass, looked at Calhoun, and proposed, "Our Union, it must be preserved." The Vice-President rose with the rest of the audience and drank the toast, but his hand trembled visibly.

Everybody knew that the President's words were a direct challenge to the Vice-President. "An order to arrest Calhoun where he sat," wrote one of the diners, "could not have come with more staggering, blinding force." After the shock had passed, it was the Vice-President's turn to toast. "The Union— next to our liberties, most dear!" he said. Then he added, "May we always remember that it can only be preserved by respecting the rights of the states and by distributing equally the benefits and burdens of the Union."

The issue was clear. In brevity as well as sentiment, Jackson had won the day. The news of the dinner and of Jackson's toast was soon out, and a wave of nationalism swept the country. Calhoun was observed in the Senate looking "crinkled and careworn."

A month later Calhoun was struck by another blow. He received a letter from the President asking if it was true that Calhoun had favored punishing Jackson for his Florida campaign back in 1818 (p. 172). The report was, in fact, correct. But Calhoun had been able to conceal his old attitude until now. When Calhoun was unable to explain himself, Jackson ceased speaking to him. At that point, Calhoun realized that his chance to become President was gone. Calhoun and his loyal southern followers knew as never before that their interests within the Union were in danger.

Indian policy. Like most frontiersmen and Indian fighters, Andrew Jackson felt that the best place for the Indians was somewhere else. He believed that the only way to handle the Indians who lived on the eastern side of the Mississippi was to move them all to the other side of the river. Settled on lands forbidden to the whites, they could be forever separated from the people of the United States. In that way, according to Jackson, there would be no more battles with the Indians. Presidents Monroe and Adams had proposed the same "solution" to the Indian problem. But it took President Jackson, who was no aristocrat from Virginia or Massachusetts but a rough man of the frontier, to carry out the brutal program to uproot the Indians from the land of their ancestors.

During his two terms in office, by fair means and foul, 94 Indian treaties were signed. Tribes agreed for varying amounts of compensation to give up their lands and go west. Some tribes went peaceably, though all went unhappily, to the lands west of the Mississippi. Other tribes dared to fight against superior forces of United States troops. In 1832 a few hundred Sauk and Fox Indians under Chief Black Hawk bravely tried to return to their homelands in Illinois and Wisconsin. Pursued by a United States force of regulars and militia, they were disastrously defeated on August 2, 1832, in the Battle of Bad Axe.

The courageous Seminole Chief Osceola in Florida led his people in the most successful Indian opposition the United States regulars ever had to face. The Seminoles hid their wives and children deep in the swamps. Helped by runaway slaves, but with meager supplies, they showed a surprising power to resist. Osceola was finally captured when the United States violated a flag of truce, and he died in Fort Moultrie at Charleston, South Carolina, in 1838. The Seminoles continued to defy the regulars into the 1840s. During these years many were captured and forcibly transported west of the Mississippi.

The Cherokees, more than any other Indian tribe, had adopted the ways of the white man. They were mostly settled in Georgia, where their farms, factories, and schools were not much different from any others. But they had no alphabet for their language until the brilliant Sequoya actually invented one. With this new alphabet the tribe

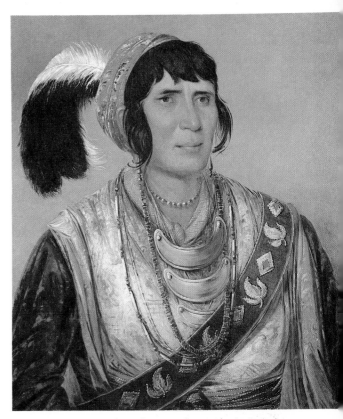

National Portrait Gallery, Smithsonian Institution

Self-trained George Catlin painted 600 portraits from life of Indian leaders like this one of the Seminole chief, Osceola.

printed its first newspaper. It was fitting that this Cherokee hero would later be commemorated in the great California redwoods, which are called "Sequoias."

The Cherokees went to court to retain their lands. In the case of *Worcester* v. *Georgia* (1832) the Supreme Court led by John Marshall ruled that the state of Georgia had no jurisdiction over Cherokee lands. But Georgia ignored the Court, and Jackson refused to intervene. "John Marshall has made his decision," Jackson was reputed to have said, "now let him enforce it." Jackson really hoped that the Indians would quietly leave Georgia as soon as possible. He feared that Georgia's clear resistance to the law of the land would encourage South Carolina's efforts to nullify the acts of Congress.

The Cherokees did not give in. Finally, in 1838, the army under General Winfield Scott rounded up those remaining in the East. During that October and November the soldiers drove 15,000 Indian men, women, and children westward. Through cold and rain the troops forced these innocent and bewildered Cherokees away from their homeland to the new "Indian Territory." This would later be called Oklahoma. The Cherokees called this path their "trail of tears." And it was the right name, for 1500 of their tribe died on the way.

The nullification controversy.
In 1832 Congress enacted a new tariff to replace the Tariff of Abominations. Though the rates were lower than those of 1828, this was still a high protective tariff. The planters of South Carolina were outraged. They were especially frightened because this tariff had passed by big majorities, which meant that the government's tariff policy would not soon change.

Meanwhile in Virginia in August 1831 a black preacher named Nat Turner led a slave rebellion during which 60 white men, women, and children were killed. The terrified whites put down the rebellion by killing at least 100 blacks, many of whom had no part in the revolt. The situation was so serious that the Virginia Assembly in 1832 lengthily debated the issue of abolishing slavery (p. 236). South Carolinians too were in a mood to review the threatening past—the Missouri Compromise, the uprisings of Denmark Vesey and Nat Turner, the radical debates in the Virginia Assembly. In several southern states where the blacks outnumbered the whites, the whites saw no way to

handle this situation except by keeping the blacks in slavery. Now this peculiar institution seemed especially vulnerable to hostile federal laws. The new tariff offered no hope that the federal government would cease tampering with property within the states. Would the next step be to free the slaves?

South Carolinian planters decided that they must protect their property—which to them meant their institution of slavery. They imagined that Calhoun's procedure for "nullifying" federal laws might be their salvation. That way not only could they get rid of the burdensome tariffs, but they would be prepared to void any federal laws that might interfere with slavery. A state convention was called to meet in November 1832, and delegates were elected. The nullifiers swept all before them.

The South Carolina convention voted by a margin of five to one that the tariff acts of 1828 and 1832 were unconstitutional and therefore null and void. They forbade South Carolinians to pay the duties required by these laws. The convention went even further and stated that any attempt by federal authorities to enforce tariff laws in South Carolina would be "a just cause for the secession of the state from the Union." Still the convention did leave one opportunity for compromise, for nullification was not to go into effect until February 1, 1833.

Jackson's response to nullification.
Meanwhile, at the very time of that convention, the national presidential campaign was under way. On December 5, 1832, Andrew Jackson was reelected by an overwhelming majority. Jackson, always a nationalist, reacted immediately to the challenge from South Carolina. Within days of his reelection his words to the nation posed the issue loud and clear. "I consider the power to annul a law of the United States, assumed by one state, incompatible with the existence of the Union." Since the nation was supreme over the states, no state could refuse to obey any federal law. And, of course, no state had the power to secede from the Union. "I will meet treason at the threshold," he wrote to the customs collector of the port of Charleston. "In forty days I will have 50,000 men in South Carolina to enforce the law."

The people of the nation rallied around Jackson, who was now at the height of his power. His

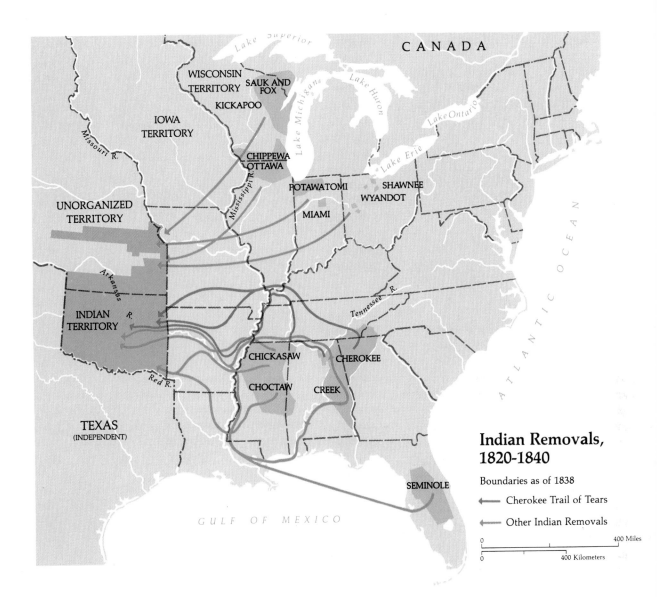

**Indian Removals,
1820-1840**

Boundaries as of 1838

← Cherokee Trail of Tears

← Other Indian Removals

0   400 Miles

0   400 Kilometers

unhesitating leadership had given new courage to all who loved the Union. Even Georgia, which was ignoring the Supreme Court's order concerning the Cherokees, supported the President. The uncompromising John C. Calhoun, who had resigned the Vice-Presidency in December in order to be elected to the Senate by South Carolina, now saw that his state must retreat. So he turned to Henry Clay — the man most responsible for the hated tariffs. Calhoun and Clay were united by their dislike of Jackson, and they shared a desire to avoid bloodshed. But Clay was also moved by his devotion to the Union.

Clay drew up a new bill that reduced the tariff rates but still preserved the protective system. Calhoun reluctantly went along with Clay's bill. Since it was offered as a compromise under pressure from South Carolina, it seemed to give Calhoun a way to save face, to stay in the Union, yet not give up his principles. The new bill reduced tariffs over a nine-year period until they finally were brought back down to the levels of 1816. It was signed into law by Jackson on March 2, 1833.

When the South Carolina convention met again a few days later, the domineering Calhoun advised the delegates to accept the new compromise tariff and rescind the nullification. This they did by an overwhelming vote. But then in a proud, if empty, gesture they turned around and nullified the "Force Bill" by which Congress had authorized the President "to employ the army and navy of the United States to collect duties in South Carolina."

Both sides now claimed victory. South Carolina planters felt they had compelled Congress to lower the tariff. Union supporters believed that Congress had forced South Carolina to back down and repeal nullification. Unfortunately this compromise bought time but offered no long-term solution. Since neither side had changed its principles, they had settled nothing. The day of battle was only postponed. The fighting language of nullification and secession would not be forgotten.

SECTION REVIEW

1. Identify or explain: Peggy Eaton, "Kitchen Cabinet," Denmark Vesey, Robert Y. Hayne, Black Hawk, Osceola, Sequoya, *Worcester* v. *Georgia*, Winfield Scott, "trail of tears," Indian Territory, Nat Turner, Force Bill.

2. How did Martin Van Buren win Jackson's favor? Why did Calhoun fall out of favor?

3. Explain Calhoun's theory of nullification.

4. What was the *chief* issue in the Webster-Hayne debate? Where and how did Jackson take a stand on this issue?

5. Describe the treatment of the Indians under Jackson.

6. How did South Carolina respond to the tariff of 1832? What was the outcome of the tariff controversy?

4. Banks and money

A successful plantation owner and land speculator, Andrew Jackson was a practical, self-made man with strong prejudices. He distrusted banks. He disliked the cheap and sometimes worthless paper money they printed. The only money he trusted was hard money—gold and silver. He was especially bitter against the Bank of the United States, which with its monopoly of the government's business was a symbol of all hated special privilege. He thought it was evil as well as unconstitutional, and he loathed it.

The war on the Bank. The charter of the Bank of the United States was not due to expire until 1836. Its president, Nicholas Biddle, was aware of Jackson's feelings. So he felt that the Bank should lie low and try to arrange a truce with the President. The ambitious Henry Clay thought he saw in the Bank an issue that might defeat Jackson in the 1832 election. Clay was the unanimous choice of the National Republicans to oppose Jackson and the Democratic Republicans.

To bring the issue to a head, and reap the political benefit, Clay induced Biddle to apply for a new charter for the Bank early in 1832. He believed that if Jackson dared to veto the recharter bill, as he hoped he would, the President would lose enough votes in the East to cost him the election.

The recharter bill went to President Jackson on July 4, 1832. Jackson was sick in bed at the time, and he said to his running mate, "The Bank, Mr. Van Buren, is trying to kill me, but *I will kill it.*" Six days later he returned the bill to Congress with a veto which, in Nicholas Biddle's words, "had all the fury of a chained panther biting the bars of his cage."

Jackson could have sent Congress a brief message stating his objections to the bill. Instead he sent a long message that was shrewdly designed to garner votes. Jackson stressed that the Bank and its stockholders were claiming special privileges and wanted a democratic government to treat them like aristocrats. Of course in any human society there were some natural distinctions which God himself had made—"of talents, of education, or of wealth." But the government must not make laws that added to the "natural and just advantages artificial distinctions." When laws made "the rich richer, and the potent more powerful," the people had to protest.

Henry Clay and Nicholas Biddle thought that Jackson's demagogic appeal would have the opposite effect from that he intended. Jackson's words revealed how little he understood the Bank. Still he proved that he did understand what the people wanted. To the mass of voters it seemed that "Old Hickory" was the champion of all the little people against the money-kings. On election day Clay carried only six states with 49 electoral votes, while Jackson carried sixteen for a whopping 219.

The removal of the deposits. After this decisive victory over "the Monster," Jackson was impatient to kill the Bank at once. But its charter ran till

Jackson, armed with his veto, attacks the many-headed monster, the second Bank of the United States and its branch banks. Bank president Nicholas Biddle is the large, top-hatted head in the center. Helping Jackson is Major Jack Downing (right), the legendary backwoodsman in many Jacksonian cartoons. Martin Van Buren, piously declaiming that he dislikes dissension, eagerly congratulates those on both sides.

1836. He was determined not to wait four years until the charter expired. He decided to deposit no new funds in the Bank and to pay the nation's bills with the funds already on deposit there. These actions would rapidly remove all the government's money from the clutches of the hated Bank. It was not easy to find a Secretary of the Treasury who would help him murder the bank. After two unsuccessful tries he finally appointed his Attorney General, Roger B. Taney (pronounced Tawney), who agreed to do Jackson's bidding. On October 1, 1833, Taney began depositing government funds in certain "pet banks" around the country. The whole nation would soon suffer from this vindictive act.

The Bank of the United States had been a wholesome influence on the nation's economy. Its officers had made sound loans that aided business. Now, using the vast government deposits, the imprudent "pet banks" lent their funds wildly and without counting the consequences. Reckless spending and uncontrolled economic growth followed. The government debt was paid off, and the surplus money that piled up in the "pet banks" spurred more and more growth. Sales of public land, which had been less than $2 million in 1830, rose to $24 million in 1836. The numerous new

Jackson, dressed as "King Andrew the First," tramples with dainty shoes on bills passed by Congress and on the Constitution. The cartoonist makes clever use of the eagle as a leg for the table next to the throne.

The Specie Circular and the distribution of the Treasury surplus.

Jackson, who shared Benton's distrust of paper money, was in a position to do something about it. On July 11, 1836, he issued his "Specie Circular," which forbade the Treasury to receive anything but gold or silver in payment for public lands. At once the land boom stopped. In that same year Congress voted to distribute to the states the surplus funds in the Treasury. Again the nation was to suffer from Jackson's ill-considered and hasty financial policies. But this time the results would not appear until his unfortunate successor had taken office.

Jackson's Presidency proved that the Chief Executive had the power to do more than simply execute the policies prescribed by Congress. He actually could make government policy and change that policy as he pleased. If the people supported him, there was little the opposition could do. His enemies were free, of course, to call him names, and they labeled him King Andrew I. To make it plain that he was a tyrant, the National Republicans renamed themselves the "Whigs," after the British party that had struggled against the king back in the 1700s.

The popular and energetic Jackson was still unshaken. One opponent confessed, "General Jackson may be President for life, if he wishes." When Jackson had enough of presidential power, he decided to retire to his beloved home, "The Hermitage," in Tennessee. As his successor he handpicked his favorite adviser, the dapper Martin Van Buren. In the election of 1836 the Whigs did not select a single candidate, but let each section choose its own in the hope of throwing the election into the House of Representatives. Still Martin Van Buren won easily over Senator Daniel Webster of Massachusetts, Senator Hugh L. White of Tennessee, and the military hero William Henry Harrison of Ohio.

The Presidency of Martin Van Buren.

Martin Van Buren had been an adroit political manager. For some reason he proved unable to exercise that skill when he became President. To make matters worse, Jackson's reckless financial policies were coming home to roost. When Jackson had removed specie from the banks through the Specie Circular and the distribution of the surplus in the Treasury to the states, the banks began to restrict

banks that sprang up throughout the West fed the spending mania. They issued more money, which was used by land speculators to buy more land. Senator Thomas Hart Benton of Missouri had hated the Bank of the United States. But now he complained, "I did not join in putting down the Bank of the United States to put up a wilderness of local banks. I did not join in putting down the paper currency of a national bank to put up a paper currency of a thousand local banks."

their loans and to stop redeeming their bank notes in gold and silver. At the same time a financial crisis in Britain caused the Bank of England to reduce the flow of specie out of that country. It was this British gold and silver coming to the United States that had helped finance the boom during Jackson's second term. So, still another support to the American economy was lost. On top of that, farmers suffered a year of bad crops.

All these influences together brought on a financial panic in 1837. By 1839 the nation was suffering a severe depression. Land sales became a mere trickle. Banks failed and factories closed their doors. The surplus in the Treasury soon disappeared. States that counted on these funds to pay for the construction of elaborate systems of roads, canals, and railroads had to stop the projects. Thousands were thrown out of work. Van Buren's whole administration was blighted by this business depression.

Van Buren achieved only one lasting change during his Presidency. On March 31, 1840, he issued an executive order that no person could work more than ten hours a day on a federal project. For the first time government workers found that they no longer had to labor from dawn to dusk. Years later Michael Shiner, a free black who worked in the Washington Navy Yard, wrote in his diary that for establishing the ten-hour day Van Buren's name should be recorded in every workingman's heart.

The election of 1840. The Whigs spent these unhappy years of Van Buren's administration preparing to put their own candidate in the White House. Just as Andrew Jackson was the first new-style President, so the first rip-snorting modern presidential campaign took place in 1840. When the Whig party held its national nominating convention in Harrisburg, Pennsylvania, on December 4, 1839, it passed over the able Senator Henry Clay. He was too well known and had made too many enemies in his years in office.

AN UGLY *MUG* OF LOG-CABIN HARD CIDER

A BEAUTIFUL GOBLET OF WHITE-HOUSE CHAMPAGNE.

With Jackson's encouragement, Van Buren
tries to stop the supply of Harrison's cider.

Democratic newspaperman sneered that Harrison
really did not care to be President but simply
wanted a barrel of hard (alcoholic) cider to get
drunk on and a log cabin to live in, the Whigs had
their clue. They eagerly took up the cry: Hurrah
for the log cabin and hard cider! Being an ordinary
man who lived in a log cabin and liked to drink
cider, they said, was no disgrace! On the contrary,
that proved Harrison was a man of the people.

The log cabin idea had great appeal. General
Harrison had really been born of an old, well-to-do
Virginia family, and he lived in a mansion. But his
supporters soon invented a log cabin that he was
supposed to have been born in. The "aristocrat"
Van Buren was pictured living in the White House
enjoying fine foods and costly wines, indifferent to
the suffering of the starving unemployed.

"Tippecanoe and Tyler too!" became the battle
hymn of Harrison's supporters. At the Whig rallies,
hard cider flowed freely from barrels on a stage-set
of log cabins. The Whigs floated to victory on a sea
of alcohol! "We were sung down, lied down,
drunk down," a Democratic paper complained.
Harrison and Tyler carried all but seven states, and
against Van Buren's 60 electoral votes they won 234.

Harrison had proved himself the perfect new-
style candidate. But it was one thing to be an
appealing vote-getting candidate, and something
else to be an effective President. As the Jacksonian
era drew to a close, the nation was beginning to
come apart at the seams. The country needed
strong, farsighted leadership. The issues could not
be washed away in hard cider. It would take more
than songs and slogans to hold the young nation
together.

Instead the Whigs chose the old soldier William
Henry Harrison, about whom most people knew
little except that he had defeated the Indians at the
Battle of Tippecanoe.

In order to pick up southern votes, the Whigs
nominated John Tyler of Virginia for Vice-President. His only reason for being a Whig was that he
shared their hatred for Andrew Jackson. The party
drew up no platform (a list of what it stood for)
because it could not agree on anything except the
desire to defeat Van Buren, whom the Democratic
party renominated.

This presidential campaign, like many to follow,
did not center on key national issues, but resounded
with empty slogans and name calling. When a

SECTION REVIEW

1. Identify or explain: Nicholas Biddle, bank
   recharter bill, Roger B. Taney, "pet banks,"
   Specie Circular, Whigs, "Tippecanoe and
   Tyler too."
2. How did Henry Clay use the Bank issue to
   influence the election of 1832? What was the
   outcome?
3. How did Jackson's financial policies first set off
   an economic boom and then a financial panic?
4. How did Van Buren make labor history?
5. Describe the election campaign of 1840.

CHAPTER REVIEW

MEETING OUR EARLIER SELVES

1. John Quincy Adams was said to have made a "bargain" to become President, but his general unwillingness to bargain hurt his Presidency. Explain by citing evidence from the text.

2. What political factors contributed to the decline of the Virginia or New England aristocrat as President and the rise of the "choice of the common man"?

3. Andrew Jackson was a man of "strong prejudices." What were some of them? How did they affect (a) his personal relationships? (b) his policies?

4. How was western land beyond the Appalachians involved in (a) changes in suffrage qualifications? (b) the Webster-Hayne debate? (c) Jackson's Indian policy? (d) Jackson's war on the Bank?

QUESTIONS FOR TODAY

1. Name some ways in which voting practices or voting qualifications differ today from what they were in the early 1800s. Which of the changes are improvements? Explain.

2. What did Andrew Jackson say about the qualifications needed to fill public office? What are some additional qualifications that ought to be possessed by persons appointed to office today?

3. Has the importance of oratory in politics declined since Webster's day? What has been the effect of radio and television on political campaigns?

YOUR REGION IN HISTORY

1. When did your state grant voting rights to nearly all adult male citizens? to adult female citizens? What steps must you take to qualify to vote today in your state?

2. What Indian tribe or tribes lived in your area before white settlement? Were they affected by removal efforts in the Jacksonian era? If so, how? If not, what happened to them?

SKILLS TO MAKE OUR PAST VIVID

1. Compute the percentage of the popular vote and the electoral vote received by each of the presidential candidates in the election of 1828. Then prepare a pie, or circle, graph for the popular vote and one for the electoral vote. Explain why the two graphs differ.

2. Assume that you were a western farmer, or a New England manufacturer, or a southern plantation owner. Write a letter to your congressman in complaint or support of the Tariff of Abominations.

3. Based on the data below and your reading, how do you account for the sharp increase in voters between 1824 and 1828, when the population increase was much slower?

	ESTIMATED POPULATION	VOTERS IN PRESIDENTIAL ELECTION
1824	10,924,000	356,038
1828	12,237,000	1,115,350

4

A nation growing and dividing 1800–1860

This painting, "Geese in Flight," was done about 1850. It reflects the interest of Americans in transportation. From the National Gallery of Art, gift of Edgar William and Bernice Chrysler Garbisch (detail).

In 1831, Alexis de Tocqueville, a 26-year-old French aristocrat, arrived here to study the new nation. By steamer, stagecoach, and horseback, he traveled for eight months over 7000 miles—as far west as Green Bay and Sault Ste. Marie and as far south as New Orleans. He saw a great deal of the United States and talked to many Americans. Back in France, Tocqueville wrote Democracy in America, *one of the best books about our country.*

"An attentive examination of what is going on in the United States," Tocqueville wrote, "will easily convince us that two opposite tendencies exist in that country, like two distinct currents flowing in contrary directions in the same channel." These two opposite forces were nationalism and sectionalism. As the nation grew, both forces would continue to grow. In these next decades national leaders and sectional leaders worked hard to hold the country together. They debated and passed laws of compromise. We will see how strenuously they tried and how sadly they failed. A divided nation was coasting down the road to civil war.

CHAPTER 10

The flourishing land

By the time of the Civil War there were distinct American ways of life. There were new ways of making houses, muskets, locks, and clocks—and nearly everything else. There were new ways of growing. The United States was the world's largest importer of people. And cities sprouted from raw western villages with a speed that startled Europeans.

But the sections did not grow all in the same way or at the same pace. Some regions were as different from others as, a century before, life in Great Britain had been different from life in the far-off American colonies. Thoughtful observers wondered if the Constitution that had been made to hold thirteen seaboard states together could really bind a continent.

1. Drawing the people together

At the time of the War of 1812 it took 75 days for a fully loaded wagon pulled by four horses to travel the 1000 miles from Worcester, Massachusetts, to Charleston, South Carolina. Letters and news traveled little faster. Could any union last if its people and their produce were so hard to bring together?

The age of roads and turnpikes. During the early years of the Republic, the land was gradually covered by a network of trails and roads. One of the most popular kinds of roads was the "turnpike." This was a road where the user had to pay a toll. It was named after a kind of revolving barrier with spikes on it that had been used on paths in England to prevent horses from passing through. The first turnpike in the United States was built during George Washington's second term to cover the 62 miles between Lancaster and Philadelphia in Pennsylvania.

The success of this Lancaster Turnpike began a wave of turnpike building in New England and the Middle States that lasted until about 1825. Most of the turnpikes were built by private companies. States and local governments sometimes helped. But the high toll-fees charged per ton discouraged their use for the farmers' bulky products.

Funds from the federal government would change the picture. In 1802 and 1803 Congress voted to use money received from the sale of the public lands for a National Road through the mountains and across Ohio. In 1806 Cumberland, Maryland, was selected as the road's starting point. This, the most important federal transportation project of the time, took a half-century. Work began in 1811. The road reached Wheeling, West Virginia, on the Ohio River in 1818 and did not reach Vandalia, Illinois, until 1852. It became a vital wagon highway to the West.

Even after the turnpikes were built, the majority of roads were just bumpy trails, many with stumps a

Major Roads about 1851

foot high in the middle. Most Americans lived on farms, and without a good cross-country road the farm family was isolated.

The canal-building boom.

The roads and turnpikes usually went to villages near the water where goods could be floated to their destination. In the West, streams and rivers led down to the broad Mississippi, which carried produce all the way to New Orleans, then out to the Gulf of Mexico and the world.

New Orleans flourished from the trade of the West which was drained into her harbors. Eastern cities wanted a larger share. New York's Governor DeWitt Clinton in 1816 came up with a daring scheme. Before becoming governor, Clinton had been five times elected mayor of New York City. Madison had defeated him for President in 1812.

Clinton was a battler for reforms. He was an abolitionist, he defended poor debtors, and he wanted Roman Catholics to have the right to vote.

Now, to promote commerce he aimed to dig the longest canal ever seen in America. It would run 363 miles through the level Mohawk Valley from Buffalo on Lake Erie to Albany on the Hudson River. Western crops, instead of floating down the Mississippi to enrich the merchants of New Orleans, would go through the Great Lakes into the canal and down the Hudson River to New York City. This was a grand and startling idea. At the time there were only 100 miles of canals in the whole United States. And none was more than 2 miles long!

There was a fight in the state legislature. Some said it would be too expensive. Farmers along the Hudson River and on Long Island feared the competition of produce from western farmers. But Clinton won. In 1817 the lawmakers voted $7 million for the project. They took it for granted that clever men would find a way to dig the long ditch. And they were right. In 1825 when the canal finally opened, the whole state celebrated.

"Lockport on the Erie Canal" was painted in 1832. As horses pull the boat toward the locks, passengers on the roof enjoy the scenery.

Munson-Williams-Proctor Institute, Utica, New York

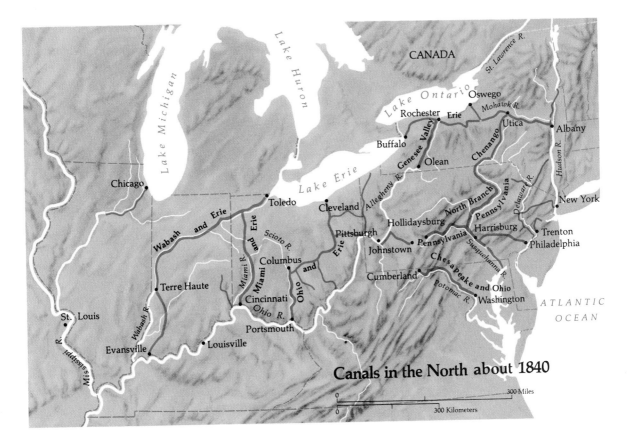

Canals in the North about 1840

Clinton proudly took national leaders down the canal and the Hudson River from Buffalo to New York City and dumped a barrel of water from Lake Erie into the Atlantic Ocean.

At once the canal was a success. Its whole cost was repaid in nine years from the tolls charged the users. The cost per ton for sending shipments from Buffalo to New York dropped from 20 cents to less than 1 cent a mile. Farm products in western New York and the Ohio Valley doubled in value now that they could so easily reach the eastern market. Cities on the Great Lakes—Buffalo, Cleveland, Detroit, and Chicago, and many more—soon rivaled the older river cities of Pittsburgh, Cincinnati, and St. Louis. New York City became the nation's commercial metropolis.

The success of the Erie Canal sparked a canal-building boom. By 1840 more than $125 million had been spent all over the North and the West on a vast canal system of 3326 miles.

Most canal projects were halted by the Panic of 1837 and the depression that followed. Some states, like Pennsylvania and Indiana, which built canals in haste without figuring how to cover their cost, were near bankruptcy. Many states now amended their constitutions to forbid use of the state's credit for canals or other internal improvements. One result was that, when railroads were built in the 1840s and 1850s, though aided by state funds, they were built by private companies.

The age of the steamboat. For all human history, boats had been driven either by manpower or by windpower. There seemed to be no other way. Then, in 1807 Robert Fulton imported a steam engine from England, put it in his boat the *Clermont,* and astonished Americans. Fulton was clever and versatile. He was an expert gunsmith during the American Revolution, and then he became a painter. He had even designed underwater torpedoes and made a kind of submarine. Now he steamed upstream from New York to Albany in 32 hours. He proved that the steamboat could be used in commerce. Only four years later the first steamboat was launched west of the mountains on the Ohio River.

Travel by steamboat could be quite luxurious. The interiors were often full of carved wood panels and elegant velvet draperies. The exterior, as shown in this 1850s photograph of steamboats crowded at a small dock, was trimmed with carved wood.

For Westerners the steamboat solved many problems. They could still float their crops on rafts downriver to New Orleans. But now they could ride back upriver in comfort in a fast-traveling, luxurious side-wheeler. Soon western rivers were alive with the tall, colorful stacks of the crowded vessels.

The steamship on western waters was unlike anything seen before. It was driven by a new type of engine—the high-pressure engine, which was light. The pioneer maker of these engines was Oliver Evans, from the neighborhood of Philadelphia, who was a genius at labor-saving devices. He had made a flour mill that used chutes and moving belts in place of manpower. And he actually had a plan for a steam-driven carriage that might have been a pioneer automobile. At first, people said he was crazy. When the gadgets worked, people stopped laughing and began stealing his ideas.

The high-pressure engines were faster than anything known before. They burned lots of wood to keep up the steam pressure, but that was not serious in the virgin forests of the West. With a full head of steam their boilers sometimes exploded. But American pioneers were willing to risk anything to get there first. Their motto was "Go ahead anyhow."

Since these steamboats had to operate on shallow western rivers filled with snags, rocks, and sandbars, they were built with a shallow draft. The engine was set on deck inside a high superstructure. In 1838 there were twenty steamboats that could operate in only 30 inches of water. Some captains joked that their ships could run on a heavy dew!

Not only were these ships light and fast, but they were inexpensive to build. That was a good thing because with the American passion for speed the boats did not last very long.

On these western steamboats the accidents were shocking. Without safety valves on the crude boilers or with the valves tied down, unlimited speed meant unlimited disaster. Europeans were appalled.

"The democrats have never liked to remain behind one another," a traveling German nobleman reported from the West about 1840. "On the contrary each wants to get ahead of the rest. When two steamboats happen to get alongside each other, the passengers will encourage the captains to run a race. . . . The races are the cause of most of the explosions, and yet they are still constantly taking place. The life of an American is, indeed, only a constant *racing*, and why should he fear it so much on board the steamboats?"

These western racers, called "brag" boats, lived a short, exciting life. Of all the steamboats built before the mid-1800s, nearly a third were lost in accidents. The main cause was explosions, which killed scores of passengers by bursts of flying wreckage and floods of scalding steam. Some steamboat owners sent the passengers who had not yet paid their fares to the back part of the vessel. Then, in case of explosion, they were less likely to be killed, and the owner could still collect his fares from them.

The triumph of the railroads.

The United States did not invent the railroad. But this country luckily was free from the artificial barriers of national boundaries that had grown up over the centuries in Europe. Here vast expanses of wilderness were filling up with people. Hordes of eager settlers wanted a speedy path to their new homes. Thousands of empty acres were suddenly populated by farmers and merchants who needed supplies brought in and who had to ship out their produce. Boston, Baltimore, and Charleston met the challenge of the Erie Canal. They built railroads to capture the commerce of the West.

It took time before everybody saw that the railroads would be the arteries that united the nation. Pennsylvania ignored the first successful railroads built in 1830. It chose instead to reach westward with a canal. But by 1840, in the country

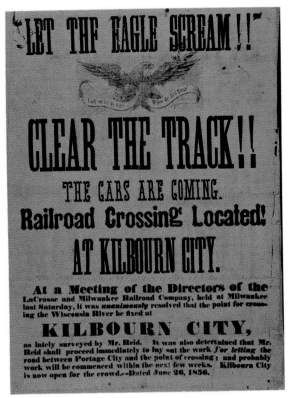

News that the new railroad would pass through your town signaled prosperity: workers to lay the rails, new settlers, lower freight costs, and new business enterprises.

as a whole, there were as many miles of track as there were of canals.

The great wave of railroad building came in the vast American West in the 1850s. In a single decade the nation's tracks increased from 8879 miles to 30,626 miles—more than enough to circle the globe. Ohio and Illinois, then still called the "West," led the nation in their miles of track. Chicago, which did not become an incorporated city until 1833, within 30 years had grown to be the greatest railroad center in the world.

Railroad building in the United States.

Cautious European railroad builders came over here in the 1840s and 1850s to see how Americans had managed to lay their tracks so fast over such vast distances. They were horrified. Just as the reckless Americans had pushed ahead on the rivers with

Railroads, 1850-1860

— Railroads in 1850

— Railroads Completed, 1850-1860

high-pressure engines on their steamboats, so now it seemed that railroading Americans were taking terrible risks. Instead of laying two sets of tracks—one for each direction—they saved time and money by laying only a single set of tracks. Of course, this increased the danger of collision. They did not trouble to level hills, to cut tunnels, or to lay their tracks in long, gentle curves. Sometimes they actually laid tracks on top of the snow—with disastrous results when the spring thaw came. No wonder the American trains so often went off the rails as they came rocketing down the steep hills or failed to maneuver the sharp curves.

By 1850 railroad wrecks were as common as steamboat explosions. Experienced travelers rode in the middle cars, rather than at front or back. Fast American trains of the middle 1800s gave all the excitement of a roller coaster, but they were much less safe.

In their headlong pursuit of speed, Americans made some discoveries. Perhaps the most important was how to design light engines that put less strain on the track and still could hold the track around sharp curves. The heavy early engines were built with large wheels mounted rigidly on axles like those of the old horse carriage. John Bloomfield Jervis, a self-taught engineer from New York, saw another way. He made a separate little truck (called a "bogie") with four low wheels and put it under the front end of the locomotive. Since the bogie wheels were low, small, and could swivel, they were not so apt to derail, even on sharply curving track.

American railroads were built by private companies with both state and private funds. The companies were aided by the federal government with free surveys and lower tariffs on iron rails. After 1850 they were given thousands of acres of public land. In England, where railroads were also being built, they usually went from one big city to another. But in the United States, where people were only beginning to fill up the continent, things were different. Here, as an amused foreign editor remarked, the railroads often went "from nowhere in particular to nowhere at all."

Laying a railroad across the vast, empty stretches of the American West was a costly business. The tracks were expensive. Whole communities of laborers had to be moved out and provided for on the prairie, on a mountainside, or in the deep forests. There the teams surveyed the track, constructed roadbeds, laid rails, cut tunnels, and built bridges. Enormous capital was required, which private firms did not yet have. The states and the federal government provided large grants of land that could be sold to make up the difference.

By 1860 steam had transformed transportation over the land and on the lakes and rivers of the United States. The railroad had opened whole new areas to settlement, spurred the growth of factories, and turned the trade of the West from the South toward the East. Instead of floating most of their produce down to New Orleans or to the southern states, Westerners now shipped their goods by rail and canal to eastern cities. These same railroads and canals brought back to them the products of the East. The economic interests of western farmers and eastern factory workers were newly united. All this would have political consequences.

Letters in every mailbox. A workable national mail system was slow in coming to the nation. The

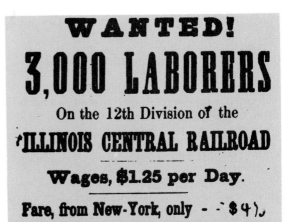

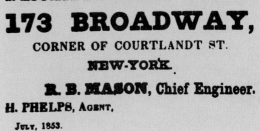

To get the tracks laid and the trains moving quickly, the railroads needed thousands of construction workers from the East Coast.

framers of the federal Constitution in 1787 had given Congress the power "to establish Post Offices and Post Roads." A post road was a main road with special stations ("posts") to provide fresh horses for the riders who carried the mail. For some years, almost all postal service was on one main post road along the Atlantic coast. People used the mail very little. When George Washington was President, the letters in the mail averaged less than one for every twelve Americans each year.

In those early years the postage on a letter was usually paid by the person who received it. If you did not want to pay the postage, you never got your letter. There was no home delivery. To get your mail you had to go to the post office.

Then in 1825 came the dim beginning of modern mail delivery. The postmaster in each town was allowed to give letters to mail carriers to deliver to people's homes. The carriers still were paid no government salary. They lived by collecting a small fee from the person to whom they delivered a letter. If you were not at home to pay, they would not leave your letters in your mailbox.

In the 1840s the growing country desperately needed a cheap and efficient postal system. The service was still so haphazard and expensive that there was widespread demand to abolish the Post Office. People called it an "odious monopoly" and said that private businesses could do better.

As a result, in 1845 Congress passed a law establishing cheap postage and tried to reform the whole system. At first each postmaster printed his own stamps, and there was chaos. Then, in 1847, the reformed Post Office Department issued the first national postage stamps—a 5-cent stamp showing the head of Benjamin Franklin and a 10-cent stamp with the head of George Washington.

Still, for most of the century, people outside of big cities had to go to the post office to pick up their mail. It was not until 1896 that Congress adopted "Rural Free Delivery"—RFD, for short. Then every family could have the mail brought to their own mailbox.

Morse and the telegraph. Some people dreamed of faster methods of communicating. But it was hard to imagine a system that did not depend on seeing signals or on sending written messages. Samuel F. B. Morse, an artist and a man of many talents, found a way to make an electric current do the job. The idea came to him on the sailing ship *Sully* coming back from a trip to Europe. After talking to a fellow passenger about electricity, he asked why it could not be used to send messages. Others before him had asked the same question—and got nowhere with their answer. But Morse did not know enough about the subject to be discouraged. He suddenly decided to make an electric "telegraph" (from the Greek words for "far writer").

On the next page is the cover for sheets of original music dedicated to Cyrus W. Field in honor of the transatlantic telegraph cable.

It took Morse five years to make a telegraph instrument that would work and six more years to convince Congress to build the first line. During that time he supported himself by giving painting lessons. Finally, in 1843, Congress appropriated $30,000. With this money Morse stretched a telegraph line from Baltimore to Washington. On May 24, 1844, he sent his famous message, "What hath God wrought?" from Washington to Baltimore.

By 1848, Morse and two partners had built a telegraphic network that stretched from Maine to South Carolina and westward to St. Louis, Chicago, and Milwaukee. Regular newspaper columns offered the latest bulletins under the heading, "By Magnetic Telegraph." Newspapermen boasted of the "mystic band" that now held the nation together.

Cyrus W. Field, a visionary New York businessman, thought there ought to be a telegraph line all the way to Europe. He formed a company to undertake the difficult task. After several years and many failures, the long line on the bottom of the ocean was finished in 1858, and telegraph messages began to pass between America and England. Within weeks the line failed, and then the Civil War prevented the laying of a new cable until 1866.

SECTION REVIEW

1. Identify or explain: turnpike, DeWitt Clinton, Robert Fulton, "brag" boats, John Bloomfield Jervis, Samuel F. B. Morse, Cyrus W. Field.

2. Locate: Lancaster Turnpike, National Road, Mohawk Valley, Erie Canal.

3. Why were state and local governments willing to finance roads and canals?

4. What was the importance of the Erie Canal?

5. Why was steamboat travel popular? Why was it dangerous?

6. How did American railroads and engines differ from those built in Europe?

7. Name some significant developments in American communication in the 1840s.

TO CYRUS W. FIELD, ESQ.

ATLANTIC TELE GRAPH POLKA.

THE NIAGARA & AGAMEMNON COMMENCING TO LAY THE CABLE.

COMPOSED BY A. TALEXY.

FULL SIZE AND APPEARANCE OF CABLE.

MAP OF THE TELEGRAPH BETWEEN AMERICA & EUROPE.

BOSTON

Published by OLIVER DITSON & CO 277 Washington St.

J. H. Bufford & Lith.

C. C. CLAPP & CO.   S. T. GORDON.   BECK & LAWTON.   TRUAX & BALDWIN.
Boston   N. York.   Philada   Cinn

Smoke from the factories of Lazell, Perkins & Company was a daily reminder to Bridgewater, Massachusetts, that the Industrial Revolution had arrived. This late 1850s hand-colored lithograph advertised the firm's "Forgings . . . Casting and all Kinds of Machinery."

2. The Industrial Revolution

The Industrial Revolution is a name for the great changes brought by the modern factory system. It came first to Britain. The British government, hoping to keep its leadership, made it a crime to take out of the country the designs of its new factory machinery. It was a crime even for workmen from one of these advanced factories to go to work in another country. But people and ideas were on the move—and America was the place for an ambitious workman.

Samuel Slater, on his own, defeated Britain's shortsighted scheme of industrial secrecy. While he worked in one of the up-to-date English cotton textile mills, he memorized the design for the machinery. Then he came to the United States—with some of the most prized industrial secrets. Helped by two American businessmen in Pawtucket, Rhode Island, he set up the first American textile factory just like the most advanced factories in England. It opened in 1792 with 72 spindles and a work force of nine children.

The rise of the factory system. In 1850 the 7th Census of the United States reported a great change in American ways of making things that soon reshaped American ways of living. Eventually this would create an American Standard of Living. The Census noted that in earlier times "the bulk of general manufacturing done in the United States was carried on in the shop and the household by the labor of the family or individual proprietors who apprenticed assistants." But now most manufacturing was being done by a "system of factory labor, compensated by wages and assisted by power." This new factory system had begun to displace the old system of household manufacturing. Before, Americans had made the things they needed in their own homes and for their own use. Now goods were produced in factories and by machines for sale to anybody willing to pay for them.

This Industrial Revolution helped bring about a Transportation Revolution. The same steam power and new techniques that made factories possible also brought the steamboats and the railroads to carry products of farm and factory out to the wider world. The Transportation Revolution reached the thousands of new customers needed to buy the masses of goods now produced in the factories. Wherever canals, railroads, or steamboats went, they provided new customers for farmers, too.

The rise of a new economy.

Now farmers began to buy factory-made clothing, furniture, kitchen utensils, and all the other output of industrial America. The pioneer family was no longer so isolated. A national economy began to emerge. Each region would specialize in what it could do best. The Northeast and the Middle States produced finished goods in their factories, the West grew wheat and corn, while the South specialized in cotton, tobacco, rice, and sugar. The produce of the South and West flowed to the Northeast, and from that region finished goods moved back to the South and West.

The United States, which only a century before was mostly an unsettled wilderness, surprised the world. Suddenly this nation became a strong competitor in the industrial marketplace. The country was lucky in its virgin forests, fertile fields, and untapped minerals. A stable government favored industry. The growing population was becoming ever more varied. People from everywhere who were persecuted, restless, or dissatisfied made the United States their mecca. They were enterprising and industrious, and they made the country stronger.

This was becoming a nation of nations. In Europe, national borders and jealous governments stopped the free flow of goods and of people over the land. But not here. The Founding Fathers had designed a great federal nation. They foresaw the need to let people and goods flow from state to state, back and forth across the whole country. "Everything new is quickly introduced here," one foreign observer remarked. "There is no clinging to old ways; the moment an American hears the word 'invention' he pricks up his ears."

The corporation.

The cost of these new factories was usually beyond the means of any one person, or even a partnership of a few people. Vast sums had to be collected. For this purpose a new social invention was at hand. The "joint stock company" had not been invented here, but had already been used in England for just this purpose. "Joint stock" ventures had brought some of the first English settlers to America. Now, when a "joint stock" company was chartered by a state, it became a "corporation." This meant that it had a life of its own and would survive in legal theory even if the shareholders died. The corporation could sue in court and in other ways was like a real person.

Shares of stock were sold to numerous investors. Each then owned a "share" in the company. Of course they might lose whatever they had invested. But a clever legal arrangement provided that they could not be held responsible for the company's debts. This was called "limited liability." Hundreds of small investors put in a few dollars each. They could share the profits but still not risk losing large sums if the company was badly managed. In this way, funds were gathered to build a great industrial nation. And not only rich people but small investors, too, could have a share of the profits.

Waltham and the factory system.

In 1813 Francis Cabot Lowell and his associates in the Boston Manufacturing Company in Waltham, Massachusetts, brought together under one roof, for the first time ever, all the processes for making cotton cloth. This required a large capital investment and a new kind of factory. It was risky business. Only bold organizers dared to take the lead—just as none but bold men would have built the Erie Canal.

Lowell came upon the idea for his factory on a trip to England during 1810–1812 when he visited the cotton textile factories. Soon after his return to the United States, the War of 1812 stopped his importing and exporting business. This gave him

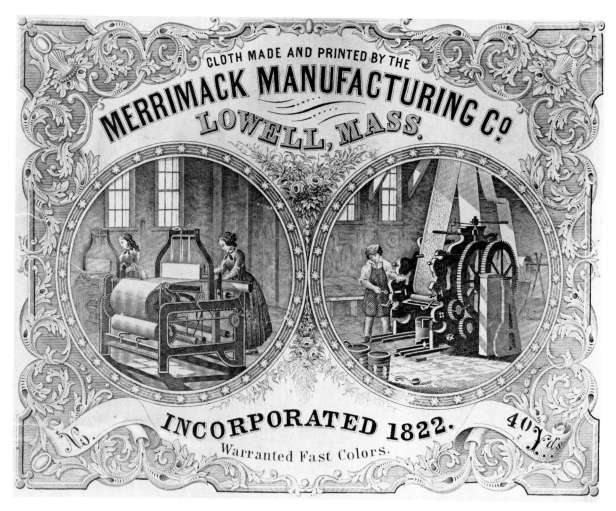

The Boston Associates named their Lowell works the Merrimack Manufacturing Company after the river that powered the machines. The women in this label are weaving cloth. The worker on the right is printing calico—a light cotton cloth once imported from Calcutta in India.

time to make plans for his Waltham factory. The factory was such a success that the Boston Associates decided to expand. They found a site on the Merrimack River, where its 30-foot falls provided power to drive the machines. There in 1822 they built a new and bigger factory. They named the town "Lowell." Soon textile factories sprouted in Massachusetts, New Hampshire, and Maine. In hilly New England they could use the waterpower of the many streams that tumbled toward the ocean.

Foreign visitors noticed that the air of American factory towns was clear. The air of European cities was filling with smoke from the fuel that fired the steam engines. But New England factories used the streams. They were built in the pleasant countryside. An Englishwoman, Harriet Martineau, in 1836 saw the fortunate American workers in Lowell. There they "might catch as beautiful glimpses of Nature's face as western settlers."

The "Waltham" or "Lowell" labor system.

What impressed European visitors even more than the landscape was the work force. They were mostly young women! Francis Cabot Lowell had not wanted American workers to become like those he had seen in the English factories and their slums.

They were, he said, people "of the lowest character, for intelligence and morals." Did the workers in a factory have to be so degraded?

Lowell and his associates noticed that the Industrial Revolution was freeing young women from many of the farm chores. Why not let them make money by working in a factory? After a few years they would move on, marry, and raise a family. Then, perhaps their daughters, too, would return to the mill to work for a while. In this way, no permanent working class would ever spring up. And people would not be stuck in a slum.

Enlisting women solved another American problem—the scarcity of workers. This would be a reason also to bring children into the factories.

With this "Waltham" or "Lowell" labor system, there grew up communities with large numbers of women and children. At Waltham, Harriet Martineau was impressed by the houses the company built for its workers. Some of the women had built houses with their own earnings—"with piazzas and green venetian blinds, and all neat and sufficiently spacious." She was impressed by the church, the library, and the lecture hall, all provided by the company.

But not all New England factories were so pleasant. Even Waltham and Lowell did not remain idyllic for long. As his mill in Rhode Island grew, Samuel Slater followed the English system of employing entire families. Everyone in the family who was over seven years old went to work in the factory. This system became usual in Connecticut, Rhode Island, and southern Massachusetts. Here was a factory working class—like that in England.

Some Southerners defended their "peculiar institution" by saying that northern "wage slavery" was worse than their own plantation slavery. Southerners, they said, at least cared for their workers when they were old or sick. But northern factory owners discarded worn-out workers just like worn-out machines. The Southerners failed to note that, if northern workers lacked security, they were free to move. If they could save their money, they could go west to open land. Free American workers could change jobs and learn new jobs.

Eli Whitney's idea. In January 1798, the nation faced the danger of war with the French dictator Napoleon, and desperately needed guns. In those days a musket was made by one man who was called

a "gunsmith." (The word "smith" came from an older word meaning to shape or cut.) Just as a goldsmith shaped pieces of gold into jewelry, so each gunsmith actually shaped all the pieces of a gun to make them fit together. Where could the United States find the thousands of gunsmiths it suddenly needed?

Eli Whitney, the inventor of the cotton gin, refused to see it that way. He had a different idea that was really very simple. Each musket was made of 50 different parts. For one man to make all these parts himself he had to be a skillful gunsmith and had to know a great deal about guns.

But suppose a worker had to make only *one* of these parts. Suppose you gave the worker a model of that one part and invented a machine to make lots of precise copies. That might be as simple as tracing out copies of a paper doll. Instead of tracing on paper, the worker would trace on sheets of iron. The worker would not need much skill at all. It might take years to train a full-fledged gunsmith. But in a single day you might be able to instruct a single worker to use a machine to make a hundred copies of that one part. Then suppose you found 49 other people and trained each one to make lots of copies of each of the other parts.

When all the workers had finished their day's work, you would have a hundred copies of each of the different parts in a musket. Of course, you would have to be very careful about your measurements. But if you could make each copy like every other copy of the same part, then any one part would fit together with any other. It would be easy to put the 50 parts of the musket together.

The test. In the wintry January of 1801 Eli Whitney went to Washington for the dramatic climax of his months of planning. Three years before, when he had first begun to figure out his new plan, he had promised the government to make 10,000 muskets. That was a fantastic number. Whitney was not a gunsmith and had never made even one gun before. Still, the government decided to finance his scheme. Even though it was a new way, it seemed quite logical. The nation was so much in need of arms—and quickly—that it seemed worth taking chances.

Before Whitney could make any muskets in his new way, he had to make the machinery for making the muskets. He spent more than two years inventing and perfecting the tools that would make precise copies of the single part that was used as a pattern. Since Whitney had spent so much time making the new machinery, he had been able to make very few muskets. Even his friends began to wonder whether his system was only a pipe dream. Would it work?

Now he had a chance to show. He had an appointment in the nation's capital with President John Adams, Vice-President Thomas Jefferson, the Secretary of War, the Secretary of the Treasury, and other members of the Cabinet. When they met, Whitney laid out separate piles of all the pieces needed to make ten muskets. The nervous Whitney watched while they followed his simple instructions: take any piece from each pile, fit them easily together, and you have a complete working musket! To do that you didn't have to be a gunsmith with years of experience behind you. Almost anybody could do it. To the astonishment of the nation's leaders in that room, the ten muskets took form in a few minutes. By this little drama the revolutionary system of interchangeable parts was proven to a doubting world.

On the battlefield there was another great advantage for guns made in this way. Since all their dimensions were uniform, if one part broke during combat it would not be necessary to send the whole gun back to the gunsmith. With a stock of standard parts you would do the job right then.

It was more difficult than Whitney had expected to make the machines to make the uniform parts of the guns. But by 1809 he had succeeded in delivering all the promised 10,000 muskets. Whitney's system soon was called the "Uniformity System" because each part in one gun was uniform (precisely the same in shape and size) with that same part in any other gun of the same design. Some called it the "Interchangeable System."

Mass production. Whitney's system came at just the right place and at the right moment. The growing United States had drawn an energetic, eager-to-learn population from all over. But there was a scarcity of immigrants who had been highly trained in the ancient skills (like gunsmithing). Oddly enough that proved to be an advantage. For if the United States had attracted thousands of gunsmiths, Whitney might never have been prodded to design his new way of manufacturing. Soon

the Interchangeable System was used to make all sorts of things. Even before the Civil War, locks and watches were actually cheaper in the United States (where they were made by this system) than they were in countries blessed by many skilled locksmiths and watchmakers.

This is what we mean by "mass production." It means producing masses of items of exactly the same kind. It means, as Whitney explained, using the skill of the machine instead of the skill of the worker. In France, for example, a young man had to work for years as an apprentice before he finally became a master gunsmith. But in America the machine became specialized, not the worker. Here what you needed was general intelligence so you could handle complicated machinery. Here the worker had to be quick to learn new ways.

Since things produced in this way were cheaper, more people could afford to buy them. When there was a wider, more prosperous market, other people were encouraged to make still more inexpensive things to sell. Each worker's time was worth more, for now he could produce more of anything—guns or locks or watches—in a single day. The employer could afford to pay him more and still make a profit. Almost anything could (and would) be manufactured in this new way. Out of all this grew an American Standard of Living that astonished an envious world by giving more things to more people than ever before.

SECTION REVIEW

1. Explain: limited liability, Waltham (or Lowell) labor system, "wage slavery," interchangeable parts, "Uniformity System."
2. What was Samuel Slater's great achievement?
3. How were the Industrial Revolution and the Transportation Revolution linked?
4. Show how the Industrial Revolution led to the emergence of a national economy.
5. How did "limited liability" foster the growth of corporations?
6. What contributions did Lowell and his associates make to the development of the factory system?
7. What role did Eli Whitney play in the development of mass production?

3. America's leading import: people

To occupy the land, to build the roads, canals, turnpikes, and railroads, to staff the factories, the United States needed people. It was not surprising, then, that the United States became a nation of immigrants.

Reasons for coming to America. While Europe became more and more crowded, America offered open air and cheap land. When families in Europe could not find food or places for their children in school or as apprentices, they naturally thought of America. In Europe, too, it was an age of turmoil. Between the time of the American Revolution and the American Civil War, there were revolutions and dictatorships in France, Spain, Germany, Greece, Italy, and Belgium. And it was an age of floods and famines. There were lots of reasons why people in Europe might want to *get away* from their old world. The disasters of Europe made refugees by the millions.

And there were plenty of reasons why someone would want to come *to* America. Of course, the old legends started in the early advertising brochures had enticed people to the colonies. These still brought people to the new nation. Now there were lots of new legends—of rich land, undiscovered mines, and fast-growing cities. And there was the real-life romance of a new nation with its doors open and its people's eyes on the future.

When you had so little to lose, why not go to America?

During the 1820s only about 500,000 people migrated to the United States. But then the pace quickened. In the 1830s and 1840s, 2.5 million men, women, and children arrived, and in the 1850s, 2.7 million.

It was lucky that the United States had so much unfilled land. The overflow of the Old World could find a place in the New. Peoples who did not know one another or who had fought against one another could now live side by side. America would be called the "last best hope of earth." The story of European hopelessness is a story of American hope.

In the years between the American Revolution and the Civil War, the two great sources of new Americans were Ireland and Germany. Events in those countries far across the Atlantic Ocean helped make the United States a world nation.

The Irish and the potato famine. Potatoes were the main food of the Irish poor. But suddenly in the fall of 1845 a blight hit the potato crop and spoiled a third of it. In 1846 the blight destroyed the whole crop all over the country. The potato blight continued until 1850.

Tens of thousands died of starvation. Weakened by hunger, hundreds of thousands died of disease. Death haunted the land.

Even before the famine, the Irish had been coming to America by the thousands. Downtrodden by English rule, they had tried to revolt many times, but they were not able to throw off their English masters. So some Irish had come to America. The United States, in the phrase of the time, was "a sort of half-way stage to Heaven." To many Irish it seemed almost as hard to get here as to reach heaven, because the cost of a steerage ticket across the ocean (between $12.50 and $25) then seemed so high.

Letters written back to Ireland made everyone want to come. "This is the best country in the world," wrote one Irish girl from New York City in 1848. One new arrival wrote back with glee that the Irish here "eat the pig themselves, and have plenty of bread to their potatoes." "Every day is like a Christmas Day for meat."

And now the Irish came by the hundreds of thousands. Through the port of New York City alone, between 1847 and 1860, from Ireland there came over a million. That was nearly half of all the Europeans who landed in New York in those years.

The Irish in America. But once the Irish had landed in Boston or New York or some other port city, they had very little choice about where to go. Few had the money or the desire to move to a lonely western farm. The farming they knew in Ireland did not make them lovers of the land. So most of them stayed in the port cities of the eastern seaboard where they could enjoy the fellowship of others recently arrived from the old country.

Many of those who did move westward in the early years used their strong arms and sturdy backs to dig canals and build railroads. When the digging of the Erie Canal began in 1817, there were not many Irish around. But before it was completed eight years later, the Irish were arriving by the thousands. On the canal they were well known for their strength, courage, and willingness to work.

The nation was growing by a great migration. And these other new Americans, like the Irish and the Germans, worked in factories and on farms. They, too, helped dig the canals and build the railroads which transformed the United States from a land of farmers into an industrial giant, a leader of the world.

SECTION REVIEW

1. Name some factors that led 5 million immigrants to enter the United States between 1820 and 1860.

2. Where did the Irish tend to settle? What part did the Irish play in the Transportation Revolution?

3. What problems in Germany led to heavy emigration? What were some special contributions of the German immigrants?

4. The rise of the West

Between 1815 and 1850 the lands west of the Appalachian Mountains became the nation's bread-basket. American workers would eat better than ever before. The farmers of the American West also fed the factory laborers of Europe. Though the South did not realize it, wheat—not cotton—was king.

The moving American. "In the United States," the young French traveler Alexis de Tocqueville noted during his visit in the 1830s, "a man builds a house in which to spend his old age, and he sells it before the roof is on." The people of the United States had become Americans by moving from other lands. They continued to move after they reached the New World. Over the next hill, round the next bend, in the next state, there they hoped to find the will-o-the-wisp "success."

In their constant movement these migratory people transformed half a continent. They cleared the forest and broke the thick turf of the prairies with the improved steel plows of the Industrial Revolution. They cut the grain with new mechanical harvesters.

In 1810 only one American in seven lived west of the Appalachians. By 1840 more than one in every three lived there. Most of these Westerners still lived on farms in the forest or on the prairies, where

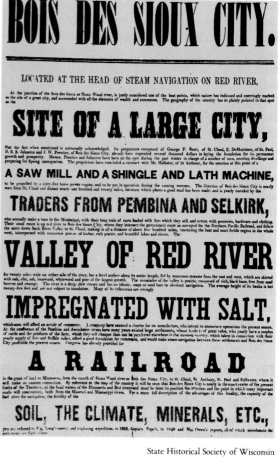

Moorhead, Minnesota, and Fargo, North Dakota, are at the river junction cited in this ad. Bois des Sioux remained only a dream.

they grew corn and wheat and raised meat for home and market. To serve them and handle their crops, new cities sprang up and began to dot the land.

Instant cities. In places where people still alive could remember the sound of the Indian war whoop and the shadow of the virgin forest, there sprouted cities. On riverways and the joining of rivers appeared Pittsburgh, Cincinnati, St. Louis, Louisville, Memphis, Minneapolis and St. Paul, Davenport, Des Moines, Omaha, and hundreds of others. On the Great Lakes and at the river entrances to the Lakes, men and women created Rochester, Buffalo, Cleveland, Toledo, Detroit, and Chicago. An astonishing crop of cities sprang up quickly in the lands west of the Appalachians.

When before had so many cities grown so fast? In the years between the Revolution and the Civil War, Americans went west to start new cities. Many hoped to make their living out of city-building. Some hoped to make money out of selling the land. The wilderness was worth very little, but once a city was there, land became valuable. Then some people would want to buy land for houses, others for farms to raise vegetables and chickens and eggs for the people of the nearby city.

The great cities of the Old World had been built on their rich past. People had come first, and then there followed newspapers to give them news, inns to house the travelers, theaters and opera houses to entertain the crowds, colleges and universities where learned men could gather and the young could be educated.

But that was much too slow and haphazard for impatient, purposeful Americans. Western city-builders wanted their city first. They wanted to see it even *before* the people were there. If they already had a newspaper, hotel, theater, and college, then surely people would come. But if they waited, then some other city might provide all those attractions first. People would then go on to Cleveland instead of staying in Pittsburgh, or they would move on from Kansas City to Omaha, or from Omaha to Denver.

The optimistic Americans were not always careful to distinguish between what had already happened and what they hoped (or felt sure) would happen. Foreigners complained that the cheery Americans did not always tell the truth. But the self-confident Americans replied that they were simply boosters. Why should they fail to report "facts" simply because they "had not yet gone through the formality of taking place"?

The families who went west in the early 1800s were often going to cities that did not yet really exist. To them a city was not just any place where lots of people happened to live. It was where people were building a community together. They built not only for their needs but also for their hopes.

For example, in Europe a city did not have a newspaper until it already had a large reading community. But in the American West, the city's own newspaper was actually founded *before* the city. Your place might never even become a city unless you *started* with a newspaper.

Hotels were constructed in the middle of nowhere. The large and elegant "Gayoso House" was built in the remote forest on the site of the future Memphis, Tennessee. It was three years before the city was even incorporated and ten years before there would be a railroad. Where were the guests? In the future, of course. When the English novelist Anthony Trollope traveled across America in the 1860s, he noted:

> When the new hotel rises up in the wilderness it is presumed that people will come there with the express object of inhabiting it. The hotel itself will create a population—as the railways do. With us [in Europe] railways run to the towns; but in the States the towns run to the railways. It is the same thing with the hotels.

Every man his own carpenter. In their instant cities Americans needed houses. And they needed them quickly. There were no grandparents or other relatives to live with until you had a home of your own. There were no old houses to rent or to buy. And out in the West carpenters were scarce or nonexistent. If you wanted shelter, you had to provide it yourself. So Americans invented a new way of building.

In England, builders of houses had got into a rut. They believed there was only one right way to build a wooden house. You built it around a frame of heavy timbers. Each long timber was a foot square, and the timbers had to be carefully fitted together by a complicated technique called "mortise and tenon." You rested your floors on these heavy supports, and closed in the sides with mud, plaster, or wood. All this produced a sturdy building, but to make it required skilled carpenters clever with the crude tools of the day. In new western towns like Cincinnati, Chicago, and Omaha, carpenters were not to be found, and people themselves did not have the skill—much less the time—to build their own houses in the old style.

All these needs produced the "balloon frame." Probably the first was built in Chicago in 1833, but we do not know who invented this new American building. Old-fashioned builders ridiculed the light "balloon-frame house" and said it would blow away in a high wind.

What was the balloon frame? The idea is so simple that it is hard to believe it ever had to be

As the photograph above shows, building a barn by old "mortise and tenon" construction required heavy beams. It was hard to put up and almost impossible to move. "Balloon frame" construction (below) was light, strong, easy to build and to move.

invented. The first notion was to forget that you ever needed a frame of heavy timbers with their ends neatly carved for a mortise and tenon to fit into one another. Instead make the lightest possible frame! Get a supply of long pieces of lumber about two inches thick and four inches wide. Then buy some long heavy nails. Stand up some of the light two-by-fours—say, eighteen inches or two feet apart—and nail other boards across them to hold them together.

Once you have your frame up, cover it outside and in with thin wide clapboards or any other material you wish. Nothing could be simpler. About three-quarters of the wooden houses in the United States are now built this way.

Of course, to build a balloon frame you need plenty of nails. In the old days nails had been extremely expensive because each one was fashioned by hand. But here again the Industrial Revolution helped the West. By 1830 New England nail-making machines were turning out nails by the thousands, better and cheaper than ever before.

The new way of building was speedy. It took less than half the time to build a balloon-frame house than one of the same size built in the old style. In Chicago, within one week in April 1834, seven new buildings of this kind appeared. By mid-June there were 75 more. By October an additional 500 were in use.

The balloon frame proved to have other advantages that nobody had counted on. It turned out to be even stronger and more durable than the old heavy-timbered construction. On top of that it helped Americans on the move because it was easily taken apart and then could be quickly put together again in some other place. St. Mary's Church in Chicago, said to be the first balloon-frame building built anywhere, within ten years of its construction was taken down, moved away, and re-erected three times. Now finally Americans on the move had the kind of house they could knock down and take along.

SECTION REVIEW

1. What were some features of city building in the West?
2. How did the "balloon-frame house" promote the growth of western cities?

5. The cotton kingdom

The South was a vast land of many different areas with different climates, different soils, different societies. It included tidewater Virginia with its dignified old families, the jungles and everglades of Florida where Seminole Indians still lived, and states west of the Appalachian Mountains that were more western than southern.

One thing drew all these states together. It was not so much that they were southern states, but that they were *slave* states.

The "positive good" of slavery. Southerners opposed internal improvements because they feared that such federal projects would provide a precedent for "interfering" within a state in other ways, too. The federal government might start tampering with slavery.

Beginning in the 1830s their fears increased as the voices of northern reformers demanding abolition of this ancient evil sounded louder and louder. Before long, abolitionist literature covered the country. It awakened Northerners to the evils of slavery. It made them hate slavery. It also made them lump together all people in the South as if all Southerners wanted slavery. More and more Northerners began to hate the South and to hate Southerners.

As these northern propagandists against slavery became more and more passionate, Southerners too became more and more unreasonable. As Northerners began to attack things about the South that were not really evil, Southerners replied by defending things about the South that were not really good. Instead of worrying over how to get rid of slavery, more Southerners began to worry over how to defend slavery, and the South and themselves, against all outside attack.

Leaders in the South stopped saying that slavery was only a "necessary evil." "Slavery is not an evil," declared the governor of South Carolina in 1829. "On the contrary," he insisted, "it is a national benefit."

One of the strongest supporters of slavery was Senator John C. Calhoun of South Carolina. The former Secretary of War and Vice-President of the United States was now the leading southern thinker. "Many in the South," he said, "once believed that it [slavery] was a moral and political evil; that folly and delusion are gone; we see it now in its true light, and regard it as the most safe and stable basis for free institutions in the world."

Calhoun was supported by many others when he called slavery "a positive good." Southern ministers said the Bible required that the blacks be slaves. Southern "scientists" said the blacks were an inferior race—the product of a "separate creation" that God made in the beginning on the African continent. Southern historians said that the glories of ancient Greece were possible only because the Greeks had lots of slaves. Astonishing nonsense was written by otherwise sane people—all to show that slavery was the greatest thing that had ever happened to the human race.

The "peculiar institution."

As Southerners began to boast of slavery, thinking about slavery began to dominate everything in the South. To avoid the unpleasant word "slavery," which freedom-loving people everywhere hated, Southerners began to call it their "peculiar institution."

What was it like, this "peculiar institution"? In the first place, it was a system of labor control. It was a way to use man-, woman-, and child-power to raise crops for sale. The largest of these cash crops was cotton, which the Southerners thought was "King" of all crops, but also important were tobacco, rice, hemp, and sugar.

It was the black slave, working from dawn to dusk, who planted, tended, and harvested these crops. Slaves did other jobs, including housework. But slavery was far more than just a labor system by which planters worked their large plantations. It was also a way of life.

The "middle passage."

In the beginning the slaves had been brought to America from Africa. In Africa they came from many different societies. Some were great empires like Songay and Melle. Some were complex cultures like Benin and Yoruba. The Bantu and the Bushmen came from societies that were more primitive. All these societies themselves practiced slavery. They enslaved people of their own color in their own land. And they made slaves of neighboring peoples. Some African chiefs sold their slaves to black slave traders, who then marched them in chains to the slave stations of the whites on the Atlantic coast. There the white men put them on ships to send to America. Some of these terrified Africans, one slave trader reported, were "so wilful and loth to leave their own country that they have often leap'd out of the canoes, boat and ship, into the sea and kept under water till they were drowned."

The "middle passage," as the voyage to America was called, was a horrendous experience. Packed tightly below decks, chained together, frightened men, women, and children died in great numbers. Those who survived the torture of this long journey to the West Indian islands, Brazil, the United States, or wherever in America, were then sold at auction to the highest bidder.

The slave trade to the United States was legally abolished in 1807. But in later years, slaves still were smuggled into the country, and a flourishing domestic slave trade continued. By the 1850s most blacks living in the United States probably had been born in this country. And most of them lived in slavery in the southern states.

Life as a "chattel."

Not all slaves were badly treated, and not all worked hard. Nor did they all work in the fields. Some were house servants, while others were skilled artisans—carpenters, metal workers, and the like. Many may not even have been terribly unhappy with their lot. But certainly some were, as the Nat Turner revolt revealed. And there were many other conspiracies that were cut off before anything happened. White Southerners lived in constant fear of slave revolts.

Some slaves resisted their owners, not violently but through careless and casual working habits. Sickness could be faked. When all else failed, some slaves tried to run away. A number actually made it to freedom and to the new trials of being a free black in a society made for whites.

Some fortunate slaves were allowed by their masters to earn money and to buy their freedom. There were a few even luckier ones who, after buying their own freedom, were able to buy that of their wives, children, and friends.

But these were the fortunate few. Most blacks lived out their lives as slaves, considered by the law to be chattels, just pieces of property, that could be bought and sold. They were at the mercy of their owners who could legally do anything they wished with them except willfully maim or kill them. Sometimes the slaves were whipped, beaten, confined, chained, and even sold away from their families.

There were some kind Southerners who loved their slaves and who were loved by them in return. The wives of plantation owners often doctored their slaves, made their clothes, and even (against the law) taught a favored black child to read and write. Rachel O'Connor of Louisiana was not alone in her reaction to the illness of a little black slave: "The poor little fellow is laying at my feet asleep. I wish I did not love him as I do, but it is so, and I cannot help it."

It was in the best interest of the owner to keep the slaves content and healthy so they would work well in the fields. But whether happy or sad, well cared for or ill, the slaves were in the absolute control of their owners and forced to do their bidding.

The effect of slavery on the South. Most white Southerners were not slaveholders. In 1860 one-fourth of the white people in the South owned all the slaves. There were only a few large plantations. Not more than 10,000 Southerners had plantations with more than 50 slaves. About one-half of all slaves were owned in groups of 20 or less. Sometimes a slave was the only slave a farmer had and managed to live much the same life as if he were the hired hand of a farm family.

The white people of the South, even though most did not own slaves, were generally convinced that slavery must continue. Some supported it because they saw no other way to control this "different" group in their midst. Even the poorest white people in the South liked to think of themselves as somehow superior to the blacks. As one poor white farmer explained, "Now suppose they was free, you see they'd all think themselves as good as we."

The South paid a high price for slavery. All craftsmen and farmers received less for their labor because of the competition of slaves. Immigrants, unwilling to compete with slave labor, avoided the South. The capital that might have gone into commerce or industry was tied up in slaves. As a result the South remained an agricultural community which exported crops and imported manufactured goods.

This made the whole South a kind of colony of the North. "With us every branch and pursuit of life, every trade, profession, and occupation, is dependent upon the North," an Alabama newspaperman complained. "In northern vessels [the Southerner's] products are carried to market, his cotton is ginned with northern gins, his sugar is crushed and preserved by northern machinery; his rivers are navigated by northern steamboats, . . . his land is cleared with a northern axe, and a Yankee clock sits upon his mantle-piece; his floor is swept by a northern broom, and is covered with a northern carpet; and his wife dresses herself in a northern looking-glass." This was only a slight exaggeration.

How had this come about? How had the home of Jefferson's small farmer become a backwater?

This lively watercolor of slaves dancing on a festive occasion was found in Columbia, South Carolina. The artist is unknown, but the painting was made about 1800.

No wonder that many Southerners, looking for someone to blame, decided to make Northerners the enemy. They began to think the backwardness of the South had been produced by a northern conspiracy. It seemed that somehow northern businessmen had been able to use the federal government for their own selfish purposes. The government subsidized northern shipbuilding. The tariff protected northern manufacturers so they could charge higher prices to southern planters.

Had not the southern states been pioneers in colonial days? They gave the nation its Washington, Jefferson, Madison, Monroe, and Jackson—its leaders in war and in peace. Now that the United States was prospering, must the South remain a colony within a nation?

SECTION REVIEW

1. Why did Southerners turn from calling slavery a "necessary evil" to calling it a "positive good"?

2. What was the "middle passage"?

3. Show how treatment of slaves differed from owner to owner. How did some slaves resist their owners?

4. What were some effects of slavery on the South?

CHAPTER REVIEW

MEETING OUR EARLIER SELVES

1. Explain how the completion of the Erie Canal might have benefited each of the following: (a) a wheat farmer in northern Ohio, (b) a merchant in Buffalo, (c) a Dutch immigrant family headed for Michigan Territory, (d) an Albany hotel owner.

2. What kinds of help did federal, state, and local governments provide in the development of (a) roads? (b) canals? (c) railroads? Why did people seek such help from government? Does such government aid strengthen or weaken the free enterprise system? Explain.

3. Identify at least three persons who played a major role in the early stages of America's Industrial Revolution. Show how each contributed to the growth of industry.

4. Compare pre-Civil War Irish and German immigration: (a) motives for coming, (b) dates, (c) numbers, (d) settlements, and (e) contributions.

5. What arguments would you expect an abolitionist to use in condemning slavery? How did some white Southerners defend slavery?

QUESTIONS FOR TODAY

1. What steps in building a wooden frame house today would be about the same as in the 1830s or 1840s? What differences would you expect to notice?

2. Has any sizable number of recent American immigrants been refugees from poverty or war in their homeland? Explain.

3. Select a modern occupation that would also have existed in the 1850s. How would the job be different today with respect to training, skills, and working conditions?

YOUR REGION IN HISTORY

1. Identify major roads, canals, and railroads built in your state or region between 1820 and 1860. How did they contribute to the industrial or agricultural growth of your region?

2. What kinds of manufacturing, if any, developed in your locality in the period 1820–1860? Why did they develop there?

3. Did any particular immigrant groups settle in your state or region from 1820 to 1860? Who were they and where did they settle? Cite particular contributions that they made.

SKILLS TO MAKE OUR PAST VIVID

1. On an outline map show the major canals built in the canal-building era. Also show cities that grew because of their location on or near these canals.

2. Draw a poster designed to recruit young women to work in the Lowell mills. Emphasize cultural, economic, and social benefits. What facts about the work would you omit?

CHAPTER 11

Reforming and expanding

⚙ The half-century before the Civil War was a time of ferment in the United States. Factories were built, instant cities were created, immigrants poured in. From Missouri, long lines of wagons headed west to their promised lands— Texas, California, and Oregon. The Americans who stayed home looked for a more perfect society where they lived. These two movements of expansion and reform forced the nation to face an issue many Americans wished to avoid. What was the future of slavery in the United States?

1. An age of reform

In a land where even cities could appear overnight it was easy to believe that a perfect world could be created. Many Americans, like the first settlers, continued to feel that they were a "City upon a hill." For the whole world to see, they wanted to create a nation where there was no injustice, where all had an equal chance to succeed, and where citizens ruled themselves. They wanted to help the insane, the orphans, the prisoners, and the blind. Americans organized themselves into groups working for peace, for temperance in the use of alcohol, for improved education, for women's rights—and for the abolition of slavery.

A religious age. There was a Christian church to suit every taste and every temperament. Unitarians tried to bring together all men and women of goodwill without any dogma or sharp theology. Millerites proclaimed that the world would come to an end in the year 1843 and urged their fellow Americans to repent while there was still time. Shakers and Rappites and others each believed they

had the one and only formula for an ideal community. Visitors from abroad came to think that there were as many denominations as there were Americans. A perceptive English lady, Mrs. Trollope, saw religious Americans "insisting upon having each a little separate banner, embroidered with a device of their own imagining."

The Protestant churches moved away from the old Puritan belief in a stern God who had decreed in advance the fate of the world for all future time. Instead churches now emphasized how close each individual was to God and how much freedom each possessed to improve the world and make his or her own future. The world of Christians seemed more democratic, more self-governing than ever before.

These ideas were stressed between the 1820s and the 1850s in the religious revivals which constantly swept the land. Perhaps the greatest single force in this movement was Charles Grandison Finney. He used every means he could to excite his listeners to their sinfulness and to save their souls. His revival meetings and those of other preachers brought many Americans to support a wide variety of reforms.

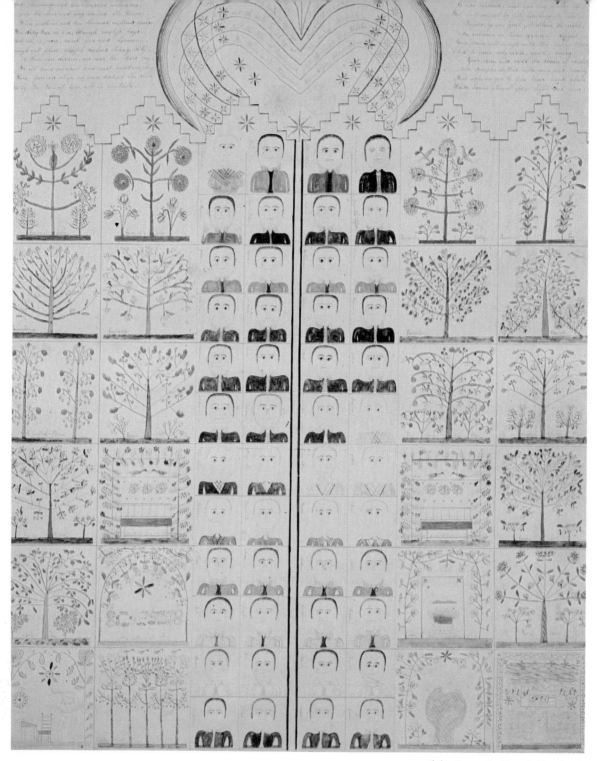

The Shakers, a religious sect founded by Mother Ann Lee, received their name from their dances during worship. The bright colors of their drawings, which the Shakers believed were divinely inspired, contrast with the simplicity of their architecture, furniture, and dress. This 1854 watercolor shows the saints, including Christopher Columbus in the top row, ranked in heaven.

The Transcendentalists.
One small group of intellectuals had an influence all out of proportion to their numbers. They called themselves "Transcendentalists." They believed that the most important truths of life could not be summed up in a clear and simple theology but actually "transcended" (went beyond) human understanding and brought together all people—high or low, rich or poor, educated or ignorant. For them God was an "oversoul" who was present showing everybody what was right and wrong. It is not surprising then that Ralph Waldo Emerson, their most eloquent voice, declared:

> What is man born for but to be a Reformer, a Reformer of what man has made; a renouncer of lies; a restorer of truth and good. . . .

Since man was good, in time the whole world would become perfect. Then, of course, there would be no need for government.

Each person had to find his or her own path to heaven. Henry David Thoreau found his lonely way to the good life in a solitary cabin on the shores of Walden Pond near Concord, Massachusetts. While he stayed there by himself for two years, he earned his living making pencils and only went to town for groceries. He found his own way to protest against the policies of his government that he believed to be evil. When the nation waged war against Mexico to add, he thought, new slave states, he simply refused to pay his taxes. For this he spent only one night in jail, since to his irritation his aunt paid the tax for him. But his explanation for his protest—in his *Essay on the Duty of Civil Disobedience* (1849)—rang down the years and reached across the world. A century later when Mahatma Gandhi led the people of India in their struggle for independence, he declared himself a follower of Henry David Thoreau.

Theodore Parker, another member of the group, was a born reformer who joined movements and attacked slavery from pulpits and lecture platforms. Bronson Alcott was a mystic and a dreamer who worked for perfection but failed at everything. His educational ideas—which included physical exercises for students, attractive classrooms, and the pleasures of learning—seemed shocking to people of those times when schools were grim and discipline harsh. Alcott's school failed as did his attempt to build a new Eden at "Fruitlands."

Alcott was never able to earn enough to live comfortably until his practical and courageous daughter Louisa May made a great success with her book *Little Women* (1868).

The Transcendentalists loved to tell what they thought. Emerson and Thoreau wrote, Parker and others preached, Bronson Alcott talked. In his popular "conversations"—wandering monologues—Alcott entertained large audiences in the East and Northwest.

The "conversation" was also used by brilliant Margaret Fuller. She gathered a group of young Boston women around her and instructed them. From this experience came her influential book, *Women in the Nineteenth Century* (1845), which spurred on the women's rights movement. Fuller also edited the *Dial,* the Transcendentalist magazine, and worked as a literary critic for Horace Greeley on the *New York Tribune.*

Reform in education.
America—a new nation, full of open land and business challenges—was a wonderful laboratory for reformers. It is not surprising that the reformers focused on education. The ability to read and write, they argued, was the foundation of a democratic life.

The modern public school movement began in the 1830s in Massachusetts. This was quite natural because the Puritan founders of New England in the 1630s had believed in education (p. 55). Now, 200 years later, the determined Horace Mann worked to fulfill the Puritan dream of an educated citizenry. He had hated the dull teaching he received as a boy, so he gave up a successful legal career to work for educational reform. Mann was appointed the first secretary of the new state board of education in 1837, and for the next twelve years he tried hard to better the training and pay of teachers, to erect new school buildings, to enlarge school libraries, and to improve textbooks. In other states crusaders followed Mann's example.

By 1860 the fruits of these efforts were impressive. The states were generally committed to providing free elementary education. Many pupils were still poorly taught, and laws did not yet require all children to attend school, but the nation had begun to realize that education was the foundation of a republic.

For students who wished more than a grammar school education, there were only 300 public high

State Historical Society of Wisconsin

Students in Milwaukee in 1846 did not have to wonder about how they should behave.

schools in the whole country and almost 100 of these were in Massachusetts. There were, however, an additional 6000 private academies, many of which charged only a small tuition to poor children. By 1860 many states were thinking of providing high schools open to all, but even by 1890 it was unusual to go to school beyond eighth grade.

Higher education. Colleges and universities were still small—few had over 100 students—and ill equipped, but their numbers had increased since colonial times. In fact, there had been a college-founding mania. Just as every instant city needed a newspaper and hotel even before it contained any people, so it needed what was loosely called a college. Usually the college was started by one of the many religious denominations, but the hopeful cities-of-the-future quickly joined in. Julian Sturtevant, founder in 1830 of Illinois College, said, "It was generally believed that one of the surest ways to promote the growth of a young city was to make it the seat of a college." So before the Civil War 516 colleges were founded—many little better than the private academies—but only 104 survived to the 1900s. These "colleges" were still chiefly concerned with educating young men for the professions and public life.

In many American cities, so-called mechanics' institutes were started for those who wished to learn the mechanical arts. And in 1824 a new kind of institution of higher learning, Rensselaer Polytechnic Institute, opened at Troy, New York, to instruct men "in the application of science to the common purposes of life."

Education for girls and women. In colonial days girls were taught the household arts but were not expected to learn to read and write. People

In some schools, students who behaved well could earn certificates of merit like this one for consistently good conduct.

American Antiquarian Society

A WINTER SCENE.

On blithsome frolics bent, the youthful swains,
Fond o'er the river crowd in various sport,
And as they sweep, swift as the winds, along,
The then gay land is maddened all to joy.

232

thought that "book learning" would put an undue stress on their delicate minds and bodies! It was a long while before women were allowed to show their full vigor. Progress came slowly and step by step. In Massachusetts girls began to attend summer sessions of the public grammar schools in the late 1700s. Still, in Revolutionary times only about half the women of New England could sign their names. By 1840 the efforts of reformers were showing results, and nearly all New England women could read and write.

But it was a while before women were given their chance at a college education. At first, small numbers of them were allowed to attend the boys' academies until secondary schools were set up especially for women. Finally in 1836 (200 years after Harvard College was founded for men) Wesleyan College in Georgia was chartered as the first college for women. Then the very next year Oberlin College in Ohio started the new era of coeducation. At last it was possible for men and women to hear the same lectures and treat each other as intellectual equals.

The mentally ill and retarded.
For centuries people who were mentally ill or retarded had been treated like criminals and stigmatized as "insane." They were feared, imprisoned, and tortured. But the American reformers felt pity for them and took up their cause. Their heroic champion was Dorothea Dix, a young Boston schoolteacher who taught a Sunday School class in the women's department of a local prison. There she found people, whose only "crime" was their mental illness, being confined and punished.

In 1843, after two years spent investigating the jails and poorhouses in Massachusetts, she submitted her epoch-making report to the state legislature. She had seen the innocent insane confined "in cages, closets, cellars, stalls, pens! Chained, naked, beaten with rods, and lashed into obedience." She asked the legislature and all her fellow citizens to share her outrage. But old ways of thought and old fears were strong. Many would not believe the shocking truth, and others accused her of being softhearted. She stood her ground.

Finally Dorothea Dix succeeded in persuading the Massachusetts legislature to enlarge the state mental hospital. She began a new crusade—which lasts into our own time—to treat the mentally ill

with compassion and medical aid. She traveled in America and in Europe pleading her humane cause. Seldom has a reform owed so much to one person.

Women's rights.
Dorothea Dix always found it best to let men present her findings to legislatures. It was widely believed that there was something unladylike about a woman speaking in public. It was difficult for women to secure permission even to attend reform meetings.

The Industrial Revolution had freed women—married and unmarried alike—from having to make many of the things necessary for the home and family. While in the early days thread had to be spun and cloth woven in each household, now cloth was mass-produced in factories. Crude, ready-made clothing could be bought in stores. At the same time, the role of the homemaker became more specialized. Now, as factory processes made the price of manufactured goods cheaper, more women could afford to buy many of the things they had once made for themselves. No longer did they have so many of the varied tasks of the frontier wife. Women found new work outside the home. The factories of Lowell and other New England towns were largely staffed by women. And the new public schools created jobs for women teachers.

This watercolor, probably painted in the first half of the 19th century, shows an evening school for girls. They are working by candlelight as their bonneted teachers watch.

Museum of Fine Arts, Boston, M. and M. Karolik Collection

233

By the rules of English law, brought here in colonial days, married women had no rights to property—in fact their only legal existence came through their husbands. All of a woman's property became her husband's when she married, including her wages if she worked. She could not even make a will without his approval!

The lowly position of women had long been obvious to some women. The strong-minded Abigail Adams, for example, had made the point again and again to her husband, President John Adams. But now in an era of reform, when women were eager to lead movements to improve education, to treat the insane more humanely, and to free the slaves, the rights of women seemed essential to a better America. A new status for women—their opportunity for an adequate education and the right to speak out in public—would mean a richer life for all.

Leaders of the women's rights movement. Two energetic and outspoken reformers, Lucretia Mott and Elizabeth Cady Stanton, organized a Women's Rights Convention that met at Seneca Falls, New

The women's rights movement included strong-minded leaders like Sojourner Truth (top), Susan B. Anthony (bottom left), and Elizabeth Cady Stanton (bottom right).

York, on July 19, 1848. The convention finally issued a clever statement based on the Declaration of Independence. The preamble stated that "all men and women are created equal." Their list of grievances was not against King George but against men, who had deprived women of their rights. They demanded that women "have immediate admission to all the rights and privileges which belong to them as citizens of the United States." They even went so far as to demand the right to vote, although many of the women delegates feared this was asking too much.

Similar conventions were held in other states. But there were plenty of people foolish enough to think that they could stop the movement by breaking up the meetings. In 1851, when the Ohio convention in Akron was disrupted, a careworn black woman of commanding stature rose and, to the surprise of all, began her eloquent appeal. The unexpected speaker, named Sojourner Truth, had been born a slave in New York. She replied to a minister's charge that women needed special assistance from men by pointing out that she had never received any help from men.

> I have ploughed and planted and gathered into barns. . . . And ain't I a woman? I could work as much and eat as much as a man—when I could get it—and bear de lash as well! And ain't I a woman? I have borne thirteen children and seen 'em mos' all sold off to slavery, and when I cried out with my mother's grief, none but Jesus heard me! And ain't I a woman?

It took a while, but within a generation Sojourner Truth's message about the equality of women began to spread across the land.

The reforming women, led by Susan B. Anthony and Elizabeth Cady Stanton, were, of course, widely ridiculed and accused of acting more like men than women. But they did make progress. New York led other states in giving women control over their own property, a share in the guardianship of their own children, and the right to sue. Divorce laws were liberalized.

But the right to vote still seemed far in the future. In 1853 a leading national journal, *Harper's New Monthly Magazine,* proclaimed that the very idea of women voting was "infidel . . . avowedly anti-Biblical . . . opposed to nature and the established order of society."

Elizabeth and Emily Blackwell braved male opposition and actually became qualified medical doctors. Maria Mitchell became an astronomer, a member of the American Academy of Arts and Sciences, and the first professor of astronomy at the new Vassar College for women when it opened in 1865. Sarah Josepha Hale edited the influential magazine *Godey's Lady's Book* for nearly 50 years, and in its interesting pages she recounted the progress of women and argued their rights to be free, fulfilled Americans.

SECTION REVIEW

1. Identify: Ralph Waldo Emerson, Henry David Thoreau, Theodore Parker, Bronson Alcott, Louisa May Alcott, Margaret Fuller, Horace Mann, Dorothea Dix, Lucretia Mott, Elizabeth Cady Stanton, Sojourner Truth, Susan B. Anthony, the Blackwells, Maria Mitchell, Sarah Josepha Hale.

2. What developments in religion were linked to the movements for social reform?

3. By 1860 what advances had been made in (a) public education? (b) the education of women?

4. Account for the rapid growth in the number of colleges in the years before the Civil War.

5. What changes did Dorothea Dix seek in the treatment of the mentally handicapped?

6. How were women's rights restricted? What gains were made?

2. The abolition movement

The first moves to end slavery had come in the North at the time of the American Revolution (p. 95). But even in the South men like Washington and Jefferson were unhappy about slavery. Jefferson had actually inserted in the Declaration of Independence an item attacking George III for promoting the slave trade to America. It was finally taken out in deference to southern prejudices. Many other Southerners of goodwill who opposed slavery comforted themselves with the thought that it was a dying institution. Then the cotton gin led to a new demand for slaves to raise cotton. More than ever before, Southerners came to believe that slavery was the very foundation of the South.

The southern antislavery movement.

Still, some Southerners continued to look for a way to get rid of slavery. In 1816–1817 the South became the center of an antislavery movement built around the American Colonization Society. Since its members believed that the blacks could never be assimilated into American life, they raised money to send all the blacks back to Africa. The Society established a colony in Africa in what is now the nation of Liberia.

In its first twenty years the Society was able to send only 4000 blacks back to Africa—and many of those were not slaves. By 1830 there were 2 million slaves in the United States, and their number was increasing through new births at the rate of 500,000 every ten years.

Most blacks did not want to go back to Africa. In 1817 a group of free blacks in Philadelphia stated positively, "We have no wish to separate from our present homes for any purpose whatever."

As the attacks of northern abolitionists became more bitter, talk of freeing the slaves became more and more dangerous in the South. Southerners like James G. Birney of Kentucky and Sarah and Angelina Grimké of South Carolina who opposed slavery felt obliged to go north. The last debates over slavery in the South were those in Virginia. By 1831 many people in Virginia were worried about slavery. The new governor, who himself owned twelve slaves, tried to persuade the state legislature to make a plan for gradually abolishing slavery. The Virginia legislature held a great debate on slavery which lasted most of the month of January 1832. Then they voted 73 to 58 to keep slavery. The vote was a tragic mistake. It made it almost inevitable that if slavery was to be abolished in Virginia, it would have to be by force from the outside.

By 1833 no reform was welcome in the South. If one reforming "ism" (even pacifism) entered their section, Southerners feared that it might soon be followed by that worst "ism" of all—abolitionism. So the South turned inward and cut itself off from the outside world, keeping out northern books, checking the mails for abolitionist literature, and even preventing the discussion of slavery in Congress (p. 245).

The movement heats up.

The problem for Southerners was that the abolitionist attacks had become so strong. Many abolitionists were devout Christians. They believed that Jesus hated slavery. "Do unto others as you would have others do unto you." You do not want to be a slave yourself. What right, then, have you to enslave others? Christianity, they said, was the religion of love—love for everyone. The abolitionists wanted to preach love. But before very long they were also preaching hate.

It was easy enough to go from hating slavery to hating slaveholders. And easy enough, too, to go from hating slaveholding Southerners to hating all white Southerners. Since abolitionists were more interested in horror stories than in statistics, they did not advertise the fact that most white Southerners were not slaveholders. In their hatred of slavery they painted a picture of the South that had no bright spot in it. If there was any virtue in the South, why had not Southerners already abolished this monstrous evil for themselves?

The abolitionists were printing all the worst facts about slavery. Of course there were plenty of horrifying facts to be told about the mistreatment of individual slaves and the separation of black families.

Theodore Dwight Weld, a New England minister, started his career on a crusade against alcohol. Then, inspired by English abolitionists, he began to fight slavery. In 1839 he published *Slavery As It Is: Testimony of a Thousand Witnesses*, put together from items he had sifted from 20,000 copies of newspapers.

The book was a chamber of horrors. His purpose, Weld wrote, was to "see the inside of that horrible system. . . . In the advertisements for runaways we detect the cruel whippings and shootings and brandings, practiced on the helpless slaves. Heartsickening as the details are, I am thankful that God in his providence has put into our hands these weapons [these facts] prepared by the South herself, to destroy the fell monster."

Nearly everybody likes to read horror stories. The book spread through the North. Within the first four months it sold 22,000 copies, within a year more than 100,000. Northerners now began to get their picture of the South from Weld's lurid book and from others like it.

The abolition movement grew larger and more outspoken. William Lloyd Garrison, editor of the abolitionist newspaper *The Liberator* and one of the

The lithograph song sheet cover for the abolitionist song "Get Off the Track" (1844) showed the freedom train coming into a station. The "underground railroad" was not really a railroad but groups of people who helped slaves escape from the South to the free states and to Canada.

most angry of the abolitionists, actually burned a copy of the Constitution of the United States. He called the Constitution a covenant with death and an agreement with Hell—because it allowed slavery. Garrison made himself so obnoxious even in the North that he was nearly killed by mobs several times. On their side, Southerners began to shout: "Death to Abolitionists!"

Elijah Parish Lovejoy was a convinced reformer like many others. He was against lots of things—including alcoholic drinks, the Catholic church, and slavery—all of which he attacked in his newspaper in Missouri. But Missouri was a slave state. So Lovejoy moved to Illinois, where slavery was not allowed, to find a safer place for his newspaper. Even there the aggressive proslavery forces reached across the border.

His printing presses were destroyed by proslavery ruffians again and again. Each time that he set up a new press the armed proslavery mob came back to destroy it. Lovejoy's press was protected by 60 young abolitionists who begged him to leave town for his own safety. But instead of fleeing he

preferred to die for a just cause. One night during an attack on the warehouse where Lovejoy was guarding his new press, the proslavery men set the warehouse on fire. When Lovejoy leaped out, he was shot dead.

Elijah Parish Lovejoy thus became a martyr for abolitionists everywhere.

Both sides were collecting their heroes and martyrs. It was becoming harder and harder to imagine that the people of the North and the South could be kept within a single nation.

SECTION REVIEW

1. Identify or explain: James G. Birney, Grimké sisters, Theodore Dwight Weld, William Lloyd Garrison, Elijah Parish Lovejoy, American Colonization Society, *The Liberator*.

2. What efforts were made to return slaves to Africa? What was their result?

3. How did northern abolitionists stir up public feelings on the slavery issue?

3. Westward ho!

The national differences over slavery might not have come to a head so soon if the nation had not been growing and moving so fast. But Americans were pushing into Texas, into New Mexico, into California, and into the vast Oregon country north of California. The transplanted Americans out there naturally wanted their new homes to become part of the United States. In the East, stay-at-home Americans dreamed of a grand Empire for Liberty stretching from the Atlantic to the Pacific Ocean.

The push into Texas. In the Mexican province of Texas, Stephen Austin started an American settlement in 1821. A Virginia-born young man only 27 years old, he had attended Transylvania University in Lexington, Kentucky, and did not look or act like a frontiersman. Seeking his fortune, he had lived for a while in Missouri before moving on to Arkansas and then to Louisiana. He had run a store, directed a bank, edited a newspaper, and officered a militia unit. Though only five feet, six inches tall, Stephen Austin had strong features and was a natural leader.

Austin's original grant from the government of Mexico allowed him to bring 300 families into Texas. Each family was to receive free of charge one *labor* of land (177 acres) for farming and 74 *labors* (13,098 acres) for stock grazing. In return the settlers were expected to become Roman Catholics and to pay 12 1/2 cents per acre to Austin for his services. At this time the government of the United States was charging $1.25 per acre in cash, and the nation was still suffering the effects of the depression of 1819. No wonder that Texas was greeted as a land of opportunity!

It seemed not too hard to reach Texas from the eastern states. If you had enough money, you could travel comfortably on a boat around the Gulf of Mexico and up one of the broad rivers. Or if you lacked money and were hardy, once you had crossed the Mississippi River you could ride your horse or bring your wagon over the rolling open prairie.

Austin had no trouble finding people to join his new colony. He was a good-natured dictator and his people prospered. The number of immigrants to Texas from the United States grew rapidly until by 1830 there were nearly 8000. More than half of them lived on Stephen Austin's grants.

Traders and trappers in New Mexico. At the same time, other daring men were pushing into a more populated part of Mexico. In New Mexico an isolated Spanish-Mexican frontier community included some 35,000 people. They lived in large towns, like Santa Fe and Albuquerque, and in scores

This handcolored lithograph of Austin, Texas, in 1840 shows the capital only four years after Texans declared their independence (p. 243). The grand house on the hill belonged to Texan President Mirabeau Lamar.

The Amon Carter Museum, Fort Worth, Texas

of remote villages. They made their living by raising sheep and growing corn. From the 1600s to 1865 these Spanish and mestizo settlers were constantly at war with neighboring Indian tribes—Apache, Ute, Navaho, and Comanche. Like the Indians they fought, they came to think of their captives as prizes of war to be kept as slaves or exchanged in commerce.

In their midst the Pueblo Indians were living and farming in their own way. Often the Pueblos and New Mexicans fought side by side against the other Indians.

Under Spain this separate society had been barred from contact with the United States. Traders who made their way to Taos or Santa Fe were most likely to end in jail and lose their trading goods.

All of this changed, however, with the Mexican declaration of independence in 1821. Suddenly contact with New Mexico was allowed. That same year Captain William Becknell of Missouri, who had gone west to trade with the Indians, happened into New Mexico. There, much to his surprise, he was given a friendly reception. The next year Becknell put together a large expedition of wagons loaded with goods for trade in Santa Fe. On this trip Becknell established the famous Santa Fe Trail. For decades to come, it would be a frontier highway for wagon trains headed west.

American influence in New Mexico grew through an influx of traders like Charles Bent and fur trappers like Kit Carson. They settled in Taos, Santa Fe, and other New Mexican towns. These men often married Spanish-Mexican women and soon formed a growing "American" faction.

The mountain men.

The trappers who traveled through the West seeking furs discovered the hidden valleys and the easy passes across the mountains. They learned the language and the customs of the Indians, who often became their friends. The fur trade had drawn explorers to the West from early colonial times, but their great days were in the years after 1825. By 1840, however, the Rocky Mountains were nearly trapped out. As one mountain man remarked, so little was left that "lizards grow poor, and wolves lean against the sand banks to howl." Meanwhile the fur-trapping mountain men, who marked off and explored the cross-country trails, became the pathfinders for later generations of westward-moving pioneers.

On to Oregon.

On the Pacific Coast in the far Northwest, the pioneers were American sailors. Soon after the Revolution they had visited the Oregon ports to pick up furs with which they sailed to China to trade for tea and other exotic goods. The first attempt by an American to set up a permanent settlement in the Oregon country was made by John Jacob Astor, a hard-driving German immigrant. He had already made a small fortune in the fur trade and was to become the richest man in America before his death in 1848. The men of his Pacific Fur Company built Astoria on the Columbia River in 1811, but during the War of 1812 they sold the fort to the British.

In 1832 Nathaniel J. Wyeth of Massachusetts, a successful 30-year-old businessman and inventor, led a small group overland to trade in the Oregon country. His route became famous as the Oregon Trail—another grand pioneer-way to the promised lands of the West. The adventures of that trail were later vividly described by another young New Englander, Francis Parkman. His book, *The Oregon Trail* (1849), soon became an American classic.

Wyeth's attempts to make money in Oregon were failures, but he blazed the way for others. On his second trip, in 1834, he escorted a party of Methodist missionaries headed by mild, easygoing Jason Lee. When Lee arrived in Oregon at the fort of the Hudson's Bay Company, he and his party were welcomed by a huge, bearded Canadian, Dr. John McLoughlin, the director of the company's fur-trading operations in Oregon. McLoughlin helped Lee, as he was to assist many American settlers, and persuaded him to settle in the Willamette Valley.

The news of the success of the Methodists in establishing a mission encouraged other denominations to follow. In 1836 the Presbyterians sent out Dr. Marcus Whitman and Henry H. Spaulding, who founded a mission at Walla Walla. The missionaries' wives, Narcissa Prentice Whitman and Elizabeth Hart Spaulding, accompanied them. Their feat as the first white women to cross the Rockies inspired other families to make the long trip to Oregon.

Father Pierre de Smet, the friendly and learned Jesuit whom the Indians called "Blackrobe," went to Oregon in 1844. During the next few years he assisted in setting up a number of Catholic missions in the Oregon country.

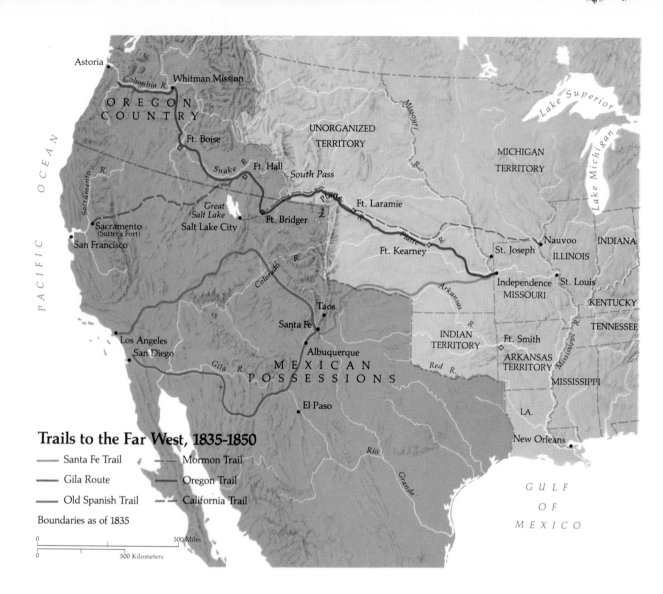

Trails to the Far West, 1835–1850

——— Santa Fe Trail   – – – Mormon Trail

——— Gila Route   ——— Oregon Trail

——— Old Spanish Trail   – ·– California Trail

Boundaries as of 1835

0   500 Miles

0   500 Kilometers

By 1843 there were about 1000 American settlers in Oregon. They had come to this promised land because of the financial depression that had begun in 1837 (p. 199) and because they had heard tall tales that Oregon was a fertile country where it was always springtime.

Since Congress paid little attention to the small settlement, they followed the example of earlier pioneer communities and made their own government. In an old barn belonging to one of the missions, on July 5, 1843, they adopted a constitution "for the purposes of mutual protection and to secure peace and prosperity among ourselves . . . until such time as the United States of America extend their jurisdiction over us."

Nearly 1000 settlers came to Oregon during the course of 1843 in the first successful mass migration. The next year brought 1500 more settlers. And the following year an additional 3000 arrived. The government back in Washington could neglect the distant "republic" of Oregon no longer.

California in the 1830s. The first Americans to reach the Mexican province of California came by boat. They traded to the missions and the ranches (p. 29) all kinds of goods in exchange for the products of the cattle ranches—tallow for their candles and hides for shoes and saddle bags. This trade and the beauties of California, as well as the life of common sailors of those days, were described by Richard Henry Dana in *Two Years Before the Mast* (1840).

The Mexican government broke up the Christian missions in 1834. The lands were supposed to go to the Indian converts but instead were carved into huge ranches. American traders, who lost some of their most reliable customers, the Franciscan fathers of the missions, now appointed trading agents in California towns. These agents, who supervised dealings with the ranchers, later became important in the drive to make California part of the United States.

In the 1830s there were only about 4000 Mexicans scattered along the California coast between the two deep-water ports of San Francisco and San Diego. Americans from the crowded eastern seaboard thronged westward in long wagon trains to the magical country that sailors and traders had extolled. Most of these found their way to the West Coast by following the Oregon Trail to Great Salt Lake and then heading southwest to California. A thriving center sprang up in the Sacramento Valley. A focus of community life was the fort built by John Sutter. A wandering Swiss citizen who had arrived in California in 1839 from Hawaii, he received an enormous grant of land from the Mexican government.

Wagon towns moving west. From the very beginning of American history, the people who came here came in groups. And when Americans decided to move farther west in the years after the Revolution, they seldom went alone. Americans traveling to Oregon and California also moved in groups. You might start out alone with a few friends and family from the settled states. But you were not likely to reach very far into the unknown West unless you soon joined with 50 or 100 others.

Most of the West was still unknown except to the mountain men and the explorers. The few wagon ways that had been marked by the explorers were the only paths through the wilderness. The most important trails started from a little Missouri town called Independence 200 miles west of St. Louis.

At Elm Grove, just outside Independence, people from all over collected because they wanted to go west. Some had never seen one another before. Just as people in Chicago, Cincinnati, St. Louis, and a hundred other places were quickly coming together and forming their instant cities, so these people with wagons were forming their own kind of instant towns. These were wagon towns, towns made to move.

It was not safe to travel alone. Indians were apt to attack a small party, but a large group might

St. Ignatius Mission, founded by the Jesuits in Montana Territory in 1845, was painted in this watercolor by Peter Peterson Tofft, a Danish immigrant who also portrayed the Oregon country.

A pioneer headed for California made this sketch of his wagon train crossing the Platte River on July 20, 1849. The broad, empty plains stretch out endlessly before them.

frighten them off. And with enough wagons in your party, you could make a kind of fort every night. The wagons would be formed into a hollow circle or square, which was like a small walled town. People were protected while they cooked their meals. They could sing and dance, or hold meetings to talk about the problems of the trip. If the Indians attacked, women and children could be safe in the hollow center while the men and boys shot back at the Indians from behind the wall of wagons.

The covered wagon used for crossing the continent was about 10 feet long and 8 1/2 feet to the top of the canvas. It was usually drawn, not by horses, but by three pairs of oxen. Even if two oxen were lost, the four that remained could still pull the wagon. When fully loaded, it could carry a ton.

Getting this heavy wagon up a hill, across rivers, and down steep inclines was never easy. But it was much easier if you were in a large party. Then the whole party could help push or pull with their teams or their muscles.

The trip across the continent was long and slow. From Independence on the lower Missouri River to Sutter's Fort in California, it was about 2000 miles on the wagon trail. The normal speed for a wagon was only two miles an hour. Even with good luck, the wagon ride from Independence to the Pacific might take five months.

When so many people lived together for so long, they had to be organized. They had to make rules for health and safety. They had to appoint commanders and judges, select juries, and punish criminals. They had to keep order, arrange marriages, and perform funerals. They felt all the needs of people in Cincinnati or Chicago or St. Louis, and had additional problems, too. If the trip was not to take forever, the group had to see that everybody did a share of the work and risked a share of the danger.

What they did was very much like what the Pilgrims on the *Mayflower* had needed to do 200 years before. They made a government for themselves. Like the first pilgrims, each wagon train made its Mayflower Compact. Each had its own do-it-yourself government. They wrote out their own laws, which everybody signed. They elected a captain, who was like the captain of a ship. He had the difficult job of assigning tasks and settling quarrels. The fate of the whole wagon train might depend on his good humor and good judgment.

The Mormons move to Utah. The best organizers were the best captains of wagon trains. The Mormons were remarkably successful. With their new American religion they looked to the West for their promised land. They set up instant cities of their own in Missouri and Illinois. When the Mormons prospered, however, their envious neighbors believed all kinds of strange stories about them and persecuted them. In late June 1844 the founder of their religion and their leader Joseph Smith as well as his brother Hyrum were killed by an Illinois mob that feared and hated these distinctive people. The Mormons had to move on.

In February 1846 their new leader, the able Brigham Young, began taking them across Iowa toward the faraway land near Great Salt Lake. There they would be hundreds of miles from the nearest settlement. They traveled in carefully organized groups, building their own roads and bridges as they went. They even planted seeds along the trail so Mormon wagon trains the next season could harvest the crops for food as they came by. One wagon train that reached Utah in October 1847 brought 1540 Mormons in 540 wagons, together with 124 horses, 9 mules, 2213 oxen, 887 cows, 358 sheep, 24 hogs, and 716 chickens.

By cooperation, discipline, and hard work, the Mormons made the dry land bloom. They dug elaborate irrigation systems and laid out a city with broad avenues. In time they were to create many towns and cities in their distant, difficult land.

The Mormons were not the only ones who expected to find a promised land in the unknown West. Hundreds of other wagon towns were held together by their own vague hopes of a prosperous future.

SECTION REVIEW

1. Identify: Stephen Austin, William Becknell, Charles Bent, John Jacob Astor, Jason Lee, the Whitmans, Francis Parkman, Pierre de Smet, Richard Henry Dana, John Sutter, Joseph Smith, Brigham Young.

2. How were the western wagon trains like towns on the move?

3. How did the Mormon migration differ from most of the others?

4. Texas and Oregon

The first opportunity for the flag to follow the American people into the new lands of the West came in Texas. But this question soon divided the nation. And it also led to war with Mexico.

The Lone Star Republic. By 1835 there were nearly 30,000 settlers from the United States living in the huge Mexican state of Coahuila-Texas. They had become Mexican citizens, but they had complaints about Mexican rule. Saltillo, the state capital, was 700 miles away from their settlements on the Brazos and Colorado rivers. These settlers from the eastern United States were in a majority in Texas proper. But they were only a small minority in the vast state of Coahuila-Texas. They had only a few representatives in the state legislature. They missed the Bill of Rights and all the guarantees of the United States Constitution, including especially the right to trial by jury.

These new Texans had come mostly from the southern United States. Since they had brought their slaves with them, they were outraged that the Mexican government tried to outlaw slavery. When that government imposed heavy customs taxes and stationed troops among the settlers, their thoughts naturally went back to the American Revolution. In 1835 they revolted and drove out the Mexican troops. Like the colonists who had revolted against George III 60 years before, the Texans declared their independence on March 2, 1836.

The convention that issued the declaration also elected a temporary government. David G. Burnet, an emigrant from Ohio who in his youth had fought for Venezuelan freedom from Spain, was elected president for the time being. Lorenzo de Zavala

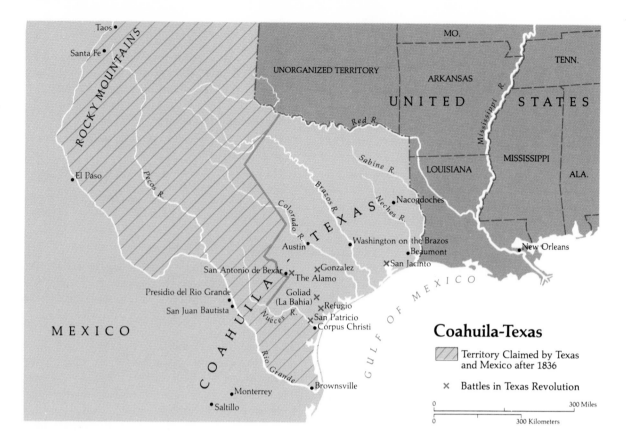

Coahuila-Texas

▨ Territory Claimed by Texas and Mexico after 1836

✕ Battles in Texas Revolution

0   300 Miles

0   300 Kilometers

was made vice-president. He was an ardent republican who had been exiled from Spain. He had fought for Mexican independence and served that new nation as a state governor, cabinet minister, and ambassador to France. In 1834 when General Santa Anna took over the government and began to rule as dictator, de Zavala fled to Texas.

General Santa Anna led an army to crush the Texas rebellion. The first battle took place at San Antonio. The Texas defenders were led by William B. Travis, a 27-year-old lawyer, and James Bowie, inventor of the bowie knife. The force included Davy Crockett, the famous frontiersman, and Hendrich Arnold, a black scout, along with nine Mexican Texans. Greatly outnumbered, they fortified themselves in an abandoned mission, the Alamo. All 187 died there, but they took 1544 of the 4000 Mexicans with them. This bloody battle, which ended on March 6, 1836, was a military defeat. But it was also a kind of spiritual victory, for it provided the battle cry "Remember the Alamo," which Texans would never forget. The fury of the Texans was kept hot when three weeks later all the defenders at Goliad were massacred after they had surrendered.

The Texan army was led by tall and magnetic Sam Houston, a veteran of the War of 1812, onetime governor of Tennessee, Indian trader, and adopted son of the Cherokees. Houston retreated with his small army until he felt the right moment had come to fight. Then he turned and attacked. In the Battle of San Jacinto on April 21, Houston's army routed the Mexican army, captured Santa Anna, and forced him to sign a treaty recognizing Texas independence. A republic was set up with Houston as the first president. A constitution modeled on those of the states of the Union was adopted. To reassure the settlers from the southern United States, the constitution of Texas forbade the Texas Congress from interfering with slavery. The new Republic of Texas offered the curious spectacle of people who had fought for their right to govern themselves—and for the right to keep thousands of their fellow Americans in slavery.

Texas at once asked for admission to the Union. But Texas was so big that there was no telling how many new states might be carved from its territory. Since all Texas was slave country, the northern states saw that the balance of North and South might be upset forever simply by creating numerous small slave states there. Some Northerners said that Texas was nothing but a slave owners' plot to smuggle a lot of new slave states into the Union.

The gag rule. Northerners were especially sensitive about slavery at this time because of the so-called gag rule in Congress. Faced with a flood of abolitionist petitions in 1836, the House of Representatives refused to receive or discuss any further petitions against slavery. Northern opponents of slavery called this the "gag rule." Former President John Quincy Adams, now a representative from Massachusetts, was a tactless and relentless enemy of slavery. He protested that such a restriction of free speech in the Congress was "a direct violation of the Constitution of the United States, of the rules of the House, and of the rights of my constituents." "Old Man Eloquence," as Adams came to be called, bored and angered southern members of the House with his lengthy orations against the gag resolution. He finally managed to secure its repeal in 1844.

Southerners tried every measure—legal and illegal—to prevent the delivery of abolitionist literature into their states. When extremists in Charleston, South Carolina, seized and burned a sack full of abolitionist pamphlets, the Congress agreed with the Postmaster General that southern postmasters did not have to deliver such mail.

The passions of the slavery issue blazed high over Texas. It seemed that to placate the slavery forces by bringing Texas into the Union would incite war with Mexico and so cost American lives. Texas was kept out of the Union. The government of the United States recognized the Republic of Texas as a separate nation in 1837 and opened diplomatic relations with the new country. First Andrew Jackson and then Martin Van Buren refused to propose bringing Texas into the Union. The question played no part in the rowdy "log-cabin" campaign of 1840 when the Whig candidates, Harrison and Tyler, were elected.

The Texas question reopened. A surprising turn of events prevented the election of the Whig President William Henry Harrison from producing

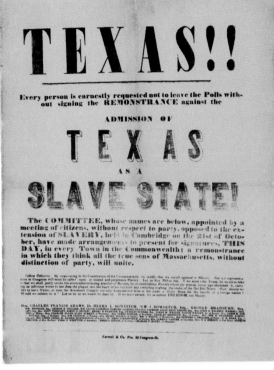

Massachusetts voters are urged to protest.

the results that voters intended. The aged Harrison caught a cold during his inauguration and died a few weeks later. Vice-President John Tyler, a states-rights Virginia Democrat, had been put on the Whig ticket with Harrison simply to attract votes. The Whig leaders expected that he, like Vice-Presidents before him, would be inactive. They never dreamed that he would do more than preside over the Senate. Now, to their shock and dismay, they had actually put him in the White House!

President Tyler left not a moment's doubt that he was a full-fledged President and would follow his own policies whether or not the Whigs liked it. He vetoed Whig bills to create a new Bank of the United States, and he opposed a higher tariff. The desperate Whig leaders could do nothing but read him out of the Whig party (to which he had never really belonged). They labeled him a "traitor" and a "President by accident." All of President Harrison's Cabinet resigned, except Secretary of State Daniel Webster. He waited until 1842 in order to complete negotiations for the Webster-Ashburton Treaty (p. 249).

Tyler as a Virginia Democrat naturally wanted to annex Texas. And of course he could expect no support from the Whigs, who by accident had put him in the White House. He was forced to look to the South. At first, he hoped to avoid a violent showdown over the slavery question. So he simply evaded the problem of Texas. But Great Britain soon made him face the issue.

Tyler learned that Texas was negotiating with Great Britain for aid and protection. The adept British diplomats saw that if they could make a firm alliance with Texas, they might block the southwestward expansion of the United States. At the same time they would secure a new source of cotton and a promising new market for manufactures. The French government, too, supported an independent Republic of Texas.

Alarmed by this unexpected willingness of Texas to enlist the great powers of Europe, Tyler saw a new urgency in the issue. He quickly began negotiating with the government of Texas. In April 1844 John C. Calhoun, who was now Secretary of State, concluded a treaty that provided for the independent Republic of Texas to enter the United States as another state of the Union.

Unfortunately for the treaty's chances in the Senate, Calhoun used it as one more time to defend slavery. This merely confirmed Northerners in their belief that the annexation of Texas was a slave owners' plot. Over all brooded a fear that annexation would bring on war with Mexico. The treaty was rejected by the decisive vote of 16 to 35.

The election of 1844. While Calhoun's treaty was being discussed in the Senate, the national conventions met to choose their candidates for President. To no one's surprise, at Baltimore on May 1 the Whigs ignored Tyler and named Henry Clay. At Clay's request, the Whig platform was silent on the subject of Texas. The Democrats also met at Baltimore, where it was expected that they would nominate their best-known leader, Martin Van Buren, who had already been President once. But Van Buren had committed himself against annexing Texas in order to gain the votes of the North. So he was passed over.

Then for the first time in American history a party nominated a "dark horse," a man who was not nationally known and who had not been thought of as a candidate. If there were few arguments in his favor, there was little to be said against him. Such a candidate, they thought, might have wider appeal than some famous man who had won loyal friends but also had made bitter enemies. The "dark horse" was James K. Polk, once governor of Tennessee and a loyal Democrat. The Whigs ridiculed the Democratic choice. Earlier that year the polka had become the most popular dance in Washington. "The *Polk*-a dance," they said, "will now be the order of the day. It means two steps *backward* for one step forward."

There was a surprise in store for the Whigs. The unknown Polk soon proved to be an adept politician. His formula for compromise was a single watchword: *Expansion!* To annex Texas all by itself expanded the slave area and seemed a menace to the North. But if at the same time you annexed the vast Oregon Territory, you had something to give the North in return. That was Polk's platform. Expand everywhere at once, and then there would be something for everybody. The very thought of stretching the nation all the way to the Pacific was exhilarating. Perhaps the nation could be united simply by marching westward together. In a divided nation, growth itself was a kind of compromise, something that everybody could agree on.

Henry Clay saw that Polk had found a popular issue. Clay had published a letter on April 27 (when he thought that Van Buren would be the Democratic candidate) opposing annexation. When he saw himself running against the expansionist Polk, he changed his tune. Clay was so anxious to be President that there were few things he would not do to smooth his path to the White House. Now he wrote that he "would be glad to see Texas admitted on fair terms" and that "slavery ought not to affect the question one way or another." But Clay misjudged the voters. His shifty behavior caused Conscience (antislavery) Whigs in New York to switch their votes to James G. Birney, the candidate of the small antislavery Liberty party. As a result Polk carried New York by a slim margin, which made it possible for him to win a close election. Henry Clay had outsmarted himself.

Ignoring the narrowness of Polk's victory, President Tyler, who had always wanted to annex Texas, called the election a "mandate" from the people. Not even waiting for Polk to come into office, in February 1845 he secured the passage of a resolution in both houses of Congress admitting Texas to the Union. The measure also provided that with the consent of Texas not more than four additional states might some time be carved from its territory, and that the Missouri Compromise line would extend westward above Texas. That was something for the South. Later that year, living up to his campaign promise, Polk claimed for the United States the whole vast Oregon Territory, which we had been sharing with Great Britain. That was something for the North.

Manifest destiny. Americans were thrilled by the vision of their Empire for Liberty reaching to the Pacific. "Why not extend the 'area of freedom' by the annexation of California?" asked the usually conservative *American Whig Review.* "Why not plant the banner of liberty there?" Then there would be no question of Old World monarchies existing in America.

The catch phrase for this whole expansive movement was provided by a New York newspaperman, John L. O'Sullivan, who wrote that it was "our manifest destiny to overspread and to possess the whole continent which Providence has given us for the development of the great experiment of liberty and federated self-government entrusted to us." *Manifest destiny!* The idea that the American destiny was clear (or manifest) challenged, elated, and exhilarated. It was an up-to-date, expanded 1800s-version of an old American refrain. The Puritan City of God, their "City upon a hill," was transformed into a continental Empire for Liberty. Both would be beacons for the world.

Fifty-four forty or fight! Polk at first demanded a stretch of Oregon that reached all the way up to the borders of Alaska (then owned by Russia). "All Oregon or none!" shouted American champions of manifest destiny. "Fifty-four forty or fight!"—the territory's northern border—became their slogan. But when the annexation of Texas brought on war with Mexico, Polk prudently decided not to risk war also with Great Britain. The two countries agreed in June 1846 to extend the 49th parallel as the border between the United States and Canada all the way to the Pacific. Western expansionists were outraged. They felt that Polk had broken his campaign promise and put the whole nation into the hands of the dreaded Slave Power.

Oregon Boundary Settlement

Disputed Area

SECTION REVIEW

1. Identify or explain: Santa Anna, Sam Houston, gag rule, John Tyler, "dark horse," James K. Polk, Conscience Whigs, Liberty party.
2. Locate: Coahuila-Texas, the Alamo, Goliad, San Jacinto, the "fifty-four forty" line, the 49th parallel.
3. How was the annexation of Texas linked to the slavery issue?
4. How did the election campaign of 1844 win support for the annexation of Texas?
5. What did the slogan "manifest destiny" mean?
6. How was the Oregon issue settled?

5. War With Mexico

The nation's troubles with Mexico were far from settled. Mexico considered the annexation of Texas (which it said was still a part of Mexico) to be an act of war by the United States. It also disputed the boundary of Texas. Meanwhile, the American settlers in California were a new trouble spot. Following the example of Texas, they too wanted to join the United States. Polk was also eager to bring California into the Union. But he hoped to find a way that would avoid war.

The declaration of war. Polk sent an agent to Mexico to offer as much as $30 million for New Mexico and California. In addition the United States would assume all claims of its citizens against Mexico if Mexico would accept the Rio Grande instead of the Nueces River as the border of Texas. But Mexico was on the brink of a revolution. Feelings against the United States ran high. Both claimants for the presidency of Mexico played upon these feelings, even refusing to meet Polk's agent.

President Polk then decided on "aggressive measures." He sent General Zachary Taylor with 2000 regular troops to the Rio Grande. The Mexicans ordered Taylor to withdraw from the disputed territory. When he refused, a Mexican unit crossed the Rio Grande and ambushed a scouting party of Americans, killing or wounding sixteen men (April 25, 1846).

Polk had already drafted a message asking Congress for a declaration of war against Mexico. Upon receiving news of the attack upon Taylor's troops, he tore up his first draft and wrote a new one. Now he declared that, in spite of his efforts to keep the peace, the war had already begun "by the act of Mexico." He asked Congress to recognize that a state of war existed and then to provide funds and troops to fight it.

Northerners feared that victory over Mexico might add still more territory and lead to even more slave states in the Southwest. But once the fighting had begun, patriotic passions prevailed. The opposition proved weak, and Congress voted for war.

Northern fears proved to be well founded. After United States victories by General Taylor's army at Monterrey in northern Mexico (September 21–23, 1846) and at Buena Vista (February 22, 1847), Mexico City was captured by an army commanded by General Winfield Scott (September 14, 1847). The helpless Mexican government then gave in to all demands of the United States. In the Treaty of Guadalupe Hidalgo (1848), Mexico gave up all claims to Texas and agreed that Texas belonged to

The Mexican War, 1846-1848

⟵ U.S. Forces

⟵ Mexican Forces

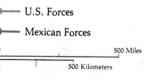

Growth of the United States to 1853

Names of the Thirteen Original States
are Underlined: <u>GA.</u>

the United States. This was only a beginning of Mexican losses.

The conquest of New Mexico and California.

American forces under Colonel Stephen Kearny marched 1800 miles from Fort Leavenworth to Santa Fe and raised the American flag over New Mexico. Then they tramped on to California. Meanwhile, in June 1846, upon hearing of the war with Mexico, the explorer John C. Frémont and his band of frontiersmen helped American settlers in California to set up a republic under the famous "Bear Flag." Shortly, however, the navy arrived and the flag of the United States replaced the Bear Flag. To complete the conquest, when Kearny and his men came out of the mountains in December 1846, all they had to do was to put down scattered Mexican resistance in southern California.

The peace treaty and the Gadsden Purchase.

In the peace treaty, Mexico handed over all the lands between Texas and the Pacific to the United States. That included California, New Mexico, and most of the present states of Utah, Nevada, Arizona, and Colorado. In return, the United States paid Mexico

$15 million and assumed claims of our citizens against Mexico for some $3 million.

After the Webster-Ashburton Treaty (1842) had finally resolved the long-disputed border between Maine and Canada, the Treaty of Guadalupe Hidalgo (1848) nearly filled in the outlines of the present United States except for Alaska and Hawaii. The final piece, a small strip of land south of the Gila River in Arizona and New Mexico, was bought from Mexico in 1853 for $10 million in the Gadsden Purchase (p. 258). This piece of land was believed to offer the best rail route across the southern Rockies to the Pacific.

The lands (including Texas) taken from Mexico after the war were larger than all the Louisiana Purchase or all the United States when the Constitution was adopted. This should have satisfied any American's yen for expansion. Yet when President Polk asked the Senate to approve the Treaty of Guadalupe Hidalgo, a dozen senators voted against it because they wanted to annex the *whole* of Mexico. "We believe it is a part of our destiny to civilize that beautiful country," the *New York Herald* proclaimed. Antislavery men also opposed the treaty, as did Whigs who envied Polk and the

Democrats their success. So the treaty only squeaked through the Senate by 38 to 14, just 3 more votes than the necessary two-thirds.

It took no prophet to predict that more western lands spelled more trouble. Every new acre was a subject for debate, for a quarrel—or even for a battle. Southerners and Northerners alike thought of nothing but whether the new lands would spread the Slave Power.

In the bitterly divided nation, every stroke of national good luck struck a note of discontent. Each section somehow was afraid that the other would gain more. Ralph Waldo Emerson wrote in his journal as the United States invaded Mexico, "The United States will conquer Mexico, but it will be as the man swallows the arsenic, which brings him down in turn. Mexico will poison us."

SECTION REVIEW

1. Identify or explain: Zachary Taylor, Winfield Scott, Stephen Kearny, John C. Frémont, "Bear Flag," Webster-Ashburton Treaty.
2. Locate: Nueces River, Rio Grande, Monterrey, Buena Vista, Mexico City, Fort Leavenworth, Gadsden Purchase.
3. List the terms of the Treaty of Guadalupe Hidalgo.

CHAPTER REVIEW

MEETING OUR EARLIER SELVES

1. A chief feature of American Protestantism was its division into many denominations and sects. Identify some of these divisions. Was such diversity beneficial or harmful? Explain.
2. Name some changes in American life between 1790 and the 1840s that led reformers to demand better schools. Show how improvements in education were linked to these changes in American society.
3. Humanitarianism—concern for human welfare and human dignity—was at the heart of the reform movements. What were some common violations of human welfare and dignity in this period? What reforms were proposed to deal with them?
4. Why would defenders of slavery be wary of social reformers?

5. How did the slavery issue complicate the idea of manifest destiny?
6. Individualism has long been regarded as an American trait, but it had to be limited on the western wagon trains. Why?

QUESTIONS FOR TODAY

1. Compare the women's movement of the mid-1800s with that of our own time.
2. What are some chief reform movements in the United States today? Which of them deal with issues similar to those of the mid-1800s?
3. What are the chances of either major party nominating a "dark horse" candidate for President in our day? Justify your answer.
4. Cite a modern example of people following the principles of Thoreau's civil disobedience. What was the outcome?
5. If Horace Mann could return to evaluate the modern educational scene, what reforms might he advocate in the public schools?

YOUR REGION IN HISTORY

1. From your locality in the 1830s or 1840s trace the route a family might have traveled to reach Texas, California, or Oregon.
2. Find out if the reform movements discussed in this chapter had any particular impact in your state. For example, what changes—if any—did your state make in public education, care of the mentally ill and retarded, women's rights, etc.?
3. Identify local or state "heroes" who were connected with the westward expansion of this period.

SKILLS TO MAKE OUR PAST VIVID

1. On an outline map show the land obtained by the United States from 1842 to 1853. Label the map to show when and how each piece of territory was obtained.
2. List items that a wagon train would need to take on the trip west from Independence, Missouri. Then arrange the items in your list into several categories: food, tools, etc.
3. Write a paragraph about life in the period of 1830–1850 using information found in the illustrations in this chapter.

CHAPTER 12

The failure of the politicians

The poison pill of the western lands soon began to do its work. The organization of every inch was disputed between the North and South. And the problem always was whether—and where—slavery should be allowed in the vast new West. Over this question Americans would kill each other in Kansas, political parties would collapse or split, and finally the nation itself would divide.

1. The Compromise of 1850

Emerson spoke for many Americans when he foresaw that the millions of acres acquired from Mexico—all raw material for new states—would produce strife and tragedy for the nation as a whole. The first act of this drama would end in a great "compromise." Many optimistic Americans, north and south, mistakenly believed this might settle the slavery question for good. But the moral issue of slavery was not a subject for compromise. The only question for a nation "conceived in liberty" was when and how slavery would be abolished.

The gold rush. By an astonishing coincidence, gold was discovered near Sutter's Fort in California in the very same year when Mexico handed over California to the United States. Gold rushers flocked to California.

Thousands went west by wagon train across the plains, through mountains and desert. Their trail was marked by broken wagons, dead animals, and human skeletons—relics of pioneers who had the spirit but lacked the strength or the equipment to carry them through. Others sailed to Panama and walked across the malaria-ridden isthmus to battle for a place on a steamer going up the California

coast. Some came all the way by sea, surviving an eight-month journey around Cape Horn. Often they formed companies to purchase old vessels. Then, like the members of the westward-going wagon towns, they drew up rules, elected officers, and sailed for the gold fields.

The clipper ships. Among the ships that sailed for California were some of the most splendid sailing vessels ever built. The swift clipper ships (so called because they could "clip" time off a passage) were built in New England, spurred by the need to speed to California. Huge profits rewarded the fastest ships. The grandest of the clippers were made by the master shipbuilder Donald McKay. As a young man he had emigrated from Nova Scotia. With a rare sense of design and a fine eye for detail, working in East Boston he turned out the speediest, most beautiful ships of the age. He became a hero for his generation, like the great designers of automobiles or airplanes for a later age. In April 1851 the Flying Cloud, the finest of McKay's many vessels, set a record of 89 days from New York to San Francisco.

Many clipper captains brought their wives. Mary Brown Patten took command of *Neptune's Car* when her husband became ill. At the age of 19, while caring for her sick husband, she navigated an

Daily Rations

FOR

BARK GOLD HUNTER.

Bread every meal. Coffee or Tea for Breakfast and Supper, with the following:

SUNDAY.
Soused Tripe.
Flour Duff with Raisins.
Pickles.

MONDAY.
Boiled Beef.
Cranberries.
Pickles.

TUESDAY.
Boiled Pork and Beans.
Pickles.

WEDNESDAY.
Boiled Mackerel.
Flour Duff.
Pickles.

THURSDAY.
Boiled Beef.
Flour Duff.
Pickles.

FRIDAY.
Tongues & Sounds & Boiled Peas.
Rice.
Pickles.

SATURDAY.
Boiled Codfish.
Indian Pudding.
Cranberries or Pickles.

BOILED BEEF'S TONGUES ONCE IN TWO WEEKS.

The menu for passengers on the *Gold Hunter* shows the limited choice because of the lack of ovens and ice. "Flour duff" is steamed pudding. The advertisement for *Neptune's Car* boasts of the speedy 97-day sail to California. This hopeful young prospector (bottom) was one of those who traveled by land to California in 1849 to mine gold.

EMPIRE LINE FOR
SAN FRANCISCO

THE CELEBRATED AND FAVORITE CLIPPER SHIP
NEPTUNE'S CAR
J. A. PATTEN, Commander,
IS NOW RECEIVING CARGO at PIER 9, E. R

The sailing qualities of this SUPERIOR CLIPPER are *unsurpassed* having made her first passage to San Francisco in 105 days, and the last in **97 days**, (beating every vessel which sailed from New-York or Boston during the year 1855,) and delivering her cargo without damaging a single package. A large portion of her cargo being already engaged, an early sailing day will be named.
For balance of Freight, apply to
WELLS & EMANUEL,
(Successors to JAS. SMITH & SON,)
NESBITT & CO. PRINTERS.   **96 WALL STREET**

1800-ton clipper for the remaining 52 days on the way to California.

In the 1850s, after a railway was built across Panama, the day of the clipper ships was on the wane. British steamships, larger and more dependable than the clippers, brought the great age of sail to an end.

California asks for admission to the Union.

People rushed to California from everywhere. Nantucket lost a quarter of its voting population in nine months. French soldiers and government officials deserted the Marquesas islands in the Pacific. Thousands came from the Mississippi Valley. Americans—north and south—sang

> Oh Susannah, don't you cry for me.
> I've gone to California with my wash-bowl on
> my knee.

During 1849 more than 80,000 people arrived in California. It was no surprise that these Americans wanted to join the Union as a new state. But in 1849 there were 30 states altogether, and the national score showed 15 slave and 15 free states. To admit California as a free state, as its people requested in 1849, would break the precarious tie.

The Wilmot Proviso.

And what was to be done with all the rest of the newly acquired lands? How was slavery to be dealt with out there? That question had been raised early in the Mexican War when President Polk asked Congress for money to negotiate a Mexican boundary settlement. Antislavery congressmen knew that this would lead to demands for more territory from Mexico. So David Wilmot, a Democrat from Pennsylvania, offered an amendment to Polk's bill. Wilmot proposed that "neither slavery nor involuntary servitude shall ever exist in any part of the territory" acquired from Mexico. Antislavery men and Westerners who were bitter over the failure to take all of Oregon joined to support this amendment. It passed several times in the House in 1846–1847, but the Senate always voted it down. Americans were now divided by the problems of expansion.

The South through its leaders, John C. Calhoun of South Carolina and Jefferson Davis of Mississippi, opposed the Wilmot Proviso. Congress, they said, had no right to interfere with slavery in the territories. More than that, they insisted that

Congress had a positive duty, under the Constitution, to protect the property of Southerners in the territories. This meant their right to own slaves. Slavery might be forbidden only when a territory achieved statehood, and then only by act of the state itself.

Between the extremes—those who would bar slavery altogether and those who would protect slavery—many compromises were proposed. For example, some suggested that the Missouri Compromise line of 36° 30' be extended all the way to the Pacific, dividing California and New Mexico into free and slave sections (map, p. 174). Others urged "popular sovereignty," which meant leaving the slavery question up to the settlers of each territory.

The election of 1848.

As the election of 1848 approached, both political parties wanted to avoid all divisive questions. Since President Polk decided not to seek reelection, the Democrats nominated Governor Lewis Cass of Michigan. He was a strong expansionist, sympathetic to the South, and cared little about slavery one way or the other.

The Whigs, though they had opposed the war, nominated the hero of the Battle of Buena Vista, General Zachary Taylor. A professional soldier and a Louisiana sugar planter, he was the owner of 300 slaves. He had no experience in politics. This easygoing southern gentleman had not even voted for some years. The Whigs counted on his war record to sweep their "Old Rough and Ready" into office. To be doubly safe against the accusation that they really did stand for something, the Whigs had no party platform.

Voters who had strong feelings on the slavery issue were angered that the major parties offered them no real choice. As a result the "Free-Soil" Democrats combined with Conscience Whigs and abolitionists to form the new Free-Soil party. They nominated Martin Van Buren for President and Charles Francis Adams, the son of John Quincy Adams, for Vice-President. Their party supported the Wilmot Proviso and called for "Free Soil, Free Speech, Free Labor, and Free Men."

The Free-Soilers took away enough votes from Cass to give New York's 36 electoral votes to Taylor, who won a close election with 163 electoral votes to Cass's 127. The Free-Soilers won no state, but 291,263 people voted for them, and they elected 13 members to the House of Representatives.

time to grow stronger—in manpower, railroads, and factories. For those who loved the Union, Clay and Douglas had performed a valuable service. They had bought time. When the evil day of armed conflict would come, that strength would help decide the issue for the North and for Union.

The revolt against the Fugitive Slave Act.
The Fugitive Slave Act of 1850 kept tempers hot in the North. It provided that state and city authorities and even plain citizens should assist in the capture and return of runaway slaves.

Harriet Tubman was called "Moses" by fugitives whom she led from slavery to freedom.

Library of Congress

State after state passed Personal Liberty laws. These forbade state officials or private citizens to assist federal courts in enforcing the Fugitive Slave Act. The laws also tried to guarantee protection and a fair trial to runaways.

Northerners showed their defiance of the Fugitive Slave Act dramatically and effectively by expanding their efforts to help slaves escape. The "Underground Railroad" was a well-organized series of routes and stopovers (stations) leading north to Canada for runaway slaves. By 1861 this scheme had helped some 75,000 slaves escape to freedom.

The most famous of all the "conductors" on the Underground Railroad was Harriet Tubman, herself an escaped slave. From 1849 to the Civil War she risked her life many times on trips into the South. During her long courageous career she helped spirit away to freedom her own elderly parents and some 300 other slaves.

The election of 1852.
There was no chance of preventing the two great national political parties from splitting into northern and southern factions unless the Compromise of 1850 was really "final" and somehow the discussion of slavery was itself abolished. But could so great an issue be simply wished away?

The Democrats, in their convention of 1852, pledged themselves to abide by the compromise measures. They nominated Franklin Pierce of New Hampshire. He was a pleasant man lacking force or decisiveness. But he had a good record as a politician and as a general in the Mexican War.

The Whigs were in a worse condition than the Democrats. President Fillmore had the backing of the southern wing of the party but was opposed by northern Whigs because he had supported the compromise. At the Whig convention it was not until the fifty-third ballot that they settled on a military hero, Virginia-born General Winfield Scott, who had captured Mexico City. The Whig platform also accepted the "finality" of the compromise measures.

But the Whigs failed to repeat the triumphs of General Harrison in 1840 and General Taylor in 1848 with this their third military hero. The Democrat Franklin Pierce won in a landslide carrying all but four states and receiving 254 electoral votes to Scott's 42. The bitter divisions in the

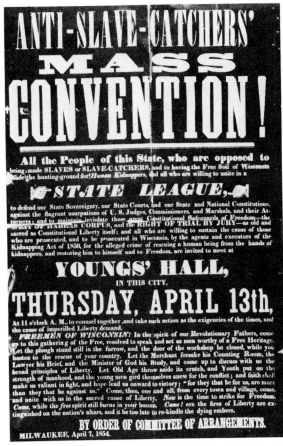

Organizers of this rally called the Fugitive
Slave Act the "Kidnapping Act of 1850."

nation were revealed in the fact that Pierce was the
only President to win a popular majority between
1840 and 1864. With this defeat the Whig party
began to fall apart.

Harmony was the key word of Franklin Pierce's
inaugural address on March 4, 1853. The compromise measures of 1850, he said, were "strictly
constitutional and to be unhesitatingly carried into
effect." He sincerely hoped that no sectional
ambition or radical excitement might again "threaten the durability of our institutions or obscure the
light of our prosperity."

A book forces the issue. But an event had already
occurred during 1852 that made Pierce's hope
unlikely. It was the publication of a book, *Uncle
Tom's Cabin*, by Harriet Beecher Stowe.

Mrs. Stowe found much of the ammunition for
her antislavery novel in Theodore Dwight Weld's
Slavery As It Is. In her book the Christ-like black,
Uncle Tom, finally is flogged to death by the brutal
slave dealer Simon Legree, because he will not give
away the hiding place of two escaped slaves.

The book quickly sold more than 100,000 sets of
an expensive two-volume edition. Then it was put
out in a single cheap volume for 37 1/2 cents.
Within a year it had sold a total of 300,000 copies.
It was made into plays and musical comedies.
Uncle Tom skits at fairs and circuses showed the
escaping slave "Eliza Crossing the Ice" with her
baby in her arms, and then Little Eva was yanked up
to heaven by pulleys. "Uncle Tom's Cabin played
here last night," said one newspaper. "The blood-
hounds were good." The book sold enormously in
England. It was quickly published in translation all
over Europe. *Uncle Tom's Cabin* became America's
all-time worldwide best-seller.

Mrs. Stowe gave one of the first copies to her
congressman one day as he was about to board the
train for Washington. He started reading the book
on the train. The story was so sad that he began to
cry. He attracted the attention of the other

257

Brown Brothers

Harriet Beecher Stowe posed for this Mathew Brady daguerreotype in the 1840s. Brady, who learned the process from Samuel F. B. Morse, became the great photographer of the Civil War.

passengers as he wiped the tears from his face and blew his nose. To avoid embarrassment, he got off the train at the next stop, where he rented a hotel room and sat up all night finishing the book. There, in the privacy of his room, he could weep to his heart's content. Many other people, too, reported that the book had upset them. There must have been thousands of tear-stained copies of *Uncle Tom's Cabin*.

It is possible that, without this book, Lincoln never could have been elected President. During the Civil War, Mrs. Stowe went to see President Lincoln. "Is this the little woman," Lincoln asked her, "whose book made such a great war?"

2. How the compromise collapsed

In his inaugural address President Pierce had boldly declared that his administration would not be controlled "by any timid forebodings of evil from expansion." This proved to be the understatement of the age. He went full speed ahead searching for new territories. He sent James Gadsden to buy the northern part of Mexico and all of Lower California. He sent Pierre Soulé as minister to Spain with orders to buy Cuba. He then reached out for Hawaii, sought a naval base in Santo Domingo, and explored the purchase of Alaska from the Russians.

Mexico had no interest in selling any large stretch of land. But Gadsden did succeed in arranging the purchase of a small tract south of the Gila River. Even then northern congressmen, wary of adding new territory for the slave power, were opposed. The Gadsden Purchase was approved only after 9000 extra acres Mexico was willing to sell were removed from the treaty. Expansion was no longer a means of compromise.

The Ostend Manifesto. The climax of aggressive nationalism came over Cuba. Southerners and their friends, including President Pierce, believed the island would add a large and profitable slave territory to the United States. But Spain did not want to sell.

In response to instructions from Secretary of State William L. Marcy, during the summer of 1854 the American ministers to Spain, England, and France met at Ostend in Belgium to shape the United States policy on Cuba.

The "Ostend Manifesto" which the ministers drew up was supposed to be a confidential dispatch to Marcy. But it soon reached the press and created an uproar. The possession of Cuba, the American ministers asserted, was essential to the welfare of the United States. And if Spain would not sell the island, they advised the United States to take Cuba by force. Pierce and Marcy said at once they had not had anything to do with the Manifesto. But that was no help. President Pierce was now branded as a proslavery man and a warlike expansionist. The Ostend Manifesto had now firmly identified slavery with expansion.

The Kansas-Nebraska Act.

The only hope for the success of the Compromise of 1850 was to keep the question of slavery out of Congress. The advance of technology and the growth of industry and commerce soon made that impossible. By an ironic twist of fate the man who was destined to revive the slavery issue in Congress and so disturb the delicate balance was a main architect of the Compromise of 1850, Senator Stephen A. Douglas.

In the 1850s, of course, Americans had not yet begun to dream of reaching the moon. They had their own grand dream—to build a railroad all the way across the continent to unite East and West. No American city could want a greater prize than to be chosen as the eastern terminus of the nation's transcontinental railway. New Orleans, Memphis, St. Louis, Chicago, and many smaller towns all hoped they would be selected and so become the bustling headquarters for reaching the wealth and commerce of the West.

Douglas wanted his home city of Chicago to receive the prize. But a railroad through the empty land of the West could only be built with the aid of government land grants. And these land grants could be made only if the region the railroad passed through was already organized politically and surveyed. With this in mind, Senator Douglas introduced a bill to organize the lands west of Iowa and Missouri. In its final form the bill provided for a Kansas Territory and a Nebraska Territory. But Southerners would never vote for a railroad through

American Antiquarian Society

Stephen A. Douglas, the "Little Giant," is shown carrying off the White House.

land that was forever closed to slavery. And Douglas could not pass his bill without southern votes.

In order to win southern support, Senator Douglas, the wizard of compromise, concocted two special provisions. The Missouri Compromise of 1820 would be repealed and replaced by the Compromise of 1850. The decision whether Kansas and Nebraska should be free or slave would be made by popular sovereignty—the vote of the

259

people living there. Douglas knew, as he said, that there would be "a hell of a storm" over the repeal of the 34-year-old Missouri Compromise. But he had to have the southern votes and that was the only way. He believed also that he could survive the storm and finally pass his bill with the help of the pro-South Pierce administration. Then, he imagined, the whole problem would quickly go away.

Douglas, an experienced politico who knew the ins and outs of Congress, actually managed to get his controversial Kansas-Nebraska bill passed in 1854, after nine months of debate. This was a great victory for Douglas, but it was an even greater victory for the South. For the whole Kansas-Nebraska territory was north of the old freedom-line of the Missouri Compromise. "Popular sovereignty" now might open those lands to slavery.

Angry rallies were held across the North in protest over the Kansas-Nebraska Act. The question of slavery in the United States had now been transformed into a battle over whether slavery should be allowed to spread into the territories.

Expansion and slavery. There was one odd but significant truth about the bitter congressional battle over the spread of slavery into the territories. It was a battle over slavery where it did not exist and might never go. This did not make the struggle any less heated. Yet it did conceal an important fact. Many Northerners, of course, were against the expansion of slavery because they hated the "peculiar institution." But many others opposed its spread into the territories not so much because they disliked slavery as because they did not want to live near or compete with blacks. Several midwestern states such as Illinois and Indiana had even put in their constitutions a ban against blacks moving into their states. These restrictions were seldom enforced. Many Northerners would have been willing to guarantee slavery where it already existed in order to be sure they would never run into blacks—slave or free—in the western territories.

Southerners failed to recognize the extent to which the opposition to the spread of slavery was actually opposition to blacks. They saw it as an attempt to bar them and their property (slaves) from the territories. To them it appeared to be just one more way the power of the North was being used to injure the South and prevent it from growing.

The new Republican party. The Kansas-Nebraska bill was greeted by anger in the North. Public meetings were held in many states. At one such meeting at Ripon, Wisconsin, the members decided to organize a new party to resist the *extension* of slavery. To show their connection to Jefferson's Democratic-Republican party, they now chose the name "Republicans," which had been dropped by the Democrats.

On July 6, 1854, the party was launched at a meeting in Jackson, Michigan. Its platform (1) declared that slavery was "a great moral, social, and political evil," (2) demanded the repeal of the Kansas-Nebraska Act and the Fugitive Slave Act, and (3) resolved to sink all political differences and unite in the battle against the extension of slavery until the fight was won. During the summer and fall of 1854, conventions in Maine, Vermont, Massachusetts, Ohio, and New York organized units of this new Republican or "Anti-Nebraska" party.

The congressional elections in November 1854 produced a revolution in American politics. The old Whig party—which in recent years had been held together by nothing but the desire for office—was shattered. Its northern members deserted and moved into the ranks of other parties. The Democratic party staggered but did not collapse. Of the 42 northern Democrats who had voted for the Kansas-Nebraska Act, only 7 were reelected to Congress in 1854. The Democrats had held a substantial majority in the 1852 Congress, but in 1854 there were only 83 Democrats to face 108 of these new Republicans and 43 representatives of another new party—the Know-Nothings.

The Know-Nothing party. Numerous parties quickly appeared and as quickly disappeared during the active year of 1854. Only two of these new parties proved significant—the Republicans and the Know-Nothing party. The Know-Nothings were a reaction to the ever-increasing flood of immigrants into the country. The party grew out of the Order of the Star-Spangled Banner. This was a secret association formed in 1849 to combat the political influence of "foreigners," especially Roman Catholics. Its real name was the American party, but everyone called it the Know-Nothing party because its members evasively replied, "I don't know," when asked about the party's activities. Ever since then, "Know-Nothing" has been a name for people who refuse to face the real issues of their day and instead seek refuge in hate and prejudice.

In the election of 1854 the Republicans and the Know-Nothings together won enough seats to control Congress. It was not always clear, in fact, who was a Republican and who a Know-Nothing, since the Know-Nothings were still partly secret. It appears that nearly a majority of the members of the House were *both* Republican and Know-Nothing.

Bleeding Kansas.
When the Kansas-Nebraska bill became law, Douglas boasted that "the struggle over slavery was forever banished from the halls of Congress to the western plains." He was wrong about the halls of Congress but right about the western plains. For the Kansas-Nebraska Act would bring bloodshed to Kansas.

The major problem with the doctrine of "popular sovereignty" was that it did not say *when* a territory could decide about slavery. As a result, there was a race for Kansas from South and North. The first to gain control, the first to create a majority—of Northerners or Southerners—would decide the fate of slavery in the territory.

Antislavery New Englanders organized and raised money to rush Free-Soil emigrants to Kansas. On the suggestion of the eminent minister Henry Ward Beecher, Mrs. Stowe's brother, these emigrants were supplied with rifles—"Beecher's Bibles." Armed proslavery men from neighboring Missouri and elsewhere in the South also flocked to the territory. "Popular sovereignty," it seemed, would be decided not by votes but by guns.

Acts of violence were inevitable in Kansas, but only twice did the situation become critical. In May 1856 a proslavery sheriff led a mob into antislavery Lawrence, sacking and burning the town. In revenge the self-proclaimed antislavery messiah John Brown led a party including his four sons to a proslavery settlement on Pottawatomie Creek. They dragged five men from their beds in the dead of night and murdered them by splitting their skulls with broadswords. Somehow Kansas avoided becoming a territory of total anarchy and civil war. Still, bands of armed men were killing each other over slavery.

Charles Sumner is attacked.
The mounting violence reached even into Congress. Charles Sumner of Massachusetts—intelligent, vain, outspoken, and tactless—delivered a speech in the Senate that he called "The Crime Against Kansas." He attacked the South and several of its senators with every insulting word he could command. Representative Preston S. Brooks of South Carolina was the nephew of a senator from that state who had been insulted. In the southern tradition he avenged the "honor" of his uncle and the South—not with words but with a

During the 1850s Kansas was known as "Bleeding Kansas." In this lithograph, the Battle of Hickory Point, a village about 25 miles north of Lawrence, is shown. A band of proslavery men, armed with a cannon, are attacking the settlement of Free-Soilers.

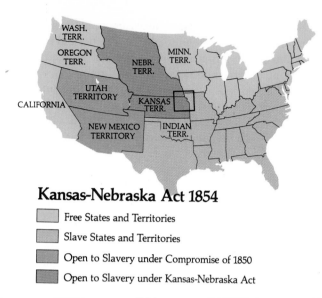

Kansas-Nebraska Act 1854

- Free States and Territories
- Slave States and Territories
- Open to Slavery under Compromise of 1850
- Open to Slavery under Kansas-Nebraska Act

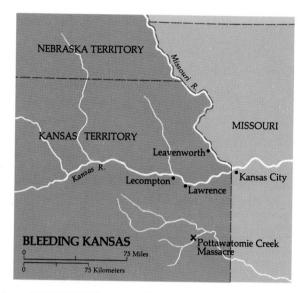

cane. On May 22, 1856, Brooks went up to Senator Sumner while he was seated in the Senate Chamber and beat him senseless. When Brooks was censured by the House, he resigned. But he was thereupon reelected by the people of his congressional district with only six dissenting votes. Brooks became a southern hero. Senator Sumner never regained his health and became a northern martyr. For several years his empty seat in the Senate proclaimed that northern and southern leaders were no longer on speaking terms.

SECTION REVIEW

1. Identify or explain: James Gadsden, Pierre Soulé, William L. Marcy, Ostend Manifesto, American party, "Beecher's Bibles," John Brown, Charles Sumner, Preston S. Brooks.

2. Locate: Lower California, Santo Domingo, Gila River, Kansas Territory, Nebraska Territory, Lawrence (Kansas).

3. What moves did President Pierce and Secretary Marcy make to expand United States territory? How was the slavery issue involved?

4. What was the Kansas-Nebraska Act? Why did Douglas want it?

5. Why were the Republican and Know-Nothing parties formed? What success did they have in 1854?

6. Name the events in May 1856 that further inflamed the slavery issue.

3. The nation comes apart

The word of God could no longer hold Americans together. Even churches were dividing. In 1844 the Methodists had split into northern and southern wings, and the Baptists followed in 1845. One of the great national parties, the Whigs, had now nearly disappeared. In its place there stood a purely sectional party—the Republicans. They were looked upon with fear and loathing in the South.

The election of 1856. In the week following Brooks's attack on Sumner in the Senate, as violence convulsed Kansas, the Democratic national convention met at Cincinnati. The delegates were careful not to nominate any candidate who could be held responsible for what was happening in Kansas. They passed over both Pierce and Douglas. Instead, they chose James Buchanan, a dignified and conservative Pennsylvanian. He had had the good fortune to be out of the country during the past four years as the American minister in Great Britain. His "availability" consisted chiefly of two negative facts: He had no connection with Kansas and no abolitionist leanings that would offend the South.

The Republicans chose as their candidate John C. Frémont, the romantic "Pathfinder of the West" and "Conqueror of California." Their slogan was "Free speech, Free press, Free soil, Free men, Frémont." The Know-Nothing party split over the issue of slavery. Its southern wing nominated Millard Fillmore. But its northern wing, the

"North Americans," joined the Republican party in nominating John C. Frémont to keep from dividing the anti-Democratic vote.

The campaign then became not national but sectional. Buchanan ran against Fillmore in the South and against Frémont in the North. Buchanan's greatest strength was in the South where he carried every slave state except Maryland, which went for Fillmore. In the North and West he carried five free states to Frémont's eleven. Buchanan's electoral vote was 174 to 114 for Frémont.

Still the Republicans in this their first national campaign had made a remarkable fight and shown astonishing strength. They polled 1,339,932 votes to 1,832,955 for Buchanan. Fillmore had received 871,731. So Buchanan had won mainly on the basis of votes given to Fillmore. Frémont had received no electoral votes in the South, where the Republican party seemed the instrument of the devil. As one southern newspaper said, "If they should succeed in this contest . . . they would repeal the fugitive slave law . . . they could create insurrection and servile war in the South . . . they would put the torch to our dwellings and the knife to our throats." Some Southerners had counseled the South to secede from the Union if Frémont was elected.

Dred Scott v. Sanford, 1857. In his inaugural address President Buchanan expressed the ill-founded belief that the long agitation over slavery was now "approaching its end." And he expressed his hope that the Supreme Court would use its authority to settle the slavery issue for good. Two days later (March 6, 1857) the Supreme Court handed down one of the most momentous and most controversial decisions in its history. It dealt with the case of the slave Dred Scott. Some years before he had been taken by his master to Illinois, where the Northwest Ordinance of 1787 had forbidden slavery, and then to Minnesota, where slavery had been prohibited by the Missouri Compromise. Afterwards he had returned to Missouri. Now he sued for his freedom.

The case finally came up to the United States Supreme Court, which had to review the decision of the federal circuit court for Missouri. That court had declared that Scott remained a slave despite his travels and that, as he was not a citizen of Missouri, he did not even have the right to bring suit. To review this decision, the justices had to decide whether Scott was a citizen. That, of course, meant deciding whether he was free—which was what the case was all about. So the court decided to answer these two questions—was Scott a citizen and was he free?

The decision against Scott was 7 to 2. Its clarity was confused by the fact that each judge wrote his own opinion to support his vote. But the opinion of Roger B. Taney (pronounced Tawney) as the Chief Justice was the most important. Blacks, according to Taney, could not be citizens. The Constitution had been made by and for white men only. So Scott could not bring suit in court. And Scott was not free either. The Missouri Compromise (and by inference the Northwest Ordinance of 1787 and the Kansas-Nebraska Act as well) was unconstitutional. Why? (1) A slave was the property of his owner. (2) The Constitution nowhere gave Congress the right to deprive a citizen of the United States of his slaves in the territories, lands which were the common property of all the states.

What the Dred Scott decision meant was that Congress could do nothing about slavery in the territories. The people there had no power to restrict or abolish slavery until they applied for admission as a state.

The Dred Scott decision evoked many protests.

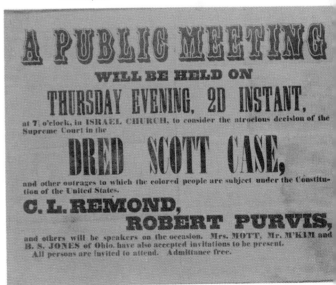

A PUBLIC MEETING WILL BE HELD ON THURSDAY EVENING, 2D INSTANT, at 7 o'clock, in ISRAEL CHURCH, to consider the atrocious decision of the Supreme Court in the DRED SCOTT CASE, and other outrages to which the colored people are subject under the Constitution of the United States. C. L. REMOND, ROBERT PURVIS, and others will be speakers on the occasion. Mrs. MOTT, Mr. M'KIM and B. S. JONES of Ohio, have also accepted invitations to be present. All persons are invited to attend. Admittance free.

The South rejoiced that at last the highest court in the land had endorsed the proslavery doctrine of John C. Calhoun and Jefferson Davis. It now seemed that slavery would be able to spread into all the territories. The North was outraged. Some Northerners vowed to overturn the decision. Stephen A. Douglas and others who had hoped to bury the slavery issue through popular sovereignty were embarrassed. The Supreme Court, which was supposed to settle constitutional issues, had now deepened the nation's divisions and moved the nation's politics to the brink of war.

The Lecompton Constitution.

To make matters worse, the trouble in Kansas boiled up again. In November 1857 a convention met at the small town of Lecompton to draw up a constitution under which Kansas might come into the Union as a state. Most of the delegates favored slavery, since the Free-Soilers had refused to take part in the election of delegates. They had feared that proslavery men from Missouri would cross the border and vote illegally. The proslavery convention, realizing that the constitution they framed might be rejected in a popular vote, allowed a popular vote only on the question of whether the constitution would be adopted "with slavery" or "without slavery." If it was adopted with slavery, slaves might be brought into Kansas without limit. If without slavery, then no more slaves could be brought in. In either case the 200 slaves already in Kansas would remain slaves.

The Free-Soilers refused to go to the polls to vote on this tricky proposition. The result was that the Lecompton Constitution was adopted with slavery. It was clear, however, that the great majority of the people of Kansas did not want slavery. When a newly elected legislature submitted the Lecompton Constitution *as a whole* to the people, the Kansas voters (this time with the proslavery forces not voting) rejected it on January 4, 1858. The Free-Soil vote was much greater than the slavery vote had been.

Douglas breaks with Buchanan.

President Buchanan had pledged himself in his inaugural address "to secure to every resident inhabitant of Kansas the free and independent expression of his opinion" on the subject of slavery. But now, in spite of the fact that the voters had just rejected the Lecompton Constitution, he sent it to Congress. He asked that Kansas be admitted as a slave state. Despite the advice of the governor whom he had appointed for the Kansas Territory that the constitution was a "fraud," Buchanan called on party loyalists to support its adoption.

This was simply too much for Douglas, who had staked his political future on the doctrine of popular sovereignty. He immediately protested the Lecompton Constitution as a "travesty and mockery" of popular sovereignty. Douglas wanted a new constitution to be framed in Kansas and then submitted to an honest vote of the people there. The government had no right to force either slavery or freedom upon them. That was a question they should decide for themselves.

Buchanan used all the force of the Presidency to induce Congress to admit Kansas as a state with the Lecompton Constitution. He even withdrew all official patronage from Douglas. But the plucky Illinois senator fought back. He joined forces with the Free-Soil Republicans to defeat the admission of Kansas under the Lecompton Constitution. Kansas remained a territory until the withdrawal of the southern members of Congress on the eve of the Civil War. On January 29, 1861, Kansas was finally admitted as a free state.

Lincoln against Douglas.

Douglas's second term as senator was now about to expire. So he returned to Illinois in the summer of 1858 to seek reelection. His Republican rival was a self-educated lawyer from Springfield who had served four terms in the Illinois legislature, one term in the Congress, and had already been defeated once before in his try for the United States Senate. His name was Abraham Lincoln. A former Whig, Lincoln had joined the new Republican party on the Kansas-Nebraska issue and had risen to be their leading politician in Illinois. But he was still unknown to the nation. When Lincoln announced against the famous Douglas, who had caught the national spotlight during his fifteen continual years in the Congress, there was little doubt who would win. No one could predict that this campaign would set Lincoln on the path to his great career as hero and symbol of what was most American.

Douglas believed that the free and slave states could continue to live together in peace. He cared not at all whether slavery was "voted up or voted down." Lincoln was certain that slavery was a moral wrong. In his acceptance speech in June 1858, at the Illinois convention that nominated him as the Republican candidate for senator, Lincoln said:

"A house divided against itself cannot stand." I believe this government cannot endure permanently half slave and half free. I do not expect the Union to be dissolved—I do not expect the house to fall—but I do expect it will cease to be divided. It will become all one thing, or all the other.

The Lincoln-Douglas debates, 1858. On Lincoln's challenge, Douglas agreed to a series of debates. The difference between the candidates was striking. Douglas was scarcely five feet in height, thickset, quick, volcanic in speech and in gesture. Lincoln, six feet four, lank and awkward, was a superb stump speaker. Slow, hesitant, and thoughtful at first, he captured his audience and carried it with him to share his beliefs.

Douglas kept referring to Lincoln's "house divided" speech as an incitement to civil strife. He contrasted the fairness, the democracy, and the "Americanism" of his own policy of "popular sovereignty." Lincoln, on the other hand, insisted that the territories be kept free from slavery. He denounced the Dred Scott decision as a southern conspiracy. At the same time he made it clear that he did not want to interfere with slavery in those states where it was established.

The high point of the debates was reached at Freeport, Illinois, on August 27. There Lincoln asked Douglas whether the people of a territory could lawfully exclude slavery before they had become a state. Douglas was caught on the horns of a dilemma. If he answered "Yes," he would seem to defy the Dred Scott decision. If he answered "No," he would oppose his own doctrine of "popular sovereignty."

Douglas tried to find a way to support both. Even though the Supreme Court had decided that slavery was lawful in a territory, the institution "could not exist anywhere for a day or an hour," he said, without the support of "local police regulations."

This was Douglas's famous "Freeport Doctrine." It was his way of evading the central, moral

National Portrait Gallery, Smithsonian Institution

This miniature was painted of Abraham Lincoln in 1860. Lincoln said that the portrait was "an excellent one. To my unpracticed eye, it is without fault."

issue of slavery. By failing to pass laws for the protection of slavery, he said, the legislature of any territory could in fact exclude it. Lincoln challenged: "Then a thing may be legally driven away from a place where it has a legal right to be."

In those days senators were not elected by popular ballot. Douglas won by eight votes in the Illinois legislature. But his Freeport Doctrine had made him many enemies in the South. Southerners would oppose his nomination for President on the Democratic ticket. At the same time he had helped make a national reputation for Abraham Lincoln.

John Brown's raid, 1859. At this time a man made of the stuff of saints and martyrs produced a drama that underlined all the worst fears of the South. John Brown, who had led the Pottawatomie massacre in Kansas, now decided that he would invade the South, arm the slaves, and let them fight for their own freedom. The most famous of black abolitionists, the eloquent Frederick Douglass, gave Brown some advice but refused to join him. And when Brown talked to a colony of fugitive slaves in Chatham, Ontario, he could not persuade them to join him either.

But Brown pursued his wild plan. In October 1859 with his little band of 22 followers (17 white and 5 black) he seized the United States arsenal at Harpers Ferry, Virginia. Then, raiding the estates of a few nearby planters, the party forcibly "freed" about 30 slaves. Taking these reluctant people with them, Brown and his men retreated to the arsenal. Ironically, the first person to die in the affair—killed by John Brown and his men—was an already-free black gunned down by these "liberators."

The countryside immediately rose against the "invasion." Five of Brown's followers escaped, but the rest were trapped in the arsenal, surrounded as it was by rivers and mountains. A detachment of United States Marines commanded by Colonel Robert E. Lee arrived on the scene. After battering down the doors, they easily made captives of the seven surviving members of Brown's band. The remaining ten had been killed or mortally wounded in the raid. The survivors, including two blacks, were all hanged by the state of Virginia for their part in the raid.

Brown, who had been only slightly wounded, was promptly tried in a state court for treason to Virginia. That was his finest hour. After being sentenced to be hanged, he said, "Now if it is deemed necessary that I should forfeit my life for the furtherance of the ends of justice and mingle my blood . . . with the blood of millions in the slave country whose rights are disregarded by wicked, cruel, and unjust enactments, I say let it be done." One month later, John Brown was a corpse on the gallows. But his spirit marched on. Celebrated in song and legend, the impractical John Brown, who had not the force to hold a single arsenal, became a spirit leading thousands to risk their lives against slavery. Emerson compared him to Christ on the cross.

No other single event alarmed white Southerners more than Brown's deed. In their eyes his rash exploit at Harpers Ferry seemed part of a widespread abolitionist plot, supported by the "black" Republican party, to incite slave rebellion throughout the South.

SECTION REVIEW

1. Identify or explain: Dred Scott, Roger B. Taney, Lecompton Constitution, Freeport Doctrine, Harpers Ferry.
2. Why might the young Republican party have been encouraged by the election results in 1856?
3. How did the Dred Scott decision widen the split between North and South?
4. Why did Douglas break with Buchanan?
5. How did Lincoln and Douglas differ on the issue of the extension of slavery? How did his "Freeport Doctrine" hurt Douglas?
6. What were the effects of John Brown's raid?

4. The election of 1860

As late as 1860, some people still thought the nation might avoid a civil war. Even if Americans could not agree on the issues, maybe they still could agree on a man. Perhaps the right American President—a man elected by all the people—could hold the Union together.

When the presidential election year of 1860 approached, the Democrats were still a national party. A tug-of-war was going on inside their party, but they still had support all over the country. If only the political battle could be fought out *inside* the party! Then perhaps there would be no more need for John Browns, no more Bleeding Kansas! Perhaps free debate—a battle of words—and friendly compromises at the party convention could settle matters. Perhaps the politicians from the North and South would stick together (as politicians often do) in order to be able eventually to share the rewards of a political victory. Could the good-natured game of politics take the place of the bloody game of war?

The Democrats divide. When the political parties met in their national conventions during the spring and summer of 1860, it quickly appeared that politics was not the road to reunion. By an evil fate the convention of the Democratic party was scheduled to meet at a traditional capital of the slave-holding South, Charleston, South Carolina. There the southern delegates demanded that the party declare its support for slavery in the territories. Douglas and other Northerners rejected this proposal. Bitter arguments followed. When Northerners finally refused to adopt the southern program, the delegates from eight southern states left the convention.

The great Democratic party was coming apart. The convention adjourned, and after a month it met again (without the delegates of the eight southern states). Then yet another group of Southerners withdrew. What was still left of the Democratic party, of course, was not a national party at all. As its candidate for President of the United States this northern remnant nominated Senator Stephen A. Douglas of Illinois.

The southern Democrats who had left the convention gathered at Richmond, Virginia. There they named their own candidate, John C. Breckinridge of Kentucky, who was then Vice-President of the United States. He believed in protecting slavery, and he thought states had a right to secede. The damage was done! Even the "national" political parties were no longer national.

Constitutional-Unionists and Republicans. The Constitutional-Union party also appeared. It was made up chiefly of former Whigs and Know-Nothings, conservatives who feared the breakup of the Union if the Republican candidate was elected. This party sought to avoid the slavery issue entirely and ran on a single-plank platform for "the Constitution of the country, the Union of the states, and the enforcement of the laws." John Bell of Tennessee and Edward Everett of Massachusetts carried its standard.

The main opposition to the Democrats, however, was the six-year-old Republican party. The antislavery party of the West and the North, it had been founded for the very purpose of opposing the spread of slavery. Still vainly hoping for some national appeal, the Republicans named one of the most conservative men they could find in their party. He had not made any radical statements, and he sounded like the soul of easygoing common sense. Abraham Lincoln, nicknamed "The Rail-Splitter," came from Illinois.

"Honest Abe." At the moment when the nation was coming apart, it was a stroke of rare good luck that Lincoln happened to be here. For there never was a better symbol of all America. Lincoln's own life was a capsule history of the whole nation. His restless family had come from England to New England and then to Pennsylvania. Lincoln's great-grandfather had lived in Virginia, where he had five sons. Four of them moved west. In 1786 Lincoln's grandfather, who had gone to Kentucky, was killed by Indians while clearing his farmland in the forest. There in Kentucky Abraham's father was raised, and there the future President was born in 1809.

Unlike other "log-cabin" candidates before him, Lincoln really was born in a log cabin. When he was only seven, his family moved again—on to Indiana. And when he was twenty-one, he moved with them once more, still farther west to Illinois. Working his way up in the world, he did a little of everything. He built a flatboat and navigated it down the Mississippi to New Orleans. For a while he worked as a surveyor, managed a mill, ran a country store, and served as a village postmaster. He was elected captain of the militia that chased Chief Black Hawk and his Indians back into the Wisconsin wilderness.

This oil painting showing a beardless Lincoln splitting rails was done about 1858.

Lincoln educated himself, and made himself into a lawyer. He was especially successful before juries. His political career had been brief and not impressive. After serving in the Illinois legislature, he had one term in Congress (1847–1849), where he opposed the Mexican War. Then in 1858 he was defeated for the United States Senate by the much better known Stephen A. Douglas.

Lincoln had magic in his speech. With his slow backwoods drawl, using the simple words of the Bible, he uttered the wisdom of a cracker-barrel philosopher. He sometimes told slightly vulgar jokes, and yet he had the uplift power of a first-class preacher. He spoke the way the average man could imagine himself speaking.

On the slavery issue Lincoln was firm, but he was no fire-eater. He was no abolitionist. In his debates against Douglas in 1858 he showed that he was about as conservative as an antislavery man could be. He tried to narrow down the whole slavery question into how to prevent slavery from spreading westward into the territories.

Himself of southern ancestry, and married to a Southerner, he did not hate the South. He believed in making every possible concession—short of allowing the spread of slavery. If anyone could have held the Union together, it would have been Lincoln. If an Abraham Lincoln—with Lincoln's shrewdness, with his charity, with his generous understanding of the South and its problems, with his feeling for compromise—could not do it, the Union was surely beyond the help of politics.

Lincoln is elected.

The fateful presidential election of November 1860 confirmed fears that there were no longer any *national* parties. It convinced the South that their hope was not in words but in weapons. From ten southern states, Lincoln received not a single electoral vote. In the electoral college, Lincoln carried all eighteen free states, and Breckinridge carried eleven slave states. Douglas received many popular votes in the North, but carried only Missouri and a minority of New Jersey's split electoral vote. John Bell, the Constitutional-Union candidate from Tennessee, carried three border slave states.

Although Lincoln easily won in the electoral college (with 180 votes to 123 for all the others), he received only 39 percent of the popular vote. This was the smallest proportion ever for a successful candidate and far less even than many unsuccessful candidates had won. His opponents all together had received nearly a million votes more than Lincoln. But strangely, Lincoln would have won even if the votes for the other candidates had been combined, for he received his votes in just the right states.

When word of Lincoln's election reached South Carolina, that state seceded from the Union. It was quickly joined by six other states from the lower South: Mississippi, Florida, Alabama, Georgia, Louisiana, and Texas. Each state declared its own independence. Then their delegates met in Montgomery, Alabama, in February 1861, even before Lincoln was inaugurated. They wrote a new constitution and announced that a new nation, the Confederate States of America, was born.

Attempts to prevent war.

Meanwhile confusion reigned in Washington. President Buchanan did not know what to do. He hoped that his term might come to an end before the storm broke. He believed secession was illegal. But he also thought the government had no right to compel a state to remain in the Union. Northern abolitionists such as William Lloyd Garrison were glad to see the "sinful" South separate itself from the Union. Pacifists like Horace Greeley, editor of the influential *New York Tribune,* would let the cotton states "go in peace" rather than engage in a war to "pin" them to the rest of the states "by bayonets."

In Congress even after the election, during December of 1860, desperate last-minute attempts were made to work out another compromise between the sections. Senator John J. Crittenden of Kentucky proposed a set of "unamendable amendments" to the Constitution. The most important of these would extend the Missouri Compromise line of 36°30' to California as the dividing line between slavery and free soil. It would forbid the federal government ever to interfere with slavery in the states.

But the Republicans, on orders from President-elect Lincoln, held firmly to their refusal to allow slavery to go into any territories, even below 36°30'. Lincoln was convinced this would only lead to attempts to seize more territory south of the line in order to make more slave states. So the compromise—a compromise the South probably would have accepted—was defeated by the votes of

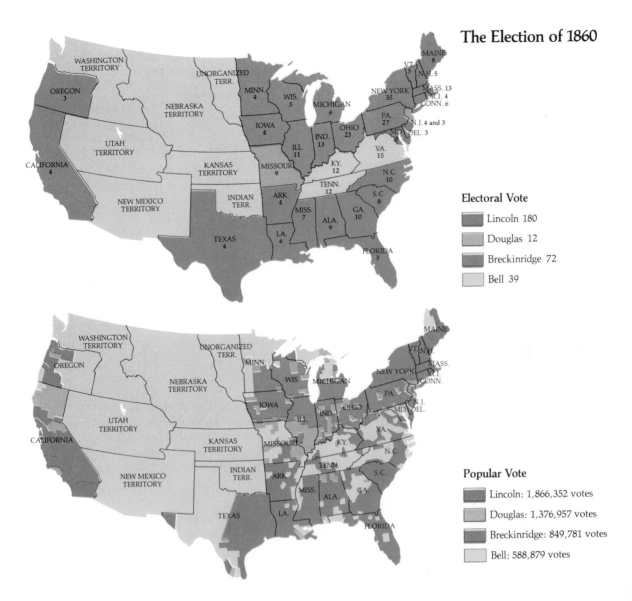

The Election of 1860

Electoral Vote
- Lincoln 180
- Douglas 12
- Breckinridge 72
- Bell 39

Popular Vote
- Lincoln: 1,866,352 votes
- Douglas: 1,376,957 votes
- Breckinridge: 849,781 votes
- Bell: 588,879 votes

the Republicans. They had heard the threats of the southern hotheads for so many years. They believed a confession of northern weakness would simply encourage the Southerners to make even bolder demands. The North must stand firm. If it did, they believed, many southern Unionists would flock to the Union banner and form common cause against the secessionists.

Lincoln faces a crisis. The Confederate States of America viewed the United States as a foreign nation. The seceded states therefore could no longer allow the United States to keep its arsenals and forts inside their borders. Using their own state troops, they at once began seizing federal posts. To avoid bloodshed, United States troops gave up all but a few strong positions. One of the strongest was a place right in Charleston Harbor called Fort Sumter.

As soon as Lincoln was inaugurated, on March 4, 1861, he had to make one of the great decisions in American history. He discovered that if Fort Sumter did not receive food soon, it would have to surrender. What should he do? Should he let the South have Fort Sumter and go its own way? That would mean no civil war. But it would also mean the end of the Union. Or should he send the needed supplies and risk a fight that might go on for

A job for the new Cabinet-maker.

In this 1860 cartoon Lincoln as repairman seeks to bind North and South together once again with "union glue."

A Currier and Ives lithograph showed the shelling of Fort Sumter in 1861. Nathaniel Currier and James M. Ives became partners in 1857. Their lithographs were popular when photographs were rare and in black and white.

years to keep all the states inside one great nation?

Lincoln decided to stand firm for the Union. He would not give up Fort Sumter. He would fight if necessary. But he would let the South fire the first shot. He notified South Carolina that he was sending supplies to Fort Sumter. South Carolina then decided to take the fort. At 4:20 A.M. on April 12, 1861, Confederate General P. G. T. Beauregard, a West Point graduate who had once fought for the Union in the Mexican War, began bombarding Fort Sumter from the Charleston shore batteries. At 2:30 the next afternoon Major Robert Anderson, also a West Point graduate who had fought alongside Beauregard in the Mexican War, surrendered the fort. No one had been wounded, but war had begun. The first, the quickest, and the most bloodless battle of the war was over. It was not a fair sample of what was to come.

SECTION REVIEW

1. Identify: John C. Breckinridge, John Bell, Black Hawk, John J. Crittenden, Fort Sumter, P. G. T. Beauregard, Robert Anderson.
2. How did Lincoln and his family typify the nation's history?
3. How did Lincoln manage to win in 1860 with only 39 percent of the popular vote?
4. Describe the founding of the Confederacy.
5. What attempts were made to prevent war?
6. What was the situation at Fort Sumter? How did Lincoln handle it?

CHAPTER REVIEW

MEETING OUR EARLIER SELVES

1. Some optimists saw the Compromise of 1850 as a "final solution" to the slavery issue. Name at least two features of the Compromise that would keep it from being a solution.
2. Some Northerners not opposed to slavery in the South wanted to keep it out of northern states and territories? Why?
3. Show the influence of the slavery issue on the presidential elections from 1848 to 1860. Consider the choice of candidates, party platforms and slogans, and the rise of splinter parties.

4. How did each of the following further inflame the slavery issue: Mexican Cession, Wilmot Proviso, Fugitive Slave Act, *Uncle Tom's Cabin,* Ostend Manifesto, raids in Kansas, attack on Charles Sumner, Dred Scott decision, Lecompton Constitution, John Brown's raid on Harpers Ferry?

QUESTIONS FOR TODAY

1. Has any political issue since 1960 aroused feelings as intense as those over slavery? Did the issue lend itself to a compromise solution? What efforts were made to seek a compromise? Did the issue give rise to any violent or illegal activities?
2. Do our two major parties today make special efforts to assure that they will have a national appeal? If so, how do they do this?

YOUR REGION IN HISTORY

1. If your state was in the Union in the 1850s, who were its political leaders? What role did they play in trying to resolve the slavery issue?
2. What important events in your state took place in the 1850s? Which, if any, of these events were linked to the slavery issue?
3. How would a person from your locality probably have tried to go to California in 1849 to prospect for gold?

SKILLS TO MAKE OUR PAST VIVID

1. Prepare an outline for a speech defending or opposing the doctrine of popular sovereignty as the way to resolve the issue of slavery in the territories.
2. Read several pages of *Uncle Tom's Cabin* and jot down words or phrases that would tend to arouse strong feelings on the slavery issue.
3. Prepare a vertical timeline of the 1850s. On one side of the line record events that proslavery people would regard as good news. On the other side write events that seemed to favor the antislavery cause.
4. Explain the cartoons in this chapter by telling whom the cartoonist is praising or criticizing, by pointing out the symbols used, and by suggesting a title for each.

5

The rocky road to Union 1860–1890

Abraham Lincoln, at the end of his Second Inaugural Address on March 4, 1865, movingly summed up the meaning of the nation's four years of bloody civil war. And he forecast the hopes and the problems of the postwar years:

> *Fondly do we hope, fervently do we pray, that this mighty scourge of war may speedily pass away. Yet, if God wills that it continue until all the wealth piled by the bondsman's two hundred and fifty years of unrequited toil shall be sunk, and until every drop of blood drawn with the lash shall be paid by another drawn with the sword, as was said three thousand years ago, so still it must be said, "The judgments of the Lord are true and righteous altogether."*
>
> *With malice toward none, with charity for all, with firmness in the right as God gives us to see the right, let us strive on to finish the work we are in, to bind up the nation's wounds, to care for him who shall have borne the battle and for his widow and his orphan, to do all which may achieve and cherish a just and lasting peace among ourselves and with all nations.*

Yankee snipers aim at a party of Confederates in this detail of an 1862 oil painting by Albert Bierstadt, from The Century Association, New York.

CHAPTER 13

The Civil War

The American Civil War was not quite like any war that had ever happened before. Half a nation fought against the other half over the freedom of a small minority. This itself was something new. It was as new, as strenuous, and as unpredictable as everything else in America. Leaving more than 600,000 dead, the Civil War would be the bloodiest in all American history—and the bloodiest war in the whole world during the nineteenth century. Of every ten men who fought, four became casualties (dead or wounded). No other modern nation paid so high a price to hold itself together.

Southerners did not see themselves simply as slave owners fighting to preserve their property, or as rebels trying to tear the Union apart. Instead they imagined they were fighting the American Revolution all over again. White Southerners, they said, were oppressed by Yankee tyrants. The people of the South were now playing the role of the gallant American colonists. Northerners were the oppressive British, and Abraham Lincoln was another George III. If the British government had no right to force American colonists to stay inside their empire, why did the United States government have any right to force Southern states to stay inside the Union?

Southerners said they were fighting for self-government. One flaw in this argument was that it left out the whole question of slavery. Self-government—*for* whom and *by* whom? White Southerners who said they were fighting for their own right to govern themselves were also fighting *against* the right of millions of blacks to have any control over their own lives. Of course, Calhoun and other defenders of slavery had not seen it quite that way. Self-government, they said, was for white people only.

1. A new kind of war

Shocked by the fall of Fort Sumter, Northerners sprang into action. President Lincoln at once called for 75,000 militia to help put down what he termed an insurrection. With Lincoln's call for troops the states of the upper South seceded. They had hesitated to leave the Union, but they felt they could not fight against the other Southern states. The North and the South now hastened to prepare for war.

The sides compared. The two sides were vastly different from each other. If we ignore Maryland, Kentucky, and Missouri, which were still in doubt, the Union had 20 million people. The Confederacy had 9 million, which included 3.6 million slaves. In other resources the North was way ahead, too. It had 22,000 miles of railroad tracks to the South's 9000. It had far more factories and factory workers, more money, more bank credit, more ships, more locomotives, more steel and iron, more farm machinery, more firearms. The North grew many kinds of crops, while the South was glutted with a few staples—tobacco, cotton, and rice—which it had to export in order to obtain all the things it lacked.

The North also had lots of labor-saving devices like the reaper to free men for the army, while the South depended for labor on its slaves. These slaves might at any moment turn out to be a "fifth column"—an enemy force behind the lines—because they had very good reasons for helping the North. Every third Southerner was black. White Southerners therefore lived in fear of a civil war all their own—if the blacks ever decided to take up arms.

Because Southerners did not see slaves as people, they also failed to use them well in the war. Even if it seemed too dangerous to give slaves arms, they might have helped in the army as a labor force and so have released whites to fight. The North, on the other hand, decided in December 1862 to use blacks in its armed forces. It was strengthened by more than 185,000 who fought on its side.

Worst of all for the South, it suffered from delusions which prevented it from seeing the facts. Southerners believed that the North was so divided that it would not be able to put up a strong fight. In fact, Southerners were astonished that any power on earth dared make war on the world's greatest producer of cotton. They had long told themselves "Cotton is King," and they believed Great Britain and France would break the Northern blockade and come to the South's aid just to get the cotton needed to keep their textile factories going. The South imagined too that only Southerners were civilized and that one Southerner "could whip a half-dozen Yankees and not half try." The South's grandiose dreams turned into nightmares.

In the end the substantial advantages of the North would produce victory. The South, unable to replace its losses of equipment, would finally die of economic strangulation. But it was a very near thing. The South came close to victory too many times for anyone to say that the leaders of the Confederacy should have foreseen the result.

The "short war." When Southerners said that they merely wanted to secede from the Union, they also gave themselves a military advantage. To win their point all they had to do was to declare their independence and go their own way. On the other hand, the North would have to *force* the Southern states to stay in the Union. The North would have to invade the South, occupy it, and subjugate it. The North had to attack.

At the beginning, many Northerners optimistically called it "the six months' war." They expected it to be over in short order. For the North seemed stronger in every way. Also the military men had been taught that the attacking army always had a great advantage. The textbooks used at West Point explained that the way to succeed was to mass your forces, invade the enemy's land, and win the war by a decisive battle or the decisive capture of the enemy's capital.

The rifle. The old-fashioned weapons had given almost no advantage to the defenders. For the old smoothbore flintlock musket (which was standard equipment in the British army during the Revolution and in European armies even later) was inaccurate. It had a short range, and it was slow to reload. That meant that the attacking forces could come very close before the defenders could shoot them down, and most of them would get through before they could be hit. If, as the Union generals at first imagined, the North could only keep the advantage of the attack, they could win a few decisive battles, capture the enemy capital at Richmond, Virginia, and then the war would be over.

These generals were wrong, though some never realized it. The war lasted four blood-soaked years. This new warfare would be as different from earlier American wars as an elephant is different from a mosquito.

A number of great changes made the difference. While the standard British weapon in the American Revolution was the flintlock musket, many American backwoodsmen had begun using the rifle. But it was not until the Civil War that the rifle became the standard American army weapon. All the textbooks that the Civil War generals had read at West Point came from the earlier age of the smoothbore flintlock.

The rifle was so called because the inside of its barrel was "rifled"—cut with spiral grooves. Then when the bullet was pushed out, it was set spinning. This gave it a longer range (500 yards instead of 50 yards) and a much more accurate aim. Another improvement was the "caplock," which used a new chemical (fulminate of mercury) enclosed in a cap to make the explosion that sent the bullet. The caplock was reliable even when the old flintlock—which struck a piece of flint against steel to make a spark—would not have worked because of wet weather. Also the old muskets had been "muzzle loaders," but some of the new rifles were "breech-loaders." This meant they loaded more quickly from the back near the trigger.

Soldiers learn to dig in. Now, with their accurate long-range rifles, the defenders sat protected behind battlements in well-supplied positions. They could pick off the attackers before they even came close. They could fire again and again because of the range of their weapons. The attacking force then had to keep moving. If they stopped to reload, they were sitting ducks.

Virginia State Travel Service

The accurate long-range rifle made defensive positions all-important. Confederate troops defended this wall near Fredericksburg in some of the bloodiest fighting of the war in 1862. The elaborate fortifications below were erected near Atlanta in 1864.

Library of Congress

In time the generals would learn that armies could no longer confront each other in solid ranks. Everyone had to take cover. Attackers had to spread out into small parties of skirmishers to make more dispersed targets. Now the "Indian" tactics, which Americans had used with success in the Revolution, would become common. Attacking soldiers had to make instant forts—of logs, bales of hay, rocks, anything in sight—so that they could get some of the advantages of defenders.

Most important, soldiers learned to make the earth itself into a fort by using the spade. This was the start of trench warfare. In the old days, generals thought it made soldiers cowardly to hide in a hole in the ground. Now the soldiers had no choice. When General Robert E. Lee ordered his men in the Army of Northern Virginia to work hard at digging trenches, at first they laughed at him as the "King of Spades." But they soon thanked him for giving them protection against enemy rifles. The spade was now as important as the gun.

The importance of railroads.

The attacking army had to carry enormous supplies of ammunition, food, and bandages. It had to build its own fortifications as it advanced. The railroad, which had never been used much in wars before, was now a great help. But once the supplies left the rails, they still had to be carried by horse or mule over bumpy roads, through mud, and across streams.

In this kind of warfare, railroads were lifelines. They were slow and hard to build, but quick and easy to cut. If you could cut the rails, the enemy would eventually have to stop fighting. The Civil War therefore became more and more a war aimed at the enemy's communication lines. The first Battle of Bull Run (July 1861) was still very much like the old-fashioned warfare, with solid lines of soldiers standing up against each other to fight a "decisive" battle. By the time of the Battle of Petersburg three years later, the Union army was aiming at the Confederate railroads.

The war of exhaustion.

This new kind of warfare was a war of exhaustion. It was not enough to cut off the enemy's supplies by railroad. You also had to stop supplies from coming in by water. The ocean and the Gulf of Mexico surrounded the Southern states. They had few deep-water ports, but there were many places on the 3500-mile coast where supplies could be landed. The South still had many highways to the world. The North therefore had to capture or blockade the Southern ports and coast if the South was to be strangled.

The South did wonders with small fast ships which constantly pierced the blockade at many points. Still the scores of Union ships offshore made it difficult for the South to export cotton and kept large merchant ships or Confederate naval vessels from reaching Southern ports.

The war of exhaustion hit everybody in the South, civilians as well as the military. The same ships that would have brought arms and ammunition to the armies also would have brought locomotives for the railroads, machinery for the factories, food and clothing and medical supplies for all. The Northern blockade against the South worked slowly but it worked surely. People called it the "Conda" after the anaconda, a huge snake that kills its prey by squeezing.

The war of exhaustion was slow. It was not won by a few knockout blows like the Battle of Waterloo, but by slowly taking away everything the South needed. In this war all the enemy's resources had to be destroyed until the will to resist was gone. European experts, who had never seen this kind of war before, began to think it was not a war at all. One Prussian general in 1864 sneered that he would not even study the battles of the war because they were nothing but "the combats of two armed mobs." Another Old World critic compared the North and South to two lunatics playing chess—both knew a few moves, yet neither understood the game.

But this kind of war was no longer a game. The old rules of war which the generals had learned at West Point were not of much use. This was all-out war, with no holds barred. The winning generals turned out to be those, like U. S. Grant, who had never believed the old rules, or those, like William T. Sherman, who were good at forgetting them.

Everybody's war.

The Civil War was everybody's war. In both the North and the South nearly every family lost a soldier. And in quite new ways the gore was brought into every home. For the first time in history, the battles were thoroughly covered by newspaper correspondents. They telegraphed back eyewitness accounts so that civilians could read the horrors next morning at breakfast.

The Union man-o-war (left) is shown overtaking a Confederate blockade runner in this oil painting. Rather than surrender, blockade runners sometimes ran their ships aground in the hope that part of the cargo might be carried ashore.

The *New York Herald* alone once had forty men in the field, and spent a half-million dollars on them. Northern reporters, who would have been shot as spies if discovered, smuggled themselves behind Southern lines disguised as women or as Confederate soldiers. When some generals objected that the newspapers were giving away valuable information to the enemy, the *New York World* protested that this was a "people's war."

The pioneer photographer Mathew Brady and his large crew took photographs at the risk of their lives and sent them back home to show everyone the battle action. Soldiers sometimes ran away from Brady's camera because they had never seen a camera before and imagined it to be a new kind of gun. Brady's photographic buggy, which soldiers called the "What-is-it?", was a conspicuous target. On several occasions, Brady barely escaped being killed.

Women at war. In the "people's war" women played a new and important part. Dorothea Dix, the courageous New Englander who had braved public opinion before (p. 233), arrived in Washington right behind the first troops. On June 10, 1861, she was appointed the first Superintendent of Women Nurses with the job of selecting and assigning women to hospitals. It took gumption to find any place for women in the army, and she was the pioneer.

Louisa May Alcott, later to make her name as the author of *Little Women*, came to Washington and worked in a hospital for Miss Dix until illness forced her to leave. She was appalled when the first group of dirty, injured soldiers appeared. But, she wrote, "I drowned my scruples in my washbowl, clutched my soap manfully, and, assuming a business-like air, made a dab at the first dirty specimen I saw." Luckily, he was a cheery Irishman, and with a good

Women played an important role in nursing the wounded on both sides. Clara Barton (top) helped the injured on the battlefield and later founded the American Red Cross. Harriet Douglas Wheaton (bottom left) served on hospital ships sailing from New York and Philadelphia. Sallie Tompkins (right) received a commission as a captain in the Confederate army for her work.

279

THE RECRUITING QUESTION—A HINT TO RAILCAR COMPANIES.

FASCINATING CONDUCTRESS of City Car (to surprised Passenger)—"Yes! you see my good man has gone to the war, and as the Company continue half his wages, I've come along to earn the other half—hurry up, sir, if you please."

This drawing suggested a way women might be employed on streetcars during the war.

deal of laughter the job was done. Louisa May Alcott went more confidently on to her next patient.

Clara Barton, one of the first female clerks in Washington, left her job to help the injured troops. So began a career of caring for the sick and the wounded that lasted throughout the war. Clara Barton was never an official in the war effort. As a volunteer this brave woman brought food, bandages, and supplies to the wounded out on the battlefield. Then, for four years after the war, she was in charge of the search for missing Union soldiers. She identified thousands of graves at the Confederate prisoner-of-war camp at Andersonville, Georgia. In 1877 Clara Barton founded and became president of the American Red Cross. It would serve the nation and the world in later wars.

Women helped set up the voluntary United States Sanitary Commission. It assisted the military by creating hospitals, caring for the injured, promoting sanitation in military camps, and distributing all kinds of supplies "from currant wine to canton flannel underwear" to the troops. Supplies and money for this ambitious program were raised by women's groups throughout the Union.

Female clerks were rare in 1860, but that too changed with wartime. Soon there were large numbers of women in the Treasury Department, while others worked at the government printing plants or made cartridges in the arsenal and the navy yard. Women were usually paid less for this work than men, and several times groups of women went on strike for higher pay.

In the South, as well, women did many jobs in the government. They too made cartridges in munitions factories. They nursed the wounded in hospitals, and sewed soldiers' clothes or rolled bandages at home. "Ladies who never worked before," one Southern woman observed, "are hard at work making uniforms and tents."

In North and South, as the men went off to war, women had to take over businesses, farms, and plantations. Some women were so anxious to do their part in the war that several hundred of them pretended to be men and served in the ranks as soldiers wearing men's uniforms until they were discovered.

The border states. Like the generals, the political leaders of the opposing sides had to be able to forget peacetime rules. And here Lincoln was wiser than the Confederate president, Jefferson Davis. When the war began, Lincoln was not even sure who was on his side or whether Washington could be held. The city was surrounded on three sides by Maryland, a slave state. If Maryland seceded, Washington would be lost. When the first Union troops, the 6th Massachusetts militia regiment, passed through on their way to protect the capital, they were mobbed. Four soldiers were killed.

Lincoln now showed his instinctive grasp of the deeper meaning of the conflict for this nation. He felt that the Constitution could not contain the seeds of its own destruction. If he had to bend the Constitution in order to save the Constitution and the Union, he would do so. If he hesitated or retreated from the harsh words of Southern sympathizers in the North, the Union might be lost before a battle was fought.

So Lincoln moved swiftly. He imposed martial law in Maryland, suppressed newspapers, arrested civilians, and even refused to let them appear before

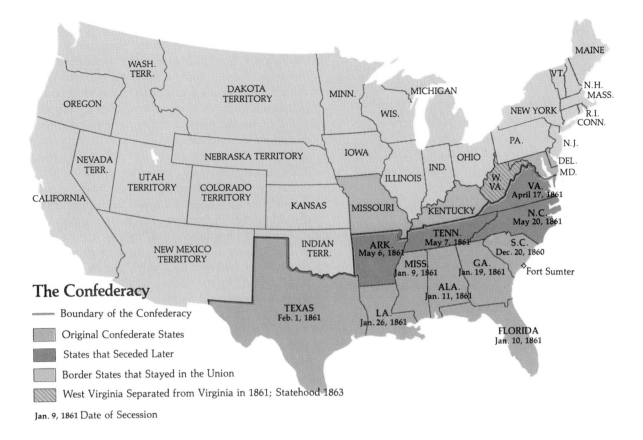

The Confederacy

— Boundary of the Confederacy

Original Confederate States

States that Seceded Later

Border States that Stayed in the Union

West Virginia Separated from Virginia in 1861; Statehood 1863

Jan. 9, 1861 Date of Secession

Map labels:
WASH. TERR.
OREGON
DAKOTA TERRITORY
MINN.
MICHIGAN
MAINE
VT
N.H.
MASS.
NEW YORK
R.I.
CONN.
NEVADA TERR.
NEBRASKA TERRITORY
WIS.
IOWA
OHIO
PA.
N.J.
DEL.
MD.
CALIFORNIA
UTAH TERRITORY
COLORADO TERRITORY
KANSAS
ILLINOIS
IND.
W. VA.
VA. April 17, 1861
NEW MEXICO TERRITORY
INDIAN TERR.
MISSOURI
KENTUCKY
N.C. May 20, 1861
ARK. May 6, 1861
TENN. May 7, 1861
S.C. Dec. 20, 1860
Fort Sumter
MISS. Jan. 9, 1861
GA. Jan. 19, 1861
ALA. Jan. 11, 1861
TEXAS Feb. 1, 1861
LA. Jan. 26, 1861
FLORIDA Jan. 10, 1861

civilian judges to hear why they were being held. This is called suspending the *writ of habeas corpus*. This writ, or court order, gives a judge the power to free a person who is being held illegally or without just cause. It serves to keep people from being held in jail without a fair trial. When Chief Justice Taney issued a writ of habeas corpus for a secessionist named Merryman, the military commander of the area refused to free the man. Taney then issued an opinion that the President had no right to suspend the writ of habeas corpus, only Congress could do that. Lincoln believed that he must act to save the Union—even if he had to break the law to do so. So he ignored Taney's decision.

It was by actions such as these that Maryland was held in the Union and Washington was saved. Union sentiment within the state had time to grow. By June 1861, Maryland was filling its quota of enlistments in the United States Army.

Missouri and Kentucky were crucial too. If they seceded, the Confederate border would be pushed to the Ohio River, and then even southern Illinois might be lost. Lincoln handled each state differently. In Missouri, he moved swiftly to seize control. In Kentucky, he moved slowly in order to allow Union sentiment to develop. The result was the same in both states—they were saved for the Union.

The question of emancipation. Lincoln was a strong leader. As a politician, he knew how important it was, in everybody's war, to keep everybody's support. At the beginning of the war, in order to keep in the Union the border slave states—Delaware, Maryland, Kentucky, and Missouri—he refused to emancipate the slaves. When General Frémont, commander of the Western Department, on August 30, 1861, freed the slaves of rebels in Missouri, Lincoln stepped in firmly and overruled him.

Lincoln's priorities were always clear. Much as he might have liked to free the slaves, his first job was to save the Union. When told that freeing the slaves would put God on the Union side, Lincoln replied, "We would like to have God on our side, but we must have Kentucky."

281

SECTION REVIEW

1. Identify or explain: "war of exhaustion," Mathew Brady, Dorothea Dix, Louisa May Alcott, Clara Barton, Sanitary Commission, writ of habeas corpus, border states, emancipation.

2. What advantages did the North have in the Civil War? the South?

3. How did the rifle give defenders an advantage? How did it make the spade a tool of war?

4. What was the Union strategy with regard to Confederate railroads and seaports?

5. Describe the role of women in the war.

6. How did Lincoln manage to hold the border states in the Union?

2. The first year: 1861–1862

The Civil War was fought mainly in three areas: (1) between Richmond and Washington, (2) in the valley of the Ohio, Cumberland, and Tennessee rivers, and (3) in the Mississippi River valley. The eyes of much of the world were on the classic battle in the East where two great armies maneuvered and fought in the small area between the Potomac and the James rivers and from the Atlantic to the Blue Ridge Mountains. Here the able Southern generals Robert E. Lee and "Stonewall" Jackson, though always outnumbered, faced and usually defeated the poorly led Northern Army of the Potomac in a series of titanic battles. The decisive war, however, took place beyond the Appalachians in the West.

The first Battle of Bull Run (Manassas). Northerners thought the war would be short and easy. They urged General Irvin McDowell to move with the main army of 30,000 men against the rebels, to seize Richmond, and so (they hoped) to end the war quickly. Since McDowell's volunteer troops and militia were not yet properly organized or drilled, and their three months' term of enlistment was about to expire, they had to be strengthened by some units of the regular army. But the Confederates were also untrained. So McDowell, thinking his forces stronger, asked to be allowed to attack.

General Winfield Scott, commander of the United States Army, protested. He outlined to the Cabinet another more long-term plan. He doubted that this war could be won in the lightning stroke of a single battle. Scott offered a plan to blockade the South, to seize New Orleans and the Mississippi River, and so "envelop the insurgent states." In this way, Scott thought, the South could be brought to terms with little bloodshed. He was wrong on the last point, and the strategy would take much longer than he expected. But at age 75, and having served in the army since Jefferson's time, "Old Fuss and Feathers" knew the realities of war. It was his plan, later called the "anaconda," reinforced by some bloody and brutal years of fighting, that would finally bring victory to the North.

The North was not yet ready to face the realities of the military situation. So Scott withdrew his opposition to McDowell's plan for a quick knockout blow to the Southern capital. Lincoln and the Cabinet then agreed to allow McDowell to move forward—"On to Richmond!"

McDowell's "grand army" met General Joseph E. Johnston's force of 22,000 on July 21, 1861, at Manassas Junction, a little town near Bull Run, a creek 35 miles from Washington. The untrained federal troops had the more difficult job of attacking, but they did well until mid-afternoon. Then fresh Confederate troops arrived by train and turned the tide of battle. Shouting loud "rebel yells," the Confederates broke the attack and sent the Federals fleeing in terror back toward Washington. Upon hearing the news of the retreat, hard-driving Southern General Thomas J. Jackson, who earned the name "Stonewall" for the firm stand of his men in the battle, shouted, "Give me 5000 fresh men and I will be in Washington tomorrow." But the disorganized Confederate forces were in no position to seize the strategic moment. Their President Jefferson Davis did not order an advance.

In the long run the South was actually hurt by this first victory. Now the Southerners made the mistake of believing that it would be easy to defeat the North. For the North, on the other hand, the defeat at Bull Run made people realize that the war could not be won in a few days. And they steeled themselves for the hard years ahead.

Command in the East was now turned over to red-haired General George B. McClellan, who was not yet 35 years old. Like most of the generals— North and South—he had gone to West Point and had fought in the Mexican War. He had then used his talents for discipline and organization to help survey the difficult route for the Northern Pacific Railroad through the Cascade Mountains. He had also been a railroad president in the Middle West. Returning to the army at the outbreak of the Civil War, his able command of Union troops in western Virginia had saved for the Union the area that two years later became the state of West Virginia. McClellan insisted on precision in drill and demanded ample supplies for his troops, who trusted and loved him for it. He spent the remainder of 1861 training the Army of the Potomac to meet his high standards of readiness for battle.

The Civil War, 1861-1865

United States

Border States (Slaveholding Union States)

Confederate States

✕ Union Victory

✕ Confederate Victory

0   200 Miles

0   200 Kilometers

The Trent affair. In November 1861 a Union warship stopped the British steamer *Trent* bound for London. Two Confederate diplomats, James M. Mason and John Slidell who had boarded the ship in Cuba, were removed from the vessel. They were on their way to England and France to seek recognition of the Confederacy.

The British people were outraged at this violation by the United States of the freedom of the seas for neutral vessels. Many called for war, and 8000 British troops were rushed to Canada. It was a dangerous moment for the United States, since war with Britain would have made it impossible to conquer the South. Fortunately, President Lincoln and Secretary of State Seward recognized the danger. Mason and Slidell were freed and allowed to continue on their way, and the United States admitted it had acted wrongly. This ended the crisis.

The war in the West. The Tennessee and the Cumberland rivers pointed like pistols at the heart of the Confederacy, while the Mississippi River cut it in two. On these rivers the fate of the Confederate States of America would be decided.

The operations in the West brought to prominence the greatest Union general, Ulysses S. Grant. Also a West Point graduate who had served with credit in the Mexican War, he had resigned from the army in 1854 when he was accused of being a drunk. The outbreak of the Civil War had found him, at the age of 39, working as a clerk in his father's hardware and leather store in Galena, Illinois. Military success was to make him the hero of the Union and later President of the United States.

Grant soon revealed that he had the special talents needed to succeed as a general. He had a genius for seeing the whole scene—and then quickly deciding what needed to be done. He possessed a silent, grim, cool courage and persistence. General Sherman later wrote to Grant, "My only points of doubt [about you as a general] were as to your knowledge of grand strategy, and of books of science and history; but I confess your common sense seems to have supplied this." Perhaps because he was not a "book" soldier, but a man of supreme common sense, Grant recognized early that this was a new kind of war. "The art of war is simple enough," he said. "Find out where your enemy is. Get at him as soon as you can. Strike him as hard as you can, and keep moving on."

Henry, Donelson, and Shiloh. Grant's first successes came in Tennessee. There he showed that by a clever combination with naval forces he could make the riverways of the South serve as highways for Northern victory. Confederate forts guarded the lower Tennessee and Cumberland rivers. On February 6, 1862, with the vital aid of a fleet of ironclad gunboats under Flag Officer A. H. Foote, Grant captured Fort Henry and so opened the Tennessee River all the way to Alabama. Within ten days Foote had taken his gunboats back to the Ohio and up the Cumberland. In another joint military and naval operation, Grant compelled the

This vivid lithograph of the Union charge at Shiloh appeared on the title page of a song.

surrender of Fort Donelson with all its 14,000 defenders. Then defenseless Nashville fell without a blow to another Union army under General D. C. Buell.

Next Grant moved an army of 40,000 men up the Tennessee River to Pittsburg Landing near the Mississippi state border. They kept on moving inland as far as a country meetinghouse called Shiloh Church. Here his men, who had not yet learned to dig defensive positions, were surprised on April 6, 1862, by a Confederate army under the able and experienced General Albert Sidney Johnston, (not a relation of Joseph E. Johnston of Bull Run fame). The Union troops were driven back to the edge of the river, where they dug in and held. The Confederates had won the day, but at a heavy cost. When General Johnston was killed in that battle, they lost one of their boldest and most seasoned military leaders.

Grant was not so easily stopped. The very next day, strengthened by reinforcements, he attacked and drove the Confederate troops from the field. There were appalling losses on both sides—13,000 dead and wounded for the North and 11,000 for the South.

At Shiloh, Grant learned that he was in a war far different from what he had counted on in the beginning. He had thought at first that the rebellion would collapse "suddenly and soon, if a decisive victory could be gained over any of its armies." But he had actually won such victories at Fort Henry and Fort Donelson. Then instead of collapsing, the Southern forces turned around, took the offensive, and nearly defeated him. Now he knew that this would be a war to exhaustion. There would be no Northern victory unless his forces were allowed to "consume everything [in the South] that could be used to support or supply armies."

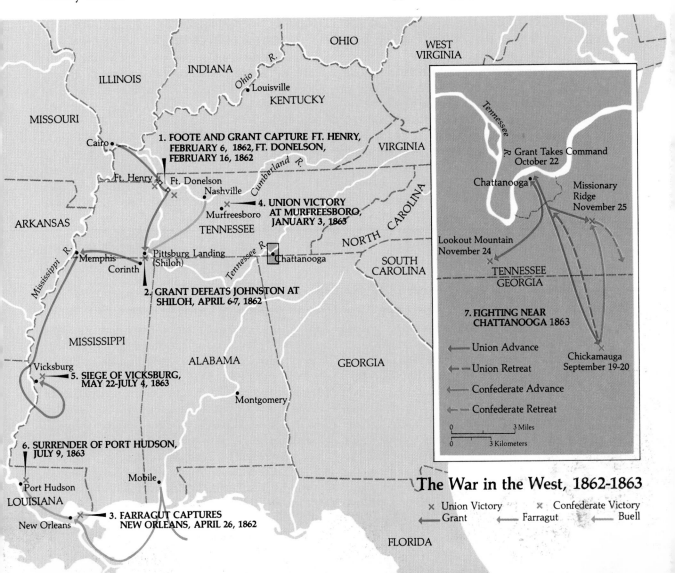

The War in the West, 1862-1863

New Orleans. Meanwhile Foote and General John Pope were working down the Mississippi River, opening it as far as the Confederate bastion at Vicksburg. At the other end of the river a bold move by the amazing David Glasgow Farragut captured New Orleans for the Union.

Farragut, the son of a naval officer, had been commissioned a midshipman at the age of nine. He had seen action in the War of 1812 when he was only eleven. His orders commanded him as he entered the river from the Gulf of Mexico first to capture the two forts at the mouth of the Mississippi that protected New Orleans. But disregarding orders he raced past the two forts (losing only three of his seventeen ships). He defeated an astounded Confederate fleet, sinking eleven of its ships. Then at one blow he seized the coveted prize—New Orleans, queen city of the South. Farragut took the city on April 26, 1862, almost before anyone knew he was in the neighborhood. Now the South could no longer support its troops in the West with supplies brought in from the Gulf of Mexico.

The war in the East. In the East, however, the prospects of the Federal forces were not nearly so rosy. Northern operations were paralyzed by the caution and indecision of General McClellan. He did not move forward. Although he actually commanded an army grown to 180,000 men, which was twice the size of the forces under General Joseph E. Johnston, he still believed he was outnumbered. And he blamed the "imbecile" administration at Washington for not sending him more reinforcements. General Johnston had his men well entrenched on the old Bull Run battlefield.

The Monitor and the Merrimac. While McClellan was hesitating, a historic sea battle was taking place. A new chapter in naval warfare was being opened. On March 8, 1862, a strange-looking ironclad vessel with sloping sides covered by four-inch iron plates and with a powerful iron ram on its bow came steaming out of Norfolk into Hampton Roads to attack the Federal blockading squadron there. This was the C.S.S. *Virginia,* usually known by its old name as the U.S. frigate *Merrimac.* To the astonishment and dismay of Northern sailors, their shots just bounced off her sides. She proceeded to destroy with ease the wooden sailing ships of the Federal fleet—including the 50-gun frigate *Cum-*

berland and the 30-gun sloop *Congress.* When the *Merrimac* returned to Norfolk, it seemed that the next day she would easily destroy the rest of the Federal fleet. Then what would prevent her from going right up the Potomac and shelling the Northern capital?

Before dawn on March 9, however, an even stranger craft steamed into Hampton Roads from the open sea. This was the *Monitor,* one of the small Union ironclads that the clever Secretary of the Navy, Gideon Welles, had ordered early in the war. From the deck of the *Monitor,* which was almost flush with the water, rose a revolving turret within which were two eleven-inch guns. This made the ship look like "a tin can on a shingle." When the seemingly "unbeatable" *Merrimac* appeared later that day, the *Monitor* was there ready for the challenge. A spectacular duel took place in which neither ironclad did much harm to the other. Then the *Merrimac* withdrew again to Norfolk.

The Union blockade of the South was not to be broken. The Confederacy's one day as ruler of the seas was over. And this first fight in history between ironclads marked the end of navies of wooden ships.

The peninsular campaign. After continual prodding by Lincoln, McClellan finally made up his mind to move. Following the West Point textbooks, he decided to try to take Richmond by a classic maneuver. He transported his large and well-equipped army by water to the peninsula between the James and the York rivers. Proceeding slowly, he worked his way to within a few miles of Richmond. The church towers of the town were visible from the Union front lines.

Then McClellan's weakness showed again. Instead of advancing swiftly to fulfill his plan before the enemy could get their bearings, he halted long enough to give the Confederates time to figure out how to beat him. In a series of battles, during which General Joseph E. Johnston was injured and General Robert E. Lee took command, McClellan saved his army from a near defeat. He finally ended up in a strong defensive position—protected by the Union navy and with his back to the James River, but surrounded by Confederate troops.

The Confederate Army of Northern Virginia was now in the command of the tactical genius of

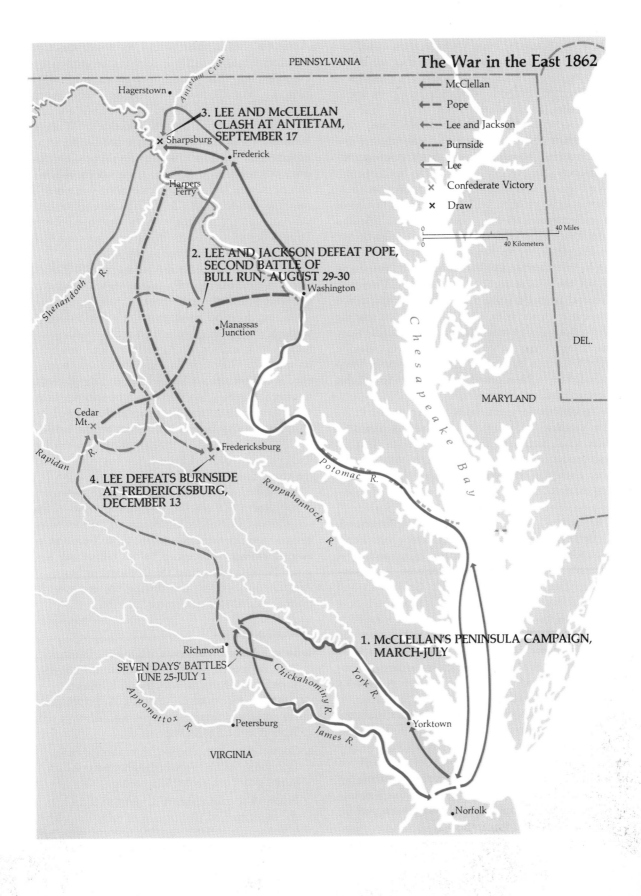

The War in the East 1862

← McClellan
←-- Pope
←- Lee and Jackson
←·-· Burnside
←— Lee
✗ Confederate Victory
✗ Draw

0 — 40 Miles
0 — 40 Kilometers

PENNSYLVANIA

Antietam Creek

Hagerstown •

3. LEE AND McCLELLAN CLASH AT ANTIETAM, SEPTEMBER 17

✗ Sharpsburg

• Frederick

Harpers Ferry

Shenandoah R.

2. LEE AND JACKSON DEFEAT POPE, SECOND BATTLE OF BULL RUN, AUGUST 29-30

✗ Washington

• Manassas Junction

Cedar Mt. ✗

Rapidan R.

• Fredericksburg ✗

4. LEE DEFEATS BURNSIDE AT FREDERICKSBURG, DECEMBER 13

Rappahannock R.

Potomac R.

Chesapeake Bay

MARYLAND

DEL.

Richmond •
✗

SEVEN DAYS' BATTLES JUNE 25-JULY 1

Chickahominy R.

York R.

1. McCLELLAN'S PENINSULA CAMPAIGN, MARCH-JULY

Appomattox R.

• Petersburg

James R.

• Yorktown

VIRGINIA

Norfolk •

287

the Civil War—the man who has been called the greatest general of the age. A man of noble character, Lee felt his first love and first loyalty was for Virginia. But, oddly enough, he was no friend to secession or to slavery.

Robert E. Lee, a true Southern blue blood, was a descendant of one of Virginia's finest families and had married Martha Washington's great granddaughter. He had graduated first in his class from West Point and later served as superintendent there. In his character the honor and the loyalty of a soldier prevailed over everything else. He had commanded the Marines who captured John Brown at Harpers Ferry in 1859. When the Civil War broke out, Captain Lee had been offered command of all the Union forces by his fellow Virginian, General Winfield Scott, under whom he had served brilliantly in the Mexican War. Lee felt that he could not fight against Virginia. When that state asked him in April 1861 to command its armies, he agreed. Then in June President Jefferson Davis called him into Confederate service to be his personal military adviser.

As commanding general of the Army of Northern Virginia, Lee knew that he must act promptly and with daring if the South was to win its independence. Since General Lee's talents were well known in the North, his name there inspired respect and fear.

The second Battle of Bull Run (Manassas).

General McClellan was now replaced. John Pope, who took over the command, had led an army that successfully cleared important points on the Mississippi. Lincoln hoped that this new brash and boastful leader would live up to his boasts and show a boldness that McClellan never had. Before Pope could march on Richmond and "end the war," he was attacked by Lee and Jackson at Bull Run (August 29–30, 1862). There his army was defeated. General Pope was speedily removed and his troops again placed under McClellan.

These reverses stirred resentment against Lincoln and his administration. Enlistments fell off, and desertions increased. People hesitated to buy Union war bonds. The congressional elections were in doubt. England considered recognizing the Confederacy. Southern hopes were high. The tide seemed to have turned for the South. Now perhaps Washington could be captured.

Antietam.

After Bull Run, Lee moved quickly. His army of 55,000 battle-hardened men crossed the Potomac into Maryland on September 4, 1862. Singing "Maryland, My Maryland," his troops expected soon to be joined by Southern friends. But somehow no one came to join them. When a Federal force at Harpers Ferry was not evacuated as expected, Lee divided his army and sent a unit to drive out the Union troops. Then a copy of Lee's orders, showing where his soldiers were located, fell into the hands of McClellan. If McClellan had moved rapidly, he might have destroyed Lee's army. But as usual, McClellan took his time and gave the enemy the chance to organize.

The two forces met at Sharpsburg, near Antietam Creek. Lee was heavily outnumbered, and the Potomac River was at his back.

All day long on September 17, in the bloodiest battle of an appallingly bloody war, the battle lines moved back and forth. At nightfall, Lee still held his position. The next day, although badly weakened, Lee's men faced McClellan's and dared them to attack. Once again, McClellan hesitated. That night Lee crossed the Potomac and returned to Virginia, leaving behind 2700 dead on the battlefield. The Union had lost 2100 killed. Each army had more than 9000 wounded. For both sides it was the worst single day of the war.

The battle, so far, was a draw, but Lee's invasion of the North had reached its farthest point. This was the high tide of the Confederacy. When news of Antietam reached England, the British decided to await further developments before taking any action. Never again would the Confederate States of America be so close to receiving the recognition from abroad that it desperately needed.

SECTION REVIEW

1. Identify or explain: Irvin McDowell, Winfield Scott, anaconda policy, J. E. Johnston, Thomas J. Jackson, George B. McClellan, Ulysses S. Grant, A. H. Foote, D. C. Buell, A. S. Johnston, David Glasgow Farragut, *Merrimac, Monitor,* Robert E. Lee, John Pope.

2. Locate: Manassas Junction, Fort Henry, Fort Donelson, Shiloh, Vicksburg, Hampton Roads, James and York rivers, Sharpsburg.

3. List six key engagements in 1861–1862 and tell the outcome and significance of each.

3. The widening conflict

Abraham Lincoln had long been under pressure to make the war into a crusade against slavery. But he had resisted. To Horace Greeley, whose newspaper strongly criticized him for not freeing the slaves, Lincoln had written in August 1862:

My paramount object in this struggle *is* to save the Union, and is *not* either to save or destroy Slavery. If I could save the Union without freeing *any* slave, I would do it; and if I could save it by freeing *all* the slaves, I would do it; and if I could do it by freeing some and leaving others alone, I would also do that. What I do about Slavery and the colored race, I do because I believe it helps to save this Union; and what I forbear, I forbear because I do *not* believe it would help to save the Union.

Abraham Lincoln and slavery. For putting the Union ahead of everything else, Lincoln has sometimes been criticized. But there is no doubt that Lincoln felt deeply that slavery was "a moral, social, and political wrong." He said:

Let us discard all this quibbling about this man and the other man—this race and that race and the other race being inferior and therefore they must be placed in an inferior position. . . . Let us discard all these things and unite as one people throughout this land, until we shall once more stand up and declare that all men are created equal.

Abraham Lincoln was every inch a politician. He was not a crusader. The passionate reformers—the John Browns and William Lloyd Garrisons—also had their role. The nation needed them, too, if it was to fulfill its mission as "the last best hope of earth." Lincoln realized that his job was not to express his feelings but to shape the real world. The people of the North had entered the war mainly because of their love of the Union. Lincoln knew that if the South were allowed to secede and become a nation based on slavery, all would be lost. In the long run only if the Union was saved would the reformers in the North be able to abolish slavery in the South. While the result of the Civil War was still in doubt, Lincoln realized that people cared more deeply for morals than for politics. As the casualties increased, he saw that the North would have to pay a high price in blood and tears. To pay that price they would have to be persuaded that this was a war against slavery.

The Emancipation Proclamation. Lincoln had, in fact, already drafted his *Preliminary* Emancipation Proclamation when he wrote to Horace Greeley in August 1862. But he felt it could not be issued without some kind of victory on the battlefield. He did not want it to look, he later said, like "our last *shriek* on the retreat."

Antietam now gave him his chance. On September 23, 1862, Lincoln issued his Preliminary Emancipation Proclamation. He warned that on January 1, 1863, anyone held as a slave in any state or part of a state where the people were "in rebellion against the United States, shall be then, thenceforward, and forever free."

Neither in this early warning nor even in the Emancipation Proclamation itself, which was issued on January 1, 1863, did Lincoln free a single slave. That would only come with the success of the Union armies. The South viewed Lincoln's proclamation as a "fiend's" act that "destroyed $4 billion worth of property and bid the slaves rise in insurrection." Jefferson Davis said it made reunion "forever impossible."

The North was divided over the proclamation. Abolitionists were delighted—though they regretted that Lincoln had not freed the slaves everywhere. Many Northerners were displeased because they wanted to fight only for the Union. In Europe antislavery feeling was so strong that the Emancipation Proclamation helped to kill any chance of recognition of the Confederacy. Now this was not merely a war for a political Union, but a war against slavery, an evil that had afflicted the world.

Ending slavery. Early in the war Lincoln had attempted to persuade the Union states of Missouri, Kentucky, Maryland, and Delaware to free their slaves and be compensated for it by the federal government. To his great disappointment, he had failed. Congress had approved his plans, and in April 1862 it had abolished slavery in the District of Columbia and provided payments to the owners for the loss of their property. Two months later it had ended slavery in the territories without giving any compensation. But Congress could not do anything about slavery in the states.

"The Emancipation Proclamation," an allegorical painting made about 1863, shows Lincoln holding his proclamation and following the goddess of liberty.

West Virginia entered the Union in 1863 with a constitution that provided for gradual emancipation. Maryland ended slavery in 1864, and a state convention in Missouri abolished it within that state in January 1865. But Delaware and Kentucky refused to act. The peculiar institution lingered in those states until the ratification of the Thirteenth Amendment was completed in December 1865.

Gloom in the North. For a while after Antietam the war did not go well for the North. A new general in the East, Ambrose Burnside, (whose name supplied the word "sideburns"!), showed that he had learned nothing about the new warfare. He attacked Lee's fortified position at Fredericksburg (December 13, 1862). The North suffered 10,000 dead and wounded to fewer than 5000 for the South. Out west, Grant and Sherman also suffered reverses. They had not yet found a way to take Vicksburg. Only in the middle theater, in central Tennessee, did a Union success at Murfreesboro lighten the gloom.

This was a bad time for Lincoln. There were demands that he reorganize his Cabinet. In the fall elections, the Democrats (who were no enthusiasts for the war) gained 32 seats in the House. Defeatism was widespread. Carloads of civilian clothing were being smuggled into the Union lines to aid deserters to escape. Voluntary enlistments fell so low that, in March 1863, the government was forced to pass its first draft law. It made all men between 20 and 45 liable for service in the national forces for a term of three years. But service could be avoided by payment of $300 or by finding a substitute to enlist for three years. The first drawing of names provoked four days of rioting in New York City in July.

The draft provided only a small proportion of total Union troops. More important were the bounties (as high as $1000) paid by federal, state, and local governments for voluntary enlistment. But this system suffered from "bounty jumping," enlisting and deserting again and again. The South had turned to conscription in 1862. But a clause

Union recruiters published posters in German to attract immigrants. American Indians (top right) were photographed as they enlisted in the Union army. The chromolithograph (below) was part of an advertisement published to urge blacks to volunteer for the Union army.

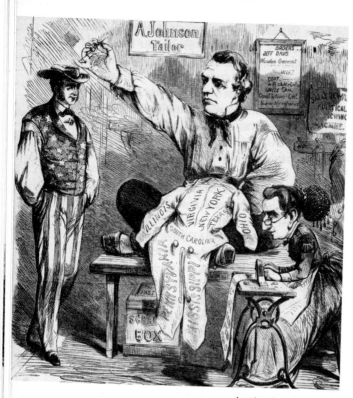

American Antiquarian Society

Andrew Johnson, once a tailor, sews up the Union in this cartoon from about 1865.

2. Andrew Johnson and the Radicals

Andrew Johnson, the new President, was in some ways like Lincoln. Both had been born in the South to poor parents. Both had served in the state legislature and in Congress. With no schooling, Johnson began life as a poor tailor. His wife, Eliza, taught him to write. Though he came from Tennessee, he had stood against secession. As Democratic senator from Tennessee, he was the only Southern senator to support the Union after the Confederates fired on Fort Sumter.

Still, Johnson was no Lincoln. He lacked Lincoln's tact and warmth and wit. He did not know how to use a joke to make a serious point. Just as Lincoln was gentle, generous, and compromising, so Johnson was crude, stubborn, and argumentative. His weaknesses would not have been serious in an ordinary citizen. But in a President they were disastrous.

When Johnson became President in April 1865, Congress was not in session and was not due to meet

again until December. Many Republicans distrusted Johnson because he had been a Democrat. In 1864 they had picked him for Vice-President on their "Union party" ticket, hoping that he would draw Democratic votes.

The Republicans wanted President Johnson to call Congress into special session to make new rules for the South, but he refused. Johnson declared his intention to follow the rules already announced by Lincoln. He alone—not the Congress!—would decide when the Southern states had satisfied Lincoln's requirements and so could govern themselves.

The Southern state conventions. Northerners were impatient to hear the South say "Uncle" and admit their defeat. The Southerners needed to be told what they had to do.

President Johnson now suggested that the Southern conventions gathered under his plan ought to repudiate (refuse to pay) their war debts, nullify their ordinances of secession, and adopt the Thirteenth Amendment freeing the slaves. These conditions were the least the North would accept as a signal that the South knew it was beaten.

But Johnson did not actually demand these terms. So South Carolina repealed rather than nullified its ordinance of secession. This implied that secession had been legal all along. Mississippi refused to adopt the Thirteenth Amendment. Instead, it announced that the slaves were free by the force of Northern arms. South Carolina and Mississippi refused to repudiate their wartime debts. Lacking firm direction from Andrew Johnson, those Southerners who were willing to give in and start life anew felt abandoned. Meanwhile the Southern fire-eaters—the extremists—were gaining strength.

The "Black Codes." Northerners were disturbed by the action of these Southern state conventions. They were even more shocked when the legislatures of the new state governments, at their first meetings, promptly adopted "Black Codes." These were based on old slave codes, Northern vagrancy laws, and laws passed in the British West Indies after emancipation was enacted there. These laws were supposed to provide for the new situation of the blacks now that they were no longer slaves. The laws strictly limited the freedom of the blacks. They could not vote. They were not allowed to

This store in Richmond, Virginia, was decorated to celebrate "Liberation Day," the anniversary of the Emancipation Proclamation.

marry whites. In some states they could be witnesses only in trials involving other blacks.

Many former slaves were using their newfound freedom to travel about and see something of the nation. This did not suit white planters who wanted to grow cotton again. So the Black Codes restricted the newly freed people to agricultural jobs or domestic service. And to keep them hard at work, harsh vagrancy laws were passed. Then they could not look for a new kind of job. In Mississippi, for example, if a black man was convicted of being a "vagrant"—a wandering person without a job—he could be fined $50. If he could not pay the fine, he could be hired out against his will to anybody who would pay the fine in return for his labor.

Northerners began to wonder if their young men had died in a Civil War merely to preserve slavery under a new name.

Confederates elected to office. On top of all this, the Southern states proceeded to elect important former Confederates to Congress. Instead of opposing this and warning the South of Northern reactions, President Johnson pardoned these men of the crime of rebellion after they had been elected to Congress.

By the time Congress met in December 1865, Andrew Johnson, a Democrat and a former slave owner, had been President for seven months. All the old Confederate states except Texas had formed new governments. In Washington, waiting to take their seats in Congress, were former leaders of the Confederacy. Among them were the Vice-President, six Cabinet members, 58 members of the Confederate Congress, and a number of high-ranking army officers. In no Southern state had steps been taken to give blacks the vote. Instead a new

Before long, certain Old Confederates in the South had organized a secret army. Its purpose was to carry on the Civil War under another name. Although slavery was abolished by law, many Southerners still hoped to preserve as much as possible of their former way of life.

This secret army called itself the Ku Klux Klan—from the Greek word *kyklos,* meaning circle. Soon many branches, or circles, appeared all over the South. Klan members traveled the countryside flogging, maiming, and sometimes killing blacks who tried to vote or who in other ways presumed to be the white man's equal. The Klan uniform was a pointed hat with a white hood to conceal the face, and a long white or black robe.

Scores of other organizations joined in the bloody work—the Tennessee Pale Faces, the Louisiana

The viper Ku Klux Klan, about to devour the messenger dove sent by the goddess of Peace, destroys chances for reconciliation.

American Antiquarian Society

KU KLUX

Knights of the White Camelia, the North Carolina White Brotherhood, the Mississippi Society of the White Rose, the Texas Knights of the Rising Sun, the Red Jackets, and the Knights of the Black Cross. In 1871 alone, in a single county in Florida, 163 blacks were murdered, and around New Orleans the murders came to over 300. These organizations kept the lists of their members secret to save them from punishment for their crimes. Thousands of blacks were driven from their homes, maimed, or tortured. Whole communities were terrorized by masked thugs on parade, by burning crosses, by kidnapping and tar-and-feathering.

Under pressure from Northern Radical Republicans, some Southern states passed laws against these outrages. On December 5, 1870, President U. S. Grant delivered a special message to Congress. "The free exercise of franchise," he warned, "has by violence and intimidation been denied to citizens of several of the States lately in rebellion." Congress then passed the Ku Klux Klan Acts to outlaw these organizations and to protect all citizens. But these laws had little effect. The state governments set up in the South by the Radical Republican Congress were replaced by old-fashioned Southern state governments. Confederate heroes were back in charge. Despite all the bloodshed of the Civil War, land and factories were still owned by white Southerners.

The work that first had been done by terrorists was now done "legally" by the state governments. Although the Southern states had approved the Civil War amendments (Thirteenth, Fourteenth, and Fifteenth) to the Constitution, although they had abolished slavery and their laws "guaranteed" the blacks their rights in the South, all these guarantees proved to be mere technicalities. Before long it was plain that slavery itself was just about the only thing the Civil War had abolished.

Thaddeus Stevens died in 1868, and soon enough his avenging spirit—along with his special concern for the rights of black people—was dead. Now more and more Northerners were anxious to "leave the South alone." In practice this meant putting the South back in the hands of white Southerners. And the South then remained divided into the same two nations—a "superior" race and an "inferior" race.

The South would not really become united with the rest of the United States until the South itself had become one. And this would take time.

312

1. Identify or explain: Joint Committee of Fifteen, Command of the Army Act, Tenure of Office Act, impeachment process, Grant, Seymour, scalawags, carpetbaggers, Ku Klux Klan, Civil War amendments.

2. What did the Southern states under military rule have to do to rejoin the Union?

3. What "illegal" act led to Johnson's impeachment? How did the trial turn out?

4. Describe the election of 1868.

5. What were some provisions of the new Southern state constitutions?

6. How did some white Southerners fight back against Radical Republican rule in their states?

4. The North withdraws

In the election of 1872, Grant ran for a second term against Horace Greeley, the candidate of the Democrats and of a new Liberal Republican party. Greeley was the editor of the *New York Tribune*. He was best known for his advice, "Go West, young man, go West!" Right there in New York City, Greeley himself had found it possible to be a pioneer. He had organized the printers on his newspaper into a union. He had stood against slavery and championed women's rights.

But the nation was in no mood for reform. President Grant was easily reelected. Then his troubles began. Although Grant could pick the best lieutenants on the battlefield, in the world of politics he was as gullible as a child. He was an honest man himself, but he could not recognize crooks even when they appeared in his own Cabinet.

The Crédit Mobilier scandal. Soon after Grant's reelection, the first of a string of major government scandals broke. The transcontinental railroad had been authorized by Congress in 1862. The Union Pacific Railroad was to build westward from Omaha while the Central Pacific worked eastward from Sacramento. To build its part, the Union Pacific founded another company named the Crédit Mobilier of America. Using federal funds, the Union Pacific paid the Crédit Mobilier Company huge fees for work done—or not done. The Union Pacific officers, who were also the owners of Crédit Mobilier, made enormous sums from this swindle.

To persuade Congress not to look into the situation too closely, Vice-President Schuyler Colfax, Representative James A. Garfield (later to be President), and several other members of Congress were bribed with Crédit Mobilier stock. All this had taken place, in fact, before Grant became President. But Grant's administration was blackened by the exposures, which supported a growing popular belief that all politicians were crooks.

Other scandals. The same year of the Crédit Mobilier exposures, 1873, there occurred the notorious "salary grab." Greedy congressmen voted themselves a 50 percent increase in salary. On top of that they made it apply to the two preceding years. They also raised the pay of Supreme Court justices. The President, who signed the bill into law, had his salary doubled from $25,000 to $50,000. Under the Constitution a President's salary may not be increased during the term for which he has been elected. Grant avoided this provision by signing the bill the day before his second term began. The public outcry against the

Uncle Sam has a hard time reaching the bottom of the barrel in this Thomas Nast cartoon on the scandals under Grant. Rings of corrupt officials hold the barrel together.

Culver Pictures

IN FOR IT.
U. S. "I hope I shall get to the bottom soon."

salary grab brought about its repeal—except for the increases for the President and the Supreme Court.

The following year brought the whiskey frauds. A large number of distillers conspired with Treasury officers to avoid the tax on whiskey. They cheated the government out of hundreds of thousands of dollars.

Scandal even reached into Grant's Cabinet. The Secretary of the Navy was shown to have received favors from men who stood to win government contracts. The Secretary of War, W. W. Belknap, was impeached by the House in 1876. He was accused of accepting bribes from a War Department agent charged with providing supplies to the Indians. He was saved from conviction in his trial by the Senate only because Grant was tricked into allowing him to resign.

The panic of 1873. Along with scandal and corruption, the country suffered a severe financial panic. After the war, the rapid growth of railroads and factories had strained the nation's financial resources. Two major fires—in Chicago in 1871 and in Boston the next year—cost insurance companies $273 million, and laid a colossal burden on these pillars of the financial community. The collapse of Jay Cooke's investment firm, which had put too much of its money in railroad construction, began the panic in 1873.

Soon a full-scale depression, one of the worst in the nation's history, was under way. It lasted for five years, shutting down mills and factories, bankrupting railroads, closing banks, bringing unemployment and starvation to thousands of workers, and spreading despair across the country.

The disputed election of 1876. Under this cloud of depression and scandal the Republicans were badly beaten in the congressional elections of 1874. A large majority of Democrats won seats in the House, giving them control for the first time since the Civil War. No longer could the Republicans win elections by "waving the bloody shirt" of war.

In their convention of 1876, the Republicans passed over their "Plumed Knight," the eloquent Speaker of the House James G. Blaine of Maine. He was suspected of granting illegal favors to a railroad, and in the climate of the times this made him an impossible choice. Instead, they picked a little-known Union general, Rutherford B. Hayes, who

Museum of the City of New York (detail)

The Boston Fire of 1872 was stopped near the State House, atop Beacon Hill, on the right of this Currier and Ives lithograph.

had built a solid reputation as a reform governor of Ohio. He was an honest man with moderate views on the Southern issue.

The Democrats named Governor Samuel J. Tilden of New York. He had an even more impressive reform record than Hayes, for it was his political courage and cleverness as a lawyer that had exposed the Tweed Ring. "Boss Tweed," a self-made, warmhearted man, had used Tammany Hall, a clique inside the Democratic party, to become the

most powerful politician in New York City. He and his friends stole more than $45 million by having contractors on city jobs charge double what the work actually cost and then having the extra amount paid over to them. Tilden was helped to destroy the Tweed Ring by Thomas Nast, a clever German-born cartoonist. Nast stirred up outrage against Tweed by his drawings in *Harper's Weekly* showing Tweed as a vulture or a fat, rich thief. Nast kept up his attacks even after Tweed offered him $500,000 to stop.

The 1876 election campaign was one of the most bitter in United States history. The Democrats saw a good chance to gain the Presidency for the first time since 1860, and the Republicans fought to retain power. The finale was even more exciting because the electoral votes were so close. Late in the evening of election day it appeared that Tilden had been chosen. He had carried states with 184 votes—only one less than a majority. Hayes had 165. Then came confusion. The three Southern states (South Carolina, Louisiana, and Florida) that were still ruled by Republicans sent in two sets of returns. The Republican set certified that Hayes electors had been chosen. The Democratic set said that a majority of the state votes had been cast for Tilden. Also Oregon had one disputed vote. In all, 20 electoral votes were in question.

October 21, 1871

Boss Tweed's head is a moneybag in this Nast cartoon. Thomas Nast made Tweed's diamond tiepin famous.

There was no provision in the Constitution or any law of Congress for deciding which set of returns was legal. The Constitution simply says (Amendment XII), "The president of the Senate shall, in the presence of the Senate and the House of Representatives, open all the certificates, and the votes shall then be counted." The president of the Senate was a Republican. If he had the right to choose which set of votes he would *count,* as well as "open," he would naturally take the Hayes votes and declare him elected by a vote of 185 to 184. If, however, the disputed votes were thrown out, or even one of them counted for Tilden, he would be elected President.

The electoral commission. A few weeks before the date for inaugurating a new President, Congress created a commission of fifteen members—five representatives, five senators, and five members of the Supreme Court—to determine which of the disputed returns should be accepted. It turned out that the commission included seven Republicans, seven Democrats, and one independent, Justice David Davis of Illinois. But then Davis was elected to the Senate, and a new justice had to be chosen. As there were only Republican members left on the Supreme Court to choose from, the commission was finally made up of eight Republicans and seven Democrats. It was no surprise, when the commission counted the disputed electoral votes, that it split along party lines and announced that Hayes had 185 to Tilden's 184.

The compromise of 1877. The crisis was not yet over. The nation seemed once again on the verge of civil war. Both houses of Congress had to approve the commission's report before a President could take office. Since the Democrats controlled the House of Representatives, they could prevent a Hayes victory. But a group of conservative Southern Democrats there, seeing the chance to use the crisis for their political advantage, had meanwhile been talking with spokesmen for Hayes. For the first time in many years, the politicians were trying the art of compromise.

The upshot was an agreement that these Southerners would break with their party and vote to accept the commission's report. In return, Hayes would grant four favors. (1) The last federal troops would leave the South. This would mean the end of the Radical Republican state governments in Florida, Louisiana, and South Carolina. (2) At least one Southerner would get a post in the Cabinet. (3) Hayes would give conservative Southern Democrats control of part of the local patronage. (4) He would support generous spending for internal improvements in the South.

On March 2, only two days before Inauguration Day, the conservative Southern Democrats voted with the Republicans to approve the commission's report. The Republican Senate of course at once agreed, and the crisis at last was over.

In April 1877, after only a month in office, President Hayes withdrew the last of the federal troops from the South. In May he decorated the graves of the Confederate dead at Chattanooga. But "reconciliation" between the whites of the North and of the South—the end of Reconstruction—only occurred because the North no longer cared to protect the rights of black Southerners.

Tilden had actually won a large majority of the popular votes, and he knew that he had been cheated out of the nation's highest office. But he proved a good patriot and a good sport. He treated the whole matter as settled and retired from politics. When he died in 1886, he left his fortune to found the great New York Public Library.

SECTION REVIEW

1. Identify or explain: Horace Greeley, Crédit Mobilier, "salary grab," W. W. Belknap, James G. Blaine, Rutherford B. Hayes, Samuel Tilden, Tweed Ring, Thomas Nast, electoral commission.

2. Describe the scandals of the Grant administration.

3. What factors led to the panic of 1873? How did it and the scandals affect the 1874 elections?

4. How was the disputed election of 1876 settled? What bargain was made by Hayes?

5. Abandoning the blacks

Peace and reunion had brought an end to slavery. But the roots of slavery ran deep. They reached into every nook and cranny of Southern life.

One of its roots was racism—the belief that one race was naturally better than another. This belief had helped keep slavery alive. At the same time slavery had kept racism alive. Under slavery, nearly all blacks in the South did lowly tasks. Therefore, it was easy for white people—and sometimes even for the blacks themselves—to believe that God had meant it that way.

Slavery could be abolished simply by changing laws. But it was much harder to abolish the belief that one race was better than another. Many generations of Southerners had taught that to their children. After the war, it was still rooted in their minds and hearts.

And after the war it became clearer and clearer that the South was still split into two "nations." Much of the time these two "nations" lived at peace. Some of the time they lived in a nervous truce. Occasionally they were actually at war. Obviously the United States could not be truly united until the races ceased to be divided. And while this was a national problem, at first it belonged largely to the South because most blacks lived there.

Black voting. When Hayes withdrew the federal troops from South Carolina and Louisiana, the last of the Reconstruction governments finally collapsed. (Florida's had already fallen.) This did not mean that throughout the South blacks no longer voted or held office, or that segregation ("Jim Crow") laws suddenly appeared. It took time for the white South to come to a fixed conclusion about the place of blacks in Southern society.

Most white Southerners assumed that blacks were inferior. At the same time, many Old Confederates believed that they had a responsibility to the blacks. They believed that the "superior" white and the "inferior" black could work together to the advantage of both. So there were attempts by conservatives to bring blacks into the Democratic party. Blacks continued to hold political office in both state and nation. There were black members in every Congress but one from 1877 to 1900.

The rise of "Jim Crow" laws. Segregation was practiced in the new public schools of every Southern state except Mississippi and South Carolina from the beginning. But blacks and whites shared trains, hotels, and other public places. Then more and more in the 1880s informal segregation began to appear. At last, with the drive to remove blacks as a political force during the Populist period (p. 528), there also came new segregation laws.

The expression "Jim Crow" to describe the forced segregation of the races originated in a popular old minstrel song. Some white Southerners were shocked by the Jim Crow laws. One sensible South Carolina editor showed how absurd the whole idea was:

> If there must be Jim Crow cars on the railroads, there should be Jim Crow cars on the street railroads, also on passenger boats. . . . If there are to be Jim Crow cars, moreover, there should be Jim Crow waiting saloons at all stations, and Jim Crow eating houses. . . . There should be Jim Crow sections of the jury box, and a separate Jim Crow dock and witness stand in every court—and a separate Bible for every colored witness to kiss.

The Supreme Court approves "Jim Crow." What this editor ridiculed soon came to pass. And when "Jim Crow" became a reality, surprisingly few in the North or in the federal government spoke out against it. The Supreme Court, in 1896, in the case of *Plessy* v. *Ferguson* actually approved segregated facilities that were "separate but equal." The majority even argued that if blacks saw this as "a badge of inferiority" it was "solely because the colored race chooses to put that construction upon it." Justice John Marshall Harlan, a Kentuckian, spoke out in a bold dissent. He "regretted that this high tribunal . . . has reached the conclusion that it is competent for a state to regulate the enjoyment by citizens of their rights solely upon the basis of race."

The problem, of course, was that there really could never be such a thing as "separate but equal" facilities for the two races. When any race was kept apart from another, it was deprived of its equality— which meant its right to be treated like all other citizens. And the slogan became an excuse for providing inferior schools and washrooms and everything else for the race regarded as inferior.

Few blacks received any land after they were freed. Most had no choice but to go to work for whites. Since few whites had any cash after the war—or wanted to spend it if they had any—the system known as sharecropping soon appeared. A black or white family would be given a section of land to cultivate and then allowed to keep a share of whatever they grew while they paid the rest as rent. Ideally, this would have meant that in a good year the sharecropper would have received a share of the extra profits.

In fact, after the Civil War there were few good years. The price of cotton stayed low until 1900. Sharecroppers earned barely enough to stay alive. In bad years they could not even buy groceries. So to feed their families they borrowed from their landlord or from the local storekeeper. The landlord and the storekeeper, in turn, often had to borrow at high rates of interest. To repay their own debts, they made the sharecropper stop growing food and instead plant a crop that could be sold for cash. In practice this meant cotton. As a result landowner, storekeeper, and sharecropper were all kept in bondage to that piece of land and to that single crop.

The Reconstruction scorecard. Radical Reconstruction had increased white Southerners' fears of blacks. It had also helped to make the Two-Nation South into a One-Party South. When the Old Confederates once again took charge of the Southern states, they had no love for the Republican party. That was the party of Yankees, the party

"The Cotton Pickers," painted in oil by Winslow Homer in 1876, shows an endless field ready for harvesting. Homer tried to capture the true look of outdoor light.

that had made war on the South and had then ruled the South with an army. By controlling the state governments, the Confederate heroes gave new strength to their old Democratic party.

The Radical Republicans had seen the evil of slavery. But they had not seen that the roots of slavery could not be pulled up in a year or two—nor perhaps even in a generation. Still, they had attempted to deal with the question of the place of blacks in the Southern states. The new, more liberal constitutions that Radical Reconstruction brought to the Southern states actually benefited the poor of both races. They laid the foundation of free public education for whites as well as blacks. Reconstruction gave the blacks a new role in political life—and valuable political experience. It was under Reconstruction that the Fourteenth and Fifteenth amendments were passed. And these would become the bulwark of equal rights.

SECTION REVIEW

1. What is racism? How did it continue to split the South into two "nations"?
2. What were "Jim Crow" laws? What effect did they have on some early attempts to treat black people fairly?
3. Why was the *Plessy* v. *Ferguson* case important?
4. What groups of people did sharecropping keep "in bondage"? How did it do so?

CHAPTER REVIEW

MEETING OUR EARLIER SELVES

1. Show that the Reconstruction policies of Congress were motivated (a) by a desire for vengeance, (b) by concerns for the rights and welfare of black Southerners, and (c) by political party ambitions.
2. With the advantage of hindsight, list and defend four or more provisions of a model Reconstruction Act for getting the Southern states back into the Union and back on their feet.
3. Was it reasonable for Northern leaders to try to exclude the Old Confederate leaders from leadership positions? Why? How might their exclusion have affected the South?
4. Explain the term "Radical Reconstruction." How did it both harm and help Southerners?

5. How was the treatment of black Southerners by 1890 similar to and different from their treatment in 1850?

QUESTIONS FOR TODAY

1. Name some laws and Supreme Court decisions of the past 30 years that overturned the Jim Crow laws and other enforced segregation.
2. How might the civil rights struggle of the past 30 years have been different if the Supreme Court in 1896 had nullified state segregation laws?

YOUR REGION IN HISTORY

1. If you live in one of the former Confederate states, make a time line of important events in Reconstruction history (1865–1877) in your state.
2. What political leaders, if any, of your state played a role in the Reconstruction era? Describe what they did.

SKILLS TO MAKE OUR PAST VIVID

1. Make a chart showing the key provisions of the Reconstruction plans of (a) Lincoln, (b) the Wade-Davis bill, and (c) the military district plan finally adopted by Congress. Next to each plan write its advantages and disadvantages from the point of view of (1) white Southerners, (2) black Southerners, and (3) Radical Republicans.
2. Draw a vertical timeline from 1860 to 1895. On one side list major events that Southern blacks would view as helpful, and on the other side list events that blacks would consider harmful.
3. Draw a cartoon expressing the view on military reconstruction of a Southern black or of an Old Confederate.

Chapter 15

The passing of the frontier

By the time of the Civil War, more than two centuries after the first colonist arrived in New England, half the nation's land was still nearly empty. The frontier—a ragged line of settlements from the East—ran through part of Minnesota, along the border of Iowa, Missouri, and Arkansas and then swung westward into Texas. Reaching in from the West Coast there was also a thin line of settlement in California, Oregon, and Washington. Between these two frontiers there were only a few islands of settlers, such as the Mormons in Utah, the miners in Colorado, and the Mexican Americans in New Mexico. Even in the "settled" areas on the edge of the open land, it was often a long way between neighbors.

In that vast open space between the two frontiers there lay an empire. A land as large as all the rest of the occupied United States. A half-known land as large as all of western Europe. It had often been passed through by trappers hunting furs, miners seeking gold, and settlers hurrying on to California, Washington, and Oregon. But the highest mountains were still unclimbed, the swiftest rivers still unmapped.

During and after the Civil War, the American people pushed into the unknown. They settled the land even before it was discovered by the explorers, geographers, painters, and naturalists. And the fact of settlement before discovery allowed Americans to dream big dreams. It fostered an optimistic, competitive, booster spirit. It produced a new kind of American. The Go-Getter out there helped find and develop the riches of the new American empire. New American ways of life were invented by a wide assortment of Go-Getters—cattle ranchers and cowboys, miners, farmers and their families.

1. Indian wars and resettlement

Today the Old West is a place of romance—the scene for an exciting book, or movie, or TV program. But for a long time the West between California and the Missouri River was a place to avoid. Until just before the Civil War the area between the line of settlement in the East and the Rocky Mountains was marked on maps as the "Great American Desert." In 1856 the *North American Review* described the area of plains and

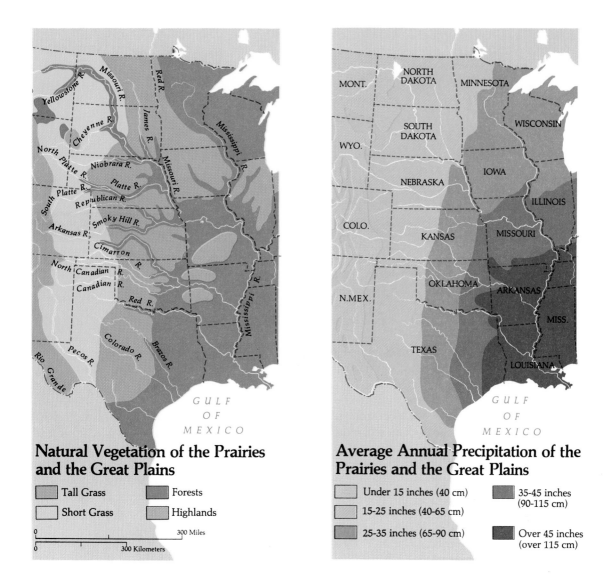

Natural Vegetation of the Prairies and the Great Plains

- Tall Grass
- Short Grass
- Forests
- Highlands

0 — 300 Miles
0 — 300 Kilometers

Average Annual Precipitation of the Prairies and the Great Plains

- Under 15 inches (40 cm)
- 15-25 inches (40-65 cm)
- 25-35 inches (65-90 cm)
- 35-45 inches (90-115 cm)
- Over 45 inches (over 115 cm)

mountains between California and Iowa as "a country destined to remain forever an uninhabited waste." Yet this area included some of the richest grasslands in the world. And it was not deserted. Thousands of Indians made their living off the land which was still the home of millions of buffalo.

In time, cattle ranchers, cowboys, miners, farm families, soldiers, and railroad construction crews would all begin to move into or through the Great Plains and the mountains. Then they would come face to face again with the land's first occupants—the Indians.

The Indians of the Great Plains. Spread over the whole inland empire between the frontiers were some 225,000 American Indians. Of these, perhaps half were the fierce occupants of the Great Plains. Seldom have people adapted more perfectly to their environment. The buffalo was the basis of the Indians' way of life. This was the American name for a shaggy kind of ox technically called the bison, which had also once roamed Europe but was no longer common there. It gave them food, clothing, shelter, and fuel.

When Europeans first reached the Great Plains, they had only single-shot long rifles. They were no match for the Plains Indians. Wonderfully at home on horseback, an Indian warrior could hold on by his heel and use the horse's body as a shield while he fired a barrage of arrows under his horse's neck.

Jules Tavernier, a French immigrant who was for many years an illustrator for *Harper's Weekly*, painted "Indian Camp at Dawn" while on a cross-country trip in the 1870s.

Carrying a short bow, he could shoot twenty arrows while galloping a distance equal to three football fields. His shield of buffalo hide was so hard that a bullet could pass through only if it hit straight on.

Not until Samuel Colt invented the six-shooter—a revolver designed to hold six bullets at a single loading—did the white invader have a weapon equal to the Indians'. Even then, according to General William Tecumseh Sherman, 3000 United States soldiers could be halted by 50 Indians.

The old Indian policy.

Beginning in the 1820s the government's policy was to push the eastern Indians westward across the Mississippi River. Let the Indians live on the "Great American Desert"! That would be their "one big reservation." If the land was not good enough for white settlers—or if white settlers did not have the skills to make their living there—leave it to the Indians!

In the 1850s (although they never planned it that way) white men, women, and children began to move into these areas once reserved for Indians. Some settled in Kansas and Nebraska, others moved on to Oregon, and still others went from place to place searching for gold. At first, the army in the West tried only to keep the trails open so that settlers, traders, trappers, and miners could travel across the land. Forts were built across the plains and treaties arranged with Indian tribes. Still the Indians, desperate to stop the invasion of their lands, organized deadly raids on the settlers and their wagon trains.

At the same time, numerous tribes who had lived for centuries on the edge of the plains were persuaded to give up their lands and move west. This stirred discontent among the tribes already there. Times were ripe for war.

Indian wars and a new policy.

Although there were some good government agents who wanted to help the Indians, many were inept and some were corrupt. Supplies promised the Indians were often slow to reach them. The Sioux went on the warpath in 1862 because they had not received the regular payments they expected and so were unable to buy food.

The many conflicts of the following years led the government to rethink its Indian policy. In 1865, when there were 25,000 soldiers armed against the Indians, a congressional investigation concluded that a new approach must be found. A Peace Commission sent out west held two large meetings and then signed treaties with the Indians in 1867 and 1868. There the Indians were told that they would be gathered together in large areas that would belong to them and where they were not to be bothered by the whites. Although the Indians did not realize it at the time, these treaties really announced the beginning of the end of the old Indian way of life.

New battles and smaller reservations.

The Indians naturally resisted. So for twenty years after the Civil War the American West was plagued by a quite different kind of war. In one sense it was another kind of civil war—between two groups of Americans both trying to make their living off the North American continent, the earliest settlers against the latest settlers.

White Americans did not understand what the Indians had achieved. With their spears and bows and arrows and different manner of living, they had mastered the ways of the American wilderness. The Indians had learned to get along with nature by following in the footsteps of their forefathers. Most of them lived a wandering way of life because they needed large areas to support even a few people. Against them were the latecomers who had brought with them all the modern equipment of European civilization. In this unequal war it was not hard to predict who would win in the long run.

Before the issue was decided, thousands died and more thousands lived in fear while blood and tears were shed on both sides. The wild American West had become a battlefield. In 1864 a militia force under Colonel John M. Chivington slaughtered about 450 Cheyenne and Arapaho men, women, and children who had thought they were under the protection of the United States. Only a few years later, soldiers under Captain W. J. Fetterman were ambushed by a group of Sioux, and all 92 troopers were killed. It was all-out war.

These battles and many others led to a new policy of even smaller "reservations." Here the Indians were too confined and the lands too unfamiliar for them to carry on their hunting and foraging way of life. No longer could they roam the plains in pursuit of the buffalo or other wild game. Deprived of their ancient ways of making a living, the Indians were forced to look to the United States government. In 1871 the government even ceased dealing with the tribes as independent nations. No more treaties would be made. Now they were considered wards of the state, and they would be dealt with by acts of Congress.

Strangely, the same Congress that was trying to bring equality and integration to the blacks of the South approved the destruction of the Indians. General William T. Sherman, who had done much to free the slaves, now set about either killing the Indians or making them "beg for mercy."

The defeat of the Indians. The next years were marked by many battles until, in 1874, peace finally seemed to have arrived. Then unexpectedly in the Black Hills (an area which had been given to the Indians "forever") gold was discovered. Hordes of settlers rushed in from East and West. Once again the Indians were crowded out. The fearless Sioux under the leadership of Chief Crazy Horse and Chief Sitting Bull made another desperate effort to hold back the flood. This battle in June 1876 came to be called "Custer's Last Stand," because when General George A. Custer got himself trapped near the Little Big Horn River in Montana he and his 264 troopers from the 7th Cavalry were killed to the last man. But it might more accurately have been called the Sioux's Last Stand, for in other battles Crazy Horse was captured, Sitting Bull fled to Canada, and the desolate Sioux were left conquered and leaderless.

The reservation policy produced a saga of Indian courage in the face of overwhelming odds and certain defeat. As the Nez Percés in Oregon were about to go to a new reservation, some whites stole their horses. This provoked a group of young braves to go on the warpath. Chief Joseph, who had wished all along to avoid a fight, now tried to lead his people to safety in Canada.

There followed one of the great stories of the West. Chief Joseph led his tribe, defended only by

The sadness of a lost cause creases Chief Joseph's face in this old photograph.

Indian Reservations, 1875 and 1890

▢ Reservations in 1875

◺ Reservations in 1890

Map labels: Little Big Horn 1876; ✕ Fetterman Massacre 1866; Sioux War 1862 ✕; ✕ Wounded Knee 1890; ✕ Chivington Massacre 1864

their 300 warriors against a well-equipped United States army, on a spectacular 1300-mile trek. On their way across Oregon, Idaho, and Montana the warriors fought a series of amazing battles, regularly defeating much larger army forces. Finally, after several months of marching and fighting, Chief Joseph and his depleted tribe reached a point only 30 miles from the Canadian border. Thinking they were already safe, they paused to rest. Then suddenly a United States army group galloped in from an unexpected direction. After suffering a five-day siege, it was plain to Chief Joseph and his courageous people that they had to surrender. Chief Joseph said,

> I am tired of fighting. Our chiefs are killed. Looking-Glass is dead. Too-hul-hut-sote is dead. The old men are all dead. It is the young men now who say "yes" or "no." He who led the young men is dead. It is cold and we have no blankets. The little children are freezing to death. My people, some of them, have run away to the hills and have no blankets, no food. No one knows where they are, perhaps freezing to death. I want to have time to look for my children and see how many of them I can find. Maybe I can find them among the dead. Hear me, my chiefs. My heart is sick and sad. From where the sun now stands I will fight no more, forever.

The final act in the tragedy of the Indian wars came on December 29, 1890, at Wounded Knee in South Dakota. There, shortly after the killing of their famous leader Chief Sitting Bull, a band of men, women, and children was arrested by the 7th Cavalry. Somehow a fight broke out. The soldiers opened fire upon the unarmed Indians and left more than 200 dead.

The buffalo slaughter. Whether the Plains Indians won or lost battles did not, in the long run, matter. They were doomed to defeat, not only by the guns of the army and the ever-increasing number of settlers who occupied their land, but most of all by the destruction of their food supply—the buffalo.

At the close of the Civil War the buffalo roaming the Great Plains numbered about 15 million. Sometimes a single herd would spread over 50 miles. The first force to endanger these clumsy, slow-moving beasts was the railroad. It split the herd into a northern and a southern group and at the same time brought hunters into their midst. The most famous of the buffalo hunters was William Cody, better known as "Buffalo Bill." At first he and the other hunters shot the buffalo for meat to feed the large crews of railroad workers. Later, city slickers who went west for adventure and for sport shot thousands from the safety of railroad cars. In 1871 a commercial method was found of treating the skins to make them usable as robes. The slaughter was on. Hunters roamed the range killing every buffalo in sight. The kill finally reached three million a year. The southern herd was gone by 1878, and the northern herd had disappeared by 1884. In 1889 all that was left of the millions of these noble animals was about one thousand.

With the animal that supplied their food, clothing, fuel, and shelter gone, the Plains Indians had to give up. These people who knew the plants and animals of the West better than any who came after them were condemned to reservations. Though wonderfully skillful and knowledgeable at wresting their living from the land, they now depended on the charity of the invaders.

Indian policy reform. In the West most settlers saw the Indians only as a menace. But many Americans, especially those raised back east away from the battles, were troubled by the sad plight of the Indians and wondered what they could do to help. Just as 30 years earlier Harriet Beecher Stowe had stirred the nation's conscience for the slave in her book *Uncle Tom's Cabin* (1852), now another eloquent woman awakened white Americans to the sufferings of the Native Americans. Helen Hunt Jackson, who came from Massachusetts before she moved to Colorado Springs, wrote *A Century of Dishonor* (1881) and *Ramona* (1884) to dramatize

In his oil painting "Herd on the Move," painted in the early 1870s, William Hays showed an endless stream of buffalo flowing across the barren plain. Hays, who died in 1875, would have found it hard to believe that by the end of the 1880s almost all the buffalo would be gone.

The Thomas Gilcrease Institute of American History and Art, Tulsa

"Mountain Jack and a Wandering Miner" (top), painted in oil by E. Hall Martin in 1850, evokes the majestic grandeur of the Rocky Mountains. Below, a supply train headed for a nearby mining company is ready to set out from Georgetown, Colorado, in the late 1800s.

Cherry Creek gold rush, Virginia City sprouted and prospered with its silver rush. Soon, where nothing had stood, according to Mark Twain, "Money was as plenty as dust." Newly rich citizens built showy houses where everything seemed to be silver plated. One man even had silver shoes made for his horses.

This rich silver find was called the Comstock Lode. Henry Comstock had not himself made the great discovery, but somehow he managed to claim the property. When he sold the mines, in bits and pieces, he received a total of only $11,000.

To extract great wealth from the mines required the energy and organizing ability that Comstock lacked. The person who had those talents, and was lucky enough to be on the spot, was John W. Mackay. He was a poor Irish boy whose parents had brought him to this country when he was nine. Eleven years later, in 1851, he decided to seek his fortune in the California gold fields. Mackay worked in various gold and silver fields, making little money but learning a lot about mining. He used his earnings to buy an old mine on the Comstock Lode. By ingenuity and new equipment he extracted more silver than anyone had thought possible. With these profits he bought other mines that were thought to be worked out. In 1873, using these new methods, he began to mine the amazing "Big Bonanza" from which he would take more than $100 million.

The Oakland Museum

Miners working the California rivers for gold hoped to get rich, but most were lucky if they found a little gold dust.

The Mining Frontier

- Gold-mining
- Silver-mining

Mackay made his millions from mines that others had given up. He was willing to invest more capital and dig deeper than others. Not many people were as lucky—or as enterprising—as John W. Mackay. Still, in the years after the Civil War thousands of impatient, ambitious, hopeful Americans on the move rushed out to new mines. Mackay's example lured them on. Behind them they left Last Chance Gulch and its Crab City (later Helena, Montana), Boise, Silver City, Centerville, Leadville, and finally, as the dead end of the miner's frontier, Deadwood, South Dakota.

"One Sunday in July, Forbestown, California" was painted by an amateur artist about 1850.

Law in mining fields and towns. The mining towns were wild, but they were not without law. For the miners, like all the people who were on the front edge of America, made their own laws.

We have seen how the people on the *Mayflower* formed a community. And in the same way each wave of men and women who moved west into places that had no organized government had to make their own rules. In the mine fields and mining towns laws had to be made about the size, staking, and defense of mining claims. Where there was still no government, the first comers had to decide what was a crime and how it was to be punished.

These laws seemed so natural, following the traditions and customs of the mines, that many miners thought they actually did not have any law. When Congress passed its first major Mining Act in 1866, it enacted the rules that had been adopted by the miners themselves.

The significance of the mining frontier. The mining frontier, the first of the last frontiers, opened up the country from the Rocky Mountains to the Sierra Nevada. It taught Americans something of the natural wealth of this continental heartland. The finding and the getting of copper, iron ore, lead, zinc, coal, molybdenum, uranium, and oil were all still to come. The mines and the miners out there created new needs for railways. And by quickening the invasions of Indian lands they brought the Indian problem to a head. In some areas, especially in Idaho and Montana, the mining frontier opened up a new farming frontier because, when the gold ran out, miners remained to work the land. And, of course, mining towns demanded meat and so stimulated the cattle business.

Between 1860 and 1900 the mining frontier produced more than $2 billion in gold and silver. Much of this went into the pockets of people who had never before seen so much money. The quick-paced life of the mining West, so full of surprises, left a wonderful legacy of folklore—and the stories of Mark Twain and Bret Harte.

SECTION REVIEW

1. Identify: William Larimer, Henry Comstock, John W. Mackay.
2. Locate: Pikes Peak, Black Hills, Cherry Creek, Virginia City, Last Chance Gulch, Deadwood.
3. How did later mining ventures differ from the earlier ones?
4. How was the mining frontier significant?

3. The cattle kingdom

While the miners were opening up the mountain and intermountain West, cattle ranchers were opening up the Great Plains. As the cowboy and his cattle moved onto the Great Plains the Indians were forced onto smaller and ever less desirable reservations and the buffalo were killed off.

The cattle frontier and the mining frontier mainly attracted men. Cowboys driving herds or riding the range, miners chasing from one spot to another after gold, soldiers pursuing Indians—all these were men on the move who had not the time or the opportunity to settle down to family life. A few hardy women did live on the lonely ranches, in the mining towns, or at the army forts, but they were far outnumbered by the migratory men.

Only as families began to settle the plains and cultivate farms did this situation change. The farming West, too, was a difficult and often frightening place for man, woman, and child. We can still share their troubles and their delights in the great novel *Giants in the Earth* by the Norwegian immigrant Ole Rölvaag, who helped build the Scandinavian community as a professor at St. Olaf College in Minnesota. Rölvaag described a new settler viewing the treeless plains where she must make her home: "How will human beings be able to endure this place, she thought. Why, there isn't even a thing that one can *hide behind.*"

To survive and build a family on the Great Plains, a woman had to be many things. She had to be a soldier holding off Indians, a farmer and a rancher, a parent and a teacher. Without women's courage and their efforts the vast open West might never have grown its permanent settlements. It is not surprising, then, that in 1869 Wyoming Territory became the first place in the nation to give women the vote and that western states were among the first to elect women governors.

Cattle and cowboys. About the time of the Civil War, the western cattle trade became big business. The men who made money from it were as different as possible from the European peasant who kept his few cattle at night in the room where he slept. The peasant could keep only a few because his house was small and he had to feed his animals by hand in winter.

By the 1890s, when this picture of women branding was taken on the Fritz Becker ranch in southeast Colorado, cattle ranching had become a family enterprise.

Colorado Historical Society

The western cattleman numbered his stock by the thousands. He did not have to give them a roof, for western cattle were tough enough to look after themselves on the range. And on the great western plains there grew "buffalo grass" which survived drought and provided free food right on the ground throughout the winter.

Raising cattle on the northern plains. Western cattlemen were bold and adventurous, willing to take big risks in a wild country. One of the first and most energetic of these Go-Getters on horseback was John Wesley Iliff. Though his parents offered to set him up on a farm in Ohio, Iliff wanted to go west to seek his fortune. He did not find gold in the Colorado mountain streams. But he did find it in the cattle that came there with Americans pushing westward.

Iliff bought oxen from the people seeking gold who wanted to lighten their load before they headed up into the mountains. In Colorado he fed these cattle free on the open range that belonged to nobody and to everybody. He also bred more cattle. When his animals were fattened, Iliff sold them to butchers in the mining camps, to travelers returning east who needed oxen to pull their wagons, or to the government to feed the army and the Indians on the reservations.

When railroads—promoted by eastern Go-Getters—pushed west, they opened another new market. Now western beef could be shipped to the growing eastern cities. At the same time, hardworking crews building the railroads had to be well fed, and what they most wanted was meat. Iliff agreed to deliver cattle by the thousands to the Union Pacific Railroad construction gangs and to the United States troops guarding them against the Indians.

This was easier said than done. He had to find more beef than anyone had ever yet seen in one place. And he had to bring it to the middle of nowhere, where railroads were still to be built.

Iliff was helped by still another brand of Go-Getter, the western trailblazer. In 1868 a remarkable man with the unlikely name of Charles Goodnight agreed to deliver to Iliff's camp near Cheyenne, Wyoming, $40,000 worth of cattle from Texas.

To get the cattle from Texas to Wyoming, Goodnight had to find his own way over some of the driest and most unfriendly land in the whole continent—what maps before the Civil War called the "Great American Desert." It was a risky business, but it seemed worth trying when a steer, bought for $4 in Texas, sold for $40 in Wyoming. Multiply that by 3000 (the number of cattle Goodnight hoped to take on each trip), and it added up to a handsome profit. Goodnight succeeded because of the skills of Texas cowboys and the nature of long-horned cattle.

Texas longhorns. When Americans had come to Texas in the 1820s, thousands of long-horned cattle were running wild. These were the descendants of a few animals brought over by Spanish explorers. The first cattle raising on the plains was started by Mexicans whose herds flourished on the rich grass. When later Americans arrived, they learned many things and borrowed much of their way of life from the Mexicans already there. These included the Mexican saddle, the lariat, along with the chaps, boots, spurs, and big hat, all suited for the rough life of the range. Many of the new words they used—"sombrero," "rodeo," "lariat," and "chaps" (chaparajos)—were borrowed from Mexico, too. The six-gun was also part of their outfit. All these things which made the cowboy picturesque to others were only his working weapons, clothes, and tools.

The cowboys' work was risky. The long-horned cattle of Texas, it was said, were "fifty times more dangerous than the fiercest buffalo." Armed with sharp horns which sometimes spread as much as eight feet from tip to tip, these bold beasts could not be managed by workers on foot. The longhorns made the Texas cowboy get on his horse, and they kept him there.

The long drive. The Texas longhorns were well equipped for long trips. Their sense of smell, the cowboys said, was as much superior to that of an ordinary eastern cow as the bloodhound's was to that of a parlor poodle. Where water was hard to find, the longhorn's nose for water could make the difference between life and death.

The real problem was how to keep all those 3000 cattle together and moving at just the right speed. If they were allowed to stop or dawdle, they might never reach their goal. But if they were allowed to trot, they might get out of control or exercise off the weight that was worth money in Wyoming. Even with no problems and the cattle moving smoothly it would take from two to four months to reach their destination.

The crews who drove the cattle usually were made up of sixteen or eighteen cowboys for a herd of 3000. They were led by a trail captain. There was also a cook driving a chuck wagon and a boy to take care of the eight or ten horses needed for each man. Often a few of the cowboys were freed slaves.

Stationed at the front, or "point," of the herd were two of the most experienced men, called "pointers." They navigated for the whole herd, following the course set ahead by the foreman. Bringing up the rear were three steady cowboys whose job it was to look out for the weaker cattle—the "drags." To prevent the herd from straggling out for miles, the whole party moved no faster than the weakest "drags" at the rear. The rest of the cowboys were stationed along the sides to keep the herd compact and all the same width.

Communication between the front and rear of the herd was difficult. The rumbling of hoofs smothered words. The cowboys, then, borrowed a clever system of hand signals from the Plains Indians.

Apart from Indian raids, the greatest peril was a stampede. The cowboys sang to the herd at night to try to keep it calm. But suddenly a quietly dozing herd might rouse into a thundering mass. To stop a stampede, experienced cowboys on their horses drove the cattle in a circle, always round to the right. Then by tightening their circle they squeezed the stampeding cattle tighter and tighter together till they had no place to run. The milling herd was forced to halt.

If the encircling tactic failed, all was lost. The stampede would get out of control. Then the cattle would fly out like sparks into the night, and they might never be seen again.

The cow town. At the end of the long drive came the "cow town," which was as American as the cowboy. It was simply another smaller kind of "instant city" like those already dotted over the West. The cow town was where cowboys delivered their herd to the cattle dealers and the railroads. There, after long lonely weeks on the trail, cowboys enjoyed the company of strangers, bought liquor, and gambled away their money.

Go-Getting cattlemen made these instant towns prosper. One cattleman, Joseph G. McCoy, picked

Frederic Remington won fame for his paintings, illustrations, and sculptures of the "Wild West." He painted "The Stampede" in 1908.

Cattle Trails and Cow Towns

▨ Original Home Range of Texas Longhorn

▢ Range and Ranch Cattle Area

a place along the Kansas Pacific Railroad. In 1867, when he first made his plans for Abilene, it was a village of about a dozen log huts with sod roofs.

It was not much of a town, but there was open land around it and plenty of good grass and water for the cattle. So McCoy bought the whole town for $2400 and quickly built a shipping yard, a big barn, and a three-story hotel. It was all finished in 60 days, and by September 1867 the first shipment (twenty carloads of cattle) left Abilene for Chicago. Soon Abilene was sending thousands of cattle

east, and the town was booming. McCoy was offered more for a single city lot than he had paid for the whole town. And before the end of the second year the Kansas Pacific owed him $250,000 in commissions for the cattle shipped.

Other prosperous cow towns followed Abilene. There were Schuyler, Fort Kearney, North Platte, Ogallala, and Sidney in Nebraska. In Wyoming there were Pine Bluffs, Rock River, Rock Creek, Laramie, Hillsdale, and Cheyenne. Montana had Miles City, Glendive, and Helena.

The cow towns did not suffer from modesty. More than one boasted she was the "Queen of Cow Towns." Dodge City, in Kansas, and others competed for the title of the "Wickedest Little City in America."

Western cattlemen and cowboys were among the first and bravest of the Go-Getters. They tried the impossible and succeeded in making something from nothing. They captured wild cattle which belonged to nobody. Then they fed the cattle on the free open range on buffalo grass which nobody had even imagined could be food. And finally they transported the cattle on their very own feet for thousands of miles to places where they could become beef.

Who could have imagined that the "Great American Desert" would become the greatest beef factory in the world?

The end of the open range. The success of the ranchers was also their ruin. Everyone wanted to invest in cattle. As more and more ranches were started, more and more cattle were put out to feed on the range. In 1885, there came a hard winter, followed by a dry summer. This destroyed some of the grass and weakened the cattle. Then another bad winter in 1886 wiped out whole herds.

At the same time that cattle ranches were multiplying, farm families were pushing in, trying another way to make their living on the Great Plains. To protect their cattle the ranchers had been stretching miles of fence—even around land that they did not own. The newly arrived farmers had gone to great trouble to secure legal ownership of the lands they settled. Naturally enough they demanded government help against the high-handed ranchers.

All these forces—too many cattle, bad weather, farmers, and government intervention—would bring an end to the cattle kingdom of the open range. As farmers moved in, the ranchers could no longer graze their cattle free on the public lands. Now ranchers had to develop new methods. They actually had to buy their grazing land. Pastures were divided up and fenced. Better cattle were bred. Food was grown for winter feed. Water was supplied by well and windmill so that cattle would not have to walk far and lose weight. The cowboy became a cowhand working year-round and round the clock. No longer could he, as one recalled, "sit

around the fire the winter through" doing no work "except to chop a little wood to build a fire to keep warm by."

Some people specialized in breeding cattle, others in fattening them for market. Cattle raising became a scientific business. It was no longer the wild, romantic adventure it once had seemed. The day of the cattle kingdom was gone. The new era belonged to the ranch hand and the farmer.

SECTION REVIEW

1. Identify or explain: Ole Rölvaag, John W. Iliff, Charles Goodnight, Joseph G. McCoy, long drive, open range.

2. Locate: Abilene, Dodge City, Cheyenne.

3. Why were women a small minority on the cattle and mining frontiers? What roles did women play in the development of the West?

4. How did Mexicans influence the cattle frontier?

5. What forces brought an end to cattle raising on the open range?

6. How did cattle raising change with the end of the open range?

---

4. The farmers' frontier

The American farmer and his family had avoided the Great Plains. It was a strange place, and at first they did not like it. They were accustomed to the wooded lands of the East. Some had become acquainted with the flat prairies that stretched from Illinois to Iowa and from Canada to Texas—land known for its rich soil, regular rainfall, and tall grass. But the Great Plains were different. Out there, trees were rare. The grass was short. Worst of all, there was very little rain. It is not surprising, then, that for a while the farmer had gladly left the West to others.

Problems on the farmers' frontier. When finally farmers decided to move onto the plains, they faced new problems. Since there was no wood for houses, they had to learn to make houses of sod. To their astonishment they found that sod houses could be warm and cozy in winter, cool in summer. These did not blow down in high winds. And they were wonderfully fireproof, which was welcome protection against the prairie fires that threatened the Great Plains. But these sod houses were dark, and

The Jerns family posed on their farm in Dry Valley, Nebraska, in 1886. By that time they had all the necessities for living on the plains. They had built several sod houses, erected a windmill, and strung barbed wire to keep their cattle from wandering away.

the ceilings dripped with rain. The old familiar wooden buildings had a lot to be said for them. Nearly every pioneer family looked forward to the day when it could build a frame house.

Whether in sod houses or frame houses, every farm family needed fuel for their fireplaces to cook food and to keep warm in the bitter winters. At first buffalo chips (dry manure) could be used, but soon the buffalo were gone. Then, at one time or another they tried everything in sight—cow manure, sunflower stalks, and hay. Until the railroads came carrying coal, nothing was quite satisfactory.

Then the weather offered new problems, for it brought only extremes. In the spring there were floods, in the summer searing heat, in the winter raging blizzards and sub-zero cold. And there were occasional prairie fires, started by lightning, which destroyed everything. Sometimes grasshoppers blackened the sky in countless numbers and in a few hours ate a whole year's crops. One very hot summer 30,000 people abandoned the Great Plains for places where life was easier. One refugee wrote on the side of his wagon that he was returning "From Kansas, where it rains grasshoppers, fire, and destruction."

Getting a farm. It has been said that civilization approached the Great Plains on three legs—water, wood, and land. But on the Great Plains only land could be found in abundance.

The railroads helped to make life easier by bringing in coal and other supplies and taking crops out to market. In addition, they encouraged settlers to come to the West. For the railroads had land to sell. To persuade the railroad companies to lay their tracks across the empty lands of the West, the state and federal governments gave them wide strips of land along the tracks. So every time these companies sold a piece of land and brought out a new family of settlers, they created customers for their railroads.

At the same time, there was free land for the asking all over the West. In 1862 President Lincoln had signed the Homestead Act, which offered everybody who could get there the chance to be a landowner. To the European peasant it must have seemed a dream. The whole American West was begging for people. All you had to do was come. You only needed to be 21 years of age and to say that you intended to become a citizen. Then you picked a 160-acre plot of "homestead" land somewhere on the vast public domain which belonged to the United States government. If you simply lived on it and cultivated a part, then the whole 160 acres would be yours at the end of five years. You paid nothing but a small registration fee.

This was an Old World dream come true. Everyone a landowner!

It took lots of wood to build the balloon frame houses of the nation's fast-growing cities. This photograph was taken in 1892 of a special train loaded with lumber for Omaha, Nebraska.

State Historical Society of Wisconsin

The mess shanty of a lumber camp in Brill, Wisconsin, was photographed in 1902. Colorful posters, many of them advertising the play *Uncle Tom's Cabin,* decorate the walls.

But the "free" land was not really as free as it seemed. In the western plains, where most of the best homesteads were found, it cost labor and money to make wild land into a farm. Before anything could be planted, the ground had to be broken. The prairie grass had roots that grew in thick mats, unlike anything known in Europe. The familiar Old World plow would not cut through but was quickly twisted by the heavy sod. It was slow work to plow up enough land to support a family, and it was expensive to hire a worker with the right tools to do the job.

Then you needed to find water. Where streams and springs were rare, the only answer was to dig a well. And to pump up the water, you had to build a windmill. On the treeless plains you had to buy the lumber for your house. Posts and barbed wire for fencing had to be brought from great distances. All this added up. You needed about $1000 to make your homestead livable. That was a big fortune for a landless peasant.

Still, if you were healthy, and willing to work year-round, and not afraid to spend a few winters in a crude sod house, you might manage. The Homestead Act allowed you to be away from your land for six months each year without losing your claim. Some energetic homesteaders used this time to earn money by working as lumberjacks in the pine forests of Minnesota, Wisconsin, and Michigan. Others helped to build the short "feeder" railroads that branched off through the countryside. Or they worked as farm laborers.

The railroads, of course, tried to persuade people to come. They sent agents to Europe to tell them about the wonderful lands along their tracks. Their agents helped with information and loans. Sometimes the railroads actually provided newcomers with a house while they were getting settled.

Often the railroad builders were granted the best lands in the West. And, anyway, once the railroads were built, the land nearest the tracks—since there were no automobiles and few roads—would be the most valuable. While railroad lands sold at higher prices, they were usually much more attractive than the more remote lands left over for distribution under the Homestead Act. In addition, in the arid West 160 acres could not support a family, so more land had to be bought somehow.

Fencing the Great Plains. Neither the railroad nor the Homestead Act was enough to bring settlement. Pioneer farming could not really come to the Great Plains until the land could be fenced to keep out the cattle. There was no wood for fences, so various methods, such as the thorny, fast-growing "Osage orange" hedges, were tried to provide an inexpensive natural fence. But you had to wait some seasons till the hedges grew, and they were never quite tight enough. Then in the early 1870s, the answer was found in barbed wire. People tried all kinds of outlandish designs. There are still examples of at least 100 different kinds of barbed wire which show us how hard the inventors tried. As was true with other important discoveries, several people seem to have come up with the right idea at the same time. The most successful of these was an Illinois farmer, Joseph G. Glidden. He designed a wire that could be easily manufactured, was durable, and not too hard to string on posts. By 1875 he was making his fortune selling this new product. And by 1883 one company alone was turning out 600 miles of barbed wire a day!

Water and "dry farming." Of course fences did not solve all the farmer's problems. He still needed water. Even today the lack of water plagues farmers on the Great Plains.

The water under the plains could be reached only by deep wells. When drilling for oil, people learned to dig deep for water, too. To bring up the water that their steam engines needed, the railroad companies used windmills. The ranchers, and soon after them the farmers, followed their example.

The first windmills could supply only enough water for family use or for the stock. Irrigation of the fields was not possible. New methods of farming that preserved the scanty rainwater had to be developed to raise crops on the Great Plains.

"Dry farming," this was called. Developed by the Mormons in Utah, it was a way of keeping and using the moisture already in the soil. First the land was plowed deep to increase its ability to hold water. Then the topsoil was firmed so the moisture below could not escape. After every rain the farmer stirred the surface to keep a blanket of soil over the moisture in the ground.

This system needed a large area and big machines. It required the tractors, harrows, disks, and cultivators turned out in large numbers by factories

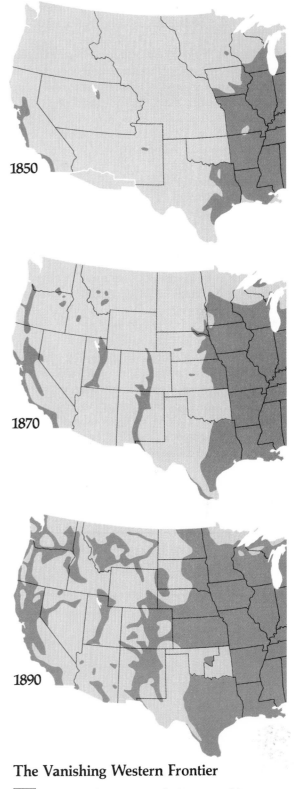

1850

1870

1890

The Vanishing Western Frontier

▓ Settled Area (2 or more people per square mile)

339

after the Industrial Revolution. Now farming, like mining and ranching, had become big business.

The growth of the West. Spurred by the discovery of gold, the open land, the Homestead Act, the railroads, and the flood of immigrants from Europe, the settlers in the West multiplied. Kansas had a population of 364,000 in 1870; it reached 1,428,000 by 1890. In those twenty years Nebraska grew from 123,000 to 1,063,000; Dakota Territory from 2000 to 540,000.

Senator Peffer of Kansas noted in the *Forum* of December 1889 that "a territory greater than the original area of the United States was peopled in half a dozen years." Kansas became a state in 1861, Nevada in 1864, and Nebraska in 1867. These were followed by Colorado in 1876, North and South Dakota, Montana, and Washington all in 1889, and Idaho and Wyoming in 1890. And new territories were established: Arizona in 1863 and Oklahoma in 1890. Each of these would become a new state before many decades had passed.

Oklahoma had been set aside for the Five Civilized Tribes. In 1834 these unfortunate Indians—the Cherokees, Chickasaws, Choctaws, Creeks, and Seminoles—had been forced to move there from their ancestral lands in the Southeast. At first when white "Boomers," as they were called, illegally entered Oklahoma Indian Territory, the army sent them away. When the pressure of new white settlers became too great, the government purchased some Indian lands and announced that on April 22, 1889, this land would be opened to homesteaders.

The Huntington Library, San Marino, California

About 1900 the people of Tonopah, Nevada, celebrate the fact their town is no longer a desert (top). The campers below await the signal to join the Oklahoma land rush in 1889.

Western History Collections, University of Oklahoma Library, Norman

At noon a shot was fired, and thousands of hopeful homesteaders who had been held back by troopers rushed across the border for the new land. When they arrived, they were astonished and disappointed to find that the lands were already occupied by illegal settlers who were "Sooner." These had eluded the army guards and staked their claims ahead of time, leaving the law-abiding land seekers behind. Ever since then the people of Oklahoma have jokingly called themselves "Sooners." The sooner and later comers by the evening of that first day numbered 10,000 in Oklahoma City and 15,000 in Guthrie.

The next frontiers would be in cities, in factories, and in shops all over America.

SECTION REVIEW

1. Identify or explain: Joseph Glidden, Homestead Act, public domain, dry farming, "Sooners."
2. Describe the hardships facing pioneer farm families on the Great Plains.
3. How did each of the following influence the development of the farming frontier: railroads, Homestead Act, barbed wire, windmills, mechanized farm equipment?
4. Describe population growth in the Great Plains after 1870.

CHAPTER REVIEW

MEETING OUR EARLIER SELVES

1. Look at the map of Indian reservations on page 324. Suppose that five or ten times as much land had been set aside for them. In which decade—the 1830s or 1870s—would such a policy have been easier to adopt? Why? How might such a policy have affected our national economic development? social development?
2. Imagine your class as a mining town with no organized government. What kinds of laws would be needed right away?
3. Why was the price of cattle in the 1860s ten times higher in eastern markets than in Texas? What factors influenced supply in both markets? demand?
4. How did the railroad land grants benefit (a) railroad stockholders? (b) pioneer farmers and ranchers? (c) the nation?

5. In what specific ways were the buffalo important to the Plains Indians?
6. Identify three mining boom towns in the 1870s and 1880s. As a traveler at that time what differences would you see from towns of a similar size on the East Coast?

QUESTIONS FOR TODAY

1. Brazilian settlers and businesses are encroaching on the homelands of the Amazon Indians to get at the rich resources of the tropical rain forest. Suggest alternative policies for the government of Brazil to deal with the problem. What groups in Brazil—and elsewhere—would you expect to support each policy you name?
2. Locate the reservations of one or more Plains Indian tribes. Try to find out how they live and earn a livelihood today.
3. Do any of the hardships faced by pioneer farm families on the Great Plains still exist for farm families there today? Describe the ways in which some of the old hardships have been eased.

YOUR REGION IN HISTORY

1. To what extent, if any, has mining influenced the development of your state? What industries now use or have used the resources of these mines?
2. During what period of history was your locality a part of the American (or Spanish) frontier? How was frontier life in your locality similar to and different from life on one of the frontiers described in this chapter?
3. If you live in one of the "last frontier" states, find out how your locality is linked to events and developments described in this chapter.

SKILLS TO MAKE OUR PAST VIVID

1. Find some pictures of a particular aspect of life in the Old West. Then prepare a five- to ten-minute talk on your subject, making use of the pictures you have selected.
2. On an outline map show the area and significant features (settlements, trails, etc.) of one of the frontiers discussed in this chapter.

6

The new industrial age
1865–1900

After the Civil War the United States was as large and varied as all western Europe. Immigrants from everywhere would find someplace to feel at home here—on lands not so different from where they had lived in the "Old Country." The English could settle on the rolling landscape of "New" England, the Swedes could farm the flat, snowy stretches of Minnesota and the Dakotas, and Italians could plant orchards and vineyards in sunny California. Imported people spread across the land.

From Chicago to New York was as far as from London to Rome. How could these scattered people become a nation? They would have to invent ways to bring everybody closer together. American know-how came to the rescue. The world was startled to see how Americans used railroads, telegraph wires, and bridges to bind a vast nation.

The nation of many cities remained a nation of many centers. Before 1900, Boston, Philadelphia, and New York—the old capitals of the eastern seaboard—were rivaled by Chicago and St. Louis, Denver and San Francisco.

The continent did not yet seem overcrowded when Americans used materials and techniques borrowed from everywhere to send skyscrapers high in the air. For the first time in history, thousands came to live and work in a single towering building. In American cities, people would be close packed and piled up together as never before. Could so many varied city people still find national leaders to speak for them?

As the nation grew stronger and richer, it was becoming more and more citified. Could the voice of the farmer still be heard? Could the families who fed the nation also find champions? Would a nation where everything was becoming bigger still care for the little people?

New materials and new methods for using them transformed the nation during the Industrial Age. This detail from an 1895 painting, courtesy of Bethlehem Steel Corporation, shows workers making steel from a Bessemer converter.

CHAPTER 16

The nation transformed

The everyday life of the American people was transformed in the generation after the Civil War. This nation would be not merely a democracy of people but also a democracy of things. It became easier for more and more Americans to share the good things of life. Farmers and ranchers found ways to make the American land yield more and better food. And many others played their parts in creating the American standard of living. A peculiarly American breed were the Go-Getters. These were men and women of all races and from all nations. The Go-Getters found new opportunities here, saw new ways to make a living for themselves, and at the same time helped build a better life for others. Without even intending it, they were bringing the whole nation together.

1. Railroads and big business

To make a profit from their land, farmers had to send their crops to market. To work their land, they needed tools from city factories. As factories grew to supply the nation's wants, the factories consumed more and more raw materials—iron, wood, and cotton. To keep the whole process going, the vast nation, spread across a continent, needed transportation. The nation was already served by its broad rivers, its many canals, and roadways. But there had to be easier, speedier ways.

Railroads gird the nation. To meet the demand, Go-Getters pushed railroads into every nook and cranny of the United States. As many miles of track were laid in the 1880s alone as in all the years from 1828 to 1870. By 1900 the nation had more miles of railroad track than all of Europe, including Russia.

When the first transcontinental railroad was completed in 1869, the time required to cross from ocean to ocean dropped from one month to one week. Within another 25 years four more transcontinental railroads were built. All but one of these railroads received generous land grants from the federal government to encourage them to build across the vacant West. Altogether, American railroads received 131 million acres from Congress and 49 million acres from the states. At the time they were given to the companies, the lands were worth little or nothing. They only became valuable after the railways were built. Then these lands would become prosperous farms and profitable sources for the nation's iron, copper, and oil.

Standard time. Americans loved speed. And railroads made it possible for them to race across the continent faster than ever before. The trains that sped from city to city brought strange new problems. One trouble which had not been noticed till then was that every town had its own clocks set to its own particular time. The astronomers said that

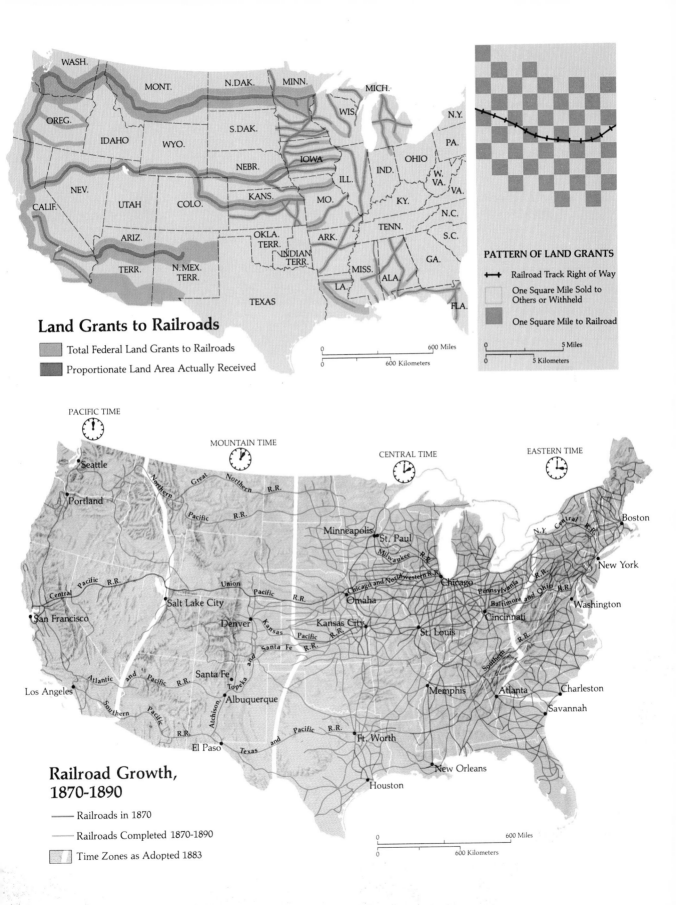

Land Grants to Railroads

- Total Federal Land Grants to Railroads
- Proportionate Land Area Actually Received

0 | 600 Miles
0 | 600 Kilometers

PATTERN OF LAND GRANTS

- ⊢─⊢ Railroad Track Right of Way
- One Square Mile Sold to Others or Withheld
- One Square Mile to Railroad

0 | 5 Miles
0 | 5 Kilometers

WASH. **MONT.** **N.DAK.** **MINN.** **MICH.** **N.Y.**
OREG. **IDAHO** **S.DAK.** **WIS.** **PA.**
WYO. **IOWA** **OHIO** **IND.** **W. VA.**
NEV. **NEBR.** **ILL.** **KY.** **VA.**
CALIF. **UTAH** **COLO.** **KANS.** **MO.** **TENN.** **N.C.**
ARIZ. TERR. **OKLA. TERR.** **ARK.** **S.C.**
N.MEX. TERR. **INDIAN TERR.** **MISS.** **ALA.** **GA.**
TEXAS **LA.** **FLA.**

Railroad Growth, 1870-1890

- —— Railroads in 1870
- —— Railroads Completed 1870-1890
- Time Zones as Adopted 1883

PACIFIC TIME   MOUNTAIN TIME   CENTRAL TIME   EASTERN TIME

Seattle
Portland
San Francisco
Los Angeles
El Paso
Salt Lake City
Denver
Santa Fe
Albuquerque
Ft. Worth
Houston
New Orleans
Minneapolis
St. Paul
Omaha
Kansas City
St. Louis
Memphis
Chicago
Cincinnati
Atlanta
Charleston
Savannah
Washington
New York
Boston

Northern Pacific R.R.
Great Northern R.R.
Central Pacific R.R.
Union Pacific R.R.
Kansas Pacific R.R.
Atlantic and Pacific R.R.
Southern Pacific R.R.
Atchison, Topeka and Santa Fe R.R.
Texas and Pacific R.R.
Chicago and Northwestern R.R.
Milwaukee R.R.
Pennsylvania R.R.
Baltimore and Ohio R.R.
Southern R.R.
N.Y. Central R.R.

0 | 600 Miles
0 | 600 Kilometers

In their hurry to lay track, transcontinental railroads often built temporary wooden bridges. The permanent bridge over the Green River in Wyoming is already under construction (left) in this 1868 photograph. Citadel Rock is in the background.

it was "noon" when you saw the sun reach its zenith—the highest point in the heavens. Since the earth was constantly in motion, and since the sun rose sooner when you were more to the east, then whether it was yet noon obviously depended on *where* you were.

Imagine what this meant for a railroad! The Pennsylvania Railroad tried to use Philadelphia time on its eastern lines. But that was 5 minutes earlier than New York time and 5 minutes later than Baltimore time. In Indiana there were 23 different local times. In Illinois there were 27, and in Wisconsin 38.

Most railroads used the local time for their arrival in each station. In between cities there was the greatest confusion. Yet for speeding trains a few minutes could make the difference between a clear track and a fatal collision.

Finally it was suggested that instead of using "sun time" they should use a new kind of "railroad time"—which would be "standard time."

For the United States as a whole, you could mark off on a map a few conspicuous time belts—up and down the whole country. You would only need four—eastern time, central time, mountain time, and Pacific time—each several hundred miles wide. Standard time would be exactly the same for all the places within each zone. At the edge of each belt the time would change by a whole hour. These time zones would be marked on maps, and then everybody could know exactly what time it was everywhere.

In the oil painting above, Chinese workers cheer as a Central Pacific train heads into a snowshed built to protect it from heavy snow in the Sierras. The poster (right) shows how new railroad lines sprang up as demand grew.

This was a sensible plan, but it took a long time to convince everybody that they ought to tamper with "God's time." Finally, at noon on November 18, 1883, the plan for standard time was adopted, and people everywhere set their watches to the new time.

Standard gauge. Standard time helped to draw all the nation's railroads together. But other steps were needed too. In 1860 there were about 350 different railroad companies and about 30,000 miles of railroad tracks in the United States. Yet there was not really a national railroad network. The main reason was that the many railroad lines were not on the same "gauge." The gauge is the distance between the two rails measured from the inside of one rail to the inside of the other. There were many different gauges. Some railroad builders put their tracks six feet apart, but some put them closer together. There were at least eleven gauges in general use. A railroad car that would just fit one gauge would not run on narrower or wider gauges.

If you wanted to send a package any distance by railroad, it had to be taken out of the car that fitted one gauge and moved into a car to fit the gauge of

the next railroad. In 1861 a package sent by railroad from Charleston, South Carolina, to Philadelphia had to change railroad cars eight times.

From the beginning, quite a few lines happened to have the same gauge. George Stephenson, the English railroad inventor, had designed his locomotive to measure 4 feet, 8 1/2 inches between the wheels—the usual distance between wheels on a wagon. When Stephenson locomotives were imported to the United States, they had this "standard gauge." And of course many early railroad lines built their tracks to fit the imported trains.

During the Civil War, in order to ship arms and troops quickly from place to place, many railroads changed to standard gauge. And then when the transcontinental railroad was completed with the standard gauge in 1869, that settled the question. Now if a railroad wanted to join the traffic across the continent, its rails had to be set 4 feet, 8 1/2 inches apart.

By 1880 about four-fifths of the tracks in the United States had been converted to standard gauge. Most of the other gauges were in the old Confederate South. Finally, in 1886, the southern railroads decided to change all their 13,000 miles of track to the national standard. A month in advance, crews went along loosening the old track. They measured the distance for the new standard gauge and put spikes along the wooden ties. On May 31 and June 1, the men worked frantically. One record-breaking crew on the Louisville and Nashville Railroad changed eleven miles of track in 4 1/2 hours. June 1, 1886, was a holiday along the southern tracks. By 4 P.M. the southern railroads had joined the Union.

Businesses compete.
As the railroads crisscrossed the land, the nation's businesses grew in number and size because they could reach more people. These were challenging times for businessmen. Competition in certain fields—like oil, steel, and the railroads—was fierce. On top of that, thirteen of the

years from 1873 to 1897 were years of recession or depression. John D. Rockefeller, who made a fortune in the oil business (p. 351), once looked back on those years and marveled that he had managed to survive them.

> How often I had not an unbroken night's sleep, worrying about how it was all coming out. . . . Work by day and worry by night, week in and week out, month after month. If I had foreseen the future, I doubt whether I would have had the courage to go on.

Rockefeller did go on, and he prospered by devising ways to limit competition. He organized "pools" in which a group of companies agreed not really to compete but instead to keep their prices the same. The law often treated these agreements as a kind of conspiracy. Since there was no legal means to enforce the pools, they usually collapsed.

Then Rockefeller and some other big businessmen tried another device. They figured out a clever new way to use an old English institution. This was the "trust." In early times in England the "trust" was invented for charities. Money would

The front and back covers of this menu from the Santa Fe railroad reveal the change in transportation across the continent that took place between 1868 and 1888. The comfortable passengers in the dining car had a gourmet menu to choose from.

The Huntington Library, San Marino, California

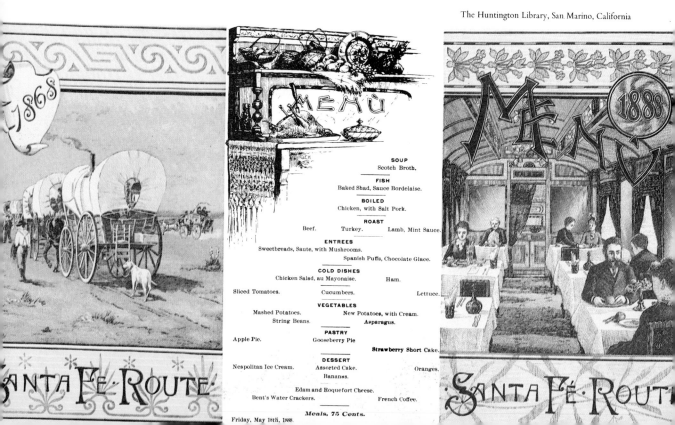

be given to "trustees" who invested it and gave the profits to the poor and the needy. The trustees controlled the money for the benefit of others. Now business firms set up "trusts"—not for charity, but to get around the laws against conspiracy. A group of companies would hand over all their stock to a board of "trustees" and receive trust certificates in return. The new trustees would then control all the companies, but the original owners—the holders of the trust certificates—would still get the profits. Still another ploy they used was the holding company. Its only purpose was to "hold" the stock, and so the control of other companies.

For some years the trust proved to be an effective way to get around the law, to combine companies, limit competition, and increase profits. The first and most famous was Rockefeller's Standard Oil Trust, but there were also trusts in cottonseed oil, linseed oil, lead, whiskey, sugar, and other products. By 1890 Congress began to pass "antitrust" laws, and the courts decided that business combinations formed to limit competition were illegal (p. 393). But many trusts continued to operate, and their powers lingered on.

J. Pierpont Morgan and Andrew Carnegie.
In the railroads, as well, combination became the answer to over-expansion and cutthroat competition. Here the main actor was the giant of finance J. Pierpont Morgan. Born to wealth, he was trained in the London office of his father's bank. His swashbuckling in the money world led people to call him a pirate. Actually he did not mind that. He had the look of a pirate, with his great frame, piercing eyes, and bulbous red nose. He named his luxury yacht (302 feet long!) the *Corsair*, which was the old French name for a pirate ship. Once, when Morgan was asked by a would-be yacht owner what it cost to run the *Corsair*, he replied, "If you have to ask, you can't afford it." But Morgan was also a man of culture. He built a great collection of rare books and works of art from all over the world which he gave to the public.

Morgan was an amazing organizer. When hard times bankrupted many railroads during the late 1800s, Morgan put them back on their feet by reorganizing them. He often combined several weak companies to make a single strong one. In time he controlled eleven railway systems with 19,000 miles of track. He also organized the biggest

Sturdy J. P. Morgan, with his hawklike stare, was known as the financier extraordinary. Astute Andrew Carnegie (bottom) created the nation's largest steel company.

steel company of all. But to do so he had to take over Carnegie Steel.

Andrew Carnegie, controlling partner in Carnegie Steel, was a talkative, intelligent steel industrialist who had been born of a poor family in Scotland. His family came to the United States in 1848, and Andrew at age 13 went to work as a bobbin boy in a cotton factory for $1.25 a week. But instead of settling for that, he educated himself by reading books and rose rapidly to better jobs. By his energy and his power to enlist the talents of others, he built the Carnegie Steel Company and became one of the richest men in America. In 1900 alone he made $25 million. And since there was no income tax in those days, he kept it all! Meanwhile, he never forgot the power of books. He devoted much of his fortune to founding libraries all over the United States in order to give others the chance to educate themselves and rise in the world. More than any one person, Andrew Carnegie was responsible for the spread of the free public library. Along with the public school, it became a keystone of American democracy.

Now Morgan wanted to buy Carnegie's company and bring his own "system" to the steel industry. Carnegie asked almost half a billion dollars for his share—and Morgan paid. Carnegie Steel and several other steel companies then were merged to form the United States Steel Corporation. It soon produced 60 percent of the nation's steel. Morgan's banking house made money, too, by selling the stock and bonds of the company to the public for a billion and a half dollars.

The new mighty corporations alarmed many people. They were richer and more powerful than any state government. These huge impersonal concerns were run by managers who were quite separate from the thousands of stockholders who really owned the business. The stockholders, each of whom owned "shares" in the company, were spread across the land. Most never even saw the factories of which they were part owners. The factory workers, instead of working for a single human boss who owned the company, now felt that they were employed by an inhuman giant. It was these companies and many smaller ones that made the United States, by 1890, the greatest industrial nation in the world. Their products, as well as the wealth they created and the salaries they paid, transformed American life.

SECTION REVIEW

1. Identify or explain: time zones, narrow gauge, John D. Rockefeller, pool, holding company, J. P. Morgan, Andrew Carnegie.
2. How did both the railroads and the public benefit from (a) the railroad land grants? (b) the switch to standard time? (c) the change to standard-gauge track?
3. Explain how a dozen big sugar companies might have formed a trust. Why would they want to do so?
4. In what sense did the giant corporations become more impersonal and inhuman?
5. How did the wealth accumulated by Morgan and Carnegie benefit the public?

2. Rock oil lights up the world

Americans before the Civil War, before anyone heard of an electric light, had to light their houses and their factories with oil lamps. People tried all sorts of mixtures hoping to find an oil that was cheap and safe, that burned well, and did not smell. They tried oils from the sap of trees, from vegetables, from fish, whales, or other animals. One oil called "camphene" was a mixture of turpentine (from pine trees) and alcohol. Another, invented in 1850 and made from coal, was called kerosene (from *keros*, the Greek word for wax). Camphene gave off good light but emitted an explosive gas. All except kerosene were smelly. Kerosene worked best, but it was expensive. So most homes were not lit at night. And people went to bed when the sun set.

Drilling for oil. In the mid-1850s George H. Bissell formed the Pennsylvania Rock Oil Company to buy lands in western Pennsylvania where oil was found floating in ponds. At that time rock oil (what we call "oil") was used mostly for medicine. Bissell found that he could not make enough money selling the oil for medicine to pay the expenses of collecting it. So he hired a famous Yale professor of chemistry, Benjamin Silliman, Jr., and agreed to pay him $500 to find out what else rock oil might be good for.

Professor Silliman's report opened a new age for rock oil. He found that rock oil—by now also called "petroleum" from *petrus*, Latin for rock, and *oleum* for oil—would make an excellent oil for lamps. His process was cheap. He simply distilled the rock oil—that is, heated it and collected the gas that came off. When the gas cooled down into a liquid, it formed a lamp oil that was just as good as kerosene made from coal. Kerosene made from rock oil gave a bright, white light, with almost no smoke, and would not explode.

The rock oil itself also had wonderful lubricating powers. It would keep the wheels and gears of machines from wearing out and would make them run quietly and smoothly.

Rock oil, with these valuable uses, could surely be sold in large quantities. But until then the only known way to collect it was to find it on the surface or by accident in a salt well. Sometimes people would dig a shallow ditch to increase the flow where it was already bubbling up.

Then one day, the story goes, Bissell saw an advertisement for rock oil from an old salt well. It was a sheet printed to look like paper money that featured the numeral 400. "A.D. 1848," it read. "Discovered in *boring* for salt water . . . about FOUR HUNDRED FEET below the Earth's surface." Boring! If oil could be obtained when you bored for salt water, why not simply bore for the oil?

"Oil coming out of the ground!" exclaimed a friend. "Pumping oil out of the earth the way you pump water? Nonsense! You're crazy."

But Bissell and other Go-Getting businessmen in the Pennsylvania Rock Oil Company decided to try. From New Haven, Connecticut, they sent Edwin L. Drake out to the oil fields. One reason they picked him was that since he had been a railroad conductor, he still had a free pass on the railroads. He could go out to western Pennsylvania without it costing anybody anything.

When Drake reached Titusville, the town closest to the biggest finds of surface oil, he decided to drill for oil. At first he could not find a driller willing to do the job. The drillers all thought that boring for oil was silly.

Then, luckily, he found an old salt driller, "Uncle Billy" Smith, who was also a skilled blacksmith and knew how to make drilling tools. Uncle Billy began drilling in June 1859, and on August 29 the hole still reached down less than 70 feet. When Drake and Smith came back two days later, the hole was full of oily black stuff.

"What's that?" Drake asked.

Uncle Billy replied, "That's your fortune!"

Soon there was an oil mania. Everybody wanted to get rich from oil. The map of northwestern Pennsylvania was dotted with such new names as Oil City, Oleopolis, and Petroleum Center.

John D. Rockefeller sets up the Standard Oil Company.

One of the most spectacular of all American Go-Getters was John D. Rockefeller. He was not an inventor or an explorer. Like J. P. Morgan and Andrew Carnegie, he was an organizer.

Young Rockefeller went to school in Cleveland, but he never went to college. His father, who traveled through the West selling patent medicines, left young John in charge of the family long before he was grown. John D. Rockefeller was ambitious. "I did not guess what it would be," he recalled. "But I was after something big."

American Antiquarian Society

This sheet music cover celebrates the Tarr Farm Oil Creek in Pennsylvania.

Even as a boy in Cleveland, young Rockefeller was systematic and well organized. While still struggling to make his way, he gave one-tenth of his income to the Baptist church and to charities. But when it came to organizing his oil business, he did not always use Sunday school methods.

Cleveland was a good place to organize "something big" in the oil business. At the receiving end of two railroads that came from the western Pennsylvania oil fields, Cleveland was on a lake big enough for large ships as well as on two major east-west railroads. Rockefeller determined to make Cleveland the center of the oil business and from there to command the biggest oil company in the world. Beginning with a small sum he had made in a grain-trading business, in 1865 he bought a Cleveland oil refinery. There crude oil from the fields was made into kerosene for lighting and oil for lubricating. Then he bought up other refineries in Cleveland and many oil wells in Pennsylvania.

As other oilmen went out of business, the railroads that carried the oil needed Rockefeller's freight more than ever. He was clever at making the two big railroads passing through Cleveland compete for his business. He bargained with one railroad by threatening to give all his business to the other. And he finally forced them to charge him lower prices than they charged anybody else. By secret arrangements he pretended to pay the regular rates. Then the railroads gave him back a "rebate"—a refund on each barrel of his oil that they had hauled. Soon they even gave him rebates on what opposing oil companies shipped.

After he perfected these tactics, he went to the small refiners in other parts of the country and asked them to sell their companies to him. "If you don't sell your property," he would say, "it will be valueless, because we have advantages with the railroads." He would then offer a price far below what the owners thought their refineries were worth. But they usually sold because they knew that Rockefeller could drive them out of business.

When it became cheaper to pump oil through pipelines instead of carrying it in barrels, Rockefeller organized his own pipeline. Then, when a different kind of oil was found in Ohio, Rockefeller hired chemical engineers to invent new kinds of refineries.

Rockefeller's Go-Getting business reached around the world. To the Chinese, his Standard Oil Company sold inexpensive lamps by the millions—and then sold the oil to fill them. Before long, people on all continents were using lamp oil from American wells. Between the Civil War and 1900 over half the American output went abroad. In those years Rockefeller, the Giant Go-Getter, helped light up the world. Now Americans could afford a lamp in every room, and they did not have to go to bed at sunset.

In the 1900s, Rockefeller's business would grow in ways even he had never imagined. After the automobile was invented, petroleum was refined into gasoline—and rock oil made it possible for a whole nation to move on wheels.

A dour John D. Rockefeller (center) along with his lawyers and other "followers" was photographed on his way to court in 1910 during an investigation of Standard Oil.

Brown Brothers

SECTION REVIEW

1. Identify or explain: rock oil, George H. Bissell, Benjamin Silliman, Jr., Edwin L. Drake, Titusville, rebates.

2. How did Rockefeller organize and build the giant Standard Oil Company? What part was played by the railroads?

3. City goods for country customers

During the colonial years, an American farm family made for themselves almost everything they needed. They built their own house (with the help of a few neighbors), and they made their own furniture. The wife and daughters spun the thread, wove the cloth, and then sewed the family's clothes. The pots and pans and metal tools which they could not make for themselves they would buy from a peddler. But they bought very few things. There were not many ready-made things for them to buy.

Then, in the years before the Civil War, American know-how drew upon ideas from Europe's Industrial Revolution to develop a new kind of manufacturing. Lots of new things were produced in vast new quantities. The new American System of Manufacture, which Eli Whitney and Samuel Colt had organized to make guns and revolvers, also turned out clocks and locks, and countless other items—both better and cheaper. Now farmers could afford to buy them.

But when farm families wanted any of these things, they had to go to the nearest village and visit the general store. Children loved the place because there you could buy candy and toys. Since the storekeeper kept a good fire in the stove, the store was where you could stay warm in winter. There you could meet friends and exchange ideas year-round.

But it was no place for bargains. The country storekeeper, who bought only a little bit of everything, could not command the best wholesale prices from the big-city manufacturers. Things would get dusty and out of date before they could be sold. And on top of that there were costly freight charges. Each item had to be hauled by wagon over bumpy backwoods roads.

Montgomery Ward. Soon after the Civil War an inventive young salesman, who had covered the West selling goods to the owners of general stores, began to think of a new plan. His name was A. Montgomery Ward. He had done all sorts of things, from working in a barrel factory and in a brickyard to selling dry goods. Often in his travels he had heard farmers complain about the small choice of goods and the high prices.

Young Ward's idea was to sell goods in an entirely new way. Instead of the old general store

Brown Brothers

The spread of mail delivery to the rural countryside enabled farm families to buy goods from mail-order firms in the cities.

which had stocked only a few of each item, Ward imagined a mail-order store. The storekeeper would stay in the big city where it was easier to collect a large stock of all sorts of goods. He would send out to farmers lists of his goods with descriptions and pictures. The farmer would not need to come to the store because the store—in the form of a catalog—would go to the farmer. And the farm family would order by mail, picking out whatever they wanted from the catalog. Then the storekeeper would mail the family the goods they had ordered.

If this new scheme worked, the storekeeper would be selling not only to the few customers in one village. He could sell all over America—to anyone within reach of a mailbox.

The possible customers of this new kind of store would not be just a few hundred, they might be millions! And then Ward could buy his goods from the manufacturer by the hundreds and thousands. The manufacturer could afford to give him a lower price.

For the customers, too, there were advantages. They had a much wider selection of goods. And they paid a lower price because the mail-order storekeeper, with so many more customers, could take a smaller profit on each item and yet would make more money in the long run.

"NOW I GUESS I'VE GOT THE BULGE ON THE MIDDLEMAN."

C.R.BUEK & CO. LITH. N.Y.   OVER.

All who are desirous of making three dollars do the work of four should not attempt to keep house without a copy of M.W.&Co's 500 page buyers guide and Catalogue.
Sent upon receipt of 15 cents to pay postage (no charge for the book itself)
Montgomery Ward & Co.
111 to 116 Michigan Avenue
Chicago. Ill.
We buy all goods from first hands, hence save you middlemens profits

Ward's boasted that buying from them would save the customers money.

Young Montgomery Ward had lost nearly all his savings in the Chicago fire of 1871, but in the very next year he managed to scrape together enough to make a start with his new idea. He put in $1600 and a partner added $800. They rented a small room over a stable, and started modestly. Their single price-sheet listed the items for sale and told how to order. Within two years Ward was issuing a 72-page catalog with illustrations. By 1884 the catalog numbered 240 pages and listed nearly 10,000 items. Within another 30 years it was over 1000 pages and included just about anything a person could imagine for animals or people.

Trust was the most important thing for a mail-order store. If you bought in a general store, you were buying from a storekeeper you knew. You could see the goods and handle them to satisfy yourself. But when you bought from a mail-order store, you had to trust somebody you had never seen. You had to believe that the storekeeper would really send you the exact thing described in the catalog.

Ward was a spectacular success. The first secret of his success was not a secret at all. It was simply to be honest, give good value, and always let the customer be the judge. On everything Ward's gave an ironclad guarantee. "Satisfaction or your money back!" If you did not like the goods when they arrived, you could always return them. If something arrived damaged, you could send it back to Ward's to be replaced. The company paid the postage both ways.

Of course there had to be trust on the company's side, too. The company had to be willing to cash the customers' checks, to believe their complaints, and to replace damaged goods without a lot of investigating. Ward was willing to do this, and to take the risks.

The catalog showed pictures of Ward himself and of the men in charge of the different departments. This was to convince the customers that they were dealing with real people. Some customers wrote in to say how pleased they were to deal with such "fine looking men." Some even named babies after Ward, and said he would be an inspiration to their children.

Ward saw that their letters were promptly answered—even if they were not ordering goods but only asking advice. One customer asked how to find a baby to adopt. Parents asked how to handle disobedient children. Some wrote him simply because they were lonely and had nobody else to write to.

Just as the tobacco planter in colonial times had asked his London agent to send him whatever he needed, now the lonely farmer asked Ward's. One customer wrote asking them to send him "a good wife." Ward's answered that it was not a good idea to select a wife by mail. "After you get the wife and you find that she needs some wearing apparel or household goods," Ward's added, "we feel sure we could serve both you and her to good advantage."

Sears and his catalog. It is not surprising that the mail-order store was a roaring success. Of course, in an age of Go-Getters, Ward was not the only man who tried his hand at building a mail-order store. One of the most creative of these others was a young man named Richard Sears. He began selling jewelry by mail. He found a partner in Alvah Curtis Roebuck, a watchmaker who ran a print shop where they could turn out their catalogs.

Sears was a clever man, and a near-genius at selling by mail. He was always improving his catalog. He developed a new quick-drying ink, new systems of color printing, and thinner paper that would take color but was cheaper to mail. He found, for example, that four pages of advertisements in color would sell as much of the same goods as twelve pages in black and white. His improvements were widely copied by other advertisers and by publishers of newspapers and magazines.

As the mail-order catalog reached more and more people on remote farms and in small villages, it became more and more important in their daily lives. While the family kept the Bible in the living room, they kept the Sears or Ward catalog in the kitchen. That was where they really lived.

There were all sorts of stories about how much faith people put in this big book. When one little boy was asked by his Sunday school teacher where the Ten Commandments came from, he said he supposed they came from Sears.

Just as Puritan boys and girls in colonial times had studied the *New England Primer* with its stories about God and the Devil, now Americans on farms studied the Sears catalog. In country schoolhouses, where there were few textbooks, teachers made good use of the catalog. They used it to teach reading and spelling. For arithmetic, pupils filled out orders and added up items. And they learned geography from the catalog's postal-zone maps.

Nothing did more than the new mail-order stores to make rural life in America something new. Before the 1900s most Americans still lived on the farm. Now that the American farm family could order from Ward or Sears, their lives became even more different from that of European peasants. Their view of the good things in the world was no longer confined to the shelves of the little village store. The up-to-date catalogs brought news of all kinds of new machines, new gadgets, and new fashions. Now American farm families could buy big-city goods at prices they could afford and from someone they could trust.

SECTION REVIEW

1. Identify: Montgomery Ward, Richard Sears.
2. What advantages did mail-order buying have over the rural general store?
3. How did the mail-order firms inspire trust? How did they transform rural America?

4. Buyers' Palaces

Meanwhile other Go-Getters were inventing ways to attract the new millions of city customers. The big stores that now grew up in American cities were as different from the little London shops as the grand new American hotels were different from the modest Old World inns.

The new American hotels were People's Palaces. Anybody could meet friends in the elegant lobby or, if you had the money, entertain them in a dining room with a crystal chandelier. The new department stores were Buyers' Palaces. And they, too, were democratic.

In London, only people who looked like "gentlemen" or "ladies" were admitted to the elegant shops. Unless the shopkeepers knew who you were, they would not let you in. You had to be a "person of quality" (as the upper classes were called) to see "goods of quality."

Department stores changed all this. Suddenly there were vast Buyers' Palaces, some large enough to fill a whole city block—specially designed to display goods of every shape, price, and description. Anybody could walk in. Now everybody could look at stylish jewelry, clothing, and furniture of the kind once reserved for the eyes of the rich.

Stewart's department store in New York was one of the first of the new buyers' palaces. This 1876 engraving shows the Broadway front of the block-large cast-iron building.

Stewart's new store.

This department-store revolution, which began shortly before the Civil War, changed the lives of American customers within a few decades. Stewart's Cast Iron Palace, completed in 1862 in New York City, was one of the first big department stores. It was the product of two different kinds of Go-Getters—a businessman and an inventor.

A. T. Stewart, the merchant who built up the business, came to the United States from Ireland at age 17. He started by selling the Irish laces he had brought with him. But he soon branched out into all kinds of goods. He was a bold, ambitious businessman. And he decided to spend a fortune on an enormous building in an entirely new style. To help him plan his grand new store, he picked an inventing genius who was sure to try something new.

James Bogardus, the man Stewart chose, had started as a watchmaker's apprentice in upstate New York. He first became famous by his design for an eight-day clock. Then he invented all kinds of new machines—for making cotton thread, for mixing lead paint, for grinding sugar, for metering gas, and for engraving postage stamps. He patented a metal-cased pencil with a lead that was "forever pointed."

His most important new idea was to construct buildings of cast iron. Bogardus's own five-story factory, built in 1850, was probably the first cast-iron building in America. The store he built for Stewart overwhelmed everybody at the time by its height—eight stories. It quickly became famous as the biggest store in the world.

Bogardus used cast iron to make an impressive Buyers' Palace. On the ground floor the outside walls no longer needed to be thick—as they had to be when a tall building was made of stone. Now there could be larger windows on every floor. Slender iron columns held up the high ceiling of display rooms a city-block wide. The ground floor was made even more palatial by a grand central staircase and a great rotunda reaching up the full height of the building, topped by a glass roof through which the sunlight streamed. You could enjoy long indoor vistas of appealing merchandise— gloves, umbrellas, suitcases, coats, furniture, all kinds of things in all shapes and sizes and colors. All the people busy looking, buying, and admiring helped make a splendid spectacle.

Naturally the Go-Getting department store-keepers wanted to display their goods to everybody who walked down the street. The thin cast-iron building frames made this easier, but it would not have been possible without a new kind of window. Before the age of the department store, glass was expensive. Windows had to be small. They were made to admit a little daylight or to look *out of.*

Then, not long before the Civil War, an Englishman invented an inexpensive way of rolling out glass in large sheets. These large sheets of glass now at last made possible the "show window." Americans invented this expression for the new kind of window that was made to look *into.* Now the goods could advertise themselves. The department store was a new, very American, and very democratic kind of entertainment where the admission was always free.

SECTION REVIEW

1. Identify: A. T. Stewart, James Bogardus.
2. What was "democratic" about the new grand department stores?
3. What made Bogardus's cast-iron building so successful as a store?

5. Things by the millions

On July 4, 1876, the nation celebrated its hundredth birthday with a Centennial Exposition held at Philadelphia. On the fairgrounds there were no rifle ranges or roller coasters or freak shows. There was no need for any. American products of all shapes and sizes—from shiny new bicycles to Alexander Graham Bell's strange machine that sent your voice over a wire—were themselves quite enough to entertain and amaze.

Visitors from Europe were astonished at how fast the United States had moved ahead. It was now threatening to take England's place as the leading manufacturing nation in the world. Machinery Hall, which drew the biggest crowds at the fair, was dominated by the gigantic Corliss steam engine. The largest ever, it was 40 feet high, weighed 700 tons, and produced over 2000 horsepower.

But it was not only size and quality that impressed visitors from the Old World. They were astonished by how cheaply Americans could make so many different things. Early in the 1800s one ingenious Connecticut manufacturer, Eli Terry, had already managed to turn out clocks that sold for so little it was not worth having an old one repaired. By the time of the Civil War good American clocks sold for less than 50 cents each, and New England factories were producing a half-million clocks each year.

Now in 1876, Europeans who saw the Philadelphia exhibits were convinced that Americans would change the world. The American machines, one Swiss engineer predicted, would "overwhelm all mankind with a quantity of products which, we hope, will bring them blessing."

Machine tools. To make things by the millions, Americans first had to create whole new industries and whole new ways of thinking. Newest and most essential was the industry for making machine tools. Machine tools were the parent machines— the machines for making the sewing machines, the gun-making machines, the clock-making machines, and all the rest. Since all these machines themselves were made of metal, machine tools were mostly metal-cutting tools.

One of the most remarkable of the American machine-tool makers was William Sellers of Philadelphia. By the time of the Centennial Exposition his work was already famous. He had invented machines that could measure and cut metal at the same time. These were essential for turning out standard-size screws and bolts.

And now these fasteners were more important than anyone could imagine before. They held together the millions of metal parts of the new machines. In the old days each bolt had been specially made for use at one place in one particular machine. If you took a piece of machinery apart, you had to label each bolt so you could put it back in the same place.

Now that would not do. What good was it to make guns or clocks with standard-size parts unless you could hold them together with standard-size fasteners?

In his *System of Screw Threads and Nuts* (1864), William Sellers offered his own standard designs for the tiny grooves. After that, if you said your machine used a "Sellers Number 6," then everybody knew exactly what you meant. The United States government adopted Sellers's system in 1868. Before the end of the century an international congress in Switzerland made it the standard for Europe, too.

Efficiency experts. While Sellers was pioneering in standard design, other Americans were inventing a whole new way of thinking about factories. In the old days, the individual craftsman in his shop would simply do things the way they had always been done before. This was called the "rule-of-thumb." You did the job in a rough, practical way, using your thumb instead of a precise measure.

But the new American factory could not be run that way. If the old gunsmith's handiwork was crude or inefficient, it meant simply that he made less money or that people stopped buying guns from him. But in a factory where hundreds of people labored elbow to elbow, everybody suffered if one worker blundered. If your work was not precise, your mistakes were carried all over the country in the thousands of misshapen parts that came off your machine.

Now there was need for a new science—a science of avoiding waste. "Efficiency" was another name for it. The Go-Getting engineer who invented it called it the "Science" of Management.

The efficiency pioneer, Frederick W. Taylor, was born in 1856 in Philadelphia. His mother, a fervent abolitionist, wanted to liberate men and women from slavery. Taylor hoped to liberate men and women from waste. He was astonished that people who worried about conserving forests and water-power and soil and minerals paid so little attention to conserving human effort.

He believed that there was one best way to do anything. But the one way that was least wasteful was not necessarily the way it had always been done.

The Bethlehem Iron Company hired Taylor to help make their huge plant more efficient. Every year millions of tons of coal and iron ore were shoveled into furnaces. Paying the men to shovel was one of the largest expenses of making iron.

This scene, engraved in 1886, shows steel being made in blast furnaces. Work in the mills was hard and the hours long.

Each man brought his own shovel and shoveled any way he wanted. But wasn't it possible, Taylor asked, that there was actually only one best way to shovel?

Taylor and his crew went into the factory and wrote down exactly what the men were already doing. Each worker was using his one favorite shovel no matter what he was shoveling. A shovelful of "rice coal" weighed only 3 1/2 pounds, but a shovelful of iron ore weighed 38 pounds.

"Now," Taylor asked, "is 3 1/2 pounds the proper shovel load or is 38 pounds the proper shovel load? They cannot both be right. Under scientific management, the answer to the question is not a matter of anyone's opinion; it is a question for accurate, careful, scientific investigation."

Taylor experimented until he found the right-sized shovel for each job. Taylor had discovered a Science of Shoveling! He designed different shapes and sizes of shovels and then tested each one to see that it was best suited to the stuff it had to carry. His small flat shovel was for the heavy ore, and his immense scoop was for light rice coal. Soon there were fifteen kinds of shovels in the Bethlehem toolroom, and the number of men needed to do the work dropped from 600 to 140. Taylor had abolished the waste.

This system, said Taylor, made it possible to pay each shoveler 60 percent more in wages. The wages of workers did rise somewhat. But, naturally enough, many workers were afraid they would lose their jobs. Others were afraid that, even if they kept their jobs, they would have to work harder. Many were afraid they would be regimented. They liked their own shovels. They did not like anybody telling them how to do their simple job.

Still, all over the country, "Scientific Management" became more and more popular with employers. They discovered that by making a science of the simplest jobs, they usually could find a better way.

Soon the American factory took on a new look. Instead of having the worker walk around to pick up parts and bring them to a workbench, the management engineers designed a workbench that moved. Then each worker could stay in one place. The bench (now a moving belt) would carry along the heavy parts from one worker to another.

This type of moving workbench was called an "assembly line," because on it the whole machine was put together, or "assembled."

Edison and his invention factory.
Thomas A. Edison invented a new kind of factory—an "invention factory." Its purpose was to invent new kinds of things to make. In the 1870s Edison set up his first "invention factory" with $40,000 he received from his own early inventions.

Edison and the clever people he brought to his "invention factory" were tireless testers and imaginative mechanics. One of their first feats was to help make electric lighting possible. The hardest problem had been to find the right thread, or "filament," to put inside the bulb. It had to be one that would give light when electricity was sent through it and yet would not quickly burn out.

They tried all sorts of materials—carbon, bamboo, hair, platinum, copper, and scores of other substances. They finally discovered that a filament of carbonized thread served well if it was in a vacuum. This made possible in 1879 the commercial production of light bulbs, which soon replaced Rockefeller's oil lamps.

Edison and his fellow inventors, looking for a way to record the human voice, invented the phonograph. They worked on a way to use the new art of photography to show "moving" pictures. In 1891 Edison patented a "kinetoscope"—a kind of peep show which showed moving pictures inside a box.

Edison fired the imagination of the American people. He was nicknamed the "Wizard." When

This photo of bustling Herald Square in New York City was taken about 1910. Note the large advertisement for Edison's phonograph.

The Museum of the City of New York

Born in London, Gompers left school at age 10 to begin work as a cigarmaker. He was age 13 when his family came to the United States. Finding work in New York City, he became a member of the cigarmakers' union that took part in a strike that failed in 1877. Then he set about reorganizing the union on a nationwide basis. He charged high dues to build up cash reserves for strikes, and he strengthened discipline within the national union. Strikes were only allowed when the union had the money to support the workers so they could hold out long enough to succeed.

Gompers had developed a special American approach to the problems of labor. In those years many workers in Europe were organizing to make

The Longshoremen's membership card (top) bears several patriotic emblems and inspiring mottoes. The colorful poster (bottom) from the Locomotive Firemen's union honors English inventor George Stephenson, who is known as the "father" of the locomotive.

revolutions. Over there desperate workers were trying to abolish capitalism and take over the factories themselves. But Gompers was no revolutionary. A hardheaded, practical man, he believed that in the long run American workers would be better off if they organized swiftly for a larger share of the profits. They should be as businesslike as the employers themselves. This was "bread and butter" unionism—aimed at higher wages, shorter hours, and safer working conditions.

This approach was so successful that other trades followed the example. Gompers became the father of national unions in the United States. In 1881 he brought many unions together in the Federation of Organized Trades and Labor Unions. In 1886 this was reorganized as the American Federation of Labor. With Gompers as president, the AF of L grew steadily in size and power. By 1904 it had 1.75 million members.

Still, most workers remained unorganized. As late as 1923, steelworkers were laboring twelve hours a day, seven days a week. Labor had a long way to go. Unions would not come into their own until the days of the New Deal and World War II.

Taylor experimented until he found the right-sized shovel for each job. Taylor had discovered a Science of Shoveling! He designed different shapes and sizes of shovels and then tested each one to see that it was best suited to the stuff it had to carry. His small flat shovel was for the heavy ore, and his immense scoop was for light rice coal. Soon there were fifteen kinds of shovels in the Bethlehem toolroom, and the number of men needed to do the work dropped from 600 to 140. Taylor had abolished the waste.

This system, said Taylor, made it possible to pay each shoveler 60 percent more in wages. The wages of workers did rise somewhat. But, naturally enough, many workers were afraid they would lose their jobs. Others were afraid that, even if they kept their jobs, they would have to work harder. Many were afraid they would be regimented. They liked their own shovels. They did not like anybody telling them how to do their simple job. Still, all over the country, "Scientific Management" became more and more popular with employers. They discovered that by making a science of the simplest jobs, they usually could find a better way.

Soon the American factory took on a new look. Instead of having the worker walk around to pick up parts and bring them to a workbench, the management engineers designed a workbench that moved. Then each worker could stay in one place. The bench (now a moving belt) would carry along the heavy parts from one worker to another. This type of moving workbench was called an "assembly line," because on it the whole machine was put together, or "assembled."

Edison and his invention factory. Thomas A. Edison invented a new kind of factory—an "invention factory." Its purpose was to invent new kinds of things to make. In the 1870s Edison set up his first "invention factory," with $40,000 he received from his own early inventions.

Edison and the clever people he brought to his "invention factory" were tireless testers and imaginative mechanics. One of their first feats was to help make electric lighting possible. The hardest problem had been to find the right thread, or "filament," to put inside the bulb. It had to be one that would give light when electricity was sent through it and yet would not quickly burn out.

They tried all sorts of materials—carbon, bamboo, hair, platinum, copper, and scores of other substances. They finally discovered that a filament of carbonized thread served well if it was in a vacuum. This made possible in 1879 the commercial production of light bulbs, which soon replaced Rockefeller's oil lamps.

Edison and his fellow inventors, looking for a way to record the human voice, invented the phonograph. They worked on a way to use the new art of photography to show "moving" pictures. In 1891 Edison patented a "kinetoscope"—a kind of peep show which showed moving pictures inside a box.

Edison fired the imagination of the American people. He was nicknamed the "Wizard." When

This photo of bustling Herald Square in New York City was taken about 1910. Note the large advertisement for Edison's phonograph.

The Museum of the City of New York

Congress awarded him a special gold medal in 1928, it was announced that his inventions had been worth $15,599,000,000 to humanity! But this was only to say that there really was no way of measuring his enormous contribution to American life. By the time of his death at the ripe age of 85, in 1931, he had become an American hero—a truly democratic hero because his work benefited every living American.

SECTION REVIEW

1. Identify or explain: Centennial Exposition, Eli Terry, William Sellers, assembly line.
2. Why was it important to have standard threads on bolts?
3. What is "Scientific Management"? What was Frederick Taylor's role? What fears did it arouse in workers?
4. Describe the career of Thomas Edison.

6. Labor begins to organize

The growth of American business—the development of "scientific" ways of shoveling, of new kinds of stores, of bigger factories, of assembly lines, of huge corporations—transformed the lives of work-ers. They became cogs in a great machine. No longer were they skilled craftsmen, the masters of tools. Instead they were becoming servants of the expensive tools of their employers. Workers no longer labored at home or in small groups alongside a boss who was both the owner of the business and their friend. Of course, even in those days they had worked from dawn to dark. But now they started and ended work when the factory whistle blew, and they worked twelve to sixteen hours a day in badly lighted and poorly ventilated buildings. Women and children made up more than half the work force. And the pleasant conditions of the early factories located in the countryside—in places like Waltham and Lowell—had disappeared under pressure of competition.

The rise of trade unions. Trade unions had ex-isted for a long time. In the 1790s in New York, Philadelphia, and other cities, certain skilled work-ers such as shoemakers, printers, and carpenters organized to protect their interests. But the pros-pects for organizing more of the nation's workers were not good. At first the courts held that unions were illegal because they were conspiracies. Then the Massachusetts Supreme Court in *Commonwealth v. Hunt* (1842) opened the path for unions when it declared that they were just as legal as any other club organized to help members for a legitimate purpose. Some states followed, but many still treated strikes, the unions' weapon for survival, as illegal.

In a few cities the trade unions joined together in federations. But the largest of these, the National Trades Union, collapsed with the Panic of 1837. By the time of the Civil War a small number of skilled trades—printers, iron molders, hat finishers, stonecutters, and cigarmakers, among others—had organized national unions to improve their wages and working conditions. But most American workers were not members of unions. It was harder here than in Great Britain, France, and other European countries to persuade workers to take the trouble and the risks of joining a union. For generally speaking, American workers were already better off than those abroad and had more hopes of rising in the world. Even with the arrival of large numbers of immigrants during the 1840s and 1850s and the increased competition for jobs, wages in the United States remained above those in other indus-trial nations.

Labor strife. As the size of factories increased and more and more businesses became large corpora-tions, the gap between worker and employer grew wider. Especially in large cities, it became easier to think of labor as merely a commodity to be bought at the lowest possible cost. A big company with lots of money could afford to close its factory when times were bad and wait for conditions to improve. But a worker still had to eat every day—in good times or bad. If workers complained, or went off the job on strike, the company could bring in new workers—strikebreakers. Of course, workers resented this treatment. The nation that had recently been a military battle-ground between North and South now became a scene of industrial battles between workers and their employers. Large numbers of workers (even many not organized into unions) were willing to go on strike. They were risking their jobs to improve their lives. Their aim was shorter hours and better wages. Workers also wanted more of a feeling of independence, of control over their own lives and working conditions. To win this, peaceful means were sometimes not enough.

Beginning in the 1870s labor battles became more frequent. In 1872 nearly 100,000 builders and mechanics in New York City went on strike. They refused to work longer than eight hours in one day. After several months, they won their point.

Miners in the eastern Pennsylvania coalfields organized a secret society called the "Molly Maguires." In 1875, on flimsy and possibly false evidence that private detectives had gathered for the employers, ten Molly Maguires were hanged for murder. Then in 1877 a railroad strike that began on the Baltimore and Ohio Railroad spread across the country bringing death and destruction in its wake (p. 385). The industrial battleground was becoming a place of bloodshed.

In 1886 came the so-called Haymarket Massacre in Chicago. A bomb killed 7 policemen and wounded 70 more after they tried to break up a meeting of workers called by anarchists and communists. In a fight at the steelworks at Homestead, Pennsylvania, in 1892, seven men were killed. The Pullman Strike in 1894 again tied up the railroads. In the Middle West, American troops, trying to keep the trains moving, were actually fighting American workers.

The Knights of Labor. Laborers tried a variety of ways of getting together to solve their problems. In 1869 the garment cutters of Philadelphia organized the Knights of Labor. Its idealistic aim was to bring all workers, skilled and unskilled, black and white, into one big union. They hoped that this union would give workers "a proper share of the wealth they create," more leisure time, more of all the benefits of society. They tried to set up companies owned by the workers themselves. They opposed child labor and demanded the eight-hour day.

The Knights were against strikes. But some of their radical members went on strike anyway when the railroads cut wages in 1884. After they won this fight for better wages, membership in the Knights boomed to 700,000. But then the Knights of Labor were involved in the Chicago strikes at the time of the Haymarket Massacre. Although they were not radical at all, a fearful public opinion lumped them together with anarchists and communists. Their membership then rapidly declined.

MOLLY MAGUIRE WARNING, No. 1

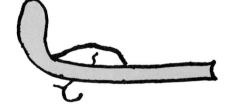

MOLLY MAGUIRE WARNING, No. 2

MOLLY MAGUIRE WARNING, No. 3

MOLLY MAGUIRE WARNING, No. 4

Brown Brothers

The Molly Maguires tried to help members by harassing the mine bosses.

Samuel Gompers and the AF of L. Labor leaders learned a good deal from the collapse of the Knights of Labor with its idealistic program and its attempt to combine all workers in one big union. One of them was a Go-Getter organizer named Samuel Gompers.

revolutions. Over there desperate workers were trying to abolish capitalism and take over the factories themselves. But Gompers was no revolutionary. A hardheaded, practical man, he believed that in the long run American workers would be better off if they organized swiftly for a larger share of the profits. They should be as businesslike as the employers themselves. This was "bread and butter" unionism—aimed at higher wages, shorter hours, and safer working conditions.

This approach was so successful that other trades followed the example. Gompers became the father of national unions in the United States. In 1881 he brought many unions together in the Federation of Organized Trades and Labor Unions. In 1886 this was reorganized as the American Federation of Labor. With Gompers as president, the AF of L grew steadily in size and power. By 1904 it had 1.75 million members.

Still, most workers remained unorganized. As late as 1923, steelworkers were laboring twelve hours a day, seven days a week. Labor had a long way to go. Unions would not come into their own until the days of the New Deal and World War II.

Library of Congress

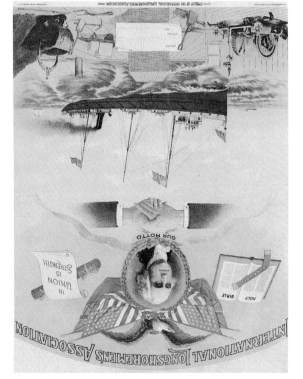

Born in London, Gompers left school at age 10 to begin work as a cigarmaker. He was age 13 when his family came to the United States. Finding work in New York City, he became a member of the cigarmakers' union that took part in a strike that failed in 1877. Then he set about reorganizing the union on a nationwide basis. He charged high dues to build up cash reserves for strikes, and he strengthened discipline within the national union. Strikes were only allowed when the union had the money to support the workers so they could hold out long enough to succeed.

Gompers had developed a special American approach to the problems of labor. In those years many workers in Europe were organizing to make

The Longshoremen's membership card (top) bears several patriotic emblems and inspiring mottoes. The colorful poster (bottom) from the Locomotive Firemen's union honors English inventor George Stephenson, who is known as the "father" of the locomotive.

Library of Congress

Culver Pictures

Practical and businesslike Samuel Gompers was the founder of the American Federation of Labor. Here he is seen about to cast his vote in a union election.

SECTION REVIEW

1. Identify or explain: *Commonwealth* v. *Hunt,* National Trades Union, Molly Maguires, Haymarket Massacre, Homestead Strike, Pullman Strike, Samuel Gompers, AF of L.

2. What progress had labor unions made by the time of the Civil War?

3. Describe labor-management conflict after 1870.

4. What were the aims of the Knights of Labor? Why did their membership decline?

5. Explain Gompers's "bread and butter" unionism.

CHAPTER REVIEW

MEETING OUR EARLIER SELVES

1. Had Hamilton and Jefferson been able to see the United States in 1900, one of them would have celebrated and the other would have wept. Who would have celebrated? Who would have wept? Why?

2. The key to the rapid industrialization of the United States was not so much the invention of machines and gadgets as it was standardization. Discuss, giving examples.

3. How did each of these developments help transform the United States between 1865 and 1900: railroad growth, trusts and other business combinations, new methods of merchandising, standardization in manufacturing, scientific management, labor unionism?

4. List some personal traits of the captains of industry and finance like Rockefeller, Carnegie, and Morgan. Do you think the same traits characterize leaders of industry and finance today? Explain.

QUESTIONS FOR TODAY

1. What businesses today, besides the railroads, benefit from standard time zones? In each case show why the standard time zones are needed.

2. The adoption of a standard gauge helped to create a national rail network. What standards exist today to aid interstate highway transportation? Can you think of ways in which more uniformity might be helpful? How might such rules make new problems?

3. What types of American stores or other merchandising techniques have been invented in this century?

4. Rockefeller's legacy was more than a thriving oil empire. His son and grandsons managed the family fortune and donated vast sums to education and philanthropy. Three descendants have served as state governors. Report on one or more of the Rockefeller descendants.

YOUR REGION IN HISTORY

Identify and describe the achievements of some business or labor leader in your state or locality between 1870 and 1900. How was this person linked to developments described in this chapter?

Maurice Prendergast's pen, ink, and watercolor, "Madison Square, New York," was done in 1901.
His use of flecks of brilliant color reflects the influence of the French Impressionists.

cities. Outside of cities many of them would have felt lonely and lost. They loved the friendly bustle and wanted to be close to people like themselves. And some of them had no choice. They had spent everything to cross the ocean and had no money left for a trip west.

Within the big American cities there sprouted little immigrant cities. By 1890 New York City held as many Germans as Hamburg, twice as many Irish as Dublin, half as many Italians as Naples. And besides, there were large numbers of Poles, Russians, Hungarians, Austrians, Norwegians, Swedes, and Chinese. Four out of five New Yorkers either were born abroad or were the children of foreign parents. The Germans and Irish who had come before 1880 were found nearly everywhere in the United States. There were also lots of Canadians in Boston and Detroit, Poles in Buffalo and Milwaukee, Austrians in Cleveland, and Italians in New Orleans.

The urban mixture. Cities were sometimes called the nation's "melting pots." Perhaps they should have been called "mixing bowls." The adult immigrant sometimes became Americanized only slowly. But very quickly a whole colony found its special place in American life. Just as the new United States had first been made from thirteen different colonies, now a great nation was being made from countless colonies of immigrants.

Wherever you came from, you could find a neighborhood in New York or in the other big cities where you could feel at home. Whether you were from Germany, Italy, Hungary, or Poland, you could shop in your own old-country language, buy familiar old-country foods, and attend a church offering your old-country services. By 1892 nearly a hundred newspapers in German were published in American cities. And there were dailies in French, Italian, Japanese, Polish, Yiddish, and a dozen other languages.

Although these immigrant colonies tried to keep separate, they could not stay separate forever. The people from different colonies became more and more alike. Children went to school and learned English. They stopped speaking their parents' language and sometimes stopped going to their parents' church. They were afraid to seem foreign. Then, too, a young man from the Italian colony might marry a young woman whose parents spoke German. In the city, people could not help feeling closer to one another.

City slums.

If the crowds were the joy of the city, crowding was the curse. New York—the nation's biggest city and busiest seaport and the magnet for the world's immigrants—was where the problem was worst. And in New York, American know-how, which at the same time was building grand cast-iron palaces for department stores, produced another, but unlucky, American invention. This was the "tenement house."

New Yorkers, of course, did not invent the slum. European cities had their streets of ancient rickety buildings and evil-smelling hovels where the poor were tumbled together. But in the years after the Civil War, New York City produced a new kind of slum—the tenement-house slum.

Most newcomers to the city could not afford to pay much rent. Back in the early years of the 1800s the poorer people of New York had lived in shacks on the swamps at the edge of Manhattan Island. But as the island filled with people, specially designed buildings went up for the city's new poor.

Immigrant women gather in the market square of a middlewestern town in the 1890s. One (far left) has adopted an American-style hat.

Tenement houses were buildings six or seven stories high designed to hold the largest possible number of families. They were solid blocks of deep buildings whose inside rooms had no windows or ventilation. There were also helter-skelter buildings of many other kinds.

The dumbbell building.

Then in 1878, to help find something better, *The Plumber and Sanitary Engineer*, a builders' magazine, announced a contest for architects. The editors offered a $500 prize for the best plan for tenement apartments for the poor.

The winning plan was the "dumbbell" tenement. It was called that because the whole building, looked at from above, was thin in the middle and bulged at both ends like the dumbbells used in gymnasiums. This plan had a good deal to be said for it compared with the plan of the flimsy firetraps that were common before. The dumbbell tenement, usually built of brick, was supposed to be fireproof.

It was designed to fit on a narrow lot. On each of the seven floors there were four sets of apartments—two in front and two in back. Since the stairway ran up the middle, the front and back rooms got some light and air from their windows on the street. Many people could be crammed into a small space.

367

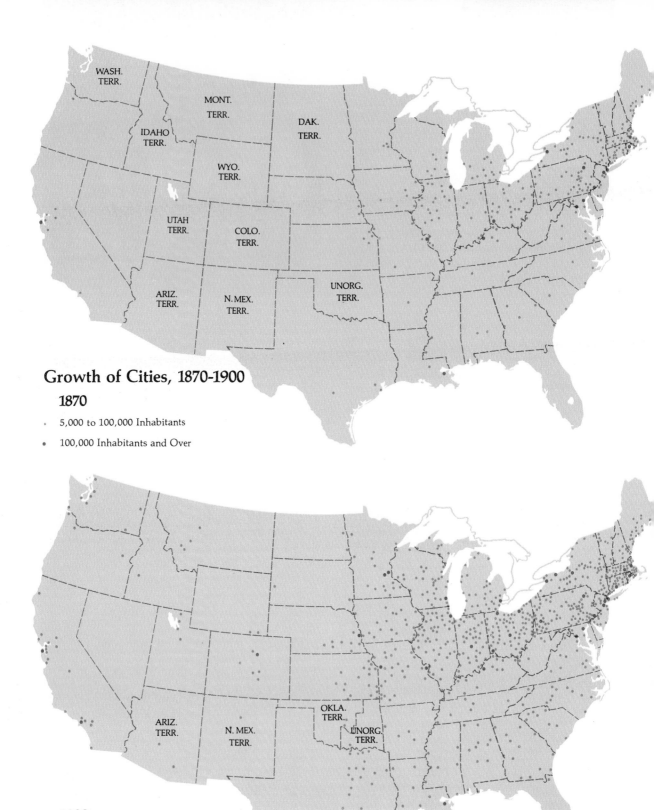

Growth of Cities, 1870-1900

1870

· 5,000 to 100,000 Inhabitants

· 100,000 Inhabitants and Over

WASH.
TERR.

MONT.
TERR.

IDAHO
TERR.

DAK.
TERR.

WYO.
TERR.

UTAH
TERR.

COLO.
TERR.

ARIZ.
TERR.

N. MEX.
TERR.

UNORG.
TERR.

1900

· 5,000 to 100,000 Inhabitants

· 100,000 Inhabitants and Over

ARIZ.
TERR.

N. MEX.
TERR.

OKLA.
TERR.

UNORG.
TERR.

DATA: CARNEGIE INSTITUTION OF WASHINGTON.

Everett Shinn, who began his career as a newspaper artist, painted "Cross Streets of New York" in 1899. He was one of the group of painters known as the "ashcan school" because they chose scenes from everyday city life as subjects for their canvases.

What was new about the plan was that the inside rooms were also supposed to get some light and air. When another tenement like it was built alongside, between them there was a narrow air shaft on which each inside room had a window. This became the standard plan for tenements.

By 1900 on the island of Manhattan alone there were more than 40,000 buildings of this type, holding 1,500,000 people. A prizewinning plan had produced the world's prize slum!

The air shaft between the buildings was only 56 inches wide—so narrow that it did not really bring in light. Instead the foul air brought up smells from the garbage piling up at the bottom. If there was a fire, the air shafts became flues which quickly inflamed all the rooms around. Up the air shaft resounded the noise of quarreling neighbors. There was no privacy.

Dirt, disease, and crime. The primitive plumbing in the hallway on each floor was shared by four families. It bred flies and germs. Sometimes the toilets became so disgusting that the tenants would not use them but depended on the plumbing at work or at school. There were no bathtubs with running water. Nearly every one of these tenement houses had at least one sufferer from tuberculosis, and sometimes there were many more.

When Theodore Roosevelt was governor of New York, he appointed a commission in 1900 to report on the tenement-house slums. They were not at all surprised that these buildings festered with poverty, disease, and crime. But they were surprised that, in spite of it all, so many of the people raised there managed to become decent and self-respecting. And the commission reported that the slums were even worse than they had been 50 years before.

Slum neighborhoods were given names like "Misery Lane" and "Murderers' Alley." This was hardly the America that the thousands of hopeful immigrants were looking for.

LOOKING BACKWARD.
They Would Close to the New-Comer the Bridge that Carried Them and their Fathers Over.

Culver Pictures

Austrian-born J. Keppler's lithograph cartoon from the magazine *Puck* shows a group of well-to-do Americans barring the entry of a new immigrant. The Newcomer sees what the Oldcomers cannot-- the shadows looming behind them of their own immigrant fathers.

But in their proposed law they did not dare list particular countries. There already were many people in the United States from those countries. They would be insulted—and they, too, elected members of Congress.

Year after year the Immigration Restriction League tried to persuade Congress to pass a literacy test. But even when they finally pushed their bill through Congress, they did not manage to make it into a law. One President after another vetoed the bill. President Grover Cleveland called the law "underhanded," because it did not say what it really meant. President William Howard Taft said the United States needed the labor of all immigrants and should teach them to read. President Woodrow Wilson agreed.

All three Presidents said the law was un-American. The United States had always been "a nation

of nations." It made no sense to keep out people simply because they had been oppressed. America was a haven for the oppressed. Here the starving could find bread, and the illiterate could learn to read.

In 1917, however, when the war in Europe was frightening Americans, the literacy test finally had enough votes in Congress to pass over President Wilson's veto.

Out on the West Coast, Oldcomers feared Newcomers from Asia. They worried about imaginary hordes that might come across the Pacific. And they had persuaded Congress to pass a Chinese Exclusion Act in 1882. Then, in 1907, President Theodore Roosevelt without the use of any law against the Japanese persuaded the Japanese government to stop their people from emigrating. This un-American agreement came to be called the

"Gentlemen's Agreement." And this became the slang expression for any agreement to discriminate against people when you were ashamed to admit what you were really doing.

SECTION REVIEW

1. Identify or explain: "melting pots" and "mixing bowls," dumbbell building, Tweed Ring, political machines, aldermen, Turner's frontier thesis, Immigration Restriction League, Chinese Exclusion Act, Gentlemen's Agreement.

2. What movements accounted for the growth of cities after the Civil War?

3. Why did immigrant colonies form in the cities? Why did they lose their separateness?

4. Describe a typical tenement house.

5. How did political bosses (a) enrich themselves? (b) win votes?

6. Why and how was a start made on limiting immigration?

Chinese immigrants, dressed in traditional clothes and with their hair in long pig-tails, walk down a street in San Francisco's crowded Chinatown about 1880.

Louis Stein Collection/California Historical Society

Culver Pictures

Jane Addams was a kind and gentle woman whose concern for needy newcomers led her to open Hull House settlement in Chicago. Many others were later to follow her example.

2. Reformers and self-helpers

Not all the Oldcomers were frightened. Some became reformers. If the country had too many strikes and too much crime, they said, that could not be blamed on those who had just arrived.

It was mainly the fault, they said, of the Americans who had been here longest and who had had the most chance to make the country better. Who had built the cities and the slums where the poor were condemned to live? Who were the members of Congress and the leaders of business and the police officers? It was not the immigrants' fault if the nation was not prepared to receive them.

Jane Addams. One of the most remarkable of the reformers and one of the most original Americans of the age was Jane Addams. She was born with a deformity of the spine which made her so sickly that after graduating from college in 1882 she had to spend two years in bed. When she was well enough to travel, her wealthy family sent her abroad to study art and architecture. What she really learned in Europe was something quite different.

373

Jacob Riis, a Danish immigrant, helped to improve the lot of New York City's poor with his books and striking photographs. This one showed Christmas Eve at a settlement house.

In June 1888, when she happened to visit the famous Toynbee Hall in London, she discovered her life's purpose. There in the poorest section of the city lived a group of Oxford and Cambridge graduates helping the people of the neighborhood. Why not try something like that in the United States?

Jane Addams's plan was simple. In the poorest, most miserable city slum she would settle a group of educated young men and women from well-to-do families. Like Toynbee Hall, the place would be called a "settlement house." The well-bred young men and women newly "settled" in the midst of a slum reminded her of the early colonial "settlers" who had left the comforts of English life to live in an American wilderness.

The young men and women who came to live in the slum, seeing the struggles of the poor, would learn things they could never learn from books. At the same time, the people of the slum would use the settlement house as a school, a club, and a refuge.

Hull House. Since she knew Chicago, she decided to do her work there. In the neediest neighborhood she persuaded the owner of a large old house to let her have it free. That became her settlement house—between an undertaker's parlor and a saloon. She called it "Hull House" after the man who had built it for his home years before.

In the neighborhood of Hull House there were Newcomers from all over Europe—Italians, Germans, Polish and Russian Jews, Bohemians, French Canadians, and others. For the young, Jane Addams set up a kindergarten and a boys' club. And she paid special attention to the very old people whom nobody else seemed to care about.

Jane Addams's work became famous. All sorts of unexpected projects started at Hull House. The Little Theater movement, of amateur actors putting on plays to entertain themselves and their friends, developed there and spread all over the country. She started a book bindery and a music school.

Settlement houses on the Hull House model appeared in big cities everywhere. Future playwrights, actors, composers, and musicians who had happened to be born into poor slum families now found their chance.

Thousands of lonely immigrants discovered that somebody else cared about them. Jane Addams—without the aid of governments or politicians—had helped make America the promised land.

Other reformers. In Hull House and other settlement houses the first social workers—many of them women—were trained, and they became a growing force for change. They moved beyond private charity to use the power of the state to improve conditions. Their first activities produced laws limiting child labor and governing the hours and conditions of labor for women.

Frances Willard was an Oldcomer who fought for reform in another way. In the Wisconsin wilderness, where she grew up, she became a good hunter. The only schooling she received came from her mother, but she learned enough to attend a college in Illinois and become a teacher. Then she was caught up by the temperance movement. Abstinence in the use of alcoholic beverages, she felt, would protect the home and Christian life. With her talent for organization and for oratory, in 1874 she was made president of the Women's Christian Temperance Union in Chicago and five years later was elected national president.

From that position Frances Willard worked also for women's right to vote. It was not surprising

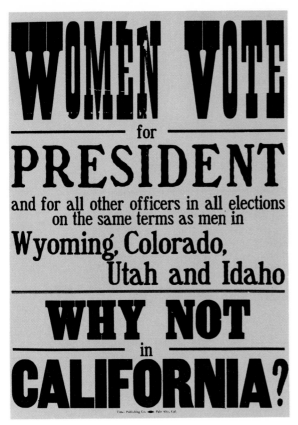

A women's suffrage amendment was sent to a narrow defeat by California's voters in 1896 after a strenuous campaign.

that the first progress came on the western frontier. There it was plain that new communities depended on pioneer women. Why shouldn't they be allowed to vote? Wyoming came into the Union in 1890 with women's suffrage. Then other western states gave women the right to vote—Colorado (1893), Utah (1896), and Idaho (1896). But the movement stalled, and little progress was made for over a decade.

Out of the South, too, there came other women reformers. Ida B. Wells-Barnett, who had been born a slave in Mississippi, became a newspaper writer in Tennessee. But when she wrote fearless stories exposing the facts about a lynching, she was driven out of the state. Then she went to New York City where she helped set up black women's clubs which became the foundation of the National Association of Colored Women in 1896. In 1909 she helped to organize the National Association for

the Advancement of Colored People. And in 1913 she established a settlement house in Chicago to help black newcomers from the South find jobs and homes in the big city.

SECTION REVIEW

1. How did the settlement houses help the urban immigrants?
2. Describe the work of Frances Willard and Ida B. Wells-Barnett.

---

3. The spread of learning

In the city and on the countryside the public schools helped make Americans. They were free, and the states passed laws requiring all children to attend. There the children of Irish, German, Italian, and all sorts of other families learned and played—and sometimes fought—together. They came to know one another better than their parents knew people from other countries. And some of these young people went on to study at new colleges and learned to become leaders.

The schools make Americans. At home many families spoke Polish or Italian or some other language, but in school everybody spoke English. Even if the parents spoke English with a foreign accent, soon the children sounded like other Americans. At home the children taught their parents English and all kinds of American customs. One little girl in New York City who had learned to use a toothbrush brought it home from school. She showed it to her mother, who had been born in a peasant hut in Poland and had never seen such a thing. Her mother, too, was soon brushing her teeth like an American.

Now many children could go on to the free public high school, which was an American invention. After 1870 these new public high schools spread across the country. By 1900 there were 6000 high schools attended by nearly 520,000 students, more than two and a half times the number attending only ten years before.

The flourishing schools made the United States one of the world's first literate nations. Thousands of the peasants and poor city workers who arrived from Europe had never learned to read. But in the United States the proportion of people who could

Jacob Riis took this picture of immigrant children saluting the flag at the Moss Street Industrial School in New York City in the early 1900s. In rural areas the one-room schoolhouse was usual. The photograph (below) taken at the end of the 19th century shows pupils from a school near Black River Falls, Wisconsin, assembled with their teacher for their annual school picture.

read and write steadily increased after the Civil War. Unfortunately in the South the promising start made during Reconstruction was not followed by the Old Confederates when they took office.

Growth of the colleges.

America had always been a land of help-yourself. But it was not easy for Newcomers to become leaders. So many respectable institutions remained in the hands of the Oldcomers whose families had been here for a century or more. For example, Harvard College—our oldest college, where young blue bloods had learned their ideas of Anglo-Saxon superiority—was run by Oldcomers. It was hard even to become a student there if you were not one of them.

New institutions offered the best chance for Newcomers who wanted to become leaders. Among the most remarkable and most American were the scores of new colleges and universities.

At the outbreak of the Civil War there were only seventeen state universities. Then, in 1862 an energetic Republican congressman, Justin S. Morrill

from rural Vermont, secured the passage of the Morrill Act. This act granted lands to the states from the public domain—30,000 acres for each of the states' senators and representatives in Congress—to support new state colleges. In these "land-grant" colleges students would be taught to be better farmers. The land-grant colleges also often offered solid courses in engineering, science, and literature. So here Newcomers, too, found an opportunity to learn.

After the Civil War, hundreds of other colleges and universities were founded. In the later years of the 1880s, some of the wealthiest Go-Getters gave millions of dollars to found and endow still more institutions of higher learning. In 1876 Johns Hopkins University was established from the fortune left by a Baltimore merchant. In 1885 a railroad builder, Leland Stanford, in memory of his son, set up Leland Stanford, Jr., University. In 1891 John D. Rockefeller, the Go-Getting oil millionaire, created the University of Chicago. And there were scores of others.

Many of these college founders had themselves never gone to college. But they shared the American faith in education. Even before the end of the 1800s, the United States had more colleges and universities than there were in all western Europe. And a larger proportion of the citizens could afford to go to college here than in any other country. The children of poor immigrants, along with millions of other Americans, now had a better chance to rise in the world.

Women's colleges multiplied rapidly in the years after the Civil War. In 1861 Matthew Vassar, who had been born in England and had made his fortune as a brewer and in whaling, founded Vassar College. When Vassar advertised to attract students to his college, he also publicized the importance of higher education for women. Before long there were more women's colleges, including Wellesley (1870), Smith (1875), and Bryn Mawr (1880). Many other new colleges, especially in the Middle West, were open to women as well as men. And the number of women in college grew from 9000 in 1869 to more than 20,000 in 1894.

Education for black Americans. Wealthy men and women, mostly from the North, also gave millions of dollars to help educate black people. By 1900 there were already about 30,000 black teachers. John D. Rockefeller, for example, had contributed over $50 million, most of it to train more teachers for black schools. The South spent less money than other parts of the country on education of all kinds. And blacks there had to attend separate, and inferior, schools. How then were they to get ahead? Black leaders could not agree.

One way was proposed by Booker T. Washington. Born a slave, Washington worked his own way upward until he was famous throughout the world. His own story of his life, *Up from Slavery* (1901), was read by millions.

In 1881 Washington founded Tuskegee Institute in Alabama. There he trained thousands of blacks to be better farmers and mechanics, to make a good living, and to help build their communities.

Frances Benjamin Johnston, a prominent turn-of-the-century photographer, caught this senior American history class at Booker T. Washington's Tuskegee Institute.

He believed in a step-by-step way "up from slavery." He did not want blacks to spend their efforts learning history and literature and foreign languages and science and mathematics. Instead, he said, they should train quickly for jobs—and mostly for jobs they could do with their hands. The vote, which had been taken away from them in the 1890s (p. 528), could wait. Self-respect, self-education, and self-help, he said, would bring blacks the opportunities they desired.

Many who admired Booker T. Washington still did not agree with him. Why should blacks have to wait for their rights? Twenty-five years after Booker T. Washington started his Tuskegee Institute in Alabama, a group met at Niagara Falls.

Their black leader was W. E. B. Du Bois. His life had been very different from that of Booker T. Washington. Born in Massachusetts after the Civil War, he studied at the University of Berlin in Germany and then received a Ph.D. degree from Harvard in 1895. Du Bois was a poet and a man of brilliant mind and vast learning. Why should anyone try to tell Du Bois and others like him to be satisfied to work with their hands?

In 1905 the declaration by Du Bois's Niagara Movement expressed outrage. It demanded for blacks *all* their human rights, all their rights as Americans, and *at once*. It opposed all laws and all customs that treated blacks as if they were different from other people. And of course, it demanded the right to vote.

SECTION REVIEW

1. Identify or explain: Justin Morrill, Matthew Vassar, Tuskegee Institute, Niagara Movement.
2. How did public schools help to Americanize the immigrants?
3. What was the importance of the Morrill Act?
4. Trace the growth of colleges for women and for blacks.
5. Contrast the views of Booker T. Washington and W. E. B. Du Bois.

---

4. Bridge-building heroes

Many of the fast-growing American cities were on the banks of rivers—the highways of the pioneers. As immigrant families and farm families pressed in,

the cities had to expand. They had to find ways of carrying thousands of daily passengers out beyond the old city limits. This meant that in order to hold their citizens together they had to span the neighboring waterways. Go-Getting engineers transformed the ancient art of bridge building to reach out to the new city frontiers.

Bridging the Mississippi. Something about bridge building attracted and inspired the American inventive genius. James Buchanan Eads, the man who would build the bridge for St. Louis, had proven himself during the Civil War. In 1861, as an adviser to the Union navy, he proposed a fleet of ironclad gunboats to control the Mississippi River. Then, when the government took up his suggestions, he built the needed ships in 65 days.

After the war the people of St. Louis, which was on the west bank of the Mississippi, saw that they had to bring the railroad across the wide river and into their city if St. Louis was to grow. Many schemes were offered. But all were rejected until Eads appeared. As a boy he had worked on a river steamboat. When only 22 years old, he had invented a diving bell to salvage ships that had sunk in the river. And then he had done a lot of walking underwater on the very bottom of the Mississippi. He knew that river bottom almost as well as other men knew the city streets.

What Eads had learned was important. Building a bridge across the Mississippi depended first on finding solid support under the sandy river bottom. As Eads had moved along 65 feet below the surface of the water, he had seen the currents churning up the sands. He knew that the supports for his bridge would have to go far below those river sands—all the way down to bedrock.

In 1867, when Eads began construction, his first problem was to lay the foundations of the two stone towers that would hold up the arches of the bridge in midstream. The towers would rise 50 feet above water level. The foundation of one would have to go down 86 feet below water level, and the other, where bedrock was deeper, would have to go down 123 feet. But was this possible?

Working underwater. Eads's plan was to use his own diving bell together with some new caissons—watertight working chambers—that had recently been perfected in England. The 75-foot-wide caissons would keep out the water while the men dug beneath the river sands to reach solid rock.

When Eads's men finally reached bedrock, they were working ten stories below the surface of the water! Because of the great pressures at that depth, the men could stay down only 45 minutes at a time. They had to come up slowly, and they rested long periods between shifts. Despite all precautions thirteen men died of "caisson disease" (sometimes called "the bends") from too rapid change in air pressure.

The bridge completed. Steel had never been used in such a large structure, but Eads decided to use it for the three vast arches of the bridge. When the standard carbon steel did not meet his tests, he ordered large quantities of the new chromium steel, and then supervised its production. While chromium steel was more costly, it was rustproof and needed no covering.

It took Eads seven years to bridge the Mississippi. Finally in 1874 in a grand ceremony the former Union general, William T. Sherman, pounded the last spike of the double-track railroad crossing the bridge. Then fourteen locomotives, two by two, chugged triumphantly across the river. President Grant came to St. Louis to proclaim Eads an American hero.

A bridge to Brooklyn. And there were other heroic bridge builders who helped open ways to the suburban frontiers. Few cities were quite so hemmed in by water as New York. Manhattan Island, heart of the city, was surrounded by the East River, the Hudson River, and the Atlantic Ocean. For a half-century there had been proposals for a bridge across the East River, connecting lower Manhattan Island to Brooklyn. When the fierce winter of 1866–1867 stopped all ferry service and isolated Brooklyn from Manhattan for days, it was plain that something had to be done.

John Roebling was ready with a plan. When he came to the United States from Germany as a young man, he opened the first factory for making wire rope out of many strands of wire twisted together. This new material was wonderfully suited for reaching over wide rivers where it was difficult or impossible to build masonry towers in midstream. From high towers on both ends you could suspend the strong wire rope to hold up the bridge.

If the Niagara River, for example, was to be spanned near the Falls, it would have to be by such a "suspension" bridge. In 1855 Roebling completed a wire-supported bridge over the Niagara—strong enough to carry fully loaded trains. This feat made John Roebling famous. In 1860 he completed another suspension bridge, just outside Pittsburgh, reaching 1000 feet across the Allegheny River. And by 1867 he had completed still another outside Cincinnati across the Ohio River.

A bridge from Manhattan to Brooklyn would have to stay high above water level in order to allow the sails and smokestacks of large ocean-going vessels to pass underneath. Could a suspension bridge, Roebling-style, solve New York's problem? Roebling's ambitious plan in 1867 proposed towers at both ends 271 feet above water level, holding up a main suspension span of 1595 feet. That was far longer than any suspension bridge ever built before.

Washington Roebling carries on. During the very beginning of construction in 1868, a ferry crushed John Roebling's foot against the dock, and he died from tetanus infection in two weeks. John Roebling's son, Washington Roebling, was ready to carry on. He too was a man of courage and had proved himself on the Gettysburg battlefield.

On his father's death, Washington Roebling at once took over the building of the bridge. In 1872, when fire in the Brooklyn caisson threatened the whole project, Roebling stayed below for seven hours in the compressed-air chamber. As a result he acquired "caisson disease."

Washington Roebling never fully recovered. Too weak to supervise the bridge on the spot, he would sit in a wheelchair in his apartment and watch the work through field glasses. Then he would give instructions to his wife, Emily, who carried them down to the bridge. All his communications with the world were through her. Efforts were made to remove him from the job, but his mind remained active, and he would not give up the command.

The dedication of the bridge. At 1:30 on the afternoon of May 24, 1883, fourteen years after John Roebling had begun the job, President Chester A. Arthur and his Cabinet joined with Governor Grover Cleveland of New York for the formal

THE GRAND DISPLAY OF FIREWORKS AND ILLUMINATIONS

AT THE OPENING OF THE GREAT SUSPENSION BRIDGE BETWEEN NEW YORK AND BROOKLYN

ON THE EVENING OF MAY 24th, 1883.

VIEW FROM NEW YORK, LOOKING TOWARDS BROOKLYN.

The grand opening of the Brooklyn Bridge on May 24, 1883, was celebrated with gun salutes and fireworks as this colorful Currier and Ives lithograph reveals.

opening of the Brooklyn Bridge. Six warships anchored below the bridge fired a resounding salute, and from the center of the bridge came a dazzling display of fireworks. The orator of the occasion declared that this, the world's greatest bridge, was a triumph of "the faith of the saint and the courage of the hero."

The "saint," Emily Warren Roebling, attended the celebrations. But Washington Roebling, the heroic bridge-building son of a heroic father, was too ill to leave the room from which he had overseen the work. The President of the United States went to Roebling's simple apartment at No. 110 Columbia Heights to give his congratulations.

SECTION REVIEW

1. How did bridge building contribute to the growth of cities?
2. What contributions did Eads and the Roeblings make to bridge construction?

5. Going up! elevators and skyscrapers

After the Civil War, Americans were not only stretching *out*. They began using their own know-how—together with materials and know-how from all over the world—to stretch their cities *up*. Although some Americans were moving to the suburbs, more people than ever before wanted to live and work right in the center of the city. Businessmen wanted to be where the action was. And many people who could afford to live in the suburbs still preferred to live downtown.

Solving problems. With old kinds of construction the tallest buildings had seldom been over five or six stories high. There were two problems that had to be solved before buildings could go higher.

The first problem—how to get the people up and down—was beginning to be solved even before the Civil War. In a few luxury hotels, elevators already carried guests up to the fifth and sixth floors. And in some early department stores the elevator was an attractive curiosity. Still, people were afraid to use them. Elisha Graves Otis invented a brake that would automatically clamp the elevator cage to the sides if the rope broke. To calm people's fears, Otis staged a sensational demonstration. He rode the elevator to the top. Then while an attendant cut the rope, Otis waved nonchalantly to the astonished spectators. Otis's early steam-driven elevators were slow, but before 1880 the improved "hydraulic" elevators (pushed up by water pressure in a long vertical cylinder) were climbing at 600 feet a minute. By 1892 an electric motor was carrying passengers up so fast that it "stopped" their ears.

The second problem—how to hold up the building—began to be solved when James Bogardus and others used cast iron for their Buyers' Palaces. No longer was it necessary to build a tall building like a pyramid, with thick supporting walls on the lower floors.

From dreams to reality. The time was ripe for the "skyscraper." Of course Bogardus was only dreaming when he forecast buildings "ten miles high." But he was not far wrong when he told American builders that only the sky would be the limit.

Bogardus himself constructed one of the first buildings of true skyscraper design. Its frame was a tall iron cage. If the cage was strong and rigid, and solidly anchored at the bottom, then the building could go up high without needing thick walls at the bottom. This was "skeleton" construction. The building was held up, not by wide foundations but by its own rigid skeleton.

Library of Congress

By the 1890s the new steel-framed skyscrapers were going up everywhere. Here is the Syndicate Building in New York City.

The first time Bogardus actually tried this, in 1855, he built a skeleton-framed tower eight stories high for a factory.

It was one thing to build a tower but quite another to trust the lives of hundreds to such a newfangled way of building. The first real try was

381

The Carnegie Steel Company's enormous plant at Homestead, Pennsylvania, in the 1890s had facilities for turning iron ore into pig iron—and mills for rolling steel into rails, bars, sheets, and rods. Employees lived nearby in the company-built town.

Library of Congress

in Chicago, where the pioneer was William Le Baron Jenney. An adventurous man of wide experience, he had helped build a railroad across Panama before there was any canal. In the Civil War he served on General Sherman's staff as an engineer.

In 1884 when the Home Insurance Company decided to construct a new office building in Chicago, they gave him the job. Jenney, who had probably heard of Bogardus's tower built 29 years before, decided himself to use an iron skeleton. In the next year his building was completed.

Steel and the age of the skyscraper. Even before Jenney's first skyscraper was completed, a better new material had been perfected. This new material, steel, like wrought iron, was made from iron ore, but was far superior. While wrought iron was easily shaped into beams, it bent too readily to be suitable for a skyscraper frame. Steel was the answer. And it was the material that made higher and higher American skyscrapers possible.

Though people had known how to make steel for centuries, the process had been difficult and time consuming. Therefore steel was so expensive that it was used only for small objects. The swords used by knights in the Middle Ages were made by endlessly hammering and reheating and then again hammering the blades. Until the mid-1800s this was the usual way to harden iron to make it into steel.

Then an Englishman, Henry Bessemer, invented his new mass-production steel furnace. By blowing air through the molten iron mass, the carbon in it was burnt out much more quickly. Now it was possible to produce 100 tons of steel from a single

furnace in twelve hours. Better, cheaper steel meant more tall buildings. The age of the skyscraper had arrived.

SECTION REVIEW

How did the work of the following contribute to the growth of cities: Elisha Graves Otis, James Bogardus, William Le Baron Jenney, Henry Bessemer?

6. New towns in the country

As the whole country became more citified, there grew up new kinds of instant cities. At first their aim was not to grow big, but to stay small—and so escape the troubles of the crowded metropolis.

Business firms were looking for new places to put their factories. Workers were anxious to escape the tenements and the darkened, crowded cities. Prosperous merchants and lawyers and doctors were eager to raise their families out in the open air.

Company towns. With the new railroad network there was less reason than ever for factories to stay in big cities. Almost any spot along a railroad line would do. Raw materials could be brought in from anywhere and finished products could be transported to any place.

If an industrialist built a factory away from a big city, the workers would not have to live in slums. Then why not build a "company town"? Out where land was less expensive, each worker could have a neat little house with a garden. The employer could provide parks and playgrounds, and workers might be more content. After the Civil War many energetic businessmen had this idea.

In 1881 Andrew Carnegie built a steel plant and a whole new town called Homestead seven miles up the Monongahela River from Pittsburgh. Besides small houses for the workers and their families, Carnegie provided a library and even bowling alleys. Homestead was not beautiful, but at least it lacked the crowds and the filth of the city slums.

George M. Pullman, inventor of the Pullman sleeping car for railroads, also decided to build a new town ten miles outside Chicago. In 1884 he bought a tract of land on the shores of Lake Calumet. He named it after himself and hoped it would be a model for other company towns. Pullman's architect designed the whole town, including a central square with town hall, churches, a library, and parks. All the buildings, including the small houses for the workers, were of dark-red brick.

In the company towns that sprang up all over the country, workers could escape the worst horrors of the big city. But they found some new horrors. Living in a company town was something like being a feudal serf in the Middle Ages. The company not only controlled your job, but it also decided where you would live, where (and at what price) you could buy your food. The company controlled your schools and even hired your police.

Some of the most violent strikes were in these company towns. When the Carnegie Steel Company cut wages at its Homestead plant in 1892, the angry workers went on strike. In the resulting violence a dozen men were killed.

Garden cities. But the company town was not the only new-style city that grew up at the end of the 1800s. On the "suburban frontier" there appeared the garden city. The first of these had been started even before the Civil War when, in the 1850s, Llewellyn Park in New Jersey was created. It was followed in the 1860s by Riverside, Illinois, outside Chicago. There Frederick Law Olmsted and his partner Calvert Vaux laid out a planned, garden-like community along the winding Des Plaines River. Olmsted and Vaux had also helped bring the country to the city when they designed and created Central Park in New York during the 1850s.

Soon other towns followed the pioneer garden cities. Some rich families who owned summer houses in the country near cities began living out in the suburbs year-round. For example, some businessmen who worked in New York City preferred living in Old Greenwich, Connecticut, forty-five minutes away on the railroad. These rich suburban pioneers set up their own country clubs and tried to keep their communities "exclusive"—for Old-comers only and not for any of the Newcomer immigrants.

The push for new garden cities was encouraged by an English reformer. Ebenezer Howard had come to America as a young man and had spent five years around crowded Chicago. Then in his book, *Garden Cities of Tomorrow* (1898), he offered his blueprint for a suburban utopia. He urged people to group together to build garden cities—new small towns out in the country. These towns, he said, should be planned with a garden belt all around. Then, if the garden city was connected to the big city by a railroad, it gave its residents the best of both worlds.

Other Americans followed Howard's advice and built garden cities. These were no longer only for the very rich, but they were not yet for people of modest means. Lake Forest outside of Chicago and

Shaker Heights outside of Cleveland tried to make the garden city more romantic than the big city. Instead of the monotonous parallel streets of checkerboard city blocks, the garden city streets wound across the countryside. Wide lawns separated the houses from the roads and from one another. Before long, garden cities like Radburn, New Jersey, were being specially planned for people of modest income. In 1910 a New York architect made a new design for space-saving "garden apartments" with "kitchenettes" (a new American word for a compact kitchen and pantry). Now you no longer needed to be rich to live out in a garden suburb.

SECTION REVIEW

1. What were the good and the bad features of company towns?

2. Identify some early suburbs and some pioneers in suburban development.

CHAPTER REVIEW

MEETING OUR EARLIER SELVES

1. While some rural villages almost vanished in the farm-to-city movement, the number of rural towns and villages (places under 2500 population) increased decade after decade until about 1930. How did the rural villages serve the farm population? How were the rural villages similar to and different from the larger towns and cities?

2. Some rural villages and the surrounding farms were also immigrant colonies. Which kind of immigrant colony—rural or city—would have an easier time clinging to its old-country ways? Why?

3. Rapid city growth required a rapid expansion of public services. What were some of these? How was the expansion of such services linked to political corruption?

4. Suppose that you were an Oldcomer in a big city in the 1890s. What changes taking place might upset you? Which of these changes might be easy to blame on the Newcomers?

5. Between 1870 and 1910 total U. S. population increased about 230 percent, high school graduates per year rose 950 percent, and college enrollment jumped about 700 percent. How did the growth of cities help to bring about this rapid rise in educational attainment?

QUESTIONS FOR TODAY

1. In 1975 our big cities (250,000 and over) had a smaller percentage of total U. S. population than in 1960. Urban growth was occurring in the suburbs and the smaller cities. Why did people flock to the big cities in the late 1800s and to the suburbs in the mid-1900s?

2. Think of the services provided by the settlement houses. How are similar services provided today? Why and how has the change occurred?

3. Building codes today tend to prevent the construction of the kinds of unsafe urban housing that prevailed in the late 1800s. Yet urban slums have not entirely vanished. Can you suggest some reasons?

YOUR REGION IN HISTORY

1. How did the rapid growth of cities after the Civil War affect your state? your county or parish?

2. To what big city or cities does your community have close ties? When did those cities grow most rapidly? What were the causes of that growth?

SKILLS TO MAKE OUR PAST VIVID

1. The table below shows the growth of rural and urban population (in millions) from 1860 to 1920. Show the same information in a line graph or a bar graph.

YEAR	RURAL	URBAN
1860	25.2	6.2
1870	28.7	9.9
1880	36.0	14.1
1890	40.8	22.1
1900	45.8	30.2
1910	50.0	42.0
1920	51.6	54.2

2. Imagine that you are a member of a six-person staff running a settlement house in 1900. Draw up a list of weekly activities that you will provide for immigrant families in the neighborhood.

CHAPTER 18

Politics in the Gilded Age

In American history the years between 1865 and 1900 are known as the Gilded Age. And for a good reason. Anything "gilded" is covered with a thin layer of gold. It glitters on the surface. But what is underneath is seldom so attractive. In this Gilded Age the surface of American life shone with many kinds of new wealth, made by adventurous and enterprising Go-Getters. That glitter covered a multitude of sins. It was a world of crowded cities, mammoth businesses, and extremes of wealth and poverty.

1. Parties in balance

The two main political parties were nearly even in strength between 1876 and 1892. In three of the five presidential elections during those years the difference in the popular vote between the Republican and the Democratic candidates was less than 1 percent. In 1876 the Democrats had a popular majority of 3 percent but lost the election. And again, in 1888, the Democrat Cleveland had 100,000 more votes than the Republican Harrison, but Harrison won. Garfield in 1880 defeated Winfield Scott Hancock by only 7000 votes in over 9 million cast. Victory seemed almost an accident.

During these years Presidents seldom had their own party in control of both houses of Congress. This inability to win both houses, combined with the closeness of the presidential vote, made an age of timid Presidents. Any new step might lose the few votes that meant a lost election and lost power.

Rutherford B. Hayes. Rutherford B. Hayes was a cold, honest, and straightforward man whose position as President was weakened by the way he came to office. His enemies referred to him as "His Fraudulency" or "Rutherfraud" B. Hayes. But Hayes himself never doubted that by a fair count he deserved to be President. Hayes further weakened his position, however, by announcing that he would serve only one term. This meant that his enemies within the party were willing to oppose him, since they knew that he would not be the party's candidate in 1880.

The great railway strike. Hayes took office in March 1877 during the deep depression that had begun in 1873. Labor strife erupted almost at once. The trouble began on the Baltimore and Ohio Railroad where the workers had suffered a series of pay cuts. In July the trainmen of the B & O went on strike. They were soon followed by railway workers in other states. Strikes, rioting, and looting shook Baltimore, Pittsburgh, Chicago, St. Louis, and many other cities. At the request of the state governors, Hayes sent federal troops to Martinsburg, West Virginia, and to Pittsburgh to protect property. He did not like using troops as strikebreakers, but he felt that he had no choice but to agree to the governors' requests.

The money question. The depression that brought the "year of violence" of 1877 brought demands for an increase in the amount of money in circulation.

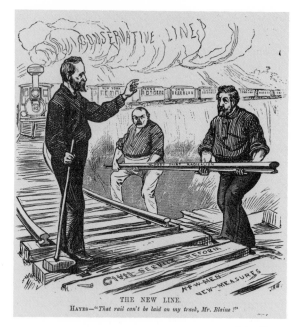

THE NEW LINE.

HAYES—"*That rail can't be laid on my track, Mr. Blaine!*"

This 1878 political cartoon shows upright and honest President Hayes pursuing a conservative course and building a solid new railroad line with civil service reform. He rejects James G. Blaine's rail of bloody-shirt radicalism.

This demand would come time and time again in the Gilded Age. Between 1865 and 1896 prices were falling. It was a time of *deflation*, which meant that a dollar would buy more every year. So farmers and people in business who had borrowed money had to pay back their loans in dollars that were worth more than the dollars they had borrowed. For example, a debt that could have been paid off in 1890 with the sale of 1000 bushels of corn took 2320 bushels in 1896. As a result, farmers and others who borrowed money pushed for "cheaper money." Money became cheaper when there was more of it. So the "borrowing classes" demanded that the government either issue more "greenbacks"—paper money that had no backing in silver or gold—or coin silver in large quantities.

Increasing the supply of silver dollars was the favored approach. If the government was required to mint all the large supplies of silver then being mined in the West, the quantity of money would be much increased. A rise in the supply of money tends to lift the general level of prices. This is called

inflation. If the price of wheat and cotton and corn went up, the farmers' problems might be solved. This proposal for minting silver was called "free silver" because it meant the "free"—that is, unlimited—coining of silver dollars.

The farmers were unable to persuade Congress to go that far. The most they could get was a bill for a limited coining of silver. In 1878 the Bland-Allison Act, named for its sponsors, Representative Richard "Silver Dick" Bland of Missouri and Senator William Allison of Iowa, passed both houses of Congress. It required the government to buy and coin at least $2 million worth of silver a month. Hayes vetoed the bill because he thought that coining silver dollars that were worth less than 90 cents in gold was dishonest. The bill passed over his veto. But it only partially satisfied the demand for a larger money supply. The question would return to haunt other Presidents.

The spoils system. Since Andrew Jackson's day, government jobs had been given to people who had worked hard to help the party win the election. "To the victors belong the spoils" was the motto of both parties. Every change of administration was marked by a wild scramble for government jobs. These were simply rewards for party loyalty. Thousands of offices were filled by people who had no other qualification. After they were on the government payroll, they were still expected to work for the party in election campaigns. They even had to hand over a part of their pay to support the party.

Some people believed that the problems of government might be solved if this system was changed. Their slogan was "Out with the party hacks." Only qualified people should hold government jobs. This program was called civil service reform. After the Civil War, influential citizens like Carl Schurz and George W. Curtis, the editor of *Harper's Weekly*, worked hard to abolish the "spoils system." Finally in 1871 Congress passed a law authorizing the President to make rules to reform the civil service. President Grant appointed a commission. But the "Stalwarts"—the old-fashioned Republican bosses—managed to prevent the commission from getting anything done. Their leader was the clever and knowledgeable Senator Roscoe Conkling, the New York State boss whose power was based on the spoils system.

The vain, handsome Conkling walked with "a turkey-gobbler strut" and was a master of ridicule. He called it "snivel" service reform. He sneered that the reformers "forget that parties are not built up by deportment or by ladies' magazines or by gush!"

Hayes and civil service reform.
President Hayes did not agree. Wanting to abolish the spoils system, he revived the Civil Service Commission. He ordered that government employees must not work in political campaigns and must not be assessed for party "contributions."

In the opening battle of his war against the spoils system, President Hayes aimed to control the hiring in the New York customshouse. The 1000 people employed there collected two-thirds of all the nation's tariff revenue. First he asked Conkling's aides in New York, Collector of Customs Chester A. Arthur and Naval Officer Alonzo B. Cornell, to resign. But Conkling needed to control those jobs to keep himself and his party in power. So Conkling fought back.

Senator Roscoe Conkling appears still triumphant in 1878 during his fight with Hayes over the customshouse. But Conkling was soon to lose.

THE NEW OFFICIAL DOOR-KEEPER.

CONKLING—"Well, just at this moment, I feel as though I was a bigger man than old Hayes!"

Hayes won this battle of the customshouse, but he did not win the war for civil service reform. Cornell went on to become governor of New York, and Arthur, only a year later, was nominated for the Vice-Presidency. Now the professional politicians in his own party were Hayes's enemies, and Democrats controlled the House of Representatives. It is not surprising, then, that Hayes accomplished little during his last two years in office.

The Republicans name Garfield and Arthur.
Hayes had been an honest, hardworking President who deserved the people's respect by his firm stands for what he believed was right. Although he had improved the Republican party's tarnished image from the days of Grant, he had made too many enemies among the leaders of his own party. They looked for a different kind of candidate to run in 1880.

The battle was between the Stalwarts led by Roscoe Conkling, who wanted a return to the "good old days" of President Grant when the bosses had their own way, and those whom the Stalwarts called the "Half-breeds." The party regulars sneered at these so-called "Half-breeds." Those people were only half loyal to the old-time Republican policies. They did firmly support the business interests, but they also were for civil service reform and took a hands-off policy toward the South. Their leader was the most magnetic politician of the age, James G. Blaine. He had the knack of making any cause seem a noble crusade, and so was called the "Plumed Knight."

The convention deadlocked between the Stalwart candidate U. S. Grant and the Half-breed Blaine. In the end it chose a "dark horse"—the popular James A. Garfield of Ohio. He had served gallantly in the Union army during the Civil War. Since then he had been a loyal Republican party leader in the Congress, but he had no particular program. In an attempt to please Roscoe Conkling and the disappointed Stalwarts, the convention named Chester A. Arthur for Vice-President. The angry Conkling tried to persuade Arthur to refuse the second-place nomination. Arthur accepted because, as he explained, "The office of the vice-presidency is a greater honor than I ever dreamed of attaining."

The party platform did plump for civil service reform but clearly avoided other issues. "What are we up here for?" a Texas delegate complained. "I mean that members of the Republican party are entitled to office, and if we are victorious we will have office."

Also aiming to win votes by avoiding the troublesome issues, the Democrats decided simply to prove their loyalty to the Union. They nominated General Winfield Scott Hancock, a professional army officer who had graduated from West Point. He was famous for fending off an attack by General Lee at Gettysburg but had no experience in politics.

Garfield is elected.

The politicians fought a hard campaign without facing the nation's problems. By waving the "bloody shirt," Garfield managed to squeak into office—with a bare 7000-vote plurality out of more than 9 million votes cast. His electoral college vote was 214 to 155.

This campaign ribbon for Garfield and Arthur in 1880 was fittingly the color of the "bloody shirt" they waved during the campaign.

The southern states, now free of all federal interference for the first presidential election since 1860, cast a solid vote for the Democrat Hancock. The "solid South" became a new expression and a new institution in American politics. For the next years in every local, state, and national election the South was found solid in the Democratic column. Not until 1920 would a Republican candidate for President win a state of the former Confederacy.

Garfield was an intelligent, adaptable man. During his long career in the House of Representatives he had shown skill in party politics and parliamentary maneuver. But he had not escaped the taint of the Crédit Mobilier scandals. Many people did not believe him when he denied that he had been bribed with stock in the company.

His brief Presidency is remembered mainly for its violent end. The big issue right from the start was who would get what jobs. Garfield began by naming a Conkling rival to head the New York customshouse, and this move led to his death. On July 2, 1881, as the President entered the Washington railroad station for a trip to New England, Charles Guiteau, a crazed Chicago lawyer, shot him in the back. Guiteau was one of the thousands of party loyalists who had failed to get the government jobs they thought that they deserved. "I am a Stalwart," he shouted, "and Arthur is President now." For eleven weeks, Garfield lingered in pain before dying on September 19.

Arthur as President.

Many people were shocked at the thought of Conkling's henchman, the Stalwart Arthur, in the White House. The dapper, wealthy Arthur was, in fact, an able organizer who had brought improved systems to the huge New York customshouse. But he also managed to take care of the party faithful. Even after his accidental rise to the White House, many voters continued to think of him as just another Stalwart, a high-class party hack.

The party regulars had a surprise in store for them. When President Arthur sent his first annual message to Congress, in an astonishing turnabout he called for civil service reform! The assassination of a President by a partisan office seeker outraged public opinion. Even Stalwart Republicans now had to go along. They feared defeat in the election of 1884 and saw "reform" as the only way to keep their own followers in office.

As a result, the Civil Service bill sponsored by Democrat George H. Pendleton of Ohio passed both houses of Congress in January 1883. Certain government jobs were "classified." This meant that they would be filled by the winners in competitive examinations to test "the fitness of applicants for the public service." A nonpartisan Civil Service Commission would do the examining and grade the candidates. The Pendleton Act forbade appointments to office for political reasons and made it illegal to assess jobholders to support the party.

Arthur named a strong head for the new Civil Service Commission and made strict rules to prevent evasion of the law. Fifteen thousand government employees (15 percent of the total) were put into the "classified" service.

President Arthur's whole administration showed that the office of President could actually lift a man above sordid party politics. He fought against wasteful "pork barrel" bills that would have spent the nation's money on unneeded river and harbor projects. He worked for tariff reform. He began the much-needed modernization of the navy. Before his term of office was over, he had surprised both his supporters and his opponents. But the people in both camps never stopped wondering how reliable he would be. They asked, "Can a leopard change his spots?" The eloquent perennial candidate, James G. Blaine, opposed Arthur for the Republican nomination in 1884 and was nominated on the fourth ballot.

SECTION REVIEW

1. Identify or explain: Gilded Age, deflation, inflation, "cheap money," "free silver," "Stalwarts," Roscoe Conkling, Alonzo B. Cornell, "Half-breeds," James G. Blaine, James A. Garfield, W. S. Hancock, Charles Guiteau, Pendleton Act.

2. How did Hayes respond to the railway strike of 1877? Why?

3. Why did demands for "cheaper money" arise in the 1870s? What was the response of Congress?

4. Who favored civil service reform? What steps toward it were made under Hayes? under Arthur?

5. How did a tragedy hasten civil service reform?

2. The Democrats come and go

Blaine had been around for a long time, and he had made many enemies. So to oppose him the Democrats shrewdly chose a political newcomer, Governor Grover Cleveland of New York.

Grover Cleveland, the "reformer." Cleveland was the son of a poor Presbyterian minister, and his early life was spent in a small-town parsonage. There he learned the virtues of honesty, hard work, devotion to duty, and obedience to law. At the same time he was a jovial man. He weighed 250 pounds, which showed how much he loved good food and drink. He never went to college but became a self-trained lawyer. After serving as assistant district attorney and sheriff, in 1881 he was elected as a "reform" mayor of Buffalo. There he became known as the "veto mayor," for he opposed any measures that smacked of favoritism or waste.

In an age of shady political bosses, he stayed independent. He was just what honest Democrats wanted in their candidate for governor of New York. So they nominated Cleveland for governor in 1882, and he was elected in a landslide. He did not disappoint the reformers who supported him. For he lived up to his reputation as the sworn enemy of Tammany Hall—the organized bosses in his very own party. And he annoyed the bosses more than ever by his nonpartisan courage in the statehouse. There he supported the laws to clean up the government of New York City which were proposed by a bumptious 24-year-old Republican legislator named Theodore Roosevelt.

Blaine versus Cleveland. Grover Cleveland's political career was one of the speediest in American history. Only three years after serving as mayor of Buffalo, he was nominated for the Presidency. Suddenly this reforming upstart from New York was plunged into a mud-slinging national election campaign.

When the "Plumed Knight" Blaine was nominated by the Republicans, the Democrats advertised the bribe he had once received in Congress to favor an Arkansas railroad. This charge had kept him from being nominated in 1876 and 1880. The Republican machine bosses were against him, too. Some nasty remarks he once made against Boss Conkling had turned Conkling into his enemy. Although Blaine had helped make his party modern and responsible, many Republicans still considered Blaine himself to be little better than a Stalwart. He had a talent for inspiring intense personal dislike. Carl Schurz, George W. Curtis, and other reformers left the party and filled the newspapers with their onslaughts.

Now the Republican regulars answered with their own name-calling. They ridiculed the reformers for being pompous and self-important. So they cleverly picked up an old Algonquin Indian word for chief or high-muck-a-muck and called them "Mugwumps." This name was so appealing that no one could forget it. And they went on with personal attacks on Cleveland for being immoral and a drunkard.

The election on November 4, 1884, was another close one. Cleveland received 29,000 more votes than Blaine. A swing of only 600 votes in New York would have carried that state for Blaine and made him President.

Two trivial events during the campaign may have cost Blaine the election. In his presence a New York minister said that the Democrats were the party of "rum, Romanism, and rebellion." Blaine may not even have heard the remark, or perhaps he was just not paying attention. Anyway the unlucky Blaine did not disagree on the spot. The alert Democrats quickly advertised this insult to the religion and the drinking customs of thousands of Irish Catholic voters. Many of these were recent immigrants still struggling to make ends meet. On that same day, some of the city's richest men gave a dinner in Blaine's honor. The *New York World* portrayed Blaine feasting while "thousands of children in this great city whose fathers labor twelve hours a day, went to bed hungry and many supperless."

The Interstate Commerce Act of 1887.

Grover Cleveland accomplished little during his first two years in office—partly because the Senate remained Republican, but also because he did not believe a President should be very active. Without guidance from the President, Congress tried to get fair treatment from the railroads for the small customers. Senator Shelby M. Cullom had helped his home state of Illinois to pass legislation regulating the railroads. As governor he had strictly enforced those laws. But Cullom was convinced that only the national government could control the rail-roads. Individual states were not strong enough to deal with the rich and powerful interstate railroads. So in 1887 Cullom oversaw the passage of the Interstate Commerce Act.

The railroads had given special low rates and also offered rebates to large companies like Standard Oil. They did not set their rates according to the distance the freight had to be carried. Where there was no competition, their rates were exorbitant. Since the railroads kept their rates secret, the small farmers could not know what it would cost to take their produce to market. And they could not count on the rates being fair. The new law banned rebates and the other favors given to powerful shippers. New rates would be proportional to distance. Rate schedules would be public and open to inspection by the new Interstate Commerce Commission.

This was the first of many attempts of Congress to solve the problems of the new industrial age by regulating "big business."

Pension vetoes.

President Cleveland, determined to reduce government spending, was at his best when he could oppose something. In 1886 he vetoed many Civil War pension bills for people who really did not deserve pensions. Then, in January 1887 Congress passed a bill awarding a pension to any needy veteran who had served in the ranks for more than 90 days. Refusing to let the pension list become an excuse for fraud, Cleveland vetoed the bill.

The issue of the tariff.

Finding that the United States Treasury was taking in $100 million a year more than it spent, President Cleveland aimed to stop the "unnecessary taxation" that produced this surplus money. In December 1887 he devoted his entire annual message to the need to reduce the tariffs—the customs duties that raised the price of goods that were imported. Both business and labor leaders had favored the high tariffs as a way to protect Americans against foreign competition.

With this message Cleveland threw down the gauntlet to the Republican party. Now, for the first time in many years, a presidential campaign would have a real issue. Many Republicans welcomed the challenge. James G. Blaine had long wanted his party to take a bold stand in favor of a high tariff.

PUCK.

A HYDRA THAT MUST BE CRUSHED—AND THE SOONER THE BETTER.

Culver Pictures

Joseph Keppler sided with Grover Cleveland on the tariff issue. In this imaginative cartoon of March 1888 Keppler showed the tariff as a "hydra"—a many-headed monster from Greek mythology. The heads were the trusts that supported the tariffs that made them thrive.

The presidential campaign of 1888. The tariff was debated in Congress for months. It became the "burning issue" of the day. The Democrats nominated Cleveland for another term and declared in their platform that "all unnecessary taxation is unjust taxation." When Blaine's poor health convinced him not to run again, the Republicans settled on Benjamin Harrison of Indiana. Their platform stressed the need for a high tariff to protect "the general business, the labor, the farming interests of the country."

The Republican candidate was the great-grandson of a signer of the Declaration of Independence and a grandson of President William Henry Harrison. He entered the Civil War as commander of a volunteer regiment from Indiana, then rose to become a general. He was an aloof, unfriendly man, unwilling to take the courageous positions that might have made outspoken enemies or firm allies.

After a career as lawyer for corporations, he had served one term as senator from Indiana.

The campaign was waged almost entirely over the tariff issue. Harrison wanted to avoid making mistakes that Blaine had made in New York by going out and mingling with the crowds. He stayed home and conducted a traditional "front porch" campaign. Delegations would come to see him, and he would make harmless short speeches promising to help them if they helped send him to the White House. Now at last the Republicans abandoned the old hatreds of the Civil War and stopped waving the "bloody shirt." Instead they tried appealing to everybody's pocketbook. This brought the Knights of Labor to their side. Wealthy businessmen, too, now gave millions of dollars to put the party back in power.

In one of the most corrupt campaigns in American history, the Republicans spent a fortune buying votes in the big doubtful states like New York and Indiana. Those states had gone for Cleveland in 1884. The Republicans did not succeed in buying a popular national majority, for Cleveland received almost 100,000 more votes than Harrison. But with the crucial support of those two states Harrison won the electoral vote by 233 to 168. The Republicans also carried both houses of Congress. Cleveland's strength was largely in the farm states. In the key industrial states, the Republicans convinced business people and laborers that the tariff really did work in their favor.

"Czar" Reed and Congress.

Harrison, unbending and abrupt, made enemies even when he tried to do the right thing. Senator Cullom said, "I suppose he treated me about as well in the patronage as he did any other senator, but whenever he did anything for me it was done so ungraciously that the concession tended to anger rather than please."

Oddly enough, the first session of Congress under Harrison produced more important legislation than any session since Reconstruction. This was due not so much to the man in the White House as to a powerful leader in the House of Representatives. The Republicans had only a thin margin of votes in the House, and this slight edge made the leader's role more important than ever. Representative Thomas B. Reed from Maine was an overpowering man in more ways than one. Standing six feet, three inches tall, he actually weighed 300 pounds. He ruled the House so firmly that he was nicknamed the "Czar." He forced the House to adopt the "Reed Rules." These prevented the minority from blocking bills and gave the Speaker and the majority the power to push through their program.

Electoral reform.

One of the first measures that the House considered was the electoral reform bill that Harrison had called for in his inaugural address. It was a pioneer civil rights bill. President Harrison was disturbed over the way Southerners often prevented blacks from voting. Since the blacks were usually Republicans, Republican Representative Henry Cabot Lodge of Massachusetts drew up a bill that allowed the federal government to see that there were fair elections.

The House passed the Lodge bill. But the rules of the Senate (unlike the House) allowed a senator to stop the regular business and prevent a vote by talking endlessly and refusing to "yield the floor." "Filibuster," the name for this practice, came from a Spanish word for the troublemakers who stirred up revolution in Latin America. Southern senators used the filibuster to block action on the tariff bill that many Republicans wanted to pass. So in order to get their tariff, the Republicans had to put aside the Lodge bill. When it was brought up later, Republican senators from the silver-producing states themselves helped to defeat it in return for southern support for a new silver coinage bill. The time for equal voting rights had not yet come.

A new tariff.

The McKinley tariff bill, named for Representative William McKinley of Ohio, raised the duty on almost every article produced outside the country that competed with American production. The list included food, clothing, furniture, carpets, fuel, tools, kitchenware, thread, and countless other items. Articles such as tea, coffee, spices, and drugs that were not produced in the United States were admitted free. Sugar also was put on the free list. But a bounty or subsidy of 2 cents a pound was to be paid to domestic producers of raw sugar. McKinley boasted that his bill, which passed the House in May 1890, was "protective in every paragraph and American in every line and word."

The senators from silver states were willing to help pass the tariff only if something was also done for silver. They said that under the Bland-Allison Act of 1878 the government still was not buying enough silver to inflate the currency or to keep the price of silver from falling. These Westerners wanted "free and unlimited" coinage of silver at the old ratio of 16 to 1 (that is, 16 ounces of silver was to be equal in value to 1 ounce of gold). Many Republicans wanted to avoid free silver, but at the same time they were determined to pass the McKinley tariff. So on July 4, 1890, the Sherman Silver Purchase Act (named after its author, Senator John Sherman of Ohio) provided that the government would purchase 4 1/2 million ounces of silver every month. This was more than double the amount required by the Bland-Allison Act. It equaled the whole current production of silver at the time. In addition, the bill provided for the issue of paper money (Treasury notes) to the full amount of the silver purchased. This would inflate the currency. And it would help farmers who wanted to pay off their mortgages in cheap money.

The bargain over silver won western votes for the McKinley tariff bill, which now finally passed the Senate. President Harrison signed the bill into law on October 1, 1890, only 35 days before the mid-term elections.

The Sherman Antitrust Act.
Congress also faced the growing demand that they do something to help farmers and small businesses against trusts like the Standard Oil Company. Everywhere big companies seemed to be taking over. Bigness meant monopoly. And monopoly meant that a few people had the power to dictate to everybody else.

By 1880 the Standard Oil Company, by fair means and foul, had captured control of 90 percent of the lamp-oil refining in the United States. In the 1890s, if you wanted sugar for your table, you had to buy it from the E. C. Knight Company. Your tobacco was controlled by the American Tobacco Company.

How could small businesses and buyers in general be protected against these tyrants of "unlawful restraint and monopoly"? Many states passed laws outlawing trusts. Still the most powerful monopolies were organized in nationwide networks. This was a national problem.

In 1888 both major parties wrote antitrust planks into their platforms. President Harrison called for legislation in his annual message to Congress in 1889.

The result in July 1890 was the Sherman Antitrust Act (also named after John Sherman). This epoch-making law aimed to punish "restraint of trade or commerce." Now it was a crime for business firms to combine to prevent competition. But the language of the law was vague. And the law would not be effective at all unless the government worked hard to enforce it.

Yet any President who wanted to be reelected had to be careful not to offend powerful business leaders. It is not surprising that Presidents usually pretended that the law did not exist. If a President dared prosecute a trust, the Supreme Court often came to the rescue by technicalities. In 1895, for example, the Attorney General prosecuted the E. C. Knight Company, which controlled 98 percent of the nation's sugar refining. But the Supreme Court held the company *not* guilty under the Sherman Antitrust Act—because it was in "manufacturing" and not in "commerce." Only a fearless President

Cartoonist Edward Kemble saw the trusts as evil vultures feeding off the Senate. Seats were advertised for sale because senators were still chosen by the state legislatures.

like Theodore Roosevelt would be willing to use the act to smash monopolies (p. 421).

The billion-dollar Congress.
This busy Republican Congress also passed many bills that were costly for the Treasury. They voted funds for river and harbor improvements, for steamship subsidies, and even to return the federal taxes paid by the northern states during the Civil War. Tight-fisted President Cleveland had vetoed the Dependent Pension Act, which old soldier Harrison now willingly signed into law. Pension outlays rose from $81 million in 1889 to $135 million in 1893. The "billion-dollar" Congress, as it came to be called, rapidly depleted the Treasury surplus which had worried President Cleveland. The surplus was gone by 1894, and there has never been one since.

In the congressional election campaign after this session the Republicans told the voters that they had accomplished a great deal. Many Americans did

The Oakland Museum

Improved farm machinery of the sort advertised here helped farmers boost production.

"business prostrated, homes covered with mortgages, labor impoverished, and the land concentrated in the hands of capitalists." The major parties seemed interested only in "power and plunder."

The Populists called for sweeping reform. They demanded the free coinage of silver and an increase in the money supply to $50 per person. They wanted an income tax to put a larger share of the burden on the wealthy. The government, they said, should take over ownership of railroads, telegraph, and telephone. The platform also called for a shorter working day for industrial laborers and the direct election of senators.

The farmers' leaders were not afraid to shock the rich and comfortable people. One of their best was the handsome, outspoken Mary Elizabeth Lease of Kansas, the mother of four. "What you farmers need," she urged, "is to raise less corn and more Hell!" She also went on:

Wall Street owns the country. It is no longer a government of the people, by the people, and for the people, but a government of Wall Street, by Wall Street, and for Wall Street. The great common people of this country are slaves, and monopoly is the master.

Then, also from Kansas, there was "Sockless Jerry" Simpson. Once when he ran for Congress, he accused his well-dressed opponent of wearing silk stockings. A reporter then sneered that Simpson was so crude that he wore no socks at all. Simpson made this into a boast. Always after that he was known as "Sockless Jerry."

Crusaders like the rabble-rousing Tom Watson of Georgia spoke for them in Congress and spoke loud and clear. "Before I will give up this fight," Watson warned, "I will stay here till the ants tote me out of the keyhole."

The election of 1892. The two major parties had held their conventions in June. The Republicans had picked Harrison again. The Democrats had chosen their strongest candidate, Grover Cleveland. He had the support of many business leaders because he opposed free silver and inflation and therefore was "sound" on the money question.

The Populists, with the eloquent and honest General James B. Weaver as their candidate, conducted a vigorous campaign. In the South they made common cause with all the poor, both white and black. Conservative southern Democrats, desperate to defend themselves against reform, raised the cry for white supremacy. They denounced all Populists as the enemies of law and order.

A cartoonist for *Puck* pictured the Farmers' Alliances as a windmaker causing the U.S. Treasury windmill to turn out worthless money by the wagonload.

THE GRANGERS' DREAM OF CHEAP MONEY.

General Weaver, an outspoken man of courage, declared:

> There is but one issue in the South. That is competition to see who can most hate the Negro. The man that wins gets the nomination. The whole thing is a dead-drag on the country. . . . Slavery must be the greatest of crimes. Here we are, all these years after it has been abolished, and we are still paying the penalty for it.

During the campaign summer of 1892 the nation was torn by labor strife. First came the bloody Homestead Strike (p. 361). When striking miners rioted in Coeur d'Alene, Idaho, President Harrison sent in federal troops at the governor's request. In these stormy times, people put their faith in Grover Cleveland. He had already proved once that he could be a competent, pacifying President. Cleveland received 373,000 more votes than Harrison and won with an electoral vote of 277 to Harrison's 145. The Democrats also won both houses of Congress. The Populist General Weaver actually received over a million popular votes, but he carried only four states—Colorado, Kansas, Nevada, and Idaho. The Populists elected three United States senators and eleven members of the House.

Cleveland's second term. Grover Cleveland's second term was as much a disaster as his first had been a success. It began with one of the nation's worst depressions, one that lasted his entire four years in office. Negative policies were no longer enough.

One major problem was that the Treasury was rapidly losing gold. Under the Sherman Silver Purchase Act, the Treasury notes issued to buy silver could be redeemed for gold. Since gold dollars were more valuable than silver dollars, people naturally turned in their silver Treasury notes for gold dollars. But the Treasury had to reissue the Treasury notes—which were then turned back in for gold again. It is not surprising that the Treasury was about to run out of gold.

Cleveland called a special session of Congress in August 1893 to demand repeal of the Sherman Silver Purchase Act. He wanted the government to stop spending $50 million a year taking in "cheap" silver for valuable gold. After some hard fighting that split both parties, his measure passed.

nation's ills. When Bryan arrived at the Democratic convention in Chicago on July 7, 1896, he was 36 years old—one year over the minimum age for a President. He had served only four years in Congress and was barely known outside of Nebraska. Unlike the other leading candidates, he did not have rich supporters.

As the convention met, it was still not decided whether the Democratic party would stay with the gold standard or whether they would join the farmers for free silver. Until Bryan came to the rostrum, the speakers at the Chicago convention had been dull and long-winded. Since there was no public-address system, most of the speakers could hardly be heard. Bryan was the final speaker for free silver.

This was young Bryan's great chance. The first sound of his ringing voice awakened the perspiring audience. They responded to his words with laughter and applause "like a trained choir," as he said, down to his last syllable. He spoke without hesitating, for he had given much the same speech many times before—to farm audiences all over Nebraska. "We will answer their demand for a Gold Standard," he ended, "by saying to them: You shall not press down upon the brow of labor this crown of thorns. You shall not crucify mankind upon a cross of gold."

The crowd went wild. Their yelling and cheering lasted for an hour. This one speech had transformed a Nebraska small-town lawyer into a front runner for President!

On the next day, the Democratic convention named him to lead their ticket. Then the Populists at their national convention also nominated him for President.

The campaign and election of 1896. The campaign offered one of the most spectacular contrasts in American history. The "Boy Orator of the Platte" hurried about the country by train, making speeches far into the night at every little town and often in between. On some days he made 36 speeches. Meanwhile, his conservative Republican opponent, William McKinley, remained calmly seated on his front porch in Canton, Ohio. McKinley made almost no speeches. When he did, he was careful to say nothing in particular—except that he was in favor of "sound money" (the gold standard) and "restoring confidence."

McKinley's campaign ribbon of 1896 showed him with his running mate, Garret A. Hobart.

Mark Hanna, a clever Cleveland businessman and political boss who had secured the Republican nomination for McKinley, managed McKinley's campaign. Hanna counted on letting Bryan talk himself to defeat. And he used every trick to convince voters that Bryan was a dangerous radical. For example, he persuaded some factory owners, as a stunt, to pay their workers in Mexican dollars (worth only 50 United States cents). This was supposed to show the workers what their wages would really be worth if Bryan won. Employees in some factories were actually told that the businesses would shut down if Bryan won.

Hanna's tactics succeeded. McKinley overwhelmed Bryan by 600,000 votes, the greatest margin since 1872. The Republicans retained their control of both houses of Congress. Despite all this,

Bryan's performance had really been spectacular. With little money or organization, deserted by the "gold wing" of his party, Bryan had polled some 6.5 million votes, more than had ever before been cast even for a winning candidate. The change of about 19,000 votes, distributed in six states, would have won him the election in the electoral college.

Bryan's fatal weakness was his inability to carry a single one of the urban-industrial states. He was a one-issue candidate, and his one issue—free silver—did not appeal to factory workers or city people. Still, he had attracted so many votes that the Democratic leaders could not ignore him. Twice again—in 1900 and 1908—he would be named the Democratic candidate for President. Bryan never won.

SECTION REVIEW

1. Why did the Democrats and Populists choose Bryan as their candidate for President in 1896?

2. Who managed McKinley's campaign? What were his tactics?

3. In 1896 why did the Republicans win?

CHAPTER REVIEW

MEETING OUR EARLIER SELVES

1. Show that control of the national government was closely divided between the two major parties from 1876 to 1896. How did this situation make for "an age of timid Presidents"? How did it stimulate the rise of the Populist party?

2. President Arthur's administration proved that the office of President can lift a person above narrow party politics. Suggest reasons why.

3. In the 1880s and '90s what stand on the "cheap money" vs. "sound money" issue would you expect each of the following persons to take and why: (a) an elderly city couple living on their savings? (b) a Kansas wheat farmer? (c) a factory worker? (d) a merchant selling chiefly to farmers? (e) a banker?

4. Grover Cleveland has been criticized for being more concerned with managing the government and controlling spending than with facing the issues of the day. What evidence can you find for or against this criticism? Which is more important for a President—to be a good manager or to be a political leader?

QUESTIONS FOR TODAY

1. Suppose that the Lodge bill (p. 392) had been passed and then enforced effectively and that Populist efforts to unite black farmers and white farmers had succeeded. How might race relations in the past 20 to 30 years have been different?

2. Getting or handing out government jobs was an important motive for taking an active part in politics prior to civil service reform. What motivates people to go into politics today?

YOUR REGION IN HISTORY

1. What leaders from your state or region were active in national politics and the struggles of the Gilded Age? What were their accomplishments?

2. Can you identify a great-grandparent or other relative who lived in America's Gilded Age? How did he or she earn a living? What reforms might he or she have supported or opposed? Why?

SKILLS TO MAKE OUR PAST VIVID

1. Study the table below. About how much did wholesale prices rise between 1860 and 1865? How does the price rise compare with the increase in the supply of currency?

2. In what five-year period did wholesale prices reach the level they had been at in 1860?

3. When did the currency supply reach the level that it had been at in 1865?

4. What conclusion can you draw from the data below about the link between money supply and prices?

DATE	TOTAL CURRENCY (in millions)	WHOLESALE PRICES (1910–14 = 100) All Products	Farm Products
1860	$ 442	93	77
1865	1,180	185	148
1870	900	135	112
1875	926	118	99
1880	1,186	100	80
1885	1,537	85	72
1890	1,685	82	71

Source: Historical Statistics, Series X 420, E 52–53

7

Democratic reforms and world power 1890–1920

Until the Civil War the United States had seemed a world of its own. Almost every needed crop or animal or mineral was found somewhere within the nation and its territories.

Then after the Civil War, more and more Americans discovered that the nation did need the world. There was still room to import people by the millions. American farmers and factory workers and business owners depended on faraway customers. At the same time, American factories and homes wanted silk from Italy and China, rubber from Ceylon and Sumatra, coffee from Brazil, tin from the Malay peninsula, chrome from Rhodesia—and a thousand other items from across the oceans.

The United States became the world's know-how center—for trying new ways of making and doing. People everywhere expected to learn from America. And Americans wanted to help the whole earth become a New World.

The years from 1890 to 1920 would test anew the belief of Americans in democracy. At home they worked to make government and business answer to the needs of the people. When neighboring Cuba suffered tyranny, Americans wanted to help. How could the United States assist other nations to become democratic without choosing their governments for them?

Could Americans take their place in the world without joining the wars of Europe? Europe suffered from intrigue, tyranny, and old-fashioned monarchs. War was that continent's disease. Would our powerful nation be tempted to try to run the affairs of people everywhere? How could Americans keep their ideals in this different kind of world? These years would offer many new challenges, and a few new answers.

Childe Hassam's "Allies Day" captures the beauty of American, French, and English flags fluttering over 5th Avenue in New York City in May 1917. From the National Gallery of Art, Washington, gift of Ethelyn McKinney in memory of her brother, Glenn Ford McKinney.

CHAPTER 19

The United States and the world

During the Gilded Age, the United States filled its land with farms, factories, and cities. Busy in their vast nation, most Americans felt no need to go abroad. Protected by broad oceans, they paid little attention to events elsewhere. Then, in 1898, war with Spain suddenly thrust the United States upon the world stage. "The guns of Dewey at Manila have changed the destiny of the United States," the *Washington Post* observed. "We are face to face with a strange destiny and must accept its responsibilities. An imperial policy!"

1. Looking outward

From time to time, earlier in the 1800s, a few traders, whalers, missionaries, and diplomats did look outward.

Early expansion to the distant East. The expansion of other nations gave the United States the chance—and the excuse—to seek American advantages overseas. American merchants had been visiting Canton to trade with China since 1785. After the Opium War of 1839–1842, Great Britain secured special privileges in China. Then President Tyler sent out Caleb Cushing, the able champion of expansion, to secure the same privileges for Americans. In the Treaty of Wanghia (1844), Cushing won for the United States "most favored nation" status. This meant that in China the United States was to receive the best treatment offered any country. Four new Chinese ports in addition to Canton were opened to American merchants for the first time. Magnificent American clipper ships and other grand trading vessels also went venturing out to the Philippines, Java, India, and other distant lands. In 1833 a commercial treaty was signed with faraway Siam.

The rulers of Japan, fearing corruption by foreign ways, kept out the foreigners. They allowed only a small colony of merchants of the Dutch East India Company to live on an island at Nagasaki. United States merchants wanted to trade with Japan, but this was not easy to arrange. It required a man of adventurous spirit and imagination. Luckily, in 1852, President Millard Fillmore found that man. He was Commodore Matthew C. Perry, a bold naval officer. He had an interest in ideas and the courage to risk danger. Perry tried to improve the education of midshipmen. He had fought pirates in the West Indies and had helped suppress the slave traffic from Africa. Now he would try to open trade with Japan. He awed the Japanese with his great "Black Ships"—bigger than any ever seen there before. When his ships arrived off the coast of Japan, he was firm and skillful in his diplomacy. He refused to deal with minor officials. He demanded that the Japanese respect the Americans. And he secured the Treaty of Kanagawa (1854), opening two ports to ships from the United States.

Meanwhile, American traders had already arrived in Hawaii in the 1790s. They were followed in the 1820s by whalers and missionaries. As early

This scene from a Japanese scroll shows the ceremonies upon Commodore Perry's arrival in Japan in 1854. The artist omitted the stripes and stars on most of the American flags flying from the longboats that had brought the delegation ashore.

as 1849, the United States declared that it could never allow the Hawaiian Islands to pass under the dominion of any other power.

When President Pierce had tried to annex Hawaii in 1854 (p. 258), the treaty was not even sent to the Senate. Every question was bedeviled by the issue of slavery. The same problem defeated his efforts to buy Cuba, Alaska, and all of Lower California. Now the slavery issue was out of the way. Expansion was no longer stopped by sectional rivalry. The whole nation's factories and farms hungered for new markets. Steamships and telegraph cables were drawing Americans out toward the world.

Seward pursues expansion. After the Civil War, Secretary of State William H. Seward became the champion of these expansionist hopes. When the Russians asked whether the United States might want to buy Alaska, he jumped at the chance. He could expel one more monarchy from the American continent. Seward also believed that a strong United States outpost on the other side of Canada would help to force the British out of Canada. Then Canada, too, could be added to the American Empire for Liberty!

But many sensible congressmen had their doubts. Was Alaska anything but a frozen wasteland? The eloquent Senator Charles Sumner of

Massachusetts shared Seward's hope to include Canada within the United States. He finally persuaded the Senate to approve the Alaska treaty (April 19, 1867). Opponents never ceased to call it "Seward's Folly." In order to secure approval by the House of Representatives of the $7.2 million purchase price, the Russian minister to the United States had to bribe some members of Congress.

When the federal government was still burdened by a Civil War debt of $3 billion, it did seem a wild extravagance to spend millions for "Seward's icebox." Few then imagined what a bargain they had made. The gold taken from the Yukon Valley since 1897 has paid for Alaska many times over. Besides, there would be North Slope oil. Best of all, this vast, untamed wilderness was a new frontier for all Americans.

The Caribbean, too, would offer its own kind of tropical frontier. Seward negotiated a treaty in 1867 to pay $7.5 million for the Danish West Indies (now the Virgin Islands). Since the Senate was slow to approve, the islands did not become part of the United States until they were purchased for $25 million in 1917.

The Alabama claims.

Secretary of State Seward could not give all his efforts to the future. The Civil War had left him problems from the past. One of the knottiest concerned the so-called *Alabama* claims. These were claims for damages to Union shipping by a number of Confederate vessels that had been built in Great Britain. British law forbade anyone in the realm from arming a ship to be used by a foreign state against any nation at peace with Great Britain. The Confederate navy had evaded this law by having ships built in Great Britain and then taking them elsewhere to be armed.

By 1863 many of these commerce raiders were on the high seas menacing the Union. Our minister to Great Britain, Charles Francis Adams, objected in vain. Then the British government changed its policy, to favor the Union cause. Two powerful ironclad vessels, the "Laird Rams" (built for the South by the Laird shipyard in Liverpool), were not allowed to go to sea.

During the war the British-built ships already at sea destroyed 257 Union vessels. Union shipowners tried to escape this threat by a technicality. They "registered" their ships under foreign flags. More than 700 vessels were shifted to foreign registry. By 1865 only 26 percent of our foreign trade was carried in ships of United States registry.

The British-built *Alabama* alone destroyed more than 60 merchant ships. Finally in June 1864 the United States ship *Kearsarge* caught up with and sank the *Alabama* off the coast of France.

The United States demanded that Britain pay for the damages done by the *Alabama* and the other ships that had been made in Britain for the South. Seward claimed only $19 million. Charles Sumner, head of the Senate Foreign Relations Committee, had other ideas. He presented a much larger bill of damages against Great Britain. In an hour-long Senate speech he demanded $15 million for vessels destroyed and $110 million for driving our commerce from the ocean. This was only a beginning. Sumner asked $2 billion more for "indirect damages." That was half the Union's cost for the Civil War! The British owed so much, said Sumner, because the British-built vessels had made the war last twice as long. They could pay this enormous bill easily enough just by handing over Canada to the United States.

The Treaty of Washington.

Of course, the British refused to take Senator Sumner's claim seriously. But many Americans approved. Finally in 1871, American and British commissioners signed a treaty at Washington. The *Alabama* claims would be submitted to an arbitration court at Geneva, Switzerland. In 1872 this panel of eminent judges from Switzerland, Italy, and Brazil found that during the Civil War Great Britain had violated the international laws of neutrality. They awarded $15.5 million in damages to the United States.

This peaceful way to settle differences was a happy precedent for later years.

Napoleon III's Mexican "empire."

Another troublesome legacy of the Civil War was the many French troops in Mexico. Napoleon III, like his uncle Napoleon I, had dreamed of a French empire in North America. In 1863, when the United States was fighting the Civil War, Napoleon III sent an army to Mexico. He overthrew the Mexican government. On the Mexican throne he seated his puppet "emperor," the young Austrian archduke Maximilian.

The United States objected. But during the war it was in no position to use troops to put down this flimsy Mexican emperor. After Appomattox, the 50,000 federal troops in Texas could easily move into Mexico. They were President Johnson's and Secretary Seward's message that the French had better go home. In the summer of 1866 Napoleon III removed the French troops. But the foolish and romantic emperor actually thought he could hold onto his throne alone. Maximilian was the only one surprised when, in the summer of 1867, he was executed by a Mexican firing squad.

The United States and Samoa. A wide variety of reasons led the nation to reach across the world. When steamships were powered by coal, coaling stations were needed everywhere. On the remote Samoan island of Tutuila, American sailors had long been interested in the fine harbor of Pago Pago. In the South Pacific Pago Pago had a strategic importance like that of Pearl Harbor in Hawaii in the North Pacific. The United States Navy tried, and failed, to set up a protectorate over the Samoan Islands. Germany also tried to seize control.

After narrowly evading war over Samoa, delegates from Germany, Great Britain, and the United States met in Berlin in 1889. They agreed to establish a joint protectorate. Ten years later Great Britain withdrew. The islands were divided between Germany and the United States. The tiny Samoan Islands enticed the United States onto the stage of world diplomacy.

The joint protectorate, our Secretary of State observed in 1894, was "the first departure from our . . . policy of avoiding entangling alliances with foreign powers in relation to objects remote from this hemisphere."

Problems with Chile. But Latin America was in this hemisphere. And Secretary of State Blaine aimed to capture trade with our neighbors to the south. In 1889 at the 1st International American Conference in Washington the nations founded the International Bureau of American Republics—now called the Organization of American States. The idea was to encourage more cordial and more equal relations among these unequal countries.

The United States was an overpowering neighbor. It was not easy to enforce a neighborly spirit. In Chile, in October 1891, American sailors on shore leave from the cruiser *Baltimore* were attacked by a mob on the streets of Valparaiso. Two sailors were

killed and eighteen injured. The Chilean government refused to apologize and put the blame on the Americans.

On January 25, 1892, President Harrison sent a special message to Congress that seemed to invite a declaration of war on Chile. When a squadron of eight United States cruisers was readied in the Pacific, the Chilean government yielded. They apologized and agreed to pay damages to the families of the killed and wounded sailors.

SECTION REVIEW

1. Identify or explain: Caleb Cushing, Matthew Perry, Treaty of Kanagawa, Charles Sumner, "Laird Rams," *Kearsarge,* arbitration, Napoleon III, Maximilian.

2. Locate: Canton, Siam, Nagasaki, Yukon Valley, Virgin Islands, Pago Pago, Valparaiso.

3. What kind of United States "expansion" to the Far East took place before the Civil War?

4. Why did Seward favor the purchase of Alaska? How did it turn out to be a bargain?

5. Explain the dispute that was settled by the Treaty of Washington.

6. What diplomatic problems arose in Samoa, Mexico, and Chile? What was the outcome of each?

2. Expanding on the seas

By 1900, without thinking of the consequences, the United States had become the third-ranking naval power in the world. This large navy was no solution to the problems of depression, farm revolt, labor unrest, free silver, and Populism. If the nation continued to build its costly navy, there must be some grand purpose. What was it?

Mahan and sea power. Captain Alfred Thayer Mahan, a scholarly naval officer who helped set up the Naval War College in Newport, Rhode Island, had an answer. To be strong in the modern world, he said, the United States must sell its products on all continents. To secure and protect these foreign markets, the nation needed a powerful navy. Drawing on his study of ancient and modern times, he wrote *The Influence of Sea Power upon History* (1890). It was sea power "that made, and kept a nation great." Captain Mahan called for a strong

Culver Pictures

Captain Alfred Thayer Mahan, naval officer and eloquent historian, persuaded Theodore Roosevelt and others that the United States must become a great power.

navy, a canal across the Isthmus of Panama, United States dominance in the Caribbean, and control of Samoa and Hawaii.

Among the many who read and believed Mahan's message was Senator Henry Cabot Lodge of Massachusetts. He came from one of the oldest New England families and had inherited wealth. His upper-class background did not keep him from being a skillful politician. With a Harvard Ph.D. degree in history and a talent for writing history, he knew the American past and was fascinated by the struggle for power. During the 1890s again and again Lodge called for a bigger navy, annexation of Hawaii, a canal across the Isthmus of Panama, and the purchase of the Danish West Indies to protect the approaches to the canal. He also wanted to bring Greenland and Cuba under United States control and to dominate the Caribbean.

Lodge's colorful friend, Theodore Roosevelt of New York, was another follower of Mahan. He believed a nation should grow strong and be ready to fight. He shared Mahan's hopes and Lodge's plans for American expansion. As Assistant Secretary of the Navy under President McKinley, he worked for these goals.

Lodge and Roosevelt believed that a great nation must be strong. The world was full of weak nations. The American empire builders said that American power was only a force for good. Other nations should be glad to be ruled by us. And the American people would profit by reaching abroad. According to Senator Albert J. Beveridge of Indiana:

American factories are making more than the American people can use; American soil is producing more than they can consume. Fate has written our policy for us; the trade of the world must and shall be ours. We will establish trading posts throughout the world as distributing points for American products. We will cover the ocean with our merchant marine. We will build a navy to the measure of our greatness. Great colonies governing themselves, flying our flag and trading with us, will grow about our posts of trade.

Renewed attempts to annex Hawaii. The people who lived in those potential "great colonies" did not all agree with Senator Beveridge. When Queen Liliuokalani came to the throne of Hawaii in 1891, she tried to shake off the control by American settlers. She wanted to restore the royal rights that her brother had given up. But she was frustrated in her struggle for freedom. In January 1893 the settlers, encouraged by the Harrison administration and assisted by United States Marines from the cruiser *Boston,* overthrew the queen. The new pro-America government drew up a treaty of annexation which President Harrison sent to the Senate for approval. The Democrats prevented Senate approval before Harrison left office.

Grover Cleveland, back in the White House again, was against expansion. Upon coming to office in 1893, he sent an agent to Hawaii to find out what had happened. The agent reported that the American minister to Hawaii had fomented the revolution. Cleveland withdrew the treaty to annex Hawaii. Instead he tried to restore "Queen Lil" to her throne. Not until after the Spanish-American War was Hawaii finally annexed by joint resolution of Congress (July 1898). Would the United States follow the European example and build an empire by conquest? Or could the Empire for Liberty in North America add states in the far Pacific?

The strong United States Navy, advocated by Mahan and supported by Lodge and Theodore Roosevelt, defeated the Spanish in the Philippines and in the Caribbean. Commodore Dewey commanded the American ships at Manila, so this painting is called "Dewey? We do!"

The Venezuelan boundary dispute. It was not easy for the growing United States to find its proper role. The new Latin American nations had only recently been colonies of European empires. The Venezuela-British Guiana boundary question was a test. President Cleveland thought the Monroe Doctrine (p. 176) was at stake. Great Britain claimed that 23,000 square miles of disputed borderland belonged to its colony of British Guiana (now the nation of Guyana). Venezuelans relied on the United States guarantees under the Monroe Doctrine. They begged the United States to defend them and save their land.

The United States urged arbitration of the dispute. But Britain refused. Then Cleveland's Secretary of State, Richard Olney, saw his chance to establish the right of the United States to intervene in Latin America. In a new version of the Monroe Doctrine he warned Great Britain. He said that the United States, "practically sovereign on this continent," would "resent and resist" any attempt by the British to take Venezuelan soil. The vast ocean between England and America, he said, made "political union between a European and American state unnatural and inexpedient." Again he called for arbitration. The British Prime Minister, Lord Salisbury, replied that the Monroe Doctrine was no part of international law. This boundary dispute was no business of the United States.

President Cleveland responded with threats. He asked Congress to vote $100,000 for a boundary commission, which was only a start. He would defend his extension of the Monroe Doctrine—even if it meant war. Congress agreed.

But many Americans feared the consequences and rose in protest. The bellicose Theodore Roosevelt was disgusted. "The clamor of the peace faction," he wrote to his friend Senator Lodge, "has convinced me that this country needs a war."

Fortunately, calmer heads prevailed. The British already had enough troubles of their own, fighting for control of South Africa. Why turn the United States into an enemy over a petty border dispute? The British agreed to submit to arbitration. In October 1899 a tribunal in Paris (generally favoring Great Britain's claim) peacefully settled the boundary that had been debated for more than half a century.

The Venezuelan affair had expressed a more aggressive American spirit. "It indicates," Captain Mahan wrote, "the awakening of our countrymen to the fact that we must come out of our isolation . . . and take our share in the turmoil of the world."

SECTION REVIEW

1. Identify: Alfred T. Mahan, Theodore Roosevelt, Albert J. Beveridge, Queen Liliuokalani, Richard Olney.
2. What was Captain Mahan's "message"? How did it influence Lodge and Roosevelt?
3. What was Senator Beveridge's "message"?
4. How was Hawaii obtained by the United States?
5. What was the importance of the Venezuelan boundary dispute to the United States?

3. War with Spain

Many Americans who never read Captain Mahan's history books had their own reasons to reach out across the world. Some were crusaders who wanted to spread Christianity. Others wanted to teach the lessons of American democracy to faraway peoples. Still others thought that the nation would not be secure without bases in every ocean. And some wanted adventure—escape from economic hard times and the humdrum life at home.

Problems in Cuba. The United States had long been interested in Cuba. As early as 1823 John Quincy Adams called Cuba a natural appendage of the North American continent. Later Presidents, too, tried to acquire the island from Spain. In 1868, just after the Civil War, rebels in Cuba began agitating for independence.

In the United States many people felt sympathy for this latest American revolution. In February 1895 when Cuban rebels declared their independence, the Spanish government sent in troops. Their ruthless general was Valeriano "Butcher" Weyler. He ordered "all inhabitants of the country" to "concentrate themselves in the towns." Anyone found outside a town after February 10, 1896, would be shot. Cuban towns were made into "concentration camps." Cuban rebels were tortured. Innocent men, women, and children—including some United States citizens—were herded together, to die of disease and starvation.

The "Yellow Press." American newspapers splashed "Butcher" Weyler's atrocities on their front pages. The new speed presses flooded the cities with six editions each day. By 1896 rural free delivery of mail brought one of these editions daily even to remote farms. The larger a paper's "circulation"—the more copies it sold—the more it could charge for advertising.

Joseph Pulitzer, an adventurous Hungarian immigrant, had secured passage to America by enlisting in the Union army. His energy and enterprise made him a fortune in the newspaper business. He built circulation by championing the interests of his "American aristocracy"—the aristocracy of labor—and by printing sensational stories. If there was no startling news, he would invent some. He once sent Nelly Bly traveling around the world to beat the legendary record of 80 days.

To make his *New York World* interesting for readers of all ages, he invented the comic strip. He hired a clever cartoonist, Richard F. Outcault, to draw the adventures of a bad boy called the "Yellow Kid." Then when these comics appeared regularly in the Sunday *World,* Pulitzer's leading competitor, William Randolph Hearst, hired Outcault to do another Yellow Kid series for his own *New York Journal.* Because both of these sensational newspapers featured the Yellow Kid, they were soon called the "Yellow Press." And the Yellow Press was more interested in selling papers than in keeping peace.

The United States readies for war. American business firms had invested more than $50 million in Cuban sugar. Hoping to prod the United States to intervene, in 1895 the rebels destroyed these sugar plantations and their mills. Then, in 1896, William McKinley was elected President with his twin promises: Protect American business! Free the Cuban people!

When Spain began to negotiate with the United States about the freedom of the Cubans, it seemed that there would be no need to fight. But the Yellow Press now cleared the path to war. On February 9, 1898, the *New York Journal* printed a stolen letter. The Spanish ambassador, Dupuy de Lôme, had written that President McKinley was "weak and a bidder for the admiration of the crowd, besides being a would-be politician who tries to leave a door open behind himself while keeping on good terms with the jingoes of his party." Though de Lôme quickly resigned, Americans were angered by his insults. Before they could calm down, a more serious incident occurred.

To protect American lives and property, the United States battleship *Maine* had been sent to Havana Harbor. At 9:40 on the night of February 15, 1898, the *Maine* was shattered by an explosion, and 260 officers and men were killed. The Navy's court of inquiry reported that the cause was an underwater mine. (Later investigations seem to indicate it was an internal explosion.) Still they could not say for sure whether or not the Spanish were to blame. Anyway the Yellow Press called for war against Spain, and headlined the slogan, "Remember the *Maine*!"

On the day after the formal United States declaration of war on Spain, Hearst's *San Francisco Examiner* called "to arms" and ran the navy signal flags for "Remember the Maine" and "Commence Firing."

When the excitable Assistant Secretary of the Navy, Theodore Roosevelt, heard that McKinley was hesitating, he said the President "had no more backbone than a chocolate éclair." On February 25 the Secretary of the Navy made the mistake of taking the afternoon off. That left impatient Teddy as Acting Secretary—in charge of the whole United States Navy. Without consulting anyone, he cabled his friend Commodore George Dewey, who commanded the United States fleet in Asian waters. Make sure, he ordered, to have your ships ready for sea. In case of war attack the Spanish fleet in the Philippines.

When the Secretary of the Navy returned to his office next day, he was astonished. "Roosevelt," he wrote in his diary, "has come very near causing more of an explosion than happened to the *Maine*." But it was too late to change the order. So even *before* war had begun in nearby Cuba, Teddy had arrayed the United States fleet for war on the other side of the world.

The United States goes to war. If McKinley had been a stronger man, he would not have been afraid to keep the peace. The government of Spain now told him they would give Cuba its independence. But the Yellow Press was still demanding Spanish blood. The "jingoes"—the people who loved to see a fight—wanted war. Their name came from a line of British song of the 1870s, "We don't want to fight, yet by Jingo! if we do, We've got the ships, we've got the men, and got the money too." The jingoes had their way.

On April 11, the day *after* President McKinley learned that Spain would agree to do everything Americans said they wanted, he asked Congress to declare war.

The war lasted only a few months—but that was long enough to create the greatest confusion. At the training camp in Tampa, Florida, commanding officers could not find uniforms. Yet for weeks fifteen railroad cars full of uniforms remained on a siding 25 miles away. The commander of United States troops in Cuba, Major General W. R. Shafter, weighed 300 pounds and was therefore "too unwieldy to get to the front." Unprepared for combat, the Army committed every kind of foolishness.

The Navy was in better shape. On May 1, when Commodore George Dewey, following Roosevelt's

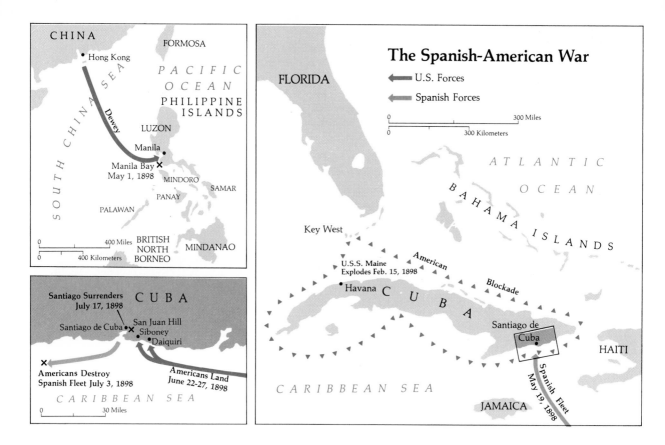

The Spanish-American War

CHINA • Hong Kong
FORMOSA

PACIFIC OCEAN

PHILIPPINE ISLANDS

SOUTH CHINA SEA

Dewey

LUZON

Manila •

Manila Bay
May 1, 1898 ✕

MINDORO

SAMAR

PANAY

PALAWAN

BRITISH NORTH BORNEO

MINDANAO

0 — 400 Miles
0 — 400 Kilometers

CUBA

Santiago Surrenders
July 17, 1898

Santiago de Cuba •✕ San Juan Hill
Siboney
• Daiquiri

✕
Americans Destroy
Spanish Fleet July 3, 1898

Americans Land
June 22-27, 1898

CARIBBEAN SEA

0 — 30 Miles

The Spanish-American War

← U.S. Forces
← Spanish Forces

0 — 300 Miles
0 — 300 Kilometers

FLORIDA

ATLANTIC OCEAN

BAHAMA ISLANDS

Key West

U.S.S. Maine
Explodes Feb. 15, 1898

American

Blockade

• Havana **CUBA**

Santiago de
Cuba

HAITI

Spanish Fleet
May 19, 1898

CARIBBEAN SEA

JAMAICA

---

impulsive orders, attacked the Spanish warships in the Philippines, he finished off the Spaniards in seven hours. The rest of the Spanish fleet, which was in North American waters, was bottled up in Santiago Harbor on the southeastern tip of Cuba.

Roosevelt and the Rough Riders. Meanwhile Teddy Roosevelt had himself named lieutenant colonel of a new regiment of cavalry. At a training camp in San Antonio, Texas, he gathered cowboys, sheriffs, and desperadoes from the West, and a sprinkling of playboy polo players and steeplechase riders from the East.

On June 22, Roosevelt's Rough Riders arrived in Cuba. They were given the job of storming San Juan Hill, which overlooked Santiago Harbor. Without their horses, which in the confusion had been left in Florida, the Rough Riders had to take the hill on foot. "I waved my hat and went up the hill with a rush," Roosevelt recalled. After a bloody fight they reached the top.

Theodore Roosevelt never suffered from modesty. When Roosevelt published his book *The Rough Riders,* the humorist "Mr. Dooley"—Finley Peter Dunne—said Teddy should have called it "Alone in Cuba."

The decisive naval battle occurred even before the Americans could place their big guns on San Juan Hill overlooking Santiago to bombard the enemy navy below. When the Spanish fleet tried to run for the open sea, the United States Navy sank every one of their warships. All over the United States, cheering Americans celebrated their victory.

The "splendid little war." By the standards of American history, this had not been a full-sized war. There were 385 battle deaths—less than one-tenth the deaths in the American Revolution, and only one-twentieth the deaths at the Battle of Gettysburg alone. While the American Revolution had lasted nearly eight years and the Civil War had lasted four years, the Spanish-American War lasted only four *months.* Secretary of State John Hay called it a "splendid little war." Even this "little" war cost a quarter-billion dollars and several thousand deaths from disease.

CELEBRATING JULY 4th, 1898 – "THE TRIUMPH OF THE AMERICAN BATTLE-SHIP."

Keppler portrays all European powers but England as disturbed by America's new naval power.

The little war marked a big change in the relationship of the United States to the world. The tides of history were turned.

The defeated Spain gave up to the United States an empire of islands. And this nation, born in a colonial revolution, would now have its own colonies. All were outside the continent; some were thousands of miles away. The United States acquired Puerto Rico at the gateway to the Caribbean along with Guam, important as a refueling station in the mid-Pacific. The Philippine Islands (all 7000 of them, of which more than 1000 were inhabitable!) off the coast of China were sold to the United States for a bargain price of $20 million.

These new American colonies added up to 100,000 square miles, holding nearly 10 million people. That was not much, compared to the vast empires of England, France, or Germany. But for the United States it was something quite new.

The meaning of this Spanish-American War in American history, then, was actually less in what it accomplished than in what it proclaimed. The American Revolution had been our War of Independence. Now the Spanish-American War at the threshold of the 1900s was our first War of Intervention. We had joined the old-fashioned race for empire.

Americans opposed to empire. Many Americans were worried. Some were saddened, and even angry. They called themselves "Anti-Imperialists," for they hated to see the United States become an empire. To be an empire, they said, meant lording it over people in faraway places. They also feared that seizing land in the Pacific might someday lead to war with Japan. Some felt Asians could never be part of a democracy. And most wondered how the United States could uphold the Declaration of Independence if it became an empire. Anti-Imperialists included Democrats and Republicans, of all sections and classes—labor leader Samuel Gompers, industrialist Andrew Carnegie, President Charles W. Eliot of Harvard and President David Starr Jordan of Stanford, philosopher William James,

413

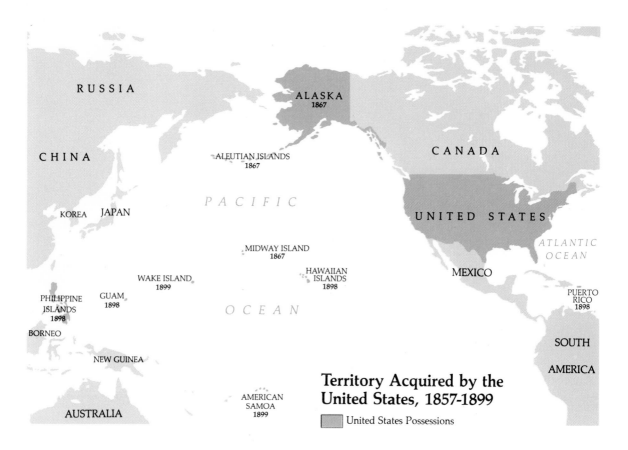

Territory Acquired by the United States, 1857-1899

United States Possessions

social worker Jane Addams, and popular writer Mark Twain. William Jennings Bryan was also opposed to America's new imperialism.

The Anti-Imperalists were especially disturbed by the situation in the Philippines. The Filipinos did not want to be ruled by the United States any more than by Spain. Led by Emilio Aguinaldo they fought against the Americans. Guerrilla warfare went on for three years. The United States used more troops and spent more money than in the entire war against Spain. Many Americans were shocked by the brutal methods we used to put down the Filipinos.

It was not until April 1902 that the last rebel surrendered and the Philippines were officially declared "pacified." Even before then, however, in 1900 under the direction of William Howard Taft, first as head of the Philippine Commission and then as civil governor, the large land holdings of the Catholic friars were distributed to the people. Under Taft's wise direction roads were built, harbors and sanitation improved, and the Philippines started on the path to self-government.

McKinley was renominated by the Republicans at Philadelphia with a unanimous shout. Theodore Roosevelt, governor of New York and "Rough Rider" hero, was the vice-presidential candidate. Once nominated, Roosevelt threw himself into the campaign with his usual boyish vigor. Up and down the country he denounced the "mollycoddles" who would have us "scuttle" out of the Philippines.

The Democrats met at Kansas City on Independence Day and nominated William Jennings Bryan. Although Bryan insisted on a free-silver plank in the platform, the campaign was not fought on that dead issue. The Republican Congress had already passed an act making gold the only standard of currency. The issue was imperialism. A huge American flag hanging from the rafters of the Democratic convention hall proclaimed, "The flag of the Republic forever, of an Empire never."

In 1900 that slogan was already too late. People did not like what they heard about the Filipinos fighting against American control, even though censorship kept them from hearing the worst. Still,

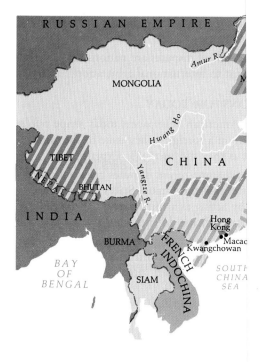

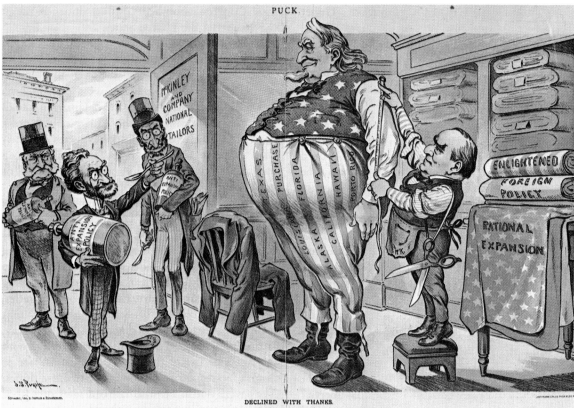

DECLINED WITH THANKS.

THE ANTIS.—Here, take a dose of this anti-fat and get thin again!
UNCLE SAM.—No, Sonny! I never did take any of that stuff, and I'm too old to begin!

influence" to other nations. Every nation
have equal commercial treatment thro
China.

When Hay addressed the Great Powe
avoided giving a direct answer. Hay wen
anyway. On March 20, 1900, he announc
their consent had been "final and definitiv
this very casual way, without realizing w
"Open Door" in China might mean, the
States plunged deeper into world affairs.

The Boxer Rebellion.
Meanwhile many (
would not let their country and themse
treated like foreign property. They rushed t
patriotic society called the "righteous Fists (
mony" (shortened to "Boxers"). In May 19(
rose up against the "foreign devils" hoping t
them out of China. The Boxers killed missi
and their families. They besieged the fore
neighborhood in Peking. It took seven weel
makeshift army of American, British, French
man, Russian, and Japanese troops to reach
and drive off the mob.

The foreign powers doing business in
wished to take their revenge and preve
happening again. They wished to overthr(
government and divide China among them

An expanding Uncle Sam turns down reducing
medicine as McKinley fits him with larger
clothes (top). McKinley ran for reelection in
1900 promising continued prosperity (bottom).

the war had helped to return prosperity to the
United States. McKinley, "the advance agent of
prosperity," was easily reelected by 292 electoral
votes to Bryan's 155.

The reorganization of Cuba.
For better or
worse—and without much thought of what it all
meant for the future—the United States was now
running a colonial empire.

The administration had already begun setting up
governments for the former Spanish islands. The
Teller Amendment was attached to Congress's war
resolution of April 20, 1898. It pledged that the
United States would not exercise sovereignty over
Cuba. We would leave government of the island
to its people.

A WINNER.

Still, United States troops did not lea[ve]
the military governor General Leor[ard Wood]
(1899–1902) the ruins wrought by the[war]
were repaired. A school system was[established.]
The finances of the island were set in or[der and]
lasted while the Cubans drew up a ne[w constitu-]
tion. But what use was a new con[stitution to]
people weakened and dying of the tropic[al disease]
yellow fever? A commission headed [by Dr.]
Walter Reed of the Army Medical C[orps found]
that yellow fever was carried by a mo[squito (the]
female *Aëdes aegypti*) which bred [in stagnant]
waters. Reed helped to stamp out th[e disease so]
Cuba could prosper.

The United States wanted certain[things]
before it withdrew its army from Cuba. [Cuba must]
make no treaties with foreign powers [that would]
limit its independence. It should not [allow any]
foreign power to acquire Cuban territ[ory. It]
should sell or lease to the United Stat[es certain]
coaling or naval stations. Cuba should [not incur]
debts whose interest could not be met ou[t of its]
revenues. And, finally, Cuba should [allow the]
United States to step in whenever necess[ary for the]
protection of life, property, and individu[al liberty.]

The Platt Amendment, named for S[enator Or-]
ville H. Platt of Connecticut, attache[d these]
provisions to an army money bill. Th[ey also]
would have to appear in any constitu[tion the]
Cubans. And they would also be in[cluded in a]
treaty with the United States. Oth[erwise the]
United States would not withdraw its t[roops.]

The Cubans protested these terms [but finally]
wrote them into their constitution. [American]
troops were then withdrawn. The Pla[tt Amend-]
ment became a "permanent" treaty wi[th Cuba in]
1903.

A new status for Puerto Rico. Th[e people of]
Puerto Rico, with a population of almos[t a million,]
willingly came under the rule of the U[nited States.]
The Foraker Act of April 1900 organi[zed Puerto]
Rico as a compromise between a col[ony and a]
territory. The President would appoint [a governor]
and a council of 11, including 5 Pue[rto Ricans.]
Puerto Ricans would elect a legisla[ture of 35]
members. The Spanish courts were swe[pt away and]
replaced by a court system like that of [the United]
States. Works of sanitation, education, [road build-]
ing, and agricultural development were [undertaken.]

The ever-ebullient TR gives a rousing speech
in New Castle, Wyoming, in 1903.

His father built a gym for the boy at home.
There Teddy worked with a punching bag and did
pull-ups on the horizontal bars. He also took
boxing lessons. By age 17 he was expert in such
track events as running, pole vaulting, and high
jumping. On his grandfather's country estate at
Oyster Bay on Long Island, he became an enthusiastic horseman and a crack shot. All his life Teddy
Roosevelt felt that he had to make up for the
childhood weakness of his body.

Roosevelt never lost his boyish excitement. He
kept up his boxing. After he was hit in the eye
while boxing with a young army officer, his left eye
became blind. He managed to keep this a secret,
and he devised ways to prevent people from
knowing that he could see in only one eye. In spite
of it, he became world famous as an explorer and
big-game hunter in Africa and South America.

From the White House he preached "The Strenuous Life." Some genteel European diplomats
dreaded being assigned to Washington when TR
was in the White House. They could not do their
diplomatic duty by sipping tea and making polite
conversation. TR expected them—along with
panting Cabinet members and generals—to join his
exhausting tramps through the countryside. "You

must always remember," a British ambassador once
explained, "that the President is about six years
old."

Dynamic energy was the key to Roosevelt's
character. The variety of his interests and curiosities was enormous. His published works on history,
politics, ethics, travel, and sport fill twenty volumes. Though born to wealth and an old family,
he was no snob. Cowboys, ambassadors, social
workers, labor leaders, senators, clergymen, writers,
and prizefighters were his friends. They met one
another in the reception room of the White House
and sat down at his table together. He loved
power. And he used it with confidence that his
policies were right. He was certain that they would
benefit the American people. He believed the
President had all the powers not forbidden in the
Constitution. He also saw the Presidency as a
"bully pulpit" from which in his high-pitched,
squeaky voice he spread his ideas. He was the first
President since Lincoln to use fully the powers of the
office.

TR believed the President should lead. And he
liked a good fight—not only in the boxing ring, but
also in politics. He had been shocked that earlier
Presidents and the Supreme Court had not enforced
the laws against monopolies. Their growing power
worried him. "Of all forms of tyranny," he
complained, "the least attractive and the most
vulgar is the tyranny of mere wealth."

The coal strike. Hardly had TR moved into the
White House when he had his first chance to show
how a President should lead. The owners of the
nation's anthracite (hard coal) mines were reckless
of the safety of their men. Workers were dying
needlessly each year. In 1901 alone, 441 men were
killed in mining accidents in the anthracite fields of
Illinois, Ohio, Pennsylvania, and West Virginia.

The men had received no raise in wages in
twenty years. They were paid by the weight of the
coal they dug, but the companies were not weighing
honestly. A man might have to dig 4000 pounds
before getting credit for a ton. Miners were
sometimes paid in scrip that could only be used in
"company stores" which charged high prices.

By 1902 the miners could endure no more. The
union leaders decided to take action. John Mitchell, then the energetic young president of the United
Mine Workers, was the son of a miner who had lost

his life in the mines. Mitchell himself had begun mining at age 12. His union—150,000 strong—included thousands of immigrant newcomers who spoke over a dozen languages.

The coal miners went on strike in May 1902. But the mine owners refused to deal with the union. They tried to force the miners back to work. George F. Baer, the president of the Philadelphia and Reading Coal and Iron Company, was the chief spokesman for the owners. "The rights and interests of the laboring man," he declared, "will be protected and cared for not by the labor agitators, but by the Christian men to whom God in his wisdom has given the control of the property interests of the country."

By October with winter coming on, people feared that the railroads would have to stop running and that they would freeze without coal to heat their homes. Then the President came to the rescue. No matter who owned the mines, Roosevelt insisted that nobody owned the miners. He called the mine operators and John Mitchell to the White House. When the owners refused to arbitrate, he let them know he might send the army into the mines. At last on October 13 the owners gave in and agreed to deal with the union. The miners went back to work and later won most of their demands. When the strike ended, TR had shown how, in the new age of big business, it was possible for the federal government to help. He had proven himself a champion of the ordinary American. He

had seen that the miners received a "square deal." That was what he wanted for all Americans.

The Northern Securities case. The coal strike was only the beginning of TR's flamboyant defense of the public interest against the trusts. His most famous target was the Northern Securities Company. It was a holding company, a corporation set up to hold a controlling part of the stock of other companies. It had been formed by railroad builder James J. Hill of the Great Northern, the Rockefellers, J. P. Morgan, and E. H. Harriman of the Union Pacific to control the four big railroads of the Northwest.

After a fierce battle over the control of the stock of one of the railroads, this holding company had brought peace between the competitors. But the people in the Northwest were now at the mercy of one big railroad combine. They depended on the railroad to bring in supplies and to take their produce to market. Now they would have to pay whatever rates the railroads wanted to charge.

The Northern Securities Company gave TR his perfect issue—and his chance to prove that he was a master of public relations. He used it skillfully to revive the Sherman Antitrust Act and to show the power of the federal government. These men of great wealth had plagued a whole region and disrupted the nation's stock market by their fight for monopoly. So the President had the company sued under the Sherman Act.

This 1903 cartoon called for new legislation to expose the activities of the trusts.

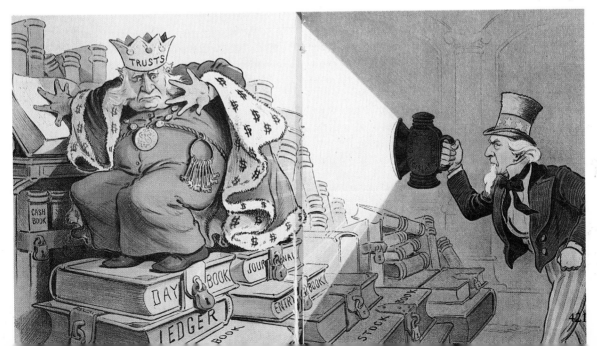

J. P. Morgan was shocked. He went to the White House and told TR, "If we have done anything wrong, send your man [meaning the Attorney General] to my man [one of Morgan's lawyers] and they can fix it up." The President later remarked of this incident, "That is a most illuminating illustration of the Wall Street point of view. Mr. Morgan could not help regarding me as a big rival operator, who either intended to ruin all his interests or else could be induced to come to an agreement to ruin none."

But Roosevelt pushed the case, and in 1904 the Supreme Court, by a vote of 5 to 4, held that the Northern Securities Company did violate the Sherman Antitrust Act. The Court ordered the company to dissolve. After this first victory, TR moved against other unpopular trusts—the beef trust, the oil trust, and the tobacco trust.

In his own mind Roosevelt always made a distinction between "good" trusts and "bad" trusts. The law should be used to break up the bad trusts, those that were formed to gouge the public by trying to end competition. Good trusts should only be regulated. A good trust might simply beat its rivals because its prices were lower, its products better, or its management more efficient. By getting Congress to add a new Department of Commerce and Labor to the Cabinet, TR showed that he meant what he said. A Bureau of Corporations within the Department was formed to help judge which trusts were good and which were bad. The government, the President declared, must be "the senior partner in every business."

President in his own right.

Roosevelt's battles for labor and against the trusts made his first term a smashing success. He easily won the election of 1904 against the Democrats' dull and conservative candidate, Judge Alton B. Parker of New York. Roosevelt carried the entire North and West with 336 electoral votes. Parker was left with only 140 votes from the "solid South." For every two popular votes for Parker, Roosevelt collected three.

Now that Roosevelt was President in his own right, he moved swiftly for major reforms. His first goal was to strengthen the Interstate Commerce Commission so it could really regulate the railroads. But he had to be both inventive and persistent to overcome the opposition of the railroads and the big businesses that benefited from

their rebates. Finally, in 1906, after a sixteen-month battle in the Senate during which he used all his skills as a leader, the Hepburn bill became law. It gave the ICC power over pipelines, express and sleeping car companies, bridges, ferries, and terminals. Railroad rebates and free passes were forbidden. If a shipper complained about any unfair rate, the Commission could reduce the rate until a federal court ruled on its fairness. To Roosevelt the Hepburn Act marked a major step on the path to effective federal regulation of business.

Other reform legislation.

Roosevelt went on to prove that a free society was not powerless against large corporations. The Meat Inspection Act gave federal officials the right to inspect all meat shipped in interstate commerce to see whether it came from healthy animals and was packed under sanitary conditions. Upton Sinclair had written a popular novel, The Jungle, showing the miseries of workers in the stockyards—and describing the rotten meat packed for sale. When the law passed in 1906, Sinclair said his book had tried to hit people in their heart, and instead had hit them in their stomach.

The year 1906 was a banner one for reform. A Pure Food and Drug Act was passed. The manufacture and sale of impure foods, drugs, and liquors was forbidden. Labels on patent medicines had to list the contents. The Employers' Liability Act provided accident insurance for workers in the District of Columbia and on interstate railroads.

Conservation of natural resources.

President Roosevelt gave a new meaning to "conservation"— the movement to conserve the nation's resources for future Americans. His own experience had shown him the need. As a young man out west he had enjoyed the open spaces. On his ranch in Dakota Territory he had ridden the range and explored the wilderness. He loved everything about the West— the cowboys, the life of the trail, fishing, and hunting. When he became President, he was shocked to see lumber companies wasting forests that had taken centuries to grow. He knew that the untouched wilderness could never be put back.

He saw some parts of the country troubled by floods while others lacked water. Saving rivers and streams and using their water wisely were just as important as protecting the land or the forests. In June 1902 his strong support helped to secure the

Photographer Carleton Watkins made an extensive record of life and development on the Pacific Coast. He was probably the first person to take pictures of Yosemite Valley. The one below was made in the 1860s. The works of painters and photographers sparked tourist interest in the Far West. In the 1880s the Denver & Rio Grande advertised the beauty of its route across the continent (left).

The wild American West gave painters exciting new subjects. Thomas Moran, an Englishman, painted this striking canvas of "The Grand Canyon of the Yellowstone" in 1871. Partly influenced by such inspiring landscapes, Congress established Yellowstone National Park in 1872.

German-born Albert Bierstadt, who went west as early as 1858, was renowned for his heroic canvases of natural subjects. Here (left) he painted the giant redwoods and the native Indians. Author-naturalist John Muir (right) was a leader in the drive to make Yosemite a national park. He also helped to persuade Theodore Roosevelt of the importance of conserving forest land.

passage of the Newlands Reclamation Act. Money from the sale of public lands in sixteen western states and territories was to be used to build large dams and canal systems to conserve water for irrigation. Vast stretches of arid lands in the West were once worth just a cent or two an acre because they were good only for cattle grazing. Now they were worth hundreds of dollars an acre for growing crops.

In 1891 Congress had given the President power over "public lands wholly or in part covered with timber." He could set them apart as forest reserves. Presidents Harrison, Cleveland, and McKinley had set aside 50 million acres. Now Roosevelt increased the number of national forests to 149 totaling over 190 million acres, an area equal to Great Britain and France combined.

TR also withdrew from sale millions of acres of public land having waterpower sites and deposits of coal, oil, and phosphates. He took steps to prevent illegal use of the public lands by lumber companies and cattle raisers. He transferred forests from the Public Land Office to the United States Forest Service, headed by his enthusiastic supporter, Gifford Pinchot. For Pinchot, "conservation" meant scientific land management. So he planned "reforesting"—the planting of trees—to go along with the cutting of trees. He saw the nation's forests as a living resource that always had to be renewed.

The panic of 1907. In the summer of 1907, when prices fell sharply on Wall Street, a number of banks and businesses failed. Some newspapers blamed Roosevelt. Even many of his supporters urged him to "go slow" against the large corporations. Roosevelt did not relax his efforts for reform.

But he was willing to compromise. He agreed when J. P. Morgan explained the need for United States Steel to purchase its largest competitor. The

Tennessee Coal and Iron Company was near collapse. Without making "any binding promise" not to prosecute under the antitrust laws, TR told Morgan to go ahead.

Further efforts for reform. Prosperity soon returned. Then Roosevelt's messages to Congress in December 1907 and January 1908 called for still more reforms. On his list were income and inheritance taxes, federal rules for the stock market, limits on the use of labor injunctions, and more effective control of business. The panic, he insisted, had been caused not by enforcement of the law but by the corporations' refusal to obey the law.

Roosevelt's interest in social reform and his outspoken attacks on "predatory wealth" led conservatives to call him a socialist. But he really had no sympathy with socialist doctrine. He did not believe in public ownership of the means of production and distribution. His large purpose, he said, was to "avoid the extremes of swollen fortunes and grinding poverty." He believed in capitalism, but he wanted to make it benefit all the people. Always the reformer, he hoped to save the United States he knew by making capitalism work.

SECTION REVIEW

1. Identify or explain: John Mitchell, holding company, Alton B. Parker, Hepburn Act, Upton Sinclair, Newlands Act.
2. Describe Roosevelt's view of the Presidency.
3. What role did TR play in the coal strike of 1902?
4. Why and how did TR fight the Northern Securities Company?
5. What measures were passed to provide (a) improved transportation regulation, (b) consumer protection, (c) accident insurance, (d) conservation of resources?
6. What other reforms did Roosevelt seek?

2. Middle-class reformers

The movement Theodore Roosevelt led was broad and deep. It reached out to states and cities across the nation.

The main centers were medium-sized cities and small towns. Support came from doctors, lawyers, ministers, small-business owners, merchants, white-collar workers, social critics, and intellectuals. Mostly Americans of old families, they had been disturbed by the strife and violence of the 1890s. They disliked the city political bosses and distrusted the great business corporations. They wanted to help the poor and the needy.

The Progressives no longer believed it was good enough for the government to be only an umpire. Even in a democracy, the powers of a citizen and a corporation were not equal. In the 1900s more and more Americans expected their government to be their guardian.

Reform in the cities. Beginning in 1889, reform mayors were elected in many cities. But bosses soon took over again. Still, some reformers managed to stay in office. Among them were some wealthy business leaders. For example, Hazen S. Pingree brought good government to Detroit. And there was Toledo's colorful Samuel M. "Golden Rule" Jones. He said, "I don't want to rule anybody, each individual must rule himself." Jones had already given his factory workers unusual benefits when he entered politics. Angered by his early reforms, the Republican machine dropped him as their candidate for mayor. But he easily won reelection as an independent.

In some cities the reform movements petered out. And then the old political machines would return to power. To prevent this, some reformers changed the form of city government. Under one plan, first used in 1900 in Galveston, Texas, the mayor and city council were replaced by a small commission usually elected on a nonpartisan ballot. Each of its members ran a city department. The commission passed laws and decided policies for the city. By 1912 more than 200 cities were using the commission plan.

Many more cities turned to a city manager. On the model of other large businesses, a trained manager was hired to run the city. A small council set the policies, and the manager carried them out. The manager was not a politician. The city manager system was most successful in small cities. It was harder to find skilled managers for big cities as well as more difficult to keep politics out. So, though city managers still run some large cities, among them the old mayor-council form of government is most common today.

State government reform. Reformers in the cities soon found that to reach their goals they had to reform the state governments, too. The earliest and ablest of the reform governors was Robert M. La Follette. In 1900 the people of Wisconsin elected "Battling Bob." After fierce fights he brought the state legislature under his control. And in his three terms it enacted a wide range of "Progressive" measures. The direct primary gave the voters the right to choose the candidates for public office. A commission was formed to control railroad rates. A competitive civil service was set up. Restrictions were put on lobbying. Laws were passed for conservation, for supervision of state banks, and for higher taxes on corporations. TR later called Wisconsin "a laboratory for democracy," and other states followed its lead.

By 1912 three-fourths of the states had passed child-labor laws barring the employment of young children and regulating the working hours of all young people. Workmen's compensation laws made the employer pay for injuries caused by defective machinery or dangerous tasks. In many states compulsory insurance systems created funds for the sick, the disabled, and the aged. In 1912 Massachusetts passed the first minimum-wage law for women. Other states regulated women's hours and conditions of work. State after state outlawed intoxicating liquors. By the beginning of World War I, 26 states were "dry."

The reformers changed the tax laws to put a heavier burden on the rich. New charges were laid upon the profits of corporations, on the inheritance of fortunes, and on large incomes. At the same time most states formed railroad and public utility commissions to keep down rates and keep up the quality of services.

Direct democracy and women's suffrage. Time after time the efforts of the reformers were blocked by political bosses and "the special interests." So the Progressives looked for ways to break their power. If the people's representatives would not respond to the calls for reform, let the voters themselves play a more direct role.

The reformers started with the ballot. In most states voters were still using colored ballots printed by the parties (p. 186). Reformers felt that if voting was made truly secret, elections would be more honest, and better representatives would be elected. Political bosses would no longer be able to tell by the color of a ballot which way a person

"Battling Bob" La Follette (left) and his wife, Belle Case La Follette (right), were vigorous battlers for reform. She influenced many as a magazine editor, speaker, and organizer. He served as the progressive governor of Wisconsin, as a U. S. Senator, and ran for President in 1924.

voted. In 1888 Massachusetts became the first state to print and distribute ballots containing the names of all those running for office. The secret ballot was soon adopted by most of the states.

But the secret, or Australian, ballot (named for its place of origin) did not break the power of the political bosses. The Progressive reformers then tried to give the voters the right to choose the party candidates for public office. The *direct primary* might break the power of party bosses to dictate who would run. Mississippi in 1902 and Wisconsin the next year led the way. In some southern states, however, the Democrats said their party was a private club open only to white voters (p. 528). It would be many years before the Supreme Court outlawed this barrier to black voters.

A second reform was direct election of United States Senators. But the "rich man's club," as the Senate was called, blocked the proposal time after time. Oregon in 1904 began to allow voters to name their choice. Then the legislature "elected" the person so chosen. By 1910 more than enough states to ratify an amendment were electing their senators this way. So at last the Senate gave in. The Seventeenth Amendment, ratified in 1913, took the election of senators away from the state legislatures and gave it to the voters.

The reformers found two other ways to deal with balky lawmakers. The *initiative* allowed 5 to 8 percent of the voters to "initiate" or start a bill by petition. In some states the bill was then put on the ballot for the voters to pass or defeat in a *referendum*. In other states there would be a referendum only if the legislature failed to pass the bill by a certain time. South Dakota in 1898 was the first of about 20 states to adopt these two measures.

A dozen states and many cities and counties adopted the *recall*. By petition, voters could force an official to stand for reelection at any time.

Some Progressives took up the cause of women's suffrage. They thought women would be more inclined than men to support reform legislation. By 1896 four western states had granted women full voting rights (p. 375). Between 1910 and 1914 seven more states—all west of the Mississippi—granted women the ballot.

The muckrakers. With reform politicians came reform journalists and novelists. Roosevelt called them "muckrakers," and the name stuck. He compared them to the man in John Bunyan's *Pilgrim's Progress* who was so busy raking the filth on the ground that he never lifted his eyes to heaven.

The muckrakers looked everywhere—in government, in Wall Street, in labor unions, in the trusts—for crime and corruption. Where they couldn't find a crime they might invent one. The new speed presses and cheap paper carried their message in the new daily newspapers and mass magazines to millions in the cities. Rural free delivery of mail took the word to remote farms.

The great wave of muckraking began in October 1902 when *McClure's Magazine* carried "Tweed Days in St. Louis." The author of this exposé was the young Lincoln Steffens, one of the most fearless journalists of modern times. He was the pioneer investigating reporter. He wrote articles on misgovernment in the cities. Later he brought them together in his book *The Shame of the Cities* (1904).

The clever Ida Tarbell published her angry attack on the Standard Oil Company. Her father believed that Rockefeller had ruined him and had driven his partner to suicide. Since she had spent five years collecting materials for her articles, she was well armed with facts. Then she wrote about the Standard Oil Company not as a business enterprise but as Public Enemy Number One.

A new force—media power—had entered American politics. To read the shocking stories, true, half-true, and sometimes false, readers flocked to *McClure's*. Other mass magazines like *Munsey's*, *Cosmopolitan*, and *Everybody's* went into this profitable business of exposing evil. Finley Peter Dunne's witty and philosophical newspaper character "Mr. Dooley" complained that whatever magazine he picked up he always got this one message: "Ivrything has gone wrong."

But the muckrakers' message got through. Within six years after Steffens's *The Shame of the Cities,* reform movements appeared in Philadelphia, Chicago, Kansas City, Minneapolis, Los Angeles, and San Francisco.

The muckrakers wrote some sensational and persuasive novels, which we can still enjoy. Frank Norris wrote about the powerful railroads in California (*The Octopus,* 1901) and the wheat exchange in Chicago (*The Pit,* 1903). Theodore Dreiser used muckraking themes for novels which outlived the Progressive Era. His books were epics of wealth, power, success—and poverty. *The Financier* (1912),

This photograph of Ida Tarbell was taken in 1904, when her *History of the Standard Oil Company* caused a sensation. Her exposé had first appeared in nineteen installments in the popular *McClure's Magazine*.

The Titan (1914), and *An American Tragedy* (1925) became classics.

Painters, too, found a way to join the muckrakers. A new "ashcan school" of artists chose some unusual subjects. John Sloane, George Luks, Robert Henri, and others filled the respectable galleries with high-priced canvases showing alleys and tenements. The bold Danish immigrant photographer, Jacob Riis, published shocking pictures of starving children in garbage-ridden slums.

Social workers, sociologists, and historians also did their bit for reform. John Spargo described the horrors of child labor in *The Bitter Cry of the Children* (1906). Gustavus Myers made his *History of the Great American Fortunes* (1909) a rogues' gallery of crooks. Ray Stannard Baker told the story of racial discrimination in *Following the Color Line* (1908). Burton J. Hendrick's disclosures in *Story of Life Insurance* (1907) led to laws regulating New York's large insurance companies.

SECTION REVIEW

1. Identify or explain: commission plan, Robert La Follette, direct primary, initiative, referendum, recall, Lincoln Steffens, Ida Tarbell, Frank Norris, Theodore Dreiser, "ashcan school," Jacob Riis.
2. How did reformers try to improve city government?
3. Why was Wisconsin called "a laboratory for democracy"?
4. Name some state reforms designed (a) to improve politics and government, (b) to regulate business, (c) to aid workers, (d) to help the needy.
5. Who were the "muckrakers"? How did they advance the reform movement?

3. Taft in the White House

Theodore Roosevelt had said that he would not run for a third term. His hand-picked successor was his Secretary of War—the jovial 300-pound William Howard Taft. The Republicans in Chicago in June 1908 chose Taft on the first ballot. The Democrats, meeting at Denver, decided to try again with William Jennings Bryan.

Taft won by over a million votes and an electoral vote of 321 to 162. But the election was more an

Lewis Hine was hired in 1908 by the National Child Labor Committee to travel the country to record the plight of child laborers. In 1911 he photographed (above) this young cotton mill spinner in Virginia. Jacob Riis made the shot (below) of New York waifs between 1880 and 1910.

endorsement for Roosevelt's candidate and policies than it was for the Republican party. The Democrats gained new strength from farmers and from workers organized in unions. Several states that voted for Taft elected Democratic governors. The Republicans also lost seats in the House, but they still retained control.

The new President. William Howard Taft took office on March 4, 1909. He was a comforting and comfortable man. But he was no cowboy and no crusader. He had served as United States Solicitor General and as a federal judge. As governor of the Philippines he had brought reforms without stirring up resentment. TR had appointed him Secretary of War, but he had never before been elected to office. Besides being a proven administrator, he was a learned and successful lawyer. By temperament

4. Woodrow Wilson and the New Freedom

Woodrow Wilson's father was a Presbyterian minister. Born in Staunton, Virginia, Woodrow absorbed from his parents a devout, unbending spirit. He decided against becoming a minister himself, but in some ways he always thought and talked like one.

Like Theodore Roosevelt, Wilson was a literary President, the author of many books. In almost every other way he was TR's opposite. While TR's first book was on sea power, young Wilson wrote about moral questions for the North Carolina *Presbyterian*. While TR adored "The Strenuous Life," Wilson lived in the world of ideas, "longing to do immortal work." At the age when TR was out west learning to ride broncos and was hunting with cowboys, Wilson was sitting in political science classes at Johns Hopkins University in Baltimore. Though Wilson wrote a book called *Congressional Government,* he had never even bothered to make the short trip to Washington to see Congress in session.

Wilson was an indoor sort of man. After a brief career as a professor, he was elected president of Princeton University. His educational reforms there won him national fame. They also angered the alumni and some of the faculty, so he was glad to be asked to run for governor of New Jersey in 1910. It was his success as governor—his only political experience—that brought him the nomination for President in 1912. He could inspire people in large groups or from the printed page. But face to face he was stiff and standoffish. He had trouble making close friends.

While Wilson had some of William Jennings Bryan's religious appeal, his tone was very different. Bryan sounded like a preacher at a country tent meeting. Wilson could have been the minister of the richest church in town. Both could persuade voters that they were joining the Army of the Lord. Wilson, like Bryan, championed the struggling farmers and underpaid workers. As a more moderate kind of Bryan, Wilson had a wider appeal.

A new dedication. Woodrow Wilson set the tone for his Presidency on the day he took office. In his inaugural address he announced that he had come to Washington "to cleanse, to reconsider, to restore." Certain new laws were needed—tariff revision, currency and banking reform, breaking up the trusts. Beyond that, however, he had come "to lift everything that concerns our life as a Nation to the light that shines from the hearthfire of every man's conscience and vision of the right." Arriving at the White House was his moment of high dedication. He allowed no inaugural ball.

Wilson's kind of leadership was useful at this moment in the nation's history. He could both describe what needed to be done and then had the eloquence to rally people to the job. While he was riding the wave of Progressive reform, he could also enlist the enthusiasm of loyal Democrats. Their party had been out of office so long that now the Democrats in Congress were glad to follow Wilson. He would help them build a stronger party.

Tariff reform. Wilson immediately called a special session of Congress to enact his urgent program. Laws must be passed to break down the barriers to individual enterprise. In the recent past, Presidents had sent a written message to open each session of Congress. The message was then droned out by a clerk. Instead, Wilson made a ceremony of this occasion. He went to the Capitol and became the first President since Washington and Adams to deliver his address in person.

In a brief and forceful speech Wilson dramatized his personal leadership. At the same time he focused the nation's attention on Congress. He made it clear that it was the duty of Congress to take action. Instead of scattering his shots, in this address he spoke only of the reform of the tariff. It was not "free trade" that he desired, but free opportunity for American business. The proposed duties would provide some revenue for the Treasury but would not enrich industries that no longer needed tariff protection.

Representative Oscar W. Underwood, who had spent his life studying the tariff, worked closely with Wilson. The new tariff bill reduced duties about 11 percent from the Payne-Aldrich Act. To make up for the lost revenue, an income tax with low rates was included. As usual, there was a bitter fight in the Senate. Then Wilson stepped in to denounce the "insidious lobby" at work in Washington. The Senate began its own inquiry that revealed how the business interests of some senators affected their attitude toward the tariff. An aroused public opinion now helped clear the road for major cuts in

Wilson and Taft rode together to Wilson's inauguration in 1913.

the tariff rates. After months of wrangling, the Underwood-Simmons bill was signed into law on October 3, 1913. It was the first real tariff reform since the Civil War.

Currency and banking reform.

Even before the tariff bill was passed, Wilson called for currency and banking reforms. There was wide agreement on the need to create a currency that would expand and contract as the economy required. Ever since the 1870s the money supply had failed to keep pace with the rising output of goods and services. And this had led to the calls for "cheap money."

The nation still had no banking system that could help a bank stop a "run" on its deposits. At the start of a business panic, most of the depositors might run to their bank to take out their money. But a bank keeps only a small cash reserve. For the bank to earn a profit, it must lend out most of its deposits. A "run" could force a bank to shut down in a few hours.

Bank "runs" in a number of places at the same time could start or worsen a panic. In addition to its small cash reserve, a bank would keep part of its required (legal) reserves in a big-city bank. And the big-city banks, in turn, kept part of their reserves in New York City banks. Thus much of the nation's deposit reserves tended to move to Wall Street, New York's financial district. The New York banks would lend large amounts "on call." This meant that the borrower had to repay the loan as soon as the bank called for its money. Many of the "on call" loans went to stock-market speculators. When small-city banks demanded their reserves, the big banks called in their loans. Then a wave of selling in the stock market—by the speculators to get money to repay their loans—caused further panic and "runs" on more banks.

The Progressive-Bryan faction wanted a system of reserve banks under federal control—that is, central banks that would hold part of the deposits (legal reserves) of the private banks. Conservative Democrats feared Bryan. To them Bryan always seemed radical. They also wanted a federal reserve system free from Wall Street control, but they wanted it to be owned and controlled by private interests. Wilson steered a middle course. Under his skillful prodding a compromise emerged.

The Federal Reserve Act.

The Federal Reserve Act was signed into law in December 1913. It divided the country into twelve districts, each with a Federal Reserve bank owned by the member banks. All were supervised by a Federal Reserve Board, whose members were appointed by the President. Every national bank had to become a member of the Federal Reserve System. Each subscribed some of its capital and surplus to form the capital of the reserve bank in its district.

These Federal Reserve banks were the central banks for their regions. They were the "bankers' banks." They held the member banks' reserves, lent money to a member bank when it was needed, and performed other services for the member banks. In case of a "run" on a bank, the member bank could pay its depositors by borrowing from the Federal Reserve bank. The "run" might not even start if the depositors believed that the bank could surely meet its obligations.

The Federal Reserve Act also created a flexible new national currency, *Federal Reserve notes*. These

In 1909, when Scott Joplin, a leading composer of ragtime, wrote this dance music, Wall Street was already the financial heart of the nation. Ragtime, a precursor of jazz, was popular until about 1915.

could be issued according to the needs of the business community.

This act provided a way to mobilize the banking reserves in time of panic. When bank withdrawals caused loans to be called in, threatening the closing of businesses and even of the banks themselves, the Federal Reserve banks could rush to the rescue. The Federal Reserve Act was a perfect example of the New Freedom. Private interests did the job, but the public supervised.

Regulating business. After the Federal Reserve Act became law in December, Wilson at last let the weary lawmakers go home for a month's recess. When they returned in January, he offered his program to regulate business. The Sherman Anti-trust Act had been aimed at certain business practices that tended to limit competition. Wilson said that was not enough. He asked Congress for a law to break up monopolies.

"To supplement existing laws against unlawful restraints and monopolies," Congress passed the Clayton Antitrust Act of 1914. It prohibited one company from taking over the stock of another if it created a monopoly. It forbade anyone to serve as a director of two or more corporations when the effect was to lessen competition. This was to prevent "interlocking" directorates, like those used by J. P. Morgan & Co. The law exempted labor and farm groups from prosecution as combinations in restraint of trade. But later court decisions undercut this exemption.

No law could spell out in advance all the unfair practices that wily businessmen might dream up. Then what should the government do? A Boston lawyer, Louis D. Brandeis, had made a reputation for fighting what he called "the curse of bigness." He helped Wilson with an answer. The law should not just outlaw unfair trade practices in general. It should set up a Federal Trade Commission with powers to stop any unfair practices whenever they occurred. This was more like TR's "New Nationalism" than the "New Freedom," but Wilson now decided he had no other choice. After a hard fight the Federal Trade Commission Act was passed in September 1914, and the federal government was committed to regulate business.

The Federal Trade Commission (FTC) had five members. Advised by experts from different industries, they drew up fair trade rules. When the FTC found a company engaging in a practice that was unfair or in restraint of trade, it could issue a "cease and desist" order. And if the company disobeyed, it was punished. The main purpose of the commission was to help individual businesses obey the law.

More Progressive legislation. With these measures, Wilson's reforms were complete. For a moment, he turned against further reforms and even blocked a bill that forbade child labor. The mid-term elections of 1914 brought some gains for the Republicans. But the Democrats kept control of Congress. Wilson saw that he must continue Progressive reforms if he was to be reelected in 1916. So he offered a new program. Much of what he asked for came from Roosevelt's "New Nationalism." In 1915 the La Follette Seamen's Act improved the quarters, food, and wages in the merchant marine. The following year several important laws were passed. A Federal Farm Loan Act provided farmers long-term loans at low interest rates. A child-labor law finally limited employment of young children in factories, mines, and quarries. And an eight-hour day was enacted for workers on the railroads.

President Wilson's first term showed the most far-reaching legislative program ever passed in a single administration. The Democrats, he boasted, had not only carried out their own platform. They had "come very near to carrying out the platform of the Progressive party."

THE ART CRITIC

Culver Pictures

SECTION REVIEW

1. Identify or explain: "bankers' banks," Federal Reserve notes, interlocking directorates, "cease and desist" orders, La Follette Seamen's Act, Federal Farm Loan Act.

2. How were Woodrow Wilson and Theodore Roosevelt alike? How were they different? Consider their backgrounds, experiences, and personal traits.

3. How did the Underwood-Simmons bill reform the tariff?

4. What chief weakness of the banking system was the Federal Reserve Act designed to correct? How did the new law help solve the currency problem?

5. What kinds of business practices did the Clayton Act declare illegal?

6. How was the Federal Trade Commission supposed to promote fair dealing and business competition?

7. What other Progressive legislation did Congress enact in Wilson's first term?

5. Seeking a world role

Progressive leaders, who showed concern for the poor at home, sent the nation in search of power abroad. The United States played a new commanding part in Latin America.

TR and foreign affairs. Theodore Roosevelt had a clear view of the new role he wanted for the United States. Although he distrusted the power of large corporations, he loved power for the nation and for himself. He wanted the United States to hold the center of the world stage. For practical purposes he was his own Secretary of State. Though he never shrank from a good fight, he saw himself as a champion of peace. His motto was "Speak softly and carry a big stick." Still, he seemed to enjoy bellowing while waving his big stick at home and abroad.

He wanted this two-ocean nation to become a power on the sea. An enthusiastic disciple of Admiral Mahan, he wanted the United States to have a great navy. In the Spanish-American War we had only 5 battleships and 2 armored cruisers. Before Roosevelt left the White House in 1909, we had 25 battleships and 10 heavy cruisers. We had become, next to the British, the strongest naval power in the world.

The United States and the Far East.

Events in the Far East offered TR a welcome chance to play the delicate game of power politics. Soon after he took office, the Russians began to move to control Manchuria. This was against our Open Door policy. But Roosevelt saw that there was little we could do to stop them.

In that part of the world Russia's great rival was Japan. When these two powers began to fight, Roosevelt drew the United States to the side of Japan. But Roosevelt did not want to see Russia driven out of the Far East, for Russia could keep the lid on Japan. Roosevelt aimed to insure a balance of power there. Only in that way, he thought, could China stay independent. So Roosevelt helped bring the Russo-Japanese War to a close before Japan could crush Russia. At Portsmouth, New Hampshire, the envoys of Russia and Japan met with him, and in August 1905 they announced the terms of peace. For this he was awarded the Nobel Peace Prize.

The peace had been won only by a bargain in which the United States, too, played a part. It was agreed that Japan would be allowed to annex Korea and to pursue its own interests in Manchuria. In return, Japan assured the United States that otherwise things would remain the same in the Pacific. Japan would not meddle with our colonies. The Root-Takahira Agreement of 1908 outlined these understandings.

Most Americans believed that all people should be allowed to govern themselves. They objected that in this pact we were bartering the independence of others. They recalled George Washington's warnings against "entangling alliances." In fact, the agreement only recognized the existing situation.

Theodore Roosevelt was a realist. He was in favor of the Open Door policy as long as it could be maintained by diplomacy. But in Manchuria the Japanese were willing to risk war to get their way. He believed that the United States should take a firm stand only when it was in our national interest to fight for our position.

Roosevelt thought the United States should stay on good terms with Japan. But we should not let the Japanese think we were weak. In 1907 he sent around the world our navy's "great white fleet" of 28 ships—chiefly to impress Japan.

The Panama Canal.

In the Caribbean, TR would be more aggressive. For here he saw the vital interests of the United States. He thought that the United States should dominate the Caribbean. And he favored building an isthmian canal.

As a world power, the United States had to be able to move its navy speedily from one ocean to another. Besides the old reasons of commerce, this was an urgent new reason to cut a waterway through Central America.

For years Americans going westward had tried to find ways to shorten the voyage to California. When TR came to the White House, a French company had already been working on a canal for twenty years. They were plagued by tropical disease. And early in 1902 they agreed to sell their canal rights for $40 million. The United States still had to get a lease on the land for the canal route. It was in Colombia's province of Panama.

TR would let nothing stop him. First, Secretary of State John Hay drew up a treaty with an envoy from Colombia. We agreed to pay Colombia $10 million at once—and later, $250,000 a year. In 1903 the senate of Colombia balked. They wanted $20 million—and another $10 million from the French company.

Then suddenly a revolution broke out in Panama. A lucky coincidence for the United States! But there was evidence that the United States had helped start the revolt. And the United States Navy had prevented Colombian troops from landing to put it down. Quickly the new "independent" Republic of Panama made a treaty leasing the Canal Zone to the United States.

Work began in 1904 but halted the next year because the workers in the swamps came down with yellow fever. To build the canal, Americans first had to stop the sickness. Under the direction of Dr. William Gorgas, who had worked with Dr. Walter

Relations with Our Southern Neighbors, 1898–1933

- U.S. Posssession
- U.S. Military Intervention
- U.S. Financial Supervision
- Special U.S. Relationship under 1903 Treaty

0   600 Miles

0   600 Kilometers

Reed in Cuba to prevent yellow fever, the breeding places of the mosquitoes that carried the disease were destroyed. Once the mosquitoes were gone, the battle against the disease was won. Gorgas made the canal possible—and helped conquer yellow fever around the world.

Work resumed in 1906, and within eight years ships were passing through the canal. The Panama Canal had cost more than a half-billion dollars, but its benefits were beyond measure.

"I took the Canal Zone and let Congress debate," TR later declared, "and while the debate goes on the canal does also." Wilson's Secretary of State, William Jennings Bryan, negotiated a new treaty with Colombia. The United States agreed to pay $25 million for the loss of Panama, with "sincere regret that anything should have occurred to mar the candid friendship" between the two nations. Roosevelt denounced the treaty as "a crime against the United States and an attack on its honor." The Senate rejected the treaty twice. In April 1921, after Roosevelt's death, the treaty was ratified by a Republican Senate with the expression of sincere regret left out!

The Roosevelt Corollary. After the Panama Canal was opened, the United States worried about the governments in that neighborhood. When the Dominican Republic (formerly Santo Domingo) went bankrupt, European creditors threatened to use force to collect their money. Roosevelt then declared a new American policy. In his message to Congress in December 1904, he explained what the United States would do in case of the "chronic wrongdoing or impotence" of a Latin American state. He said that we were bound to intervene, "however reluctantly," and to "exercise our international police power."

Construction of the Panama Canal began in 1903, and "The Big Ditch" was opened to ships in 1914. By June 1913, when this photograph was taken, workers were still excavating at Culebra Cut, the deepest part of the canal.

With the consent of the president of the Dominican Republic, the United States took over the financial affairs of that country. Soon the debts were paid, and the creditors in Europe were then satisfied.

In the past the United States had told European powers not to interfere in the Americas. Now TR declared that the United States would police a whole continent. Though nobody else was allowed to, forces of the United States might intervene in Latin America. The nation that had inspired the world by its Declaration of Independence now shook the world with a new declaration of intervention! This was the "Roosevelt Corollary" to the Monroe Doctrine. TR meant what he said, and later Presidents agreed. Under this policy, the United States would intervene—sometimes more than once—in the Dominican Republic, Cuba, Panama, Haiti, and Nicaragua.

The Algeciras Conference.

It seemed unlikely that the restless, aggressive TR could stay out of the international politics of Europe. France and Germany were on the point of war over control of Morocco. At first TR hesitated to do anything.

Then "to keep matters on an even keel in Europe" he stepped in. He persuaded the two nations to attend a conference in 1906 at Algeciras, Spain. There United States delegates helped France and Germany come to a peaceful settlement. Could it be said anymore that America had a set of interests separate from those of Europe?

Foreign affairs under Taft.

TR never cared much about the economics of foreign affairs. Commerce was not nearly as dramatic as clashing navies or expanding boundaries. But for his successor, President Taft, money was the measure of diplomacy. "Dollar diplomacy"—the nickname for his foreign policies—meant using United States ambassadors (and armed forces) to promote business. Taft and his Secretary of State, Philander C. Knox, urged Americans to invest abroad to build American influence. Then our government would protect United States investors.

Taft pushed American bankers to invest in China. And there, as a response to Taft's dollar diplomacy, Japan and Russia enlarged their own spheres of interest.

"Dollar diplomacy" explained Taft's actions in Latin America, too. When civil war broke out in Nicaragua in 1912, United States Marines were sent in to protect American business interests. While there, the marines supervised the national elections. A small detachment stayed until 1925. Latin Americans began to wonder whether the people of the United States had forgotten their own Declaration of Independence.

A "moral" foreign policy.

President Wilson's first foreign policy test came in Mexico. Then and there he would set the moral tone that was to dominate his foreign policy.

Just before Wilson took office, a liberal government in Mexico, headed by Francisco Madero, had been overthrown by a cruel general, Victoriano Huerta. Madero was murdered while being taken to jail—probably on Huerta's orders.

Other Mexican revolutionaries opposed Huerta. But he controlled four-fifths of his country. Twenty foreign governments recognized Huerta as Mexico's president de facto. This meant that they did not judge whether Huerta's government was really legal. They only recognized that in fact he was in control.

Woodrow Wilson—the preacherly President—had other ideas. Formerly the United States had recognized *de facto* governments whenever they came to power. Now Wilson declared that he would not "extend the hand of welcome to anyone who obtains power in a sister republic by treachery and violence." He called upon Huerta to step down, and Huerta refused. Then Wilson turned to a policy of "watchful waiting."

Problems at Tampico and Veracruz.

After a time Wilson plotted to force Huerta from power. He allowed arms to be sent to Huerta's chief rival, Venustiano Carranza. Soon a crisis arose. A shore party of American marines collecting supplies in Tampico, Mexico, was arrested and sent to jail. The marines were soon released and Huerta apologized, but he refused to fire a salute to the United States flag as we demanded.

On April 20, 1914, Wilson asked Congress to approve the use of armed force "to obtain from General Huerta the fullest recognition of the rights and dignity of the United States." The next day a wireless message came from the navy. It reported that a German steamer loaded with arms for Huerta was expected to dock at Veracruz in a few hours. So before Congress had even acted, the President ordered the seizure of the city to prevent their delivery. A detachment of marines was landed, and 19 Americans and 126 Mexicans were killed before the marines controlled the city. Mexicans—including Huerta's chief rival, Carranza—united against the United States, and it appeared that war was near.

The large republics of South America—Argentina, Brazil, and Chile, known as the ABC powers—now offered to mediate between the United States and Mexico. They recommended that Huerta give way to a provisional government. Huerta refused, but they had so undercut his position that he could no longer keep control. He stepped down in July, Carranza entered Mexico City in triumph, and in November Wilson withdrew American troops from Veracruz.

Chasing Pancho Villa.

Still Wilson's Mexican troubles were not over. Carranza's most successful general was Pancho Villa, a former bandit and a brilliant cavalry leader. When Villa began a new revolt, civil war raged again. Villa's raiders killed people on both sides of the border. Finally, when he burned Columbus, New Mexico, in March 1916, many United States citizens were killed.

Wilson, with Carranza's reluctant permission, sent out General John J. Pershing and an expedition of 15,000 men to get Villa "dead or alive." The National Guard, 150,000 strong, was ordered to the border. A West Point graduate, Pershing had commanded cavalry against Chief Geronimo and had fought in the Spanish-American War and in the Philippines.

The pursuit of Villa and the mobilization of the National Guard soon showed how ill-prepared the United States was for war. Villa struck again in the United States, and another force of 8000 men was sent into Mexico in pursuit, only to end up in a clash with Carranza's forces. Once again war with Mexico seemed near. But by now the thunder of the great powers fighting in Europe put a bandit general in a new perspective. The United States might soon be drawn into a global conflict. Seeing this prospect, in January 1917 Wilson withdrew the forces from Mexico. With the entrance of the United States into World War I in April 1917, the Progressive Era would end.

Pursuing the Mexican rebel Pancho Villa in 1916, General Pershing leads American troops across the Santa Maria River.

Culver Pictures

SECTION REVIEW

1. Identify or explain: Root-Takahira Agreement, "great white fleet," William Gorgas, Roosevelt Corollary, Algeciras Conference, Philander C. Knox, *de facto* recognition, Victoriano Huerta, Venustiano Carranza, Pancho Villa, John J. Pershing.

2. Locate: Manchuria, Isthmus of Panama, Colombia, Dominican Republic, Morocco, Veracruz, ABC powers.

3. How did Roosevelt try to advance the interests of the United States in the Far East?

4. Trace the steps leading to the construction of the Panama Canal and the settlement with Colombia.

5. How did TR stretch the meaning of the Monroe Doctrine?

6. Cite instances of Taft's "dollar diplomacy."

7. Why and how did the United States intervene in Mexican affairs in 1914 and 1916?

CHAPTER REVIEW

MEETING OUR EARLIER SELVES

1. What traits in the youthful TR showed up in President Theodore Roosevelt? Explain.

2. The text names or implies many business abuses. Which chiefly affected workers? consumers? business competitors? Were there other victims? Explain.

3. Which of the abuses listed for item 2 above would you expect to be less severe or extensive if there was a business climate of vigorous competition? Explain.

4. Would reforms have been as likely to occur without the "muckrakers"? Explain.

5. How did Roosevelt "carry a big stick" in both domestic and foreign affairs? Cite examples. Did he observe the first part of his motto "Speak softly"?

6. Assume that United States intervention in the Dominican Republic in 1904 and in Nicaragua in 1912 helped those countries straighten out their economic and/or political affairs. Would the "good results" justify the action taken? Explain.

QUESTIONS FOR TODAY

1. Try to describe the leadership style of today's President or some other recent President. How does it compare with the style of Theodore Roosevelt, Taft, or Wilson?

2. Are any of the reform issues of the Progressive Era still relevant issues today? Cite examples and describe the issues as specifically as possible.

3. Can the United States wield "a big stick" in its relations with Latin America today? Why or why not?

YOUR REGION IN HISTORY

1. Did any big city in your state or region experience major reform in the early 1900s? Describe how it happened.

2. List some Progressive measures passed by the legislature of your state between 1900 and 1914.

SKILLS TO MAKE OUR PAST VIVID

1. List some reform measures adopted by the states or the federal government in the Progressive Era. Under each one tell what abuse or condition the reform was designed to correct.

2. Outline the provisions of a new state law that you propose to introduce by the *initiative* process. Then summarize the provisions so that they will be clear to voters who are asked to sign the petitions.

CHAPTER 21

Germany
the slow-
action. G
teed" Belg
into Franc
agreement
many. T
Central P
Later, Japa
By the tin
Norway,
Switzerlan

The Unit
not surpri
vast and t
topple kin
They took
fifty years
Americans
the Progre
good reas
been only
sevelt a h
miseries o

In 19
ing t
Hou
venti

NRS.

The United States and World War I

The First World War began as an Old World war. Everything about it expressed the world that Americans hoped they had left behind. That Old World was a battlefield of national ambitions, religious persecutions, and language barriers. European armies had fought over whether a nation's boundary should be on one side or the other of a narrow river. Old World monarchs had transferred land from one flag to another, bartering people as if they were mere real estate.

In the 1800s the empires of Great Britain, France, and Germany had expanded over the whole world to the deserts and jungles of Africa, the high mountains of Asia, and the islands of the Pacific. Each empire sent out its own merchants and colonial settlers. Each built its strong navy to protect and police the ocean highways. Each built a vast army to guard the homeland and to suppress colonial uprisings anywhere on the globe.

At the same time in Europe national hopes had been growing and stirring up new conflicts. Ordinary citizens who had learned to read became proud of their own languages and their own national heroes. Daily newspapers now alerted citizens to their "national honor," awakened political hopes and ambitions, and nourished pride in the nation's exploits in faraway places. Kings and queens, princes and princesses, czars and czarinas—who were cousins and uncles and aunts—added their own family loves and hates to all the other reasons for peace or war.

1. A spark ignites Europe

By 1914, a world war might have begun almost anywhere. It happened to be sparked in the most confused part of Europe. In the mountainous Balkans of southeastern Europe, small nations jostled and offended one another with their ancient feuds and jealous princes. For centuries these mini-nations had been dominated by Turkey, Russia, Austria, and other major powers. The word "Balkan," in fact, came to describe any community that was broken up into small warring groups.

We cannot be surprised that this was where World War I began. It started in Sarajevo, the

443

World War I, 1914-1917

Central Powers
Allied Powers
Neutral Nations
German Submarine Zone

Stabilized Fronts, 1915-1917
········ Farthest Advances of Central Powers
Eastern Front Armistice Line, December 1917
Boundaries as of 1914

Map labels: ATLANTIC OCEAN, NORWAY, SWEDEN, FINLAND, Petrograd (St. Petersburg), IRELAND, NORTH SEA, DENMARK, GREAT BRITAIN, London, Hamburg, EAST PRUSSIA, Tannenberg, Minsk, RUSSIA, NETH., BALTIC SEA, Berlin, GERMAN EMPIRE, Ypres, The Somme, Le Havre, BELG., LUX., The Marne, Paris, Verdun, Dresden, Prague, POLAND, Brest-Litovsk, Kiev, FRANCE, Bern, SWITZ., Munich, Vienna, AUSTRIA-HUNGARY, Budapest, UKRAINE, Lyon, Odessa, Marseilles, ROMANIA, SPAIN, CORSICA, ITALY, Sarajevo, SERBIA, MONTENEGRO, Danube R., BULGARIA, Sofia, BLACK SEA, PORTUGAL, Rome, SARDINIA, Naples, ALBANIA, Constantinople, Gallipoli, GREECE, TURKEY, SICILY, Athens, AEGEAN SEA, CRETE, CYPRUS

Map annotations:
5. RUSSIAN REVOLUTION, MARCH 1917 RUSSIANS SIGN ARMISTICE, DEC. 1917
1917
3. RUSSIANS DEFEATED, AUG. 1914
2. GERMAN ATTACK AUG. 1914
4. ITALY ENTERS THE WAR, MAY 1915
1. ARCHDUKE FERDINAND ASSASSINATED, JUNE 28, 1914

Legend (upper left):
Europ[e]
Alli[ed]
Cent[ral]
Neu[tral]

Early losses in the war. In the opening battles in 1914, even before the trenches were dug, each side lost a half-million men—more than there had been in the entire German army 50 years before. Then, during 1915, the British and French did not advance more than three miles at any point. Still the French lost a million and a half men in 1915 and a million in 1916. At the Battle of the Somme—which lasted for five months in 1916—the Germans lost more men than had been killed during the whole four years of the American Civil War. On one bloody day nearly 20,000 British soldiers were killed.

Never before had so many men been slaughtered so rapidly or so senselessly. Before the war was over, the soldiers killed on both sides would number 10 million, and another 10 million civilians would die from disease, starvation, and the revolutions that grew out of the war.

When the United States finally plunged in, both sides were weary and sick of the bloodshed. The Germans were near victory. They had made peace with the Russians and now could concentrate all their forces on the western front. In May 1918 the German trenches were within 50 miles of Paris.

capital o
patchwor
28, 1914,
Austro-H
a state vis
by young
boring kin
governme
crime, an
dispute.
and bomb

Troops from the United States played a key role in the battles of 1918. A company of engineers digs a trench in France (left). Another group of Americans charges (above). Men of the 18th Infantry (below) march through the ruins of a small French town near St. Mihiel.

There were many ways to help the war effort (top). The 1919 French poster (below) shows war-damaged Verdun.

The Germans hoped that when they reached Paris they would force the Allies to surrender before American troops could make a difference.

The American Expeditionary Force. But the Americans came in time. At the end of May, the Second and Third divisions of the American Expeditionary Force (AEF) were sent into action. They fought bravely at Belleau Wood and Vaux near Château-Thierry. In July, 85,000 Americans were there to help save Paris. By August an American army of a half-million under General John J. Pershing advanced against the Germans on the southern front. Before the end of September a million and a quarter Americans were fighting in France.

After a bloody battle in October, the Americans advanced to Sedan, 50 miles behind the trenches that the Germans had held for three years. The Americans then cut the railroad that had supplied the German army in their sector. The German defense opposite them began to fall apart. At the same time, the French and the British were advancing all along the line.

The German generals and their emperor had made a bad mistake. They had not imagined that American help at the last moment could turn the tide. Though the Americans arrived late in the battle, they actually did make the difference that decided the war. The United States lost 50,280 men in action. But this was nothing compared to the 4 million lost by Russia, France, and Great Britain and the millions lost by the lesser powers. They had done the real dirty work.

The bloodiest war yet in history—a first "World War"—ended with the armistice on November 11, 1918. In New York and San Francisco and Dallas and Chicago and Atlanta, Americans danced in the streets.

SECTION REVIEW

1. Identify or explain: John J. Pershing, American Expeditionary Force, armistice.
2. Locate: Belleau Wood, Château-Thierry, Sedan.
3. How was World War I different from earlier wars?
4. How did the AEF turn the tide?

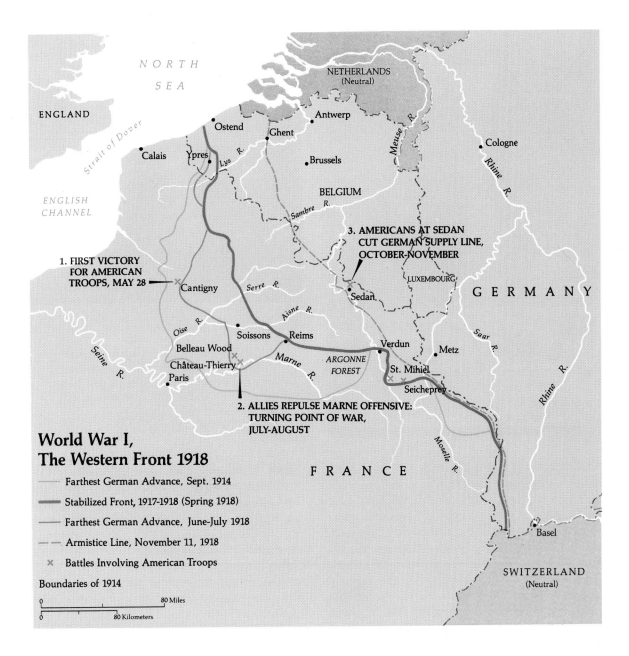

**World War I,
The Western Front 1918**

― Farthest German Advance, Sept. 1914

― Stabilized Front, 1917-1918 (Spring 1918)

― Farthest German Advance, June-July 1918

--- Armistice Line, November 11, 1918

× Battles Involving American Troops

Boundaries of 1914

0 ————————— 80 Miles

0 ————————— 80 Kilometers

1. FIRST VICTORY FOR AMERICAN TROOPS, MAY 28

2. ALLIES REPULSE MARNE OFFENSIVE: TURNING POINT OF WAR, JULY-AUGUST

3. AMERICANS AT SEDAN CUT GERMAN SUPPLY LINE, OCTOBER-NOVEMBER

3. The home front

American troops had tipped the scale for the Allies. But it had been a near thing. The United States preparedness program had been inadequate. With the outbreak of the war the nation suddenly found that it had to mobilize men, money, machines, and minds to aid its struggling friends. To get this task done, the President was given new and sweeping powers. The government, acting through scores of boards, commissions, and committees, regulated daily life. It dictated what (and how much) people should eat. It rationed their sugar and their fuel, and discouraged their travel. It even tried to tell them what to think. The free enterprise system that business was accustomed to came to a halt. The government told industry what it could buy, what it could produce, even where it could build factories. This was the first experiment in total war. Never before had the nation been so organized for a single purpose.

Back our girls over there

Y.W.C.A.

United War Work Campaign

A YWCA poster (left) reminded Americans that women were "over there," too. Some women, like the Broadway chorus girls shown above, signed up for military training to serve in the Home Guard.

Mobilization of men and women. First of all the nation needed an army. The American tradition, expressed in the Constitution, distrusted a large standing army in peacetime. Experience since ancient times showed that ambitious rulers could use the army against the people. Congress passed a Selective Service Act on May 28, 1917, by a nearly unanimous vote in both houses. The law required all men between the ages of 21 and 31 to register for military service. During the Civil War, a person who was drafted could hire a substitute—if he could afford it. But not now.

Despite fears of draft riots like those during the Civil War, draftees were registered peaceably on June 5. Nearly 10 million men were listed. It was decided that a lottery would be the fairest way to choose whom to draft. Each man who had registered was given a number between 1 and 10,500. On July 20, 1917, these numbers were placed in a bowl, and blindfolded officials withdrew enough numbers to call 687,000 men into the army. Before the war was over 24 million men between the ages of 18 and 45 entered the Selective Service rolls.

Almost 3 million of these were called into service. The militia, now called the National Guard, was also brought into federal service. By the time of the armistice in 1918 nearly 4.8 million people—enlistees, draftees, and National Guard—were serving in the armed forces. Among them were women in the Nurses Corps of the army and navy. About 11,000 female yeomen enlisted for office jobs when the Navy Department decided that its right to enlist "persons" included women.

This vast army had to be fed, clothed, equipped, and armed. In the beginning, of course, there were shortages. Before many months American factories were supplying the needed pistols, rifles, machine guns, shells, and bullets. The heavy equipment—the artillery, the tanks, and the airplanes—was still provided by the French and the English.

The war at sea. To move American troops and supplies to Europe there had to be "a bridge of ships." German submarines were sinking ships faster than they could be replaced. "They will win," the British admiral Sir John Jellicoe warned, "unless we can stop these losses—and stop them soon."

Luckily, at the start the United States Navy was in better shape than the army. Fast destroyers were thrown into the battle against the U-boats. Rear Admiral Sims insisted that all ships headed across the Atlantic should travel in convoys. A convoy was an organized group of merchant and passenger ships surrounded and protected by naval vessels armed to ward off submarine attacks. This system worked so well that the German submarines did not kill a single member of the huge AEF on its way to France.

To provide the bridge of ships, the United States began a mammoth shipbuilding program. The government contracted for 10 million tons of ships and built shipyards to construct them. In fact, few of these vessels would be delivered in time to help the war effort. But by seizing the German vessels that happened to be in American waters in April 1917 and by impressing into service almost everything that could float, the government partly filled the gap. Meanwhile more than 1 million American soldiers and millions of tons of equipment were carried to France by the British merchant marine.

Mobilizing money. The expenses of the army and navy, and credit and materials for the Allies, ran into billions of dollars. Money, too, had to be mobilized for war. At least $23 billion was spent for the American war effort, and more than $10 billion went in war loans to the Allies.

In new shipyards like the one in the poster, the United States began an all-out shipbuilding program during World War I. Few ships were finished during the war, but by 1921 the United States had the world's largest merchant fleet.

ON THE JOB FOR VICTORY

· UNITED STATES SHIPPING BOARD · EMERGENCY FLEET CORPORATION ·

Brown Brothers

Brown Brothers

The nation's effort in World War I was spurred on and supported by war bonds. Women sold them on the street (top left). A parade in New York City (top right) helped raise support for the fourth of the Liberty Loans. Below a poster asks support for the last, or Victory, Loan.

Library of Congress

THEY KEPT THE
SEA LANES
OPEN

INVEST IN THE
VICTORY LIBERTY LOAN

458

The government used both taxes and loans to pay these huge expenses. Increased taxes brought in $10.5 billion. The rest was borrowed from the people through the sale of government bonds. Four Liberty Loans and a Victory Loan, "to finish the job," brought in $23 billion.

The government takes control. Of course, a nation geared to peace could not all at once meet the demands of war. Under the pressure of war, the government took over some private businesses. In December 1917, when the overburdened railroads were near collapse, the government took them over. Secretary of the Treasury William McAdoo became director-general of the railroads. He ran them as a single system but left day-to-day operations in the hands of the private managers. Half a billion dollars was invested in improvements and equipment. Soon the railway express companies and the inland waterway systems also came under McAdoo's control. Before the end of the war, government control was extended to telephone, telegraph, and cable companies.

To mobilize industry and agriculture, the preparedness legislation of 1916 had provided for a Council of Defense. In May 1917 this Council set up a national food-control program. It was headed by a hard-driving mining engineer who had run the Belgian War Relief program. His name was Herbert Hoover. Born a Quaker, he combined engineering efficiency and Quaker charity to bring help to the starving Belgians without offending their self-respect.

Hoover's board had no legal power to do its task. Wilson therefore asked Congress for broad powers over the production and distribution of food, fuel, fertilizer, and farm machinery. Hoover was named head of the new Food Administration. All sorts of measures were tried. There were voluntary "wheatless, meatless, heatless days." Hoover urged men and women to plant "war gardens." Prices on farm crops were set high enough to encourage farmers to raise more food and fiber. The use of grain to make beverage alcohol was banned. Coal was rationed for home use. Fuel and food output rose as home consumption went down.

While American "doughboys" were mired in trenches overseas, not all Americans were suffering equally from the war. The big rise in demand for

KEEP *it* COMING

"We must not only feed our Soldiers at the front but the millions of women & children behind our lines"
Gen. John J. Pershing

WASTE NOTHING

UNITED   STATES   FOOD   ADMINISTRATION

Herbert Hoover's Food Administration urged Americans to waste no food.

food—for our soldiers and for the armies and the civilian population of the Allies—sent food prices skyrocketing. Farmers could pay off their mortgages, paint their barns, and buy new farm machinery. The price of land rose, too. But higher crop prices enabled farmers to extend their acreage. They began to plant marginal land that would not have paid off under ordinary conditions. When the war was over, and American farmers were no longer expected to feed European armies, food prices would plummet. Farmers would have to pay a peacetime price for their wartime prosperity.

The War Industries Board. The Council of National Defense set up in July 1917 to mobilize industry actually lacked the authority to do its job. As a result, by January 1918 the industrial war effort was on the verge of collapse. As heavy snows fell it seemed even the weather would not cooperate. The chairman of the Senate committee investigating the war effort saw "inefficiency in every bureau of the government." Republican senators called for a War Cabinet of three men. This would make President Wilson a mere figurehead.

Wilson fought to keep control and put the mobilization on track. He submitted a bill that gave him wide powers to reorganize the government and expend funds as he wished. Even before the Overman Act giving him these powers was passed in May 1918, Wilson created the War Industries Board. Bernard M. Baruch, a Wall Street financier of great energy and vision, was put in charge. He showed how a statesman of the business world could bring his wisdom to the national service.

The job of the War Industries Board was to decide what goods should be produced. It could also set prices for government purchases of supplies. For two years Bernard Baruch was the economic dictator of the country. But he seldom had to use force. He had other means of "persuasion." One day Baruch was having trouble getting the automakers to cut down on the output of automobiles. He had them listen in while he phoned the railroad office to stop train service to their plants. Next he called on the army to seize the auto firms' stockpiles of steel. The automakers promptly gave in. Under Baruch's direction the WIB soon gained control of the industrial war effort. Production went up, waste went down, and criticism lessened.

The labor force. The 4 million men enlisted in the armed forces were withdrawn from the nation's labor supply. A million women helped to fill the gap, doing jobs that they had never been allowed to do (nor known that they could do). The war helped them discover themselves as they streamed into mills and factories. They became furnace stokers, managed assembly lines, and wore the uniforms of railroad and streetcar conductors.

Some reformers announced that economic freedom for women had at last arrived. They were wrong. After the war, women were asked to leave their jobs as an act of "patriotism" so the men could return. By 1920 the proportion of women in the labor force had dropped below the level of 1910.

Blacks by the thousands moved north to take advantage of the new chances for jobs. After suffering in the South from wages that dropped to as low as 75 cents a day in 1914–1915, they saw the North as a promised land. Within a few years there were more than 75,000 blacks in the coal mines and 150,000 on the railroads.

The shortage of labor sent wages up as the government and private firms bid against each other. To fill essential jobs in vital industries, there was a United States Employment Service.

"This is labor's war," said AF of L president Samuel Gompers, and he pledged labor's support. In return for a promise not to strike, unions would get some direct support from the government. Early in April 1918, a National War Labor Board was created to arbitrate labor disputes. Some 1500 cases were submitted to this board. In the few instances in which labor refused to accept the decisions, the President used the pressure of public opinion to compel workers to return to their jobs. In extreme cases, he took over the plant.

Employers, on their part, were forbidden to discharge workers for union activities. Wherever possible, the government insisted on reducing the workday to eight hours. As a result of government support, the membership of labor unions doubled. In spite of a 50 percent rise in prices between 1914 and 1918, labor's *real* income rose 20 percent above the prewar level.

Mobilizing minds. The government also wanted to enlist the minds of the people in the war effort. Millions of Americans had opposed our entry into the war. Some German Americans, naturally enough, did not want to fight against the land of their ancestors. Some Irish Americans felt themselves traditional enemies of the English. Socialists declared that the war was only a capitalist dogfight. Midwest Progressives said the nation should devote itself to reform rather than war. And then there were the pacifists who said that war—only murder under another name—could never be justified.

How could the government convert these reluctant citizens? How could it whip up enthusiasm for our friends and hatred for our enemies? How could it sell war bonds and keep people hard at work? For these tasks President Wilson created the Committee on Public Information. George Creel, a journalist, was appointed chairman, assigned to "sell the war to America." In May 1917 the Creel Committee began publishing a daily *Official Bulletin* of the war news that the administration wished to make public. The committee hired professors, writers, artists, and lecturers by the thousands. Their job was to convince and to reassure Americans that the war was a crusade for freedom and democracy. The Germans were portrayed as hateful beasts, barbarous "Huns" out to dominate the Western world.

This effort helped create a war fever with sad aftereffects which long outlasted the war. It stirred up spy scares and a frantic hunt for traitors. Otherwise sensible Americans now refused to play Beethoven or Wagner. They dropped German courses from the schools. They turned "sauerkraut" into "liberty cabbage" and converted "hamburger" into "Salisbury steak." But this anti-German madness was really anti-American. For without the hundreds of thousands of immigrants from Germany the nation would have been much poorer. The United States—"a nation of nations"—had been created by people from everywhere and was enriched by all their languages and cultures.

The attack on civil liberties. The Espionage Act of 1917 gave the President powers of censorship. It enacted heavy penalties against anyone who handed out information about any place connected with the national defense. To urge resistance to the laws of the United States, to refuse to do military duty, or to hinder the draft now became crimes punishable by prison terms. The Trading with the Enemy Act of 1917 obliged any newspaper printed here in a foreign language to furnish the Postmaster General with English translations of everything it published about the war.

The Sedition Act of 1918 went even further than the infamous Sedition Act of 1798 against which Jefferson and Madison had protested. For the 1918 law imposed penalties on anyone who used "disloyal, profane, scurrilous, or abusive" language about the United States government, flag, or uniform. It empowered the Postmaster General to refuse to deliver mail to anyone who, in his opinion, was using the postal service in violation of the act.

With this barrage of propaganda and new laws, Americans who disagreed in any way with the activities of the government were hounded and harried. In 1917 more than 1100 striking copper miners who were members of the radical Industrial Workers of the World were taken forcibly from Arizona to New Mexico, where they were in-

terned. IWW leaders were thrown into jail. Eugene V. Debs, the many-time Socialist candidate for President, was sentenced to jail for ten years for denouncing the war in 1918. While still in jail he ran for President in 1920. His sentence was finally commuted in 1921.

This was a strange way to fight a war for freedom and democracy. How could the nation improve its war effort if citizens were not allowed to criticize the government or the armed forces? In fact, opposition to the war was slight and scarcely hampered the war effort. But the mania of these times would last even after the war. The virus of witch-hunting and super-patriotism was not easy to cure.

SECTION REVIEW

1. Identify or explain: Selective Service Act, Liberty Loans, William McAdoo, War Industries Board, Bernard Baruch, Herbert Hoover, National War Labor Board, Committee on Public Information, George Creel, Espionage Act, Trading with the Enemy Act, Sedition Act, IWW, Eugene Debs.
2. How did the armed services grow? the merchant marine?
3. How was industry mobilized for war?
4. How did the war affect consumers? farmers? women workers? organized labor?
5. How did the government encourage patriotism? What were some results?
6. Describe wartime attacks on civil liberties.

4. Losing the peace

When the Germans agreed to the armistice in November 1918, they believed that the peace would be generous—and based on Wilson's high-minded Fourteen Points. They were in for a brutal shock.

The Versailles Treaty. President Wilson, announcing that he would go to the Peace Conference in Paris, gave ammunition to his critics. He said his only purpose was to help achieve the goals of his Fourteen Points. They said he was more anxious to be the Preacher to the World than to be the Protector of the United States. No President while in office had ever before gone to Europe.

ICELAND

ATLANTIC
OCEAN

NORTH
SEA

NORWAY

SWEDEN

FINLAND

Leningrad

ESTONIA

DENMARK

LATVIA

LITHU-
ANIA

Danzig

EAST
PRUSSIA

SOVIET
UNION

IRISH
FREE
STATE

GREAT
BRITAIN

BALTIC SEA

London

NETH.

Berlin

Warsaw

Brest-
Litovsk

BELG.

GERMANY

POLAND

Versailles
Paris

LUX.

Rhine

CZECHOSLOVAKIA

FRANCE

AUSTRIA

BESSARABIA

CASPIAN SEA

HUNGARY

SPAIN

ITALY

YUGOSLAVIA

ROMANIA

BLACK SEA

Rome

ALBANIA

BULGARIA

GREECE

Constantinople
(Istanbul)

TURKEY

PERSIA

**Europe and the Near East
after the Treaty of Versailles
and Other Peace Settlements**

MEDITERRANEAN
SEA

CYPRUS
(Br.)

SYRIA
(Fr. Mandate)

Baghdad

Territory Lost by

Russia

Germany

Austria-Hungary

Turkish Empire

Boundaries as of 1926

LEBANON
(Fr. Mandate)

PALESTINE
(Br. Mandate)

IRAQ
(Br. Mandate)

TRANS-JORDAN
(Br. Mandate)

LIBYA
(Ital.)

EGYPT

RED SEA

HEJAZ AND NEJD

Riyadh

0   600 Miles
0   600 Kilometers

Medina

NETHERLANDS

BELGIUM

Rhine

GERMANY

LUX.

RHINELAND

SAAR

FRANCE

ALSACE LORRAINE

SWITZ.

In Paris the three Allied leaders whom Wilson had to bargain with were clever and tough. They were Prime Minister David Lloyd George of Great Britain, Premier Georges Clemenceau of France, and Premier Vittorio Orlando of Italy. Each of them remembered the enormous cost of the war to his country. Each wanted to get as much as possible in lands and wealth and power for his own country. Each hoped to punish the enemies so that they would never rise again.

Wilson irritated the other members of the "Big Four." They saw him as a self-righteous leader who always said he was worrying about "all mankind." They compared the Points that Wilson had announced from Washington with the Commandments given to Moses on Mount Sinai. "Mr. Wilson bores me with his *Fourteen* Points," Clemenceau sneered. "Why, God Almighty has only ten!"

The treaty that came out of the Paris Conference was not as selfish or as vengeful as the European leaders would have wished. Nor was it nearly as just and noble as President Wilson might have hoped. Each victor got land it had been promised in secret treaties. The German colonies were parceled out among the Allies. Yet, at the same time, some new smaller republics—like Czechoslovakia and Poland—were created so that at last these people could govern themselves.

The provisions most poisonous for the future of Europe had to do with "reparations." These were payments the Allies demanded from Germany to "repair" all the war damage. When the Germans signed the armistice, they knew they might have to pay for the damage to civilians.

The British and the French raised the damages to include the *total* cost of the whole war to all the Allies. This meant not only the homes and farms and factories destroyed, but also the cost of guns and ammunition, the uniforms and pay for soldiers, and even the pensions to wounded Allied soldiers and to their relatives. This sum was so vast and so hard to estimate that the Allies refused to name a figure—or even to name a time in the future when the Germans would be allowed to stop paying.

President Wilson did manage to put his own scheme for permanent peace—the League of Nations—in the very same package with all those things the other Allied powers really wanted. He believed that, even if the treaty was not perfect, his new League of Nations could correct the mistakes later.

Crowds cheered President Wilson on July 8, 1919, when he returned from the Paris Peace Conference. Watchful Secret Service men in white straw hats accompanied him.

The fight over the treaty begins. When President Wilson returned to the United States, he was greeted like a hero. An escort of festive warships led him into New York Harbor. Ten thousand people welcomed Wilson at Union Station in Washington.

His triumph was short. Now his political mistakes came home to roost. When Wilson had chosen the American Peace Commissioners to go to Paris, he had snubbed both the Republican party and the Senate. Yet the Republicans held the majority in the Senate. And before any treaty became law, the Senate would have to approve it by a two-thirds majority.

President Wilson simply could not believe that there were reasons why sensible Americans might not want to approve his treaty. What frightened Americans most was the plan for a League of Nations—especially Article 10. Wilson, with typical obstinacy, said that Article 10 was the heart of the League, and that the League was the heart of the whole treaty.

In Article 10 each League member promised to respect and preserve all the other members of the League against "external aggression." At first sight that looked harmless enough. But the real purpose of the Article was to make each member of the League regard an attack on any other member as an attack on itself. In that case, each League member would be expected to prepare for war and then presumably fight to protect all the other members.

To agree to this would overturn one of the oldest American traditions. Should the United States let itself be *required* to plunge into some future European war?

Borah and Lodge lead the opposition. Two able, contrasting Republicans led a relentless battle against allowing the United States to join Wilson's League. One was Senator William E. Borah of Idaho. Borah, like Wilson himself, was the son of a Presbyterian minister who had wanted him also to go into the ministry. A graduate of the University of Kansas, he was as eloquent as Wilson but had more experience in politics. Although a Republican, he supported many Democratic measures when he happened to agree with them. He had worked for the income tax and had fought against the trusts.

Senator Borah's own rule in politics was to stay independent, and then support whatever measures seemed best. In the same way, he believed that the United States should not be dependent on other countries. He bitterly opposed our joining the League of Nations for fear it would take away our independence.

The other leader of the anti-League forces was the learned Senator Henry Cabot Lodge of Massachusetts. He, too, had had a long career as a politician. At the time of the World War he was chairman of the Senate Committee on Foreign Relations. That committee had the power to recommend to the Senate whether or not they should adopt the treaty. Unlike Senator Borah, Lodge was a man of strong personal hates. He distrusted Woodrow Wilson, and so he feared Wilson's League.

The failure to enter the League. Then President Wilson made his fatal decision to appeal directly to the American people. In early September 1919, though already in ill health, he traveled 8000 miles, visited 29 cities, and gave 40 speeches in 22 days. At Pueblo, Colorado, he collapsed and had to be taken back to the White House. There he suffered a stroke. For nearly eight months he could not even meet his Cabinet. Edith Wilson, his wife, carried messages back and forth from everybody else to the President. It was never quite clear which messages actually reached him.

Before the election of 1920 Wilson made another grave blunder. If he had been willing to work with Senator Lodge, he still might have found some compromise. Then he might have succeeded in steering the treaty and the League through the Senate. Instead Wilson once again became the preacher. "Shall we," he asked "or shall we not, redeem the great moral obligation of the United States?" He declared that the election of 1920 would be a "solemn national referendum" on the League of Nations.

The Democratic candidate for President, Governor James M. Cox of Ohio, stood up for the League. The weak, but likable Republican candidate, Senator Warren G. Harding of Ohio, opposed the League. He said vaguely that he favored some sort of "association of nations." Americans chose the Republican Harding by a resounding majority of 7 million votes.

The United States never joined President Wilson's League of Nations. Wilson was saddened that the American people chose a "barren independence." But he did not give up his hope that what a union of states had accomplished in North America, a union of nations might someday accomplish for the whole world.

SECTION REVIEW

1. Identify or explain: David Lloyd George, Georges Clemenceau, Vittorio Orlando, "Big Four," reparations, William E. Borah, Henry Cabot Lodge, James M. Cox, Warren G. Harding.

2. Describe the main issues treated in the Treaty of Versailles.

3. What political mistake by Wilson made it hard for him to secure Republican support for the treaty?

4. What feature of the League of Nations was most opposed by Americans?

CHAPTER REVIEW

MEETING OUR EARLIER SELVES

1. In his War Message President Wilson said that the German government's January 31, 1917, announcement of unrestricted submarine warfare was "in fact nothing less than war against the government and people of the United States." Then he spoke about a moral crusade to make the world "safe for democracy." Do you think he needed to make our entrance into the war a moral issue? Explain.

2. Senator Norris of Nebraska was one of 56 members of Congress to vote against the declaration of war. He explained how the United States had violated its status as a neutral nation. What were some of the unneutral actions of the United States prior to 1917? Were they justified? Explain.

3. Critics of the war pointed to huge gains made out of the war by Wall Street and big business. Who were other "winners" on the home front? Who may have been "losers"?

4. What kinds of freedoms were curtailed during the war? Which of these acts were most necessary? least necessary? Why?

5. What are some lessons that future Presidents might have learned from Wilson's efforts to persuade the United States to take a leading role in world affairs?

QUESTIONS FOR TODAY

1. Much of the conflict in the Middle East in recent years has had its origin in decisions made during World War I and the peace conference. What were some of these decisions? Are there other conflicts in the world today that have strong links to World War I and the treaties?

2. The job of the Creel Committee was to "sell the war" to the public. What programs or policies today or in recent years has the government tried to "sell"? What techniques has it used?

YOUR REGION IN HISTORY

1. What contributions did your community make to the war effort in 1917–1918?

2. What World War I memorials exist in or near your community? What contributions to the war effort do they commemorate?

SKILLS TO MAKE OUR PAST VIVID

1. Draw a poster enlisting support for food or fuel conservation or some other home-front aspect of the war effort.

2. Prepare a vertical timeline of the war years of 1914–1918. On one side list military and diplomatic events. On the other side list events on the home front.

3. Prepare a list of questions to use in an interview with someone who has recollections of World War I. If possible, use these questions in an actual interview and report on what you learned.

8

From boom to bust
1918–1932

Thomas Hart
Benton's painting
"Boomtown"
with its oil wells
evokes the spirit
of the 1920s.
Memorial Art
Gallery of the
University of
Rochester, New
York; Marion
Stratton Gould
Fund (detail).

President Calvin Coolidge reported to Congress on the State of the Union in early December 1928. "No Congress of the United States ever assembled," he said, "on surveying the state of the Union has met with a more pleasing prospect than that which appears at the present time. In the domestic field there is tranquility and contentment . . . and the highest record of years of prosperity. In the foreign field there is peace, the goodwill which comes from mutual understanding. . . ." The twenties, most Americans agreed, had been a wonderful decade.

Before the next year was out, the stock market had crashed, and the ranks of the unemployed had begun to swell. The following years would see banks and factories close and find millions out of work. Most distressing of all to Americans, the government of the able engineer Herbert Hoover seemed unable to solve the nation's pressing problems. "In Hoover we trusted," placards read, "now we are busted." The President constantly made encouraging statements. He said the country was basically in good shape and the crisis would soon pass.

But the crisis did not pass. From the euphoria of the booming "Jazz Age," Americans were plunged into the Great Depression. They no longer would wonder how high up women's skirts and the price of stocks on the market would go. Instead it seemed that the entire American system might collapse.

CHAPTER 22

Return to normalcy, 1918–1929

In the 1920s the sound of radios and phonographs began to fill the air. For the first time motion pictures opened fantastic vistas for the millions. Americans started their love affair with the automobile. Women's skirts—which had once been thought dangerously high when they revealed a glimpse of the ankle—now suddenly shot up to the knee. Long hair had been called a woman's "crowning glory." Now respectable women cut their hair short in a "boyish bob"—and actually wore lipstick. Some even smoked cigarettes in public!

At the same time there were still many old-fashioned Americans. They were shocked by what they saw. Women, they said, ought to be put on a pedestal, where they had neither the freedom nor the temptations of the rest of the human race. In this and other ways the twenties was an age of conflict, confusion, excitement, and experiment. Never was the nation more American. This was still a New World where people might try anything—at least once.

1. The postwar reaction

The cease-fire in Europe did not bring a quick end to the problems of war. The war itself had created new problems. It had left a trail of starvation and death and opened the floodgates of revolution. Peace on the battlefield brought another sort of warfare—in parliaments and factories. All over Europe, dissatisfied people seized the chance to turn their nations upside down. In the United States there was worry that the virus of revolt would infect Americans.

Allied intervention in Russia. In March 1917 a revolution in Russia toppled the government of Czar Nicholas II. Then the new liberal Provisional Government led by Alexander Kerensky had in turn fallen in November before radical Bolsheviks (Communists) led by V.I. Lenin. They promptly took Russia out of the war. Hoping to keep German troops from moving to the western front, the Allies stepped in. They said their purpose was to help Russia form a stable government. Some Western leaders, however, no doubt hoped that they could "strangle Bolshevism at its birth," as Winston Churchill later put it. Japan, for its part, hoped to secure control over eastern Siberia.

As a result, when the armistice came in 1918, many American troops stayed in Europe. They

A Poor Fish Out of Water

This cover of a 1926 issue of the original *Life* magazine was done by John Held, Jr., whose drawings captured the flavor of the 1920s.

were fighting a new kind of war—a war against communism. Earlier that year the United States had joined Britain, France, and Japan in sending troops into northern and eastern Russia. The Allies lifted the hopes of the enemies of the Bolsheviks within Russia and so prolonged the "Great Russian Civil War" of 1918–1920. In the new Russia—now called the Union of Soviet Socialist Republics—the distrust of the Western powers would fester for many years.

During World War I, the Creel Committee had made the people of the United States suspicious of anything un-American. Now the mysterious Communists seemed to threaten to overturn the governments of Europe. They had even formed a party in the United States. It was small and harmless, but many Americans were still jittery, and other events in the country increased their fears.

Labor strife. Within the United States the truce between employers and workers came to an end as soon as the war was won. Workers were anxious to keep the wartime benefits they had gained and felt threatened by soaring prices. In 1919 some 4 million workers went out on strikes costing $2 billion in lost sales and wages. Union violence at home frightened the public.

In the autumn of that year, after the Boston police walked out in a labor dispute, looting and violence spread across the city. When the mayor asked for help, Governor Calvin Coolidge called out the National Guard to keep order. He declared that there was "no right to strike against the public safety by anybody, anywhere, anytime." This statement—and his prompt action against the striking policemen—brought him the Republican vice-presidential nomination in 1920.

A strike against United States Steel, during which eighteen workers were killed, failed. A coal strike, which President Wilson called "not only unjustifiable but unlawful," was broken by a court injunction. These defeats forecast the decline of the unions during the 1920s. Opposed by business, government, the courts, and popular opinion, union membership fell from 5 million in 1921 to 4.3 million in 1929. In these same years total nonfarm employment rose by nearly 7 million.

Urban riots. The end of the war was also marked by an increase in racial friction. Though blacks had served bravely on the battlefield and skillfully in the factories, anti-black feeling had increased. During the year after the armistice 70 blacks, including at least 10 soldiers in uniform, were lynched. "Lynching" was named after a Colonel Charles Lynch of Virginia. It was the barbarous act of a mob that hanged a person without a legal right to do so.

In the summer of 1919 there were more than 25 race riots. The worst occurred in Chicago, where a dispute at the beach set off six days and nights of rioting. Hundreds were injured, and 15 whites and 23 blacks were killed. The trigger-happy Attorney General A. Mitchell Palmer was haunted by Bolshevik ghosts whom he imagined to be everywhere. During that "Red Summer," without reason he accused the Chicago rioters—along with anybody else he disliked—of being Communist agitators.

followers, who made a career of harassing blacks, Jews, Roman Catholics, and all "foreigners." Somehow they were able to enroll about 4.5 million "native born, white, gentile Americans." These included many who wanted someone to blame for lack of jobs and many who were worried by the turmoil of postwar Europe. Somehow the Klan came to dominate the politics of several states.

To enlist and keep its members, the Klan shrewdly used all sorts of hocus-pocus. They had passwords, marched about in white sheets, and held secret meetings. But they were no laughing matter. They whipped and killed innocent citizens. They burned buildings and brought terror to whole communities. Yet they seldom went to jail for their crimes, because they bullied sheriffs and judges into joining them.

The conviction in 1925 of the Indiana Grand Dragon for murdering his secretary marked the beginning of the end of the "new" Klan. The newspapers then began to expose the crimes of the Klan, and respectable Americans avoided it like the plague.

Sacco and Vanzetti. Every epoch of American history has had its martyrs. Their names enter the folklore. John Brown was a willing martyr of the fight against slavery. In this later age Nicola Sacco and Bartolomeo Vanzetti, two Italian-born immigrants, became unwilling martyrs in the struggle for equal justice to all.

In 1920 a holdup took place at a South Braintree, Massachusetts, shoe factory. A paymaster and guard were killed. Shortly afterward Sacco and Vanzetti were arrested. They were both gentle men with no criminal record. But they believed the philosophy of anarchy. They were tried, found guilty, and sentenced to die. There was no solid evidence against them. It was widely thought that they were really victims of the frenzied fear of radicals and aliens.

The belief in the innocence of Sacco and Vanzetti was so widespread that in 1927 the governor of Massachusetts finally had to appoint a committee to review the fairness of their trial. But the committee itself was loaded with prejudice. The author of its report was Harvard President A. Lawrence Lowell, long an officer of the Immigration Restriction League, who was well known for his belief in the "superiority" of the Anglo-Saxon peoples. It is not surprising that this committee reported that the trial had been fair.

When Sacco and Vanzetti were executed, millions of Americans mourned. They believed that the two gentle Italian immigrants were victims of fear and prejudice.

Ben Shahn's grim 1930s painting of Nicola Sacco and Bartolomeo Vanzetti shows them handcuffed together as they stoically await their fate.

The disillusioned writers. Some of the brightest American writers did not like what they saw. The brilliant H. L. Mencken, a Baltimore journalist, used his acid pen to ridicule American follies in phrases that would not be forgotten. He laughed at democracy and called the American people the "Booboisie." The American-born poet T. S. Eliot, who had moved to England, described the postwar world as *The Waste Land.*

Yet the age produced the greatest crop of writers ever to light up an American generation. Novelists Sinclair Lewis, Sherwood Anderson, F. Scott Fitzgerald, William Faulkner, and Ernest Hemingway, along with playwright Eugene O'Neill, made their criticism of their own age into enduring literature.

The nation goes dry. The temperance movement—to discourage the use of intoxicating liquors—was as old as the Republic. Ever since the 1830s it had won the support of some reformers and industrial leaders. As early as 1851, the state of Maine passed a model temperance law. More and more citizens believed that control of liquor was necessary to decrease gambling, organized crime, and political corruption. They were troubled to see workmen wasting their paychecks at saloons while their families went hungry. In the new industrial age, too, a drunk at a machine could injure himself and many others.

By World War I, half the states of the Union had passed laws banning the sale of alcoholic beverages. Then came the war, and all at once "Prohibition" became a national concern. It would conserve grain. It would strike at the German Americans who brewed beer. And it would insure sober, clearheaded workers and soldiers. The wartime Congress passed a Prohibition amendment to the Constitution and sent it to the states. It became the Eighteenth Amendment when it was ratified by three-fourths of the states by January 1919. The sale of beer, wine, and distilled liquors was to stop in January 1920.

In theory, the whole nation was now "dry." All but two states ratified the amendment, yet many Americans had no intention of giving up drinking. Millions of Americans who could see nothing "criminal" about enjoying a glass of beer or wine suddenly became lawbreakers. Only 1520 federal agents were hired to try to stop the flow of liquor. Prohibition could not be enforced. So it bred a

disrespect for all law. Since law-abiding citizens could no longer deal in liquor, the trade became a source of wealth and power for gangsters. "Booze" became the plague of the nation.

Women's suffrage. A more successful by-product of World War I was women's suffrage. Like the temperance campaign, the move to give women the vote had long been a goal of reformers. The war finally brought them success. "The services of women during the supreme crisis have been of the most signal usefulness and distinction," Woodrow Wilson wrote. What good reason could there be for depriving half the nation's adults of the right to vote? President Wilson's support, in 1919, helped the suffrage amendment pass Congress with little opposition. Only fourteen months later, the thirty-sixth state ratified the Nineteenth Amendment. At last women became first-class citizens.

SECTION REVIEW

1. Identify or explain: Bolsheviks, Calvin Coolidge, immigration quotas, Sacco and Vanzetti case, temperance movement, Eighteenth Amendment, Nineteenth Amendment.

2. What action in 1918 brought Russian distrust of the Western powers?

3. Describe the main developments in labor relations and race relations after World War I.

4. What events were troubling Americans in 1919–1920? How did Attorney General Palmer react?

5. How did the National Origins Act restrict immigration?

6. Describe the goals and methods of the new Ku Klux Klan.

7. Why and how was the Prohibition amendment approved? What were some of its results?

2. Searching for the good old days

The rash of postwar fears and headaches—bombs, Bolsheviks, riots, and strikes—made many Americans yearn for the "good old days." The nation was tired of their preacher-President. They wondered whether the United States should try to settle the problems of turbulent old Europe and the world. Their election of the Republicans' Warren G.

Harding and Calvin Coolidge showed the desire of Americans to turn inward. "America's present need," Harding explained, "is not heroics, but healing, not nostrums but normalcy, not revolution but restoration, not surgery but serenity."

Warren G. Harding. President Harding had started as the owner of a weekly paper in the small town of Marion, Ohio. His newspaper grew and prospered with the town, and he became a power in state politics. He had served in Ohio's senate and as lieutenant governor and had just completed a term as a United States Senator. When he was nominated for the nation's highest office, he had little training and even less capacity to be President of the United States. But he was friendly and likable. Silver haired and dignified, he looked so much like a President that voters easily imagined he had other qualifications, too. The Republicans picked him because the party was badly divided between its abler men—General Leonard Wood, Governor Frank Lowden of Illinois, and Herbert Hoover. The little-known Harding had few enemies.

Harding got off to a promising start. He seemed to know his own limitations and said he would choose some of the "best minds" to help him. And that he did. Charles Evans Hughes, one of the wisest Republicans in the country, was named Secretary of State. Herbert Hoover became Secretary of Commerce. Andrew W. Mellon, one of the nation's richest men and a wizard of finance, headed the Treasury. He would remain there for twelve years under three Presidents. Henry C. Wallace, widely known as the editor of a farm journal and a champion of conservation, became Secretary of Agriculture.

Some of Harding's other appointments were less wise, and a few were disastrous. Albert B. Fall of New Mexico, an old friend from Harding's Senate days, was named Secretary of the Interior. But he was opposed to conservation. That seemed an odd qualification for the head of a department founded to conserve the nation's resources. For Attorney General the President chose Harry Daugherty of Ohio. His only recommendation for the job was that he had "groomed" Harding for the Presidency and managed his campaign. It soon appeared that this would be a government by "cronies." The least able and more self-seeking officials seemed to be in charge. Harding's old friends, who spent more time

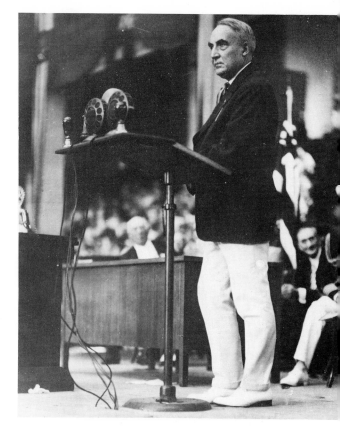

In 1923 Harding became the first President to address the American people over the radio.

playing cards together than planning the national welfare, came to be called the "Ohio Gang." They were not ashamed to use their offices to enrich themselves. Their crimes would make the weak Harding a synonym for incompetence, and their activities would help bring about his death.

Foreign affairs. As President, Harding was out of his depth. The affairs of the larger world were really too much for him, but he tried to seem decisive. In his inaugural address he declared that he wanted nothing to do with the League of Nations. "We seek no part in directing the destinies of the Old World," he said. "We asked the sons of this republic to defend our national rights, not to purge the Old World of the accumulated ills of rivalry and greed." As a result the Versailles Treaty was ignored, and the United States made a separate peace with Germany. It was signed by Harding on July 2, 1921.

The First World War had shown that when the world was at war no one could feel at peace. The great island-nations, Great Britain and Japan, needed strong navies—both for commerce and to protect their shores. And the United States was a two-ocean nation. After the war, each of these nations built up its navy. The world was supposed to be at peace, but these countries seemed to be preparing for war at sea. Where would it end?

Few Americans wanted to pay the cost of an arms race. At the call of President Harding, delegates from nine great powers with interests in the Far East met in Washington in the fall of 1921.

From their meetings three treaties emerged in 1922. In the *Five Power Treaty*, Great Britain, Japan, the United States, France, and Italy agreed to limit the number of their capital ships (vessels over 10,000 tons displacement). They would scrap 2 million tons of ships. The two biggest powers—Great Britain and the United States—each were allowed to keep 500,000 tons, Japan 300,000 tons, and France and Italy 175,000. In addition the powers agreed not to build any more forts or naval bases on their possessions in the Pacific—except for Hawaii.

Once the treaty was concluded, the Western powers feared that they had given Japan a free hand in the Pacific. They then managed to obtain the so-called *Nine Power Treaty*. This protected Western interests by binding all to observe the Open Door in China. They promised to respect China's integrity and not seek land or special privileges there.

To free Great Britain from its military alliance with Japan, a *Four Power Treaty* was signed between the United States, Great Britain, Japan, and France. They agreed to respect one another's possessions in the Pacific. Any issue that seemed likely to disturb the peace of the Far East would be sent to a joint conference. The Senate, though still fearing entangling alliances, accepted this treaty. But the senators did so with the reservation that the United States assumed "no commitment to armed force, no alliance, no obligation to join in any joint defense."

The Washington Conference was the first successful disarmament conference in modern history. But there was no way to enforce the agreements. Japan, with expanding industry and a growing population crowded onto its islands, was determined to become a great power. These treaties provided a decade of peace. They also gave Japan the time to organize and to become a great Asian power without interference. Still, our nation's relations with Japan could not be happy so long as the Immigration Act of 1924 was in effect as an insult to the Japanese people.

Harding's domestic program. The way back to "normalcy," as Harding found, was a rocky road. A sharp decline in business began in 1920. To deal with the problems of depression and conversion to peacetime, the President called Congress into special session in April 1921. He asked for higher tariffs, lower taxes, less government spending, and aid to disabled soldiers and to farmers.

One of his proposals would open a new era in planning federal spending. He asked Congress to create a bureau to sift the money demands of each department. All requests would go into a single budget to be sent to Congress for its review and approval. For the first time, Congress and the people would be able to see all at one time and in one document how the government intended to spend the people's money. In response, Congress passed the Budget and Accounting Act. This set up the Bureau of the Budget. At the same time a General Accounting Office headed by a Comptroller General would check to see that the money was spent for the legal purposes and would recommend economies.

The President proposed new high tariffs to protect farmers from Canadian competition. An emergency tariff raised duties on 28 farm products. The next year the Fordney-McCumber tariff gave industrialists, too, the protection they wanted.

The effects of these trade barriers were not good. The Fordney-McCumber Act clogged the flow of foreign trade. Europeans needed to sell their goods here in order to get dollars to buy our products. To no one's surprise, then, European nations retaliated by raising their tariffs against goods from the United States. American business firms had trouble selling their products abroad. The tariff race, like the arms race, would be costly to everybody.

Secretary of the Treasury Mellon asked that the high wartime taxes (to support the armed forces) at once be reduced. Industry would not grow without more capital investment, which he believed the wartime taxes were preventing. In 1921 Congress repealed the wartime excess profits tax on industry. It also reduced the top level of taxes on the wealthy from 65 percent to 50 percent. (Mellon had wanted it to be 25 percent.) Congress also lowered taxes for middle- and lower-income people, which Mellon had not asked for. Mellon finally had his way in 1924 when a new tax bill reduced the top tax to 25 percent. In the next few years it was cut even more. During one tax debate someone observed that Mellon would receive a larger personal reduction than all the taxpayers in the state of Nebraska put together.

The bonus bill. When a war veteran was discharged, he received a "bonus" of $60. Disabled veterans could get hospital care and other special benefits. Veterans' organizations were demanding that those who had served in the armed forces in wartime deserved special treatment when the nation enjoyed the peace they had helped to bring. They asked for another and larger "bonus." Harding argued that the soldiers had never expected a bonus. He said that serving in the army was only their patriotic duty. He vetoed the "bonus" bill, and Congress failed to override his veto.

The veterans' groups kept up their pressure. In the spring of 1924, after Calvin Coolidge had become President, a new bonus bill (the Adjusted Compensation Act) was passed. This gave a veteran an insurance policy totaling in value $1.25 for every day spent overseas and $1 a day for service in the United States. Veterans could borrow up to 25 percent of the value of their policies. Coolidge vetoed the bill, but Congress easily passed it over his veto.

The war debts. The $9 billion in war debts owed to the United States by its former allies—Great Britain, France, and Italy—created a baffling problem. This money had been mostly spent in the United States to finance the war against Germany. The Allied powers argued that the United States should cancel the war debts because the money had been spent also in defense of the United States.

The Harding administration insisted that the war debts should not be canceled. So they were paid back in installments. The money came from the huge reparations the Versailles Treaty forced Germany to give the victorious European nations to repair the damage caused by the war. And the only way Germany could pay was by borrowing from the United States. With the depression of the 1930s, this whole merry-go-round stopped. Only Finland ever paid its entire debt.

The death of Harding. While the whole world was trying to find a way out of these vast and puzzling problems, Americans were plagued by corruption and by the bad judgment of their President. In 1923 Harding began to hear stories about what some of his "Ohio Gang" had been up to. He had made the mistake of appointing a chance acquaintance, Colonel Charles R. Forbes, head of the Veterans Bureau. This was a huge enterprise that had charge of the hospitals and all other forms of veterans' relief. In two years $250 million was wasted or stolen from these programs. Even after Attorney General Daugherty told Harding of the rumors about Forbes, the President, ever loyal to his friends, let Forbes leave the country. From Europe, Forbes resigned. When the Senate began a probe of the Forbes case, the Veterans Bureau's legal adviser, Charles F. Cramer, committed suicide.

Soon after hearing about Forbes, Harding learned that Jesse Smith, Daugherty's close friend and aide in the Justice Department, had been selling his influence. Smith himself committed suicide in May 1923.

The stories about Harding's "friends" revealed a scale of corruption not known since the days of President Grant. The pleasant, easygoing President was shocked. "I have no trouble with my enemies," Harding said. It was his friends who kept him "walking the floors at night."

The saddened President left Washington for a trip to the West Coast and Alaska in June 1923. During the trip he asked Secretary Hoover and others again and again what a man should do when he had been betrayed by his friends. During his travels Harding was taken ill. He died suddenly in the evening of August 2, 1923.

The Harding scandals. The nation mourned Harding's death. Soon the truth about his administration began to come out. At first the probes were called mere efforts at "character assassination" of Harding. But not for long. Forbes was sent to Leavenworth prison for two years. Thomas W. Miller, Alien Property Custodian, was also sent to

MILL END REMNANT SALE
A Whole Lot of Junk, such as Moral Responsibility, Honor, Ethics, etc., to be practically given away.
A Triumph of Merchandising!

SOLD

SOLD

ARMY

SOLD

WELCOME GHOULS

Sight Seeing Tours Ruins of Washington

EXTRAORDINARY SALE!
Capitol, Army, Navy, White House, etc., Remarkable Values at only 19¢ each
Thursday Only
No phone or Mail Orders

AMERICAN INSTITUTIONS
CABINET MEMBERS
LAWYERS, ETC.
BOUGHT, SOLD & QUOTED.

SPECIAL TODAY
THE MINT
(In A1 Condition)
was $2.50
now $1.98

Ellison Hoover in *Life,* March 6, 1924

The attempt of Harding's associates to enrich themselves by selling and leasing public property for their own profit brought this reaction from a cartoonist. Everything—from Cabinet members to the Mint—could be bought at bargain prices. Honor and ethics were "practically given away."

jail for selling for the profit of the Ohio Gang valuable property taken from the Germans during wartime. Attorney General Daugherty was tried, but he was not convicted.

The most sensational of the scandals was the attempted theft of the national oil reserves. Oil had taken the place of coal to power the ships of the navy. It had become a prime need for commerce and national defense. The government in 1912–1915 had set aside three promising oil fields as reserves for the nation's future. But Harding's Secretary of the Interior, Albert Fall, leased two of these—Teapot Dome in Wyoming, and Elk Hills in California—to private interests in return for $325,000 in gifts and "loans." Fall ended up with a year in prison, and the leases were later canceled by the Supreme Court.

SECTION REVIEW

1. Identify or explain: Charles E. Hughes, Andrew Mellon, Henry C. Wallace, Albert B. Fall, Harry Daugherty, "Ohio Gang," Budget and Accounting Act, General Accounting Office, Fordney-McCumber tariff, bonus bill, war debts, Teapot Dome, Elk Hills.

2. Describe the outcome of the Washington Conference. What was lacking to make the treaties effective?

3. What did the Harding administration accomplish in (a) control of spending? (b) tariff revision? (c) tax cutting?

4. What scandals took place during Harding's administration? Was Harding to blame?

3. "Keeping cool with Coolidge"

Vice-President Calvin Coolidge was spending his vacation at his father's home in the little village of Plymouth Notch, Vermont, when he was awakened with the news of Harding's death. By the light of a kerosene lamp his father, John Coolidge, a justice of the peace, administered the oath of office.

Coolidge had never even seen Washington, D.C., before he became Vice-President. He had hardly ventured beyond the borders of his native state of Vermont or neighboring Massachusetts, where he had built his political career. He had been mayor of Northampton, lieutenant governor, and then governor of Massachusetts. Home for Coolidge, his wife, Grace, and their two sons was half a double house in Northampton. This he rented for $27 a month.

President Coolidge. If a playwright had invented a character to contrast with Harding, he could not have done better. Harding was a genial, unbuttoned good fellow who liked to sit around the White House smoking cigars and playing cards with his cronies. This new President was reticent, plain, and thrifty. A man of few words, "Silent Cal" was not one to warm the cockles of your heart. He naturally tempted comedians to make jokes about his quiet manner and his immobile face. Once when a rumor started that he had died, a wit remarked, "How would you know?"

But Coolidge was like Harding in one way. He too was an admirer of American business. His best-known utterance was: "The business of America is business." Like Harding, he was anxious not to trouble business with government rules. In the 1900s Calvin Coolidge still shared Thomas Jefferson's belief that the government is best which governs least.

The election of 1924. This let-alone policy fit the temper of the times. Most Americans were tired of the rules and rationing of the war years. Coolidge followed the Harding policies. Only a year after Coolidge had been thrust into the White House, the Republicans meeting in Cleveland chose him to run for President in the next election. Charles G. Dawes, a banker who had served ably as Director of the Budget, was named for Vice-President.

When photographers began to follow Presidents everywhere, they took pictures of them in all sorts of situations. "Silent Cal," who never appeared comfortable in front of a camera, can be seen here posed stiffly in a hayfield. It seems doubtful that he intended to do any real work.

Brown Brothers

When the Democrats met in their convention, the party was deeply divided. The split in the party mirrored a split in the nation. The Americans who still made their living on farms were troubled by the new ways of life in the growing cities. City dwellers believed they were the vanguard of progress. By a vote of 542 to 543 the convention actually refused to denounce the Ku Klux Klan (p. 471). There were dozens of candidates who took advantage of the confusion.

Finally the main battle was between William G. McAdoo of California and Al Smith of New York. McAdoo, Woodrow Wilson's son-in-law, had served as Wilson's energetic and able Secretary of the Treasury and wartime director of the railroads. He was the candidate favored by the rural South and West. The colorful city politician Alfred E. Smith had left school at eleven. He had received his education on the sidewalks of New York, which was easy to tell because he spoke with a resounding New York accent. He was opposed to Prohibition, and he was a devout Roman Catholic.

Between Smith and McAdoo the convention deadlocked. After 102 ballots, the weary delegates settled on the safe and colorless John W. Davis. He was a conservative New York corporation lawyer. For Vice-President the Democrats chose William Jennings Bryan's brother, Governor Charles W. Bryan of Nebraska. At last the delegates could go home after sixteen days spent in the hot Madison Square Garden in New York City.

The Republicans, like the Democrats, would also suffer from the division between the city and the country. When the Republican convention adjourned, "Battling Bob" La Follette of Wisconsin broke with his party. Coolidge, he said, "had literally turned his back on the farmers." Senator La Follette himself then ran for President as the candidate of a new Progressive party. Both Republicans and Democrats attacked La Follette as a dangerous radical.

When the votes were counted, it was plain that most Americans preferred to "keep cool with Coolidge." He received 15 million votes to Davis's 8.5 million and La Follette's surprisingly large 4.8 million. During that election 123 women won seats in state legislatures. And two women, Miriam A. "Ma" Ferguson of Texas and Nellie T. Ross of Wyoming, wives of former governors, were elected governors of their states.

Grace Coolidge (left) and the President appear on the platform of their train as they travel to the summer White House in 1928.

Government helps business. "If the federal government should go out of existence," President Coolidge once said, "the common run of the people would not detect the difference for a considerable length of time." That was the way he thought it ought to be. For him "free enterprise" simply meant the freedom of business from government rules. Regulation, he believed, would make business less profitable. And, according to Coolidge, it was profitable businesses that made the whole nation happy and prosperous. "The man who builds a factory builds a temple," he declared. "The man who works there worships there." Some people said the President was making business into a religion.

Regulatory agencies, like the Federal Trade Commission and the Federal Reserve Board, were put in the charge of men who would help the businesses they were supposed to regulate. The FTC urged whole industries to agree on trade policies. Some of these agreements tended to create monopolies. Secretary of Commerce Hoover also promoted these "fair practice" agreements so that industries could share information on products and markets. Hoover believed that the day of cutthroat competition was over. Now, he thought, the Department of Commerce should help them cooperate for better products and higher output.

The Supreme Court helped this process along. In 1920 the Court ruled that United States Steel was not a monopoly even though the company controlled 40 percent of the steel industry. This still did not, the Court said, "unreasonably restrain trade." With this green light—and with the help of Hoover and the regulatory agencies—companies all across the land merged to create larger units. By 1929, only 1289 firms produced three-fourths of all goods turned out by corporations. In many industries a few big firms were setting prices through trade associations. The Supreme Court still said that these industrial trade groups were not restraining trade.

And the country prospered. Most Americans were doing better. The price of shares on the stock market was going up rapidly. The economic picture looked promising.

The farm problem. There were a few areas that were slow to recover after the war. The textile, leather, and soft coal industries were weak. Blacks, Indians, and Mexican Americans still had little share in American prosperity. The obvious big problem was the distress on the farms. Now no one could ignore this problem, because the farmers had learned to speak up.

Farmers were growing poorer while much of the rest of the country was growing richer. It seemed that the more they produced, the less they were paid for their crops. At the same time their clothes, their farm implements, their fuel, and the other products they had to buy were going up. Their taxes were rising. When the farmers demanded help, they did get higher tariff protection. But this did little good. High tariffs on farm products could not keep prices up when there were surplus crops.

Now the farmers demanded more direct aid. Senator McNary of Oregon and Representative Haugen of Iowa devised a scheme to use government money to save the farmer from the free market. The idea behind their complex plan was to keep up the price of staple crops regardless of what happened to other prices. The federal government would buy the surpluses that would have driven down farm prices if they went on the open market. The government then would either hold the produce until the market for it improved or it would sell the produce abroad. The McNary-Haugen bill failed to pass Congress in 1924 and 1926. In the next two years it did pass, but Coolidge vetoed it each time. "Farmers have never made money," he said. "I don't believe we can do much about it."

The election of 1928. Near the end of his fourth year in office, Calvin Coolidge announced (in one of his *longer* speeches), "I do not choose to run for President in 1928." In his place the Republicans named the able and ambitious Secretary of Commerce, Herbert Hoover.

The Democrats nominated the "Happy Warrior," Alfred E. Smith. Smith had made a superb record as governor of New York. He had been opposed by many bigoted Democrats from the small towns and from the South who feared that a Catholic President would be only an agent of the Pope. But this time they were not strong enough to deny him the nomination he deserved.

Party platforms were not important in this election. Instead it was what the candidates seemed to stand for. Al Smith, with his New York East Side accent, his brown derby and cigar, and his Roman Catholic religion, was the image of the big city. City people liked his call for the repeal of Prohibition and the return of liquor control laws to the states. Hoover, on the other hand, seemed to stand for big business, for small town and rural America, and for Protestantism and Prohibition.

Prohibition and Smith's Catholic religion were the chief issues of the campaign. Smith met the religious issue squarely. He said that his devotion to his church meant as well devotion to the Constitution and the principle of separation of church and state. But his nomination stirred up much prejudice and fear, especially in the rural South and Middle West where the new Ku Klux Klan had been strongest.

Even without the Catholic issue Hoover could scarcely have failed to win in 1928. Although he lacked personality, his humanitarian record in the war and his policies in the Department of Commerce had made him popular. The country was prosperous, and most Americans were still Republicans. Few observers were surprised when Hoover trounced Smith. He received 21 million votes to Smith's 15 million and captured all but eight states. He even carried five states in the formerly solid South—the first Republican to do so since the days of Reconstruction.

Hoover's easy victory hid some trends that were important for the Democrats. Smith had attracted many new votes in the twelve largest cities, which had formerly been strongly Republican. For the first time since the Civil War, these population centers showed a net plurality for the Democrats. The key to future elections would be in these cities that could carry the big states with their large electoral votes. But for now this crucial fact was hidden by the rosy glow of Republican prosperity.

SECTION REVIEW

1. Identify or explain: Charles G. Dawes, William G. McAdoo, Al Smith, John W. Davis, Charles Bryan, Progressive party, Miriam Ferguson, Nellie T. Ross, regulatory agencies, McNary-Haugen bill.

2. What were some unusual features of the campaign and the election of 1924?

3. In the 1920s how was business "helped" by (a) Coolidge's attitude toward business? (b) the regulatory agencies? (c) the Supreme Court?

4. Why were farmers in trouble? How did Congress propose to help them? What was Coolidge's response?

5. Who were the candidates for President in 1928? How did they differ?

Herbert and Lou Henry Hoover along with Hoover's secretary greet the crowds at a "whistlestop" during the 1928 campaign.

The Bettmann Archive, Inc.

Ever the "happy warrior," Al Smith waves to his enthusiastic supporters who line the streets of New York City in the midst of his race with Hoover.

Culver Pictures

4. Life in the Jazz Age

During the 1920s the United States seemed a land of miracles. Never before were factories making so many new things. Never before had the daily life of a nation been so quickly transformed.

New products for living. At the opening of the 1900s the automobile was still such an oddity that in Vermont the law required a driver to send someone an eighth of a mile ahead with a red flag. By 1918 there were nearly 7 million cars on the road. Auto and truck production topped the 2 million mark in 1922 and climbed to more than 5 million in 1929. With the spread of automobiles came the building of new highways and the paving of the roads. Now Americans no longer had to live close together and near their jobs and shops. They could work and shop in places too far to walk to, and out of reach of a streetcar. The first "shopping center" for the newly mobile American was built in Kansas City in 1922.

Back in 1900 the closest thing to a movie was the crude "nickelodeon." In return for your nickel you looked into a box to see pictures move for a few minutes. In 1929 one hundred million tickets were being sold to the movies every week, and the movies could actually talk!

Until World War I most Americans had not even heard of the radio. The first broadcasting station—KDKA in Pittsburgh—did not open until 1920. Its first broadcast carried the Harding-Cox election returns. By 1929 the annual turnout of radio sets numbered 4 million. Television was still in the future. It seemed amazing enough that voices could be sent without wires.

The phonograph was a commercial success by 1905, and within ten years half a million phonograph records were being sold annually. By 1921 production had reached 100 million a year, and a music new to many Americans was sweeping the land. Blacks moving north during World War I brought with them their jazz and blues, and soon recording companies began making records of these surprising sounds. Blacks were now giving the United States a fresh kind of original American music. New heroes and heroines appeared on the scene—Louis Armstrong, "Duke" Ellington, "King" Oliver, Earl "Fatha'" Hines, Ferdinand Joseph La-Menthe Morton, known as "Jelly Roll," Bessie Smith, and many others.

During the 1920s everyone began to want a refrigerator to replace the inconvenient old ice box. At the beginning of the decade only about 5000 mechanical refrigerators were made each year. By 1931 over a million a year were being produced by the nation's factories. Now even city people could easily keep milk and fresh fruit and vegetables in all seasons.

Health and education. With advancing medical knowledge now at last the diseases that most threatened children—typhoid, diphtheria, and measles—were coming under control. Americans were healthier and were living longer than ever before. They were also making the highest wages in history—and working shorter hours.

Education in the United States was better and reached a larger proportion of the people than in any other country. By 1928 the money that Americans spent each year for education was more than that spent by all the rest of the world put together. In most European countries only a grade school education was free. But in the United States a free high school education was normal, and millions could hope to go to college.

"The Roaring Twenties." The 1920s have been called "the Roaring Twenties." And with good reason. There were the speakeasies (the illegal bars) and the flappers (girls with short hair and short skirts). There was the new music—jazz, ragtime, and blues suddenly blaring out of millions of phonographs and radios. For the first time in our history huge crowds gathered to watch sporting events. In a single ball park on many afternoons 50,000 fans cheered Babe Ruth as he was breaking all records with his home runs. One hundred forty-five thousand people paid $2.6 million to watch the second fight between Gene Tunney and Jack Dempsey. And a charming young southern gentleman from Georgia named Bobby Jones delighted the nation by defeating the world's best at golf.

The climax of national pride and excitement came May 21, 1927. That night the handsome Charles A. Lindbergh, "Lucky Lindy," landed in Paris. He had made the first solo nonstop flight from New York to Paris in 33 1/2 hours. The nation was inspired to see how courage and the airplane could shrink the Atlantic Ocean. Millions

John Held, Jr., helped to create the image of "flappers" and "flaming youth" in the 1920s.

of New Yorkers roared their admiring welcome when he returned. As he was paraded through the streets, 1800 tons of shredded paper rained down from the surrounding skyscrapers. Americans admired Lindbergh's modesty as much as his bravery. He called his book *We* and always shared credit for his feat with his airplane, with those who built it, and with all the Americans who had made his adventure possible. The nation had a new hero—and a new kind of hero. He toured the nation to encourage the rise of air mail and to promote air travel.

The roar of the factory. More than the roar of music or crowds, the sounds that marked the twenties were the hum of the electric dynamo, the clatter of machines, the rhythm of the factory assembly line. The nation was finding and making new ways to manufacture radios, refrigerators, airplanes, automobiles, and all sorts of gadgets by the millions. Now a great new force—electric power—was added to the steam power that drove the first modern factories.

The ideas of Frederick W. Taylor on "scientific management" (p. 358) became more and more popular with employers. By making a science of the simplest jobs, they could find a better way to do them.

Charles Lindbergh was the first person to fly nonstop between New York and Paris and the first to fly across the Atlantic alone. He is shown here with his plane in which he made the flight. "The Spirit of St. Louis" can be seen at the National Air and Space Museum, Washington, D.C.

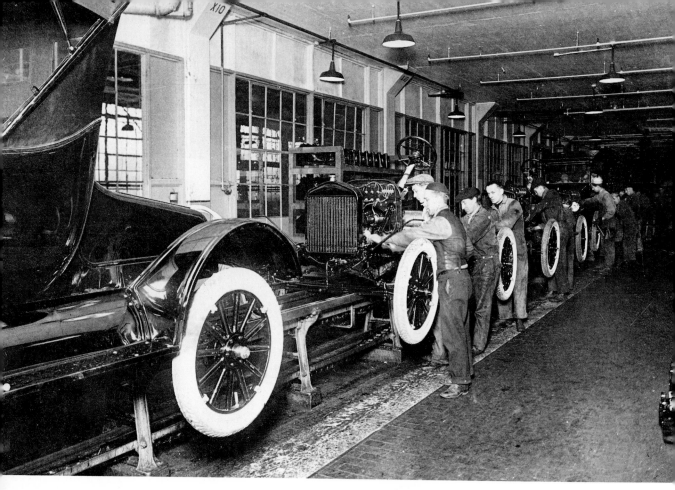

Henry Ford's assembly line introduced a new standard for efficiency in mass production. Instead of going from task to task, workers stayed in place and a moving belt brought their work to them.

In an astonishingly short time the American factory took on a different look. Scientific management engineers invented a whole new way of organizing a factory. Instead of having you walk around to pick up parts and bring them to your workbench, the management engineers designed a workbench that moved. Then you could stay in one place and keep your mind on your proper job. The bench (now a moving belt driven by electricity) would carry along the heavy parts from one worker to another.

This new kind of moving workbench was called an "assembly line" because on it the whole machine was put together or "assembled."

In April 1913 a bold mechanic named Henry Ford decided to try an assembly line for making automobiles. He wanted to make cars so cheaply that he could sell them by the millions. He made

some improvements of his own in the assembly line. For example, he arranged the moving belt so that it would always be "man-high." Nobody had to waste energy bending down or reaching up.

Ford also varied the speed of the belt. He explained:

The idea is that a man must not be hurried in his work—he must have every second necessary but not a single unnecessary second. . . . The man who puts in a bolt does not put on the nut; the man who puts on the nut does not tighten it. On operation number 34 the budding motor gets its gasoline. . . . On operation number 44 the radiator is filled with water, and on operation number 45 the car drives out.

Henry Ford opened his new plant with its electric-powered conveyor belt in 1914, and the time it took to put together a Model T dropped from 14 hours to 93 minutes. By 1925 the process was so perfect that one car rolled off the assembly line every 10 seconds. Machines that had not been imagined 50 years before now cost so little that they changed the lives of ordinary Americans.

Selling the products of the factories. There grew up a powerful American business to sell this outpouring of new products. Advertising had been around for a long time, but only about $1 billion a year was spent on it before World War I. By 1929 more than $3 billion a year was spent for advertising through newspapers, magazines, billboards, direct mail, and—fastest growing of all—the radio. Advertisements for consumer goods promised comfort, health, beauty, status.

Even more important in selling goods was buying on credit. Now you did not have to wait to buy what you wanted until you had saved enough money. "Buy Now, Pay Later," the ads screamed. By 1928 Americans owed more than $1 billion for the automobiles they had bought on the installment plan.

Buying "on time" can help keep business booming so long as people can afford to buy all that the factories produce. But in the 1920s wages did not rise as fast as output. The real wages of American workers rose 26 percent between 1918 and 1929 while their productivity was going up 40 percent. Without more money, workers could not buy—even "on time"—all the automobiles, refrigerators, radios, washing machines, vacuum cleaners, and other expensive items that fueled the economy.

Most Americans were unaware of any problems. They agreed with Herbert Hoover who caught the spirit of the time in his inaugural address in March 1929:

Ours is a land rich in resources, stimulating in its glorious beauty, filled with millions of happy homes, blessed with comfort and opportunity. In no nation are the institutions of progress more advanced. In no nation are the fruits of accomplishment more secure. In no nation is the Government more worthy of respect. No country is more loved by its people. I have an abiding faith in their capacity, integrity, and high purpose. I have no fears for the future. . . . It is bright with hope.

"The supreme combination of all that is fine in motor cars"

Color. Nature abounds in beautiful and harmonious color combinations. The birds, the flowers, the sunset skies, set perfect examples—and point the way to brilliant color schemes all in perfect taste.

Yet what artistry is required in the selection of shades and tones to satisfy the modern vogue for color in motor cars! Packard has a special Board of Color made up of men of long experience and artistic judgment. These men create the standard color combinations which charm the eye in such wide variety on today's Packard Six. And they advise on the special requirements of those who buy the Packard Eight.

Whether Six or Eight is your choice you may be as sure of the charm and good taste of the Packard's color scheme as you are of its lasting beauty. For Packard lavishes as much care and effort on the unusual processes which preserve the car's color and finish as upon the selection of the shades which will appeal to Packard's discriminating clientele.

Nothing finer is offered anywhere in the world than the enduring brilliance of Packard cars —long in life and long in beauty of lines and finish.

P A C K A R D
ASK THE MAN WHO OWNS ONE

Culver Pictures

Some automakers emphasized color and style. Henry Ford said his customers could have *any* color—so long as it was black!

SECTION REVIEW

1. What kinds of new consumer goods and services became widespread in the 1920s?
2. Why was "roaring" a good description of the 1920s?
3. What changes were making factory production more efficient?
4. What factors helped producers sell their rising output of new products?

CHAPTER REVIEW

MEETING OUR EARLIER SELVES

1. Many Americans in the early 1920s yearned for a return to the calmer prewar era. What postwar changes would they find disturbing? What changes occurring later in the 1920s might most Americans find agreeable? From your lists of the two kinds of changes, what conclusion can you draw about the kinds of social and cultural change that a people will resist and the kinds they will welcome?

2. Identify some groups who suffered from the fears and hysteria of the early 1920s. How did they suffer? Why were they the targets?

3. The radicals in the 1920s included anarchists, socialists, and communists. Find out how their beliefs differed. Should they have been regarded as equally dangerous? Explain.

4. Following World War II the United States spent billions to promote European recovery (p. 586). Contrast this policy with the war debts and reparations policies of the 1920s. How do you account for the differences? Which was the better course? Why?

5. Compare postwar corruption under Grant and under Harding. Consider the nature and extent of the fraud, the parties involved, and the President's role in it.

6. In regulating business, government has to act like a referee in a boxing match. It has to prevent dirty fighting (cutthroat competition) while seeing that the boxers actually fight (compete). How would you rate the federal government in the 1920s as a "business referee"? Cite examples to support your judgment.

QUESTIONS FOR TODAY

1. What recent efforts has the United States government made to obtain arms limitations? Compare these efforts with those in the early 1920s with respect to (a) nations involved, (b) types of armaments, (c) assurance that the parties abide by the agreement, and (d) public support.

2. Name some Roman Catholics who have sought the nomination for President in recent elections. Was their religion a political handicap? Why was it more of a handicap for Al Smith in 1924 and 1928?

YOUR REGION IN HISTORY

1. Trace the migration of black Americans from or to your region, state, or locality during and after World War I. If substantial numbers moved in, what kinds of jobs did they get? How were they treated?

2. How did your state vote in the elections of 1924 and 1928? Try to account for the results.

SKILLS TO MAKE OUR PAST VIVID

1. The postwar era was more upsetting to the older generation than to youth. What changes in American culture in the Roaring Twenties would have worried the elders? What kinds of changes would both young people and their elders have welcomed?

2. Which illustrations in this chapter suggest the *Roaring* Twenties? Write a sentence about each such illustration pointing out "the roar."

CHAPTER 23

The coming of the Great Depression

When Herbert Hoover took the oath of office in March 1929, trade was booming, industry was flourishing. Unemployment was low, wages were up, prices were steady, and corporations were making big profits and paying fat dividends. Some people had not felt this tide of prosperity, but even they seemed to take it for granted that their time would come.

Yet before the end of Hoover's first year in office, the stock market had collapsed. The nation was beginning to slide into the worst depression in its history. And by the time Hoover left office in 1933, many citizens had lost faith in their business leaders. Some had begun to question the American economic system and even democracy itself.

1. A prosperous nation

Most Americans were confident that with Hoover, the Great Engineer, at the helm, their country's growth and prosperity would never end. Progress, it seemed, must go on forever. Then, in late October 1929, came terrifying signs that the success story might have an unhappy ending.

Herbert Hoover, engineer. Herbert Hoover was a perfect symbol of the ideals and hopes of the American business community in the 1920s. He showed that to succeed in the United States and to be elected President you did not have to come from a rich, upper-class family. His life proved that in America character, intelligence, and hard work could make a national leader. Born of Quaker parents on a small farm in Iowa in 1874, he had been orphaned at the age of ten. He worked his way through Stanford University, where he studied engineering. Then he made his fortune as a mining

engineer—in Australia, Africa, China, Latin America, and Russia. He was a millionaire by the time he was 40.

When World War I broke out, Hoover was living in London. His Quaker heritage and his desire to soften the miseries of war drew him quickly into relief work. He did a speedy and spectacular job as head of the Commission for Relief, which fed 10 million starving people in Belgium and northeastern France. When we entered the war, he came home to lead the Food Administration. And at the war's end, Wilson put him in charge of economic relief for all Europe. Hoover and his team, as English economist John Maynard Keynes observed, "not only saved an immense amount of human suffering, but averted a widespread breakdown of the European system."

"The ungrateful governments of Europe," Keynes added, "owe much more to the statesmanship and insight of Mr. Hoover and his band of

to lend to needy banks, railroads, insurance companies, and farm credit associations. Congress also passed at Hoover's request the Federal Home Loan Bank Act to help people with mortgages from losing their homes. As Hoover said, that was "one of the tragedies of this depression."

Hoover's limitations. Hoover did more than any other President before him had ever done to check a depression. But he refused to provide direct relief for individuals. He said it was dangerous to get people in the habit of receiving charity from the national government.

What Hoover did helped, but it was not enough. The disaster was more far-reaching than he realized. And it required remedies more novel than he could imagine.

Then to complicate his problem, one of the worst droughts in recent history hit the nation in 1930. On half a million farms in eighteen states from Virginia to Oklahoma crops withered and cattle died of thirst. Hoover went along when Congress voted $45 million to help farmers feed their livestock, but he opposed giving $25 million to feed the farmers and their families. Finally he allowed Congress to vote $20 million for loans. To give the money, the President said, "would have injured the spiritual response of the American people." But the times called for new measures. The American spirit would have to be lifted by a more adventurous American willing to try new ways.

SECTION REVIEW

1. Identify or explain: Black Tuesday, Federal Farm Board, Hawley-Smoot Tariff Act, Agricultural Marketing Act, public works, Reconstruction Finance Corporation.
2. Who tried to stop the collapse of the stock market? How? What happened?
3. Why did it matter that the stock market crashed?
4. What steps did Hoover and Congress take to stop the business decline? Why did these steps fail?
5. What factors put severe strains on the banking system?
6. How did hard times affect needy people during the early 1930s?

3. Foreign affairs in a gloomy world

The depression also left its mark on foreign affairs. American banks had made large loans to banks in Europe. As panic and depression spread, European banks also came under pressure from their depositors. In June 1931 Germany and Austria were on the verge of financial collapse. Hoover said that we would postpone for one year any payments on the war debts owed to us by our former allies. And he asked them to do the same on their debts to one another and on the German reparations.

Even this *debt moratorium* did not save the situation. Nation after nation was forced to give up the gold standard. They refused any longer to tie the value of their money to gold. Still, the President, supported by American business opinion, refused to allow the war debts to be canceled. Nations should follow the same rules as private individuals! President Coolidge had said, "They hired the money, didn't they?" Anyway, all the debtor nations except Finland ended up defaulting, or not paying. Many Europeans felt that their own depression and unemployment were caused by these war debts and by the high American tariffs against their goods. They expected the United States to be more charitable than other nations.

The Kellogg-Briand Pact. Not only the war debts but the memory of battlefield horrors haunted Americans. During the Coolidge years the United States along with Great Britain, France, Italy, Germany, Japan, and some 60 other nations had signed a peace pact. They had promised to "renounce war as an instrument of national policy in their relations with one another." They agreed to seek the solution of all disputes or conflicts, "of whatever nature," by peaceful means. This Kellogg-Briand Pact—named for Secretary of State Frank Kellogg and French Foreign Minister Aristide Briand—was signed in Paris in August 1928.

Some hardheaded Americans said that the Kellogg-Briand Pact did no more than express a pious hope. They warned that Americans should not feel secure simply because they hated war. Others had more confidence in the peace pact. They even thought it would now be safe to agree to reduce the size of the costly American navy.

In January 1930 a new naval conference of the United States, Great Britain, Japan, Italy, and France met in London. The United States, Great

MARRIED AGAIN

Library of Congress

After World War I, according to this cartoon, the Kellogg Pact remarried Peace to the wicked world.

Britain, and Japan agreed to continue the limits on the number of large capital ships (p. 475). They also accepted fixed ratios for cruisers, destroyers, and submarines.

But new forces were rising in Europe. A few farsighted writers saw another world conflict brewing. The belligerent Mussolini had brought fascism to Italy in 1922. And it was the old tragedy—only with new villains—all over again. Fearing Italy, France refused to limit its naval power. Italy, openly warlike, refused to sign any agreement. Finally the whole purpose of the London naval treaty was frustrated by an "escalator" clause. This allowed any country to build more ships if another power threatened its "national security." Still, Secretary of State Henry L. Stimson said he looked forward to further conferences "confident that we shall obtain ever increasing security with ever decreasing armaments."

Coolidge and Latin America. United States relations with Latin America during the Coolidge years had been a strange mixture. At times we seemed interested only in "dollar diplomacy." Then again, we would seem to be a sincere "good neighbor." In 1916 the United States Marines were sent into the Dominican Republic to protect the sugar and fruit holdings of United States businesses. Then in 1924 these troops were pulled out. A treaty was agreed upon that ended our military rule there, and the troops were brought home.

The United States had long shown a special interest in Nicaragua. It was a possible site for a canal between the oceans. And American business had invested there in coffee, banana, and sugar plantations. But Nicaragua's main crop seemed to be revolutions. In 1912, marines were sent there to protect American interests. Hardly had they been withdrawn in 1925 when another revolution broke out. The United States sent back the marines, who put a friendly party in power. But the Nicaraguan guerrillas had their own ideas. The drama of civil war followed. The United States finally gave up armed intervention and withdrew the marines in 1933.

In Mexico it was oil that attracted special United States interests. The Mexican constitution of 1917 had declared that all oil deposits now belonged to the state. This was true even if they had been granted earlier to private companies. The name for this takeover was *expropriation*. Oil companies were supposed to apply for oil leases on land they thought they had already purchased. The United States protested, and it was not until 1925 that Mexico began to enforce its control over the oil. President Coolidge objected that Mexico was "confiscating property legally owned by American citizens."

In January 1927 Congress called for the peaceful settlement of the issues. Coolidge sent a former Amherst College classmate, the shrewd and able Dwight W. Morrow, as ambassador to Mexico. Morrow, a partner in J. P. Morgan's firm, showed what could be done by tact and sympathy. With his understanding of Mexico's problems he won the confidence of the government and the people.

When America's hero Charles A. Lindbergh made a nonstop goodwill flight of 2200 miles from Washington to Mexico City in December 1927, he too became an "ambassador of goodwill." There Lindbergh met Ambassador Morrow's brilliant and attractive daughter Anne. They married in 1929. Sharing a love of the airplane, they flew around the nation and the world exploring new air routes. They awakened enthusiasm for the Air Age. The Lindberghs also wrote popular books about their experiences and cheered the country by their romantic collaboration.

Hoover and Latin America.

President Hoover and his Secretary of State Stimson were determined somehow to improve our relations with the countries of Latin America. For 30 years the United States had been intervening in their affairs, and now it was no easy matter to remove their suspicions. Before taking office, Hoover had shown that he meant business when he spent ten weeks on a goodwill trip. In Argentina he announced that the United States would no longer interfere in the domestic affairs of those nations.

By the Roosevelt Corollary to the Monroe Doctrine (p. 439), the domineering TR had declared the right of the United States to intervene in Latin America when United States interests were threatened. Now, it was announced, the Roosevelt Corollary was no longer our policy. "The Monroe Doctrine," Secretary Stimson said, "was a declaration of the United States versus Europe—not of the United States versus Latin America."

The Hoover administration declared that it would respect the facts of South American political life—whether we liked them or not. Any "de facto" government, that is, one that in fact controlled a country, would be recognized by the United States.

Japan ends the peace.

On the other side of the world in 1931, the Japanese army seized Manchuria and the next year turned it into the puppet state of Manchukuo. Americans were shocked but could not be surprised. The firm agreements in the Nine Power Treaty and the high hopes of the Kellogg-Briand Pact were shattered. What could Americans do?

Secretary of State Stimson sent a note of protest. The United States, he said, would not recognize such changes made by force. The Council of the League of Nations, with an American "observer" present for the first time, invoked the Kellogg-Briand Pact to outlaw Japan. In January 1932, Japanese forces attacked Shanghai and bombed the city, killing thousands of civilians. But neither the League of Nations nor the people of the United States would risk war to restrain this aggression. Americans were more troubled by their depression than by the sufferings of the distant Chinese.

Stimson urged economic sanctions—a trade boycott—against Japan. Hoover refused, for he feared that sanctions would be the first step to war.

Meanwhile, war-loving leaders were rising to power in Italy and Germany. Mussolini and Hitler would remember the timidity of the United States and other peaceful nations. If the high-sounding agreements had no power against an aggressive Japan, why should other aggressive powers hold back? Fascist Italy and Nazi Germany—the forces of tyranny and barbarism—saw their green light.

SECTION REVIEW

1. Identify or explain: debt moratorium, Kellogg-Briand Pact, London Naval Conference, Henry Stimson, expropriation, Dwight Morrow, economic sanctions.

2. Locate: Dominican Republic, Nicaragua, Manchuria, Shanghai.

3. How did Hoover try to ease financial stress in Europe?

4. Between 1920 and 1932 what were the signs of our friendlier relations with Latin America?

5. What were some results of Japanese aggression in China in 1931–1932?

4. The election of 1932

By 1932 industrial production in the United States was only half what it had been in 1929. Countless Americans were working only part-time, and 12 million more were out of work. President Hoover was the handiest person to blame, even though the depression had actually begun almost before he had moved into the White House. One folk song of the unemployed declared, "Hoover made a soup hound out of me." A man's empty pocket turned inside out was called a "Hoover flag." People looked forward to a change in the White House.

The conventions.

Still, the Republicans felt they could not reject Hoover or his policies. When they met in the Coliseum at Chicago in June 1932, they renominated Hoover and Vice-President Curtis on the first ballot. The platform stood firmly on the merits of the Hoover administration. It warned against the dangers to business if the Democrats came to power. It supported Prohibition. In a word, it stood "pat"—hoping that natural forces would solve the nation's problems.

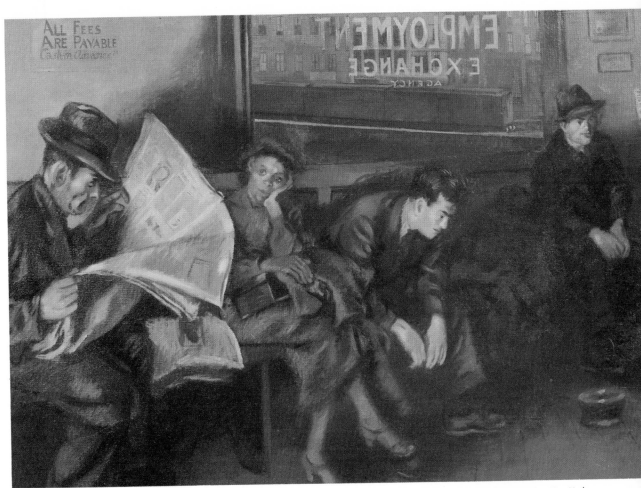

Isaac Soyer, the son of a Russian immigrant, knew from personal experience the trials of poverty in the big city. In realistic paintings, such as this one done in 1937, he tried to capture the despair of life during the depression years.

When the Democrats met in the same building a few days later, the leading candidate was Governor Franklin D. Roosevelt of New York. He had been Assistant Secretary of the Navy under Wilson and had run for Vice-President in 1920. His main rival was Al Smith, former governor of New York, who had the support of Tammany Hall. After a hard fight, the Roosevelt forces won the delegates of California and Texas, who had favored Speaker of the House John Nance Garner of Texas. Roosevelt won the nomination on the fifth ballot, and Garner was named for Vice-President.

FDR was no radical, but he loved to try new things. He was not afraid to break precedent by flying from Albany to Chicago to deliver his speech of acceptance. "Let it be from now on," he declared, "the task of our party to break foolish traditions."

The campaign. FDR loved campaigning. And his campaign delighted him with cheering crowds everywhere. The unlucky Hoover was often booed and heckled. "I've been traveling with Presidents since Theodore Roosevelt," one Secret Service agent remarked, "and never before have I seen one actually booed, with men running out into the streets to thumb their noses at him. It's not a pretty sight."

During the campaign Hoover argued that the real causes of the depression were world conditions

The urbane Franklin D. Roosevelt, here reaching to shake hands, and his running mate the homespun "Cactus Jack" Garner of Texas (right) were greeted with cheers and applause as they toured the nation during the 1932 campaign. Baltimore's mayor is in the middle.

that the United States could not control. He condemned Roosevelt's experimental ideas. He said they would destroy American free enterprise and the American system of government. If the Democrats were elected, he predicted, grass would grow in the streets of a hundred cities.

Roosevelt attacked the Republicans for encouraging the reckless stock market speculation that had brought on the panic. He was eloquent, persuasive, and smilingly confident. He promised a "New Deal" and a rapid recovery of prosperity for business and agriculture. But he did not produce a blueprint for recovery. He offered proposals that seemed to appeal to all the nation's varied groups. He supported many Progressive policies. He called for repeal of Prohibition, and he declared that everyone had a right to a comfortable living. The products of industry, he said, should be distributed more fairly. Except on a few issues, Roosevelt's speeches were so general that it was hard to disagree with them. Hoover thought FDR kept shifting his positions and called him "a chameleon on plaid." The usually wise commentator Walter Lippmann criticized FDR as "a pleasant man who, without any important qualifications for the office, would very much like to be President."

But it did not matter much what Roosevelt said. Almost anybody could have beaten Hoover. Who wanted to vote *for* the depression? To no one's surprise, the Democrats won a mighty victory. FDR received some 23 million votes and carried 42 states. Hoover, with fewer than 16 million votes, carried only 6 states. In the electoral college the count was 472 to 59. The Democrats won a majority of 191 in the House and 22 in the Senate. The American people had given their mandate to change the policies of government. Could FDR meet the challenge?

SECTION REVIEW

1. Who were the opposing candidates for President and Vice-President in 1932?

2. What were the issues in the election campaign?

3. Why did the Democrats win a mighty victory?

CHAPTER REVIEW

MEETING OUR EARLIER SELVES

1. Buying stock in corporations always involves some risk. How does "buying on margin" increase the risk? Is there a difference between *investing* in stock and *gambling* in the stock market? Explain.

2. Hoover responded to the depression by proposing small temporary adjustments here and there rather than by calling for some basic economic reforms. Find evidence in the chapter for this conclusion. How did Hoover's responses to the depression match his beliefs?

3. A business recession has a "snowball effect"— growing in size and picking up speed as it rolls downhill. Show how the 1929 crash sent the economy spinning downhill. How did a collapse in one part of the economy lead to other failures?

4. Although peace was their goal, many post-World War I treaties and pacts carried the seeds of future violence. Using evidence in this chapter, identify the weaknesses of the postwar agreements and discuss why they alone were unable to prevent the coming of war.

QUESTIONS FOR TODAY

1. Hoover in 1920 and Eisenhower in 1948 were considered "presidential timber" by *both* major parties. Why? Can you name any public figures today who might be almost equally attractive to both major parties? Why? What do your answers suggest about differences between the two parties?

2. Could Hoover's personal credo on page 488 apply today? If you agree, provide some reasons why. If you disagree, construct a credo that you believe fits today's world.

3. Contrast the help available for an unemployed worker in the early 1930s with today's.

YOUR REGION IN HISTORY

1. Interview two or more persons who lived in your community or nearby between 1930 and 1932. How were their families affected by the depression? Find out as many details as you can about lay-offs, bank failures, mortgage foreclosures, and so on.

2. Find out how a particular business in your area fared in the early years of the Great Depression.

SKILLS TO MAKE OUR PAST VIVID

1. The table printed below shows year-to-year changes in eight aspects of the American economy from 1928 to 1932. Which item best shows the deep decline in business activity? Why?

2. Which three items show the setback in farming? How are they related?

3. How are items B and F related?

4. How did the depression affect factory workers who held on to their jobs? What additional information would help you answer this question?

5. Would you have expected government spending to drop between 1929 and 1932? Why or why not?

SOME ECONOMIC CHANGES BETWEEN 1928 AND 1932
(Figures in millions unless otherwise noted.)

	1928	1929	1930	1931	1932
A. United States exports (merchandise)	$5,030	$5,157	$3,781	$2,378	$1,576
B. Spending for new housing	$4,195	$3,040	$1,570	$1,320	$485
C. Farm spending for lime and fertilizer	$318	$300	$297	$202	$118
D. Federal spending	$2,933	$3,127	$3,320	$3,578	$4,659
E. Cash receipts from farming	$10,991	$11,312	$9,055	$6,331	$4,748
F. Lumber production (billions of board ft.)	36.8	38.7	29.4	20	13.5
G. Unemployment (in thousands)	2,080	1,550	4,340	8,020	12,060
H. Average weekly earnings of production workers in manufacturing (actual dollars)	$24.97	$25.03	$23.25	$20.87	$17.05

9

Depression at home and aggression abroad 1933–1945

On March 4, 1933, when Franklin Delano Roosevelt became the thirty-second President of the United States, the nation was in the deepest depression in its history. Poverty stalked the land. Some observers believed a revolution was at hand. But FDR was not discouraged. "We do not distrust the future of essential democracy," he asserted in his inaugural address. "The people of the United States have not failed. In their need they have registered a mandate that they want direct, vigorous action."

Roosevelt gave the nation action aplenty during the next twelve years as he served longer than any other President. He did not always find solutions to problems, but he kept trying. The majority of voters never lost their faith in him or in their democracy.

In war, too, FDR would lead the nation with zest and confidence. When he took office he could not know that he would have to organize the nation for its greatest defensive effort in history. His eloquent, strong leadership inspired his fellow Americans. He enlisted farmers and factory workers to overwhelm the forces of barbarism with American arms and supplies. As Commander in Chief he would send the army, the navy, and the air force to far corners of the earth. And he enlisted other world leaders in a grand strategy for victory.

power. He called for a "soak the rich" tax and the breakup of certain holding companies. The First New Deal had been directed mainly toward recovery from the depression. This Second New Deal aimed at reform.

Social Security.

The United States was far behind the industrial nations of Europe in protecting citizens against the risks of unemployment and old age. Under prodding from Dr. Townsend and his followers, from the AF of L, as well as some members of Congress, Roosevelt in January 1935 asked for an insurance plan. But until the *Schechter* decision, Congress had failed to act. Now the President pushed hard for his new idea of social insurance. While people were working, each of them would pay a small amount every month, with their employers paying the same amount, into a national Social Security fund in the Treasury. Then when a worker was too old to work, he or she would receive a monthly payment. The pay-outs would not start until 1940, since workers would have to build up some credits in their Social Security account. And only workers in trade and industry were covered at first. So the law also had a plan to take care of those in need.

This second part of the Social Security Act came to be known as *public assistance*. It was not social insurance, since the persons getting the monthly welfare checks did not pay into an insurance fund. Public assistance was a federal-state program. Any state that accepted the plan would get federal funds covering about half of the costs. The money would come from general state and federal revenues. The aged, the blind, and the dependent children covered by public assistance would have to prove their need for aid.

Unemployment insurance was a third part of the new law. It was also a joint federal-state program. The plan was to give laid-off workers some income for a number of weeks while they were hunting for a new job or waiting to be rehired. The money would come from a payroll tax paid by employers of eight or more persons. Each state would set up its own system under standards set by federal law.

The Social Security Act meant that millions of people would not have to live in fear of starving. And since persons getting old-age insurance would have put some of their own hard-earned money into the fund, they would not have to feel like charity cases. "Social Security" was a good name for the plan. It made millions feel more secure.

Moving against concentrated wealth and power.

The Social Security Act took the wind out of the sails of Dr. Townsend. The President's series of "soak the rich" taxes helped him win away followers of "Kingfish" Long. FDR asked for higher estate and gift taxes, higher income taxes on the largest incomes, and a corporate income tax graduated to the size of the profits of businesses. The President said the bill would help "to prevent an unjust concentration of wealth and economic power" and reduce "social unrest and a deepening sense of unfairness." These measures were passed in a Revenue Act in August 1935.

Roosevelt also moved against the powerful utility companies that provided the nation's gas and electricity. Just thirteen holding companies controlled 75 percent of all the country's electric power. The Public Utility Holding Company Act was designed to restrict each company to operating a single system in a single area. A "death sentence" clause—enacted only after a bitter fight—empowered the SEC after January 1, 1940, to dissolve any utility holding company that could not prove that it was saving the consumers money. Under this law most of these great holding companies were broken up within the next three years. The law also gave federal agencies the power to regulate companies that sold natural gas or electric power across state lines.

Helping labor.

FDR was the greatest friend of organized labor who had ever lived in the White House. His Second New Deal included the National Labor Relations Act. Senator Robert Wagner of New York had first proposed this act as early as 1934, but then FDR thought that section 7a of the NRA would give labor all the help it needed. After the Supreme Court killed the NRA, the President threw his support to Wagner's labor bill.

The new Wagner Act guaranteed the right of workers to join unions and to bargain collectively. It set up the National Labor Relations Board (NLRB) to oversee elections by which workers would decide which union, if any, would bargain for them. The Board could also stop unfair practices by employers against unions. Since the law put no obligations at all on the unions, it is not surprising that many employers thought the act was unfair and one-sided. Passed in July 1935, the law was upheld by the Supreme Court in 1937. The unions called it "Labor's Magna Carta."

By the time the second hundred days of the New Deal came to an end, in August 1935, the President found that most business leaders and wealthy people were against him. But he saw his reform program as nearly complete. Now, he said, there would be a "breathing spell."

More trouble with the Supreme Court.

During 1936 the Supreme Court struck down the AAA. The judges declared that the so-called "processing tax" could not be collected because it was not really a tax at all. Instead, they said, it was an unconstitutional way to limit farm output. Did this mean that the federal government could do nothing at all to solve the problem of farm surpluses? To get around the Court's objections, Roosevelt had Congress pass a Soil Conservation and Adjustment Act (February 1936) that restricted production under the name of conservation. The government paid farmers to plant soil-conserving crops on part of their land.

In April the Supreme Court limited the powers of the SEC. It also struck down the Guffey-Snyder Coal Act of 1935, which had tried to set up a "little NRA" by enacting the NRA coal code into law.

The President was concerned to find a constitutional way to protect workers by setting minimum wages. But the conservative Court ruled (5–4) against a New York state law that had set minimum wages for women. The majority argued that the Fourteenth Amendment left the state "without power by any form of legislation to prohibit, change, or nullify contracts between employers and women workers as to the amount of wages to be paid." In 1923 the Court had already struck down a federal wage law for women in the District of Columbia. Now the Court seemed to be saying that neither the states nor the federal government could set minimum wages. Still, FDR did not give up. He asked Congress for a law that he hoped the Court might accept. In the Government Contracts Act of June 1936, Congress gave the Secretary of Labor power to set minimum wages and maximum hours for workers in firms doing business with the federal government. It also prohibited them from employing boys under 16 or girls under 18. Since thousands of firms wanted to sell part of their output to the government, the new law improved the lot of many workers.

The election of 1936.

In early 1936, of course, FDR focused his attention on the coming presidential election. He believed that his New Deal had already proven itself a substantial success and that he deserved to be reelected. By June industrial production had returned to the level of 1923–1925. Factory employment was up. Farm income and weekly wages for workers had risen. The unemployed, who numbered more than 10 million in the winter of 1934–1935, had now dropped to 7 million. National income had increased 60 percent over 1933. Although the depression was far from over, Franklin D. Roosevelt was the most popular President since his cousin Teddy.

When the Republicans met at Cleveland in June, they had the impossible task of naming someone who could defeat the attractive "miracle worker" in the White House. To be named the Republican candidate that year was like being handed a lottery ticket that was sure to lose. On the first ballot they chose Governor "Alf" Landon of Kansas, a liberal Republican and onetime Bull Moose progressive. Despite the opposition of conservative Republicans to the New Deal, he ran on a surprisingly liberal platform. The Republicans seemed to have little choice but to endorse most of the New Deal programs. It was difficult to attack old-age and unemployment benefits, the right of labor to organize and bargain collectively, minimum-wage and maximum-hour laws for women and children, and soil conservation. The depression, FDR, and the New Deal had somehow changed the point of view of a whole nation. And despite lingering suspicions of "big government," the Republican party, too, came right along.

It was no surprise when the Democrats nominated Roosevelt and Garner again. FDR used his acceptance speech to set the tone of the campaign. He considered much of the criticism of business leaders to be mindless. And he directed all his considerable talents of wit and irony against them. He called them "economic royalists." He said they were anxious to build their personal dynasties, to control the government, and to exploit the workers—rather than to serve the nation's interests.

Shoppers on Main Street in 1936 saw campaign banners like these. The cartoon below was drawn after Harry Hopkins said that the needy numbered "one person out of every ten."

"They denied the Government could do anything to protect the citizen in his right to work and his right to live." It was time, he said, to destroy their anti-democratic power. "This generation," he proclaimed, "has a rendezvous with destiny."

The Democratic platform spelled out the far-reaching duties it believed the government should fulfill. Among these were to protect the family and the home, establish a democracy of opportunity for all, and aid those overtaken by disaster.

To the left of Roosevelt there were other candidates. The mild-mannered intellectual Norman Thomas, who had led the Socialists in 1928 and 1932, was again their candidate. The Communist party as usual put up Earl Browder. A new "Union party" drew together several unhappy groups—the followers of Father Coughlin, of Dr. Townsend, and of Huey Long. (Senator Long had been assassinated on the steps of the Louisiana state capitol in September 1935.) Their candidate was Representative William Lemke of North Dakota.

But it was Roosevelt all the way. His margin of 11 million votes over "Alf" Landon was the largest in history until that time. He carried every state but Maine and Vermont. "I knew I should have

ONE PERSON OUT OF EVERY TEN

gone to Maine and Vermont," he joked. "But Jim Farley wouldn't let me." All together the Socialists, Communists, and Unionists polled only about 1 million votes.

The new majority party. The election of 1936 revealed that, for the first time since the Civil War, Roosevelt had succeeded in making the Democrats the party of the majority. The party's enlarged support came mostly from those whom the New Deal had been able to help. FDR would be spokesman for "the Forgotten Man." This meant the immigrants and their children, the farmers and the laborers—Americans who somehow had not won the race for money and success. Teachers, social workers, and reformers of many sorts felt that FDR was their leader. Blacks were swinging to the Democrats in ever larger numbers.

Many of these "forgotten people" lived in the big cities, and they provided him a solid following.

Their votes could carry the largest states, which themselves had nearly enough electoral votes to win the election for President.

A new kind of Presidency. Roosevelt's success was not all due to his programs. Now his personal charm and his warm resonant voice could reach the whole nation. FDR was our first radio President. In his fireside chats over the radio, he came right into everybody's living room. He explained what he was doing in simple language that anybody could understand. Even his paralysis somehow became an advantage. He had to sit down while he talked. This meant that when he spoke to the nation he did not sound like a politician making a speech but like a member of the family in friendly conversation. When he began a radio talk, he did not say "Fellow citizens," but "My friends."

He also held many press conferences, which pleased the newspaper reporters. In all his four

FDR was our first President to use the radio effectively. His friendly, mellifluous voice was able to reach right into the homes of the three out of four families who owned radio receivers in 1936.

years President Hoover had offered only 66 press conferences. FDR met the press 337 times during his first term. He made the reporters his friends. This was plain in the stories they wrote about their President.

SECTION REVIEW

1. Identify or explain: WPA, NYA, American Liberty League, Huey Long, Father Coughlin, Francis Townsend, William Green, *Schechter* v. *United States,* social insurance, NLRB, Government Contracts Act, "Alf" Landon, Union party.

2. Explain the importance of the WPA.

3. Who were the critics of the New Deal? What were their complaints?

4. Describe the three main programs set up by the Social Security Act.

5. Why would the tax law, the holding company law, and the labor law in 1935 displease business leaders?

6. How were laws to aid farmers and wage earners written to avoid Supreme Court objections?

7. Who ran against Roosevelt in 1936? Why were their chances of winning so poor?

3. The end of the New Deal

When FDR began his second term, everything pointed to more success in his effort to give the nation a New Deal. His inaugural address on January 20, 1937, admitted that much still remained to be done: "I see one-third of a nation ill-housed, ill-clad, ill-nourished." He promised to do something to help them. But soon he was involved in a struggle that wasted his energies and undercut his influence with Congress.

The attack on the Supreme Court. On February 5, 1937, without consulting his Cabinet or the Democratic party leaders, Roosevelt sent to Congress a plan to reorganize the federal courts. Although he did not say so, nobody doubted that his target was the Supreme Court. FDR proposed that the President should have the power to increase the number of justices on the Supreme Court from nine to fifteen if the justices refused to retire at the age of 70.

What he offered as a plan to "reform" the Court really was a way to make the Supreme Court approve the New Deal laws. If he had come out and declared his purpose, he would have lost much support. So he pretended that the nation needed his "reforms" because the courts were behind in their work. His plan came to be called a scheme for "court packing." And the name was not unfair.

Roosevelt's "court packing" message split the Democratic party and the nation. He had grown overconfident because of his great victory at the polls. He made the mistake of thinking that the nation would follow wherever he pointed.

Chief Justice Charles Evans Hughes was adroit in his opposition. He pointed out that the Court was up to date in its work and that a larger Court would be inefficient. He even timed a Court decision to help his cause. The Court upheld a Washington state minimum-wage law, reversing its decision of just ten months before, and showing that the Court did not always strike down reform legislation. One headline proclaimed, "A Switch in Time Saves Nine." Then the Court upheld the Wagner Act and the Social Security Act.

The Senate rejected Roosevelt's plan to pack the Court. In its place, Congress passed a law that allowed federal judges to retire at age 70 with full pay. One conservative justice retired while the debate was going on. Another retired the next year. FDR claimed that he had really gained what he wanted. It was more accurate to say that he won his battle but he lost the war. To win that battle he had lost much of the goodwill of Congress.

The Roosevelt recession. During 1937 the President learned a harsh lesson in economics. Business was booming. There were still 7 million unemployed, but some of his advisers feared a runaway inflation. In his first election campaign Roosevelt had promised to balance the budget. He now took the necessary steps. The Federal Reserve Board began to put the brakes on credit. Then the government cut the WPA by 1.5 million people. Now, when Social Security taxes were collected for the first time, still more money was drained out of the economy. At the end of 1937, business had slumped, and the number of unemployed had risen to 10 million. To stimulate the economy the President saw that he would have to resume his large-scale spending.

In April 1938 Roosevelt sent to Congress a message asking for an increase of the WPA work force—this time by 1.5 million, the same number who were cut in 1937. He said he would need $3 billion more for recovery and relief. The act was passed in June. Only by these means did the Roosevelt recession come to an end.

New farm and labor reforms. In 1938 the President also asked Congress for new measures to help the farmer and to control wages and hours in industry. The second Agricultural Adjustment Act (which Secretary of Agriculture Wallace called the best program of farm relief ever enacted) provided an "ever-normal granary." This meant putting farm products in storage in years of surplus and then releasing them in years of scarcity. Prices could then be stabilized around the "parity" level of 1910–1914. The second AAA continued giving to farmers the benefits of the Soil Conservation Act. And it allowed growers of certain crops to set marketing quotas if two-thirds of them agreed. A new Federal Crop Insurance Corporation insured wheat crops against natural disasters like drought, flood, and plant disease. Wheat itself could be used to pay the insurance premium.

Congress also passed a Fair Labor Standards Act. In all industries involved in interstate commerce, the length of the work week would gradually be reduced to 40 hours. The minimum wages (first set at 25 cents an hour) would increase over eight years to 40 cents an hour. Time and a half was to be paid for overtime. The law also forbade labor by children under 16.

The purpose of this Fair Labor Standards Act was to boost the buying power of wage earners. Also, the cut in the work week, along with the overtime pay rule, would induce employers to hire more workers. People were astonished when they learned that 750,000 workers had to receive raises to bring their wages up to 25 cents an hour.

The attempted "purge." FDR's fight over the Court had soured his relations with Congress. At the same time, the demands of the unions (p. 516) and the new government-spending policy upset the conservatives in both parties. Roosevelt's pet measures—such as his proposal for six regional projects similar to the TVA—were defeated by an alliance of Republicans and conservative Democrats.

The "ever-normal granary" program helped to fill huge grain elevators like these shown in 1941 by FSA photographer John Vachon.

521

Then the angry President decided to try to "purge" his party of his conservative opponents. Most of these were from the South. In 1938 he made the mistake of intervening in primary elections by writing letters, attending conferences, and making speeches. This effort boomeranged. In nearly every case where he interfered, the conservative candidate won.

Republicans saw their chance to take advantage of the splits in the Democratic party. And they profited from the rising tide of conservatism. They gained 75 seats in the House and 7 seats in the Senate. They elected 11 governors and polled 51.5 percent of the vote outside the "solid South."

The election of 1938 really marked the end of the New Deal. Republicans and conservative Democrats now had enough votes in Congress to block any more New Deal laws. And the President turned to problems abroad. Fascist Italy, Nazi Germany, and Imperialist Japan were on the march.

The New Deal—an appraisal. So the New Deal came quietly to a close. What had it accomplished? Many Americans were not sure. Millions were still out of work. Prosperity would not return until the nation was forced to try the Keynesian approach in a big way by World War II. Then massive government spending would put all the factories back to work.

Still the experimental Franklin D. Roosevelt had magically lifted the nation's spirit. "It was this administration," he said, "which saved the system of private profit and free enterprise after it had been dragged to the brink of ruin." The President had avoided the extremes. He had taken a middle course. Rejecting the dogmas of socialism, he yet increased government control over the economy— over banking, agriculture, and public utilities. The federal government played a new role in setting standards for wages and hours of work and in providing some income support for farmers, the aged, and the unemployed.

Americans discovered new strength. On the whole, the federal Constitution proved remarkably adaptable to the needs of a new age. Americans had survived their worst peacetime disaster—without spreading hate, without inciting civil war or abridging liberties. And they had not been seduced by a dictator. Freedom had proved the best atmosphere in which to keep freedom alive.

SECTION REVIEW

1. Identify or explain: Charles E. Hughes, Roosevelt recession, second AAA, ever-normal granary, crop insurance, Fair Labor Standards Act.
2. What was Roosevelt's plan to "reform" the Supreme Court? Why was it called a "court packing" plan?
3. Name some government actions that helped to bring about a recession in 1937–1938. What steps were taken to end the recession?
4. Describe additional measures that were enacted by Congress in 1938 to help farmers and industrial workers.
5. How did FDR try to regain firm control of his party in 1938? What was the result?

CHAPTER REVIEW

MEETING OUR EARLIER SELVES

1. Compile a list of New Deal laws and programs named in this chapter. Which of these were "experimental" in that they represented new or greatly broadened areas of federal activity?
2. Identify and describe New Deal measures designed to help (a) workers, (b) consumers, (c) owners of businesses.
3. Compare the first and second "hundred days" of the New Deal.
4. What did Keynes say a nation should do to lift itself out of a depression? How did Roosevelt respond to this idea?
5. What Supreme Court decisions disrupted Roosevelt's program? What arguments against his "court-packing" plan would you expect an opponent to use?
6. How do you account for the increasing congressional opposition to Roosevelt's proposals in his second term?

QUESTIONS FOR TODAY

1. Name some federal agencies and programs begun under the New Deal that are still operating today.
2. How would you expect your life to be different today and in the future if the Social Security Act had never passed?

3. Compare FDR's leadership style with that of the President today.
4. Find out how the federal government provides financial support for some college students today. Compare these programs with the help provided by the National Youth Administration in the 1930s.

YOUR REGION IN HISTORY

1. Identify buildings, roads, parks, or other projects in your locality that were built or improved under the WPA, PWA, or other work-relief programs of the New Deal. Are the works of any artists or writers employed by the WPA on display or in your local archives?
2. Find out what efforts were made by your state government to deal with the problems of the Great Depression.
3. Name some New Deal measures that you think would have received wide support in your community in the 1930s and tell why. Which measures would probably have had little support? Why?

SKILLS TO MAKE OUR PAST VIVID

1. Prepare a series of questions to use in an interview with someone who worked under the NYA, WPA, or CCC program. Then arrange an interview and report on your findings.
2. Using the list of New Deal measures prepared for item 1 in "Meeting Our Earlier Selves," arrange them in three categories: relief, recovery, reform. Some items can fit more than one category.
3. Write a contemporary editorial—or draw a cartoon—supporting or opposing a particular New Deal measure.

CHAPTER 25

Reshaping American life

In 1933 another Bonus Army descended on Washington. This time, instead of being driven away, they were housed and fed by the government. Their leaders talked to the President. Then one day these veterans were startled to meet a tall, gawky woman with appealing eyes and a wide, toothy smile trudging through the mud to the old army barracks where they were housed. The visitor was Eleanor Roosevelt, wife of the President of the United States. She sat and talked with them, listened to their troubles, and joined in their singing. And she carried her sympathy back to the White House.

Eleanor Roosevelt personified the change in the government. Her humane spirit represented to many groups—blacks, immigrants, migrant workers, the aged, and the unemployed—the hope that through the New Deal they, too, might somehow someday enjoy the plenty of American life.

1. Problems on the farm

But it was far easier for Eleanor Roosevelt to join their singing or for FDR to speak warmly to "my friends" over the radio than for the government to change the daily lives of people in trouble. The problems of the farmers, for example, were varied and complicated. No single law could give all they needed. Some farmers needed electricity. Some were fighting dust storms. Others, working as tenants, were not getting a square deal from their landlords and had no way to share in the government's bounty. Many could not afford to buy the tractors or combines to make their land profitable. Still others, who lived on worn-out land, had no money to buy fertilizer. Nor did they know how to renew their land by planting diverse crops. Their problems seemed as overwhelming and unmanageable as nature itself.

The dust storms. In the 1930s the Great Plains began to blow away. Bountiful rains in the 1920s had encouraged farmers to plow the fragile grasslands without worrying about the future. Then the rains ceased. Drought cursed the whole mid-continent from Canada to Mexico.

The sun baked the land into a brittle, powdery crust. Nineteen states in the heart of the nation became one enormous "Dust Bowl." Crops shriveled. Cattle died. When the wind blew, the topsoil—with no living roots to hold it in place—swirled into the air. Great, dark, yellowish clouds filled the sky, choking the nose and throat, blotting out the sun and causing street lights to be turned on at midday. The precious soil of the Great Plains blew all the way to the East Coast—even sifting into the White House—and on out into the Atlantic Ocean.

William C. Palmer's 1934 painting "Dust, Drought, and Destruction" shows the ravages wrought by the great dust storms of the 1930s. The farm has been abandoned, the windmill has fallen, the tree has died, and the wind swirls the soil away through the air.

Many families, whose fields grew only dust, gave up. They loaded their old cars with what they could carry and left the land where they had been raised. The "flivver" which Henry Ford had invented no longer carried them to a holiday in town. Now instead it took them on their desperate quest for a better life—anywhere. They moved in all directions, without a clear destination and with no real plan. The "Okies" from Oklahoma and the "Arkies" from Arkansas headed west. A third of a million people from those states and from Texas, the Dakotas, Kansas, and Nebraska hit the road. Thousands ended up in California as migrant laborers picking fruit and vegetables and living in squalid camps. Their hard journeys and their frustrated lives can never be forgotten, for they became the long-suffering heroes of John Steinbeck's powerful novel, *The Grapes of Wrath*.

The mild climate and the legend of its golden land made California the number one goal of the migrants. In 1939 that state tried to stem the tide by passing a law forbidding poor migrants to enter. But two years later the Supreme Court declared the law unconstitutional.

A quarter-million Mexicans seeking work went to California during the 1930s. Other Mexicans, along with Filipinos, Okies, Arkies, and other migrants—at least another 100,000—moved north into Colorado, Wyoming, and Montana to work in the sugar beet fields. But, unlike the Okies, they had no Steinbeck to tell their story.

Conserving the land. FDR's own experience had shown him the need for soil conservation. The land on his ancestral estate at Hyde Park, New York, had been worn out by centuries of unscientific farming.

The depression forced many families to go on the road in search of work. A large number headed for the West Coast, where they hoped to find jobs in the orchards and vineyards. In this photograph by Dorothea Lange in November 1936 a family in California uses their car for a home.

He renewed that land by planting thousands of trees "in the hope that my great grandchildren will be able to try raising corn again—just one century from now." Trees would help stop the dust storms on the Great Plains. Farmers across the nation followed their President's example. With seedlings from the government they planted 200 million trees across the expanse extending from the Dakotas to Texas. For years experts had said no trees would grow on the western plains. But these trees took root. Their growth surprised the experts and helped other farmers, too, by making new "shelterbelts," conserving water and holding in place the precious topsoil.

The New Deal, from its start, tried new ways to help the farmer. As early as 1933 a Soil Erosion Service was set up to preserve the farmer's most valuable resource. Farmers and CCC boys were taught terracing and contour farming. Then the Soil Conservation Act of 1936 aimed to reduce surpluses and also to promote soil conservation (p. 517). Today we still profit from the New Deal experiments—the TVA, the great dams in the West, reforestation, and grazing control—all ways to preserve and renew the American land.

The lot of farm tenants. After the Civil War, there were no longer slaves to till the soil in the South. Their place was taken by a new class, the *sharecroppers* (p. 318). These farmers—white and black—did not own the land they lived on, and they were not paid wages for their work. Instead they received a share of the crops, and the owner of the land got the rest.

Sharecroppers were not legally slaves, but they were tied to their plot of land by the bonds of debt and despair. Since they had no capital, the only way they could secure the seed for the next year—and the food and clothing for their family—was to pledge their share in advance. One year of bad crops was enough to drown them in debt. They could not survive on their land, yet they dared not leave.

Although it was not planned that way, the condition of the sharecroppers was made even worse by the first AAA. The law paid landowners to take some acres out of production, and this was often the marginal land the sharecroppers farmed.

To help the poor sharecroppers and other tenants who still could work their land, Harry Hopkins under the Federal Emergency Relief Act loaned them money and gave them seeds and equipment. When their land was too poor to support them, he tried to resettle them on better lands. In 1935 FDR moved these activities to the Resettlement Administration under Rexford Tugwell.

But all these efforts hardly made a dent in the problem. Senator John Bankhead of Alabama proposed a new approach. The Bankhead-Jones Farm Tenant Act of 1937 provided long-term loans to help tenants buy the farms they worked. Blacks and whites were treated alike. And the unfortunate Okies and the Arkies who became migratory farm laborers, following the ripening crops, were at least

"Roasting Ears" was painted by Thomas Hart Benton of Missouri in the 1930s.

The Metropolitan Museum of Art, The Arthur H. Hearn Fund, 1939

provided with clean camps. The Farm Security Administration replaced Tugwell's agency to carry out these programs.

The problems of American farmers—of the poor tenants, sharecroppers, and migrants—were as broad and as varied as the continent. These were not to be solved in a few years, nor by a single farm program in Washington. Still, the New Deal efforts could give them hope and cheer them with the news that they were not forgotten.

Rural electrification. By the mid-1930s electricity had reshaped the daily lives of Americans in cities. It was lighting their homes at night, running their radios, cooling their refrigerators. But not for farmers. They fed an electrified nation, but they themselves had not yet entered the electric age. Only one farm family in ten had electricity.

On May 11, 1935, President Roosevelt set up the Rural Electrification Administration to help bring electric power to the farms of America. The REA could loan money at low interest to help private companies or farmers' cooperatives build their own generators and install power lines. This produced an electrical revolution. By 1941, four out of five American farms were enjoying the comforts that only electricity could bring. More than any other transformation, this showed that their government, which now remembered them, could draw them into the mainstream of modern America.

SECTION REVIEW

1. Identify or explain: Eleanor Roosevelt, "Dust Bowl," John Steinbeck, sharecroppers, Rexford Tugwell, Bankhead-Jones Farm Tenant Act, Farm Security Administration.

2. How did the dust storms affect the farmers on the Great Plains?

3. What soil conservation programs were begun under the New Deal?

4. How did the New Deal try to help poor tenant farmers?

5. How did the REA help most farm families?

2. Helping black Americans

In 1930 around 80 percent of all black Americans were still living within the borders of the old Confederacy. There they were not allowed to vote. Little money was spent on their education, and they went to separate and inferior schools. They found it hard to borrow money to buy houses or farms. In some southern states the blacks made up more than half the population. Yet the paths to wealth and political power were closed to these black citizens.

It was no wonder then that, in 1938, President Roosevelt called the South "the nation's No. 1 economic problem." By almost any measure—health, housing, schools, auto ownership, farm equipment, or family income—the South was the worst-off section of the whole United States. And in the impoverished South, the blacks were the poorest of all.

Yet new forces were at work in America. Among them were black leaders themselves. Even under slavery there had been brave rebels like Nat Turner and Denmark Vesey. The persuasive Frederick Douglass had been a leader in the abolition movement. During the Civil War he had helped recruit blacks for two regiments in the Union army. After the war he became marshal of the District of Columbia and United States consul general in Haiti. In the early 1900s, too, there were many kinds of black leaders who offered different views of American life and the doors to opportunity. Booker T. Washington and W. E. B. Du Bois, each in his own way, pointed in new directions for black Americans (p. 377).

Black Southerners lose the right to vote. When the Populists had tried to unite all the poor—black and white—behind economic reforms in the South (p. 397), they provoked an extreme reaction. White Democrats defeated the Populists by pointing with alarm to the fact that they worked with blacks. And soon white Populists admitted they could never win elections if the race question was used against them. Southern whites combined their energy and ingenuity to find ways to keep blacks out of the polling booths. This was no easy task. The Fifteenth Amendment, adopted during Reconstruction, had plainly declared that the right of citizens to vote should not be denied "by the United States or by any state on account of race, color, or previous condition of servitude."

Southerners tried using the "grandfather clause." A state would simply pass a law giving the right to vote to those persons who did have the right to vote on January 1, 1867 (before the Fifteenth Amendment) and to those persons' descendants. Anyone else who wanted to vote had to pass all sorts of impossible tests. Of course that included blacks. They would not be allowed to vote simply because their grandfathers did not have the right to vote! Beginning in 1895 seven southern states passed "grandfather" laws. Not until 1915 did the United States Supreme Court declare that these laws violated the Constitution.

Another trick was the so-called literacy test. It pretended to limit the vote to people who could read. But when blacks came to vote, the white election judges gave tests that they themselves probably could not have passed. They would ask a black to explain the most difficult part of the Constitution. A white person only had to read out a simple sentence.

Some southern states also used the poll tax. That was a tax that everybody had to pay before going to the polls to vote. Most blacks in the South were so poor that they really could not afford the few dollars for the tax. And even if a black person paid the tax, the election judge could always find some mistake in the tax receipt, and so keep the black person from voting.

The craftiness of some white Southerners seemed endless. They even went so far as to pretend that the great political parties in the South were not political parties at all, but only private clubs. Therefore, they said, nobody except white "members" had a right to vote in the primary election when their "club" picked its candidates for public office.

Since the Democratic party was in complete control in most of the South, winners in that party's primary would win the offices. By keeping black people from voting in the primary, then you would take away their votes.

Working for rights for blacks.

Thoughtful citizens all over the country became ashamed that the nation had been so slow to give all Americans their simple rights. The Niagara Movement, sparked by W.E.B. Du Bois, grew stronger (p. 378). To help prevent shocking race riots like the one in Springfield, Illinois, (Lincoln's burial place) in 1908, a new organization, the National Association for the Advancement of Colored People (NAACP), was founded in 1909 on Lincoln's birthday. Dr. Du Bois

became the impassioned editor of the NAACP magazine, *The Crisis.*

Americans of all races and religions, from all parts of the country, joined hands. People like Jane Addams, who already were working for the poor of all races in the northern city slums, gave money to pay for lawyers to help blacks secure their rights in the South. The president of the NAACP, Boston lawyer Moorfield Storey, argued the case when the Supreme Court in 1915 set aside the "grandfather" laws. The NAACP also won other important cases. One of these declared that no trial of a black could be a fair trial (as the Constitution required) if blacks were kept off the jury. During the next years the NAACP was the most important group trying to awaken all Americans to the rights of blacks.

Things were getting better for blacks. But the progress was painfully slow—and there was a long way to go.

Failures of the New Deal.

For millions of black Americans—especially in the South and in the big city slums in the North—there still seemed almost no change. Black workers were the last hired and the first fired. Black children still had less money spent on their education. Blacks were not allowed to live wherever they could afford, but had to live in special neighborhoods. Even under the New Deal, blacks were not always given their fair share. For example, they were not allowed to live in the model towns built with government money in the Tennessee Valley.

Most of those blacks whom Du Bois called the "Talented Tenth" still had to take lowly jobs. When the NRA codes allowed blacks to be paid less than whites, blacks began to say that NRA just meant "Negroes Ruined Again." *The Crisis* said in 1935 that blacks "ought to realize by now that the powers-that-be in the Roosevelt administration have nothing for them."

Yet more and more blacks voted for FDR and the New Deal. In Chicago, for example, where in 1932 only 23 percent had voted for Roosevelt, 49 percent favored him in 1936, and 56 percent in 1940. But the New Deal had done nothing to remove the poll tax. In most of its programs, blacks were still treated unequally. And when an anti-lynching bill was introduced to Congress, FDR refused to support it. "If I come out for the anti-lynching bill now," Roosevelt told

In spite of the high unemployment in the nation's cities in the 1930s, black families from the rural South continued their farm-to-city migration. In Chicago they had no choice but to live in the black belt on the South Side—often in houses like the one in this 1930s' photograph.

Walter White of the NAACP, "they [southern senators] will block every bill I ask Congress to pass to keep America from collapsing. I just can't take that risk."

Blacks in government. Despite the failings of the New Deal, Roosevelt did convince most blacks that he sided with them in their fight for equal treatment. He spoke out against lynching as "collective murder." Under Woodrow Wilson and his Re-

publican successors, blacks in government jobs were segregated. Now those who were brought into the growing bureaucracy were given their rightful place with other Americans. A "Black Cabinet" or "Black Brain Trust" became close advisers of the President. Among them were Dr. Will W. Alexander, who for a time headed the Farm Security Administration, and Mary McLeod Bethune, the forceful director of the Division of Negro Affairs of the National Youth Administration. Mrs. Bethune channeled large amounts of aid to thousands of black youngsters, helping them stay in school or learn new trades.

As usual, Eleanor Roosevelt helped blacks to feel that the administration cared about them. She was known to be a good friend of Mary McLeod Bethune's. She invited the National Council of Negro Women to tea at the White House. She was seen, and photographed, visiting black schools and other projects useful to black citizens.

A "Black Renaissance." After World War I a movement called the "Black Renaissance" or the "New Negro Movement" began in Harlem. This neighborhood in New York City became a gathering place for black poets, writers, scholars, painters, and musicians. Poets like Langston Hughes and Countee Cullen revealed whole new vistas of American experience. Also in Harlem then was Dr. Du Bois, who told the exciting story of the renaissance in *Black Manhattan* and *Along This Way*.

The Harlem Renaissance ended about 1930, but its influence spread outward. In cities across the nation there were small but active groups of poets, writers, painters, and actors. The movement was helped along by the New Deal's Federal Writers' Project.

The rights for black Americans would come gradually—but not fast enough for W.E.B. Du Bois. He lost faith in America and in democracy. He joined the Communist party and then renounced his United States citizenship. In 1961, at the age of 93, he moved to the new African country of Ghana. But, as we shall see, others of stronger faith—the Rev. Martin Luther King, Jr., for example—continued their struggle in and for America. They would bring historic victories of justice and equality, not only for blacks, but for all Americans.

SECTION REVIEW

1. Identify: W.E.B. Du Bois, NAACP, Will W. Alexander, Mary M. Bethune, "Black Renaissance," Langston Hughes, Countee Cullen.
2. Name and explain devices used in southern states to keep blacks from voting.
3. What legal victories did the NAACP help win?
4. In what respects did the New Deal fail to help black Americans? How did it help them?

---

3. The New Deal and women

Many Americans had thought that winning the right to vote would allow women to become an independent force in politics. This had not happened. Many women failed to go to the polls. And because they did not vote, politicians had little reason to respect their special demands. It would take more than the Nineteenth Amendment to bring women into the mainstream of American political life. It would take a long program of education and the slow discovery that women were not shaped by nature only for roles as wives and mothers. They were just as qualified as men for leadership and service in government, business, and the arts. In the experimental spirit of the New Deal era millions of Americans—women and men—were awakened to these opportunities.

Eleanor Roosevelt. The person best placed to help them was the President's wife. Eleanor Roosevelt's mother had died when she was eight, and her father, just before her tenth birthday. Raised by her grandmother, she had lived a lonely life. Perhaps her own unhappiness as a girl had made her sympathetic to the needs of others who felt alone and abandoned. She adopted all the nation's unhappy and neglected people as her foster children. And she dared to speak up for them in her regular press conferences. She wrote a newspaper column and gave radio talks. She traveled everywhere. In 1933 alone she covered 40,000 miles. One newspaper headlined on its society page, "Mrs. Roosevelt Spends Night at White House." FDR, in his wheelchair, could not move about as she did. She became the conscience of the New Deal and the eyes of the President. It was not unusual for him to tell the Cabinet that something needed to be done because "My Missus told me so and so."

Women in government and politics. With Eleanor Roosevelt in the White House, women for the first time gained substantial political influence and positions of power on the national scene. Women reformers came to Washington in large numbers to work for the government. Mary (Molly) Dewson, a friend of the Roosevelts', took over the direction of women's work in the Democratic party. In 1936 the Democratic convention ruled that each member of the Platform Committee had to have an alternate of the opposite sex. The

New York Times called this "the biggest coup for women in years."

Eleanor Roosevelt and Mary Dewson fought hard to get women into the government and to see that New Deal programs helped women. In 1930, women held only 17.6 percent of the postmaster positions, but six years later their share had gone up to 26 percent. The Civil Works Administration employed 100,000 women by the end of 1933.

Some of the most important positions in FDR's administration were given to women. Frances Perkins was Secretary of Labor. Florence Allen became a judge of the Circuit Court of Appeals. Other women became ambassadors and top officers of the WPA and other agencies. Formerly all the women executives in the federal government could

Among the most active supporters of a larger role for women in the government and the Democratic party during the New Deal were Eleanor Roosevelt (below) and Mary Dewson. Because FDR was unable to walk, Mrs. Roosevelt traveled everywhere, becoming his eyes and ears outside the White House.

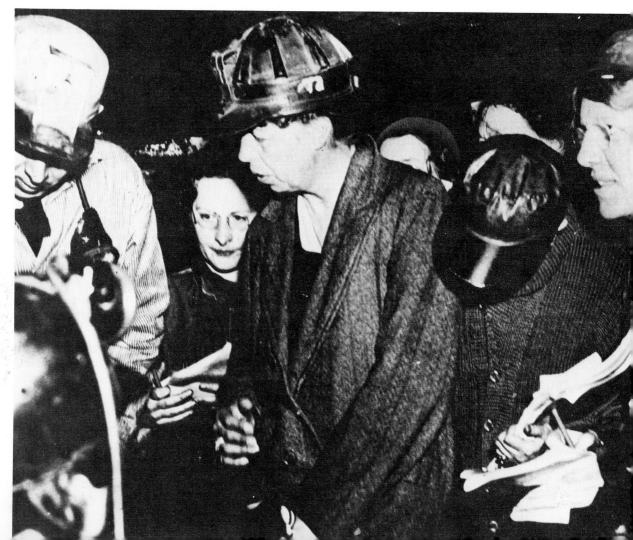

meet for dinner in a small clubroom. Now they needed a large hall.

Eleanor Roosevelt thought that women could help humanize government. The aim of the New Deal, as she saw it, was to promote "the general happiness of the working man and woman and their families." Women had something special to offer.

The economic inequality of women. Still, during these years women were usually given jobs that were considered "women's work"—as teachers, typists, clerks, nurses, and textile workers. They were seldom put in supervisory positions. Though 80 percent of the schoolteachers of the nation were women, in superintendent positions they were only 1.5 percent. One-third of all graduate degrees were awarded to women, yet they made up only 4 percent of the college professors. Even when they did the very same work, women often were paid less than men.

In those depression days of widespread unemployment, many Americans—including leading women—feared that women would take jobs from men. This would increase the unemployment of the traditional family "breadwinners." Florence Kahn, congresswoman from California, declared, "Women's place is not out in the business world competing with men who have families to support." Secretary of Labor Frances Perkins agreed.

While women were heartened by the examples of Eleanor Roosevelt, Frances Perkins, Mary McLeod Bethune, Mary Dewson, and others like them on the national scene, they still had a long road to travel toward economic equality.

SECTION REVIEW

1. Identify: Mary Dewson, Frances Perkins, Florence Allen.
2. How did Eleanor Roosevelt help women achieve political influence?
3. How did the depression affect job prospects for women?

4. The struggles of labor

The New Deal hoped to enlist the help of organized labor to improve the lot of "forgotten Americans"—blacks, women, immigrants, the poor. Through section 7a of the NRA, and then by the Wagner Act and its National Labor Relations Board, the government lent its support to the attempts of workers to organize.

The growth of the AF of L. Loss of jobs had cut union membership after the Great Crash. Then the unions began to recover in 1934. But they were still unable to organize the great mass-production industries—steel, autos, rubber, textiles. The AF of L was a federation of craft unions and so was better suited to the past than to the future. Its ways of thinking were not adapted to a world of vast factories, of power-driven machinery, and mass production.

The Carpenters' Union, for example, had grown by moving from the construction trades into any industry that dealt with things made of wood and finally anything "that ever was made of wood." In this way—and by expanding into many new and smaller fields—the AF of L had reached a membership of 3.5 million by 1936.

The birth of the CIO. Some union leaders were not happy with the craft approach. They felt that the age of crafts had gone out with the horse and buggy. John L. Lewis, the massive, shaggy-browed leader of the United Mine Workers, believed that the industrial world of the 1900s required a new kind of labor organization. The American Federation of Labor, led by Samuel Gompers and William Green, had organized the aristocracy of American labor. They believed that the skilled workers in the old crafts—carpenters, plumbers, and bricklayers— could only lose if they threw in their lot with the millions of unskilled workers in factories and mines.

Lewis had begun working in the mines when he was 16. Even after he became a high union official he never forgot that he was a miner. And he was confident that if labor was to become a great power and defend its interests it would have to organize in a new way. Unions would never get into the steel mills or auto plants if the company had to deal with a dozen craft unions. Each union would want what was best for its own members. Lewis said that a single union should bargain for all the workers— skilled and unskilled—in a giant industry. There should be one industrial union for steel, not a dozen or more craft unions.

The AF of L had never organized the steel industry. For it did not fit into the old craft pattern. Now Lewis wanted to unionize the

Wide World Photos

John L. Lewis, shown here after a trip down into a mine, was the tough and charismatic leader of the CIO in the 1930s.

leaders and their members were expelled from the AF of L, the CIO declared its independence and became an important new force in American life.

The CIO quickly stepped up its efforts. In 1937 alone production was halted by 4740 strikes. That spring the workers themselves invented an ingenious new weapon that worked for a short while. When they went on strike, instead of leaving the factory they simply stayed there and sat down at their machines. They refused to work or let others work. They had food brought in and slept on the factory floor. They said that since it was their work that made the factory valuable, the factory really partly belonged to them. But the Supreme Court disagreed, and in 1939 "sit-down strikes" were banned.

Of course, the strikers did not always simply sit down. And employers sometimes hired private police who were reckless of the rights and the lives of workers. Outside the Republic Steel plant in Chicago ten striking workers were killed. From these struggles came a new era for labor unions in the United States. During 1937, General Motors, Chrysler, U.S. Steel, and many smaller steel companies as well as Firestone Rubber, General Electric, and some major textile firms signed CIO contracts. Unions would play a strong new role in American industrial life. As never before, workers would look to them to hear their grievances and protect their rights. The power of factory owners over their workers was much reduced. Through the NLRB, the federal government supported the unions.

Challenged by the success of the CIO, the AF of L swung into action to expand its membership. Between 1936 and 1938 membership in all unions increased from 4 million to 6 million. Big business would now be opposed by big labor.

New union members. The membership of the old-line craft unions of the AF of L had been mostly Americans of the older immigration—English, Scots, Germans, Irish, and Scandinavians. Out of fear and from prejudice these unions commonly excluded the later comers from southern and eastern Europe in addition to blacks and women. The new CIO unions welcomed all these groups with their theme song, "Solidarity Forever."

Women found new openings in the factory because the CIO began to recruit workers without

steelworkers because steel mills were the largest single users of coal. Their owners also owned coal mines.

In 1935 the Committee for Industrial Organization (later the Congress of Industrial Organizations) was formed by Lewis. He was joined by other labor leaders who agreed that American labor needed a new approach—Sidney Hillman of the Amalgamated Clothing Workers, Charles Howard of the Typographical Union, and Thomas McMahon of the Textile Workers. This "CIO" quickly changed the direction of American labor organization. At first the founders said they only wanted to advise the AF of L on how to organize the giant industries. But the conservative leaders of the AF of L resisted these efforts. In 1937 when the CIO

Employees at a General Motors Corporation plant in Flint, Michigan, sat down by their machines in 1937 in the nation's first sit-down strike. They were seeking recognition of their new CIO union, the United Automobile Workers, and their tactic prevented the company from running the plant with strikebreakers. They won their demands, but the sit-down strike was soon declared illegal.

regard to sex. Within a few years nearly a million women joined the unions. But even in the unions women were not yet quite equal. For example, the liberal Amalgamated Clothing Workers still allowed women to be paid less than men for the same work.

The unions themselves showed dramatic changes. The International Ladies Garment Workers Union, whose members had been largely Jewish at the end of World War I, now in the mid-1930s was nearly half Italian. Before 1940 many of its members were Puerto Ricans. By opening their doors the unions had the power to open opportunity for new immigrants and the children of immigrants.

The labor movement continued to harbor large pockets of prejudice. Despite the example of the CIO, certain unions—especially in building trades—continued to exclude blacks, Puerto Ricans, Mexicans, and others whom they considered "different." Farm laborers, migratory workers, and domestic servants remained outside the ranks of organized labor.

Neither the unions nor the New Deal could bring an end to unemployment. Even after the mobilization for war in 1940 had provided thousands of new jobs, there were still 6 million out of work in 1941. Not until 1943 would the nation reach full employment.

SECTION REVIEW

1. Identify: John L. Lewis, Samuel Gompers, William Green, CIO, Sidney Hillman, sit-down strikes.

2. How did an industrial union differ from a craft union?

3. How did some employers try to break strikes?

4. What gains did American labor unions make in 1936–1938?

5. What groups formerly left out of unions made big gains through the efforts of the CIO?

CHAPTER REVIEW

MEETING OUR EARLIER SELVES

1. What problems were sharecroppers facing in the 1930s? Did the New Deal benefit these farmers?

2. What New Deal laws or other actions of the Roosevelt administration helped black Americans of the 1930s? (Review chapters 24 and 25.) What were some shortcomings?

3. How would you expect a leader for women's rights in 1940 to assess the 1930s—the progress and setbacks for women?

4. What tactics did labor use to improve its position in the 1930s? Which ones were the most successful? Why?

5. How did Eleanor Roosevelt represent the "spirit" of the New Deal?

QUESTIONS FOR TODAY

1. Speak with one or more persons who remember the 1930s. Compare their lifestyle then with yours today.

2. Identify some of today's black artists, writers, entertainers, and athletes. Which of these people would have had much less chance to gain recognition (and high income) in the 1930s? Why?

3. Who, according to the text, were the "forgotten Americans" of the 1930s? What groups, if any, would you call "forgotten Americans" today? Why?

YOUR REGION IN HISTORY

1. Find out how the rise of the CIO affected unionization in your state or locality from 1935 to 1940. Were there any major labor-management disturbances in your locality?

2. Some elderly women in your community probably obtained their first jobs in the 1930s. Find out from them—and from other sources—what kinds of jobs were available for women in the 1930s.

3. How did the political complexion of your city, county, or state change in the 1930s? For example, did support for Democratic candidates rise from 1932 to 1936? What happened between 1936 and 1940?

SKILLS TO MAKE OUR PAST VIVID

1. Prepare a series of questions that a journalist or radio news commentator might have used in 1938 for an interview with one of the following: Eleanor Roosevelt, John L. Lewis, W.E.B. Du Bois, or Frances Perkins.

2. Write a two-page biographical account of some person named in this chapter. Include some interesting anecdotal material.

3. Some of the illustrations in this chapter show the problems faced by America's "forgotten" people. Using several pictures, identify who these people were and describe their needs and wants.

CHAPTER 26

Clouds of war

While Americans were trying the New Deal experiments in democracy, desperate and hungry people in Europe were handing over their lives and liberties to ruthless dictators. Some of the most civilized peoples of Europe had returned to an age of barbarism. In Italy, only ten years before FDR entered the White House, Benito Mussolini and his Fascists (as his party was called) marched on Rome. They seized the government, abolished democracy, destroyed the liberties of the Italian people—all on the promise of jobs and glory. In Germany, too, in the very month when FDR took his oath of office, Adolf Hitler, with his gang of Nazis, was made dictator.

1. Foreign affairs, 1933–1939

When Franklin D. Roosevelt moved into the White House in March 1933, the world prospects were grim. The outlook for civilization was darker than at any earlier time in American history. Two decades before, when President Wilson was elected, European nations were battling for empire and for the world's treasure. Now the threats to peace came from national leaders who screamed their hatred of democracy and modern civilization. They declared war on the ideals of equality and representative government on which the United States was founded.

The rise of Hitler. During the next years, European diplomacy would be dominated by Adolf Hitler, the most destructive dictator of modern times. He was not really a German, because he was born in Austria. A high school dropout, he wanted to be an artist, but twice failed the admission examination for the art academy in Vienna. He

lived on charity and by selling copies that he made of picture postcards. In World War I he joined the German army. He was gassed and wounded, and never reached a higher rank than corporal. After the war he began to organize his own political party, aiming to seize the government and lead Germany to world power. Driven by a passionate, senseless anti-Semitism, he was determined to exterminate the Jews—whom he blamed for Germany's defeat.

In 1923, after his Nazi thugs failed to take over in the southern German state of Bavaria, where they surrounded the leading officials in a beer hall, he was sent to prison. There he wrote his 800-page *Mein Kampf* (My Struggle), which became the bible of the Nazis, and then of all Germany. He declared that the Germans were the "Master Race," entitled to rule the world. Democracy, he said, was a fraud, and the only good government was a dictatorship. The dictator should rule not by truth but by the "Big Lie." Christianity, according to him, was also a fraud, invented by the Jews to make cowards of the Master Race. Hitler's plans for a "Third Reich" to last a thousand years were so simple-minded and so immoral that few people outside Germany took them seriously.

But inside Germany, thousands, and then millions were joining his National Socialist (Nazi) party. They resented the Versailles Peace Treaty after World War I and the reparations that had been imposed on the German people. Partly as a result of these heavy payments, the economy fell apart and inflation ran wild. A loaf of bread that cost ten marks one week would be priced at one thousand marks the next week, and then would quickly skyrocket to a billion marks. Money lost its value so fast that salaries and wages had to be paid every 24 hours. Life savings became worthless.

Hitler comes to power. The democratic government within Germany after the war was weak. The German parliament, split into a dozen political parties, was unable to organize the nation's economy. Millions were unemployed, and goods were scarce. The world depression that in the United States had led Americans to try their New Deal left the Germans leaderless, hungry, and hopeless. Who could help them? Whom should they blame?

At this moment Hitler, with his mad vision of world power, came on the scene. He gave them their scapegoat—the Jews—upon whom they could blame everything. But he was not so mad that he could not organize spectacular meetings with swastika flags flying for thousands to hear his hour-long orations of hate and glory. And he was a master of the radio. He appealed to the unemployed and the rabble made up of both the ambitious and the disappointed.

Reasonable leaders in other countries found his schemes so outrageous that they would not believe they were real. Yet respectable Germans sat by watching while his thugs beat up opponents, assassinated enemies, sent innocent millions to concentration camps, and filled the newspapers with their Big Lies. Hitler showed that people were more timid than was ever before imagined.

The Germans made Hitler their God. When they greeted each other, they no longer said "Grüss Gott" (God be with you!) but "Heil Hitler!" And anyone who used the old greeting was suspected of treason. They set up their German Christian church to make Christianity serve the Master Race.

With pomp, parades of goosestepping soldiers, and huge swastika flags flying, the Nazis celebrated their Third Reich in 1938.

Wide World Photos

Adolph Hitler (above) and his followers tortured and murdered millions in concentration camps. These inmates of Dachau, a camp in Germany, greet the American troops who freed them in 1945.

Wide World Photos

The main new institution they invented was the concentration camp. To these places of torture they sent millions of Jews and countless other anti-Nazi Protestants and Catholics. There they used gas chambers to kill children, women, and men whom they considered their enemies. They extracted the gold from the teeth of the corpses to buy armaments and used human ashes to fertilize their fields. And one of the most difficult tasks facing FDR and his supporters was to persuade Americans that this was not just a nightmare.

Communist Russia, as the same time, was in the grip of the wily and vicious Josef Stalin. There, too, people who spoke up were tortured and sent to labor camps in remote Siberia. In Japan the expansion-minded army leaders were shaping the nation's policies. And the Italians under Mussolini were planning to create a new Roman Empire.

The looming threat of war. Italy, Russia, and Japan had all been American allies in the First World War. President Wilson had called that a war "to make the world safe for democracy." Now these same countries had become threats both to

democracy and to peace. Germany, risen from defeat, was building an enormous new army, making weapons at frightening speed, and menacing its neighbors. Any one of the new military powers had a better-equipped army than the old democracies had.

In 1935, pursuing its dreams of empire, Italy invaded Ethiopia and bombed innocent villages from the air. In 1936 Germany moved its army back into the Rhineland, which had been demilitarized after World War I. Seeking a base for their aggressions in western Europe, Hitler and Mussolini slipped arms and men into Spain to support the Fascist General Francisco Franco. Spain became the world's battlefield in a bloody civil war. Fascist forces from everywhere fought against the republican government, which was aided by Communist Russia and supporters from France, England, and the United States.

Except to the cheeriest optimists, it was plain that another world war was brewing. Should the United States sit by and see the forces of savagery dominate the world?

The Good Neighbor policy.

Roosevelt came into office in 1933 pledging that the United States would be "the good neighbor" in world affairs. We would be "the neighbor who resolutely respects himself and, because he does so, respects the rights of others." He meant his statement to apply to all the world, but the "Good Neighbor policy" became a label for his Latin American policy.

Roosevelt intended to continue the policies of Herbert Hoover toward our southern neighbors. We would not try to run their governments. To prove his point, FDR withdrew our marines from Haiti. But when Cuba was torn by another revolution, our pressure brought the conservatives to power. Some Latin Americans wondered then whether the United States had really changed. FDR tried to reassure them. At a Pan-American conference at Montevideo, Uruguay, in 1933, Secretary of State Cordell Hull joined in a declaration that "no state has the right to intervene in the internal or external affairs of another."

The United States gave solid evidence of the new policy. Back in 1901 our Congress had forced the Cubans to add the Platt Amendment (p. 416) to their constitution as a condition for the withdrawal of American troops from the island. Cuba promised to provide the United States with naval and coaling stations. They also gave the United States the right to intervene to preserve order and maintain Cuban independence. It amounted to a Cuban declaration of dependence on the United States. Now, in May 1934, by a new treaty the United States gave up its right to intervene. At last Cuba would be treated like a sovereign nation.

The real test of the Good Neighbor policy came in Mexico. In 1938 President Lázaro Cárdenas suddenly announced that the Mexican government was taking over all foreign oil properties. The holdings of the seventeen British and American companies were valued at nearly half a billion dollars. The British broke off diplomatic relations with Mexico. Some Americans urged us to send in our troops, but Secretary Hull was patient. He preferred to negotiate and reached a settlement in 1941. Mexico agreed to pay the oil companies for their properties and also settled other claims of United States citizens. The Roosevelt administration began to persuade our Latin American neighbors that the United States was ready to treat them as equals.

Japanese-American relations.

On the other side of the world, a military clique in control of Japan reached across the narrow Sea of Japan to conquer an empire. When the Japanese seized Manchuria in 1931, the League of Nations condemned Japan as an aggressor. The Japanese withdrew from the League and in 1937 attacked weak China. The democracies of western Europe uttered bold, brave words against the Japanese, but they were afraid to act. They preferred to let Japan enslave Asian millions rather than risk war themselves.

On December 12, 1937, the United States gunboat *Panay* on the Yangtze River in China was sunk by Japanese bombs. Two American sailors died. The United States protested. A prompt apology from Japan, with an indemnity of $2 million, closed the incident, but left Americans worried.

FDR and neutrality.

President Roosevelt warned that if aggression continued in Asia, Africa, and Europe, the whole world would be engulfed in war. The United States could not remain a mere spectator. If the democracies of Europe were conquered by the Nazis and their allies, the United States would be next on their list. He called for a "quarantine" of the aggressor nations. But for the moment he could do little more to help the free nations of Europe. Americans had not forgotten the senseless slaughter in the First World War. More and more Americans said, "Never Again!" Some were becoming pacifists, saying they would never go to war for any reason. Still others became "isolationists," hoping to fence off the New World. Naturally enough, Americans who had come from Italy or Germany did not like the idea of fighting against their old homeland. Americans of Irish descent remembered the English tyranny over their island. A few people even became American Nazis.

Some historians argued that if the United States had really been neutral during World War I, our nation would not have had to go to war at all. Might the world have been better, they asked, if the United States had remained at peace? The seeds of the world's problems, they said, were planted in World War I. Perhaps a neutral United States might have prevented the follies of the Treaty of Versailles. Some sensational hearings presided over by Senator Gerald P. Nye of North Dakota seemed to show that arms manufacturers and bankers had led us into the war for their own profit.

The obvious answer seemed to be to pass a law. If Congress had the power to declare war—why could not Congress simply declare peace? Why could not strong, clear "Neutrality Acts" keep us neutral? Some thought that the United States occupation of the Philippines might involve us with Japan in the Pacific. In 1934 the Tydings-McDuffie Act provided for the independence of the Philippines in twelve years. Early the next year, Roosevelt recommended to the Senate that we join the World Court, which had been set up by the League of Nations. But isolationists feared that even the "advisory opinions" given by the Court might draw us onto the battlefields of Europe.

As war clouds gathered, Americans' fond hopes for neutrality grew ever stronger—and more futile. Acts were passed in 1935 and again in 1936 to prevent Americans from sending arms to the nations at war. Americans were warned that they traveled at their own risk on the ships of nations at war. When the Spanish civil war broke out in 1936, the neutrality laws were extended to bar shipments of arms to either side. But this hurt only the Spanish republicans. Franco was already receiving all the arms he needed from Hitler and Mussolini.

WAKE UP! WAKE UP, UNCLE!

Daniel Bishop, *St. Louis Star-Times*

As world war approaches, Uncle Sam sleeps and is tied down by opponents of involvement.

The isolationists came up with still another "neutrality" law in 1937. This permitted sales to belligerents, but only "cash-and-carry." A country at war had to pay cash for its goods before the goods left our shores. And the country at war had to carry the goods in its own ships. The law embargoed munitions and also allowed the President to extend the embargo to other exports. The isolationists believed that at last they had passed a law that would keep the United States out of war.

Still, some isolationists sought an amendment to the Constitution that would prevent Congress from declaring war without first submitting the question to a popular vote. A poll of the American people in 1937 showed that 75 percent favored such an amendment. President Roosevelt was strongly opposed. He warned that "it would encourage other nations to believe that they could violate American rights with impunity." And the House refused to submit the amendment to the states.

Neither President Roosevelt nor a dozen acts of Congress could block the world's drift toward war. In January 1938, FDR suggested a world conference to reduce armaments and promote national economic security, but the British Prime Minister Neville Chamberlain said no.

Hitler on the march. One of Hitler's goals was to bring into the "Third Reich" all the millions of people of "German blood" in Austria, Czechoslovakia, and Poland. Of course, there was no such thing as "German blood," but some German professors supported him, and the millions of German people went along.

In March 1938 Germany invaded and annexed Austria. Hitler's next target was the strategic Sudetenland on the Czech border with Germany. It contained 3 million people of German ancestry. The Czechs mobilized, expecting aid from Great Britain, France, and Russia. But those countries would not risk war to save the Czechoslovak republic.

Prime Minister Chamberlain of Britain and Premier Daladier of France met Hitler and Mussolini at Munich, Germany, on September 28, 1938. There, in an attempt to appease Hitler, they agreed to dismember Czechoslovakia—the one democracy in Europe that survived east of the Rhine—and give a piece to Germany. As Hitler occupied the Sudetenland, Chamberlain reported to Parliament that the Munich Pact guaranteed "peace in our time."

We know today that if Britain and France had resisted at this moment, German generals were planning to remove Hitler. But Hitler was riding high. He and his German people began to think he was unbeatable. Could anything prevent a world war?

"There can be no peace," Roosevelt warned, "if national policy adopts as a deliberate instrument the threat of war." In November 1938 when Hitler increased his brutal persecution of the Jews, Americans were more horrified than ever. Now FDR demanded that the arms embargo be removed from the neutrality law so the United States could help the victims of aggression. Still most Americans were optimists. And many others were isolationists hoping that we could remain an island of peace and prosperity in a world of war and misery.

On March 15, 1939, Hitler seized the rest of Czechoslovakia. The policy of appeasement was now exposed as a failure. Great Britain pledged aid to Poland in case its independence was threatened.

United Press International Photo

A German motorized detachment rides through a Polish town already destroyed by bombs.

When Mussolini invaded little Albania on April 7, Britain gave a similar guarantee to neighboring Greece and Romania.

In a desperate effort to keep all Europe from catching fire, President Roosevelt asked Mussolini and Hitler to promise to refrain for ten years from attacking a list of 31 nations. In return these nations would promise not to attack Italy or Germany. But Hitler replied with sarcasm. In his shrieking, abusive speech before the German Reichstag (legislature) he ridiculed FDR. He knew that the democracies were not prepared for war. He was determined to have his own way and dominate the world before the democracies dared stand against him.

President Roosevelt asked Congress to repeal or modify the arms embargo because it was helping the aggressor nations, who were well supplied with

Hoping to start life anew, a family returns to its farm near Bromberg, Poland, in November 1939 after Nazi bombings have left it in ruins.

arms from their own factories. By a vote of 12–11, the isolationists in the Senate Foreign Relations Committee put off any changes in the law until the next session of Congress, which was to meet in January 1940.

Continuing problems with Japan.

Meanwhile, on July 26, 1939, the State Department moved against the Japanese war machine. Japan was told that in six months we would end the Japanese-American Commercial Treaty of 1911. This freed Congress to stop the sale of war materials to Japan. The Japanese had been invading China with arms bought in the United States. And the Japanese were disturbed by news that their new ally Nazi Germany had made a sudden alliance with Japan's old enemy Russia. For a time Japanese expansion in Asia was slowed.

War comes to Europe.

In Europe the attempts to appease Hitler seemed only to whet his appetite for more conquests. He had risen to power by telling the German people that Communist Russia was their prime enemy. Now he shocked the whole world when he announced a nonaggression pact with Stalin in 1939. The secret terms gave Germany western Poland, while the Soviet Union was free to take Finland, Estonia, Latvia, eastern Poland, Bessarabia (in Romania), and Lithuania. The Nazis believed that in this way they would protect themselves against war on two fronts. In return Russia would gain a buffer zone against Germany—and a temporary assurance against attack.

Throughout the summer of 1939 Hitler demanded that Poland return to Germany certain districts containing people of "German blood." Poland, bolstered by Britain and France, stood its ground. Then on September 1, without warning, Hitler invaded Poland. Two days later England and France declared war on Germany. Then Stalin's armies marched into Poland from the east on September 17. Within two weeks, on September 29, brave, long-suffering Poland was divided between the two tyrants.

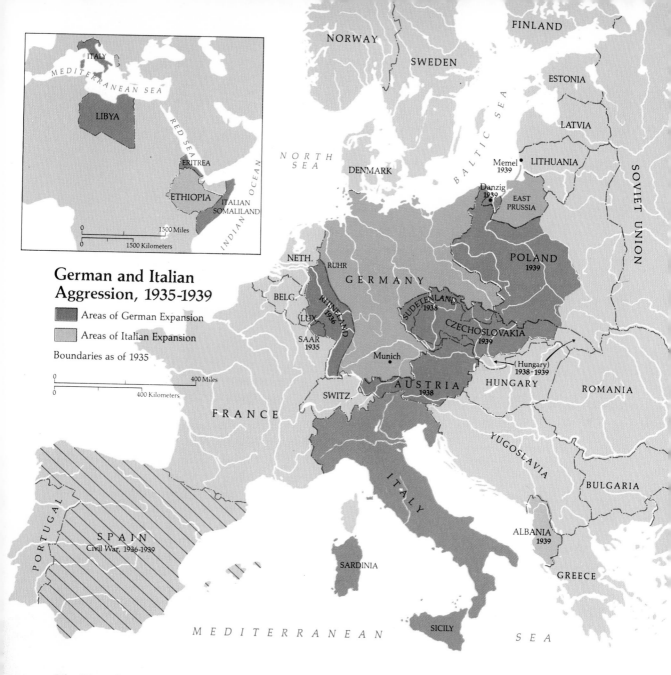

German and Italian Aggression, 1935-1939

Areas of German Expansion

Areas of Italian Expansion

Boundaries as of 1935

The United States reacts. Unlike President Wilson 25 years before, Roosevelt did not ask the American people to be neutral in thought as well as deed. He invoked the Neutrality Act of 1937 when war broke out. But in a fireside chat, he reminded the American people, "Even a neutral cannot be asked to close his mind or his conscience."

President Roosevelt called Congress into special session on September 21, 1939. He asked them to change the "cash and carry" Neutrality Act of 1937

and repeal the embargo on selling or shipping arms to the belligerents. He believed it was urgent for the United States to find ways at once to help the Allies against Hitler. If the United States waited, the barbaric forces might win, and then it would be too late. Many voices were raised against his attempt to break out of our isolation. Among them were Senator William E. Borah of Idaho and the nation's hero, Colonel Charles Lindbergh. "Preparedness" Republicans like Henry Stimson and

Frank Knox supported the President. After a bitter debate Congress voted the Neutrality Act of 1939. It helped the forces of democracy by repealing the arms embargo.

SECTION REVIEW

1. Identify or explain: Adolf Hitler, *Mein Kampf,* National Socialist party, Nazis, concentration camps, Josef Stalin, Benito Mussolini, Francisco Franco, Lázaro Cárdenas, *Panay,* Tydings-McDuffie Act, neutrality laws, Neville Chamberlain, appeasement.

2. Locate: Ethiopia, Rhineland, Montevideo, Manchuria, Yangtze River, Sudetenland, Albania, Estonia, Latvia, Lithuania.

3. What conditions in Germany led the people to accept a dictator?

4. Once in power, how did Hitler strengthen his control?

5. Cite instances where the government followed Roosevelt's Good Neighbor policy.

6. Why were many Americans "isolationists"? How did they try to isolate the country?

7. What was the Munich Pact? What was its outcome?

8. What events in the summer of 1939 led to the outbreak of World War II?

2. The battlefield is everywhere

For six months, while Germany was moving its armies back from Poland, there was no fighting in western Europe. The British were busy moving their forces to France. The French sat smugly behind their Maginot line. They thought that no enemy could pierce this 350-mile line of tunnels, concrete forts, and anti-tank fields. The headlines spoke of a "phony war." In November the giant Soviet Union began a three-month winter siege of its tiny neighbor, Finland. The bravery of the Finns against hopeless odds stirred the admiration of the free world. But part of Finland came under the Communist heel. Then, in April 1940, Hitler launched a stunning new kind of war.

The new warfare. *Blitzkrieg* (lightning war) was Adolf Hitler's surprising strategy. This depended on air power. And it was nothing like the battles that generals had read about in their textbooks. The idea was to strike with lightning speed. Using the fastest new vehicles (airplanes, tanks, trucks, and even motorcycles), the Nazis would rush quickly deep into enemy territory. The sluggish enemies would be overwhelmed.

Blitzkrieg also meant war that struck like lightning—from the sky. Air power made it possible. Leaping over "standing" armies, over water barriers

The German "Stuka" dive bombers, shown here flying in formation in 1941, served the Nazi "blitzkrieg." Swooping out of the sky, they devastated all below.

Wide World Photos

and coastal fortifications, the Nazi air force would strike at the heart of the defenseless nations.

On April 9, 1940, Hitler ended the "phony war" and shocked the world by invading Denmark and Norway. One month later he rushed into the Netherlands, Belgium, and Luxembourg. From there he quickly bypassed the "impregnable" Maginot line and lunged deep into France. On June 14 his Nazis marched into Paris. Thousands of weeping men and women lined the streets, helpless against this lightning invasion. France surrendered by the end of June.

Whether Americans liked it or not, the battlefront was now everywhere. The airplane had made old notions about war out of date. What the submarine had done to the freedom of the seas, the airplane was doing to almost all the other rules of warfare.

Billy Mitchell advertises air power. Just as Admiral Mahan had alerted Americans to the influence of sea power on history, so during World War I the bold and outspoken Billy Mitchell had begun to advertise air power.

Air power was then so new that few took it seriously. In the Civil War and the Spanish-American War, light observation balloons had been used. But "military ballooning," as it was called, was still thought of mostly as a sport or a hobby. In 1913 when Mitchell was a young officer in the Signal Corps, he began to be intrigued by the airplane's military uses. Then, during World War I, as General Pershing's Chief of Air Services, he was impressed by the deeds of British and French warplanes.

At the end of the war, American generals and admirals still considered the airplane as merely another weapon. Like a new machine gun, it was to be used by either the army or the navy in their own regular operations.

Billy Mitchell had other ideas. He was convinced that airplanes really ought to be put into an entirely new military unit, under a command all their own. So long as Americans thought of airplanes only as helpers for the army and navy, he argued, we were sure to be left behind. We would lose the next war to nations who saw that air power was something new and world-shaking.

Air power, Mitchell said, had shifted the main targets. No longer were they the enemy *armies*.

Wide World Photos

The charm of Billy Mitchell, champion of U. S. air power, shows in this early picture.

Now the targets would be the "vital centers"—the centers of industry, the centers of supply, and the centers of the enemy's will to resist. "Armies themselves can be disregarded by air power," he explained, "if a rapid strike is made against the opposing centers."

Americans could not bear the thought of a new warfare that was so horrible. They hated to believe that whole cities might have to be destroyed.

Mitchell was an expert at getting publicity. He made speeches and wrote magazine articles and books to alert all citizens to the importance of air power. Many of his fellow officers disliked him for it. Some called him "General of the 'Hot Air' Force."

Mitchell gives a demonstration. But Mitchell was not to be put off. Battleships were supposed to be "unsinkable." To prove that airplanes were effective against battleships, he planned a spectacular show. He arranged to have the German battleship *Ostfriesland*, which had been surrendered at the end of World War I, hauled to a position 60 miles off the Virginia coast. It was a ghost ship, with not a soul on board.

Just before noon on July 21, 1921, a flight of Mitchell's army bombers left Langley Field 85 miles away. As they arrived over the battleship, they dropped six 2000-pound bombs. Within twenty minutes the "unsinkable" battleship was at the bottom of the ocean. It was the first time a battleship had ever been sunk by planes.

When admirals and generals still refused to grasp the full meaning of air power, Mitchell tried other tactics. He publicly denounced the conduct of our defense by the War and Navy departments as incompetent, criminally negligent, and "almost treasonable." This was the sure road to court martial—and that seemed to be his purpose. On December 17, 1925, a panel of generals found General Billy Mitchell guilty of "conduct which brought discredit upon the military service." They sentenced him to a five-year suspension from active duty.

Building air power. Mitchell's campaign had already forced President Calvin Coolidge to take some action. The committee he appointed did not support all Mitchell's demands, but they did urge the buildup of an American air force.

Then, on May 21, 1927, Charles Lindbergh made his famous nonstop flight from New York to Paris. As the military meaning of Lindbergh's feat sank in, Americans began to realize that some of Billy Mitchell's "wild" ideas were not so wild. Now it seemed quite possible that some day the United States might be attacked by airplanes that came nonstop across the ocean. The nation began to take Mitchell, and air power, seriously.

In 1935 the new American long-range B-17 bomber (soon called the "Flying Fortress" and equipped with the super-accurate Norden bombsight) first went into the air. Now it was hard to doubt that air power would change the meaning of war. Air war against "vital centers" would be as different as possible from the old trench warfare.

The United States Navy also had its champion of air power. He was as different from Billy Mitchell as night from day. Admiral William A. Moffett, a pilot and aviation enthusiast, was quiet and diplomatic, just as Mitchell was noisy and brash. Each in his own way served the cause of air power.

Moffett became head of the Navy's newly created Bureau of Aeronautics in 1921. He worked steadily for the development of aircraft carriers and for catapult-launched airplanes on battleships and cruisers. His farsighted work would help to make possible the United States victory over Japan in World War II.

The United States prepares for war. President Roosevelt had long recognized the Nazi menace. Even before the Germans had overrun France, he had sent a special message to Congress warning the nation to rearm. He announced a bold plan to turn out 50,000 planes in the next year, 1941, and every year until the Nazis were beaten. And he asked for billions of dollars to create a two-ocean navy. In one of his most effective fireside chats over the radio, he alerted the nation:

> The Nazi masters have made it clear that they intend not only to dominate all life and thought in their own country, but also to enslave the rest of the world. . . . We cannot escape danger, or the fear of danger, by crawling into a bed and pulling the covers over our heads. . . . No nation can appease the Nazis. No man can tame a tiger into a kitten by stroking it. . . . Let not the defeatists tell us that it is too late. It will never be earlier.

Still there were those who believed they could ward off the Nazi menace by the old-fashioned magic word "Neutrality!"

The isolationists hoped the Neutrality Act of 1939 would keep us out of war. But Roosevelt saw during 1940 that if Great Britain was not to fall, it would have to receive more help from the United States. Could he convince the country in time?

The Battle of Britain. Great Britain now stood alone against Hitler and Mussolini. "The battle of France is over," the eloquent Prime Minister Winston Churchill told the House of Commons. "I expect that the Battle of Britain is about to begin." He warned that on its outcome depended the future of the world. "Let us therefore brace ourselves to our duties, and so bear ourselves that, if the British Empire and its Commonwealth last for a thousand years, men will say 'This was their finest hour.'"

Hitler sent hundreds of bombers to rain devastation and death upon London and other British cities during the summer and fall of 1940. He was determined to force the British to surrender before a rearmed America could come to their aid.

The cheerful fortitude of the English during the Battle of Britain became legendary. Here Londoners sleep between the rails or on the platform of a subway station to escape German bombs.

A key factor in the Battle of Britain—and in the entire war against Germany—was that the British had acquired a device by which they could read Germany's most secret coded messages. This was a machine nicknamed "Ultra." Through Ultra, and helped by "radar"—a word made up of *ra*(dio) *d*(etecting) *a*(nd) *r*(anging)—the British often knew when the German bombers were coming and where they were headed. In this way they were able to move the small fleet of Royal Air Force (RAF) fighter planes from place to place to intercept the incoming bombers.

The secret that Great Britain had Ultra had to be kept at all cost. Winston Churchill, then, had to make a terrible choice. Should he alert the city of Coventry to the attack that Ultra had revealed was coming? Then the Germans could figure out that Britain had the decoding machine and would

change their codes. The British might lose their advantage for all the rest of the war. So Churchill told no one. Coventry's grand old cathedral, as well as thousands of houses and hundreds of people, was destroyed by masses of German bombs on the night of November 14, 1940.

With the help of Ultra the British defense against German bombers was increasingly successful. That fall Hitler decided that he had to postpone "Sea Lion," his plan to invade England across the channel. But throughout the winter the Germans continued the bombing of British cities.

World affairs and the presidential campaign of 1940. As the Battle of Britain raged, the United States held an election campaign. The Republican convention at Philadelphia in June surprised nearly everybody. Thomas E. Dewey, the racket-busting young district attorney of New York, had been the leading candidate. But an eleventh-hour drive brought to the front a man who was no politician and had never run for office.

Wendell L. Willkie was the bright, dynamic president of Commonwealth and Southern, a large public utilities corporation. Born in Indiana, where he attended the state university, he practiced law in Ohio before becoming a man of wealth and a powerful corporation lawyer in New York City. He had a warm, boyish appeal, and his trademark was a floppy lock of hair which marked his informal approach to life. He was persuasive in a very different way than FDR. Instead of FDR's cul-

To avoid giving away "Ultra," Churchill had to let the city of Coventry and its 14th-century cathedral be destroyed in 1940.

tivated Harvard accent, he spoke with the voice of the Middle West and for the values of self-made America. He so much disliked the New Deal emphasis on government aid that, though he had been a Democrat all his life, he finally became an outspoken Republican in 1940. He had made a name for himself fighting against the TVA, which he said unfairly competed with his company. Willkie was nominated on the sixth ballot. In a bid for the farm vote, the convention chose Senator McNary of Oregon to run for Vice-President.

In mid-July 1940 in Chicago, the Democrats did not surprise many when they chose FDR. But no one in American history had ever run for a third term as President. Secretary of Agriculture Henry A. Wallace of Iowa was picked as his running mate.

Although Willkie opposed FDR's New Deal policies, he shared the President's determination to aid Great Britain and to arm the United States against the aggressor. Foreign policy was not as much an issue in the election as the isolationists had hoped. Willkie also favored conscription, which Roosevelt had asked for in June. His support helped the measure to pass in September. This draft law provided for the registration of men between the ages of 21 and 35. No more than 900,000 were to be called into the service at any one time during peace, and the act was to expire on May 15, 1945.

The destroyer deal. Roosevelt tried every legal device to help the Allies secure supplies. To get around the law, he approved selling American military equipment to private companies that were buying for the British. But offering the goods on American shores was not enough. Italian and German submarines were sending these supplies to the bottom of the sea before they reached Britain. Winston Churchill asked for American destroyers to convoy these essential supplies, to hunt down and ward off the enemy submarines. "I must tell you," the British prime minister cabled to FDR in July 1940, "that in the long history of the world this is a thing to do now."

If he did as Churchill asked, Roosevelt feared that the isolationists would accuse him of bringing the United States into the war without the approval of Congress. Candidate Willkie assured him that he would not make the transfer of destroyers an issue in the campaign. Still, to protect himself against isolationist attacks, the President shrewdly devised a "Destroyer for Bases" deal. In September the President, as Commander in Chief of the Navy, transferred 50 old, but still useful destroyers to Great Britain. In exchange, we received the use of eight British naval bases all along the Atlantic coast from Newfoundland to British Guiana (Guyana). Great Britain promised that, if conquered, it would not surrender its fleet to Hitler.

The end of the campaign. As the election campaign wore on, Willkie, desperate for a winning issue, accused FDR of leading the nation into war. When Willkie became reckless in his attacks, Roosevelt became reckless in his responses. "I have said this before," he told American parents, "but I shall say it again and again and again: Your boys are not going to be sent into any foreign wars."

FDR won handily—though not as easily as in 1936. Willkie polled 45 percent of the popular vote, but he carried only ten states with 82 electoral votes to Roosevelt's 449. The precedent-breaking FDR had broken another precedent. He was the first person to be elected President for a third term.

Helping the British. Soon after the election, Roosevelt was faced with a dilemma. The British had run out of cash and were running out of ships. If the neutrality law was not quickly changed, the United States might not be able to get help to the British before they were defeated by the Nazis.

FDR showed his usual genius for compromise and for persuasion. He offered a clever plan called "Lend-Lease." We would "lend" or "lease" to the British—or any other country whose defense the President considered vital to the defense of the United States—whatever war supplies we could make. In that way the British would not need cash, and the hesitating members of Congress might be persuaded that we were getting value in return.

At the same time, in January 1941, in his annual message to Congress, President Roosevelt proclaimed the Four Freedoms. After the war he hoped for "a world founded upon four essential human freedoms"—freedom of speech, freedom of religion, freedom from want, and freedom from fear. Later that year, after a secret meeting with Churchill on a warship off the coast of Newfoundland, the two men issued the Atlantic Charter. This was an up-to-date version of Woodrow Wilson's Fourteen Points (p. 451).

SECTION REVIEW

1. Identify or explain: Maginot line, "phony war," Winston Churchill, Thomas E. Dewey, Wendell Willkie, "Destroyer for Bases" deal, Lend-Lease plan, Four Freedoms.
2. What lands fell to the Nazis in April-June 1940? Why was the Nazi advance called a blitzkrieg?
3. Discuss Billy Mitchell's ideas on air power. What was the outcome of his campaign?
4. What steps did Roosevelt take to rearm the nation?
5. How did Hitler try to conquer Great Britain? How did "Ultra" help defeat Hitler?
6. Describe Roosevelt's steps to supply the Allies before the United States declared war.

3. War comes to the United States

Step by step the United States moved closer to war. Of course Americans did not want to send our troops into battle. But how could that be avoided? Most of the world was in flames, and the aggressor nations were everywhere triumphant. Could we let them succeed?

The war spreads. President Roosevelt extended the zone "necessary to the defense of the United States" far out into the North Atlantic. Our troops occupied the island of Greenland in April 1941 and Iceland in July. On May 7 Congress authorized our government to seize 92 ships in our ports. These ships belonged to Germany and Italy and to countries like France, Holland, and Norway, which Hitler had conquered. German and Italian property in the country was "frozen" on June 14.

Eight days later Hitler made his great blunder. In his crazy belief that all battlefields were alike, and that blitzkrieg could conquer all, on June 22, 1941, only a year after conquering France, he suddenly invaded Russia. If he had studied history, he might have learned that more than a hundred years before, Napoleon had lost his empire in the same desperate gamble. Vast, frigid Russia embraced and paralyzed invaders. At first it seemed that Hitler might conquer Russia as quickly as France. But when the Germans were deep into Russia—only fifteen miles

Europe at the Peak of the Axis Power 1942

- Axis Nations
- ······ Farthest German Advance, December 1941
- Axis-Controlled Territory, November 1942
- Vichy-Controlled Territory
- ▲▲▲ Maginot Line
- Boundaries of 1937

ICELAND

ATLANTIC OCEAN

NORWAY SWEDEN FINLAND

NORTH SEA

BALTIC SEA

Oslo

Stockholm

Helsinki

Leningrad

ESTONIA

LATVIA

Moscow

USSR

NORTHERN IRELAND

IRELAND GREAT BRITAIN

DENMARK

Copenhagen

Memel

LITHUANIA

Danzig

EAST PRUSSIA

Smolensk

Voronezh

Coventry

London

NETHERLANDS

Berlin

Warsaw

POLAND

Kiev

UKRAINE

Stalingrad

Dunkirk BELGIUM

Brussels RHINELAND

LUXEMBOURG

SUDETENLAND

Prague

CZECHOSLOVAKIA

Rostov

Paris

FRANCE

Vienna

AUSTRIA

Budapest

HUNGARY

BESSARABIA

Odessa

Kerch

Bern

SWITZERLAND

Vichy

VICHY FRANCE

ROMANIA

Bucharest

Yalta

BLACK SEA

Lisbon

PORTUGAL

Madrid

SPAIN

CORSICA

Rome

ITALY

SARDINIA

YUGOSLAVIA

Belgrade

ALBANIA

BULGARIA

GREECE

Athens

Istanbul

TURKEY

SYRIA

IRAQ

MEDITERRANEAN

SPANISH MOROCCO

Oran

Algiers

SICILY

Tunis

SEA

CRETE

CYPRUS (BRITAIN)

LEBANON

MOROCCO (VICHY)

ALGERIA (VICHY)

TUNISIA (VICHY)

MALTA (BRITAIN)

0 ——— 600 Miles
0 ——— 600 Kilometers

---

from Moscow—the Russian winter arrived. The fingers of Nazi soldiers became numb. Frozen oil crippled the motors of tanks. The Nazis had to stop. They would finish off the Russian bear with the return of warm weather.

Meanwhile the German navy stepped up its submarine warfare in the Atlantic. The United States was already convoying American merchant ships. On September 1, 1940, we began to convoy British ships, too. Then on September 4, 1941, the United States destroyer *Greer* was attacked by a submarine. The President issued new orders for our ships to shoot German subs on sight. He had not told the American people that the *Greer* had

been following the Nazi sub and reporting its position to the British. FDR now ordered our merchant ships to be armed. He let them sail to the ports of the countries at war.

On October 17 the destroyer *Kearny* was hit and badly damaged with the loss of eleven lives. Then on October 31 the destroyer *Reuben James* was sunk by a German submarine with the loss of half its crew. In the Atlantic Ocean the United States had entered an undeclared war.

Trouble in the Pacific. Still, it was not Germany but Japan that plunged the United States into the Second World War. In 1940 Japan had become a partner of Nazi Germany and Fascist Italy. Japanese aggression was building what they called the Greater East Asia Co-Prosperity Sphere. This was a fancy name for Japanese domination of the Far East. German victories in Europe had encouraged the Japanese to try to seize all the poorly protected French and Dutch lands in Asia. Perhaps they could also take the British colonies. And China, too, was on their list.

To prepare for all this, the Japanese planned to seal off the Burma Road—the Allied supply route for China. Then China could not receive aid when the Japanese attacked. The Japanese managed to occupy bases in the north of French Indochina. And in July 1941 they took the bases in the south. The United States responded with an embargo on all trade with Japan.

In the discussions that followed between Japan and the United States, the one sticking point was China. The Japanese demanded that the United States cut off aid to the Chinese Generalissimo Chiang Kai-shek. Secretary Hull not only refused to abandon the Chinese but demanded that the Japanese withdraw from China at once. Faced with the choice of giving up their dreams of empire or going to war, the Japanese militarists chose war. In mid-October a more warlike government under General Hideki Tojo came to power in Japan.

The United States had broken Japan's diplomatic and naval codes with our own Ultra, which we called "Magic." Having read their dispatches, we knew that the Japanese would attack somewhere, but we did not know where. It appeared that they were aiming at Thailand, the Malay peninsula, and the Dutch East Indies (Indonesia)—perhaps even the Philippines. United States forces there were alerted to expect attack. But the Navy did not know that on November 26 a Japanese aircraft carrier force had left Japan headed for Pearl Harbor in Hawaii.

On December 7, 1941, the majority of the United States Navy's Pacific fleet was caught unawares by the Japanese attack on Pearl Harbor. This photograph was taken when the destroyer *Shaw* exploded.

Wide World Photos

The attack on Pearl Harbor. Just before 8 o'clock on Sunday morning, December 7, 1941, while Japanese diplomats were pretending to discuss peace at the White House, a fleet of 191 Japanese warplanes attacked American airfields at Pearl Harbor. Then they dropped bombs on the ships of the United States Navy anchored in the harbor. An hour later came a second fleet of 170 Japanese warplanes.

The attack was a perfect surprise—and the greatest military disaster in American history. One hundred and fifty American warplanes—the bulk of our air force in the Pacific—were destroyed on the ground. It was a better demonstration than Billy Mitchell could have imagined, and the fulfillment of his most dire prophecies. Of the 94 American ships in Pearl Harbor at the time, all the most powerful—the 8 battleships—were put out of action, together with 3 cruisers and 3 destroyers. More than 70 civilians and 2300 servicemen were killed.

The next day President Roosevelt appeared before Congress to announce that Japan's "Day of Infamy" had plunged us into war. Three days later Germany and Italy declared war on the United States.

SECTION REVIEW

1. Identify or explain: Greater East Asia Co-Prosperity Sphere, Chiang Kai-shek, Hideki Tojo, "Magic."
2. Locate: Burma Road, French Indochina, Thailand, Dutch East Indies, Pearl Harbor.
3. Name three ways in which the United States tried to help the Allies and strengthen the defense of the North Atlantic in 1940–1941.
4. What were the Japanese war goals in the Far East in 1941?
5. Describe the attack on Pearl Harbor.

CHAPTER REVIEW

MEETING OUR EARLIER SELVES

1. Some Americans praised the European dictators for putting the jobless back to work and getting the "trains to run on time." What values were they overlooking in their praise of the dictators?

2. How did Franklin D. Roosevelt's policies toward Latin America differ from those of Theodore Roosevelt?
3. Cite actions by the world democracies in 1933–1938 that tended to encourage aggressive acts by Germany, Italy, and Japan.
4. How did the United States shift from a position of strict neutrality in 1935 to active help for the Allies by October 1941? Cite specific actions by FDR and Congress.
5. Why did Hitler and Stalin sign a nonaggression pact in 1939? Why did it surprise the world?
6. Did the election of 1940 present a clear choice to the voters? Explain.
7. Why were Americans shocked by the attack on Pearl Harbor?

QUESTIONS FOR TODAY

1. How is the United States actively involved in world affairs today? How might the lessons of the 1930s explain this involvement?
2. Where in today's world are governments disregarding the rights of individuals? Cite examples. Are other nations intervening to stop these violations? Should they?

YOUR REGION IN HISTORY

1. Through interviews with elderly residents and research of local papers published in the 1930s, try to determine the extent of isolationist sentiment in your locality in the late 1930s.
2. Which candidate won the electoral votes of your state in 1940? What particular appeal did he have in your state?

SKILLS TO MAKE OUR PAST VIVID

1. Prepare a list of pro or con arguments that might have been heard in 1938 on the issue of isolationism for the United States.
2. Write a newspaper editorial defending or criticizing Franklin D. Roosevelt's decision to run for a third term in 1940.

CHAPTER 27

A world conflict

The United States now faced war on two fronts. For the first time in our history, this two-ocean nation was threatened by enemies on both oceans. And the enemies were everywhere triumphant. In the Pacific, Japan followed the Pearl Harbor surprise with attacks on the Philippines, Wake Island, Guam, the Dutch East Indies, Malaya, and Hong Kong. In the Atlantic, German submarines were disrupting our vital supply lines. The Nazis controlled western Europe from the Norwegian Sea to the Aegean. They had overrun the Balkans and stood at the gates of Moscow. Russia seemed ready to fall. The Italians had taken Libya. In southern Russia German forces were poised to cut through the Caucasus to Iran and Iraq, hoping to meet the Japanese army in India. For the Allies it would be a long road back.

1. Mobilizing for defense

The United States was not prepared for World War II, but it was in much better shape than in 1917. The draft had been started in 1940, and by the time of the attack on Pearl Harbor the army had grown to 1.6 million. A mammoth defense program had been launched to produce a torrent of guns, planes, tanks, and ships.

Converting to wartime. Before Pearl Harbor many industries, just emerging from the depression, were not eager to convert to wartime production. Labor expected a larger share of the new prosperity. In 1941 strikes multiplied fivefold.

With the United States entry into the war, the nation turned to the urgent task of becoming the "arsenal of democracy." Again, as in World War I, government agencies were created to focus the nation's life—the work of factories, farms, and mines, the research of industries and universities—on this great purpose.

Rationing was needed to be sure that everyone had a fair share, enough but not too much, of scarce items like heating oil, shoes, meat, sugar, and coffee. Every man, woman, and child received coupons for a share of rationed items. Gasoline, too, was rationed, not because it was in short supply, but to conserve rubber in tires, which was dangerously scarce. Americans were not used to this sort of regulation. Still, daily life in the United States was less regulated than in most other countries at war. Our own armed forces and those of our allies suddenly demanded all that the country could produce. Full employment replaced unemployment. Prosperity returned on the home front.

By 1942 American production equaled that of Germany, Italy, and Japan combined. And by 1944 it was *double* theirs. Even in ships, where the

...we here highly resolve that these dead shall not have died in vain...

REMEMBER DEC. 7th!

Make the SCRAP PILE GROW for the ARMY·NAVY and AIR FORCE "Do Your Part"

Stunned by Pearl Harbor, the most crushing disaster in our history, Americans vowed not to forget. They saved rubber, metal, and paper to be made into armaments and war supplies.

United States had failed badly in World War I, production was enormous. From July 1940 to August 1945, United States shipyards produced a tonnage equal to two-thirds the merchant marines of all the Allied nations combined. Before the war was over, American factories turned out 250,000 planes, 100,000 armored cars, 75,000 tanks, 650,000 pieces of artillery, and millions of tons of bombs, shells, and bullets.

Women in the armed forces. To fight the war it was necessary to build a huge army. Ultimately 15 million men and women served—10 million through the draft and 5 million as volunteers. Now all the services began to enlist women to perform all sorts of duties except those of combatants. In 1945 there were 258,000 women serving as Army WACS, Navy WAVES, Coast Guard SPARS, and women marines. Over 1000 women flew as civilians in the Women's Air Forces Service. They performed the hazardous job of ferrying military planes to Great Britain and other theaters of war. In 1979 the Air Force belatedly recognized these women pilots as war veterans who were entitled to all veterans' benefits.

Racial segregation and the war. Of the 15 million in the armed forces, about 1 million were blacks. They suffered less discrimination than in World War I. During World War II, the Marine Corps no longer kept them out, and before the war was over there were 17,000 black "Leathernecks." It became easier for qualified blacks to become officers. The Air Force trained black officers and pilots, and more than 80 won the Distinguished Flying Cross. Even the Navy, which before had taken blacks only for kitchen work and as waiters, began to open up. The example of Dorie Miller at Pearl Harbor may have helped. Even though only an untrained messman, he grabbed a machine gun during the attack and shot down four Japanese planes. For his heroism Dorie Miller received the Navy Cross.

Blacks served in every theater of the war. After the Japanese captured the Burma Road lifeline to China, black engineering battalions helped perform the incredible feat of building the Ledo Road. They pushed this new supply line through the steaming jungles and mountainous terrain of northern Burma.

During World War II, blue stars were hung in windows to indicate that family members were away in the armed forces. Gold stars were shown for those who died in the war. This woman had three sons in the service.

One black doctor made a major contribution to the war effort that helped save countless lives of soldiers of all colors. Charles Drew developed the blood bank for collecting and storing the blood plasma which injured fighting men so badly needed. Ironically, over the strong objection of Dr. Drew, the blood plasma of whites and blacks—for no scientific reason—was kept segregated.

The long shadow of the divided South remained. At first, most blacks, once more fighting for democracy, were still segregated in the services. Some progress was made during the course of the war in breaking down segregation. All shared equally the risks of battle. Death was no racist.

Newspaper correspondents noted that there was no color line in the foxholes. President Harry S Truman in 1946 appointed a national committee to recommend action to bring racial equality into the armed services. By 1949 the Army, Navy, and Air Force had abolished racial quotas. They finally realized, as *The Crisis* had said during World War II, "A jim crow army cannot fight for a free world." In the Korean War of 1950–1953 Americans of all races fought side by side.

Black Americans and the home front. One of the most effective fighters for racial equality at home was the black labor leader, A. Philip Randolph. Born in Florida, he attended the City College of New York, founded a magazine, and became active in the Socialist party. He created the Brotherhood of Sleeping Car Porters in 1925 and after a bitter fight won recognition from the Pullman Company, which manufactured and ran the sleeping cars on American railroads. The march on Washington that Randolph organized in 1941 threatened to bring 100,000 blacks to the capital to protest against racial discrimination in wartime hiring.

Under this pressure, even before the march could take place, President Roosevelt issued his historic Executive Order 8802. This outlawed any discrimination on the basis of race, creed, color, or national origin in the federal government or in defense factories. A Fair Employment Practices Committee (FEPC) was appointed to enforce this policy. Roosevelt's order did not end discrimination. But substantial progress was made in both industry and government.

As in World War I the flood of blacks from the South to northern cities for jobs in the booming war factories increased racial tensions. In 1943 there were race riots in a number of cities. The worst of them, in Detroit, left 25 blacks and 9 whites dead.

After World War I about 80 percent of all blacks in the United States still lived in the South. But by 1950 nearly half of them lived in other parts of the country. During the war, black Americans, like other Americans, were becoming more and more citified. Outside the South nearly all of them were living in cities. And in the South they, too, were moving off the farm. Along with other Americans, they were churning quickly and easily around the country. It was harder than ever for the old South to keep its old ways.

Japanese Americans are interned. Japanese and Americans of Japanese ancestry had long faced discrimination on the West Coast. After Pearl Harbor their situation became much worse. For no good reason other citizens blamed them for what the Japanese militarists had done and even began to suspect that they might be helping the enemy across the Pacific. Western politicians and frightened military men pressured FDR to remove them from the coastal states. President Roosevelt gave in. Early in 1942 under the excuse of national security, 110,000 Japanese Americans were rounded up. There was no evidence that these Americans were disloyal. They were forced to sell their homes and businesses on short notice and at sacrifice prices. They then were confined in camps, watched by armed guards, and treated as if they were dangerous. Not until after the presidential election of 1944 did the government change its policy and begin to release these innocent citizens.

Despite this humiliating treatment, 1200 men volunteered from the camps to serve in the United States armed forces. In a segregated unit these soldiers in the 442nd Regimental Combat Team fought heroically in Italy. Another Japanese American battalion was recruited from Hawaii, where there was no internment because there were so many Japanese.

In time of war it is harder than ever for a free nation to preserve its freedoms. Defending the country becomes a matter of life and death. Dissenters are open to the charge of being traitors. This is a true testing time of democracy. In World War II, except for the disgraceful treatment of Japanese Americans, the nation's record was far better than it had been in World War I.

Women and the war effort. The need for workers opened economic opportunities for women. Now, instead of being dissuaded from taking jobs as they had been during the depression, they were urged to go to work. Six million women joined the 12 million already in the labor force. They took on a wide variety of jobs and surprised the men who had said they were too weak and delicate to be lumberjacks, blast furnace operators, stevedores, or blacksmiths. They proved that they could handle all these jobs. And they also operated complex

Ordered to leave their homes and businesses on short notice by order of the United States government, bewildered Japanese Americans wait in Los Angeles for a train to take them to an internment camp.

Library of Congress

For some, the war opened new opportunities. These two women welders worked in a Connecticut factory in 1943.

machines in shipyards and airplane factories. Many for the first time could show their talents as doctors, dentists, chemists, and lawyers. "Rosie the Riveter" became an inspiration for all Americans.

Black women benefited, too. Before the war a greater percentage of black women worked than white. But they were generally restricted to low-paying jobs as domestic servants or farm laborers. When war came, they found more interesting and better-paying jobs. Nearly half a million black women who had worked as domestics left that work during the war to take positions in factories.

When World War II ended, it seemed that once again women might be forced to leave their jobs to make places for returning servicemen. But this time a much larger proportion was offered work in peacetime production. Prodded by war, the nation discovered its women and helped women discover themselves.

Raising money. War was expensive. From 1941 to 1945 the federal government spent $321 billion—twice as much as was spent during all the years from 1789 to 1941! Even during the depression, when people were alarmed by the size of the federal budget, the government had paid out only $8 billion each year.

Americans were paying the highest taxes in the nation's history. To prevent great fortunes from being made from the war, the federal income tax reached 94 percent for the highest incomes. Still, taxes brought in only 41 percent of the cost of the war. The rest was borrowed from banks, corporations, and individuals.

When everyone was employed, when wages were high but there were few goods to buy, prices went up rapidly. This was wartime inflation. But if people loaned their money to the government for war bonds, they would have less to spend on goods. So prices might be kept down. The government therefore ran a massive campaign and sold $100 billion in war bonds.

To prevent prices going sky-high, wages and prices were frozen by the government in 1942. In spite of these efforts, in the course of the war the cost of living went up 29 percent. Manufacturing wages went up 70 percent. Farmers earned more than ever before. The depression now seemed ancient history. The needs of a world at war had brought prosperity to Americans at home.

SECTION REVIEW

1. Identify or explain: rationing, WACS, WAVES, SPARS, Dorie Miller, Charles Drew, A. Philip Randolph, FEPC.

2. In what ways did each of the following contribute to the war effort: (a) industry, (b) women, (c) blacks?

3. What special gains, if any, did the war effort bring to women? to black Americans? to all civilians?

4. How were West Coast Japanese Americans treated during the war?

5. How did the federal government (a) raise money to pay for the war? (b) try to control inflation?

World War II, The Mediterranean, 1942-1944

←— Allied Forces

× Allied Victories

▨ Axis Nations

▢ Axis-Controlled Territory, 1942

▨ Vichy-Controlled Territory, 1942

```
0                          500 Miles
|----|----|----|----|----|
0                     500 Kilometers
```

2. "The end of the beginning"—1942

Soon after the United States entered the war, the Allies agreed that the first goal was to defeat the Germans. It was clear that if the Germans won in Europe, the United States would be left to face the aggressor nations all alone. So the United States postponed the offensive in the Pacific. There we would have to be satisfied with "active defense" until we had disposed of Mussolini and Hitler.

The battle of the Atlantic. The battle of the Atlantic was being lost to the "wolf packs" of German submarines. Month after month they were sending thousands of tons of Allied supplies to the bottom of the ocean. In May 1942, for example, 120 ships were sunk. Unless the submarines were beaten soon, Allied forces would be left without food or weapons, and the war would be lost. These critical months of the battle of the Atlantic were between mid-1942 and mid-1943. By good research (and good luck) the Allies invented radar and sonar in the nick of time. Airplanes using radar could locate and destroy submarines or direct armed ships to the attack. Navy ships using sonar— so(und) na(vigation) r(anging)—could hear distant propeller noises from subs. They could also locate their targets by echo-ranging. Sharp-sounding "pings" were sent out from a submarine destroyer, which found the enemy when these sounds rebounded off the submarine hulls.

Success in North Africa. While the battle of the Atlantic was being fought, the Allies began their first offensive moves in North Africa. German and Italian forces there were commanded by the "Desert

Fox," General Erwin Rommel, one of the most shrewd, daring, and resourceful commanders of the century. His forces had reached El Alamein, only 70 miles west of Alexandria, Egypt. They now threatened the Suez Canal and the oil fields of the Middle East. At this moment of danger the British were again aided by Ultra, their secret decoding machine. It revealed Rommel's plans for his crack *Afrika Korps*. With great sacrifices of men and weapons, the British managed to hold their lines and then began to build up for a counteroffensive.

Meanwhile the Russians were pressing the Allies to open a "Second Front" in Europe with a new invasion of the continent into lands held by the Axis powers. This would divert the enemy from their attack on the Russians. Instead the Allies decided in July 1942 to use their forces to clear Africa of the Germans and Italians. They would try to divert Rommel by invading and attacking North Africa from the west.

To strengthen Allied forces in Africa, British troops were withdrawn from other fronts and sent to Egypt. Using Ultra, the British were able to destroy German supply vessels. On October 23, General Bernard Montgomery led the British Eighth Army in the attack. At first Rommel's lines held. Then, on November 4, Montgomery's army broke through. They began chasing Rommel's Afrika Korps, which had a reputation for being unbeatable. Within a week Hitler had the news that his precious Afrika Korps was in disarray. Rommel's failure to take Egypt had cost him 500 tanks, 400 guns, and 60,000 men.

At this strategic moment, United States and British forces struck their stunning surprise blow. On November 8, 1942, a huge Allied force, guarded by 350 warships, landed from 500 transports onto the west coast of Africa. Most of these had come from Great Britain, but 101 ships carrying 35,000 soldiers had crossed the 3000 miles from the United States. This gigantic operation had been planned, equipped, and launched in only four months.

The Allied landing was an immediate success. At the time, that area was ruled by the "Vichy" French, who had been conquered and were helping the Nazis. They had that name because the town of Vichy in central France was the new capital of their puppet government. But now the Vichy French in North Africa quickly sided with the Allies. Within three days all of North Africa to the borders of

Robert Capa/Magnum

Robert Capa, one of the top photographers of World War II, caught this picture of a United States paratrooper in full battle dress in North Africa.

Tunisia was in Allied hands. The Germans fleeing from the west had managed ahead of the Allies to reach Tunisia, where they met the remnants of Rommel's Afrika Korps. There the Nazis gathered and regrouped their forces hoping to counterattack.

When Montgomery's army arrived at the borders of Tunisia, the two Allied forces united to surround the Germans. So 1942 ended with Tunisia firmly held by a still-dangerous Axis force and the land around them held by the Allies.

In November 1942 the Russians had gone on the counteroffensive. After some of the bloodiest fighting of the war, they broke the siege of Stalingrad and surrounded an entire German army. After that army was captured in February 1943, the Russians swept rapidly westward. Meanwhile in January the siege of Leningrad had ended. The tide was beginning to turn.

World War II and Latin America. The "Good Neighbor policy" paid dividends in World War II. In 1939, by the Declaration of Panama, an Inter-American Conference drew a 300-mile offshore defense zone around the whole hemisphere south of Canada. The warring nations were warned to avoid combat within this zone. At a conference of foreign ministers of the Latin American countries in January 1942, twenty-one of them agreed to break off diplomatic relations with Nazi Germany and its Fascist allies.

Some of them went further. Nine Caribbean republics declared war on the German-Italian-Japanese Axis in December 1941. Mexico and Brazil joined them in 1942. All the New World nations finally declared war on the Axis. Pro-Fascist Argentina did not join the Allies until almost the end of the war.

The Latin American nations provided vital war materials—rubber, quinine, tin—along with naval and air bases. Brazil sent troops to Europe, and Mexico had an air squadron in the Pacific. The Mexican and Cuban navies patrolled the Caribbean for German subs. In return, the United States gave military equipment and loans.

Active defense in the Pacific. In the Pacific for months after Pearl Harbor the Japanese knew nothing but success. By March 1942 they controlled all the waters from the Gilbert and Solomon islands to the mainland of Asia, a distance of 4500 miles. They held every island within that area except for the southern part of New Guinea and the Bataan peninsula of Luzon in the Philippines where a doomed American force bravely fought on until May 1942. The Japanese were masters of the Malay peninsula, the British bastion of Singapore, and Thailand. They had invaded Burma. During all this fighting, the Japanese destroyed their enemies' navies while they themselves lost no ship larger than a destroyer.

The Allies had to take steps at once to prevent their being knocked out of the Pacific before they

United Press International Photo

Chinese troops cross a swaying bamboo bridge on the way to North Burma. They joined American troops there to fight the Japanese.

could finish off the Nazis. They decided on a policy of more active defense. They had to hold what little remained to them in the Pacific. Otherwise they would not have bases to start from when they finally went on the offensive. They had to be sure to keep Hawaii and Samoa, and of course they needed to protect the sea lanes from the United States to the great stronghold of Australia. Fortunately, the Japanese had fewer submarines than the Germans and tended to use them against warships, so Allied supply convoys were seldom attacked.

The raid on Tokyo. By great good luck the United States aircraft carriers had happened to be at sea when the Japanese hit Pearl Harbor. During this period of active defense the Navy used them for nuisance raids on Wake and other Japanese-held islands. Then, on April 18, 1942, General James B. Doolittle led B-25s launched from a carrier to attack Tokyo. This first raid on the Japanese capital did little real damage to the city. But it gave the Japanese people a hint of what was to come. And it lifted American morale.

After Doolittle's raid, the Japanese decided to establish a new line—a "defensive perimeter"—running from the Aleutian Islands in the north, through Midway, Wake, the Marshalls, the Gilberts, Fiji, and Samoa to Port Moresby in New Guinea and to Tulagi in the Solomons. At this line they hoped to stop air raids like the one on Tokyo. They also planned to disrupt the sea transport between the United States and Australia. Planes would patrol the waters between the scattered islands. The Japanese navy would be stationed near the center, ready to be rushed wherever needed. This would help them "save face." It was also a symptom of what a Japanese admiral later called the "victory disease."

The Battle of the Coral Sea. The skilled Japanese Admiral Yamamoto hoped to bring on a major sea battle with the Allied Pacific Fleet in 1942. Unless that fleet was destroyed, he feared that by the next year the Allies would be strong enough to launch an offensive against Japan.

Japanese Conquests in Far East to August 1942

Japanese-Controlled Territory

× Allied Victories

The first collision between the two fleets occurred in the Battle of the Coral Sea, May 7 and 8, 1942. This historic naval battle showed how modern science had changed war. For the first time in history in a great naval encounter, no ship on either side was within sight of an opposing ship. Now it was aircraft carrier against aircraft carrier.

During the battle both sides made mistakes, and both suffered heavy losses. The Japanese sank the United States carrier *Lexington*. For them this made it a "tactical" victory. "Tactics" had to do with winning the box score in a particular battle. But it was a "strategic" success for the United States. "Strategy" (from the Greek word for "general") had to do with the big picture and the war as a whole. To gain their advantage in the Coral Sea, the Japanese had to recall their invasion force headed for Port Moresby. So they were forced to stop their drive toward Australia.

The Battle of Midway. From the Japanese point of view the island of Midway was the key to the whole perimeter scheme. From there they could bomb Pearl Harbor and make it useless as an offensive base for our Pacific Fleet.

Admiral Yamamoto intended to force a showdown at Midway with the American Pacific Fleet of Admiral Nimitz, which was still suffering from the disaster inflicted by the Japanese on December 7. But the United States had the advantage of the "Magic" decoder. Our forces knew where the Japanese were going. So they were ready and waiting when the Japanese struck at Midway on June 4, 1942. During the battle that followed, United States carrier planes sank four of Japan's best carriers and destroyed some of their most skilled air groups. The United States lost one carrier, but handed Japan its first great naval defeat.

For the first time in World War II, the balance of naval power in the Pacific had now shifted to the United States. In this one decisive battle the whole strategic situation in the Pacific was transformed. The Japanese had to abandon their plans for taking Midway, Fiji, and Samoa.

The battle for Guadalcanal. The Japanese decided to risk one more try to take Port Moresby in New Guinea. To protect that gamble they seized Guadalcanal, one of the nearby Solomon Islands, and established an air base there. Under the Allied

policy of active defense, this could not be allowed. Guadalcanal was the stepping stone that the Allies needed for returning to the Philippines and finally for invading Japan itself.

The Allied attack on the position the Japanese were building on Guadalcanal was nicknamed "Shoestring." It had to be undertaken with very little in the way of men or equipment because at that same moment forces and supplies were being gathered for the invasion of North Africa. On August 7, 1942, some 20,000 marines were landed on Guadalcanal and the neighboring island of Tulagi. These landings were followed, in the early morning hours of August 9, by the Battle of Savo Island. There a Japanese cruiser force sank four out of the five United States and Australian heavy cruisers that were protecting our transports unloading on Guadalcanal. This terrible defeat forced the withdrawal of the transports, which left the marines short of supplies.

War in the steaming jungles of Guadalcanal was old-fashioned hand-to-hand fighting. There the alert dodging of an enemy's knife could mean life instead of death. The marines had been trained for this sort of combat. They never were put to a harder test. The Allied marines lived up to their reputation for heroism. On land, this may have been the only time the Japanese were ever outfought by an enemy they met on equal terms. Finally the beaten Japanese evacuated the island on February 9, 1943. At heavy cost of pain and life, it was there at Guadalcanal that the Japanese advance was finally stopped.

The end of the beginning. Early in January 1943 President Roosevelt and Prime Minister Churchill met at Casablanca in Morocco to plan future operations. There had been a striking improvement in the military outlook since their last meeting a year before. The Soviets had won the Battle of Stalingrad and were beginning to turn the tide in Russia. Egypt had been saved and Morocco, Libya, and Algeria taken for the Allies. Guadalcanal would soon be taken from Japan. The RAF and the United States Eighth Air Force were bombing Germany with deadly accuracy and increasing frequency.

"Now, this is not the end," Churchill said. "It is not even the beginning of the end. But it is, perhaps, the end of the beginning."

SECTION REVIEW

1. Identify: Erwin Rommel, Afrika Korps, Bernard Montgomery, Vichy French, James Doolittle, Admiral Yamamoto, Chester Nimitz.
2. Locate: El Alamein, Tunisia, Stalingrad, Midway, Wake, Marshall Islands, Samoa, Port Moresby, Solomon Islands, Coral Sea, Guadalcanal, Savo Island, Casablanca.
3. What inventions helped the Allies fight the "battle of the Atlantic"?
4. What successes in 1942 gave the Allies hope of winning the war?
5. Describe the Allied strategy in the Pacific in 1942.
6. What was the chief result of the battle (a) of the Coral Sea? (b) of Midway? (c) for Guadalcanal?

3. Victory in Europe

The Allies were divided on where they should go after they seized Tunisia as they confidently expected to do. At Casablanca the Americans argued for an invasion of France in 1943, but again the British resisted. They wanted first to free the Mediterranean completely by taking Sicily and then knocking Italy out of the war. The British view finally prevailed. The Allies also agreed that they could now begin to take the offensive in the Pacific. Most important, the Allies announced that they would not stop fighting until they had won "unconditional surrender" from all their enemies. Some people thought this was a strategic error and might prolong the war.

The fall of Tunisia. The Axis army in Tunisia was now trapped. They tried to fly out their best troops, and some did escape that way. But then the Allied bombers caught their transport planes on the ground and destroyed them. On March 7, 1943, Rommel was recalled to Germany, where Hitler confessed that Africa was lost. When Rommel asked him if he still believed that total victory was possible, Hitler replied, "I know it is necessary to make peace with one side or the other [Russia or the Western powers], but no one will make peace with me."

On May 7, 1943, General von Arnim surrendered the Axis forces in Tunisia. He and sixteen other generals were taken prisoner along with a quarter-million Axis troops, including some of Germany's best-trained and best-armed soldiers. This victory was as dramatic and as decisive as Stalingrad. Italian morale was destroyed, and Great Britain's Mediterranean lifeline was opened again. Now the way was prepared to act on the Allies' secret decision to invade Italy from the south.

The battle in Italy. On the morning of July 10, 1943, swiftly and suddenly 250,000 American and British troops landed along 150 miles of Sicilian coastline. It was the greatest amphibious operation of all time. Never before had so many troops been landed at once for a single attack. Unfortunately, because the plan was faulty, the German and Italian forces were allowed to escape from the island of Sicily to the mainland of Italy.

But the Italians had now had enough of war. Mussolini was forced to resign, and a new government was installed. At the end of July the Italians began to put out peace feelers to the Allies. After much bargaining, an armistice was signed on September 3 with Italian forces. But during those long negotiations the Nazis rushed reinforcements to Italy to hold the country till the bitter end.

When British and American troops landed on the toe of Italy, they ran into fierce German resistance. Not until June 4, 1944, did the Allies finally enter Rome. Still the Germans held on. For the United States this invasion of Italy was one of the deadliest campaigns in the war. Seventy thousand Americans were killed. By their courage and that of the British, Poles, and other Allied troops, they tied up 23 German divisions and weakened the Nazis everywhere else.

The air war. While the Allies were making their slow way toward the invasion of France in 1944, Germany was already being invaded by air.

The lightning strike of air power at Pearl Harbor had shocked Americans into seeing that the world faced a new kind of war. Now the battlefield was everywhere. There was no place where civilians could hide from the airborne terror. Warplanes sometimes flew so high they could not be seen and could barely be heard, to strike at homes and factories.

Robert Capa took this picture of the jubilant citizens of a small Sicilian town in 1943 welcoming the American troops who have liberated them. Capa was killed covering the Vietnam War.

The British began bombing Germany in 1941 when the RAF dropped 46,000 tons of bombs on enemy targets. British bombers flew over Germany at night and "saturation" bombed whole areas. Incendiary bombs set fire to entire cities. Since these attacking bombers could not be seen from the ground, British losses were not heavy. They hoped that by destroying cities, disorganizing labor, and shattering civilian morale, they could force the Nazis to surrender even before the Nazi armies were conquered.

The United States Army Air Force made its first raid on Germany in August 1942. It pursued another plan—"pinpoint" attacks in daylight.

When bombers could see their targets, they could focus their bombs on the crucial factories and could report whether they had hit their targets. At the same time the Germans could see the approaching planes. The Americans thought their B-17 bombers—called "Flying Fortresses" because they bristled with so many machine guns—were so heavily defended that the Germans could not deal with them. But soon German fighters were downing American bombers in disastrous numbers. In response, the United States developed new long-range fighter planes to protect the bombers and so continued their precision bombing. Soon the skies of Germany were raining bombs day and night.

United Press International Photo

This American B-17 "Flying Fortress" bomber has just made a direct hit on a huge aircraft plant in East Prussia where the Germans had thought they were outside the Allied bombing range.

The Germans responded with their V-1 flying bombs and their even more terrifying V-2 rockets, which dropped suddenly and silently from the sky carrying death-dealing one-ton bombs. Never before in the history of warfare was there so much suffering by civilians. But bombing did not end the war. German factories continued to produce airplanes and other war machines in large numbers. The military effect of Allied bombing was to force the Nazis to use up their energies on fighter planes and antiaircraft weapons for their own defense. And this drained away the Nazi power to attack.

Allied planes killed nearly a third of a million Germans and destroyed 5 million homes. Still, bombing did not have a substantial effect on the German war effort until 1944. Then the bombs were concentrated on specific war industries—airplane, tank, truck, and ball-bearing factories, oil and gas production. Since Germany had dispersed its factories to defend against air attack, the Allied attack on railroads and highways helped paralyze Nazi war production.

D-Day in France. The United States and Great Britain secretly agreed that in June 1944 they would invade France by landings across the English Channel. This was the most important—and the best-kept—secret of the war. The invasion would be directed by the American General Dwight D. Eisenhower, who became Supreme Commander of the Allied Forces in Western Europe. The Allies intended at the same time to keep maximum pressure on Italy and to invade the south of France.

The cross-channel invasion was a dangerous maneuver, for the Germans had been building up their forces to meet an expected attack. They had had four years to construct their coastal fortifications. They had brought 58 divisions to France. But the Allies could pick the time and place to attack. Allied bombings had already brought chaos to the Nazi transportation system. And the Allied invaders could count on aid from the French Resistance, men and women who at great risk gave secret help to the Allies.

To mislead the Nazis, the Allies skillfully led the Germans to believe that the attack would come in the area of Calais at the narrowest part of the English Channel. By radio broadcasts, arranged so that the Nazis would get the message, they gave the Germans the impression that a great invasion force was prepared to land there.

During the night of June 5 on the orders of General Eisenhower, a mighty force of 600 warships and 4000 supporting craft carrying 176,000 men moved toward the coast of Normandy. They were protected by an air cover of 11,000 planes. At 5:30 A.M. the navy began its bombardment of the coast of Normandy. At 6:30 A.M. the first troops hit the beach between the mouth of the Seine River and Cherbourg. The Allies had achieved tactical surprise, and despite some trouble spots the initial landings were a success.

The German generals now wanted to throw all their armored forces—the German name was "Panzer," meaning armor—against the invaders in one great counter stroke. But Hitler, who thought that he was wiser than his generals, overruled them. He still was sure that the main invasion would come at Calais. So Rommel, the army group commander on the spot, was forced to hold

General "Ike" Eisenhower gives a pep talk to a group of paratroopers about to be dropped into France on D-Day. The men's faces are darkened to lessen their chances of being seen.

United Press International Photo

back the Panzer divisions. The Allied men, armor, and supplies managed to reach shore and establish a secure beachhead. After the first few days the invading force was out of danger. It was one of the greatest Allied achievements of the war. In a single week the Allies had landed 326,000 men, 50,000 vehicles, and 100,000 tons of supplies.

The Allies on the move. The battle of the Normandy invasion lasted from June 6 to July 24, 1944. At the end of that time, the Allies had landed more than a million men and controlled 1500 square miles of Normandy and Brittany. The breakthrough and the beginning of the battle for France came on July 25 when General George Patton's Third Army struck hard at the Germans. Soon thousands of Patton's tanks were pouring through. The FFI (French Forces of the Interior—the Resistance) now came out into the open to aid the Allies. Up from the Mediterranean came the United States Seventh Army under General A. M. Patch to join the eastward-moving Allied troops. Paris was liberated on August 25, Brussels and Antwerp a few days later. Within six weeks after the breakthrough all France had been cleared of Germans. And the Germans had lost nearly half a million men and untold amounts of machinery and material.

Units of General Courtney Hodges's First Army moved onto the "sacred soil" of Hitler's "unbeatable" Thousand Year Reich on September 12, 1944. Soon six Allied armies with 3 million men were facing the powerful Siegfried line of fortifications that extended the whole length of Germany's western border.

Meanwhile from the east, huge Soviet armies were hastening toward the German border. A great Russian offensive had speedily swept 460 miles across the Ukraine and Poland to the gates of Warsaw. There, unfortunately, the Russians stopped. This gave the Germans time to crush a heroic revolt of the Polish underground in the city.

When the Russians moved toward the south, Romania and Bulgaria surrendered quickly. On October 20 the Russians reached Belgrade. In December at Budapest the Germans dug in and put up stubborn resistance.

On the western front, meanwhile, the Allies were once again divided over their strategy. Should they strike straight for Berlin, or instead advance on a broad front? One try at the sudden-thrust strategy

Trucks, guns, tons of equipment and thousands of men are unloaded on the beachhead at Normandy as barrage balloons float overhead.

was an attempt to jump the river-barriers of the Meuse, the Waal, and the lower Rhine with three airborne divisions. One British officer called it "a bridge too far." And so it proved. When this failed, the Allies settled for the slower strategy.

The election of 1944. In the United States, despite the war-to-the-death against totalitarian powers, politics continued as usual. During the summer that saw the liberation of France, Franklin D. Roosevelt was unanimously nominated for his fourth term as President. He said he only wanted to go home to Hyde Park, "But as a good soldier . . . I will accept and serve." The strains of

the Presidency in wartime had taken their toll on FDR. How long could he bear up?

The Vice-Presidency was more important than ever before. At the Democratic convention the real battle was over FDR's running mate. In the end the convention named Senator Harry S Truman of Missouri. He had begun his career as a machine-politician in Kansas City. But he made a name for himself in the Senate as the head of a committee looking into defense contracts.

Wendell Willkie hoped once again to win the nomination of the Republican party. Now his liberal international views troubled many of the party leaders. Governor Thomas E. Dewey of New York soundly defeated him in the Wisconsin primary. Then Willkie withdrew from the race, and Dewey was nominated as the Republican candidate. Conservative Governor John W. Bricker of Ohio was his running mate.

On November 7 the nation gave President Roosevelt a decisive victory. He won by 3.6 million votes and by 432 to 99 in the electoral college. The Democrats also won substantial majorities in both houses of Congress. Just as during the Civil War, when Abraham Lincoln was re-elected, the nation had decided "not to change horses in the middle of the stream."

The Battle of the Bulge. On December 16, 1944, the Germans made a final desperate bid to break the Allies. With two armies they struck a weakly held front in the Ardennes district of France intending to sweep through and seize Antwerp, the main Allied base. This would have cut the Allied army in two and left the northern half without access to its supply harbor. The German attack was favored by foul weather, which grounded Allied planes. Heavily wooded terrain screened the Nazi movements and gave them the advantage of surprise over the unwary Allies.

The German attack got off to a good start. Spearheaded by Panzer divisions of heavily armored vehicles, they penetrated 60 miles, almost to the Meuse River, creating a large "bulge" in the Allied lines. Finally they were stopped by the armies of Patton and Montgomery. There at the vital rail junction and road center of Bastogne, the 101st Airborne Division under General McAuliffe made its heroic stand. When he was surrounded by the Germans and asked to surrender, McAuliffe made his historic one-word reply—"Nuts!" McAuliffe's 101st disrupted the German timetable, halted the attack, and held out until relieved by the Third Army. By the end of January the Bulge was "pinched off" and the Germans were forced back to their Siegfried line. United States losses were heavy, but the "Battle of the Bulge" had cost the dwindling Nazis 120,000 of their best remaining men.

Conferring at Yalta. In February 1945, when the defeat of the Nazis appeared to be in sight, President Roosevelt met with the other Allied leaders, British Prime Minister Churchill and Russian dictator Josef Stalin. At Yalta, a Russian summer resort on the Black Sea, they would agree on their plans for the Nazi surrender. Germany was to be taken apart. Once again, the Germans would have to pay enormous "reparations."

Churchill, Roosevelt, and Stalin, the leaders of "the Big Three," pose for photographers in a courtyard during their important meetings at the Russian summer resort of Yalta. FDR, tired and haggard, was to die only two months later.

Stalin was a tough and clever bargainer. At first he demanded that Poland be put under a Communist puppet government. When Roosevelt and Churchill objected, Stalin promised to let the Polish people choose their government by free elections. Then, arguing that the Soviet Union had been the most devastated of the Allies, he made them agree to give Russia half of all the German reparations.

Stalin promised to declare war against Japan soon after the defeat of Germany and said that when the new United Nations was organized, the Soviets would join. In return the Soviets gained some strategic Japanese islands. Stalin would also be allowed to conquer Outer Mongolia—a vast area twice the size of Texas—on the Russian border in central Asia. At the same time, Stalin solemnly promised not to interfere in the countries along the Russian border in Eastern Europe. He said he would let the people of Poland, Czechoslovakia, Hungary, Romania, and Bulgaria elect their own governments.

Too soon the democratic leaders would discover what Stalin's promises were worth. Looking back, some historians say that Roosevelt and Churchill should have known better than to believe anything Stalin said. Again and again the Communist leaders had called democracy a fraud. But at the time, the British and American leaders did not have much choice. The Soviet armies still had unrivaled power in Eastern Europe. The Western powers thought they desperately needed the help of those armies to finish off the Nazis and Japanese. All they were able to demand from their Russian ally was promises. They felt lucky even to get those! For the next twenty years the free world would pay the price for Stalin's lies.

The failure to take Berlin. Now the Allies closed in for the kill. On March 7, 1945, the First Army crossed the Rhine bridge at Remagen. Crossings were also soon made at other locations, and by the first week of April all the Allied armies were across the river. Caught between the Russian Communist armies speeding westward and the Anglo-Americans speeding eastward, German resistance was now rapidly collapsing.

World War II, European Theater, 1944-1945

☐ Axis-Controlled Territory 1942

← Allied Forces

✕ Allied Victories

| 0   400 Miles |
| 0   400 Kilometers |

4. RUSSIAN AND AMERICAN TROOPS MEET AT THE ELBE, APRIL 25, 1945

5. GERMANS SIGN SURRENDER AT REIMS, MAY 7, 1945

1. D-DAY, JUNE 6, 1944

2. PARIS LIBERATED, AUG. 25, 1944

3. BATTLE OF THE BULGE, DEC. 16-26, 1944

| 0   150 Miles |
| 0   150 Kilometers |

General Dwight D. "Ike" Eisenhower, who had successfully directed the invasion of Europe, now faced a decision that would shape the future of Europe. If he wanted, he could quickly move his forces into Berlin, the capital of Germany, and also into Prague, the capital of Czechoslovakia. In Anglo-American hands, these capitals would be strongholds to help the democracies enforce Stalin's promise to let the people of Eastern Europe choose their own governments.

Or, General Eisenhower could wait to mop up the German troops behind his own lines—meanwhile letting the Russians overrun more of Eastern Europe and consolidate their positions in Berlin and Prague. But in Communist hands, those capitals would help the Russians to foist their dictatorship on all the surrounding peoples. The Russians could then make the border countries—Poland, Czechoslovakia, Hungary, Romania, and Bulgaria—into a group of "satellites" revolving around Moscow.

The farsighted Winston Churchill saw this threat. "I deem it highly important," he warned General Eisenhower, "that we should shake hands with the Russians as far to the east as possible." But Eisenhower was anxious to avoid the loss of more American soldiers, and FDR did not interfere. Instead of rushing the democratic forces eastward, Ike decided to stop 50 miles west of Berlin at the River Elbe. Stalin applauded this fateful decision, for now both Berlin and Prague were left to the Russians.

Until the last minute, Churchill kept trying to persuade President Roosevelt to push speedily on to Berlin and Prague. The new "mortal danger to the free world," he said, was our so-called "ally," Russia. How tragic, after the long struggle against the Nazi tyranny, to hand over half of Europe to a Communist tyranny!

The death of Roosevelt. Before Churchill's wisdom could prevail in Washington, President Roosevelt was dead. Worn down by wartime burdens, he had gone for a rest to Warm Springs, Georgia, where he often went for treatment of his paralyzed legs. On April 12, 1945, he complained of a headache, and within minutes a blood vessel had burst in his brain. The valiant, cheerful leader, who had helped raise his fellow Americans from the depth of the Great Depression and who had organized their battle against Nazi barbarism, did not live to have the satisfaction of receiving the Nazi surrender.

The nation grieved as it had grieved for few Americans since Lincoln. Men and women wept in their offices, at home, and in the streets. They felt that they had lost not only a national leader but a personal friend.

Germany surrenders. Russian and American troops met at the Elbe on April 25. Other Russian troops were fighting their way from house to house through the heaps of rubble of Berlin. Hitler committed suicide in Berlin. Meanwhile his old henchman Mussolini had been captured by Italian partisans and executed. To show their contempt for the strutting dictator who had brought their beautiful land to ruins, they hung up Mussolini's body by the heels for all to see. On May 8, 1945, the Germans signed terms of unconditional surrender at General Eisenhower's headquarters in the French city of Reims. The day was celebrated joyously in the victorious countries as V-E (Victory in Europe) Day.

Robert Capa photographed these German civilians fleeing from their farmhouse in 1945 after it was seized by American paratroopers and then shelled by the German army.

Robert Capa/Magnum

SECTION REVIEW

1. Identify: Flying Fortresses, V-1 and V-2 missiles, Dwight Eisenhower, George Patton, FFI, A. M. Patch, Courtney Hodges, Siegfried line, Harry Truman, Thomas Dewey, A. C. McAuliffe, V-E Day.

2. Locate: Sicily, Calais, Normandy, Cherbourg, Brittany, Ardennes, Bastogne, Yalta, Remagen, Berlin, Prague, Elbe.

3. What were the chief results of (a) the Allied victory in North Africa? (b) the Italian campaign?

4. How did the British air attacks on Germany differ from those by the American planes?

5. How did Germany's situation change between June and November 1944?

6. What was the importance of the Battle of the Bulge?

7. What agreements were made at Yalta? Why did it seem necessary to make them?

8. Where did the Anglo-American and Russian armies meet? Why was this meeting line significant?

4. The war in the Pacific

"The victory is but half won," President Truman warned. "The West is free but the East is still in bondage. When the last Japanese division has surrendered unconditionally, only then will our fighting job be done."

The struggle for the islands. After the fall of Guadalcanal in February 1943, a two-year struggle began to regain other islands and to prepare for the final attack on the Japanese homeland. General Douglas MacArthur and his troops would advance through the islands of the western Pacific from New Guinea to Mindanao in the Philippines. At the same time the navy and marines would have to cross the central Pacific in a series of amphibious operations by way of the Gilbert, Marshall, and Mariana islands. So long as the Japanese held these central Pacific islands, their airplanes could attack anything that moved along the New Guinea-Mindanao path of General MacArthur. Both advances had to succeed together.

United Press International Photo

General MacArthur, brilliant leader of the army in the Pacific, was generous in victory.

Japan fiercely resisted every landing and stubbornly contested every inch of ground. Our losses were high in the capture of Tarawa in the Gilberts in November 1943, and of Kwajalein and other islands in the Marshalls and of Saipan in the Marianas in February 1944. The tiny island of Iwo Jima was the scene of some of our heaviest losses and some of the most memorable American heroism. After a month of desperate fighting (February-March 1945), at the frightful cost of 5000 dead, the marines planted the American flag there on Mount Suribachi. With the capture of Iwo Jima and Okinawa (April-June 1945), where 11,000 more troops died, we were within striking distance of the Japanese homeland. Victory was in sight.

The return to the Philippines. Meanwhile in the southwest Pacific in a series of brilliant campaigns,

General MacArthur's forces were leap-frogging toward the Philippines. Two years before, when MacArthur had left the Philippines and Allied prospects were dim, he had promised, "I shall return!" Now, on October 20, 1944, he fulfilled his promise when the Americans swarmed ashore at Leyte Island on the southeast tip of the archipelago. Again and again the Japanese vainly tried to land reinforcements on Leyte.

Before the Allies could clinch their victory in the Pacific, they would have to fight the greatest sea battle of all time. They would have to end, once and for all, the Japanese navy's ability to keep the Allies off their home islands. In the Battle of Leyte Gulf on October 23–25, the Japanese were so badly defeated that their navy was knocked out of the war.

American troops were now free to land on the main Philippine island of Luzon. The first troops went ashore on January 9, 1945, and were followed by later waves. They fought toward Manila from the north and the south. When they reached the city, the Japanese stood firm. Each house became a fortress for a few Japanese soldiers who gave their lives to delay the American advance. Finally on March 9, after fierce street fighting the last Japanese soldier in the city gave up. During the battle for Manila, MacArthur declared the Commonwealth of the Philippines to be reestablished. "My country has kept the faith," he said; "your capital city, cruelly punished though it be, has regained its rightful place—citadel of democracy in the East."

On July 4, 1946, (fulfilling the promise made by the McDuffie Act back in 1934) the Republic of the Philippines was proclaimed independent. In the following March, a 99-year agreement was signed, giving the United States military and naval bases in the islands.

Splitting the atom. Upon the death of President Roosevelt in April 1945, the tremendous task of finishing the war and planning the peace suddenly fell to the courageous, peppery new President, Harry S Truman. He was a man of decision,

American infantry wade ashore from amphibious landing craft onto Leyte Island in the Philippines. The jungle still smolders from the pre-attack naval and air bombardment.

United Press International Photo

destined to make some of the most fateful decisions in modern history. And he was prepared for great decisions. Ever since he was a young man, he had been reading books of history. He especially admired President Jackson and President Lincoln. He knew how earlier American Presidents had shaped the future. When he took his oath of office, he felt overwhelmed, and he asked the nation to pray for him.

His first great decision was on a subject so secret that even as Vice-President he had not heard of it. It concerned the colossal American project that had already nearly succeeded—to build an atomic bomb. "Atom" was a word of Greek origin that meant something unbreakable. It was believed to be the smallest possible unit of matter. To create a bomb by the splitting of tiny atoms would be the most gigantic, most costly single scientific effort of the war. This startling achievement would change the relations between all nations for decades to come.

Those who made the American bomb possible (in addition to many American scientists) were a "Who's Who" of world science. From Germany came the greatest physicist of the age, Albert Einstein. Because he was a Jew, the Nazis had taken away his German citizenship and seized his property. From Italy, as a refugee from Mussolini, came the brilliant Enrico Fermi, who was one of the first to propose an atomic bomb as a practical possibility. Scientists, engineers, and mathematicians came also from Hungary, Austria, Denmark, and Czechoslovakia—refugees from all the enslaved parts of Europe. The barbarism of the enemies had brought together in the United States the greatest scientific minds of the age.

To build an atomic bomb certain theoretical questions first had to be answered. Was it really possible to achieve "the controlled release of atomic energy"? If it was possible to break the atom, and create a "chain reaction," then an enormous amount of energy would be released even from one atom. If a chain reaction could be started, then when one atom was split it would split the other atoms touching it, and a fantastic blast of energy would suddenly explode. But could it be done? And if a chain reaction was started, could it be controlled so that one exploding atom would not destroy the world? These were the two great practical questions.

The answer came at 3:25 on the afternoon of December 2, 1942, in a secret laboratory that had been a squash court on the campus of the University of Chicago. Professor Enrico Fermi supervised the experiment. When everything was prepared, he gave the signal to pull out the control rod. Suddenly the Geiger counters resounded with telltale clicks from the radiation made by the successful breaking up of uranium atoms. The dignified scientists let out a cheer. They had produced a chain reaction that transformed matter into energy. And they had been able to prevent it blowing them up! The Atomic Age had begun.

One of the physicists hurried to the telephone and gave the code message to be relayed to the President of the United States.

"You'll be interested to know," he reported with mock casualness, "that the Italian navigator has just landed in the New World. The earth was not as large as he had estimated, and he arrived in the New World sooner than he had expected."

"Is that so?" he was asked. "Were the natives friendly?"

"Everyone landed safe and happy." This meant that Professor Fermi (the "Italian navigator") had succeeded even ahead of schedule. The "New World" was, of course, the uncharted world of atomic power.

The atomic bomb. In May 1942, only seven months before the Fermi experiment succeeded, President Roosevelt had set up the super-secret Manhattan Project to prepare to build a bomb. But it took another three years and a cost of $2 billion for the Manhattan Project to do the job.

At 5:30 on the morning of July 16, 1945, on a remote desert near Alamogordo, New Mexico, the moment came to prove that the bold thinking of the scientists could be matched by the practical know-how of engineers. The answer required no delicate Geiger counter to detect it. The world's first atomic bomb exploded—with a blinding flash and a towering mushroom cloud such as had never been seen before.

By the time the bomb was perfected, the Germans and Italians had already surrendered. Of the enemies now only Japan remained. On July 26 the Allied leaders gave the Japanese a solemn warning that "the alternative to surrender is prompt and utter destruction." Still they did not surrender.

After the victory over Germany, this dramatic poster, with a map of the world as background, symbolically showed the full force of the Allies being directed at Japan.

Should the United States use the atomic bomb? President Truman alone had to decide. No one knew how long Japan would hold out. Despite the terrifying fire raids of March 1945, when much of Tokyo was destroyed, the Japanese militarists showed no signs of giving up. If the war dragged on and Americans had to invade Japan, it might cost a million lives. The atomic bomb, President Truman knew, might kill hundreds of thousands of innocent Japanese. But life for life, the odds were that it would cost less.

On August 6, 1945, three weeks after that first blinding blast on the New Mexico desert, a single American B-29 dropped an atomic bomb on Hiro-shima. About 75,000 people were killed outright. Tens of thousands more perished later from wounds or radiation. The Japanese still held on. A few days later another plane dropped an atomic bomb on Nagasaki. Then the Japanese finally caved in. They announced their surrender on August 14, 1945.

The cost of World War II. The human cost of World War II can never be finally known. The United States lost 292,000 lives in combat, over five times the toll of World War I. Without the brilliant medical advances of the war—the blood banks and wonder drugs, the skilled doctors and

In 1945 Nagasaki, Japan, like Hiroshima, was obliterated by an atomic bomb. Only reinforced concrete buildings remained standing after the blast. Everything else was blown away.

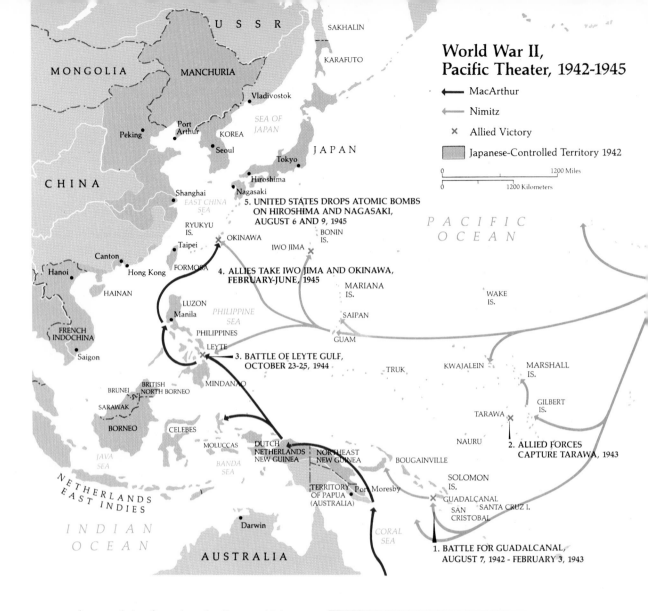

World War II, Pacific Theater, 1942-1945

← MacArthur
← Nimitz
✕ Allied Victory
▨ Japanese-Controlled Territory 1942

0 _____ 1200 Miles
0 _____ 1200 Kilometers

5. UNITED STATES DROPS ATOMIC BOMBS ON HIROSHIMA AND NAGASAKI, AUGUST 6 AND 9, 1945

4. ALLIES TAKE IWO JIMA AND OKINAWA, FEBRUARY-JUNE, 1945

3. BATTLE OF LEYTE GULF, OCTOBER 23-25, 1944

2. ALLIED FORCES CAPTURE TARAWA, 1943

1. BATTLE FOR GUADALCANAL, AUGUST 7, 1942 - FEBRUARY 3, 1943

nurses—the number of combat deaths would have been far higher.

Still, the cost for the United States was small compared to that for the rest of the world, where perhaps as many as 60 million died—18 million Russians, 4 million Germans, 2 million Japanese, and possibly 22 million Chinese. And most horrible of all, the Nazis' gigantic crime—6 million Jews senselessly exterminated in gas chambers and concentration camps.

At last World War II was over. The menace of Nazi barbarism and of Japanese militarism was destroyed. But the world was haunted by a host of new fears. These had been created by the war itself.

SECTION REVIEW

1. Identify or explain: Douglas MacArthur, Albert Einstein, Enrico Fermi, chain reaction.

2. Locate: New Guinea, Mindanao, Tarawa, Kwajalein, Saipan, Iwo Jima, Okinawa, Leyte Gulf, Luzon, Hiroshima, Nagasaki.

3. What was the Allied strategy in the Pacific in 1943-1944? Name the major battles.

4. What was the purpose of the atomic experiment at the University of Chicago?

5. Why did Truman decide to use the atomic bomb?

6. What were some costs of World War II?

CHAPTER REVIEW

MEETING OUR EARLIER SELVES

1. From 1939 to 1943 the number of workers in nonfarm jobs jumped from 30 million to 42 million. How was this rapid expansion of labor supply achieved at a time when the armed forces grew by more than 8 million?

2. For the civilian population, how did wartime hardships compare with the depression hardships a few years earlier?

3. How did technological advances change warfare in World War II from what it had been in World War I? Give examples.

4. How did the "Good Neighbor policy" pay dividends in World War II?

5. How did "the tide turn" in late 1942 and early 1943?

6. What were some major differences between the war against Germany and the war against Japan?

QUESTIONS FOR TODAY

1. Why did Churchill want to "shake hands with the Russians as far to the east as possible"? What was Eisenhower's decision? Are any world problems today linked to that decision? Explain.

2. What were the effects of the atomic experiments at the University of Chicago that reach to our own day?

YOUR REGION IN HISTORY

1. What kinds of goods were produced in your locality to aid the war effort in World War II?

2. Identify in your state any military camps or other armed forces facilities that served the war effort in 1940–1945.

3. Find out how high school students in your area helped on the home front.

SKILLS TO MAKE OUR PAST VIVID

1. Draw a World War II timeline (1939–1945) showing major military and political events.

2. On a world map trace the movement from recruitment to discharge of a relative or acquaintance who served in World War II.

3. Make a bar graph showing the following data on military and personal consumption expenditures for selected years from 1938 to 1948.

YEAR	MILITARY EXPENDITURES	PERSONAL CONSUMPTION
	(in billions of dollars)	
1938	$ 1.0	$ 64.6
1940	1.6	71.9
1942	22.6	89.7
1944	74.7	109.8
1946	42.7	147.1
1948	10.6	178.3

a. In what two years did the biggest *percentage* increase in military spending occur? personal consumption expenditure?

b. Why did spending for personal consumption continue to rise?

10

Postwar problems
1945–1960

"Ah, that instant! I felt as though I had been struck on the back with something like a big hammer, and thrown into boiling oil. For some time I was unconscious. When I abruptly came to again, everything was smothered in black smoke; it was like a dream or something that didn't make sense." So one survivor described the explosion of the first atomic bomb on August 6, 1945, at Hiroshima.

A new era in the history of the world had begun. Under the shadow of the atomic bomb, war between great powers could never be the same again. Isolation was no longer possible. Could the United States shape a foreign policy for survival in this frightening world?

In the postwar age, the American ways of living, thinking, and doing would be transformed. Magic machines would change the meaning of space and time. Faraway events would be seen in everybody's living room. Now millions, in their two-week vacations, could jet to Paris or Rome or Tokyo and see the world for themselves. Computers took over old jobs and created new jobs. Suburbs and superhighways changed the places where people lived and worked, where they went to school and shopped.

This most modern nation on earth was ruled by machines that no one had imagined a few years before. Could Americans still preserve the self-government of the simpler days of the Republic's founders? Could a machine-America keep alive the spirit of adventure that had conquered a continent?

Truman: neither war nor peace

At the end of World War II, the United States faced a world in ashes. The old order was burnt out, and nothing had arisen to take its place. Some Americans yearned to return to the former isolation of the Western Hemisphere. But world trade was more important than ever before. To prosper, the United States had to exchange goods with the nations of Europe, Asia, and Africa. Now, with airplanes and atomic weapons, the battlefield was everywhere. On this new-fashioned planet, Americans could not withdraw. The end of the war did not break our ties with Europe. And before long we would be drawn into the battles of Asia.

1. Beginnings of the cold war

The United States and Great Britain had been the allies of Soviet Russia for only one reason—to defeat Adolf Hitler. Since the two Western powers had never trusted Stalin, they had not even told him about the atomic bomb. The Communist leaders feared the capitalist nations but expected the whole world to become Communist. They hoped for the collapse of the democracies.

Still, American leaders thought that these differences would not have to bring on another war. Perhaps the Soviets could be persuaded to join a new and stronger League of Nations. And there capitalists and Communists might talk to each other instead of shoot at each other. Before long, Americans would discover that the Soviet leaders did not share their hopes.

Harry S Truman. The day after taking the oath of office, President Truman held a press conference. "Last night," he told the reporters in his midwestern twang, "the moon, the stars, and all the planets fell on me." To the surprise of many (including, perhaps, the new President himself), Harry S Truman proved equal to all his great decisions.

Harry Truman was born in Lamar, Missouri, in 1884. After high school, he worked as a bank clerk and then ran the family farm. In World War I, he served in the field artillery and rose to the rank of major. When the war was over, he started a clothing business, which failed during the postwar recession. Between 1922 and 1934 he was the elected County Judge (county commissioner) in Jackson County, Missouri. He studied law in night school.

In 1934, with the help of the political machine run by Kansas City's boss, Tom Pendergast, Truman was elected to the United States Senate. At that point he was considered only a routine machine politician. But Truman soon became known for his hard work, his intelligence, and his fairness. As

Doughty President Truman tossed out the first ball to open the 1949 baseball season.

head of the Senate Committee Investigating the National Defense Program, he held the national spotlight.

Building a new world organization. In 1943 Britain, the United States, and Russia had agreed to set up a new organization to replace the League of Nations. At the beautiful Dumbarton Oaks estate in Washington in 1944, China joined these three to make detailed plans. Then, on April 12 the next year, 200 delegates from 50 nations met in San Francisco to form the United Nations (UN). This was not a peace conference, for the war was still being fought on all fronts.

Russia and the United States disagreed over the use of the veto in the Security Council. They both thought there should be a veto so the great powers could protect themselves from unfavorable United Nations decisions. But on matters not concerning themselves directly, Russia and the United States

parted company. Russia thought that any action should be able to be vetoed. The United States disagreed, fearing that this would paralyze the new organization. Despite these differences, a charter emerged for the United Nations. After World War I the Senate had rejected the League of Nations. But now, on July 28, 1945, the Senate ratified the United Nations charter by the decisive vote of 82–2.

The UN aimed to preserve the peace and provide a better life for all. The General Assembly included delegates from every member nation. There each nation had one vote, except for Russia, which had three votes—one for itself and one each for the Ukraine and Byelorussia. This concession to Russia had been offered at Yalta to persuade the Soviets to join the UN. The General Assembly could discuss any subject within the scope of the charter. And it made recommendations to the small and powerful Security Council. The Assembly fixed the UN budget, admitted new members approved by the Security Council, and elected member nations to the many UN agencies.

The Security Council had eleven (later fifteen) members. Of these the Big Five (United States, Britain, the Soviet Union, France, and China) had permanent seats and the right to a veto. The six other members were elected for two-year terms but had no veto. This Security Council had the power to look into disputes and to act against any nation that threatened the peace.

The Secretariat, headed by a Secretary-General, would handle the UN's day-to-day affairs. Trygve Lie of Norway was the first person to head this office. An American, Dr. Ralph Bunche, the grandson of a former slave, served for many years as Under Secretary.

The International Court of Justice was the court for the UN. It could deal with legal questions that arose between members. Many other agencies were set up under the Economic and Social Council (UNESCO) to build the world community. The United Nations Relief and Rehabilitation Administration (UNRRA) was financed mainly by the United States. It supplied food and clothing to nations devastated by the war.

Controlling the atom. What could the UN do to control the menacing new power of the atom? In June 1946 Bernard Baruch, for the United States, proposed a world agency with control over atomic energy and the right to inspect atomic-energy plants anywhere. If the inspection system was set up, the United States said it would destroy its atomic bombs. Under Baruch's scheme no vetoes would be allowed. But Russia once again sabotaged the plan by insisting on its right to veto. The Soviets demanded that the United States destroy its weapons even before the new controls were created. As a result, there was no progress.

Problems with the Russians.

The dispute over the atom was only one signal of the widening gulf between the United States and Russia. Time after time the Soviets refused to live up to their promises. At Yalta Stalin had pledged to hold free elections in Poland for the formation of a new government. Instead he forced a Communist government on the Poles. The Soviets also retained their hold on the former Baltic republics (Latvia, Lithuania, and Estonia). And they supported Communist forces in Hungary, Bulgaria, and Romania. Russia's goal was to keep "friendly" states all along its borders. If those people would not vote for a Communist government, Stalin was ready to fasten it on them with guns and tanks. And if communism was crammed down the throats of the people of Eastern Europe, what about the lands that bordered those nations? Now a Communist tyranny threatened Europe.

To broadcast the new danger, Truman sponsored a speech by Winston Churchill at Westminster College in Fulton, Missouri. There on March 5, 1946, the eloquent Churchill sounded the alarm. "From Stettin in the Baltic to Trieste in the Adriatic an iron curtain has descended across the Continent," he warned. "I do not believe that Soviet Russia desires war. What they desire is the fruits of war and the indefinite expansion of their power and doctrines." Churchill's words were reinforced by Russia's failure to keep its promise to remove its troops from Iran. The Soviets were also squeezing Turkey to give them military bases and control of the straits leading from the Black Sea bordering southern Russia to the Mediterranean. Then the Russian navy could move freely back and forth.

In Greece, civil war erupted in the fall of 1946. The right-wing government was under attack by Communist insurgents supported from the neighboring Communist countries. Would the Soviets try to force their ways on the world? A Soviet spy ring in Canada (including a member of the Canadian parliament) was exposed. Atomic secrets, it was learned, had been sent to Russia.

Warnings about Russia.

Meanwhile some thoughtful American leaders were alarmed by the Soviet threat to the free world. One was the learned George F. Kennan, our minister-counselor in Moscow. Another was our Under Secretary of State, the suave and cultivated Dean Acheson. They believed that the Russian Communists intended to conquer the world. As Kennan warned in a long telegram to the State Department from Moscow in February 1946, Russia must be "contained" within its present limits. Soviet communism would then either collapse from within or the Russian people would force a change in policy.

Kennan and Acheson—and President Truman himself—believed that if Hitler had been stopped at Munich instead of being "appeased," World War II might never have happened. Now, to prevent a third world war, the United States must stand up to Russia. And they were encouraged in this belief by events in Iran. After a strong warning from Britain and the United States (and the threat of force), Russia withdrew its troops from Iran in May 1946.

The Greek civil war.

By the beginning of 1947 the situation in Greece was serious. Great Britain had been sending troops and money to the Greek government. Still the British had problems enough of their own at home. They could no longer afford to support the anti-Communist cause in Greece. Without that support the right-wing government would probably fall and the Communists would take over. Americans feared that this would put the USSR in control. "A highly possible Soviet break-through might open three continents to Soviet penetration," Acheson warned. "Like apples in a barrel infected by one rotten one, the corruption of Greece would infect" Asia, Africa, and Europe.

The Truman Doctrine.

Acheson's appraisal of the situation was probably overdrawn. In 1948 Yugoslavia's ruling Communists, under Marshal Tito, would break with Moscow. Like the Yugoslavs, the Greek Communists were not just another wing of Soviet Russia. But Acheson did not know that. From his view the withdrawal of British support

Shown next to President Truman in 1950 are Dean Acheson (left) and George Marshall (right), the main architects and managers of foreign policy in the Truman years.

meant the Communists would take command and Stalin would be in charge.

To prevent this, Secretary of State George Marshall, working with Acheson, quickly devised a program of military and economic aid for Greece. Marshall had been Chief of Staff of the Army during World War II. Truman sent the program to a special session of Congress in March 1947. He asked $300 million for military and economic aid to Greece and $100 million for aid to Turkey. He also asked Congress to allow him to send civilian and military personnel to Greece and Turkey to oversee the use of our aid and to train their people. "It must be the policy of the United States," Truman declared, "to support free peoples who are resisting attempted subjugation by armed minorities or by outside pressure. . . . We must assist free people to work out their own destinies in their own way." This was called "the Truman Doctrine."

The Greek-Turkish Aid bill became law in May 1947. Congress and the President declared that the United States was threatened wherever Communists challenged. To oppose Communist expansion, peacetime military aid to other countries would be a regular tool of our diplomacy. The Truman Doctrine would guide the foreign policy of the United States for a generation.

The Russians denounced the aid bill as an invitation to war. Critics at home (led by former Vice-President and now Secretary of Commerce Henry Wallace) did not share President Truman's distrust of the Soviets. For opposing his "get tough" policy, Truman fired Wallace. Meanwhile United States aid—especially military advisers and equipment—helped defeat Communist and other guerrilla forces in Greece and Turkey. This weakened Soviet influence there.

Marshall proposes a plan. In May 1947, while Congress was debating the Truman Doctrine, Winston Churchill described Europe as "a rubble heap, a charnel house, a breeding ground of pestilence and hate." The homegrown Communist parties of France and Italy (supported by the Soviets) became ever stronger. It seemed that nothing could prevent the Communist conquest of Europe.

The Policy Planning Staff of the State Department set itself a difficult task. Was there some way, short of war, to stop the Communist advance and "contain" the Russians? Could a new plan of economic aid somehow preserve free governments? Poverty and unemployment made people desperate and brought dictators to power. Prosperity and jobs could save democracy. But how could war-torn Europe be healed? The Truman Doctrine was a way to stop the advance of communism. But how could we advance freedom?

In his memorable speech at Harvard University on June 5, 1947, Secretary of State Marshall proposed a plan. During the next three or four years the United States ought to help Europe with substantial gifts to prevent "economic, social, and political deterioration of a very serious character." This would not be military aid but would be directed "against hunger, poverty, desperation, and chaos."

Russia was invited to join, but the Soviets refused to take part. And they kept Poland and Czechoslovakia (which was still attempting to keep free of Soviet domination) along with the other East European "satellite" nations from accepting American aid. By staying out, the Russians made it easier to persuade Congress to pass the plan.

The European Recovery Program. For ten months Congress debated the pros and cons. Supporters of Marshall's European Recovery Program (ERP) explained that it was necessary for our own defense and economic survival. Opponents, led by Senator Robert Taft of Ohio, charged that it would cost far too much. It would also expose us to new dangers abroad, which might lead to another world war. On the left, Henry Wallace denounced the plan as an attack on Russia—a "Martial Plan."

A bloodless Communist coup d'etat in Czechoslovakia in February 1948 helped the supporters of ERP. Senator Taft himself voted for the bill, and the measure was passed by large majorities in both houses of Congress. The Marshall Plan, signed into law by President Truman on April 3, 1948, provided $5.3 billion for European recovery over the follow-

After the Second World War the people of Europe carried on their lives among the ruins. This woman created a flourishing garden within bombed-out walls.

David Seymour/Magnum

ing year. The United States was now committed to save Western Europe. "Containing" Soviet Russia, as Ambassador Kennan had urged, would not only strengthen American defense. It would also create new markets for our goods.

At it turned out, ERP was a brilliant success. Of the $12 billion spent in Marshall aid, more than half went to Britain, France, and West Germany. By 1950 these nations of Europe had increased their output by 25 percent over prewar levels. As European nations became more prosperous, they could buy more of our goods. This in turn would help keep our economy booming.

The Point Four program. The Marshall Plan was later followed by another generous program of aid, also intended to fight communism by promoting economic growth. This, too, would create new markets for American farms and factories. "Point Four," it was called, because it was the fourth point in President Truman's 1949 inaugural address. This program would give economic and technical aid to the poor free nations of Asia, Africa, and Latin America. For these purposes billions of dollars were—and still are—being spent abroad.

SECTION REVIEW

1. Identify or explain: Security Council veto, "iron curtain," George Kennan, Dean Acheson, President Tito, George C. Marshall, containment policy, Greek-Turkish Aid bill, "satellite" nations, Robert Taft, Point Four program.

2. Locate: Dumbarton Oaks, Baltic republics, Trieste, Iran, Black Sea.

3. Name the chief United Nations agencies and describe their functions.

4. What was the Baruch plan for atomic energy? Why was it not put into effect?

5. Name some early signs of the widening gulf between the Soviet Union and the United States.

6. What warnings about the Soviet Union were sounded by (a) Churchill and (b) Kennan?

7. What was the Truman Doctrine? Why was it proclaimed in March 1947?

8. Describe the Marshall Plan by giving the reason for it, its provisions, and its results.

2. Dealing with a new world

The nation had to shift somehow to a peacetime way of life when World War II ended. How could we combat the threats of inflation and unemployment? How could we meet the pent-up demands of business and labor? How could we help men and women change over from the armed forces to civilian life? All this and more had to be accomplished under a new and untried President.

Bringing the boys home. As soon as the war ended, Truman faced extreme pressure to "bring the boys home." At first the plan was to decrease the size of the armed forces only slowly and stay alert to any new threats abroad. But when there were riots by troops who wanted to go home, the President gave in and suddenly reduced the army. By midsummer 1946 the armed forces had been cut back from 12 million to 3 million. Truman warned that this was "disintegration" rather than demobilization. Still the United States—the sole possessor of the atomic bomb—remained the most powerful nation on earth.

Fortunately, Congress had prepared for the return of the veterans. In June 1944 it had passed a Servicemen's Readjustment Act—usually called the "GI Bill of Rights." This provided hospitals for the sick and wounded and clinics to help the disabled. It offered payments to veterans without jobs. It gave them preference for jobs in the federal civil service. Money was earmarked to help them buy homes, farms, and businesses. Free tuition, books, and expenses for job training, college, or other advanced education were given to those who wanted them. Eight million veterans of World War II used this educational program at a cost of $14.5 billion.

The Atomic Energy Act. How could a nation at peace use the newfound power in the atom? Both political parties agreed that the federal government had to keep control of the raw materials of atomic power. These rare metals—uranium and plutonium—were called "fissionable materials" because their atoms could be split. But the two parties disagreed on whether control should be put in the hands of civilians or of the army.

A compromise, the Atomic Energy Act, was signed by President Truman on August 1, 1946. It preserved the government monopoly of fissionable materials. A five-member civilian Atomic Energy Commission (AEC) was put in control. It was to encourage private and government research and development in both military and peaceful uses of atomic energy. In less than a decade the commission would employ 7000 workers and spend $2.5 billion a year.

Converting to peacetime.

To help provide peacetime jobs, Congress passed the Employment Act in February 1946. A new Council of Economic Advisers would advise the President and Congress on how to create jobs and national prosperity. In fact, the nation adjusted swiftly to peace. There was no lack of jobs.

Instead, the nation was troubled by shortages of materials, by strikes, and by inflation. With the end of the war, labor, which had patiently kept the factories going, was keen on seeking wage increases. A nationwide railroad strike threatened to tie up transportation, and the coal miners also went out on strike. On President Truman's orders the government seized both the railroads and the coal mines. The coal strike was soon settled, but the Engineers and Trainmen refused the compromise accepted by eighteen other railroad unions.

The angry President then asked Congress for power to declare a state of national emergency whenever a strike in a vital industry endangered the national safety. Workers who continued to strike would lose all benefits of employment and seniority and be drafted into the army. The House passed this extreme measure. But the Senate had not yet acted when the strikers returned to work.

Consumer goods—refrigerators, stoves, and cars, for example—were scarce until factories could shift to peacetime production. The new prosperity gave money to people who had waited years to buy these products. Truman wanted to continue price controls to prevent runaway inflation. But Congress refused to extend wartime controls. Between 1946 and 1947, the wholesale prices of food, clothing, and fuel went up 25 percent.

The attitude of the 80th Congress.

In the midst of the strikes and shortages, inflation at home and challenges from abroad, elections for Congress took place in the fall of 1946. The Republicans campaigned on the slogan, "Had Enough?" They won control of both houses of Congress for the first time since 1928.

The 80th Congress, elected in 1946, expressed the desire of many Americans to turn back the clock to

War veterans picket a mine in 1946 claiming that they should have back the jobs filled by "outsiders" who were hired during the war.

the simpler days before World War II. They hoped to cut government spending and to undo much of the New Deal. The leading speaker for this yearning was Senator Robert A. Taft of Ohio, the son of President William Howard Taft. He was a man of sharp intelligence, high principles, and utter honesty, although he lacked a sense of humor and was not a good mixer. Senator Taft wanted to limit United States commitments abroad and to free the individual at home. He wanted, as he said, "to break with the idea that we can legislate prosperity, legislate equality, legislate opportunity. All of these good things came in the past from free Americans working out their destiny."

The Taft-Hartley Act.

The most important single piece of domestic legislation passed by this Congress was the Taft-Hartley Act of 1947. Fed up with strikes and disturbed by corruption and communism in some unions, Congress hoped to curb union power. The bill did not go as far as either Senator Taft or Congressman Hartley had wanted. But it aimed to achieve a better balance between labor and management. It outlawed the "closed shop," which had allowed only dues-paying members of a union to be hired. It did not ban the "union shop," which required workers to join a union after they had been hired. Instead the law permitted a state to enact what came to be called a "right-to-work" law. This would forbid the union shop in that state.

An interesting clause of the Taft-Hartley Act was the "cooling off" period. If the President saw that a strike might endanger the public safety, he could require the parties to "cool off" for 60 days. During this period there could be no strike or lockout, while labor and management tried to agree. The law forbade unions to make political contributions. Union officers had to sign statements that they were not Communists if they wished to bring cases before the NLRB. The law was passed over Truman's veto.

The unions bitterly attacked the Taft-Hartley Act. They called it a "slave labor" law meant to destroy their unions. But in fact the law worked quite well. In spite of the fears of union leaders, the unions continued to grow. Between 1945 and 1952 their members increased from 14.6 million to 17 million. "Big labor" now began to oppose "big business."

An active Congress.

Republican members of Congress believed that the income tax was unfair to people with higher incomes. They argued that the "soak-the-rich" taxes would destroy the profit motive. So in 1948 Congress lowered taxes all along the line, but most of all for the wealthy. When Truman vetoed the bill, it was passed over his veto. To economize, Congress cut aid to farmers and refused the President's requests to help public housing, to expand Social Security, and to aid education.

The 80th Congress was fighting an old battle. It was really attacking the New Deal and the four-term President, FDR. Congress passed the Twenty-second Amendment to limit any President after Harry Truman to two terms. This amendment was ratified by the required three-fourths of the states by February 1951.

In 1947 Congress also passed the Presidential Succession Act. Seven times in our history until then, American Presidents had died in office. In each case the Vice-President had been sworn in as Chief Executive. The next officer in line for the Presidency after the Vice-President was the Secretary of State and then on through the Cabinet in the order in which their positions were created. Cabinet members, of course, are appointed by the President. But Truman believed that the President should always be someone who had run for office and been elected by the people. The 1947 act made the succession pass from the Vice-President to the Speaker of the House and then to the presiding officer of the Senate. Cabinet members were to follow these three officials in the same order as before.

Truman tries to extend the New Deal.

In the anti-New Deal 80th Congress Harry Truman found a perfect foil for his own election campaign. During 1947 and 1948 he sent to Congress bill after bill for his "Fair Deal." Most were extensions of the New Deal, but in 1948 he also asked for far-reaching civil rights laws.

Truman had long been worried by discrimination against blacks. In 1924 he had been defeated in an election because he opposed the Ku Klux Klan. In 1946 he had set up a Committee on Civil Rights to find better ways to protect the civil rights of all the people. Their report showed the evil effects of segregation, and in February 1948 Truman called

Europe after World War II

- U.S. Zone
- British Zone
- French Zone
- Russian Zone
- Annexed by U.S.S.R.
- Annexed by Poland

0 — 600 Miles
0 — 600 Kilometers

NORWAY · SWEDEN · FINLAND

NORTH SEA

Stockholm

ESTONIA · LATVIA · LITHUANIA

U S S R

Moscow

NORTHERN IRELAND · IRELAND · GREAT BRITAIN

DENMARK

BALTIC SEA

Gdansk

EAST PRUSSIA

Moscow

London · NETH. · Berlin · Warsaw · POLAND

ATLANTIC OCEAN

BELG. · GERMANY

LUX. · Paris

Kiev

FRANCE · Nuremberg · Prague · CZECHOSLOVAKIA

SWITZ. · AUSTRIA · Budapest · HUNGARY

ROMANIA

Rhine · Danube R.

Lisbon · PORTUGAL · SPAIN · Madrid

YUGOSLAVIA · Belgrade

CORSICA · ITALY

Rome · SARDINIA

ALBANIA · GREECE · BULGARIA · Istanbul · BLACK SEA

MEDITERRANEAN

SPANISH MOROCCO

MOROCCO (FRENCH) · ALGERIA (FRENCH) · SICILY · TUNISIA (FRENCH)

SEA · TURKEY

BERLIN

— Wall Built 1961

0 — 15 Miles
0 — 15 Kilometers

WEST BERLIN · EAST BERLIN

BERLIN

---

upon Congress to act to end racial injustice. He asked for anti-lynching and anti-poll tax laws and a permanent Fair Employment Practices Committee, along with stronger and better-enforced laws for civil rights.

When southern senators threatened to filibuster, Congress refused to act on his proposals. Still the President did what he could on his own. In 1948 he began the desegregation of the armed forces (p. 556). He appointed the first black governor of the Virgin Islands and the first black judge in the federal courts. He strengthened the Civil Rights Section of the Justice Department. And he ordered the Department to assist blacks in their own civil rights cases.

The decisive Congress. Because Congress had failed to enact much of his Fair Deal, during the election of 1948 Truman called the 80th Congress the "Do-Nothing" Congress.

Yet this was actually one of the most effective Congresses in United States history. It put the Truman Doctrine and the Marshall Plan into effect. It passed the National Security Act, which placed all the armed forces under a new Cabinet department with a civilian Secretary of Defense. The Secretaries of the Army, Navy, and Air Force now served under him and were without Cabinet rank. The act also placed military leadership in the Joint Chiefs of Staff. It created the National Security Council, a super-Cabinet to plan and coordinate defense. This Council included the President and Vice-President, the Secretaries of State and of Defense, and the Director of the Office of Emergency Planning. The act also set up the Central Intelligence Agency (CIA)—the first permanent, worldwide intelligence agency in United States history.

The problem of Germany.

After Germany surrendered, it was split up into zones of occupation among France, Great Britain, Russia, and the United States. Berlin also had been divided among all four victorious powers, but it was surrounded by Soviet-controlled territory. The leaders of the Big Three wartime powers—Stalin, Truman, and Churchill—met at the Berlin suburb of Potsdam in July 1945 to discuss ending the war against Japan and solving postwar problems in Europe. They decided that the future of Germany should be worked out by the foreign ministers of the United States, Great Britain, Russia, and France.

At Potsdam the Big Three leaders confirmed that "war criminals" would be brought to justice swiftly. In October a four-power tribunal meeting at Nuremberg, Germany, began to try Nazi leaders for crimes committed during the war. Ten of these Nazis were executed. Hundreds of German soldiers were also sentenced to death by the Allies' military courts, and 500,000 other Germans were punished for their Nazi activities. Later, Japanese leaders were also tried in Japan, and Premier Tojo and six others were executed. Four thousand Japanese were sent to jail, and 400 Japanese officers were sentenced to death for committing atrocities.

The Allies could not agree on what to do with Germany. So in March 1948, the United States, England, France, and the Benelux nations (Belgium, the Netherlands, and Luxembourg) announced plans to make the Western Zone of Germany a single unit. A federal government would be set up there. And West Germany would come into the European Recovery Program.

When the Russians blockaded West Berlin in 1948–1949, the Western powers responded with a gigantic airlift which brought thousands of tons of supplies to Berlin each day.

NATO

North Atlantic Treaty Organization Nations 1949

Soviet-Dominated Countries

0   1500 Miles

0   1500 Kilometers

The Berlin blockade. Hoping to prevent the Western powers from setting up a separate West German government and to keep Germany from helping European recovery, the Russians put pressure on West Berlin. On June 19, 1948, they banned all traffic between the Western Zone and Berlin by railroad, highway, or canal. This combat without open fighting came to be called the "cold war."

Harry Truman never considered giving in. "We are going to stay, period," the feisty President said. There would be no backing down to the Russians as long as Truman was in the White House. The United States, England, and France began to supply the city by air. Food, coal, clothing—all kinds of things the people of the city needed—were flown

in. Four thousand tons of supplies reached Berlin each day.

On May 12, 1949, the Western powers approved the Basic Law for the German Federated Republic (West Germany). On the same day Stalin recognized his defeat and ended the blockade. Then in September the West Germans began to rule themselves. In military and foreign affairs they were still controlled by the occupying powers. One month later the Russians responded by setting up their German Democratic Republic in East Germany. West Germany formally was given full sovereignty in 1955. East Germany remained a Russian satellite. Hitler's "Thousand Year Reich" had become a divided nation. Could Germany ever be reunited without threatening the peace of Europe?

The creation of NATO. Out of the Berlin blockade came the North Atlantic Treaty Organization (NATO). The Atlantic Pact that established NATO allied the United States and Canada with ten Western European nations extending from Norway to Portugal. Later, when Greece, Turkey, and West Germany joined, the membership numbered fifteen. The Atlantic Pact was signed by the foreign ministers on April 4, 1949.

Under Article 5 of this pact an attack on any one of the parties would be treated as an attack on them all. Some senators argued that this committed the United States to go to war without a declaration by Congress. This same fear had defeated the League of Nations in the Senate in 1919. But now the senators approved the Atlantic Pact in July 1949 by a vote of 82 to 13. The Senate followed our long tradition by avoiding calling this an "alliance." And Congress actually did retain the right to declare war. Yet there was no doubt in anyone's mind that whatever NATO was called, the United States had made a major shift. We had joined the first peacetime alliance in our history. General Eisenhower was named commander of the NATO forces. He set up Supreme Headquarters, Allied Powers in Europe (SHAPE) at Paris early in 1951.

The Republicans scent victory in 1948. In the midst of the Berlin blockade, the United States held a presidential election. The Republicans, after taking control of Congress in 1946, thought they would easily win. Now shortages and strikes, though less worrisome than they had been, remained a nuisance. The world still seemed on the brink of war. No wonder plain little Harry Truman seemed an easy man to bring down.

Many Republicans wanted the chance to run against Truman. Among the hopefuls were Senator Robert A. Taft, called "Mr. Republican," Governor Harold Stassen of Minnesota, Governor Earl Warren of California, and the 1944 candidate Governor Thomas E. Dewey of New York. Some leaders in both parties hoped to draft the war hero General Dwight Eisenhower. But he refused to be a candidate.

The Republicans, meeting at Philadelphia, feared that an outspoken anti-New Dealer like Taft could not win. They turned again to the moderate Tom Dewey and chose Earl Warren as his running mate. New York and California! That seemed an unbeatable team. The Republican platform approved many popular New Deal reforms. It also accepted the "bipartisan" foreign policy—the policy agreed on by both parties—that had been followed ever since Pearl Harbor. There were, in fact, real questions about the policy of containment that deserved public discussion. Yet these important issues were not debated by the candidates because foreign policy was supposed to be bipartisan. In the campaign the Republicans simply insisted that they could run the country better. Their slogan said, "Time for a change."

The Democrats divide. The Democrats also met in Philadelphia. And many party leaders wanted to dump Truman. They were sure he would lose. But he was self-confident—and he loved a fight. Using his powerful position in the White House, he was able to win on the first ballot. His friend, Alben W. Barkley of Kentucky, the Democratic leader in the Senate for eleven years, took the second spot on the ticket.

The Democratic platform favored repeal of the Taft-Hartley Act. It pledged recognition of the new state of Israel, which was struggling to be born in Palestine. It came out for strong civil rights legislation—abolition of poll taxes in federal elections, a national anti-lynching law, fair employment legislation, and the end of segregation in the armed forces. The Democrats were bidding for the continued support of the black voters who now held the balance of power in the big northern cities. Their votes might well swing their states into the Democratic column.

The adoption of the civil rights plank split the party wide open. Thirty-five members of the Mississippi and Alabama delegations walked out of the building. Only two days after the Democratic convention adjourned, delegates from thirteen southern states held their own convention in Birmingham, Alabama. In a hall flanked with Confederate flags and resounding with rebel yells, they nominated Governor J. Strom Thurmond of South Carolina for President. Governor Fielding Wright of Mississippi was named his running mate.

They called themselves States Rights Democrats or "Dixiecrats." Their platform asserted the doctrine of states' rights. It condemned the civil rights plank of the Democratic convention and insisted on the segregation of blacks.

It appeared even more certain that Truman would lose when Henry A. Wallace and his followers also left the party to create a party of their own. Calling themselves "Progressives," his supporters chanted, "One, two, three, four—we don't want another war." Wallace was convinced that both at home and abroad Communists and liberals should work together. The Communist party endorsed his candidacy. The Progressive platform called for the repeal of the draft, strong civil rights laws, cooperation with Russia, banning atomic bombs (and destroying all American bombs), and freedom of speech and political action for Communists. Senator Glenn H. Taylor of Idaho, the self-styled "Singing Cowboy," was the Progressive nominee for Vice-President.

The election of 1948. People remembered that the election of 1946 had already shown a swing to the Republicans. Now the Progressives and the Dixiecrats split the Democratic vote. Public opinion polls showed strong support for Dewey. The Republicans considered their victory certain. Many Democrats privately agreed with them, and most big-city newspapers predicted that Truman was a sure loser.

Truman gleefully displays the headline that too hastily announced his defeat in 1948.

Meanwhile, Truman was not sitting still. He called the 80th Congress back into special session and challenged them to enact the platform the Republicans had issued at their convention. When they failed, the President scorned them as the "Do-Nothing" Congress throughout the election.

Truman now shrewdly could run against the Republican 80th Congress instead of against Governor Dewey. He convinced people that the Congress had done nothing but serve the powerful corporations. Through the Taft-Hartley law, he said, Congress had tried to enslave the workers. By keeping America's doors closed against the displaced persons of Europe, Congress had struck a blow against all immigrants. He continued to appeal to blacks by calling for civil rights laws.

Truman conducted a rough-and-tumble, whirlwind campaign. He traveled on a special train that made countless quick whistle-stops—just long enough for his speech and some friendly greetings from the townspeople. He gave 356 speeches, covered 30,000 miles by train, and met 12 million people. On the other hand Dewey, a reserved and dignified man, acted coolly and quietly as he thought befit the next President of the United States. One reporter quipped, "How long is Dewey going to tolerate Truman's interference in the government?"

In the 1948 campaign, for the first time, television was important. On TV and on the road, President Truman seemed relaxed and homey. Critics said that Governor Dewey appeared stiff and formal like the bridegroom on a wedding cake. Television offered a vivid new chance for American voters to size up their candidates.

On the morning after election day, based on the early returns the *Chicago Tribune* headlined that Dewey had won. In fact, the spunky Harry Truman—who never gave up—had turned defeat into victory. President Truman's favorite picture of himself showed him holding up a copy of that *Chicago Tribune.* When the later returns from the farm belt turned the tide, Truman's popular vote was 24 million to nearly 22 million for Dewey and over 1 million each for Thurmond and Wallace. In the electoral college Truman had 303, Dewey 189, Thurmond 39, and Wallace 0. In addition the Democrats won a majority of 93 seats in the House and 12 in the Senate. Nearly everybody was surprised—except Harry Truman.

SECTION REVIEW

1. Identify or explain: GI Bill of Rights, Atomic Energy Commission, Employment Act of 1946, Twenty-second Amendment, Presidential Succession Act, "Fair Deal," National Security Act, CIA, Nuremberg trials, Berlin blockade, NATO, Atlantic Pact, Harold Stassen, Earl Warren, Alben Barkley, Strom Thurmond, "Dixiecrats."

2. Describe demobilization in 1946. How were the war veterans helped?

3. How did Truman respond to the strikes and inflation in 1946? What was the result?

4. List some purposes and provisions of the Taft-Hartley Act.

5. On what measures did the 80th Congress support Truman? oppose him?

6. Describe Truman's stand on civil rights.

7. Why was Germany divided in 1948–1949?

8. How did the creation of NATO depart from American tradition?

9. Describe the campaign and election of 1948: candidates, issues, campaign styles, and outcome.

3. President in his own right

Harry Truman's second four years in office were momentous. They would be marked by hysterical spy hunts, by the "loss" of China, by Russia's explosion of an atomic bomb, by defensive alliances, and by an undeclared war in Korea. Through it all Harry Truman was courageous and decisive. But many Americans did not agree with his decisions.

Truman asks for a Fair Deal for all. President Truman interpreted his victory in 1948 as a signal that the nation approved his "Fair Deal." Instead when he tried to persuade Congress to pass his Fair Deal laws, he ran into strong opposition from both Republicans and Democrats. Still, during the next four years he did manage to persuade Congress to raise the minimum hourly wage from 40 to 75 cents and to extend Social Security to an additional 10 million Americans. He signed laws to clear slums, to renew cities, and to provide low-income housing. Congress voted more funds for the TVA, for bringing in electricity to rural areas, and for the expansion of hydroelectric, water-control, and irrigation projects. But Truman suffered defeats on civil rights, on national health insurance, on the repeal of the Taft-Hartley Act, on federal aid to education, and on his plan to keep up farm incomes.

The second red scare. The stresses of the cold war with Russia, along with the 1946 reports of spying in Canada, frightened Americans. On very little evidence, they began to suspect that there was a strong Communist conspiracy to take over the United States. Truman, who had some reasons of his own to distrust the Russians, joined the crowd. On March 22, 1947, the President issued an Executive Order for the FBI and the Civil Service Commission to check on the loyalty of all federal employees. The honest, hardworking government workers were made miserable. The order made it seem that they were guilty of disloyalty until they proved they were innocent.

Within the next four years 3 million employees were cleared, 2900 resigned, and 300 were dismissed as being of doubtful loyalty. The criteria for suspicion were so broad that it may well be that none of these people was ever a Communist or else had only been a Communist before the war. In December 1947 Attorney General Tom Clark listed 90 organizations said to be disloyal to the United States. The listed groups were not allowed to prove that they were not disloyal. Membership in one of these groups at once became cause for suspicion that the person was a Communist.

Meanwhile, the 80th Congress breathed new life into the House Un-American Activities Committee (HUAC). One of its most active members was a young congressman from California, Richard M. Nixon. The committee held numerous public hearings and treated those who refused to answer its questions as guilty. Its free-swinging actions led to many ruined reputations and produced blacklists in the movies, radio, and TV.

The most famous case to come out of the HUAC was that of the wellborn Alger Hiss. He had served in the government since 1933, had been an adviser to the President at Yalta, and then temporary secretary at the San Francisco conference to set up the United Nations. In 1946 he was elected president of the Carnegie Endowment for International Peace. In 1948 Alger Hiss was accused by

Whittaker Chambers, a confessed former Soviet courier. Chambers said that Hiss had provided him with classified documents, which then had been photographed by Communist agents and returned to government files.

Hiss sued Chambers for libel. He denied Chambers's charges before a New York grand jury. In one trial the jury could not agree. After a second trial Hiss was convicted of perjury in January 1950. High-ranking Democrats were among the character witnesses for Hiss. And President Truman made the mistake of saying that the Hiss case was a "red herring" put out by the 80th Congress to prove that it was actually doing something. Many Americans, already upset by the crisis with Russia, now believed that the Democrats were "soft on communism."

The world situation worsens. In September 1949, several years earlier than expected, the Soviet Union exploded an atomic bomb. No longer did the United States have its monopoly. Then in February 1950, Klaus Fuchs, a scientist who had helped to make the first atomic bomb, was arrested by the British as a spy. He confessed that from 1943 to 1947 he had given the Russians important secrets about the bomb.

Our former ally Chiang Kai-shek was driven from the vast mainland of China to the small island of Taiwan (Formosa). By October 1949 the Chinese Communists, led by Mao Tse-tung, were in control of the Chinese mainland. At first the United States had given Chiang large amounts of aid. We had tried to mediate between him and

Chinese Communist troops had just taken Nanking from the forces of Chiang Kai-shek in 1949 when famed French photographer Henri Cartier-Bresson took this picture.

Henri Cartier-Bresson/Magnum

Mao to form a single government. But neither of them had been willing to compromise. When fighting broke out between them, the United States had backed Chiang. Many Americans who did not want to see communism come to China still were only lukewarm supporters of Chiang. They saw him as another dictator and disliked the corruption in his government. But his fall and the loss of mainland China to the Communists seemed one more defeat for the United States.

The rise of McCarthy.

At this moment a clever and unscrupulous politician began to play upon the fear and helplessness felt by Americans. It was hard to explain how the strongest nation in the world had reached such a pass. Was this the fault of traitors inside the United States? Joseph R. McCarthy, Republican senator from Wisconsin, gave them the answer they wanted to hear. On February 9, 1950, in a speech in West Virginia he charged that the State Department was infested with Communist agents. He waved a piece of paper on which he said were listed their names. His charge, repeated over and over, increased the alarm. Even after McCarthy was unable to find a single Communist in the State Department, many troubled Americans still listened to him. McCarthy became the strongest political power in the country outside of the major party leaders. Even Presidents feared to cross him.

Protecting the United States.

Members of Congress, too, seemed panicked by the internal threat for which there was so little proof. But most of all they wanted to prove that they were not soft on communism. In 1950 Congress passed the McCarran Internal Security Act. It required Communist or "Communist-front" organizations to register with the Attorney General. These included groups that were not Communist at all but which, it was suspected, might harbor some Communists. Of course, it was impossible in practice for any large organization to prove that it had no Communists. The suspect groups had to provide membership lists and financial statements. Membership in the Communist party itself was not made a crime, but employment of Communists in defense plants was forbidden. In case of an internal security emergency, the act gave the President sweeping powers to round up and detain anyone who might even

possibly commit espionage or sabotage. President Truman vetoed the McCarran Act. He said that it was worse than the Sedition Act of 1798 and that it took a "long step toward totalitarianism." But the law was passed over his veto.

Using the excuse of "internal security," in 1952 Congress passed a new immigration law, the McCarran-Walter Act. Again Truman vetoed the bill, but again it was passed over his veto. The law kept the quota system, which favored immigrants from northern and western Europe. It provided a complicated and insulting system of loyalty checks for foreigners who wished to visit the United States. It also gave the Attorney General the power to deport immigrants for being members of Communist and Communist-front groups even after they had become citizens. The law did include one small victory for the American tradition. It finally allowed Asians living in the United States to become citizens and set a quota permitting about 2000 to enter the country each year.

The fears of Communist subversion were heightened by the arrest of Julius and Ethel Rosenberg and Morton Sobell, on the report of Klaus Fuchs that they had passed key secrets about the atomic bomb to the Russians. In March 1951 the Rosenbergs, after a lengthy trial, were sentenced to death for a crime "worse than murder." Sobell was sentenced to 30 years. The Rosenbergs were executed in 1953. As with Sacco and Vanzetti back in the 1920s, many citizens doubted that the Rosenbergs were guilty. Or they believed that even if they were guilty, the nation was not well served by inflicting this drastic penalty in peacetime.

Civil war in Korea.

Troubled by these problems at home, Americans soon discovered that from the other side of the globe the Soviets could find ways to threaten the American peace of mind. Civil war exploded in Korea in June 1950. Korea was an ancient country (the size of Mississippi and Indiana together) on a peninsula in East Asia, opposite Japan. Its borders touched Communist China and the Soviet Union. It had been annexed by Japan in 1910 and was surrendered to the Allies in 1945. At the end of the war Russian troops had moved into the country as far as the 38th parallel. American troops had freed the country south of that line.

Korea was supposed to be united under a government chosen by free elections ordered by the

Tempers rose during Khrushchev and Nixon's famous "debate" that took place at a model American kitchen display in Moscow in 1959.

"At this wondrous moment," British Prime Minister Macmillan said, "we seem on the threshold of genuine practical steps toward peace." The next meeting was set for May 16, 1960, at Paris.

Collapse of the conference. The spirit of Camp David was shattered on May 5, 1960. Khrushchev announced that Soviet forces had shot down an American U-2 plane engaged in aerial reconnaissance over the Soviet Union, and they had captured the pilot. At first the United States flatly denied the charge of spying. Many Americans assumed that the United States had been regularly flying over Russia. Still, the nation was surprised when the

President in a television address accepted personal responsibility for the aerial spying and actually defended it. He refused to apologize. Even the conservative *Wall Street Journal* was shocked: "Up until now it has been possible to say to the world that what came out of the Kremlin was deceitful and untrustworthy but that people could depend on what they were told by the government of the United States. Now the world may not be so sure that this country is any different from any other."

The heads of state gathered in Paris, but the planned conference never took place. Khrushchev bitterly attacked Eisenhower and the United States. He withdrew his invitation to the President to visit the Soviet Union. He said he would have no more meetings with Eisenhower until he apologized. The President refused.

Troubles in Latin America. The United States faced critical new problems even with our neighbors in the Western Hemisphere. Since the days of the Good Neighbor policy and World War II, the nation's attention had been directed mainly to the large challenges farther away.

The United States had tried to prevent the spread of communism by supporting governments that proclaimed their anti-communism. But this policy sometimes backfired. We often ended up helping repressive governments. We found ourselves bolstering dictatorships—merely because they were anti-Communist. This lost us friends among freedom-loving people. In many parts of the world, where free institutions were weak, we had no easy choice.

Americans were upset in 1958 when Vice-President Nixon was stoned and spat upon in Venezuela on his goodwill tour of Latin America. The people had not forgotten our earlier support of a dictator in their country.

United States weakness in Latin America was exposed by the rapid movement of events in Cuba. In 1958 the longtime dictator of that country, the corrupt Fulgencio Batista, was overthrown by a young lawyer, Fidel Castro. For three years Castro had led guerrilla forces operating from the Cuban hills. Castro seized the large foreign (mainly United States) holdings in Cuba. He collectivized the farms. He freed the country from its dependence on the United States. But he tied himself to the Soviets and set up a new police state. "Cuba, sí,

Yanqui no!" was Castro's popular rallying cry. An eloquent and long-winded speaker, he soon became a folk hero. He was famous for his big Havana cigars and his friendly manner with Cuban peasants. He outlawed all parties except the Communists and set up prison camps for his enemies. With Soviet aid, Castro built up one of the strongest military forces in Latin America. This loaded pistol was only 90 miles off the coast of the United States.

Eisenhower steps down. If it had not been for the Twenty-second Amendment, Ike could probably have run for and won a third term. Unlike TR or FDR, he had not been a strong President. But his calm and friendly way and his good-humored honesty helped ease the bad temper and quiet the jumpy nerves that troubled the nation when he took office. In addition, he had consolidated the New Deal economic and social programs. He made them all-American institutions when he adopted them as Republican programs. And most important of all, the nation was no longer involved in any foreign wars.

Outgoing President Eisenhower cheerfully posed with his young successor at the White House before Kennedy's inauguration.

Elliot Erwitt/Magnum

Before leaving office, Eisenhower followed the example of another General-President, George Washington, more than a century and a half earlier. Like Washington, Eisenhower turned his farewell address into a warning against the dangers hidden in the future. He cautioned against the "military industrial complex" that was making its influence "felt in every city, every state house, every office of the federal government." In the future, he admitted, our nation would certainly need vast military forces and enormous factories. What troubled him was "the potential for the disastrous rise of misplaced power. . . . We must never let the weight of this combination endanger our liberties or democratic processes." Still beloved by the mass of Americans, Ike retired to his farm in Gettysburg, Pennsylvania. He left the many unsolved problems of the nation and the world to a promising young President, John F. Kennedy.

SECTION REVIEW

1. Identify or explain: Aswan Dam, UN Emergency Force, *Sputnik*, *Explorer I*, National Defense Education Act, NASA, King Hussein, Anastas Mikoyan, Camp David, U-2 incident, Fidel Castro.

2. Locate: Suez Canal, Sinai peninsula, Gaza, Syria, Jordan, Lebanon, Iraq, Quemoy, Matsu, Formosa Strait.

3. Summarize the crises in Hungary and Egypt under these headings: (a) causes, (b) participants, (c) results.

4. What part did each of the following play in the development of rockets, missiles, and earth satellites: (a) Robert Goddard, (b) German scientists, (c) "Operation Paperclip," (d) Wernher Von Braun, (e) Russian scientists and engineers?

5. How did the United States react to *Sputnik*?

6. What was the Eisenhower Doctrine? Where was it applied? What were the results?

7. Describe the crises centering at Taiwan, Berlin, and Cuba.

8. What efforts were made in 1959–1960 to relax the cold war? How did they turn out?

9. What was Eisenhower's warning in his farewell address?

CHAPTER REVIEW

MEETING OUR EARLIER SELVES

1. The President needs to be a policymaker, administrator, diplomat, and leader. How did Eisenhower's career up to 1952 provide experience in these roles? Compare his background with that of earlier General-Presidents.

2. Cite instances when the Eisenhower administration made a *forceful response* (use of force or threat of force) to troublesome events in foreign affairs. On what occasions did the United States use diplomacy or make other non-threatening responses? In each case describe the response made by the Eisenhower administration and tell whether or not you think it was suitable.

3. In six of his eight years, Eisenhower had to work with a Democratic majority in Congress. How might this have influenced his move to "moderate Republicanism"?

4. What events in the 1950s gave Eisenhower chances to exert leadership for human rights? How did he respond?

5. Some observers see the Eisenhower years as a period of relaxation—after the turbulent years of depression, world war, and postwar adjustment. Is this a realistic judgment? Explain. Does the nation need a "breathing spell" after a period of rapid change?

QUESTIONS FOR TODAY

1. To what extent has today's President moved away from positions taken in the election campaign? Can you account for the changes?

2. What major domestic problems that faced the Eisenhower administration are still with us today? Study one of these persistent problems and point out how it has changed.

3. Identify major trouble spots in the world today. Which of these were also problems in the Eisenhower era? Are today's problems linked in any way to actions by the United States in the 1950s?

4. Would Eisenhower's "open skies" plan be appropriate today? Explain.

YOUR REGION IN HISTORY

1. How were schools in your state affected by the Supreme Court's 1954 school desegregation decision? If change had to take place, how was the matter handled?

2. Find out how schools in your district responded to the challenges posed by Russia's early lead in space exploration.

3. Identify changes that took place in your city or county during the Eisenhower years in such areas as housing, other construction, industry, and population. Were any of these changes stimulated by federal laws enacted in these years?

SKILLS TO MAKE OUR PAST VIVID

1. The following events mentioned in this chapter helped to produce other events or conditions. List each event under the title "Cause." Opposite it, under the title "Result," write an appropriate result: (a) end of Korean War; (b) Communist takeover of China; (c) return of Shah of Iran to power: (d) Army-McCarthy televised hearings; (e) mob violence over school desegregation in Little Rock; (f) joint U.S.-USSR support for cease-fire in Egypt; (g) Soviet launching of *Sputnik*; (h) Communist Chinese shelling of Quemoy and Matsu.

2. Find a political cartoon of the 1950s that commented on some aspect of the Eisenhower Presidency. Explain the cartoon and the cartoonist's point of view.

CHAPTER 30

Mobile people and magic machines

In every war, besides the killing and the misery, large changes are at work. Wars set people on the move. There are not only the men and women serving in the armed forces. Thousands move to the factories in distant cities making arms and tanks and planes. Wars change the way the nation grows. Families are separated. Young people cannot settle down and raise new families.

Wars also produce new machines. The nation's scientists and engineers must invent new devices to defeat the enemy. They have to find new ways to send information across great distances, to move troops, to feed and shelter people at home and at the front. Out of the machines of war eventually come machines of peace. The radio and the airplane, which were tried and proven in World War I, changed American life in the years that followed. And so from World War II came new medicines like penicillin and electronic machines like television.

The forces of mobile people and magic machines have a "momentum"—a power to keep themselves going. In this chapter we will see how the forces that gathered strength during World War II (and had started even before) gained momentum. They transformed the country during the eras of Truman and Eisenhower. And afterwards these forces continued to shape the nation.

1. A changing people

After World War II dramatic changes took place in the population—in the rate of growth, length of life, occupation, and the places where people lived. All this had far-reaching effects on the lives of every American.

Studying the population. The study of population is called "demography." This comes from the Greek words *demos* (people) and *graphein* (to write or record). Demographers point out that, at different times and places, the population grows in different ways. For example, during wartime when young men and women are away from home in the armed forces, families have fewer children. The "birthrate" normally goes down. After wars, husbands and wives are reunited, more young people marry, and the birthrate goes up. So it was after World War II.

Demographers analyze statistics about population. Such statistics are important for planning by government and business. The framers of the

Constitution back in 1787 knew that the growing nation would need up-to-date facts about the moving population. So they established the federal census (Art. I, sec. 2), requiring the national government to count the population every ten years. Then the members of the House of Representatives could be reapportioned according to the changes.

As the census became more detailed, the public could use this information to plan the water supply and roads and schools. Businesses could build factories where workers would be living. They could predict the size of the market for their product. The Bureau of the Census (now in the Department of Commerce) became an American institution. It has gathered all sorts of facts about our people. And demographers even invented ways to estimate the changes occurring between the regular decennial (every ten years) census.

The nation grows. After World War II the United States experienced a "population explosion." When the Great Depression finally ended, people had more money to support a family. And then when veterans returned home at the war's end, the birthrate increased. But this was not just the normal increase after any war. The population soared so fast that even expert demographers were astonished.

In 1940 there were 132 million people in the United States. During the decade of the 1930s our population had increased just 7.2 percent—the smallest proportionate increase in the nation's history. By 1950 there were 151 million, an increase of 14.5 percent over 1940. Between 1950 and 1960 the number of people went up even faster—by 18.5 percent—to a total of over 179 million. This was mainly due to the high birthrate. At the same time, refugees from war and nazism and communism swelled the number of immigrants coming to the United States from 1 million during the decade of the 1940s to 2.5 million in the 1950s.

By the end of 1950 one person was being added to the nation every twelve seconds. This explosive growth was equal then to another Richmond, Virginia, every month and a whole Maryland every year. It put strains on cities and states, which were forced to build bigger hospitals, to hire more police and firefighters, and especially to add new schools to cope with the large numbers of children.

Paolo Koch/Photo Researchers

During the 1950s, our population increased so rapidly that experts said we were in the midst of a "baby boom."

Slowing the boom. During the 1960s the population boom began to slow down. Still the nation grew by 13.5 percent, which meant adding nearly 24 million people to make a population of 203 million by 1970. The nation now had twice the number of people it had only 50 years before.

By the end of 1972 the baby boom was over. The Census Bureau reported then that American women were not having quite enough babies to keep the population steady. But the many male and female babies born during those years of population explosion would grow up and in time have their own children.

Moving west, north, and south. Even while the rate of growth of the American population changed,

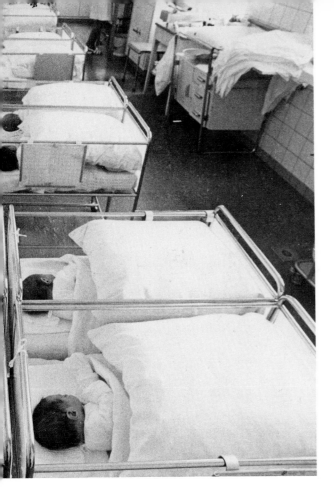

same time, one of every three Americans lived on a farm. In 1970 only one American in every 22 still lived on a farm. Each year farms held a smaller and smaller proportion of the people. The number of farms had fallen from a peak of 6.8 million in 1935 to under 3 million in 1970; and it was continuing to fall rapidly. Of course, at the same time, the farms that remained grew much larger in size. Farmers still spoke with a powerful voice in national politics. The 4.5 million American farm workers in 1970 were more numerous than all the workers in the steel, automobile, and transportation industries combined.

Back in 1820 the average farm worker could produce only enough to feed four people. Now, modern farm machinery, improved seeds, better fertilizers, and scientific methods had enormously increased what each farmer could produce. By 1950 one farm worker could feed 15, and by 1970 each one could produce enough for 45! American farmers helped feed people in Russia, India, and all over the world.

For those who remained on the farm, life became less isolated during the postwar years. The spread of telephones and automobiles meant that farm families could see or talk to their neighbors more easily. Television brought to the farmhouse the same news broadcasts, sports programs, and other entertainment seen by apartment dwellers in the big cities. Some American farmers drove large tractors equipped with air conditioning, citizens' band (CB) radios, TV sets, and high fidelity sound systems. The experiences of all Americans were becoming more and more alike.

The move to the suburbs. Meanwhile, the city people did not sit still in the centers of their growing metropolises. After 1950 they moved in large numbers out of the central cities to the nearby suburbs. In 1950, 35 percent of the nation's people lived in the central cities and almost as many—27 percent—in the suburbs. By 1970 the suburbs were winning, for 31 percent lived in the central cities and 37 percent in the suburbs. This gave many Americans a new opportunity to enjoy fresh air, to mow their lawns, to watch birds, and plant gardens of flowers and vegetables. But it also produced "suburban sprawl" and new traffic jams! Homes and factories and shopping centers were jumbled together in ugly mixes.

the people never ceased to move. After World War II, the lure of the West drew millions all the way to the shores of the Pacific. By 1964 California, with 10 percent of the nation's people, had become the most populous state in the Union.

At the same time there were north-south movements that did not fit the old pattern. Between 1920 and 1960 large numbers of blacks left the South heading north, hoping for better jobs, more equality, more opportunity. Still, in 1940 three-quarters of all blacks lived in the South. But by 1970 the South held only half of black Americans. Now there were more blacks in the North and proportionately more whites in the South. After 1960 a new migration of whites from North to South more than made up for the departing blacks.

Moving off the farms. All across the nation there was another great and speedy migration—from the countryside to the city. In 1920 the nation's rural and urban populations were equal in size. At the

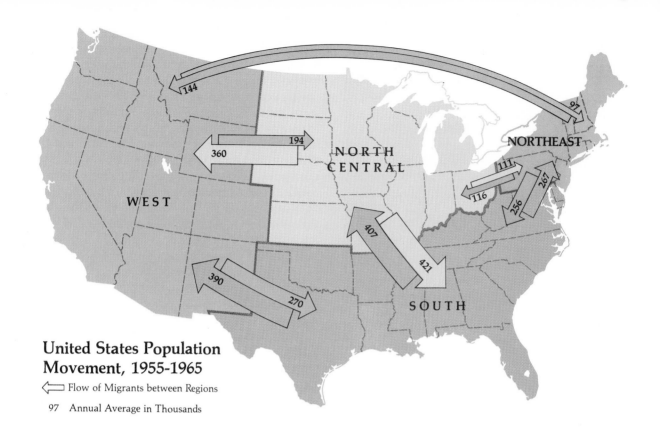

United States Population Movement, 1955-1965

⟵⎯ Flow of Migrants between Regions

97 Annual Average in Thousands

After World War II, suburban tract housing like Levittown, Pennsylvania, shown here, was rapidly built to hold the growing population.

Van Bucher/Photo Researchers

To describe this America, the census could no longer deal simply with "cities." Americans were spread across the country in new clusters. The census called each cluster a Standard Metropolitan Statistical Area (SMSA). Each SMSA was a dense population (including suburbs) surrounding a central city of at least 50,000. One of every four Americans lived in or near the ten largest SMSAs. By the 1970s the nation's 250 SMSAs contained about two-thirds of all the people. More than half of them lived in the suburbs.

Now these new-style cities—the SMSAs—were so many and so close together that it was hard to know where one ended and another began. Looking down from an airplane flying northward from Norfolk, Virginia, to Bangor, Maine, what you saw looked like one big super-city. This needed a new name, and people began calling it a "megalopolis" (from the Greek words for "monster" and for "city"). These sprawling monster-cities grew also in Texas, Florida, California, and on the edge of the Great Lakes.

One surprising fact was that—although the whole heart of the continent had been filling up for two centuries—more than half of all Americans now lived within 50 miles of the oceans, the Gulf of Mexico, or the Great Lakes.

A mobile people. Even when they reached California or Florida or arrived in their chosen city, Americans did not settle down. Every year after 1948 one American in five moved to a new place—down the street, to a nearby town, or on to another state. The census found that in a single year in the 1970s more than 36 million people had changed houses. Of course, most of them had just moved within the same city or county. Still, they had to get used to a new neighborhood with different stores and schools. In 1970 a quarter of all the people in the United States were living in a different state from where they had been born.

This moving around made problems—and opportunities—for all Americans. For example, most black Americans were transformed from rural to urban citizens. In 1940 one-third of all employed blacks worked on farms. By 1970 fewer than 4 percent were farm workers, and four-fifths of the black population lived in urban areas. Most were still prevented from moving to the suburbs by their own poverty or by white prejudice. In the half-century after the Civil War the proportion of blacks in the whole population of the United States declined from 13 to 11 percent. That proportion has remained about the same ever since.

In a fast-moving America—of Americans living close together—it was easier for blacks to demand their rights. The first successes of Martin Luther King, Jr., and Rosa Parks were in crowded Montgomery and on the buses that carried people to work (p. 614).

The concentration of this 11 percent in the cities also gave blacks an increased political power. They were a voting bloc that could be easily identified and (because of segregation) easily found. Now at last, even in the South, they were allowed to vote. Their support for Kennedy in 1960 and for Carter in 1976 helped provide the narrow margins for victory. In the cities, where they lived closer together, it was easier for them to support their candidate. Their votes brought Atlanta, Georgia, its first black mayor in 1973. By then there were black mayors in Los Angeles and Detroit and in 90 other cities.

In 1964 there were only four blacks in Congress, but by 1972 there were fifteen, including Edward Brooke, Republican senator from Massachusetts. Black influence at the polls would have been even greater if more blacks had voted. In the late 1970s only one-third of the 15 million blacks eligible to vote had registered, and only one-third of those registered bothered to cast their ballots.

As the barriers were slowly broken down, during the 1960s an increasing number of blacks began to join fellow Americans in the suburbs. There they rose from 2.5 percent to 4.2 percent, still far below their 11 percent in the total population. Political power now lay with the suburbs because more voters lived there than in either the cities or the rural areas.

An aging population. The nation was reshaped—not only by how the population moved but by how the population grew. After World War II, there was a striking increase in the number of Americans over 65. People were living longer because of better diet, advances in medicine and surgery, and the invention of "miracle drugs" (like sulfa and penicillin), which cured diseases that had often been fatal. In 1900 the average life expectancy of all Americans at birth was only 47, and people over 65 represented only 4 percent of the population. By

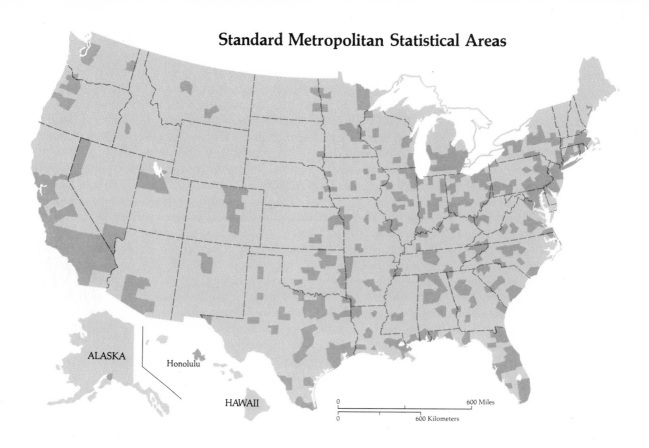

Standard Metropolitan Statistical Areas

ALASKA

Honolulu

HAWAII

0   600 Miles

0   600 Kilometers

the 1940s the average life expectancy reached 65. By 1970 it had climbed to 71.

The census showed that men generally did not live as long as women. In the 1970s men at birth had a life expectancy of 67 while for women it was nearly 75. By 1970 the number of people over 65 had grown to 20 million—10 percent of the whole population. They outnumbered the people in all the twenty smallest states combined. And they had their own special hopes. They were another new group whom the successful politician had to please. American youth usually looked for adventure and opportunity. "Senior citizens" cared more for security and leisure. In the 1960s and 1970s, could these different hopes be matched?

SECTION REVIEW

1. Explain: demography, SMSA, megalopolis.
2. Point out major trends in population growth and movement from 1945 to 1970.
3. Why did the number of farm workers decline?
4. How was population mobility beneficial?

2. Everyday life transformed

The new world of adventure was the world of science and of machines. Ever since the colonists had "invented" their nation, and devised a new kind of written constitution, Americans had loved to experiment. They also liked to buy new things. Visitors from abroad noticed that Americans were machine minded.

The famous cartoonist Rube Goldberg said the American motto ought to be, "Do it the hard way!" Americans loved complicated ways of simplifying everyday life. Why walk if you could ride? Why use a wooden pencil if you could use a metal pencil with retractable lead—including many colors that you really did not need? Why write with a pencil or pen if you could use a typewriter? Or why use a simple hand-operated typewriter when there was a much more complex electric machine? Why write it yourself at all if you could first dictate it into a machine that recorded your voice on a tape, which would be put into another machine to be played back to someone who would transcribe the words on an electric typewriter? In the machine-rich United States, everyday life was full of fantastic surprises.

A growing economy. All these machines helped create the American standard of living. They helped make life more interesting, as well as more complicated. They opened opportunities for investors, for business leaders to build factories, for skilled workers to make the machines—and for salespeople and advertising experts to sell these machines by the millions. After the war the economy expanded and prospered.

The quarter-century from the end of World War II until about 1970 brought the nation its longest period of prosperity. There were brief recessions, but the statistics of economic growth were astonishing. The Gross National Product (GNP)—the total value of all goods and services produced in the nation—measured in 1958 dollars rose from $355.2 billion in 1945 to $722.5 billion in 1970. In the same period, per capita income before taxes increased (in 1958 dollars) from $1870 to $3050. Between 1967 and 1978, the average hourly rate of pay for private nonfarm occupations more than doubled, going from $2.68 to $5.73. Most Americans prospered as they shared the highest per capita income in the world.

Prosperity—enormous government projects in war and peace, high wages, and a growing demand for everything—had its price. The terrible price, which Americans began to pay in the 1960s, was inflation. From 1948 through 1965 prices rose an average of only 1.7 percent a year. But beginning in 1966 and continuing through the 1970s prices soared upward at an average rate of 6 percent a year. This meant that $1 could buy only half as much in 1978 as it had bought in 1967.

Not knowing what inflation might bring, people were afraid to plan their future. Savings began to lose their value. If you saved money for a house or a car, maybe the price would rise faster than you could save. Then why save? Americans began to believe that they should spend their money now or borrow so they could buy goods before prices went up. This ran up the demand and raised prices even more.

Reasons for prosperity. Immediately after World War II, there was a large, pent-up demand for housing and for all peacetime products, such as

Stores encouraged their customers to "Charge it!" and the nation's economy boomed.

automobiles and kitchen appliances, that were hard to get during the war. This demand, backed by wartime savings, gave a big boost to sales. Government spending did not decline and kept the economy booming. American export trade, supported by the billions of dollars the United States government paid out for foreign aid, flourished.

All sorts of new machines—radios, high fi's, television sets, washing and drying machines, deep freezes, power lawnmowers, and countless others—kept factories busy and customers eager to buy. None was more important than the automobile. Fewer than 1 million new automobiles were produced during World War II. By 1970, 8 million a year were being turned out. These consumed one-fifth of the nation's new steel, half its malleable iron, and two-thirds of its rubber and lead.

All these cars needed highways. In 1956, then, the nation began the largest road construction program in its history. Under President Eisenhower, Congress voted $33 billion (later increased) for a ten-year program to build a whole 42,500-mile network of interstate superhighways. By 1975, because of inflation, it would cost $39 billion just to finish the last 5500 miles of the system. In 1978 President Carter signed a highway bill that

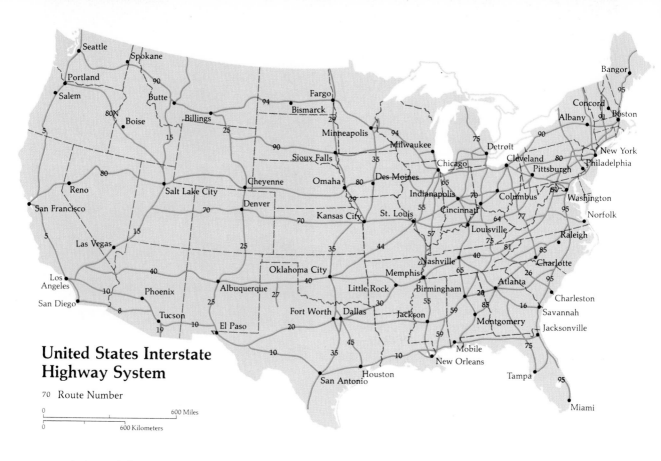

United States Interstate Highway System

70 Route Number

0 _____ 600 Miles

0 _____ 600 Kilometers

provided $9.3 billion a year for three years. Many more billions were spent by states and localities.

The automobile and the suburbs. In earlier days cities had grown up near waterways. Then railroads went to the cities, and new cities grew along the railroads. Even before the automobile, streetcars took people out to the suburbs to live and back into the center of the city to work and to shop. The automobile gave its owner a new freedom. Of course, railroads and streetcars had to stay on their special tracks. But the car would take Americans of the twentieth century anywhere there were roads. Factories, stores, and movie theaters moved out to shopping centers in the suburbs. The "downtown" of a big city was no longer the center of people's lives.

Americans had fallen in love with their automobiles. In 1971 alone, they spent the staggering sum of $180 billion to buy new and used cars. This was more than four times what they spent for their public elementary and high schools. From their homes in the suburbs Americans could drive to work every day. Life in the suburbs—shopping, going to school, visiting friends—required a car.

Living with the automobile. The automobile brought strange by-products. One of these was the "credit card." The first credit cards were offered by the large gasoline companies to attract customers. They gave out these identifying cards so that people could charge gasoline purchases anywhere on the road at one of their hundreds of stations. After 1950, other businesses picked up the credit card idea.

The parking problem was also new. To attract customers to the central city, huge parking garages were built in choice locations. So automobile traffic increased. Then the poor pedestrians had to risk their lives when they crossed the street. Cars ruled the surface of the earth. Millions of automobiles polluted the atmosphere with carbon monoxide and hydrocarbons. It was hard to live *without* automobiles, but could Americans learn to live *with* them?

Machines to do everything. Of course, the automobiles needed accessories—windshield wipers, turn

Even the large-scale construction of superhighways like this could not prevent traffic jams when the nation's automobiles multiplied after World War II.

signals, car radios. This created new industries by the hundreds. Also Americans wanted, made, and bought new electric appliances for the home, for the factory, and for the office. These included air conditioners, dehumidifiers, electric blankets, electric knives and toothbrushes, automatic washing machines and dryers, dishwashers, garbage disposals, pencil sharpeners, typewriters, cash registers, and countless other items. The factories to make these products, and the factories to make the machines that went into the factories, created new jobs by the thousands.

To produce the electricity to run these homes and factories, the nation burned the old reliable coal, which had driven the factories in the preceding century. The factories also were powered by oil and natural gas brought in by giant pipelines from the West and Southwest to the cities of the South, Midwest, and East.

Light metals like aluminum, magnesium, and titanium were combined with chromium into sparkling, rust-free new alloys. Aluminum production leaped from 287,000 tons in 1940 to 2 million tons in 1960 and over 4 million in 1970. Industrial chemists

invented "plastics"—which were cheaper than wood or metal, easier to shape into the new tools and toys and gadgets. There were man-made wash-and-wear textiles like nylon and Dacron, which never lost their press. And countless other "synthetics" were used for detergents, drugs, insecticides, and fertilizers.

All these products had to be put in packages. The packaging was as new as the product. In the 1800s, people had taken their own containers to the general store to carry home their milk or coffee or crackers. Then, after World War I, the rise of advertising, national brands, and supermarkets created a whole new "packaging" industry. As customers walked through the aisles of supermarkets to serve themselves, they bought their groceries in familiar packages. Sometimes even when they didn't really need something, they bought it simply because they were attracted by the colorful, much-advertised package.

The spread of television. Advertising these packaged products became still another big industry. This advertising supported broadcasting on radio

631

and television while it filled every American living room with "commercials."

Television, one of the most magical of American machines, conquered the nation with astounding speed. In 1948 there were only 200,000 television sets in all the United States, and of every hundred families only one owned a set. But by 1970 nearly every American home (95.5 percent) had at least one television set. After the first commercial communications satellite, *Early Bird*, was put into space in 1965, live broadcasts could be sent from Europe to the United States. In the 1970s satellites brought events from all over the world—even President Nixon's visit to far-off China—into the nation's homes.

Now Americans could see and hear events as they happened. The war in Vietnam, civil rights marches, riots in the streets—along with entertaining series, cartoons, old movies, and sports events—all appeared on the TV screen. The magic of television brought a new kind of confusion. The wonderful box in everybody's living room created the Instant Everywhere. You could stay wherever you were and see what was happening at that instant all over the United States—and all over the world. Americans felt magically close to events in Vietnam, on the civil rights battlegrounds of Alabama and Mississippi, even on the moon! They sometimes forgot how far away those fearful and exciting events really were.

"Network" programs, which cost a fortune to produce, made celebrities out of the newscasters. Citizens all over the nation could see and hear their President and watch events in Washington. There was a new danger that they would pay less attention to their mayor or their governor or the real neighbors in their own town.

Americans, for the first time, could see events "replayed." They forgot that this, too, was a modern miracle. Before photography or radio or television, an event happened only once. Then it was gone forever unless an artist painted it in a picture or a writer told the story. In the age of television, by the 1960s when you watched a sporting event, you could not only see the game played once. You could see the most thrilling moments played again and again on instant replay. With your tape recorder, also developed after World War II, you could reproduce music from radios, records, and live groups to be played again

Bruce Davidson/Magnum

Here the distant Statue of Liberty is bracketed by a new feature of the American landscape.

whenever you wanted. You could record your family gatherings at Christmas or Thanksgiving. Members of the family could send each other greetings in their own voices.

New-style pioneers. There were many American pioneers on these new machine-frontiers. The age of the Go-Getter was not over. Instead of clearing the land and building cities in the wilderness, the modern pioneer built machines no one else had imagined, to satisfy needs never before felt. One clever inventor, Edwin H. Land, devised an instant camera that not only took pictures, but developed them on the spot. Imaginative Chester F. Carlson, who had worked his way through the California Institute of Technology, invented a new copying system. Bold businessmen in Rochester, New York, supported his research and invested in his machine to make an image on paper. They renamed his process "xerography" (from the Greek words *xeros*, "dry," and *graphein*, "to write"). Soon Xerox machines were everywhere. Offices and libraries all over the country were reproducing letters and books. It was easier than ever before to make a copy of anything.

More machines, and more machines to make machines! All these required energy, which meant more electricity. Between 1940 and 1970 the production of electricity in the United States increased over sevenfold. We used far more energy than any other nation. As a result of improved machines and better working methods, between 1947 and 1970 the output of factories per working hour more than doubled!

Machines to run machines. There seemed no end to the powers of machine magic. The next step was to invent machines to run the machines. In the years after World War II, that actually happened. About 1946, Americans began to use another new word, "automation." The fantastic new machine was the "computer." Its main inventor was a brilliant Hungarian immigrant, John von Neumann, who had helped plan the atomic bomb and now was a professor at Princeton. In a few seconds the electronic computer would count and calculate what once had busied a hundred workers for days. High-speed computers could count, sort, remember, and select information—then use it to run factories or oil refineries.

In the 1960s and 1970s computers found thousands of new uses—to monitor patients in hospitals, to process checks in banks, to handle credit-card bills, and to keep track of library books. They solved problems for scientists, mathematicians, educators, engineers, and business leaders. The computer even moved into supermarkets and provided a machine that could read the lines on packages, then add up the price. The take-it-for-granted customer instantly had a neat shopping list with the name and price of each item.

In all sorts of factories, the work was transformed. In automobile factories, for example, welding machines with electronic memories made some of the decisions live workers once had to make. After a "live" welder guided the computers once through their jobs, the machines were then "programed" to remember what to weld and then they would repeat it over and over again as each car came by.

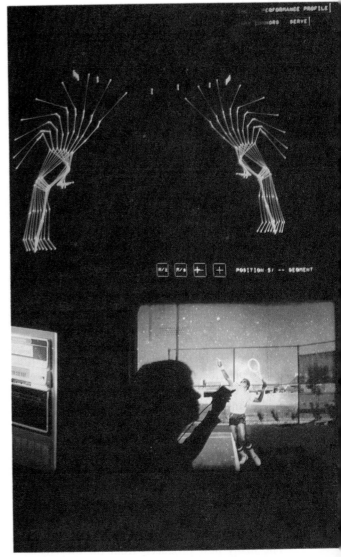

An athlete working to improve his tennis stroke uses a computer to analyze his movements and help him do better.

The advantages of these miraculous machines were obvious. They took the place of a great deal of drudgery. But, like all other machines, they had their price. They put people out of work. And until those people could be trained for new jobs created by the new machines, they might feel lost and useless. This was the kind of price that other new machines had always extracted. Here was another challenge to American enterprise, education, and government.

preacher, Billy Graham, drew hundreds of thousands to his meetings—there to make "decisions for Christ." He spoke to millions more on radio and television. And Norman Vincent Peale reached more millions with *The Power of Positive Thinking* (1952), which quickly broke all the records of the time for a best-seller.

Still, in the 1960s some theologians said that religion had lost its power in the United States. "God is Dead," they complained. But Americans by the millions went to the church of their choice. Ministers, like the automobile makers, tried using novelty to attract people to church. They found ways to make their services more entertaining. They changed the seating and brought in rock groups and guitar players. While this offended some churchgoers, it attracted many young people.

The opinion polls showed little change in American religious belief or churchgoing. In 1975 some 94 percent of the people polled said they believed in God, and 68 percent believed in an afterlife. In 1948 the figures had been almost exactly the same. Nearly half of the nation's adults went to church regularly. This was the largest proportion in any Western country. Despite automobiles, radios, television, and automation, the Americans' faith in religion remained.

SECTION REVIEW

1. Identify: John Dewey, James B. Conant, Fulton J. Sheen, Billy Graham, Norman Vincent Peale.

2. Explain some events occurring outside the United States that affected American education.

3. How did technological change affect religion in the United States?

4. Art and the machine

Meanwhile the machines and new ways of life left their mark on the arts. After the camera was invented, anybody with a camera could make a picture exactly like what he saw. It was no trick anymore to make a "likeness" of a person or a landscape. So the artists, too, tried to make something different. They experimented with new ways to paint and new kinds of statues. These were no longer pretty figures of men and women, trees or flowers. Instead they were abstract patterns showing the artist's private vision.

Adventurous artists. The most famous of these was Jackson Pollock (1912–1956), who had been born in Cody, Wyoming, and was trained to paint in the traditional style. He invented his own kind of Abstract Expressionism called "action painting." He would put his large canvas on the floor and then (he explained) paint with "sticks, trowels, knives, and dripping fluid paint or a heavy impasto with sand, broken glass and other foreign matter added." Along with Pollock came Willem de Kooning, Helen Frankenthaler, Franz Kline, Adolph Gottlieb, Mark Rothko, Barnett Newman, and Robert Motherwell, each with another new vision of how to paint. Some people wondered whether what they produced was really "art." But many more enjoyed what they saw. They believed Americans should experiment with art, just as they did with everything else.

"Blue Territory" by Helen Frankenthaler.

Jackson Pollock's "Autumn Rhythm" (above) is one of the artist's "action paintings." Robert Motherwell painted "Elegy to the Spanish Republic, 108" between 1965 and 1967.

Collectors, museums, and galleries began snatching up "minimal art" at high prices. Minimal art did little or nothing to change an object, and simply considered the object as art. Andy Warhol's "pop art" offered larger-than-life paintings of Campbell Soup cans and Brillo boxes, and Claes Oldenburg's pop art produced a huge statue of a lipstick or a canvas of a *Hamburger with Pickle and Tomato Attached*.

Still, even into the 1970s some of the most successful painters continued to compete with the camera. They, too, delighted millions of Americans. Andrew Wyeth's paintings were as precise and accurate as a photograph, but somehow seemed more real.

Writers in a complex world.

Writers also had trouble casting the new world of speedy change and all-powerful machines in the old patterns. Herman Wouk's *The Caine Mutiny* (1952) told about the problems of command in the modern Navy. James Jones's World War II novel, *From Here to Eternity* (1951), showed characters who were lonely and lost. J. D. Salinger's *Catcher in the Rye* (1951) was a story of an adolescent trying to escape hypocrisy. In *Invisible Man* (1952), Ralph Ellison's black hero gradually saw that he was powerless and that the world was out of his reach. Ellison made the black man in a white world a symbol of everyone's puzzling experience in the industrial age. Joseph Heller's *Catch-22* (1969), a hilarious tale of wartime red tape, became a name for all the no-win situations in modern America. Carson McCullers portrayed the silent world of two mutes in *The Heart Is a Lonely Hunter* (1940) and the loneliness of a young girl in *The Member of the Wedding* (1946). Eudora Welty in *Delta Wedding* (1948) and *Losing Battles* (1970) described the intimate ties that bind families together. Katherine Anne Porter described us all in *Ship of Fools* (1962).

William Faulkner wrote about how the South (and America) lost the simple ideals of the farming past. In a mythical county in Mississippi in *The Hamlet* (1940), *The Town* (1957), and *The Mansion* (1959) he told the long story of the greedy and unpleasant Snopes clan. Faulkner won the Nobel Prize for literature in 1950.

Still other writers, like Saul Bellow, who also won the Nobel Prize, described the problems that thoughtful men and women faced inside themselves. Norman Mailer, after writing *The Naked and the Dead* (1948), his action-novel about World War II, turned to writing about himself. His "new journalism" report on the anti-Vietnam march on Washington in 1967 was called *The Armies of the Night*.

In spite of all the hi-fi's and television sets and the other entertainment machines, Americans bought and read more books than ever before. Each year's new titles numbered more than 40,000. Inexpensive paperback books, hardly known in this country before the war, flooded the market. Readers could find them everywhere—not only in bookstores, but now also in drugstores, supermarkets, and airports. Millions joined book clubs. Best-selling books often went on to become movies or television shows. And sometimes movies were turned into novels.

To help it use all sources of knowledge, back in 1800 the Congress had set up its own library. By the later 1900s the Library of Congress was the largest in the world—with about 20 million books (in 468 languages!) and about 80 million other items. Besides books, magazines, and newspapers, there were photographs, motion picture films, musical recordings, art prints, maps and globes, the manuscripts of famous men and women, and braille books and "talking books" for the blind. It served all other libraries, along with writers, scholars, and all the people. Like the Congress itself, it was a symbol of democratic America that everybody could visit on Capitol Hill in Washington. And it, too, was using the magic of the computer to control its millions of items and offer them to Congress and the nation.

Americans were delighted and bewildered, frustrated and challenged by the kaleidoscope-world of new machines. Books, the movie screen and the TV tube, the works of painters and sculptors helped make sense of their world. Political leaders, the men and women whom Americans elected to represent them and to manage their government, were still the most conspicuous shapers of American life. In the next generation, could these elected leaders offer the uplift and the direction the nation needed?

The forces of mobile people and magic machines, unlike the terms of Presidents, did not end on a particular day. These forces came to a climax under Presidents Truman and Eisenhower. But the forces were rooted in World War II, and even earlier, and did not end with any President's term. The forces we have described would become stronger with the passing years. They help explain the new problems and new opportunities that the nation would face in the turbulent 1960s and after.

SECTION REVIEW

1. How did painters break with tradition in the postwar era?
2. Name and describe the work of some influential writers in the postwar era.
3. How did television and the movies affect the book publishing industry?

CHAPTER REVIEW

MEETING OUR EARLIER SELVES

1. How have farming and farm life changed since 1950?
2. What social changes would you expect to see in the United States as the proportion of young people declines and the proportion of elderly people rises?
3. Identify ways in which computers and other forms of automation affect you and your family.
4. What are some "learning by doing" school experiences that you have had in the past ten years? How do you learn history besides by reading history books?
5. What evidence do you see that religion continues to have a significant influence on American life?

QUESTIONS FOR TODAY

1. Identify gadgets and machines that you use or can buy that were not available when your parents were your age. Name some machines used by you which were also used by your parents in their youth. How do these machines differ today from the earlier models?

2. Talk to workers with 25 years or more service in the same occupation. Find out what changes have occurred in their jobs. Consider equipment used, hours of work, work procedures, relations with management and/or customers, and so on.

YOUR REGION IN HISTORY

1. Study the "Flow of Migrants" map on page 626. Did your region have an overall gain or loss of population from the migration? Which other region had the heaviest flow of migrants from your region? What particular attractions might have brought people to your region in the period 1955–1965?
2. Try to find out how the racial and ethnic composition of your city, county, parish, or borough changed from 1950 to 1970. How do you account for the changes?
3. To what extent have blacks or Hispanics gained political office and government jobs in your locality in recent years? other minorities?
4. Interview leaders of a local church or synagogue on changes that have occurred in their local or national institutions since 1950.

SKILLS TO MAKE OUR PAST VIVID

1. Study the SMSA map on page 628. Identify the SMSAs in your state by naming the central city (or cities) of each one. What are some other cities and towns in your SMSA or the one nearest to you? Locate the largest super-city, or megalopolis. Where are there others?
2. Plan an auto trip of 2000 miles or more. On an outline map show your route, drawing Interstate highways in *red* and marking their numbers (I-80, for example).

11

Turbulent times
1961–1974

"We dare not forget today that we are the heirs of that first revolution. Let the word go forth from this time and place, to friend and foe alike, that the torch has been passed to a new generation of Americans, born in this century, tempered by war, disciplined by a hard and bitter peace, proud of our ancient heritage, and unwilling to witness or permit the slow undoing of those human rights to which this nation has always been committed, and to which we are committed today at home and around the world."

So John F. Kennedy introduced his Presidency, and so began a turbulent era for the United States. During the following thirteen years one President would be assassinated. Another would decline to run again because of opposition to his foreign policy. And a third, facing impeachment, would resign. During these years, which had begun with so much hope, Americans would be distressed and divided by the actions of their government and their Presidents.

The United States not only survived. The Republic drew new strength by discovering that the people could control their government. They would not wage war without understanding the reasons. They could even replace their President. Never before had they seen so clearly how the Constitution had given power to the people.

"Thrust," by Adolph Gottlieb, seethes with energy contained and released. It foreshadows the turbulence of the new era. From the Metropolitan Museum of Art, George A. Hearn Fund, 1959

CHAPTER 31

Years of hope and promise

The White House took on a new tone when John F. Kennedy, his beautiful wife, Jacqueline, and their vigorous little children moved in. To many people the Kennedys, with their youth, good looks, charm, and culture, created in Washington something like a fairy tale with all its magic. Camelot, they called it, after King Arthur's palace and the idyllic happiness of the time. This Camelot was to last only a brief 1000 days. Then Americans would awaken again to the real, hard world.

1. John F. Kennedy wins

The 1960 campaign would be the first fought mainly on television. Both candidates were carefully "packaged" for sale to the American public. For the first time, all who wished to watch could see them face each other on TV in "great debates."

Nominating the candidates. Before the national convention there were two serious Republican contenders. The energetic Nelson A. Rockefeller, who had been elected governor of New York in 1958, represented the liberal wing. But in December 1959, finding that the party leaders would not support him, he withdrew from the race. When the Republicans met in Chicago in July 1960, the road was cleared for Vice-President Richard M. Nixon of California. He was nominated for President. Then, as a sop to the party liberals, Henry Cabot Lodge, Jr., a former senator from Massachusetts and now ambassador to the UN, was drafted for the second place.

The Democrats faced a heated contest. The main candidates were all senators—John F. Kennedy of Massachusetts, Hubert H. Humphrey of Minnesota, Lyndon B. Johnson of Texas, and Stuart Symington of Missouri. Adlai Stevenson, although not active in the race, waited in the wings hoping that the nod would come his way once more. The most important early fight was between Humphrey and Kennedy. Hubert Humphrey hoped to rally all the old Roosevelt and Truman liberals. The 42-year-old Kennedy was a proven vote-getter and had a conservative record in the House and Senate. His chief handicap was that he was a Roman Catholic. Many party leaders wondered whether a Catholic could be elected President.

The first test of this question came in the primary in West Virginia, where the voters were 95 percent Protestant. The Democrats there would choose whether their delegates to the Democratic convention would support Kennedy or Humphrey. Kennedy won a smashing victory. This knocked Humphrey out of the race and did much to quiet the religious issue. Then Kennedy went on to other victories. When the delegates gathered at the convention in Los Angeles, a last-minute push by

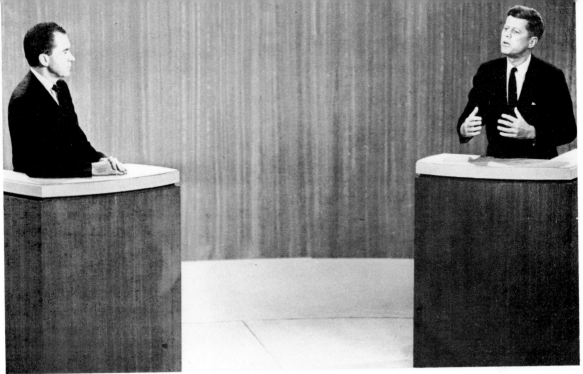

John Kennedy's performance on television in the "great debates" swung many voters to his side.

Lyndon Johnson failed, and Kennedy was nominated on the first ballot.

Kennedy, wanting to make peace with his strong rival and to unify the party, chose Johnson for his running mate. The powerful majority leader of the Senate surprised everyone by accepting. Since LBJ came from Texas, he would help "balance" the ticket and attract votes in the South and Southwest.

The "great debates."

Kennedy argued that, under the Republicans, the nation was stagnating and not moving ahead. During the 1950s, he said, the Gross National Product (the total of all the goods and services produced) had not been growing as it should. He warned of a recession. According to him, the government had neglected all those who needed special help—the young and old, the poor and minorities. Our cities were plagued by slums. Our schools were not doing their job. The general in the White House, he said, had not improved our defense. The nation was behind Soviet Russia in nuclear missiles, and our other arms could not deal with the small "brushfire wars." His slogan was, "Let's get the country moving again." He pointed the way toward a "New Frontier." "Mr. Nixon says, 'We never had it so good.' I say we can do better."

The two candidates appeared together on television in a series of four one-hour programs. People called these the "great debates." But they were not like the old-fashioned Lincoln-Douglas debates a century earlier. In those debates one man spoke for an hour, his opponent replied for an hour and a half. Then the first speaker had another half hour to reply. Now the candidates would only speak for 8 minutes in the first and last debates. All the rest of the time reporters would ask them questions. Each candidate had only 2 1/2 minutes to give his answer.

These "great debates" reached the largest audience that had ever watched a political discussion. Seventy million citizens saw each program. In earlier times the only people who could hear a candidate were those he could reach with his own voice—outdoors or in a meeting hall. Now a whole nation could see and hear both candidates at once. Kennedy seemed to gain more from the debates than Nixon. Though he was less well known, now his charm, poise, and good looks came into everybody's home. His adept handling of questions undercut criticism of his youth and inexperience.

The United States had become a television democracy. And there were new dangers. The man who showed up best on TV was bound to be the best "performer." He could give the cleverest response in 2 1/2 minutes to questions that he had just heard—and look the best doing it. But was that a good test for a President?

The election of 1960 was a cliffhanger. The final count showed the narrowest popular edge (3/10th of 1 percent of all votes cast) since 1880. Alaska had entered the Union in January 1959 and Hawaii followed in August, so there were now 50 states. In the electoral college, Kennedy carried, sometimes by razor-thin margins, enough states to give him 303 votes to Nixon's 219.

There were enough disputed ballots in key states so that Nixon might have challenged the result. But like most other losers of close presidential races, Nixon decided for the good of the nation not to contest the numbers.

John F. Kennedy. Kennedy was the youngest man ever *elected* President, although not the youngest ever to hold the office. That distinction belonged to Theodore Roosevelt. Kennedy, who had been born in Brookline, Massachusetts, on May 29, 1917, was still only 43 when he took office. He came from a large Irish Catholic family. His grandfathers on both sides had been leaders in Democratic politics in Boston. His father, Joseph P. Kennedy, made a fortune in business and finance, and supported FDR for election. FDR appointed him to the Securities and Exchange Commission and then sent him as ambassador to Great Britain. The young Jack Kennedy inherited a love of politics and of the Democratic party.

The year when Jack graduated from Harvard, 1940, was a time of crisis for the free world. The young Kennedy felt the crisis. He revised his student thesis and made it into a book called *Why England Slept.* He told how English statesmen had appeased the Nazis and let them become the menace to the peace of Europe. Then during World War II Jack Kennedy served as a naval officer for four years and won Navy and Marine Corps medals for heroism. He had risked his life to rescue the crew of his PT boat when it was cut in two by a Japanese destroyer. After the war no one was surprised to see another Kennedy enter Massachusetts politics. Of course he was a Democrat. He was elected to the

United States House of Representatives in 1946 and then was elected to the Senate in 1952 and 1958. But Jack Kennedy did not leave an impressive record as a lawmaker.

Like FDR he turned bad luck into an opportunity. He had injured his back in college playing football, and the crash of his PT boat made it worse. After a back operation in 1954 he could not leave his bed for six months. During his slow and painful recovery he wrote another book, *Profiles in Courage.* This story of brave choices by American statesmen won the Pulitzer Prize for biography in 1957.

While Kennedy was writing his book about courage, the Senate was deciding whether to censure Senator Joseph R. McCarthy for his reckless attacks on government servants. Kennedy now kept silent. He did not cast his vote on the McCarthy condemnation because he was recovering from his operation. And he never revealed how he might have voted had he been present on the Senate floor. His critics wondered whether he really understood the meaning of courage.

When Kennedy became President, he brought to the White House youth, vigor, broad culture, and a quick mind. His ability as a speed reader became a legend. He loved to sail, and people were pleased to see that their President was energetic enough to enjoy touch football.

But before he became President, Jack Kennedy had run nothing larger than his Senate office. The nation had not shown great enthusiasm for him. He had won election by the smallest of margins. Could this attractive but inexperienced young man really lead the country to a "New Frontier"?

The inaugural address. On January 20, 1961, a bright sunny day in snow-covered Washington, John F. Kennedy was inaugurated. After the New England poet Robert Frost recited a poem, JFK took the oath of office. His inaugural address was short and eloquent. Since his slim victory might make it difficult for him to get major bills through Congress, Kennedy spoke chiefly on foreign affairs. The first President born in this century, he announced that a "new generation of Americans" had taken control. "Defending freedom in its hour of maximum danger," his generation, too, would hold the line against communism. "Let every nation know, whether it wishes us well or ill, that we shall pay any price, bear any burden, meet any hardship, support any friend, oppose any foe to assure the survival and success of liberty." He called on his fellow citizens to "ask not what America will do for you—ask what you can do for your country."

Many Americans were ready for Kennedy's call after the quiet, steady General Eisenhower. But some remembered the ringing, world-resounding words of Woodrow Wilson. And some feared that Kennedy's brave words, too, might lead us into a world conflict.

The new administration. Kennedy brought into office a whole new team. The President himself clearly planned to play a leading role in foreign affairs. For his Secretary of State he appointed a calm, quiet Georgian, Dean Rusk, who was president of the Rockefeller Foundation. For Secretary of Defense he chose Robert S. McNamara, who was only a year older than Kennedy. As president of

the Ford Motor Company, McNamara had earned a national reputation for finding new ways of running a vast organization. McNamara's slick hair showed his concern for neatness and precise control. Kennedy asked C. Douglas Dillon, a Republican and a wealthy New York investment banker, to become Secretary of the Treasury. This appointment, the new President hoped, would quiet fears that he might be "unsound" in economic matters.

Family feeling was strong among the Kennedys. Now President Jack appointed his brother Robert as Attorney General. Robert Kennedy had only served a brief stint as a lawyer in the Justice Department and then as counsel for Senator Joe McCarthy, before the senator was condemned, and for other congressional committees. He had managed his brother's campaign with skill and ruthlessness. "I see nothing wrong," JFK joked, "with giving Bobby some legal experience before he goes out to practice law." Robert Kennedy remained

John and Jacqueline Kennedy brought youth and glamor to the White House. Beside them at the Inaugural Ball are John's parents, Joseph and Rose Kennedy, and Lyndon and Lady Bird Johnson.

Black Star

his brother's closest adviser and turned out to be a forceful Attorney General.

SECTION REVIEW

1. Identify the chief contenders and the eventual nominees for the two major parties in the 1960 election.
2. Describe the Kennedy-Nixon television debates. What were the dangers in such debates?
3. What qualifications did Kennedy have for the Presidency?
4. Identify four members of Kennedy's Cabinet.

2. Learning hard lessons

The new Kennedy team came to power believing that they could solve all problems. They would soon discover that both at home and abroad some issues were too complex for their hopeful, youthful energies. The first blows to their self-confidence came in foreign affairs.

Trouble in Laos. One of the nations created from French Indochina was Laos. A pro-Western faction was put into power there with the secret help of the CIA. The Communists, and those who wished to remain neutral between Russia and the United States, tried to overturn this regime. "You might have to go in there and fight it out," Ike told JFK. On March 23, 1961, Kennedy publicly warned that the United States would use armed force to prevent a Communist takeover of Laos.

Kennedy was urged by some of his advisers to send in American troops. But to avoid war he agreed to compromise. The British helped persuade the Soviets to come to a conference to set up a new government that would be neutral.

A truce was then arranged. Finally, in June 1962, the three warring factions in Laos came together. They formed a "coalition" government—in which each had a part. Then at Geneva in July, the United States, Russia, Great Britain, and eleven other countries signed a treaty promising to keep the country neutral. Without the use of American

At a March 1961 conference President Kennedy makes a point about the Laotian situation.

forces, it did prevent—or at least postpone—a Communist takeover. Two years later, to nobody's surprise, the Communist faction (the "Pathet Lao") backed out of the coalition. Laos was still a battleground.

The Bay of Pigs. President Kennedy had good reason to be cautious in Laos. For meanwhile close to home—only 90 miles off the Florida coast—the United States suffered a shocking setback. In September 1960 President Eisenhower had approved a plan proposed by Allen Dulles (brother of Secretary of State Dulles), director of the CIA. The United States would supply money and arms in Guatemala for a force of anti-Castro Cubans. This force was trained and ready to go by April 1961. Kennedy and his advisers expected that when the small invasion force landed, the Cuban people would seize the chance to overthrow Castro. So the President gave the signal for the invasion to proceed.

Some 1500 Cuban refugee fighters landed at the Bay of Pigs (Bahía de Cochinos) on the south coast of Cuba on April 17. They were not greeted by the popular uprising they expected. Instead, within hours their attack had bogged down, and they were in trouble. On April 18 Khrushchev threatened that the Soviet Union would go to Cuba's assistance if the United States did not "call a halt to the aggression against the Republic of Cuba." Soon the fighting was over, and 1200 of the anti-Castro troops were captured. In December 1962 after American companies and individuals paid Castro a ransom of $50 million in food and drugs and $3 million in cash, the unlucky refugee troops were freed.

Conference at Vienna. The Bay of Pigs disaster shook President Kennedy and his advisers. It dismayed our European allies and made further problems with the Soviets. At the peace settlement in Potsdam after World War II, the democracies had made the mistake of dividing the great capital city of Berlin and allowing the Soviets to surround it with their troops. Now once again Khrushchev called for the evacuation of West Berlin before the end of 1961 by France, Britain, and the United States and the creation there of a "free city."

Prosperous West Berlin was an outpost of democracy and free enterprise in the very heart of Communist East Germany. It was a living advertisement for freedom, which Russia and the Communist dictators of East Germany feared. The East German leaders would not allow their people to escape to the free world. Still some of their desperate and courageous citizens risked their lives to slip through to West Berlin. The democratic powers were supplying West Berlin by highways controlled by the Communists. Khrushchev again threatened to sign a peace treaty with East Germany. This would allow the East German Communists to starve West Berlin by cutting off all the food that came by land.

At the same time, the unpredictable Khrushchev also made some friendly gestures. He released some American airmen whose RB-47 plane had recently been shot down over Russia. And he told the American ambassador in Moscow that he would like to meet Kennedy. So in June 1961 JFK flew to Vienna, Austria. It was not expected that this would be a full-fledged "summit" meeting, where important treaties would be signed. Instead this was supposed to be merely a chance for discussion.

The talks did not go well. Made even bolder by the Bay of Pigs fiasco, Khrushchev stormed and threatened. But Kennedy was not adept at handling the Russian leader. Still, he did get a Soviet promise to work for peace in Laos, and he stood fast on Berlin. At the end he said to the Soviet premier, "I see it's going to be a very cold winter."

The Berlin wall. In a somber speech to the American people soon after his return, President Kennedy made it clear that, if necessary, the United States would stand and fight for Berlin. Now he increased the draft quotas. He called up reserve and National Guard units. And he asked Congress for $3.2 billion to enlarge our armed forces. At the same time Kennedy made it clear that the United States was ready "to search for peace."

In August 1961 the Russians suddenly sealed off East Berlin from West Berlin, first by erecting a fence and then by building a grim, high wall. No longer could Easterners escape to freedom through West Berlin. Kennedy responded by sending a force of 1500 men to the city as a signal that the United States would act.

The firm refusal of the Western powers to give in led Khrushchev to back down. In October he withdrew his year-end deadline. In 1963 Kennedy encouraged the free world when he went to Berlin

The Brandenburg gate is seen here from the West Berlin side of the wall built by the Soviets. The sign warns: "Attention! You are now leaving West Berlin."

and stated "I am a Berliner." This was an American President declaring that the United States would not allow free people to be strangled.

"Flexible response." During these crises spread across three continents—in Laos, Cuba, and Berlin—President Kennedy was trying to make over American foreign policy. He had been impressed by a speech of Khrushchev's in January 1961 that promised Soviet aid for "wars of national liberation." Khrushchev would use these wars of people to throw off the yoke of colonial rule to spread communism. Kennedy wanted to oppose this threat. But as McNamara put it, the United States ought to be able to use "a fly swatter where a fly swatter is a proper weapon, instead of using a sledge hammer." The President did not want to choose only between doing nothing or threatening "massive retaliation." He thought we should have armed forces capable of a "flexible response"—based on the size and the danger of the challenges.

The large purpose of our foreign policy would remain the same—to stop the growth of communism. Still, as JFK showed in Laos, when United States interests were not directly threatened, we would not use force against governments that were neutral. Kennedy believed that we should support progressive governments. Removing poverty and injustice would discourage Communist revolutions. He was friendly to the new nations of Africa. Sékou Touré, Guinea's leader, once called him "my only true friend in the outside world."

The Alliance for Progress. Kennedy proposed that we join the nations of Latin America in an Alliance for Progress. Similar to the Marshall Plan for Europe, this promised to Latin American nations $20 billion in economic aid over ten years. In August 1961 an Inter-American Conference in Uruguay accepted the plan. To receive economic aid the Latin American nations would improve their farms, reduce poverty, and promote industry.

They promised to invest $80 billion. In fact, few of these reforms were ever undertaken. Wherever possible, they avoided spending their own money. And the Kennedy administration did not insist that they live up to their promises. The United States tended to aid any government that was anti-Communist, that worked with the Alliance, and that had some popular support.

The Alliance made some friends—but it also made enemies. Critics in Latin America saw us using the Alliance to keep dictators in power. They said that the United States was more interested in stopping communism than in promoting freedom.

The Peace Corps. A favorite new program of JFK's—the Peace Corps—was designed to answer those arguments. This would show that the United States wanted to help all the poverty-stricken people in the world.

The plan was to train thousands of young Americans to work in underdeveloped countries. They would have all their expenses paid and receive some "severance pay" at the end of their two-year term. But they would not get a salary. They would be "volunteers"—like volunteers for the army in wartime—but their job would be peace. They would serve as teachers, nurses, doctors, engineers, and carpenters. Wherever they were sent, they would help the needy people raise better crops or build roads and bridges or improve their water supply. The President began the program even before Congress provided funds. By 1965 the project was costing $115 million a year.

Unfortunately, the Peace Corps was not the success all hoped it would be. Curing the ills of needy people was not so simple. Every country had its own large problems. To solve these you had to understand its language, its religion, and its history. Intelligent young Americans with high ideals seldom had enough of the knowledge or the skills required. Most of them had never before lived outside the United States. Some were lonely. It was hard to learn the customs of a remote country. Some countries even asked the Americans to leave. Yet many members of the Peace Corps helped people in ways they could not help themselves. And nearly all the volunteers learned more about the world. When it began, the program lifted the nation's spirit and helped bring a new patriotism in peacetime.

SECTION REVIEW

1. Identify or explain: Pathet Lao, Allen Dulles, Potsdam Conference, Berlin Wall, wars of national liberation, Sékou Touré.
2. Locate: Laos, Bay of Pigs, Berlin, Vienna.
3. What problems did Kennedy face in Laos? How were they resolved?
4. Explain the purpose and the outcome of the landing at the Bay of Pigs.
5. Why did the Communists want the Western powers to leave Berlin?
6. What was Kennedy's policy of "flexible response"?
7. What were the purposes of the Alliance for Progress and the Peace Corps?

3. Facing Communist challenges

Wherever they looked around the world, JFK and his advisers saw tests of America's determination to stand for peace and freedom. Responding to these challenges would call upon all the young President's will and resourcefulness.

The "missile gap." During the election campaign the candidates had disagreed over the nation's power to wage war. Were we weaker than the Russians? Were we trailing Russia in nuclear missiles? Nixon said we were not. Upon entering office, JFK found that the answer lay in whether you listened to the Air Force, the CIA, or the Navy. Only the Air Force insisted that there was a real missile gap. Secretary of Defense McNamara disagreed. Anyway, the Kennedy team decided to build more missiles. This was partly to satisfy Congress. And it was partly to have extra strength. Then we could survive a "first-strike" attack by Russia and still be able to hit back. If we had that strength, perhaps Russia would never dare launch a surprise attack.

With this purpose Congress voted new funds for the ICBMs (intercontinental ballistic missiles). Known as Minutemen, they were stored in concrete silos buried deep in the ground.

In addition there was the Polaris SLBM (submarine-launched ballistic missile), carried by nuclear submarines. Unlike earlier subs, those driven by atomic power could circle the globe without ever surfacing for fuel, supplies, or air. They carried missiles underwater. The first nuclear-powered sub, the *Nautilus*, had been launched in 1954. Then in July 1960 the first Polaris missile—weighing 14 tons with its deadly nuclear warhead—had been tested. It landed 1150 miles away right on target.

By 1964 the stepped-up Kennedy defense program had provided the United States with 1100 intercontinental bombers, 800 land-based ICBMs, and 250 Polaris missiles under the sea. In every class the Soviets were far outnumbered.

Putting a man on the moon.

But we were still behind the Russians in outer space. On April 12, 1961, they had sent up the first man in space. Yuri Gagarin went whirling around the earth in a satellite and made nearly a full orbit—in 89 minutes. The best the United States could do was a flight 115 miles into the sky by Alan B. Shepard on May 5. Some Americans feared that the Russians might use their lead in outer space to launch weapons against the United States. President Kennedy took up the challenge.

Sending a man into outer space was much more risky than exploring the arctic or another continent on earth. Could a human being survive out beyond the earth's atmosphere? Since humans needed oxygen to live and there was none in outer space, they would have to carry their oxygen with them. Could they carry enough? Also the President remembered that when we had first tried to put an object in space the missile had collapsed on the sand. The United States should not risk another fiasco.

Some Americans said that the $40 billion needed to reach the moon might be better spent. But the persuasive Vice-President Lyndon B. Johnson was a space enthusiast. And President Kennedy decided to take the grand risk. After the Russians sent Yuri Gagarin into orbit and after Shepard had made his successful flight, JFK promised that the United States would land a man on the moon before 1970. This spectacular success would make America the pioneer once more—this time out to another New World. Although Kennedy would not live to see it, his promise would be kept.

Working for disarmament and a test-ban.

If the United States led the way to outer space, what would the Russians do? Wouldn't they be tempted to build up their arsenal? President Kennedy still hoped somehow to stop the costly arms race. To halt the testing of nuclear weapons would be a first step. Beginning in the 1950s, people began to learn more about radiation. This was the deadly cancer-causing side effect of testing nuclear weapons.

In November 1958, Russia, Great Britain, and the United States—the only nations that at that time had nuclear bombs—had met in Geneva to discuss the problem. The United States promised that it would do no more testing so long as the Soviets did none. During the next two years the talks dragged on. Meanwhile Khrushchev was pushed by his own scientists and by Chinese criticism that he was "soft" toward the United States. In September 1961 he allowed testing in the atmosphere to begin again. Khrushchev boasted to a Communist party congress that Russia had exploded a 50-megaton bomb. This meant a bomb equal to 50 million tons of TNT, a bomb 2500 times bigger than the one that had killed instantly 75,000 people at Hiroshima!

JFK answered by ordering the United States to begin testing underground. The dangers of radiation there were much less. Then at the United Nations he called for complete disarmament. "Mankind must put an end to war," he told the delegates, "or war will put an end to mankind."

When Kennedy received no reply from Russia, in March 1962 he ordered new tests in the atmosphere. In fact, JFK did not believe these tests were really necessary. But he did not want the Russians to think the United States was weak or afraid.

The Cuban missile crisis.

During the summer of 1962, the Soviets stepped up the cold war. They began to move nuclear missiles into nearby Cuba. On October 14, 1962, clear pictures of Soviet missiles there were obtained by our U-2 spy planes.

As Secretary McNamara said, "It makes no great difference whether you are killed by a missile fired from the Soviet Union or from Cuba." But how should President Kennedy act against these enemy weapons on our doorstep? If the United States did nothing, would anyone believe we would ever resist the Soviets?

The Joint Chiefs of Staff recommended an invasion to seize the missiles and bring down Castro. At the very least, they wanted a general air strike—at targets all over the island. Kennedy wisely rejected this advice. Still, he did risk a

650

TRUCKS UNDER
OUFLAGE NETTING

CABLE

THEODOLITE STATION

5 TRUCKS UNDER
CAMOUFLAGE NETT

MISSILE SHELTER TENTS

Wide World Photos

This sharp photograph from a high-flying U-2 shows one of the medium-range missile sites under construction by the Soviets in Cuba. It was released by the Defense Department on October 28, 1962, the same day that Khrushchev announced that the missile sites would be dismantled.

showdown. In a dramatic television address on Monday, October 22, he denounced this "secret, swift, and extraordinary build-up of Communist missiles." He stated that he had ordered the Navy to begin "a strict quarantine [blockade] on all offensive military equipment under shipment to Cuba."

War now seemed to hang in the balance. Would the Soviet ships that were on their way to Cuba turn back? What would Khrushchev do? Of course, the Soviets denied there were any missiles on the island. Then at an emergency meeting of the UN Security Council, our Ambassador Adlai Stevenson proved with photographs that the missiles were there. On Wednesday, five Soviet ships stopped short of the quarantine zone. On Friday, the Russians began to signal that maybe the question could be negotiated. Then Kennedy received two letters from Khrushchev. He decided, on the advice of his brother Robert, to answer the one that held out some hope of peace.

On Sunday Khrushchev broadcast that he had ordered the missiles to be dismantled and removed from Cuba in return for an American pledge not to invade the island. "We should like to continue the exchange of views," he added, "on the prohibition of atomic and thermonuclear weapons, general disarmament, and other problems relating to the relaxation of international tension." The super-powers had drawn back from the brink of war.

The weakening alliances. Still, the world could see that the war of words could easily become a war of missiles. The allies of the United States in NATO feared someone's bad guess or a miscalculation. The proud president of France, Charles de Gaulle, had disliked following the lead of the United States. Now, he said, the missile crisis

Wide World Photos

JFK consulted Ike a number of times during his Presidency. This photograph was made after the Bay of Pigs fiasco in 1961.

1966 de Gaulle took France out of NATO and ordered American forces to leave his country. In 1967 NATO headquarters was moved from Paris to Brussels, Belgium.

At the same time that France was beginning to go its own way, countries in the Communist bloc (though dominated by Russia) began to show some independence. Now the Eastern European satellites, especially Poland and Romania, began to try to copy Tito. They started to follow slightly different paths from the Soviets. Much earlier, back in 1948, Tito, the strongman in Yugoslavia, had proved that a Communist country did not have to stay under Russia's heel.

The greatest split in the Communist alliance was between China and the Soviet Union. While the Russians now were willing sometimes to give in to avoid war, the Communist Chinese seemed unwilling to compromise with anyone about anything. In 1960 after a series of quarrels, the Russians withdrew their technical experts from Communist China. Then when China attacked India in a border dispute in 1962, the Soviets supported India. After Khrushchev's retreat in the Cuban missile crisis, Mao's Chinese Communists sneered at the Soviets. They said that Russia was only a "paper tiger." And Soviet leaders answered that war would not turn the world to communism.

showed how a single member of the NATO alliance could drag the other countries into war against their will.

To draw all the NATO nations closer together, President Kennedy had proposed his *Grand Design* for Western Europe in 1962 before the missile crisis. The United States would join the European Common Market in lowering tariffs. Congress approved this plan by the Trade Expansion Act of 1962. The President was permitted to reduce tariffs 50 percent and remove the tariffs entirely on articles heavily traded by the United States and Western Europe. But Congress said Kennedy could not remove the tariffs entirely unless Great Britain was admitted to the Common Market.

De Gaulle said that Kennedy's Grand Design was simply a plan for control of Western Europe by Great Britain and the United States. In January 1963 France vetoed Britain's application to join the Common Market. De Gaulle hoped to create a new power bloc—a Third Force—led by France, which was building its own nuclear weapons. In

A test-ban treaty. Once again in June 1963 President Kennedy called for an end to the arms race. Nearly fifty years earlier, Woodrow Wilson had wanted "to make the world safe for democracy." Now Kennedy expressed a more modest hope. "If we cannot end now all our differences, at least we can help make the world safe for diversity." He revived the test-ban talks. In July, Great Britain, the United States, and the Soviet Union agreed to outlaw nuclear tests in the atmosphere, in outer space, and underwater. The treaty did not touch the vast arsenal of nuclear weapons still held by the Big Three. And it allowed underground testing to continue. The treaty was signed and approved by the Senate 80 to 19 on September 4, 1963.

More than 100 nations agreed to the test-ban treaty. No one was much surprised when the French, who had recently exploded their own atomic bomb, and the Communist Chinese, who soon would have a bomb of their own, refused to sign.

Problems in Vietnam. His success with the missile crisis and the test-ban treaty encouraged JFK to think that bold diplomacy might save the world from atomic war. The civil war in South Vietnam proved a tougher problem. The Geneva peace conference of 1954 had decided that elections to unify all Vietnam would be held by July 1956. But Ngo Dinh Diem, who was now leading South Vietnam, refused to go along. He was sure that he would lose to the Communist North. The United States agreed with Diem. Neither South Vietnam nor the United States had signed the Geneva accords.

After South Vietnam refused to take part in elections, guerrilla warfare against Diem's government broke out. The war was led by former members of the Communist Viet Minh. Enormous amounts of money and supplies were already pouring into the country from the United States. Now we began to send in "advisers" to train the South Vietnamese army. In 1960, opponents to Diem—including Communists and others—created the National Liberation Front (NLF). Their goal was to overthrow Diem and reunify the country. Diem named them the "Viet Cong," meaning Vietnamese Communists.

President Kennedy continued the support of Diem begun by Eisenhower. As NLF victories increased, he resisted advice from Vice-President Johnson and others to send in many more troops. Still, the number of American "advisers" slowly grew.

These advisers urged Diem to carry out reforms to strengthen his support in the country. Instead of making reforms, Diem brutally put down all opposition. When Buddhists staged demonstrations against him, his troops opened fire on them. Several Buddhist monks—in desperate protest—burned themselves to death in public. Kennedy now began to see that outsiders could not solve the problems of the South Vietnamese. "It is their war," he declared. "They are the only ones who have to win it or lose it."

At that time the American military advisers in South Vietnam came to 16,000. The United States military leaders wanted to send more. On November 2, 1963, Diem was overthrown, with American knowledge and approval, by a military junta. Diem was murdered. The military outlook for the anti-Communists became worse and worse.

But President Kennedy would not live to make the next move.

SECTION REVIEW

1. Identify or explain: missile gap, ICBM, Polaris missile, *Nautilus*, Yuri Gagarin, Alan B. Shepard, Charles de Gaulle, Trade Expansion Act of 1962, Ngo Dinh Diem, NLF, Viet Cong.
2. How and why did the Kennedy administration step up the defense program?
3. How did Kennedy challenge the Russians in the space race?
4. What problems arose over the testing of nuclear weapons? How was the issue resolved in 1963?
5. How did the Cuban missile crisis turn out?
6. How did France disrupt efforts for strengthening NATO?
7. What splits appeared in the Communist bloc?
8. How did Kennedy respond to the problem in Vietnam?

---

4. A New Frontier

President Kennedy found that domestic affairs were just as tricky as foreign affairs. Since he had been elected by only a hair's breadth, he had no clear "mandate" for any policy. In Congress he faced an unfriendly coalition of Republicans and conservative southern Democrats.

The domestic program that JFK outlined in 1961 was mostly an extension of the New Deal. He aimed to stop the business recession, to spur the nation's growth rate, and to "get the country moving again." There were few bold new proposals in what Kennedy called the "New Frontier."

Congress refuses to act. The hardest blow was when Congress refused to pass Kennedy's ambitious bill for federal aid to education. He hoped to help make education more equal in the different states. Of the $5.6 billion he requested, the states would receive $2.3 billion for public school construction and teachers' salaries. The rest would go to needy college students. The bill passed the Senate easily enough. Then Roman Catholic leaders insisted that it be amended to provide aid to parochial schools. Though President Kennedy was himself a

Catholic, he would not yield. Enough Roman Catholic Democrats joined the Republicans to defeat the bill in the House of Representatives. A similar bill failed again in 1962.

Kennedy offered an equally ambitious plan to use the Social Security system to provide medical care for the aged. But his proposal did not receive serious consideration from Congress. The powerful American Medical Association called it "socialized medicine." JFK did not push the measure, since he knew he could not win.

Some successes. All was not disappointment and defeat. The Housing Act of 1961 provided $4.9 billion for urban renewal. The minimum wage went up from $1 to $1.25 an hour. In order to get the increase, JFK agreed to exclude 700,000 workers in laundries and small intra-state businesses. An Area Redevelopment Act offered $300 million to create new industries and retrain workers in "distressed areas" suffering from unemployment. Federal insurance under Social Security (p. 516) was extended to more of the unemployed, and federal funds were provided.

Congress also approved the Twenty-fourth Amendment to outlaw the poll tax. This tax was still being used in five southern states to discourage poor people—chiefly blacks—from voting. This amendment became part of the Constitution when it was ratified by three-fourths of the states by January 1964.

Controlling the economy. These measures, together with the large sums spent for defense and for space programs, helped end the recession that had started in 1960. But unemployment remained high. Kennedy also worried about inflation caused by rising government spending.

To control inflation, JFK proposed "wage-price guideposts." These tied any increase in wages to an increase in output. If a firm making 1000 items for $10,000 could boost output to 1100 for the same $10,000 cost, the productivity increase would be 10 percent. Wages could then rise by that amount while the company could still sell the items to its customers for the same price. There would be no price inflation.

A conflict with the steelmakers. At the large United States Steel company, the employers and the workers signed a new labor contract on March 31, 1962. To avoid inflation, the union accepted a modest wage increase well within the President's guidelines. The workers took it for granted that the company would not raise prices. Then on April 10, the president of United States Steel announced a large increase in the price of steel. Other steel companies followed.

Since steel was used in so many products, the rise in its price would push other prices up. An enraged President Kennedy denounced the company and demanded that they roll back their prices. They soon gave in. The whole business community, which had been unsure of the President's attitude toward business from the start, was shaken by his anger. In May 1962, partly as a result, the stock market suffered its sharpest decline since the Great Crash of 1929.

As it turned out, the President's quarrel with business was not deep or lasting. His first friendly gesture was a Revenue Act in September 1962. It granted $1 billion a year in special investment tax credits for business firms making new outlays for machines and equipment. He did not object when some steel companies announced price increases early in 1963. Wall Street was encouraged, and prosperity seemed on its way.

Getting the economy moving. President Kennedy still thought that the gross national product was not growing fast enough. Russia's GNP was growing more rapidly, and he feared that in time we might lose our lead.

From the start of Kennedy's term, his Council of Economic Advisers had urged a big cut in taxes. The government was already running into debt, spending more on arms and services than it brought in through taxes. Still they argued that cutting taxes would be a good idea. If people had to spend less on their taxes, they would have more to spend on other things. Business would prosper, and in the long run more taxes would come in to help balance the budget. JFK did not manage to convince Congress to make the cut.

The problem of poverty. The economy was growing during most of the postwar years. Yet certain areas of poverty seemed never to be touched by private business or government programs. There had always been some poverty in the United

States. But as the nation became ever richer, some people hoped that ours might be the first country where nobody was poor.

In his popular book, the author Michael Harrington called the nation's poor *The Other America* (1962). These were "the unskilled workers, the migrant farm workers, the aged, the minorities, and all the others who live in the economic underworld of American life." Even in the United States, he wrote, there were millions "maimed in body and spirit, existing at levels beneath those necessary for human decency. If these people are not starving, they are hungry. . . . They are without adequate housing and education and medical care." President Kennedy began to worry as much about these people as about the nation's business. He began to plan a war on poverty.

The problem of civil rights. "Civil rights" described the rights of all Americans to vote and to have a fair trial. It also meant the right to have an equal chance at any job they could handle and to live and play wherever they could afford. President Kennedy believed that the federal government should pass laws to guarantee these rights to all Americans everywhere in the country.

During the election campaign of 1960, he had criticized Eisenhower for not doing enough. Now he himself moved only slowly. He was afraid that if he demanded these reforms, he would lose the support of southern members of Congress for his "New Frontier" bills. Finally, in 1962, he signed his name to an order to desegregate public housing projects supported with federal funds.

Just as Ike had done, he appointed a Committee on Equal Employment Opportunity. It was to see that companies that worked for the government gave everybody an equal opportunity. He directed his brother Robert at the Department of Justice to support black efforts to vote in the Deep South.

JFK encouraged blacks by his appointments. He named Carl Rowan ambassador to Finland and Andrew Hacker as associate press secretary. He appointed a number of blacks as United States district judges and Thurgood Marshall as judge of a United States Court of Appeals. He tried to set up a Cabinet Department of Urban Affairs and put Robert Weaver at its head. But conservative Democrats and Republicans defeated the bill. On the other hand, to keep on the right side of southern

David Campbell/Photo Researchers.

Appalachia was a main target of the War on Poverty. A family with ten children lived on this small farm in southeastern Kentucky.

Democrats, he named several segregationist judges to federal district courts.

The black revolt. The pressures to do more were building rapidly. In 1961 "freedom riders," blacks and whites from North and South, took buses south to protest segregation of the races in bus stations. They were greeted by riots and beatings. Their buses were burned. On May 29, 1961, Attorney General Robert Kennedy called on the Interstate Commerce Commission to ban segregation in interstate bus terminals. That was finally done in September.

In the fall of 1962, a black Air Force veteran, James Meredith, tried to enroll in the all-white University of Mississippi. A court ordered that he be admitted. Still, Governor Ross Barnett personally prevented him from registering. When Meredith finally did enroll, riots followed that caused two deaths and injuries to hundreds. President Kennedy ordered 5000 federal troops to the scene to restore quiet. Meredith remained at the

University of Mississippi—protected by federal troops.

All this violence to prevent one young black man from going to college! It was seen by millions on TV across the country. Now the civil rights struggle came into everybody's living room. Television was bringing the nation together. Civil rights was the whole nation's problem.

The pressure for an end to segregation—in schools, colleges, hotels, restaurants, employment, and all American life—grew enormously in 1963. Sit-ins and demonstrations forced the desegregation of lunch counters, hotels, and theaters in 300 cities in the South. Slowly the hated signs telling people what could be used by "white" and what by "colored" were coming down.

In April 1963 Martin Luther King, Jr., and his Southern Christian Leadership Conference (SCLC) began a drive to end segregation in Birmingham, Alabama. There segregation was enforced by local laws. King insisted that the struggle should be peaceful. He and his demonstrators were opposed by Chief "Bull" Connor's police with electric cattle prods, snarling dogs, and fire hoses. Birmingham exploded with rioting and fire bombing. And all this, too, was seen on television.

In June Governor George Wallace prevented two blacks from enrolling in the University of Alabama. He promised segregation in the state of Alabama "today, tomorrow, and forever." But strong pressure from JFK finally made Wallace give in, and he allowed the blacks to register.

A new civil rights law. By now, one hundred years after the Emancipation Proclamation, it was clear that if blacks were to be treated equally with whites, new federal laws were needed. On June 11, 1963, Kennedy addressed the nation on television. "Are we," he asked, "to say to the world and, much more importantly, to each other that this is a land of the free except for Negroes; that we have no second-class citizens except Negroes; that we have no class or caste system, no ghettos, no master race except with respect to Negroes?" Later that same night Medgar Evers, head of the Mississippi NAACP, was murdered outside his home.

A week later Kennedy sent a new civil rights bill to Congress. It was not nearly as strong as many people wanted. Still, it went far beyond any civil rights law ever requested before.

The march on Washington. To put pressure on Congress to pass Kennedy's bill, supporters staged a mammoth march on Washington. It was organized by Bayard Rustin, who had helped A. Philip Randolph organize an earlier march on Washington, back in 1941. Kennedy tried to discourage the march because he feared a backlash in Congress. But on August 28, 1963, there was one of the largest demonstrations in American history. More than 200,000 black and white "Freedom Marchers" gathered in Washington before the Lincoln Memorial. The eloquent Reverend Martin Luther King, Jr., stirred the audience—and the nation watching on television—with his dream of a United States where all people are equal. A place "where all of God's children, black men and white men, Jews and Gentiles, Protestants and Catholics, will be able to join hands and sing in the words of the old Negro spiritual, 'Free at last! free at last! thank God almighty, we are free at last!'" And, led by Mahalia Jackson, they all sang the old Baptist hymn that had become the anthem of the civil rights movement, "We Shall Overcome."

But the nation was large, and prejudice had deep roots in history. In September Americans received another lesson of how far away lay the fulfillment of the Reverend King's dream. A bomb exploded at a Birmingham church, and four little black girls were killed.

SECTION REVIEW

1. Identify or explain: Housing Act of 1961, Area Redevelopment Act, 24th Amendment, "wage-price guideposts," investment tax credits, Thurgood Marshall, "freedom riders," James Meredith, George Wallace, Medgar Evers, Bayard Rustin.

2. What major Kennedy proposals did Congress reject? What were his successes?

3. How did Kennedy try to control inflation?

4. How did Kennedy propose to hasten economic growth? How did Congress respond?

5. What groups of people remained poor in spite of rising prosperity?

6. List successes and failures in JFK's civil rights record.

7. How did television affect the civil rights movement?

Bob Adelman/Magnum

Thousands in the 1963 March on Washington move past the reflecting pool toward the Lincoln Memorial.

5. The tragic end

In November 1963 President Kennedy took time out to mend his political fences. He thought of the presidential election coming in 1964. And he wanted to arouse support for himself and "New Frontier" bills that still had not been passed. Like many Presidents before him, he went out on the road. He traveled to the two southern states he hoped to carry in 1964, to Florida and then to Texas. The crowds were large and enthusiastic.

Death in Dallas. JFK had been warned that there was bitter feeling against him in Dallas. Only a month before, an angry crowd had pushed and spat upon Adlai Stevenson when he went there to speak

on United Nations day. Yet if the President visited Texas, he could not skip the state's second largest city. So he scheduled a three-hour visit for November 22, 1963.

The presidential party included Jacqueline Kennedy, Vice-President and Mrs. Lyndon B. Johnson, and Governor and Mrs. John B. Connally of Texas. Their motorcade passed through cheering crowds on its way to the Trade Mart, where the President was to deliver a luncheon address. As the President's car passed through Dealey Plaza, rifle shots were heard. One bullet ripped through Kennedy's neck and another through his brain. Governor Connally was wounded. The President was dead by the time his car reached a hospital. The dream of Camelot had ended in nightmare.

Lee Harvey Oswald, a solitary, neurotic young man was seized for the crime. Only two days later the nation watching television saw Oswald, escorted by police, being taken to the Dallas county jail. Before the nation's eyes Oswald was gunned down by a nightclub owner named Jack Ruby.

The first reaction to all of this was disbelief. Had the youngest elected President really been murdered at the height of his powers? America was stunned and could find no ready explanation. Who had killed the President, and why? One of the great tragedies of American history would also remain one of the mysteries.

The Warren Commission. A commission headed by Chief Justice Earl Warren would spend nine months trying to get to the bottom of the matter. They called scores of witnesses, took the advice of ballistic experts, and interviewed hundreds. They concluded that Lee Harvey Oswald had acted alone and so had Jack Ruby. Still the commission failed to pursue many leads and left many questions unanswered.

In 1979 a committee of the House of Representatives reported the results of their own year-long study. They used a new kind of sound analysis to tell how many shots had been fired and from where. And they concluded that more than one rifle had been fired at JFK. They also suggested that when he killed Oswald, Ruby might have been acting for others. But who held the second rifle, if there was one, and why had Oswald and Ruby fired their deadly shots? These questions were never fully answered.

The people's reaction. The shocked American people watched the tragedy played again and again on television. On their screens, in their living rooms, they mourned at the President's funeral.

John F. Kennedy was the fourth President in 100 years to die at the hands of an assassin. Was it no longer safe for an American President to move among the people?

Even JFK's political opponents were overwhelmed by the tragedy. Everyone was reminded how unpredictable was history. People who had not voted for JFK still wept at the wasted talents of a brilliant leader. After his death, his friends naturally inflated what he had accomplished in his 1000 days. "Robbed of his years," one journalist wrote, "he is being rewarded and honored in death as he

As millions watched on television, the funeral cortege of John F. Kennedy moved grimly towards Arlington Cemetery. The riderless horse symbolized the loss of a leader.

never was in life. Deprived of the place he sought in history, he has been given . . . a place in legend."

The Kennedy years, an appraisal. JFK's months in office are less important for the laws that were passed than for a new uplifting spirit. The young President was still growing and learning his job. No one could say whether he would have done better in a second term. There was always the chance. His untimely death left him a President noted more for his promise than for his achievement.

In foreign affairs, he led the cold war. He believed that the United States had to remain stronger than the Russians. He was also worried that we should not even seem to be weak. But the force of events, the power of the Russians, and the creeping spread of communism gradually changed his hopes. Whether we liked it or not, Kennedy concluded, we must accept a world that was not all free. "No one can doubt," he said, "that the wave of the future is not the conquest of the world by a single dogmatic creed but the liberation of the diverse energies of free nations and free men."

JFK always disliked "experts." He felt that they had led him into the Bay of Pigs disaster. Yet when he moved away from "massive retaliation" to "flexible response," he created new experts. The RAND (*Research and Development*) Corporation was set up by the Air Force to plan for air and space needs. And there were other new "think tanks." More than ever before, universities were drawn into research for the Defense Department and the CIA.

What remained from John F. Kennedy's brief Presidency was a lively and cheerful, but not substantial, inheritance. Humor, charm, vigor, and excitement were his trademarks. After his administration it was hard for people anywhere to think that the United States was a tired old nation. And the New World nation would not lack new young leaders.

SECTION REVIEW

1. Identify or explain: John Connally, Lee Harvey Oswald, Jack Ruby, Warren Commission.

2. How did the 1979 report of the assassination differ from that of the Warren Commission?

3. Appraise the Kennedy Presidency.

CHAPTER REVIEW

MEETING OUR EARLIER SELVES

1. How important do you think it is to elect a President who has great personal charm and the ability to attract supporters? Explain.

2. In his early months in office, where was Kennedy most successful in foreign affairs: Laos, Cuba, or Berlin? Explain.

3. In what ways did the Peace Corps succeed?

4. How did the Vietnam problem differ from the earlier one in Korea? Consider both the nature of the problem and the response of the United States.

5. What were Kennedy's most significant achievements in foreign affairs? in domestic affairs? Why?

QUESTIONS FOR TODAY

1. A Soviet military presence in Cuba in 1979 stirred debate. How did the problem differ from the 1962 Cuban missile crisis?

2. Compare Kennedy's efforts to stimulate the economy and yet control inflation with such efforts being made today.

3. How do you think people in your locality would respond to a program of volunteer service at home or abroad? Are any such programs sponsored by the federal government today?

YOUR REGION IN HISTORY

1. How did your locality respond to the civil rights activities of the Kennedy years?

2. How has the position of black people in your state or locality changed since 1963?

SKILLS TO MAKE OUR PAST VIVID

1. Read an assessment of the Kennedy administration in two other sources. Then summarize how the accounts agree and differ.

2. Find a contemporary political cartoon that provided commentary on the Kennedy administration. Write an explanation of the cartoon, citing the situation involved and the cartoonist's point of view.

CHAPTER 32

Lyndon B. Johnson—from success to failure

This would be a time of triumphs and troubles. Led by a strong President, Lyndon B. Johnson, the Congress found new ways to protect the rights of some citizens and to widen the opportunities for all. At home it was an age of fulfillment. The injustices of centuries would begin to be righted. Yet this would take time. Impatient Americans turned to violence. Meanwhile, an undeclared war on the other side of the world, in a place most Americans had never heard of, would cost thousands of American lives. There, too, the President said, Americans were defending freedom. But the nation was unconvinced. He did not persuade Americans that they needed to be fighting there—nor did he tell them all they wanted to know. One of the best-qualified, strongest Presidents became the leading figure in an American tragedy. People would forget his successes at home because of his failures abroad.

1. Taking the reins

The nation, stunned by the loss of its young President, wanted to hear a clear, commanding voice. Lyndon B. Johnson, the new man in the White House, saw what the times needed. As he later explained:

> Everything was in chaos. We were all spinning around and around trying to come to grips with what had happened, but the more we tried to understand it, the more confused we got. We were like a bunch of cattle caught in the swamp, unable to move in either direction, simply circling 'round and 'round. I understood that; I knew what had to be done. There is but one way to get the cattle out of the swamp. And that is for the man on the horse to take the lead, to assume command, to provide direction. In the period of confusion after the assassination, I was that man.

Lyndon Baines Johnson. Johnson was perfectly trained to take charge. He was not as young or as witty as JFK. But he stood a commanding six feet three—as tall as Texans are supposed to be. And he spoke with a Texas drawl which carried a charm all his own. He had spent most of his life in the House of Representatives and the Senate. He knew the members of Congress by their first names. He respected them and they respected him. Better than any other man alive, he knew how to put laws through Congress.

LBJ's life had centered around politics. His father had been a state legislator in Texas, and the young Lyndon loved to go to the statehouse to watch and listen. Even more, he enjoyed traveling around with his father, visiting the voters of their district during election campaigns. "Sometimes," he recalled, "I wished it would go on forever."

While still a student at Southwest Texas State College, Johnson worked as campaign manager in the successful reelection of a state senator. After graduating from college in 1930, Johnson taught for a year in a high school in Houston. His political skills were already recognized, and he was asked to be the aide of a Texas congressman. In 1932, at the age of 24, he arrived in Washington, where he would spend most of the remaining 41 years of his life.

One brief break came from 1935 to 1937 when he returned to Texas as state director of the National Youth Administration. Even then his sympathy for the downtrodden was clear. Years later an aged black leader recalled how "we began to get word up here that there was one NYA director who wasn't like the others. He was looking after Negroes and poor folks, and most NYA people weren't doing that."

Johnson was elected as a Democrat to the House of Representatives in 1939. In 1941 he was the first member of Congress to enlist in the armed forces. His navy career was cut short a year later when FDR ordered all senators and representatives back to Washington. He remained in the House until 1948, when he was elected to the Senate.

The Senate was the perfect stage for a man of LBJ's character and talent. Since there were only 96 senators, and each served for six years, it was a kind of club. All the members of the House of Representatives were elected every two years, and there were more than 400 of them. The Senate was a more intimate place. LBJ was a careful student of both people and issues. And he was always doing favors for others.

He earned a reputation as a superb "horse trader." Johnson used to roam the halls seeking senators whose help he needed on some bill. When he "accidentally" met one of them, he would give him "The Treatment." In his colorful Texas slang, the overpowering LBJ would plead, threaten, accuse, cry, laugh, complain—until his fellow senator agreed. "The Treatment" might last minutes or hours. A senator who knew called it "an almost hypnotic experience that rendered the target stunned and helpless." But Johnson was not just acting. "What convinces is conviction," he said. "You simply *have* to believe in the argument you are advancing. If you don't, you are as good as dead."

When he was majority leader of the Senate from 1955 to 1961, LBJ ran the place as if he owned it.

Fred Ward/Black Star

LBJ here exerts his famous powers of persuasion in the Oval Office in 1964.

Then when John F. Kennedy asked him to join his ticket as candidate for Vice-President, LBJ accepted. The tall Texan wanted to use the office to become a national figure.

He hoped it might be a stepping stone to the White House. Since the inauguration of Lincoln a century earlier, five Vice-Presidents had become President. Still, for an energetic and ambitious politician, being Vice-President was frustrating. The Vice-President had to support the President's policies, yet he had no executive powers of his

Here we see a price for the nation's spectacular industry and high standard of living. Highways crisscross the landscape and smog darkens the sky.

meant for insects. One day, she warned, we might awaken to a "silent spring." No birds would be left to sing.

Rachel Carson alerted Americans to "ecology." This was the science of the relation between organisms and their environment. President Kennedy had set up a commission to study the questions raised by Rachel Carson.

Just as the pesticides aimed at insects were killing birds, so the exhaust fumes of automobiles could pollute the air that everybody breathed. Now President Johnson persuaded Congress to pass laws to reduce pollution from the exhaust pipes of cars and trucks and from factory chimneys.

The waters of our lakes and rivers were polluted by chemicals dumped from mines and factories.

Junkyards and cemeteries for dead automobiles made a mess of the wild and beautiful American countryside. People called this "visual pollution." New laws were passed requiring fences around these eyesores. The number of billboards was limited. Pesticides were controlled.

The wonderful power of books was proved again in 1965 when Ralph Nader, a bright 31-year-old lawyer, stirred the nation with his *Unsafe at Any Speed*. In that year alone, he wrote, nearly 50,000 Americans would die in automobile accidents and more than 4 million would be injured. He argued that many of these deaths and injuries would be the fault of the automakers. He accused them of being more interested in selling cars than in saving lives. They cared too much, he said, about car styling and sales gimmicks and too little about safety features. Bumpers were not even strong enough to resist an impact of over three miles an hour, and car bodies were not much stronger. Nader's campaign helped spur Congress to pass the Highway Safety Act of 1966. It set safety standards for new cars and for tires.

LBJ and administration. Never before in American history had Congress produced so many social programs so speedily. Between 1965 and 1968 the reform laws came to 500. It was much easier to pass a law than to change the way people behaved. LBJ was a wizard in the Congress. But making all the new laws work was quite another matter. The restless President Johnson had a way of asking for more new laws even before old laws on the same subject had been tried out. For example, the standards for the Water Quality Act of 1965 had not yet been set when the Clean Water Restoration Act was passed calling for the setting of still more standards.

Administering all these new programs, finding the good people to run them, was itself a colossal job. Meanwhile the President was being distracted by some other colossal problems, thousands of miles away, in Vietnam.

"Wartime" inflation in peacetime. Just like earlier wars, the undeclared war in Vietnam suddenly increased the demand for goods. After the tax cut of 1965, citizens had more money, and the government was now spending billions on defense. Though the nation had not actually declared war, wartime inflation was here again! Prices began to shoot up. The Consumer Price Index had risen by an average of only 1 percent a year during the Kennedy years. Then it went up 3 percent in 1967 and 5 percent in 1968. The government's wage and price guidelines collapsed.

To slow down inflation and pay the ever-higher costs of the Vietnam War, LBJ asked Congress for a temporary 10 percent surcharge on income taxes in 1967. (Taxpayers would figure their regular tax and then add 10 percent to it.) But by that time Congress was becoming less cooperative. They asked whether a tax increase was really necessary. To pay for the war, President Johnson was forced to cut back on non-defense spending. "Great Society" programs suffered. Still, every year the federal government went deeper into debt. From $3.8 billion in 1966, the deficit rose to $8.7 billion in 1967, and $25.2 billion in 1968. In June 1968, when the tax surcharge finally became law, inflation was on the rise.

SECTION REVIEW

1. Identify or explain: "Great Society," Medicare, Medicaid, Elementary and Secondary Education Act, Truth-in-Packaging, Appalachia, Robert Weaver, Consumer Price Index, tax surcharge.
2. What important laws were passed under President Johnson on (a) health care, (b) education, (c) pollution, (d) consumer protection, (e) regional development, (f) housing and rents, (g) immigration?
3. How did Rachel Carson and Ralph Nader influence "Great Society" legislation?
4. Why did inflation speed up in the late 1960s? How did Johnson try to deal with it?

3. Black revolt and youth rebellion

President Kennedy and President Johnson had raised high the hopes of many Americans that injustice, inequality, and poverty could be erased. The failure to achieve quickly the difficult goals they proclaimed may have been inevitable. But among certain groups—blacks and the middle-class young especially—the result was frustration and anger and ultimately violence.

The beginnings of black revolt. Centuries of discrimination could not be wiped out in a few years. Black Americans were disappointed that the eloquent speeches and beautiful promises were not all fulfilled overnight. Disappointment became frustration. And frustration led to revolt. In the northern states that had fought to free the slaves, the discontent was most acute. There segregation continued not by law, as it did in the South, but in everyday fact.

Civil rights laws could do little for the 50 percent of the black Americans in the North. They had to live by themselves in special neighborhoods. They were not admitted to some of the best schools and clubs. Even if they were bright and well trained, they could not get jobs in the building trades, or as executives in businesses or banks, or in the best law firms. Since laws had helped so little, they flailed

United Press International Photo

Leaders of both races joined Martin Luther King in the march from Selma to Montgomery in March 1965.

about trying to find ways to awaken their fellow Americans. They staged a "stall-in" of autos to disrupt the opening of the New York World's Fair in 1964. And riots erupted in Rochester and New York City.

The Summer Freedom Project in Mississippi in 1964 aimed to register blacks so they could vote. Civil rights workers (white and black) came down from the North. Three of them were murdered and became martyrs to the cause of equality. Many of the civil rights missionaries were beaten or wounded. Black homes and churches were burned. Because of these violent tactics, blacks feared to demand their rights, and only 1200 new voters were registered.

The murders in Mississippi had their effect. But it was not what the plotters expected. The national outrage helped to push the stronger Civil Rights Act of 1964 through Congress in July. Then, even in Mississippi, public places—such as restaurants— began to serve both races. When schools opened there in September, a few white and black children of Mississippi began going to school together. The last strongholds of segregation started to fall.

The Voting Rights Act. In 1964 the Rev. Martin Luther King, Jr., received the Nobel Peace Prize. The Nobel Prizes had a strange history. They were founded by Alfred Nobel, a Swedish manufacturer of arms who invented dynamite (both the chemical and the name). He was worried that his products were used mainly by people at war to kill one another. His guilty conscience led him to leave his huge fortune to create a foundation that would give prizes in science, literature, and peacemaking. All people in the world were eligible, and there was no greater honor awarded anywhere.

Upon his return from Sweden, early in 1965, King announced his drive to register 3 million voters in the South. He began his push in Selma, Alabama, a city with 15,000 blacks, but almost no black voters. Once again black Americans were clubbed, shocked with electric cattle prods, and arrested— only for trying to exercise their rights. The horrified nation saw it all on TV screens in their living rooms.

Then King announced that he would lead a march for freedom from Selma to the Alabama capitol in Montgomery. On March 7 the freedom marchers were attacked by the police and turned back. Two days later they tried again, and again they were turned back. Governor George Wallace did everything he could to stop the march. He went to court. He told President Johnson that Alabama could not afford to protect the marchers. On March 15, LBJ called units of the Alabama National Guard into federal service and ordered federal marshals and the FBI to Alabama.

That same day President Johnson went before Congress—while the nation watched on television.

He denounced the denial of constitutional rights to the black citizens of Mississippi. He demanded a law to provide federal registrars at the polls wherever blacks were not already voting in normal numbers. These registrars would have the power to enroll new voters so that no person could be denied the right to vote on account of race. LBJ compared the battle of Selma to the battles of Lexington and Concord in the American Revolution. He repeated the slogan of the civil rights forces—"We *Shall* Overcome."

On March 21 the great march from Selma to Montgomery began under the protection of federal marshals, the FBI, and the Alabama National Guard. Ministers, priests, and rabbis from all over the country went to Selma to join Martin Luther King in the march. Four days later the demonstrators peacefully entered Montgomery. But that night a white woman civil rights worker was shot and killed.

For the first time in history all American citizens at the same time could see their fellow citizens in another part of the country demanding their rights. It was before their eyes on television. No wonder, then, that Congress now passed the Voting Rights Act. President Johnson signed it into law on August 6, 1965. Only one year later the number of blacks registered to vote had gone up 50 percent, from 870,000 to 1,289,000. Soon black officials began to be elected in communities throughout the South. At last it appeared that the dreams of Radical Republicans after the Civil War might finally be achieved.

Burn, baby, burn. Hardly had the Voting Rights Act of 1965 passed than Watts, a black ghetto in Los Angeles, exploded in violence. This was only the first of more than 100 riots that would rage in many cities across the nation during the long, hot summers of the next three years.

LBJ was stunned by Watts. He had just signed his great Voting Rights Act into law—and now this. "How is it possible," he asked, "after all we've accomplished?" Johnson was understandably bitter. For the riots hurt his Great Society programs. They seemed so aimless and only served to destroy, when what was needed was to build. They created a backlash among many whites who already felt blacks were receiving too much from the government. This was less a revolution than an explo-sion. The President tried to understand. "God knows how little we've really moved on this issue," he said, "despite all the fanfare. As I see it I've moved the Negro from D+ to C-. He's still nowhere. He knows it. And that's why he's out in the streets."

The riots drew attention to the more radical black leaders. The handsome Malcolm X was an ex-convict who had become a member of Elijah Muhammad's Nation of Islam—usually called the Black Muslims. Muhammad rejected integration. He called all whites "devils." He thought whites and blacks should be separate and that blacks should have a nation of their own. Malcolm's eloquent voice carried a message of hate. "When I speak," he said, "I speak as a *victim* of America's so-called democracy."

Malcolm X split off from Elijah Muhammad's Black Muslims and formed his own group. He did not follow Martin Luther King's Christian gospel of nonviolence. But after a pilgrimage to Mecca, where all true Muslims were supposed to go once in their lives, he began to change his view that all whites were born evil. For true Muslims believed that all races were equal. Malcolm X's career ended in a blaze of gunfire from several of his many black opponents in February 1965. His powerful *Autobi-ography,* which came out after his death in 1965, fanned both black hate and black pride.

Black Power. The summer of 1966 was a season of riots in northern cities. In the South, James Meredith, the first black to attend the University of Mississippi, tried to walk from Memphis, Tennessee, to Jackson, Mississippi, to encourage black people not to be afraid. He was shot and wounded. This provoked some black leaders to think that maybe Malcolm X was right. Stokely Carmichael, a young black radical, began to preach "Black Power." Martin Luther King had preached love and human brotherhood. Now the angry champions of "Black Power" mainly wanted to be able to "get even." They wanted their chance to lord it over others.

By the fall of 1966 the civil rights movement was divided and in disarray. White backlash grew stronger. For the first time in recent years, a civil rights measure failed to pass Congress. The summer of 1967 saw the worst rioting in United States history. Blacks went on the rampage, destroying

Massive rioting in Detroit in 1967 brought death and destruction. Federal troops and the Michigan National Guard were sent into the city to restore order.

their own neighborhoods and leaving smoking rubble in Newark and Detroit. In Detroit alone 43 died and 5000 were left homeless. The Soviet newspaper *Pravda* gleefully printed a picture of army tanks on the streets of Detroit.

Again during 1967, LBJ asked for new civil rights laws, but Congress was no longer sympathetic. About all that LBJ could do that year was to appoint Thurgood Marshall to the Supreme Court. A graduate of the Howard University Law School, he had headed the legal staff of the National Association for the Advancement of Colored People, and he had successfully argued the case against segregation in 1954. Now he was the first black ever to serve on the highest court in the land.

A new generation. This was a time of troubles and struggles. The nation's young people had been the source of hope and optimism. But now, in the 1960s, many acted as if they had been raised on sour milk. They were the product of the "baby boom"—born during and soon after World War II. Between 1960 and 1970 the number of Americans aged 15 to 24 grew by 50 percent—from 24 million to 36 million. This was more than they had increased in all the last seven decades.

This new generation was different. They were the first generation to have lived all their lives under the shadow of nuclear weapons. They were the first TV generation. Their parents were sobered by knowledge of the Great Depression. But the society that these young people knew had enjoyed almost continuous prosperity since their childhood.

They had been surrounded with countless new things—TV, high-fidelity records, stereo, FM radio, wide-screen movies with wrap-around sound, large cars dappled with chrome, superhighways and supermarkets. At the same time they heard the shrill warnings of Rachel Carson, Ralph Nader, and other prophets of doom. They could see that all the many wonderful things in American life still did not solve the ancient problems of justice and equality. And on TV they would see their young President assassinated, their cities smoldering in riots, their generation dying on the distant battlefield of Vietnam—and people of scores of new nations starving in Africa and Asia. The world seemed confusing and frustrating as never before. Where was the new frontier?

Hippies and the New Left. Different young people reacted in different ways. Most went about their business. They attended classes, read their textbooks, and prepared themselves to make a living. But a few "tuned in, turned on, and dropped out." They joined the so-called "counter-culture," which was opposed to the culture accepted by most Americans. They used drugs, they let their hair grow long, they bought army-navy surplus clothing. They wore beads, fringe jackets, and sometimes put feathers in their hair. They called themselves "hippies." They said they admired the simple, natural ways of the American Indian—about whom they usually knew nothing at all. There were not many of them, but they made the headlines and offered an interesting spectacle on television.

Then some others, aided by young faculty, organized the Students for a Democratic Society (SDS). "Do not bend, spindle, or fold," the warning on computer cards, was one of their favorite slogans. They called for a New Left—a revitalized radical movement to transform the United States. They said they believed in democracy, but they acted like anarchists. They hated what they called "the Establishment." This included the government and nearly all teachers. They blamed their parents and their teachers for the ills of the world. They were unhappy about the Vietnam War and many other things. They showed it by screaming obscene slogans and disrupting classes. They demanded "Student Power."

One of their favorite movies was *Dr. Strangelove, or How I Learned to Stop Worrying and Love the Bomb*, which ended in nuclear explosions. Their favorite heroes, in fact, were the "losers" like Malcolm X or "Che" Guevara, the Cuban revolutionary who died trying to export revolution to Bolivia.

At the University of California in Berkeley in 1964, a group of these unhappy students, in a so-called "Free Speech" movement, went on strike. Soon students at other colleges were following their example. At Columbia University in New York City in the spring of 1968 they occupied administration buildings, burned a professor's manuscripts destroying the work of a lifetime, and demanded the deciding voice in university affairs. In most universities the professors, who liked to be liked by their students, gave in. Across the country, people outside universities wondered what had happened to the American love of learning and the Jeffersonian tradition of free debate.

Frank Siteman/Stock, Boston

Hippies tried every way to show that they rejected the values of most Americans.

SECTION REVIEW

1. Identify or explain: Nobel Prizes, freedom march, George Wallace, Watts, Malcolm X, Black Muslims, Stokely Carmichael, "Black Power," Thurgood Marshall, hippies, New Left, SDS.

2. What kinds of discrimination were northern blacks facing in the early 1960s?

3. What was the Summer Freedom Project of 1964? What was its unexpected effect?

4. How did the Voting Rights Act help to assure the voting rights of southern blacks?

5. What were some effects of the urban riots of 1965–1967?

6. Describe some responses by young people to the troublesome 1960s.

4. "The most unpopular war"

During 1964 the United States sank deeper and deeper into the war in Vietnam. In the course of the campaign for President, Senator Barry Goldwater had asked LBJ to send more American troops. But the President resisted. He had promised during the campaign, "We are not about to send American boys nine or ten thousand miles from home to do what Asian boys ought to be doing for themselves." Still, Johnson would not negotiate with North Vietnam. "We do not believe in

Vietnam

— Demarcation Line of 1954

0   300 Miles
0   300 Kilometers

SOUTHEAST ASIA 1945

conferences to ratify terror," he declared. Secretary of State Dean Rusk said that just as our duties to the free world required us to stay in Berlin—so now we must defend freedom in Vietnam.

The Tonkin Gulf Resolution. Off North Vietnam in the Tonkin Gulf on August 2 and 4, 1964, two United States destroyers were attacked by North Vietnamese gunboats. This brought matters to a head. President Johnson said they were attacked without cause. (Later it appeared that they had been protecting South Vietnamese gunboats making raids on the North.) He went on television to announce "that repeated acts of violence against the United States" must be answered. At that moment, he revealed, United States planes were attacking targets in the North.

The next day, August 5, he asked Congress for a joint resolution to empower "the President, as Commander in Chief, to take all necessary measures to repel any armed attack against the forces of the United States and to prevent further aggression." It passed without a single negative vote in the House. In the Senate there was debate only because the independent Senator Wayne Morse of Oregon threatened a filibuster if there was no discussion. Morse said the resolution violated the Constitution by giving the President powers that belonged to Congress. Senator Ernest Gruening of Alaska called it "a predated declaration of war." But only these two voted No.

In fact, President Johnson did not believe that he really needed the resolution. He believed that as Commander in Chief he had the right to send armed forces wherever necessary. He said that this meant even sending troops to Vietnam. He followed the example of Truman in Korea, Eisenhower in Lebanon, and Kennedy in the Cuban missile crisis, who had not asked Congress for permission to use armed force. But LBJ wanted a resolution to protect himself from later congressional criticism. Americans agreed that the President must use troops to defend the United States. It was not so clear that he should send Americans into a civil war on the other side of the globe.

The widening Asian commitment: Vietnamese Communists. In January 1965 Johnson's advisers warned him that the United States would have to increase its aid if South Vietnam was to be saved

A desperate refugee in Vietnam carrying pots, pans, and a stove trudges past United States troops.

from the Communists. In February there was a Communist attack on a United States military unit, and 7 Americans were killed and 100 wounded. To retaliate, LBJ ordered the bombing of North Vietnam. Still, he hesitated to order all-out bombing or to commit more troops. "If there is one thing that the American people will not take," he said, "it is another shooting war in Asia." Despite his worst fears, that was exactly what Americans were in.

Could the United States now afford to "lose" South Vietnam? That was the unwelcome question. To avoid defeat more and more American power was needed. In March American planes were bombing regularly. On April 1, 1965, LBJ, against his own promises, sent American troops against the Viet Cong. A few days later, with no public announcement, he added another 20,000 men to help the 27,000 already in Vietnam. American troops were sinking into the quicksand and disappearing into the jungles of Southeast Asia.

Why we were in Vietnam. It was not easy to make clear to the American people why we were in Vietnam at all. The simplest explanation was offered by President Eisenhower (who, in fact, carefully stayed out of Vietnam). This was the "domino theory." Vietnam, he said, was like the first in a row of standing dominoes. If you toppled it over, the other dominoes (the neighboring countries) would fall, too. All Southeast Asia would quickly be taken over by the Communists.

Another reason was to stop aggression. Early in 1965 there were still only a small number of North Vietnamese soldiers in South Vietnam. But American military leaders remembered how Europe had fallen to the Nazis because Britain and France had not acted soon enough.

A third reason for going into Vietnam was to protect our reputation. We wanted other free countries to believe that we would stand by them if they were attacked by Communists. This was called our "credibility." If we did not protect South Vietnam, we feared other nations would not believe we would help them. Then our whole worldwide system of defense against the Communists might collapse.

For all these reasons in July 1965 President Johnson committed the United States to victory in Vietnam. By the year's end the American troops there numbered 185,000. Were we in so deep that it no longer mattered why we were there? The urgent task now, a State Department spokesman explained, was "to avoid humiliation." While this was seen as a patriotic duty, it was not inspiring.

The Dominican Republic.

The Communist issue was still very much alive in the Caribbean—on our own doorstep. In the Dominican Republic a revolution had overthrown the government on April 24, 1965. No one could tell who would take power. When civil war broke out, the American ambassador in Santo Domingo panicked. He feared that Juan Bosch, the last popularly elected president, was winning and that he supported the Communists. The ambassador asked Washington for troops to protect American lives and "prevent another Cuba." LBJ sent in American forces. By May 5, when a truce was arranged, the United States had 22,000 men in the Dominican Republic.

Johnson defended this intervention. "The American nation," he said, "cannot, must not, will not, permit the establishment of another Communist government in the Western Hemisphere." Later, it became plain that the situation in the Dominican Republic had not been as bad as we had thought. The Communists had not been about to take over after all.

Widening the "credibility gap."

Even after LBJ decided to commit troops to the fighting in Vietnam, he refused to admit that there had been any shift in United States policy. In July 1965, when he decided to build up our forces in Vietnam, he chose not to reveal to Congress or the people what he intended to do. He announced that he was sending 50,000 men right away, and he asked for more money to pay for that commitment. But he did not let Congress know what the full cost would be.

President Johnson later explained that he feared if he told the whole truth he would not be able to pass his Great Society legislation. He was on the verge of achieving his dream "of improving life for more people than any other political leader, including FDR." If Congress began to debate foreign policy, that might be the end of the Great Society. "I was determined to be a leader of war *and* a leader of peace."

LBJ had not fully shared his intentions or fears about Vietnam or the Dominican Republic with the American people. And in domestic affairs, when news leaked out of what he was going to do, he would sometimes change his plans and do something else. Soon there developed a "credibility gap." This was a gap between what the President wanted people to believe and what was credible (really believable). As the months of the Vietnam War went on, that gap widened. The American people began to doubt what Johnson told them about Vietnam—or anything else.

A "peace offensive."

During 1965 all across the nation there appeared signs of growing opposition to the war in Vietnam. The influential Senator J. William Fulbright of Arkansas, chairman of the Senate Foreign Relations Committee, had voted for the Tonkin Gulf Resolution. Now he argued that we were in too deep and should withdraw. At the University of Michigan students and professors staged a new kind of demonstration. Part study group, part political rally, this was the first antiwar "teach-in." In October a few young men burned their draft cards. The climax came in November 1965 when 30,000 antiwar protesters marched on Washington.

Ever since July, Secretary McNamara had been urging a halt in the bombing of North Vietnam. He said this would be a goodwill gesture to encourage the Communists to negotiate. As opposition to the war grew, Secretary of State Rusk moved to that position, too. So on December 23, 1965, LBJ announced a halt in the bombing and a "peace offensive." The President explored many diplomatic avenues. Still there was no reply from North Vietnam. Early in 1966, after a 37-day pause, the huge B-52s went back to bombing North Vietnam.

Johnson loses support.

Even while public opposition to the war increased, the United States commitment in Vietnam was also growing. By the end of 1966 there were 400,000 American men and women there. The casualties (killed, wounded, missing) were rising rapidly. There were 2500 in 1965 and 33,000 in 1966. Yet the war seemed to make no progress, and no end was in sight. All this provided opponents of the war with new arguments. Students, led by a small but loud group who called themselves the New Left, sabotaged public meetings and refused to allow debate. Many others who opposed the war were disgusted by their violence and bad manners. By late 1966 President Johnson had to restrict his public appearances.

Still a considerable number of Americans believed that, even though the war might never be "won," the United States dared not walk away from Vietnam. They feared that if the Communists from the North occupied South Vietnam they would kill thousands of innocent Vietnamese who had opposed the Communists. The feared bloodbath did not take place. But later events in many ways supported their predictions. Many Vietnamese were imprisoned, thousands were "resettled" in the countryside, and hundreds of thousands were forced out to sea to face death in flimsy boats.

As 1966 drew to a close, Secretary of Defense McNamara was becoming more and more gloomy about the war. Since the continued heavy bombing of the North did not seem to be forcing the enemy to give in, he advised that the bombing be stopped. He urged LBJ to make stronger efforts for a negotiated peace. He even suggested that we offer "a role for the Viet Cong in negotiations, postwar life, and government of the nation." But no such plans were made, and the war dragged on.

In November 1965 the opinion polls showed that 66 percent of the American people approved of the way Johnson was running the country. By October 1966 only 44 percent thought he was doing well. In elections that fall the Republicans gained in both the House and the Senate. The main reason was the voters' unhappiness over the war in distant Vietnam. The nation, puzzled over why we were there at all, was still more puzzled over why we stayed there.

Mounting opposition to the war. In May 1967 Secretary McNamara expressed the rising discontent. "The picture of the world's greatest superpower," he wrote to LBJ, "killing or seriously injuring 1000 noncombatants a week, while trying to pound a tiny backward nation into submission on an issue whose merits are hotly disputed, is not a pretty one." The United States was dropping more bombs each month on little Vietnam, which is the size of New Mexico, than had been dropped in total on Nazi Germany during all the months of heaviest bombing in World War II.

In June 1967 McNamara commissioned a study of the role of the United States in Vietnam since World War II. The study showed that the American people had been deceived about the real situation. That fall McNamara resigned. In 1971

These Americans marched in the streets proclaiming opposition to the war in Vietnam.

this report, called the Pentagon Papers, was finally leaked to the press (p. 688).

Throughout 1967 the number of United States troops in Vietnam continued to increase. They reached 475,000, and casualties that year climbed to 80,000. Opposition to the war became ever more shrill. In New York 300,000 marched in protest, and a crowd of 100,000 tried to close the Pentagon in the nation's capital. The bitter cry, "Hey, hey, hey, LBJ, How many kids did you kill today!" was heard at demonstrations in colleges across the land.

The Tet offensive. All this was just a prelude to 1968. In January, General William Westmoreland, the American commander in Vietnam, issued another optimistic report telling how the war was being won. Four days later, on the Vietnamese New Year's holiday called "Tet," the Viet Cong and North Vietnamese suddenly launched their strongest offensive. They struck at cities throughout South Vietnam, even penetrating the heavily guarded grounds of the United States embassy in

Saigon. After brutal fighting over the next month, the enemy was driven out of the cities with heavy losses. In this, the first TV war, the American public at home witnessed the killing.

General Westmoreland claimed that the Tet episode was actually a victory for the United States and South Vietnam. The Communists had suffered enormous losses. But the Communists had seized the initiative. They had driven United States and South Vietnamese forces into defensive positions around the cities. Now the Communists from North Vietnam were operating freely in the countryside. General Westmoreland asked for 206,000 more troops and more fighter squadrons. These new forces would add $12 billion to the $30 billion a year that the war was already costing.

Clark Clifford, a trusted personal adviser of LBJ, now replaced McNamara as Secretary of Defense. He was a "hard-liner" (a "hawk") on the war. This meant that he believed we should continue

Young people helped Eugene McCarthy in the 1968 campaign.

fighting in Vietnam even at great cost. But when he studied the detailed military reports, Clifford himself began to have doubts. Soon he, too, began to work for "winding down"—removing our troops and moving out.

The fall of LBJ. After Tet, at the very moment when the fighting in Vietnam was heaviest, the presidential campaign in the United States was getting under way. Senator Eugene McCarthy of Minnesota, a gentle man of poetic temperament who had enlisted some college students and other opponents of the war, challenged Johnson for the party's nomination. He called for a negotiated settlement and a prompt withdrawal of all American forces.

The first primary contest was held in New Hampshire in mid-March 1968. As the unknown McCarthy toured New Hampshire, LBJ's rating in the opinion polls continued to fall. By March the polls reported that only 36 percent of the people approved of his Presidency, and a mere 26 percent thought he was handling the war well. McCarthy made a surprisingly strong finish in the New Hampshire race against LBJ—with 42 percent of the votes. This was not a victory, but it was as good as one. A President in office was supposed to win easily.

The vote for McCarthy was, in fact, a protest against LBJ. Many who voted for McCarthy actually favored the war—but they thought it was being badly handled. When McCarthy's success showed that Johnson might be beaten, on March 16 Senator Robert F. Kennedy, a younger brother of President Kennedy's, entered the race.

Secretary of Defense Clifford, LBJ's old friend, reported that he had consulted leaders around the country. Once they had been for the war. Now they thought we ought to get out. When Johnson himself consulted his advisory group of former and present government officials, they agreed with Clifford.

On March 31, 1968, LBJ announced on television that he had ordered sharp restrictions in the bombing. He called for peace talks. Then he stunned his listeners. He declared at the end that in order to keep his actions on Vietnam from being thought of as just playing politics, "I shall not seek, and I will not accept the nomination of my party for another term as your President."

Three days later, the North Vietnamese agreed to begin talks to end the war. The next day in Memphis, Tennessee, Martin Luther King, Jr., was assassinated. The blacks in cities across the nation exploded. They burned, looted, and rioted in 100 cities. In Washington, the flames of smoldering buildings in the black neighborhoods, fired by the blacks themselves, could be seen from the White House. The problems of the United States on the battlefields of Vietnam, halfway around the world, seemed on the way to solution. But in the nation's own front yard the challenges remained.

Peace talks began in Paris in May and dragged on throughout the months of the presidential campaign. On June 23, 1968—with the count starting from December 22, 1961, when the first American serviceman had died in Vietnam—the war became the longest in United States history.

SECTION REVIEW

1. Identify or explain: Dean Rusk, Wayne Morse, "domino theory," "credibility gap," J. William Fulbright, Robert McNamara, Pentagon Papers, Tet offensive, Eugene McCarthy.

2. How did the Tonkin Gulf incident lead to our increased involvement in Vietnam?

3. What were the reasons for American involvement in Vietnam?

4. Why did Johnson intervene in the Dominican Republic?

5. Trace the decline of support for the war in Vietnam and for President Johnson.

CHAPTER REVIEW

MEETING OUR EARLIER SELVES

1. What measures that had been urged by President Kennedy did President Johnson persuade Congress to enact? Why was Johnson more successful?

2. What changes would a black person living or visiting in the Deep South expect to see when the Civil Rights Act of 1964 went into effect?

3. How did the laws passed in 1964–1966 seek to promote (a) greater equality? (b) a better environment? (c) consumer protection?

4. Summarize the philosophies of three black leaders of the 1960s. How did they differ? Which leader had the most lasting influence on the civil rights movement?

5. Which of the reasons cited for our involvement in Vietnam do you consider the most compelling? the least compelling? Why?

6. What reasons would you expect an antiwar activist in the 1960s to offer for United States withdrawal from Vietnam?

QUESTIONS FOR TODAY

1. What lessons might a President and Congress learn today by reflecting on the high volume of legislation enacted during the Johnson years?

2. Has any book published in the past five years had an impact as powerful as the Carson and Nader books? Explain.

3. Compare the values and actions of today's youth with those of the 1960s. How do you account for similarities and differences?

4. How does American foreign policy today reflect our experience in Vietnam?

YOUR REGION IN HISTORY

1. Find out how your school system was influenced by the Elementary and Secondary Education Act.

2. How was your locality directly affected by other Great Society laws and programs?

3. Did any political demonstrations or urban riots in the 1960s take place near where you live? What brought them on? What happened? If your locality remained calm, how do you account for this?

SKILLS TO MAKE OUR PAST VIVID

1. Interview (a) a 1960s voter and (b) a Vietnam veteran on their perceptions of the war at that time. Try to find out if, how, and why their attitudes on the war changed.

2. Construct a vertical timeline for the years 1963–1968. On one side put highlights of your family's history. On the other side list highlights of the Johnson Presidency.

CHAPTER 33

The rise and fall of Richard Nixon

The Presidency of Richard M. Nixon produced a crisis in the life of the nation. In 1972 he and Vice-President Agnew won a second term with a popular majority of 18 million votes, the greatest number in history. Yet within two years, Agnew had resigned to avoid trial for bribery and income-tax evasion, and Nixon himself had left office to avoid impeachment. The ordeal of the nation was without precedent. But it also offered a unique opportunity for the representatives of a free people to show that the President was not above the law.

1. Electing the President, 1968

The election campaign of 1968 brought into the open many of the hopes and fears of the American people. In its course the short, blazing political career of Robert F. Kennedy would be snuffed out. It would see armed guards, barbed wire, and rioting in the streets of Chicago during the Democratic National Convention. And its end would find Richard M. Nixon, who had barely lost in 1960, now narrowly achieving his consuming ambition to be the President of the United States.

The race for the Democratic nomination. The Vietnam War ended the long political career of Lyndon B. Johnson. It also pushed Robert F. Kennedy into the presidential race. He campaigned across the country in the primaries against Senator Eugene McCarthy of Minnesota. Campaigning in the critical race for California's 174 convention delegates, Kennedy drove himself to exhaustion. And he won that state's support in the coming Democratic convention. On the same day, June 5, he also won in South Dakota.

RFK went to the ballroom of the Ambassador Hotel in Los Angeles to thank the workers who had made his California victory possible. After his brief speech, he suddenly decided to leave the hall by the kitchen to avoid the crush of his well-wishers. There Sirhan Sirhan, a Jordanian who disliked Kennedy's support of Israel, was waiting. He fired three shots at the senator, who died the next day.

The nation had not yet recovered from the shock of the assassination in April of Martin Luther King. Now, only two months later, another prominent leader was murdered. The people who mourned their loss were also lamenting the rise of violence in American life.

When Lyndon Johnson stepped aside in March 1968, his buoyant, voluble Vice-President, Hubert Horatio Humphrey, decided to enter the race. Humphrey ran in no primaries, but he had the support of the leaders of the Democratic party.

When he arrived in Chicago for the party convention, he had enough votes to win the nomination on the first ballot.

Chaos in Chicago.
The events that occurred in Chicago during the Democratic convention of 1968 were played out on television. What people saw damaged Hubert Humphrey's chances to win the Presidency.

Inside the convention hall, protected by guards and barbed wire, there was a nasty name-calling fight over the platform plank on the Vietnam War. One side, the followers of Eugene McCarthy and the late Robert Kennedy, demanded an immediate end to the bombing and the quick withdrawal of United States and North Vietnamese troops. They called for a coalition government of all South Vietnamese parties. The other side, followers of Johnson and Humphrey, supported peace talks. But they opposed withdrawing unless North Vietnam also withdrew. They wanted to stop the bombing of North Vietnam only when it "would not endanger the lives of our troops." Finally the Johnson-Humphrey resolution won. New York State's antiwar delegates pinned on black armbands of mourning.

In most cases, national party conventions in the United States had been good-humored. Festive delegates wore colorful hats, sang, joked, and cheered. At those times the nation could see each convention end in happy unity. Now the dark shadow of the Vietnam War had turned a circus into a funeral. The bitterness and violence of European and Latin American politics had somehow infected American life.

Outside, on the streets of downtown Chicago, thousands of opponents of the war swarmed. The most obvious were the "Yippies"—the Youth International party—who made fun of the whole affair. They nominated a pig, Pigasus, for President. But the fun soon ceased, for the Yippies and other war opponents yelled at the police, taunted them, and began throwing things. Then fierce fighting broke out. The hot weather did not help. The police, provoked by the demonstrators, showed little skill or restraint at crowd control. At the same time, many demonstrators wanted to incite the police to violence in order to attract TV attention. The result was an unpleasant and unfamiliar spectacle. Much of this was seen on television just as

Fred Ward/Black Star

The 1968 Democratic nomination was won by Hubert Humphrey after a bitter contest inside the convention hall in Chicago.

Hubert Humphrey was nominated for the Presidency. Senator Edmund Muskie of Maine became his running mate.

Humphrey would never escape the scenes of Chicago. They seemed to reflect the worst side of the United States of recent years—the war, the angry young people, the rioting in cities and on college campuses. The divided, wrangling Democrats did not look like a party that was prepared to solve the nation's problems.

The Republicans choose Nixon.
The Republican fight for the nomination was, as usual, a far more gentlemanly affair. Richard Nixon had led the race all the way. Though challenges were made by Governor Rockefeller of New York and Governor Ronald Reagan of California, Nixon won easily at Miami, Florida. For his vice-presidential nominee,

During the Democratic convention in Chicago, streets teemed with youthful demonstrators: Yippies, members of SDS, and McCarthy supporters. Police, demonstrators, and bystanders finally met in a bloody clash which thousands of Americans watched on television.

he chose Governor Spiro T. Agnew of Maryland. Agnew had begun as a liberal Republican, but after a riot in Baltimore following the death of Martin Luther King, he had emerged as a strong spokesman for law and order.

In his acceptance speech, Nixon called for the support of the "silent majority." These Americans were "the non-shouters, the non-demonstrators, that are not racist or sick, that are not guilty of the crime that plagues our land." And on the war he made it clear that he would bring peace. "Those who have had a chance for four years and could not produce peace," he declared, "should not be given another chance."

The American Independent party.

A third candidate, former Governor George C. Wallace of Alabama, opposed the federal push to integrate the schools, and he spoke out against the courts that "coddled criminals." He protested the attempts of the government to halt segregation in the sale or rental of all housing: He wanted to "win" in Vietnam. "I think we've got to pour it on

there," he said. Wallace hoped to appeal to enough discontented voters to keep either of the major candidates from winning. Then the election would be thrown into the House of Representatives. There his supporters could use their votes for trading purposes to achieve Wallace's goals.

The issue of the courts.

The main issue of the campaign was clearly the war in Vietnam. Nearly as important was the question of law and order. This issue touched everyone—especially people living in the slums of the cities, where the crime rate had soared. In the country as a whole during the 1960s, while the population went up only 13 percent, violent crimes climbed 148 percent.

Some people blamed this on the Supreme Court. Under Chief Justice Earl Warren, who had been appointed by President Eisenhower, the Court seemed to be overturning old standards and interfering everywhere.

It was constantly intruding within the states. In the *Brown* case it had decided for school integration. Then it began to lay down new rules for elections. In 1962 the Court declared that federal courts could step in to guarantee equal representation to all citizens in all states. For some years Americans had swarmed from farms into cities and their suburbs. Still many states had not changed their laws that apportioned representatives in the state legislatures. City voters did not have enough representatives, while farmers were over-represented. In 1964 the Court required all state legislatures to reapportion both their houses and their congressional districts on the principle of "one man, one vote." The people who lost their over-representation naturally did not like it.

The Supreme Court also decided some hard cases involving the separation of church and state. In 1962 the use of a prayer composed by the New York Board of Regents in public school classrooms was found to violate the First Amendment, which prohibited the establishment of religion. The next year the Court outlawed Bible readings in public school classrooms for the same reason. These decisions provoked outcries from some citizens. They denounced the Court for undermining the religious faith of American young people. They recalled that in the 1950s "under God" had been added to the Pledge of Allegiance and "In God We Trust" printed on all our currency. But others applauded the Supreme Court's defense of the First Amendment and said that religion was strong in the United States because it was not enforced by the government.

Many more Americans were troubled by the decisions of the Supreme Court which, they said, showed too much sympathy for persons accused of crime. They did not like the Court's rule in *Gideon* v. *Wainwright* (1963) that the state had to furnish legal counsel to poor defendants even in minor criminal cases. They objected when the Court decided in *Escobedo* v. *Illinois* (1964) and *Miranda* v. *Arizona* (1966) that a conviction would not stand unless the police had informed the accused of the right to remain silent and to have an attorney present when questioned. Suspects also had to be warned that any statement they made could be used against them in court. And in 1968 the Court ruled that in capital crimes (punishable by death) a person who opposed the death penalty could not for that reason be kept off the jury. This meant that many of the 435 persons awaiting execution on death row would have to be retried.

To many Americans these attempts of the Court to safeguard the constitutional rights of the individual against the power of the state just seemed another way of "pampering" criminals. In July 1968 a Gallup poll revealed that three Americans out of every five were unhappy over the Supreme Court's decisions. Candidate Nixon promised that when there were openings on the Court, he would appoint "strict constructionists"—judges who would interpret the Constitution strictly.

Nixon wins. The election turned out to be closer than anyone had expected. Humphrey's campaign, which started slowly, began to pick up steam toward the end. And Wallace's drive, though weaker than he had hoped, won 10 million voters. Thirteen percent of the total cast their ballots for George Wallace and gave him five southern states. Nixon defeated Humphrey by only 510,000 votes out of the 73 million cast, and he received only 43.4 percent of the total vote. This gave him the lowest winning majority since Woodrow Wilson in 1912. The Democrats retained their control of both houses of Congress.

SECTION REVIEW

1. Identify or explain: Eugene McCarthy, Sirhan Sirhan, "Yippies," Edmund Muskie, Ronald Reagan, Spiro Agnew, "silent majority," American Independent party, Earl Warren, *Gideon* v. *Wainwright*, *Escobedo* and *Miranda* cases.

2. How did violence affect the 1968 election campaign? Give examples.

3. Describe George Wallace's strategy in the 1968 election. What was his goal?

4. What stand did the Warren Court take on (a) equality of representation? (b) school religious exercises? (c) criminal rights? Why did the Court's decisions arouse criticism?

5. Would the outcome of the 1968 election have been different if Wallace had not run?

---

2. Nixon's first term

On election night Nixon declared that the theme of his Presidency would be to bring the American people together again. He said that he would try to

also discourage Americans from buying foreign products.

After these policies were adopted, inflation fell in 1972 to 3.5 percent. With a budget that in 1971 showed a $22.3 billion deficit and with an even larger deficit projected for 1972, the economy began to thrive and unemployment dropped. For President Nixon—and the nation—these were welcome facts as he planned for reelection in 1972.

SECTION REVIEW

1. Identify or explain: H. R. Haldeman, John Ehrlichman, Henry Kissinger, Neil Armstrong, Michael Collins, Edwin E. Aldrin, Jr., *Apollo 11*, Cambodian incursion, Kent State incident, Leonid Brezhnev, SALT, Warren Burger, wage-price freeze.

2. Summarize Nixon's career to 1968.

3. In what ways was the moon-landing project different from previous explorations of the unknown?

4. Make a timeline showing key events in the Vietnam War, including responses to the war at home, from 1969 to 1973.

5. What were Nixon's goals for (a) the Supreme Court, (b) the economy, (c) foreign policy? To what extent was he successful in achieving those goals?

3. The fall

The election of 1972 was to see Richard Nixon win the greatest popular majority in the history of the United States. Yet less than two years after his great victory he would become the first President ever to resign from office.

The Nixon outlook. The destruction of Richard Nixon began long before the campaign. Perhaps it began as far back as 1960 when he lost to Kennedy by such a narrow margin. For that convinced Nixon that he must never again leave anything undone in an election campaign—no matter how certain victory might appear.

His trouble was rooted in his view of himself and his opponents. Nixon the fighter never failed to see politics as a battleground—where you used whatever tactics were needed to win. "His use of football analogies was so revealing," Cabinet member Elliot Richardson explained. "Anything was OK except what the referee sees and blows the whistle on."

Pursuing enemies. It was not surprising that Nixon had a passion for secrecy. Those who opposed him he called his enemies. His special targets were people in the antiwar movement and his newspaper and TV critics. Against them he believed that he had the right to wield all the powers of the President. To spy on them and harass them he used government agencies such as the CIA, FBI, IRS, and FCC. Even when these activities were not technically illegal, they were an abuse of his presidential powers.

Nixon was determined to find out how the news of the secret bombing of Cambodia had reached the newspapers. In 1969, then, he ordered the FBI to place wiretaps (without the court orders required by law) on certain government employees and reporters. Believing that the antiwar protesters were actually tied to the Communists, in 1970 he tried to create his own super-secret intelligence group. This group would open mail, tap telephones, and even break into private homes and offices to get evidence to prove that his political opponents—his "enemies"—were really traitors. If his personal spies were caught, the answer would be that it was all for "national security"—to protect the nation. This plan came to nothing, however, because J. Edgar Hoover, the man who had built up the FBI and was the nation's chief spy-catcher, refused to go along. "The risks are too great," he warned.

In June 1971 the *New York Times* began to publish the "Pentagon Papers." This was the secret study of United States involvement in Vietnam that Secretary McNamara had ordered in 1967 (p. 675). The document had been given to the *Times* by Daniel Ellsberg, who had worked on the report. The government said the report would reveal secret information damaging to the national security and therefore sued to stop the *Times*. When the case went to the Supreme Court, the Court refused to intervene and allowed the papers to be printed.

The Department of Justice then indicted Daniel Ellsberg for theft, conspiracy, and espionage. President Nixon remained deeply disturbed. He was determined to track down his enemies—even if he had to set up his own system of counterespionage!

Within the White House, Nixon now formed a secret special unit. Since the job of this unit was to "stop leaks" of information, it was called the "Plumbers." Their first assignment was to find some way to ruin the reputation of Daniel Ellsberg. But the Plumbers were inept. Hoping to uncover some embarrassing information, they broke into the Los Angeles office of Ellsberg's psychiatrist. They found nothing. This was only one in a series of illegal acts that would destroy Nixon and his closest aides. For the Plumbers would soon turn from "national security" to party politics. And they would finally bring down the President, whom they were supposed to protect.

McGovern wins the Democratic nomination.

One part of the Nixon campaign strategy for reelection in 1972 was to divide the Democrats against themselves. Then the Nixon group would promote the candidate who was the easiest to defeat. This scheme included giving financial support to George Wallace of Alabama, opposing middle-of-the-road Edmund Muskie of Maine, and favoring the candidacy of George McGovern of South Dakota. It also included a variety of "dirty tricks." False letters were sent out attacking one candidate under the name of another. "The idea," one of the Nixon managers explained, "was to get the candidates backbiting each other."

George Wallace's push for the Democratic nomination was cut short by a shocking act of violence. While delivering a campaign speech in Laurel, Maryland, he was shot by an angry listener. Three bystanders were also shot. At first it seemed that Wallace might not survive. He lived but became paralyzed from the waist down and was no longer a serious contender.

Muskie's campaign faltered early, and George McGovern took the lead. He had helped to reform the party rules after 1968. More women, blacks, and young people would be delegates at the convention in 1972. He made a special effort to appeal to each of these groups.

When the party met in Miami Beach early in July, Senator McGovern won the nomination easily on the first ballot. As his running mate he chose Senator Thomas F. Eagleton of Missouri. But soon it came out that Eagleton had been hospitalized for psychiatric problems. McGovern asked Eagleton to step down. As a replacement the Democratic

Dennis Brack/Black Star

President Nixon, his wife, Patricia, and Mrs. Dwight Eisenhower, widow of the former President, enjoy the 1972 Inaugural Ball.

National Committee named Sargent Shriver, a brother-in-law of John and Robert Kennedy's. McGovern's judgment and his stability were called into question by his handling of this problem. At first he had said that he was behind Eagleton "1000 percent." Then suddenly he turned around and dropped him.

The 1972 campaign.

The Republicans also met in Miami Beach and quickly renominated Nixon and Agnew. They had an easy campaign. President Nixon seldom left the White House. He took a strong stand against busing and for the local control of schools. He also opposed abortion. He was against legalizing the smoking of marijuana and against welfare payments for those who would not work. He kept the bitter Vietnam issue alive by opposing amnesty for those who had avoided fighting in the war by deserting from the armed forces or by dodging the draft. At the same time the news in late October that peace seemed to be at hand in Vietnam was a boost for Richard Nixon's campaign.

Lawrence Fried/Magnum

Despite some enthusiastic support, George McGovern was badly defeated in 1972.

McGovern was openly against the war in Vietnam. He favored allowing abortions and legalizing the smoking of marijuana. He was for a cut in defense spending. He urged reform of the welfare system. But since his proposals were not well thought out, the Republicans found them easy to attack. The Republicans called him a far-left candidate with far-out ideas.

On election day Nixon won a resounding victory. With 60.7 percent of the vote, he carried 49 of the 50 states. McGovern had hoped for strong support from the new young voters. In 1971 the Twenty-sixth Amendment had been passed allowing any citizen 18 or over to vote. But many of these 11.5 million new voters failed to vote at all, and of those who did, many voted for Nixon. Only 55.7 percent of all Americans old enough to vote went to the polls—the lowest number since 1948.

Spying on the Democrats. The result showed that the Republicans had such an easy win that they really could have played by all the rules and still gained a large majority. Yet, for some reason they would not leave well enough alone. The nervous Nixon team, to make their victory doubly sure, had turned to underhanded tactics. As early as January 1972 Attorney General John Mitchell, who was soon to resign to devote full time to heading Nixon's campaign, heard one of the Plumbers present a program of secret, illegal campaign activities. A $1 million program of kidnapping, wiretapping, and "dirty tricks" to hurt the Democrats was suggested. Mitchell rejected the plan as too expensive. Though he was the nation's chief law-enforcement official, the Attorney General said nothing about the idea being wrong.

Finally, the campaign managers agreed to spend $250,000 on a new kind of political intelligence-gathering plan. None of them really liked it. In fact, one later said, "We feared that it might be a waste of money and also that it might be dangerous." But the White House wanted to know what its political opponents were up to. John Mitchell and the others approved an elaborate criminal plan, which included "bugging" the office of Lawrence O'Brien, head of the Democratic National Committee.

The first wiretap on O'Brien's phones did not work. Then, on the night of June 16, the Plumbers once again broke into the Democratic National Committee offices in the Watergate office building. And this time they were caught! They carried evidence that might link them to the White House and so open the President to the charge of being a criminal conspirator.

Nixon orders a cover-up. President Nixon did not know about the Watergate break-in until after it happened. But then easily, almost carelessly, he moved to cover up the crime. As soon as he and his aides did that, they were committing a crime themselves.

First the President ordered his staff to tell the CIA to stop the FBI from investigating the case. They were to say that "national security" was involved. The CIA refused to go along. So Nixon saw that money was paid to the Plumbers to keep them quiet about their connection to the White House. By September 1972 these men had received $220,000 in hush money.

Somehow the Watergate affair did not really catch the public's attention when it took place. Still, newspaper reporters Robert Woodward and

Carl Bernstein kept probing the strange events surrounding Watergate. Their reports, published in the *Washington Post,* kept the time bomb of Watergate ticking. It would go off, however, only after Nixon was safely reelected. Watergate would prove to be one of the oddest—and most unnecessary—crimes in American history.

Investigating the campaign.

Soon after the Senate convened in 1973, it voted 77–0 to set up a committee to look into any "illegal, improper, or unethical activities" in the 1972 election. Senator Sam Ervin of North Carolina was to head the committee.

When the Ervin Committee began its hearings, President Nixon and his aides felt pressure from three sides. If anyone involved in the burglary told the truth to a judge or to the Department of Justice or to the Ervin Committee, the White House link to the Plumbers would be revealed. So the President and his aides tried to devise still more ways to cover up their connection to the crime.

Nixon sank deeper and deeper into a new crime—the crime of the cover-up. The American people might have excused a President for making mistakes. But they would not tolerate a President who did not take seriously his sworn duty to obey and enforce the law.

Nixon under pressure.

Hoping to lift some of the pressure, on April 17, 1973, the President issued a statement that because of "major developments in the case" he had ordered "intensive new inquiries." He said that he had not learned until March 21, 1973, that there were attempts to cover up the scandal. This was a lie, for he had known ever since late June 1972. Nixon now heard that some of the people involved in the cover-up were beginning to talk. He was desperately trying to save himself. He had been informed by Attorney General Richard Kleindienst that the Department of Justice had enough information to indict Haldeman, Ehrlichman, and John Mitchell. He knew, too, that he could be impeached. So he began to thrash about, talking of using "a million dollars" and "clemency" to end this disaster.

On April 29, Nixon told his chief aides, Ehrlichman and Haldeman, who were in deep trouble, that they were fired. The following day, he told the nation on TV that he was naming a new Attorney General, Elliot Richardson, who was empowered to appoint a special prosecutor to investigate the Watergate case.

The discovery of the tapes.

"The Greatest Show on Earth," as the Ervin Committee hearings soon were called, opened its televised proceedings on May 17, 1973. They went on for three months. Millions watched fascinated by all the strange doings of the Nixon men—"enemies lists," money drops, dirty tricks, millions raised illegally from corporations, and attempts to use the IRS to harass enemies.

Then, late in the hearings, the news came out that since February 1971 there had been tape recording machines in the White House and Executive Office Building. Unknown to all but a few, these machines had been taping everything said there by the President and his aides. Nixon had been anxious that the events of his Presidency should be amply recorded for future historians. The tapes would make history in a way he never imagined. They would finally destroy Richard Nixon.

As soon as the existence of the tapes was known, both the Ervin Committee and the new special prosecutor, Harvard professor Archibald Cox, wanted to hear certain key conversations. Nixon refused to hand over the tapes. He insisted that the President could not do his job if his records were not kept confidential. So the matter went to the courts. On October 12, the Court of Appeals ruled, 5–2, against the President. "Though the President is elected by nationwide ballot," the court declared, "and is often said to represent all the people, he . . . is not above the law's commands." Nixon had a week to decide whether to appeal the decision, to turn over the tapes, or to take some other action.

Agnew resigns.

At this moment when the net was closing ever more tightly around the struggling President, Vice-President Agnew—who had risen to power by preaching law and order—was accused of serious crimes. On August 1, 1973, he was told by the Department of Justice that he was being investigated for income-tax evasion, conspiracy, bribery, and extortion. There was evidence that he had accepted kickbacks from Maryland state contractors as governor and even as Vice-President.

At first Agnew protested his innocence. Then, after bargaining with the prosecution, he decided to

For five months of televised hearings, the Senate Committee probed the Watergate break-in and other "illegal, improper, or unethical activities" that took place during the 1972 campaign.

resign as Vice-President and to plead "no contest" to tax evasion. This meant that he would not try to prove his innocence in court and that he would accept the penalties of being guilty. In return, the government was willing to drop the other charges against him. The prosecution also asked the court for leniency "out of compassion for the man, out of respect for the office he has held, and out of appreciation for the fact that by his resignation he has spared the nation the prolonged agony that would have attended upon his trial." The court fined him $10,000 and placed him on probation for three years. The government then released in detail the evidence against him.

Fortunately, in 1967 the Twenty-fifth Amendment to the Constitution had been adopted. It came from the time of President Eisenhower's illness and was mainly intended for a situation when the President was not physically able to carry on the duties of his office. In case of a vacancy in the office of the Vice-President, the President would nominate someone who was to be confirmed by both houses of Congress. President Nixon now made the first use of the amendment. For the new Vice-President he chose Gerald R. Ford of Grand Rapids,

Michigan, the Republican floor leader in the House of Representatives. Well known and respected in Congress, he was quickly confirmed.

War in the Middle East.

To add to Nixon's troubles, on October 6, 1973, war broke out anew in the Middle East. Egypt and Syria attacked Israel on Yom Kippur, the holiest day of the Jewish year. Then, on October 12, the President decided to go all out to aid the Israelis and offset the supplies the Arabs were receiving from Russia. He ordered a massive airlift from the United States all the 6450 miles to Israel—including helicopters, howitzers, and even 50-ton tanks. In response, the Arabs embargoed oil shipments to the United States. The winter of 1973–1974 found the United States faced with its first gasoline shortage.

The Saturday Night Massacre.

President Nixon now made a move that was to lose him much of whatever support he had left in the country. First, he announced on Friday, October 20, that Watergate was sapping the strength of the nation. To resolve the crisis, he said he would compromise on the issue of the tapes. He would offer summaries of their contents. He also revealed that he had ordered Special Prosecutor Cox to stop trying to get the tapes.

The following day Cox refused to accept the President's order. He demanded the actual tapes. Nixon then told Attorney General Richardson to fire Cox. But Richardson had promised both Cox and the Senate that he would not interfere with the Special Prosecutor, so he resigned. Then Nixon asked the Deputy Attorney General to fire Cox. But he, too, resigned rather than carry out the order. Finally, Robert Bork, the Solicitor General, who believed that the President had the right to fire Cox, whatever might be the wisdom of the act, discharged the Special Prosecutor.

This was called "the Saturday Night Massacre." Elliot Richardson later said that by firing Cox, President Nixon wanted to show the world that he was still in charge of the government. "It was like the 1970 action in Cambodia," he said. "He wanted to show Moscow and Peking his determination, and to do that he would pay the necessary domestic price."

But Nixon had misjudged the American people. To them his actions seemed an admission of guilt. *Time* magazine, which had never before run an editorial in all its 50 years, now said, "The President Should Resign."

The President's troubles mount. At this point the House Judiciary Committee began hearings to decide whether the President should be impeached. Nixon finally gave in. He agreed to give up to the court the tapes that had been subpoenaed and to appoint a new Special Prosecutor.

As if Nixon did not have enough problems at this point, his personal finances were also being investigated. A House committee revealed that he had paid less than $1000 in taxes in both 1971 and 1972 even though he had earned $200,000 each year. His low taxes were based on a questionable gift of his vice-presidential papers (which he valued at $570,000) to the National Archives in 1969. This had saved him $235,000 in taxes. It also came out that $10 million in federal funds had been spent on his properties at Key Biscayne in Florida and San Clemente in California and on his daughters' houses. Even though the money was said to be for security for the President and his family, the amounts seemed to be way out of line.

By early 1974 President Nixon was under such pressure that he was no longer able to govern effectively. But still he held on, although he spent as little time as possible in Washington.

On March 1, 1974, Mitchell, Haldeman, Ehrlichman, and five others were indicted by a grand jury for conspiring to cover up the Watergate break-in, for obstructing justice, and for perjury. In a secret report the grand jury also named Nixon as a co-conspirator. He was not indicted because the new Special Prosecutor, Leon Jaworski, argued that a President could not be indicted until he had been impeached and removed from office.

Nixon made one last desperate attempt to escape his problems. On April 29, 1974, he went on television. He was seated before a tall stack of blue notebooks, which he described as the transcripts of more tapes that he had recently been asked for—and which he had refused to hand over. These, he said, contained everything about Watergate "and what I did about it."

The transcripts astounded the country. They revealed the President and his aides as petty men,

President Nixon sits before a stack of notebooks containing what he claimed to be the full transcripts of the Watergate tapes.

speaking in vulgar expletives. They were constantly scheming about how to "get" their enemies. Senator Hugh Scott of Pennsylvania, leader of the Republicans in the Senate, called the tapes "a shabby, disgusting, immoral performance."

Still the Judiciary Committee and Jaworski continued to press Nixon for the actual tapes themselves. When he refused, the question went on its way to the Supreme Court.

The House committee favors impeachment.
Under the Constitution, the House of Representatives has to vote the articles of impeachment against a President. Then the President is tried by the whole Senate, with the Chief Justice presiding.

On July 24, after nearly three months of private hearings, the House Judiciary Committee began its public televised debate over the articles of impeachment. On July 27 the committee voted 27 to 11 in favor of Article 1—that the President had followed a "course of conduct or plan" to obstruct justice in the cover-up of the Watergate break-in. Six Republicans had joined the 21 Democrats to vote against their President. Two days later, the committee voted a second article of impeachment— that the President had abused his power when he used the Plumbers, the IRS, FBI, CIA, and other government agencies in violation of the constitutional rights of citizens. Finally, on July 30, it voted 21 to 17 to impeach the President also for failing to abide by legal House subpoenas. The committee voted against attempting to impeach the President for the secret bombing of Cambodia or for evading taxes or for using government funds on his homes.

The whole nation watched in sadness—but also in awe and admiration—as they saw the men and women of the committee show such judicial fairness. The committee as a whole seemed to rise above the bitterness of partisan politics. The nation was inspired to see its representatives take such pains to cleanse the White House. As it became plain that the committee would have to vote to impeach the President, some committee members of both parties were in tears. They, too, were saddened at what they had to do.

The President resigns.
Even at this point, it seemed possible that the House of Representatives might vote not to approve the committee's report. Or, even if they did approve the three articles of impeachment, perhaps the President would not be convicted by the Senate. Some members of Congress still felt that the committee had not found the "smoking gun"—the clear, unmistakable evidence of a presidential act to cover up the break-in. Without such evidence, should a few hundred representatives in Congress vote to remove from office a Chief Executive who had been voted into office by a majority of millions of Americans? Some of the members of Congress still feared that they would set a precedent. Would some future Congress remove a President simply because they did not like him or disagreed with his policy?

The tapes (which the President himself had ordered to insure his place in history!) proved Richard Nixon's final undoing. The Supreme Court decided on July 24 that he had to hand them over. Then the President could hide no longer. On August 5, 1974, he confessed that portions of the tape for June 23, 1972, were "at variance with certain of my previous statements." That tape clearly recorded the President in his own voice ordering Haldeman to get the CIA to stop the FBI investigation of the break-in. This showed that Nixon had lied all along about when he knew of the cover-up and that he had, in fact, personally ordered the cover-up.

That night, as the fall of the President seemed certain, Secretary of Defense James R. Schlesinger took the unheard-of action of ordering all United States military commanders to refuse to accept orders from the White House unless they were countersigned by him. The President could no longer be trusted. The following day Nixon informed the Cabinet that he still would not resign. Congress would have to impeach him. But on August 7 three of the most respected Republican leaders—Senator Hugh Scott, Senator Barry Goldwater, and Representative John Rhodes—called on President Nixon and made it clear that he had no support. If he tried to stand and fight, they said, he would be impeached by the House, and then he would be convicted by the Senate.

The next day Nixon, on television to the nation, announced his decision to resign. On August 9, 1974, he signed the official letter of resignation. He was the first President ever forced to leave office before the end of his term.

While the tearful former President was flying across the nation to his home in San Clemente,

California, back in Washington Gerald Ford was being sworn in as the thirty-eighth President of the United States.

SECTION REVIEW

1. Identify or explain: wiretaps, Daniel Ellsberg, "Plumbers," George McGovern, Sargent Shriver, Lawrence O'Brien, Woodward and Bernstein, Ervin Committee, Elliot Richardson, Archibald Cox, 25th Amendment, Gerald Ford, oil embargo, "Saturday Night Massacre," Leon Jaworski.

2. How did "national security" enter into Nixon's pursuit of his "enemies"?

3. Account for Nixon's easy victory in the 1972 election.

4. Why did the "Plumbers" break into the Watergate building?

5. Recount the highlights of the Watergate affair from the break-ins to Nixon's resignation.

CHAPTER REVIEW

MEETING OUR EARLIER SELVES

1. Why have modern Presidents required a large White House staff? What problems arise from this arrangement?

2. How did the "Sense of the Senate" resolution in 1969 (p. 685) reflect popular opposition to the Vietnam War?

3. In May 1969 what conditions did Nixon rule out in the Vietnam peace negotiations? Were those conditions met? Explain.

4. Why was United States recognition of the People's Republic of China a momentous event? Why was Nixon well suited to bring about this change of policy?

5. How did two resignations bring Gerald Ford to the Presidency?

6. Opinion polls taken in 1975 and 1976 showed a sharp drop in people's "trust in government." What may have been some other by-products of Watergate?

QUESTIONS FOR TODAY

1. Is "law and order" a major political issue today? What remedies are officeholders or candidates proposing?

2. A major reason for United States fighting in South Vietnam was to prevent the fall of other Southeast Asian lands to the Communists (the "domino theory"). Have events since the peace negotiations proved or disproved the "domino theory"? Explain.

3. Considering our relations with the People's Republic of China today, how would you evaluate Nixon's "China policy"?

YOUR REGION IN HISTORY

1. Was your state legislature reapportioned as a result of the 1964 "one man, one vote" Supreme Court decision? If so, how was your county or other election district affected?

2. Was your school district affected by the 1962–1963 Supreme Court decisions on religious exercises? Explain. Describe the arguments pro and con over religious exercises in the schools.

SKILLS TO MAKE OUR PAST VIVID

1. Interview several adults about their reactions to the *Apollo 11* expedition and the moon-landing. Find out how they felt about the program before and after the landing. Prepare a survey form to guide your interviews. Then report your findings to the class.

2. Write a one- or two-page summary of the Watergate affair. Choose its essential aspects and make them clear for an uninformed reader.

12

The United States looks ahead

Richard Lippold's gold wire sculpture "Variations within a Sphere, No. 10: The Sun" is a tensely balanced expression of space and matter. The Metropolitan Museum of Art, Fletcher Fund, 1966

When the United States celebrated its two-hundredth birthday in 1976, it was already the oldest of the new nations. And even before 1987, when Americans would celebrate the two-hundredth anniversary of the framing of the Constitution, the nation was living by the world's oldest written constitution still in use.

Since the Civil War, Americans had been seeking ways to keep their country young in spirit. The nation had been kept young by always asking what it meant to be an American.

In these next years the nation, more anxiously than ever before, would seek equality of opportunity for all Americans. Congress passed laws, and citizens organized, to bring women, as well as black, brown, and red Americans, and handicapped Americans into the mainstream of national life.

Competition—within the nation and between nations—was still strenuous and demanding. The unusual American opportunities and needs to compete had made the nation strong and would keep the nation strong.

The millions of immigrants, their children and their children's children, would still seek new opportunities for themselves and all other Americans to show what they could do. "We can no longer say there is nothing new under the sun," Thomas Jefferson had written back in 1801. As the twentieth century neared its close, the United States remained a nation of experiments.

CHAPTER 34

A new world of competition

The twentieth century was a time of climax. Never before had Americans cared so much to fulfill the ideal of equality. Never before had they worked so hard to keep Americans free—to choose their President, to decide on their laws, to know what was going on in their government. It was not surprising, then, that this was a difficult time.

It was difficult, too, because the nation was built not just on the ideal of equality, but also on the ideal of freedom. Equality and freedom were twin ideals. Equality meant the right to be treated equal in the courts and by the law, and the right to vote. Freedom meant the right to have your say, to believe and worship as you pleased, to grow and be educated according to your talents, to choose your job, and to compete for the best things in life. In the two centuries of the nation's life both these ideals had widened. When President Ford took his oath of office, there was more equality and more freedom for more Americans than ever before.

Equality meant opportunity, freedom meant competition. Although the twin ideals—equality and freedom—both came from the American Revolution, as the years went on the two ideals had not always worked together. In fact they sometimes got in the way of each other.

We can understand why that happened if we think of life in America as a kind of game. Of course everyone wanted to be a winner. But to keep the factories and the farms going, and to keep life decent and pleasant, the game had to be played by certain rules. That meant, of course, that there would be winners and losers. The nation would be strong and keep its place in the world only if the rules made it possible for everybody to have a chance to play—and then let the best person win. This meant that there could be no rules to keep anyone out because of race, sex, religion, or where his family came from. This meant, too, that to keep the chances fair, everybody was entitled to education, health, and decent housing. This was the American idea of equality.

Still, everybody knows that some people are stronger than others, some are brighter, some harder workers. Freedom meant the opportunity for everyone to show his or her ability—and, if possible, win in the competition. In totalitarian countries, people were told what their jobs would be, where they had to work, and what their income would be. The winners were named by the government. But freedom was a chancy world. It meant keeping the market open for ideas to compete against each other. It meant keeping the nation open for everybody to try to become a winner. The extra rewards for special ability would have to go to those (regardless of race, sex, age, or religion) who actually were especially able.

Naturally everyone wanted a chance, and the ideal of equality had to guarantee that chance. But everybody could not be an equal winner. The ideal of freedom had to guarantee everybody's right to be as successful as that person could be.

The tradition of the two ideals goes back to the very beginning of the nation. To understand their meaning in our time we must see how those ideals have widened. We will see how Americans have tried to live happily together as they made the two ideals work together.

1. The two traditions

The Declaration of Independence had declared the right of Americans "to assume among the powers of the earth, the separate and equal station to which the Laws of Nature and of Nature's God entitle them." The British government had not allowed Americans their equal rights to govern themselves and vote on their own taxes. It had not given them the freedom to trade where they wanted and to make what they wished. The American Revolution, then, was fought to give this new nation both equality and freedom in the world of nations.

Within the nation, too, these ideals of equality and freedom would rule. "We hold these truths to be self-evident, that all men are created equal, that they are endowed by their Creator with certain unalienable Rights, that among these are Life, Liberty, and the pursuit of Happiness." According to Jefferson, the bulwark of rights was education. He preached a "crusade against ignorance." "Diffusion of knowledge among the people" was the only "sure foundation . . . for the preservation of freedom and happiness."

The "natural aristocracy." Every generation, Jefferson believed, had enough of its own bright and able people to run the government and preserve freedom. While all men were "created equal," with equal rights before the law, Jefferson did not believe that every individual person was just as clever and as talented as everybody else. He said there was a "natural aristocracy." This was nothing like the Old World aristocracy. Over there certain lucky people had high-sounding titles and power in the government only because their parents and grandparents were rich, owned lots of land, or were friends of the king or queen. Nobody had elected them, and they had not earned their wealth or their high position.

The "natural aristocracy"—a democratic aristocracy—in this country would be a different breed. They would be the ablest, most industrious, and best educated. And they would be elected to government jobs because of their very own talents and knowledge.

Jefferson outlined a system of education to train these people and prepare them to lead. All would compete, and then the people who did best in the examinations would move up to the next level of schools. In this way, he hoped, the nation would be well supplied with the kind of "aristocrats" needed in a free republic.

A neat one-room schoolhouse was caught in this watercolor made about 1900 by an unknown painter. The month was February, when Valentine's Day sentiments mingled with patriotic feelings on the birthdays of Washington and Lincoln. Students of the different grades sat together.

This was a grand idea. If it was perfected to include everyone, it would save this new nation from the prejudices and the unfair advantages that had ruled the older nations of Europe. On the whole, in the long run the United States did not do too badly in working toward the ideal. But there were some serious problems that plainly got in the way of the system, even in Jefferson's day.

The difficult dream. Thomas Jefferson himself was a wealthy Virginia aristocrat in the Old World sense of the word. From his father he had inherited a plantation of several thousand acres and slaves to work the land. His mother came from a family with high social position. He had the advantage of an excellent education at the College of William and Mary, he became a lawyer, and then was easily elected to the Virginia House of Burgesses. If he had been born in the slave-quarters, we might never have heard of him. He might never have had the opportunity. Jefferson himself believed that slavery was a curse that violated the will of God. But he lived on a plantation in Virginia where nearly all the blacks were slaves.

To make Jefferson's dream of a full-fledged "natural aristocracy" come true, many changes would have to be made in the life of that Virginia. In his time, no person would even have a chance to take the examinations without the good luck to be a son born into a white family that could send him to grammar school to learn to read and write. Jefferson did not believe that women should be taught the same difficult subjects that were taught to men.

In this book we have traced the progress, over the centuries of American history, of efforts to widen opportunity. We have seen the rise of the American public school, the free public high school, the wonderful growth of American private colleges and state and land-grant public universities.

It would take a long time to make opportunity equal for all Americans. There would never be perfectly equal opportunity, even with a whole system of free education for all. There would always be differences between families. Naturally some parents would be more anxious than others for their children to go on with their education. And, of course, better-educated parents in homes where there were lots of books would be able to give their children a head start in the competition.

Still, a great deal could be done to make opportunities more equal. In the southern states where slavery had flourished and where blacks continued to be treated as second-class citizens, the public schools were not often equal for all. And in big cities in the North, segregated black neighborhoods tended to leave their children at a real disadvantage.

When the Supreme Court of the United States in 1954 outlawed segregation in the public schools, they took a big step to insure that educational opportunities would be more equal. The 1962 law against segregation in federally funded public housing helped. After the anti-poll tax amendment to the Constitution (Twenty-fourth Amendment) was finally adopted in 1964 and the Voting Rights Act was passed in 1965, blacks in the South were able to use their votes to elect officials who would protect their rights and improve their opportunities. The years after World War II saw these and other strenuous efforts to fulfill the American dream of equal opportunity.

Immigrant problems and immigrant inequality. The blacks were not the only Americans whose opportunities had not been equal. Every immigrant group had suffered discrimination when it arrived on these shores. They all had their painful problems. They had been cut out of the best schools, the best colleges, the best neighborhoods, and the best jobs. With only a few exceptions, there had been no civil rights laws or constitutional amendments passed to protect them. In fact, as we have seen (p. 371), some of the most respectable, richest, and best-educated Americans actually formed organizations purposely to discriminate against new immigrants.

When the Irish came here in the 1840s as refugees from the potato famine and from religious persecution, they were treated as intruders by some of New England's oldest residents. Factories and offices needing employees displayed the sign saying, "No Irish Need Apply." The Know-Nothing party, beginning as a secret society in New York City in 1849, organized discrimination against Catholics and immigrants. Their special targets were the new Irish Americans and the many German Americans who had been moving into the Middle West. Hatred against Catholics was again organized in 1887 in a group that called itself the American Protective Association. They poured slanders on the thousands of recent Italian and Polish immigrants. In 1894, when the flood of immigrants came from central, eastern, and southern Europe, many leading Bostonians (whose parents had immigrated some time before) joined with professors and university presidents from Harvard, Wisconsin, and California to form the powerful Immigration Restriction League.

Among the groups most discriminated against were the Jews. Seeking refuge from ghettos and persecution in Germany, Poland, and Russia, Jews brought with them a tradition of learning, and reverence for books and education. Many were eager to pursue their studies in the best universities and medical schools. But the best universities, like Harvard, set up shameless restrictive quotas, which deprived Jews of their equal chances.

Chinese, Japanese, and Korean immigrants, too, suffered more than their share of discrimination—simply because they also wanted their full opportunities as Americans. The school board in San Francisco actually tried to force their segregation in the public schools until President Theodore Roosevelt made them stop.

At the dawning of the twentieth century there were 76 million people in the United States. Of these, more than 10 million had themselves been born in Europe, and more than one-third of all Americans—26 million—had at least one foreign-born parent. Although people boasted that this was a nation of immigrants, nearly every kind of immigrant at some time had suffered some sort of discrimination!

The social disease of discrimination, as we have seen, lasted violently into the modern century. In the 1920s the Ku Klux Klan, along with its hocus-pocus and its costume of white sheets, dared to target its terror against Catholics, Jews, and blacks in the South and the Midwest. During World War II, FDR gave in to panic and put thousands of innocent Japanese Americans into concentration camps. When the able Al Smith ran for President in 1928, he lost votes merely because he was a Catholic. And when John F. Kennedy was nominated for President in 1960, political leaders wondered whether the time had yet come when a Catholic could be elected.

Prejudice and discrimination, then, were not the monopoly of any one part of the country nor of any one period. Perhaps they would never be entirely cured. But the United States had made a good start. The traditional American open door policy at home gave refuge to oppressed peoples from the whole world. The Civil War against slavery, the Emancipation Proclamation, and the Thirteenth, Fourteenth, and Fifteenth amendments to the Constitution were long-overdue steps. In World War II the United States had fought the discrimination, barbarism, and racial superstitions of the Nazis. Now Americans were ready again to move ahead. Civil rights laws, supported by Presidents of both parties ever since Truman, declared that the American conscience had been newly awakened. In our land the twentieth century would be another century of progress for human equality.

Busing for school integration.
Righting past wrongs was not easy. Americans loved speed. They expected to accomplish in a few years what elsewhere had required centuries. And Americans, too, had a faith that laws could cure almost anything. By the Eighteenth Amendment and the laws against alcoholic beverages, Americans showed that they believed laws could cure the social ills of drunkenness. In that they were disappointed. But could laws speedily cure discrimination?

After Albert Einstein fled to the United States in 1933 to escape Nazi anti-Semitism, Ben Shahn made this painting of the white-haired physicist arriving here.

Editorial Photocolor Archives, New Jersey Community Center

Ellis Herwig/Stock, Boston

To bring about racial balance in northern schools, students were sometimes bused from one neighborhood to another.

Congress and the states passed new laws and set up new commissions. It was discovered that the problem was more complicated and deeper rooted than it seemed at first. Programs to cure past ills also created new problems.

One example was busing. After the decision of the Supreme Court in 1954 outlawing racial segregation in public schools, various means were tried to comply with the law. Often neighborhoods were racially segregated. It seemed that the only way to provide "racial balance" in classrooms was to bring pupils from one neighborhood to another. This was costly. City children had been walking to their neighborhood schools. So parents were annoyed to see their children taken in buses to schools all the way across town. In the South legal segregation had ceased by the late 1970s. Then the age-old system of separate public school systems for the races came to an end. But racism survived in the form of private schools that white parents set up to avoid integration.

and mothers was also increasing. The reasons for this included inflation, the better education of women, the rising American standard of living, the mechanizing of the American kitchen, and the desire of women to find more challenging work. Still, one-third of all female workers were employed in clerical jobs—as secretaries, file clerks, and telephone operators. Few were executives or managers. In the early 1970s women accounted for only 7 percent of the physicians and only 3 percent of the lawyers. But during these years the enrollment of women in medical schools and law schools increased rapidly. By the end of the decade they made up one-fifth of the medical students and one-third of the law students.

Even if women were not yet in the positions that their talents deserved, the American tradition of free speech and the right to organize made it possible for them to be heard. Their rising level of education was a help. In 1960 only 35 percent of American college students were women, but by 1978 the figure had risen to 48 percent. Women now demanded their share of the American tradition of equal opportunity.

The pioneer tradition also played its part. In immigrant families, or in families moving into the unfamiliar West, women had made important decisions and they bore heavy responsibilities. Ever since colonial times, foreign visitors to this country had noticed the power of American women and sometimes made fun of it. But the opportunities for women had not yet been brought into an urban age of technology and large industry.

Women seek equal rights. The new feminist movement took many forms. Betty Friedan's National Organization for Women demanded social and legal changes to bring women into "the mainstream of American society . . . in fully equal partnership with men." Small militant groups even called for female separation, the end of the family, and the end of separate masculine and feminine roles.

The first national success of the women's rights movement came by accident. When the House of Representatives was debating the Civil Rights Act of 1964, Congressman Howard Smith of Virginia offered an amendment to Title VII to bar job discrimination on the basis of sex as well as race. He did this not to assist women, but because he thought this would help defeat the entire measure. Instead, the bill with his amendment became law. This ban against sexual discrimination would be used against businesses and educational institutions.

As the movement gained momentum, Congress added its support. In 1972, two-thirds of the members of both houses of Congress approved an "Equal Rights" Amendment and sent it to the states. A similar amendment had been proposed in 1923 but had repeatedly failed to get approval by Congress. The proposed amendment now read: "Equality of rights under the law shall not be denied or abridged by the United States or any state on account of sex." It was quickly ratified by 22 states. Then it ran into strong opposition.

The feminist movement and the Equal Rights Amendment were opposed by some women and some men because they valued the privileges more than the rights of women. They believed in the old tradition. There was no more important work, they insisted, than bearing and raising children. They thought that women were intended by nature for different roles than men. Reformers in the Progressive Era had demanded special laws to protect women in factories. "Equal rights" might mean the end of special protection for women and the end of "alimony" to support them and their children in case of divorce.

Under the Constitution, to adopt the Equal Rights Amendment, ratification by three-quarters of the states was required. In 1979, when the amendment was still three states short of the needed number, Congress extended the deadline for ratification to June 30, 1982.

Aid from the government and the courts. Meanwhile the federal government found ways to use its power. In 1972, President Nixon's Secretary of Labor, James Hodgson, ordered companies that contracted with the government to set goals and timetables for hiring women and minorities. The Justice Department started suits under Title VII of the 1964 Civil Rights Act to force large business firms to end job discrimination. Colleges and universities that received federal aid were investigated to see if they discriminated against women. The Equal Employment Opportunity Act passed in 1972 required employers to pay equal wages for equal work. Other laws barred discrimination against women when they applied for credit.

American women in 1977 joined in International Women's Day to demonstrate for their equal rights

And again the Supreme Court played a role. In 1971 the Court ruled that unequal treatment based only on sex violated the Fourteenth Amendment. In one of its most controversial decisions, the Court held in 1973 that, except in the later stages of pregnancy, states could not make it illegal for women to have abortions. The new feminists hailed this as a victory. They said that a woman's most important right was control over her own body. But their passionate "Right-to-Life" opponents said that the unborn child had rights of its own and that abortion was murder.

By 1980, though there was still a way to go, women had made great progress. They were beginning to be found in nearly every occupation. The avenues of choice were widening. Women now worked as truck drivers, car mechanics, business leaders, doctors, lawyers, ministers, and even as astronauts. They were governors, mayors, and Cabinet members, as well as senators and representatives. "For the first time in modern history," a woman journalist observed, "a woman is born into a society which has acknowledged her right to the freedom to choose the role she wants." In 1979, for the first time, an American silver dollar appeared with the likeness of a real woman. Susan B. Anthony was not the most beautiful woman in American history. But her face on the coin bore an important new message.

SECTION REVIEW

1. How did Betty Friedan reawaken the women's rights movement?

2. If there were few legal barriers to the advancement of women by the 1960s, what factors held back their efforts to achieve equality?

3. Cite evidence showing (a) gains by women by the 1970s and (b) continued male-female inequality.

3. Spanish-speaking peoples

During these years of civil rights movements, other groups that felt themselves discriminated against organized for equal rights. After women and blacks, the largest such group was the Spanish-speaking people, or Hispanics. Their population was growing at such a rate that demographers predicted they would be the largest minority in the United States by the year 2000.

They had come from many places and at many different times. Some of their ancestors came to America with the Spanish conquerors in the century after Columbus, and their families have lived here for more than 400 years. Others emigrated to the mainland United States from Spain, Cuba, Puerto Rico, and other Caribbean islands, from Latin American countries, and from the distant Philippines in the Pacific.

The Mexican Americans. Three-fifths of all the Spanish-speaking people in the United States are Mexican Americans. They are both the newest of the new immigrants and the oldest of the old. The ancestors of many of them settled in the Southwest and California in the 1600s and 1700s (p. 28). These early settlers were followed over the years by millions of others. By 1980 there were at least 7 million Mexican Americans in the United States, and thousands more were entering the country every year. By far the largest number of them have continued to settle where their first settlements lay—in California, Arizona, New Mexico, Colorado, and Texas. Their language and their culture give a special rich flavor to the food and shape the music and architecture in the whole region.

Many Mexican Americans are descended from the intermarriage of Spanish and Indian peoples. They proudly trace their heritage all the way back to the great Aztec and Mayan civilizations. They generally call themselves by a variety of names: Mexican, Mexican American, Chicano (a form of *Mexicano*), mestizo, and sometimes just *La Raza* (meaning "the people"). Conservative and hardworking, the Mexican Americans are almost entirely Roman Catholic in religion, with strong family ties, and they cling to the Spanish language.

Although originally a rural people, now, like the whole nation, they are largely urban. Fully 80 percent have settled together in city neighborhoods, which they call *barrios*.

From the very beginning the differences of religion, language, skin color, and culture between the Mexican Americans and other Americans (whom they call "Anglos") created conflicts. Each group tended to view its way of doing things as superior. But Anglos were the majority and controlled the government, courts, and schools. Mexican Americans were often discriminated against. Great numbers of them ended up in the lowest-paying jobs where no training was needed.

The rise of a "Brown Power" movement. The Mexican Americans organized their own groups to voice their needs. For example, the thousands of veterans who had fought for the United States in World War II formed the Mexican G.I. Forum. Then, in the tumultuous 1960s, Mexicans began to speak out more loudly.

During the 1960s there developed a Chicano or "Brown Power" movement. Among its most outspoken leaders was Reies López Tijerina, or *El Tigre*. Born in Texas, he led a fight in New Mexico for the return of the lands he said the Anglos had stolen from the original Spanish-speaking settlers. But many of the more conservative Mexican Americans, like Senator Joseph Montoya of New Mexico, disapproved of Tijerina's radical program. And instead of the name "Chicano," which some of the young had begun to use as a symbol of pride, they preferred to be simply Americans.

Another leader was Rodolfo "Corky" Gonzales of Colorado. He was a former prizefighter and, for a short time, director of a war-on-poverty youth program. In 1965 he founded the Crusade for Justice in Denver, which aimed to build Chicano pride by giving them jobs and social services in their own communities.

Organizing farm laborers. Many Mexicans and Mexican Americans worked as poorly paid farm laborers. Some, called *braceros* (a Spanish word meaning laborers), came north under contracts to work in the fields. Others entered the country illegally by slipping across the long and difficult-to-patrol border between Mexico and the United States. They were called "wetbacks" because some of them swam or waded across the Rio Grande.

Farm workers had always been the most difficult laborers to organize into a union. Since they came to work only for a season, and were spread across the countryside, it was hard to bring them together for meetings. But the shrewd and eloquent Cesar Chavez decided to try, and he had remarkable success. He had worked as a farm laborer himself. In 1962 he began to organize the migrant laborers— brown, white, and black—into a union. In 1965, when 900 Filipino grape pickers in another union went out on strike, Chavez's union decided to go out, too. The following year, the two unions merged to form the United Farm Workers Organizing Committee.

Chavez, like Martin Luther King, Jr., believed in nonviolence. He firmly insisted on following this course throughout the long years of the strike against the owners of vineyards in Delano, California. This won him public support from church groups, from other unions, and from political leaders like Robert F. Kennedy.

A brilliant publicist, Chavez organized an effective nationwide boycott of California grapes. When some of his followers resorted to violence, he protested by fasting for 25 days—and badly injured his health. But nonviolence prevailed. Finally, the opposition of the vineyard owners started to crumble. In 1970, after five years, many of them signed contracts with Chavez's union. He had actually organized farm laborers into a union and had won better pay and working conditions. Cesar Chavez had done what had been thought impossible.

Chavez himself stayed out of politics, but other Mexican Americans won high office. Both New Mexico and Arizona have had Mexican American governors. Other Mexican Americans have been elected to the United States Senate and the House. President Nixon appointed a Mexican American woman, Romana A. Bañuelos, to be Treasurer of the United States. And President Carter appointed Leonel Castillo as Commissioner of the Immigration and Naturalization Service.

Puerto Rico and the Puerto Ricans. The Puerto Ricans were different from other Hispanics because all of them were citizens of the United States before they arrived on the mainland. The special relation between Puerto Rico and the rest of the United States allowed them to go back and forth to their home island at will.

The island of Puerto Rico had been visited by Columbus in 1493, even before any Spaniards had

Daniel S. Brody/Stock, Boston

Cesar Chavez organized migrant workers in California into a union and led them in a long, successful strike against vineyard owners.

come to mainland America. When Columbus arrived, the Arawak Indians were already there. During the colonial period the island was settled by Spaniards and by black slaves imported from Africa. The land and the climate were ideal for raising sugar cane. And from the sugar was made the famous Puerto Rican rum. In 1898, after the Spanish-American War, the United States took over the island.

One of FDR's braintrusters, Rexford G. Tugwell, was sent to Puerto Rico as governor in 1941. There he worked with Luis Muñoz Marin, a poetic and inspiring Puerto Rican political leader, and they produced "Operation Bootstrap." This was a program to improve agriculture and attract industry to

Children in New York City patiently wait for an approaching Puerto Rican Day parade.

the island. In 1947 the island began electing its own governor. Muñoz led the way toward a special "Commonwealth" status for Puerto Rico within the United States. When the Commonwealth of Puerto Rico was proclaimed on July 25, 1952, Muñoz became the first popularly elected governor. The following years showed how the resourcefulness and intelligence of people might make up for the lack of other natural resources.

Under the ingenious "Commonwealth" plan, Puerto Ricans were given powers of self-government like those of citizens of the states. Puerto Rico is represented in Congress by a resident commissioner who can speak but has no vote, except in committees. Puerto Ricans do not pay federal income tax on money earned in Puerto Rico, and they do not vote in national elections. By 1970, with the aid of "Operation Bootstrap," Puerto Rico had the largest per capita income in Latin America. Still, Puerto Rican incomes were low by comparison to the mainland United States.

After World War II, unemployment on the home island led thousands of Puerto Ricans to move to the mainland. In the 1970s about one-third of all Puerto Ricans—1.5 million—were living in the continental United States. Of these about one-half lived in New York City, where many worked in the garment trades. The city now held more Puerto Ricans than the island capital of San Juan. Though they were citizens, in other ways they were immigrants and suffered many of the problems of earlier immigrants. Since they spoke another language and felt strange, they formed their own neighborhoods where the signs were in Spanish. Strangers, without the advantages of money or education, they, too, joined the American quest for equal opportunity.

Despite the cordial political relations between the Commonwealth and the rest of the United States, many Puerto Ricans on the island were not satisfied. Some agitated for independence so that Puerto Rico could be a separate nation. Others wanted Puerto Rico to become a state in the Union. Still, in election after election the majority of Puerto Ricans voted to keep the unusual Commonwealth status. Meanwhile, Puerto Rico, with its delightful tropical beaches and its Spanish-

American flavor, became a favorite vacation spot for thousands from the mainland. And Puerto Ricans were enriching the culture of the United States, through such figures as the violinist José Figueroa and the actor José Ferrer.

A new migration. Throughout its history the United States has served as a refuge for people fleeing turmoil and repression at home. After Fidel Castro seized power in Cuba in 1959 and began to create a Communist state, over half a million islanders fled to the United States. Many went on to settle in other lands, but nearly 400,000 chose to remain here. A substantial proportion settled in Florida, especially in and around Miami.

Some of these newcomers dreamed and planned only for the day they could return to their homeland. But others became Americans and began a new life.

The Cubans who came to the United States were generally well educated, and over two-thirds were trained for white-collar jobs. Hardworking and ambitious, some of them soon rose to head banks and businesses. Large sections of Miami became almost as Cuban as Havana itself. Once again the United States had served as a haven and a land of opportunity.

SECTION REVIEW

1. Identify or explain: Chicano, *La Raza*, *barrios*, Joseph Montoya, Rodolfo Gonzales, Luis Muñoz Marin, Operation Bootstrap.

2. What chief groups make up the Spanish-speaking peoples of the United States? Locate their major areas of settlement.

3. How did Cesar Chavez work for greater equality for Mexican Americans?

4. How does the status of Puerto Ricans differ from that of other Hispanics in the United States?

5. What event brought many Cubans to this country?

4. The American Indians

After World War II when Americans tried once again to make opportunities equal, injustices of the American past came home to roost. It was one thing to give all Americans an equal chance for education and for jobs today. That was difficult, but not impossible. It was quite another thing to try to undo history.

This problem arose in regard to the very first Americans. They were here, of course, centuries before the first Europeans or Africans. As the United States grew, their own cultures had not prospered. American Indians were not immigrants, were not settled in big cities, and could not vote. They had little appeal for politicians. In colonial times and for much of the 1800s, newer Americans considered them simply part of the wilderness to be cleared away. Later they were treated as "wards" of the government and put on reservations. These were usually on land that nobody else wanted. Then during the 1900s their numbers grew. Though in 1900 they totaled less than a quarter-million, by the end of the 1970s they were nearly 1 million. Not until the Snyder Act of 1924 were all Indians born in the United States admitted to full citizenship.

The Indians had been the victims of varying whims of United States officials. Under FDR in 1934 there was an Indian "New Deal," which aimed to halt the sale of Indian land, to restore tribal land-holding, to rebuild the tribes, and to promote tribal culture. In a bold move FDR appointed outspoken and combative John Collier, the executive director of the American Indian Defense Association, as head of the Bureau of Indian Affairs. From that position, between 1933 and 1945, Collier fought to enable the Indians both to preserve their old ways and to participate fully in American life.

During World War II, 25,000 American Indians served in the armed forces. They felt they had earned their right to be full-fledged American citizens, with fully equal opportunities. But after World War II, the Native Americans still had the least education, the lowest incomes, the highest unemployment, the worst health, the shortest life expectancy, and the highest suicide rate of any large group in the country.

Termination and relocation. In the 1950s, under President Eisenhower, the federal government's policy toward the Indians changed once again. Congress enacted laws for a new program called "termination." The idea was to end all federal involvement with the Indians and leave the states to

A Navaho woman about 1900 weaves a traditional rug.

deal with them. This program had unfortunate effects because most states would not provide health, education, and welfare services that the Indians needed.

Another new program called "relocation" offered jobs to Indians to induce them to relocate in cities. There, it was hoped, they would earn a better living and become part of the larger society. This program, too, was a disaster. Many Indians were persuaded to relocate. The proportion of American Indians living in urban areas increased from 10 percent in 1930 to 45 percent in 1970. But the effects were not what was planned. Urban Indians generally had higher incomes and were better educated than reservation Indians. Yet in the cities many of them felt displaced and unhappy. They created new urban Indian ghettos. In 1972 the program was finally dropped.

New help for Indians. President Lyndon Johnson, in a special message to Congress in 1968, called the Indian "The Forgotten American." He pointed to their poor housing, their alarming 40 percent unemployment, and the fact that only half of the young Indians completed high school. He asked Congress to enact a program to give Indians a standard of living equal to that of other Americans. Congress replied by voting $510 million for Indian aid programs—the highest amount ever.

President Nixon, too, tried to find new ways to help the Indians. He called for the end of the "termination" program. He also proposed that federal programs on the old Indian reservations be turned over to the Indians themselves to run. Indians were appointed to twenty top positions in the Bureau of Indian Affairs (BIA). And the Office of Education, after a two-year study, recommended that tribal history, culture, and languages be stressed in Indian education and that Indians be given a larger role in running their schools.

Indian Power. The Indians themselves began to take violent action to call attention to their wants. During 1969 an angry group of 78 Indians seized Alcatraz Island with its deserted prison in San Francisco Bay. They demanded that it be made a cultural center. Finally, they were evicted by United States marshals in 1971.

In 1972 the militant American Indian Movement occupied the offices of the BIA in Washington. They demanded all the rights and the property that they said had been guaranteed to the Indians over many past years by their treaties with the United States government. After a week of talks—and damage estimated at a half-million dollars—the Indians finally left the building.

More than 200 armed members of the American Indian Movement during 1973 took over the village of Wounded Knee on the Oglala Sioux Pine Ridge

Deserted Alcatraz Island in San Francisco Bay was seized by Indians in 1969.

Reservation in South Dakota. They opposed the local tribal government and demanded other reforms. This town was symbolic, since it was near the site of the last battle of the Indian wars—the slaughter at Wounded Knee Creek in 1890 (p. 324). The occupation continued for two months. The Roman Catholic church, the trading post, and other buildings were destroyed. Two Indians were killed in the shooting that periodically broke out between the Indians and United States government agents.

The Indians themselves were sharply divided. The militants at the BIA and at Wounded Knee wanted to oust from positions of authority the Indians who did not do what the militants demanded. Many other Indians rejected the violence of the radicals. They, too, wanted to run their own affairs and see the old treaties carried out. But they felt that the way to gain their rights was through the courts.

The Indian Self-Determination and Education Assistance Act of 1975 assured the Indians of more say on their own reservations and on their educational programs. During 1977, President Carter created the new post of Assistant Secretary of the Interior for Indian Affairs to advance Indian interests. A member of the Blackfoot tribe, Forrest J. Gerrard, was named to the post. He promised to make the BIA an advocate of the Indian cause. And the American Indian Policy Review Commission proposed that full tribal sovereignty should be given back to the Indians.

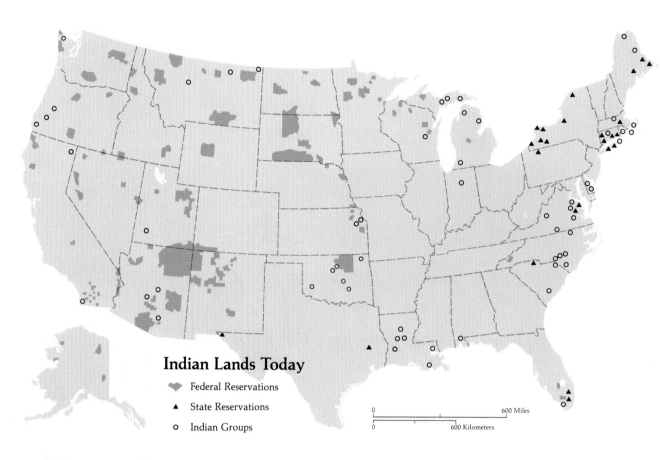

Indian Lands Today

◆ Federal Reservations

▲ State Reservations

○ Indian Groups

0   600 Miles

0   600 Kilometers

Indians turn to the courts. Indians from Maine to California went to court during the 1970s to win the return of lands taken from their ancestors centuries or decades before. They also demanded the right to raise their children on reservations, to hunt and to fish, and to control minerals, water, and grazing on the reservations.

In the mid-1970s the Department of Interior, whom they had regarded as their enemy, began to side with them. Time after time the Indians won in the courts. The state of Rhode Island returned 1800 acres taken illegally from the Narragansets many years before. The Penobscot and Passama-quoddy Indians of Maine were granted thousands of acres and millions of dollars to settle their claims. The Sioux of the Black Hills won a ruling that 7 million acres of their land had been taken from them illegally. Indian control of their lands and resources gave a new power to the tribes. Indian reservations contained an estimated 16 percent of the nation's energy resources (coal, uranium, and oil). Their new power would come from this inherited wealth.

SECTION REVIEW

1. Identify or explain: Snyder Act of 1924, Wounded Knee, Forrest Gerrard.
2. What were the "termination" and "relocation" policies? What were their results?
3. How did federal policy toward the Indians change under Presidents Johnson and Nixon?
4. What action did members of the American Indian Movement take to win Indian rights? What other strategy did Indians use?
5. Describe gains made by Indians in the 1970s.

5. New vistas of equality

Americans discovered new opportunities and new problems as they attempted to deal with the meaning of the word equality. They discovered new groups that now sought equal treatment.

Equal rights for the handicapped. The postwar American crusade against inequalities took another

716

group to its heart. This "minority" was not an immigrant group. It included Americans of all races, all religions, and both sexes. It was found in every state and every city of the nation. These were the handicapped—people who were disadvantaged by a physical disability that made it difficult for them to compete on an equal basis with other Americans. They included the blind and the deaf, and persons who lacked the use of one or more of their limbs. Some were veterans. Their numbers were large. In 1978 they were estimated at 35 million Americans—more than all the blacks, Hispanics, and Indians taken together.

The Rehabilitation Act of 1973 forbade discrimination against the physically disabled in any of the programs, activities, and facilities that were supported by federal funds. Other laws aimed to prevent job discrimination against handicapped persons. The new federal regulations for equal opportunity in some conspicuous ways eased the everyday lives of the handicapped. In 1977 federal regulations required that public sidewalks must not have a slope greater than 5 percent and could not be interrupted by steps. Every public building had to have at least one main entrance designed for wheelchairs. In public places, too, some telephone booths and toilets had to be provided for use by the handicapped. In 1978 federal specifications required that new buses have a facility for boarding passengers in wheelchairs.

To help the blind, the signs in public buildings had to be made with raised letters or numbers. Doorknobs leading to rooms not intended for normal use had to have special ridges to make them identifiable to the touch. Wherever public warning signals were given by sounds, there also had to be visual signals to warn the deaf. In public meetings and regularly on certain TV news broadcasts, programs were interpreted in signs for the deaf.

Even in 1978, when Congress was cutting other costs, it authorized $5.2 billion to be spent over the next four years to provide equal opportunities and legal protection for the handicapped.

Other kinds of handicapped persons—the mentally ill and the mentally retarded—also gained. Community mental health centers were virtually unknown in 1965. Only ten years later they numbered more than a thousand. During these years, too, education of the mentally retarded was improved. By 1979 ten states had declared that

Jose A. Fernandez/Woodfin Camp & Associates

Many handicapped citizens are entering the mainstream of American life.

their handicapped students would have a right to equal education with the non-handicapped.

Everywhere there were signs of concern. By a series of laws and court decisions during the 1970s the federal government insisted that education in the nation's schools and colleges should be opened to all qualified mentally and physically handicapped. This was called "mainstreaming"—taking the handicapped out of special institutions and bringing them into the mainstream of American life.

How many languages? Never before had a nation tried so strenuously to give all its people pride in

717

CHAPTER 35

Changing leaders in Washington

The years after Watergate offered new challenges to the leader in the White House. This was to be a time of healing and a time of recovery. When the news was no longer full of Watergate, the Congress was no longer worried by what to do about the President. They turned instead to how they could work with him. The American people had proven their power to remove their President. But it was much easier to change the nation's President than to solve the nation's long-term problems. Inflation and the energy shortage were not the fault of either political party or of any one President.

The outside world was taking new, more complicated shape. No longer did it seem a simple two-way struggle between the free and the unfree world. Soviet Russia and Communist China had become bitter enemies, and both were anxious for American support. All over the world, the United States needed the friendship, the trade, and the oil of nations that were not democratic.

The two Presidents who followed Richard Nixon were a study in contrasts. Gerald Ford had never sought the Presidency, but he knew Washington and the ways of Congress. Jimmy Carter was one of our most inexperienced Presidents. How would the nation fare?

1. Gerald Ford becomes President

Gerald Ford, the first man to become President without being elected President or Vice-President, faced an awesome task. The people's faith in the honesty and integrity of their political leaders had been shaken. Congress and the executive branch were sharply at odds over both foreign and domestic affairs. The economy was in tatters as the nation sank into the worst recession since the Great Depression, and inflation soared.

By the end of Ford's term none of these problems had been entirely solved. Yet many of the wounds left by the fall of Nixon had started to heal, and the nation had begun once again to look to the future.

The new President. Ford was not a dashing man nor an eloquent speaker, but at this moment in the nation's history he may have been something more important. There was nothing devious about him. He was honest and open. And his long experience in the Congress gave him much knowledge and some wisdom about how Washington functioned.

Gerald Ford had worked his way up in the world. He was born in Omaha, Nebraska, and when he was only two, his parents were divorced. Then he moved with his mother to Grand Rapids, Michigan, where she remarried. His stepfather legally adopted the boy and gave him his own name, Gerald R. Ford.

He used his large athletic build and his skill as a football player to help him gain an education. After graduating from the University of Michigan and playing in the 1935 All-Star game, he received an offer to play professional football. Instead he went to Yale as an assistant football coach and boxing coach. He also hoped to work his way through the Yale Law School. After three years he was admitted to the law school, from which he graduated in the top third of his class in 1941. Then he returned to his home in Grand Rapids to practice law. In 1942 he entered the navy and saw combat in the Pacific.

He returned to his law office in Michigan in 1946, and two years later he was elected as a Republican from Grand Rapids to the House of Representatives. He was reelected thirteen times in a row, and in 1965 he became Minority Leader of the House. A solid conservative, he opposed expensive welfare programs and supported the war in Vietnam. He also advocated the final passage of the civil rights laws.

When he became President in August 1974, Ford wanted to put an end to the Watergate problems, restore the people's faith in their government, and cure the nation's economic ills—especially inflation. He promised to run an open administration and to work with Congress. As he took the oath of office on television, he reminded the nation's voters that, since they had not chosen him, he had a special duty to earn their confidence.

Selecting a Vice-President.

Now that the Vice-Presidency was vacant, under the Twenty-fifth Amendment Ford had to name a new Vice-President, who would take office if confirmed by both houses of Congress. He chose Nelson A. Rockefeller, a leading liberal Republican who had been governor of New York from 1958 to 1973.

Rockefeller, a grandson of John D. Rockefeller, was a man of enormous wealth. His father and mother had given him a strong religious foundation and impressed him with a sense of duty. He graduated from Dartmouth College in 1930, and then determined to spend his life in the public

Fred Ward/Black Star

Energetic Nelson Rockefeller (left) was Ford's choice for Vice-President.

service. Many people were suspicious of anyone named "Rockefeller," but he went into politics anyway. He proved himself an able administrator and served Presidents of both parties from FDR to Nixon. He helped build the Good Neighbor policy in Latin America and was credited with inventing Truman's Point Four program to aid underdeveloped countries.

Since his income was nearly $5 million a year, before the Congress confirmed his nomination as Vice-President, they held lengthy hearings. They wanted to know where his money was invested and what he did with it. After looking into his life and character for an unprecedented three months, Congress was satisfied, and in December 1974 both houses confirmed his selection. The cheerful and dynamic Nelson Rockefeller, who had sought the Presidency himself in 1964 and 1968, was one of the most experienced Americans ever to become Vice-President.

Pardon and clemency.
Soon after taking office, Ford revealed that he was thinking of moderating any punishment for former President Nixon. At first he said that he would not do anything until the courts had acted.

Then, less than two weeks later, he went on television to announce that he was granting a full pardon for any crimes Nixon might have committed during his time as President. Ford said he feared that unless Nixon and Watergate were put behind, it would be impossible for him to govern effectively. The nation would continue to be torn apart by the events of the past. He pardoned Nixon, he said, "to heal the wounds that had festered too long."

Nixon accepted the pardon. Although he admitted that he had handled the Watergate question badly, he still failed to say that he had done anything wrong. But President Ford had been trained as a lawyer. As Ford himself later explained, before granting the pardon he had discovered what a pardon really meant. The Supreme Court had decided that in accepting a pardon a person was confessing guilt.

Ford's pardon of Nixon lost him much public support. Some people felt that the former President should have been tried for his acts. Many thought that Nixon should at least have been made to admit that he had done something wrong.

As another way to bury the past, Ford announced a program of clemency for those who had deserted from the armed forces or evaded the draft during the Vietnam War. They would not be punished if they took the oath of allegiance to the United States and then did up to two years of alternative service in jobs that would "promote the national health, safety, or interest." Since this was not an outright pardon, only about 22,500 of the 124,000 draft evaders and deserters accepted Ford's offer. Some Americans were also displeased with Ford's clemency plan. They felt that these men had shirked their duty and deserved to be punished. President Carter later pardoned nearly all the draft evaders. But this provoked less comment—perhaps because by then the passions of war had begun to cool.

Controlling the CIA and the FBI.
The Watergate and impeachment hearings had led to serious charges against the Central Intelligence Agency and the Federal Bureau of Investigation. Soon President Ford appointed a commission under Vice-President Rockefeller to study the CIA. Committees in the House and Senate began their own probes of the CIA and FBI.

It was found that under six Presidents, from Franklin D. Roosevelt to Richard Nixon, the FBI had abused its powers. Without legal permits its agents had tapped telephones, read private mail, broken into buildings, placed listening devices in homes and offices, and kept records on thousands of innocent citizens. The FBI had broken into the offices of the insignificant Socialist Workers party 90 times between 1960 and 1966. And it was found that conversations of Martin Luther King, Jr., had been monitored and taped.

The CIA had also been spying on Americans and opening their mail. It had even experimented with dangerous mind-control drugs. Abroad the CIA had worked secretly to bring down a Marxist regime in Chile and then denied doing so to Congress. It was accused of having plotted to assassinate unfriendly foreign leaders.

Clearly the nation needed to gather every kind of information from every part of the world. This was the job of the CIA. Also, to enforce federal laws and to convict criminals there had to be an FBI. Still Congress wanted to oversee both agencies. In Communist countries and in dictatorships, citizens were at the mercy of the police. But in a free country innocent citizens had to be protected from harassment and from snoopers.

Was it possible to devise a system of oversight that would neither give away our secrets nor hamstring our intelligence operations at home and abroad? President Ford set up an Intelligence Oversight Board made up of three private citizens to monitor the CIA. Both the House and Senate appointed their own committees. At the FBI, a new director promised to take firm control of the bureau's agents and activities. Congress worked on new laws more strictly defining the activities of the two agencies.

Opening up the government and protecting the elections.
There was strong feeling in Congress that the activities of all the hundreds of government

agencies had to be opened up so people could know what their government was doing and see that nothing illegal was done. A little-used Freedom of Information Act, passed in 1966, was strengthened by a series of amendments in 1974 and 1976. Government departments and agencies now had to give copies of documents in their files to anyone who asked for them. Only a few exceptions for national defense, foreign policy, and law-enforcement investigations were allowed. A Privacy Act, also passed in 1974, gave citizens the right to see the information collected about them and to correct or amend it.

By these laws, the United States government became the most open in the world. Now there was a danger that officials might spend so much of their time and energy answering the public's questions—and trying to please the newspapers—that they would have little left for the business of government.

The Watergate hearings had also revealed large-scale illegal gifts to the Nixon reelection campaign. To limit the size of political contributions—and reduce temptations—a Federal Election Campaign-funding Reform Act was passed in 1974. It also provided federal funding for candidates in presidential primaries and elections.

Problems with the economy. While President Nixon was distracted by the long agony of Watergate, he had not managed to bring inflation under control. By 1973 inflation was running annually at 8.5 percent. In 1974 inflation had increased to 12 percent and a recession had begun. By raising prices and so decreasing the amount a dollar could buy, inflation hurt every American.

When Gerald Ford came to the White House, he viewed inflation as the nation's number one problem. Government spending poured more and more money into the marketplace and kept prices going up. Repeatedly he tried to cut government spending to save the nation billions of dollars. He used his veto 66 times to try to check Congress. But Congress continued to vote expensive programs.

Oil and the economy. A large factor in inflation was the shortage of oil. Until 1953, the United States produced more oil than we could use, and regularly exported petroleum and petroleum products. As the economy expanded and everybody

Dennis Brack/Black Star

Filling-station managers found amusing ways to say "No Gas Today" during the Arab oil embargo of 1973–1974.

used machines for everything, we came to use more oil than we produced. Homes and automobiles, farms and factories needed the energy made from oil. Now we had to import oil to keep American machines going. Year after year, imported oil provided a larger proportion of the nation's needs.

President Nixon had helped Israel during the Yom Kippur War in 1973. In protest the oil-rich Arab nations of the Middle East cut off their shipments to the United States, leaving a shortage of 17 percent in our oil supply. During the winter of 1973–1974, for the first time there were long lines of cars waiting for gasoline at the filling stations.

Even after the Arab embargo ended in March 1974, the oil shortage continued. Oil-producing

OPEC

Members of the Organization of Petroleum Exporting Countries

countries, led by Venezuela, had begun to organize back in 1960. By 1974 their powerful Organization of Petroleum Exporting Countries (OPEC) was in control and began to raise prices. Now the United States would have to face the continuing problem of ever-higher prices for the ever-increasing amounts of energy it needed.

To this long-term problem there were only two possible solutions. One was to reduce our use of oil. The other was to increase the American output of oil—or other sources of energy. President Nixon proposed a number of short-term measures, such as higher taxes on oil and lower speed limits. On orders from the federal government many states lowered their highway speed limit to 55 miles per hour, because cars driving at lower speeds use less gasoline per mile. For long-term measures he proposed more nuclear plants, more use of coal, and building a pipeline across Alaska to the large oil deposits on the edge of the Arctic Ocean.

When Ford became President, the worst of the temporary oil shortage was past, but the problem remained. And by 1975, in part because of the energy crisis, the United States was in the worst recession since the 1930s. Ford now tried urgent measures to get the economy moving again. Taxes were cut, and huge government deficits running over $50 billion pumped new money into the economy. The economy did recover. In 1976 inflation dropped below 5 percent.

Running for President. The presidential campaign of 1976 was one of the longest in our history. Gerald Ford announced in July 1975 that he wanted to be President in his own right. His main opposition for the Republican nomination was Ronald Reagan, a former movie star and a persuasive public speaker, who had served two terms as governor of California. He represented the conservative wing of his party. An outspoken anti-Communist, he criticized the policy of détente with Russia. He wanted the Republican party to take strong conservative positions—on limiting government activity, on taxes, and on all public issues. Ford favored more moderate positions to broaden the party's appeal.

After a series of primaries early in 1976, the two candidates were neck and neck when the party gathered in Kansas City, Missouri, for its convention. On August 19, on the first ballot Ford narrowly won the nomination with 1187 votes against 1070 for Reagan. In a crucial decision to satisfy the party's conservatives, Ford dropped Nelson Rockefeller and instead chose Senator Robert Dole of Kansas as his running mate. He later said this was a mistake that might have cost him the election.

The Democratic campaign was even longer than the Republicans'. As early as September 1973, Governor Jimmy Carter of Georgia, a man little known outside his state, told his mother that he was planning to run for President in 1976, "and I'm going to win."

Carter's term as governor ended in January 1975. Since state law barred him from succeeding himself, he began spending all his time campaigning for the Democratic nomination for President. As late as October of that year, however, few people considered him a serious contender.

But this was soon to change. He showed a single-minded devotion to his purpose. He remembered the old saying that the first qualification for a President is the ability to get elected. He was warm, folksy, and always smiled, and he had the wholehearted help of his able and pretty wife, Rosalynn. He was not an eloquent speaker. He was at his best in small groups. A "born again" Christian and a member of the Baptist church, he impressed people with his simple manner and his sincerity.

In 1976 he began to win primary after primary over the many other Democrats seeking the nod. When the party met in New York City for its convention, Carter had won 18 of the 31 Democratic primaries and was clearly in the lead. He was nominated on the first ballot and named Walter F. Mondale, an attractive liberal senator from Minnesota, to run for Vice-President.

With the enthusiastic support of his wife, Rosalynn, Jimmy Carter rose from being a former governor of Georgia to become President of the United States.

Elliot Erwitt/Magnum

Mark Godfrey/Magnum

Farmers were among the most outspoken of the many groups in the 1970s defending their own special interests.

with congressional leaders. After Watergate, Congress was understandably sensitive about its own role in government, and this caused problems. Carter's tendency to set deadlines that could not be met also created difficulties. When he sent his energy program to Congress in April 1977, it was found that some of his hastily gathered figures were wrong. Even worse, he announced his program to Congress as "the moral equivalent of war," and then he seemed almost to forget about it. In other cases he backed down in the face of opposition—without warning his supporters on Capitol Hill. As early as May 1977 one Democratic member of Congress complained, "Even Nixon had his partisans up here, but you don't hear anyone say, 'Let's do it for Jimmy.'"

By October, congressional leaders were pleading with the President to stop sending his proposals. Congress was swamped. That same month Carter announced that he would leave well enough alone. He gave priority to energy, Social Security, a tax bill, and welfare reform.

Successes and failures. The Social Security system was in trouble. It was paying out more money than it was taking in. Unless something was done, in a few years the whole system would be bankrupt. The disabled and the elderly would no longer receive their pensions. The law that President Carter signed in December 1977 raising Social Security taxes was the largest peacetime tax increase in history. Congress also voted to increase aid to cities and for housing. By a new scheme of allocations, more funds were channeled to the older cities of the Northeast and Midwest.

Carter did not submit his promised major tax reform. A lesser measure to reduce taxes to stimulate the economy was passed. His programs for energy, for electoral reform, and for a sweeping change in the welfare system were all stymied. An effective President would have to be effective in Congress.

The rise of the special-interest state. In some measure Carter's failures in Congress were due to changes in the nation. Political party loyalty had declined. And American political parties had been forces for moderation and compromise. To elect a President or a member of Congress, people with different goals had to come together.

In late twentieth-century America, citizens tended to organize less around their political party than around their particular interests. Environmentalists, pro- and anti-gun forces, the poor, the blacks, business, labor, truckers, farmers, shipowners, mayors, governors, consumers, pro- and anti-abortion groups, and many others—each pushed for its special program. Broad issues of national concern became lost. The rise of television, opinion polls, and public relations helped all these groups attract attention. Politicians were attacked or supported not for their general political outlook, but for their stand on a single issue. In Congress, under these pressures, party loyalty declined. Members of Congress were less apt to follow the President's lead or pass measures for the good of the party.

Presidential weaknesses. The President's own lack of experience made his problems worse. At first he was contemptuous of Congress. He infuriated some members by denying them the "pork barrel"—the pet dams, canals, and other water projects for their own state or district. Then he enraged others by quickly backing down. He deluged Congress with proposals, then failed to provide the leadership needed to pass them. It was expected that Carter would have to compromise to get laws through Congress. But his hasty retreats on the water projects, on a tax rebate, and on other matters left his supporters on Capitol Hill feeling deserted.

Part of Carter's problem lay in his own character. He did not make friends easily. He was often described as a loner. The men around him, the Georgians, were mostly much younger than he and were even more lacking in knowledge and experience. The only one of a similar age was Georgia banker Bert Lance, who became Carter's director of the key Office of Management and Budget. But soon after he took office, serious charges were made over Lance's handling of his own personal finances as well as his management of the banks he had headed. In September 1977 Lance was forced to resign.

Once in the White House, the campaigner who had been so friendly with everybody became remote and hard to reach. He failed to seek the advice of older and more experienced heads who might have steered him through the thickets of Washington. While he enmeshed himself in details, the government seemed leaderless.

The problem of inflation. By 1978 inflation even overshadowed the energy crisis. The inflation that had been 4.8 percent in 1976 and 6.8 percent in 1977 now climbed to over 8 percent. At the same time, the economy was troubled by a record trade deficit. We were buying from abroad far more than we sold there. The dollar was seriously unstable on foreign exchanges. Taxpayers were beginning to revolt against ever-higher taxes. In one attempt to cool inflation, Carter called for voluntary restraints in January 1978. He vetoed several bills passed by Congress on the grounds that they would increase inflation.

Finally, in October the President announced an anti-inflation program with wage-price guidelines. This meant that the increase of prices by corporations, and of wage-demands by unions, would be kept within the limits permitted by the President. He announced that government contracts would go only to firms that stayed within his limits. But still

the rate of inflation soared, reaching 1 percent a month during the first half of 1979.

The problem of inflation was deep-seated and complex. It was produced by the rising cost of oil, a higher minimum wage enacted in 1977, the increased Social Security taxes, and costly environmental and safety regulations. The many welfare programs to aid the sick, the poor, the aged, and the unemployed played their part, too. The government's constant attempts to stimulate the economy to provide more jobs also made the problem worse. Every government program seemed to make the economy more rigid and less responsive to changing needs. The nation saw a baffling new phenomenon: stagnation of the economy and inflation of prices. People called this "stagflation."

The energy problem. The United States was the most profligate energy user in the world. With only 6 percent of the world's population, the United States used 33 percent of all the world's energy!

Gas shortages in the 1970s resulted in long lines at the pumps as stations curtailed their hours.

Robin Moyer/Black Star

Electricity from nuclear power plants would lessen the need to import foreign oil and would help reduce smog, like that hanging over Atlanta (below). An accident at Three Mile Island (top) in 1979 sparked fears about the safety of such plants.

William Weems/Woodfin Camp & Associates

Even with our own rich oil fields, by the late 1970s we still had to import over 40 percent of our oil needs. As OPEC constantly raised prices the cost of foreign oil soared. During the 1970s the annual bill went from $1.5 billion to $60 billion. Of course this pushed up the price of gas for cars and trucks and buses, heating oil for homes, and fuel to run factories—all of which increased inflation. As American dollars poured out, our trade deficit mounted. And the dollar's value abroad declined.

Energy vs. the environment. The energy problem ran head on into another concern—the environment. President Johnson signed the first laws to clean up our water. President Nixon, as he created a Council on Environmental Quality, announced a "now or never" fight on pollution. In December 1970 a new Environmental Protection Agency (EPA) brought together the existing agencies dealing with water quality, air pollution, and the disposal of the millions of tons of bottles, paper, and other solid waste that Americans threw away every week. It was also to set standards for disposal of nuclear waste and to regulate the use of pesticides.

When President Carter took office, he announced his strong support for this movement to clean up the environment. But these controls quickly collided with the need to conserve oil. Which was more important?

The United States had enough coal to supply our needs for hundreds of years. But burning coal befouled the air with sulfur dioxide, which could be removed only at great expense. To keep the air clean, factories and power plants were urged to switch from coal to oil. Then with the oil shortage, under President Nixon the electric power companies were urged to switch back again to coal. Every such switch cost money for new equipment and added more to inflation.

"Strip mining" was one of the commonest and cheapest ways to dig coal. Large strips of the earth's surface were cut away to get at the coal just below. Each strip mine left an ugly gash on the landscape where sod and trees had been torn up. Putting the land back was expensive and not always possible. President Ford vetoed laws forcing the strip miners to restore the land. He said it was so expensive that it would discourage the coal mining that the nation badly needed. President Carter, however, endorsed these laws and tried to make them even more strict. He thought restoring the land was worth the extra cost for coal.

Another cause of air pollution was the automobile. The exhaust pipes of cars emit carbon monoxide and hydrocarbons. In large quantities these gases irritate the eyes and lungs and interfere with breathing. In big cities—like Los Angeles, New York, and Chicago—thousands of cars fill the air with pollutants, which leave a blue-grey pall hovering in the heavens. "Smog" (smoke and fog) was the new word for it. Devices could be added to car engines that reduced these dangerous emissions. But the devices added to inflation by increasing the cost of the car. And they reduced the efficiency of the engine so that it went fewer miles on a gallon.

Even trying to preserve land in parks and as wilderness ran into the energy problem. Bitter arguments took place in Congress over attempts to save millions of acres of untouched land in Alaska. Some members of Congress argued that much of this land should be left open for oil exploration as well as for mining and timbering. Still President Carter worked to preserve the land.

The question of nuclear power. Nuclear power, which many thought was the likely supply for our new energy needs, was plagued by problems of pollution and of safety. No one had found a safe way to dispose of the used-up uranium. Even after the uranium no longer had the energy to run the reactor, it remained radioactive. This meant that it could cause cancer. The government stored it in temporary holding places until a solution could be found.

There were fears about the safety of nuclear reactors. If something went awry, radioactive material might be released in the air, endangering the lives of people for miles around. This threat appeared remote during the first twenty years of nuclear power. Then suddenly, in the spring of 1979, something went wrong at the Three Mile Island nuclear plant near Harrisburg, Pennsylvania. For several days there seemed to be a danger of a massive escape of radiation. After a week the problems at Three Mile Island were under control. Still, the incident raised questions about the safety of the whole nuclear power industry, which supplied 12 percent of the nation's electricity.

Opponents of any use of nuclear energy were outspoken and sometimes violent. They prevented

Tankers take on OPEC petroleum at a Persian Gulf oil depot and refinery. The cutoff of Iranian oil after the fall of the Shah in 1979 added to the nation's energy problems.

construction of new plants and blocked the roads to older plants. Such opposition was not surprising or unusual in the history of technology. New machinery and new sources of power—steam and electricity, the railroad, the automobile, and the airplane—had always sparked campaigns of fear. For every new technology has had a price.

A weak energy program.

During 1977, all that President Carter was able to accomplish of his energy program was to create a new Department of Energy. The department took over most existing federal energy agencies. The following year, Congress finally passed a weak energy bill, eighteen months after Carter had asked for it. It was far different from what he wanted. It began to free newfound natural gas from government price regulation. It required that most electric power plants burn coal. New taxes and tax credits would encourage conservation.

Energy crisis.

In 1979, once again the energy problem became critical. A revolution in Iran toppled the friendly government of the Shah and stopped the flow of oil. The new government could not control the chaos, and Iran's oil production did not return to normal. Then OPEC, which seemed reckless of the world economy and the well-being of the developing countries, again increased its oil prices.

After attending a conference of seven leading industrial nations at Tokyo, Japan, on ways to save oil, Carter hastened home to deal with the growing problem. He disappeared to Camp David to produce a program that he said would be announced in a speech on July 5. Then he suddenly changed his mind. Without explaining, he abruptly canceled the speech. To Camp David he called more than 100 American leaders—from government, business, religion, journalism, and many other fields. They discussed the energy crisis, the state of the nation, and how to improve Jimmy Carter's "image" so he could be reelected President in 1980.

Finally, ten days after it had first been planned, Carter came down from the mountain and spoke to the people on television. He was critical of his own leadership, and he said that there was a "crisis of confidence." Reporters were reminded of the campaigning Jimmy Carter, who spoke in sermons. Though the speech focused on energy, he never mentioned two crucial issues—nuclear power and government control of oil and gas prices.

The following day he announced his new proposals—"the most massive peacetime commitment of funds and resources in the nation's history." He called for a program to cut oil imports in half by 1990. He urged the nation to produce synthetic fuels in large amounts, to develop solar and nuclear power, and to conserve energy. He proposed an Energy Security Corporation to provide financial aid for private companies to develop synthetic fuels, to search for hard-to-find natural gas, and to produce oil from shale. He asked for an Energy Mobilization Board empowered to cut through any red tape which might slow the construction of new fuel facilities.

Hardly had Carter announced these sweeping proposals when he distracted attention from the energy problem by a major shake-up of his Cabinet. The press and the public were puzzled that the President congratulated Secretary of HEW Joseph Califano on a fine job—then said he was fired. Altogether five Cabinet members resigned or were fired. His closest aide, the 34-year-old Hamilton Jordan, was officially made chief of staff. Jordan had not had wide experience in government and did not have the confidence of Congress. But he was an early Carter supporter, tested in his loyalty to the President.

Some commentators referred to "Haldeman" Jordan and noted the dangerous similarities to the later days of President Nixon. The top White House staff, who had been chosen for their loyalty to Carter, stood between the President and the people.

The White House and Cabinet changes also marked Carter's attempt to get ready for the 1980 campaign for President. He was trying to return to the role of "outsider" that he had played in 1976. Carter attacked "the isolated world of Washington" and pledged to go out to speak to the people more and find out about their concerns. It was clear to all, including Carter himself, that his Presidency was in serious trouble. His refusal to take a clear position on controversial issues, his poor record with Congress, and his declining popularity as shown in numerous polls undercut his ability to lead.

SECTION REVIEW

1. Identify or explain: Hyman Rickover, Hamilton Jordan, Bert Lance, wage-price guidelines, EPA, Three Mile Island, Joseph Califano.
2. How did Carter's lack of a limited, clearly defined program hurt his efforts to achieve his goals in Congress?
3. How did Congress "rescue" Social Security?
4. Identify some special interest groups. How did they come to affect American politics?
5. What were some causes of the steep inflation? How did Carter try to halt it?
6. Show how environmental and energy concerns collided.
7. Describe Carter's energy proposals.

3. Foreign affairs under Ford and Carter

Despite the sudden turn of domestic politics and the rapid changes in the outside world, the foreign policy of the United States remained surprisingly consistent. The war in Vietnam still left its mark. But the nation continued to pursue the goal of national security and of détente. The aim was to keep our old friends and try to avoid making new enemies. If we could help relax world tensions and reduce the dangers of war anywhere, all nations—including ours—might hope for a generation of peace. No sudden moves could achieve these goals, only slow, steady diplomacy.

Henry Kissinger. During the long months while the nation struggled over Watergate and the possible impeachment of President Nixon, our foreign policy did not falter. Nor was it inactive. This was largely due to the talents of Henry Kissinger and to Nixon's willingness to put confidence in him. In 1969 Nixon chose Kissinger, then professor of government at Harvard, to be his special assistant for national security affairs, and in 1973 named him Secretary of State.

Kissinger had been born in Germany. When he was fifteen years old, his family fled to the United States to escape Hitler's persecution of the Jews. He became a citizen in 1943, served three years in the United States Army, then attended Harvard, where he received his A.B. *summa cum laude* and his Ph.D.

Marvin Newman/Woodfin Camp & Associates

Henry Kissinger arrives in Israel on one of his "shuttle diplomacy" missions.

A brilliant and profound student of history, he was author of books on the relation between national power and world diplomacy. He never entirely lost his German accent, and he joked about that, as he did about much else. Unlike the solemn diplomats, he was witty and outspoken about himself and other world figures. But he was good at keeping diplomatic secrets and was constantly surprising the press and the public by turning up in unexpected places. He had made a secret trip to mainland China to prepare for President Nixon's history-making visit. Newspaper reporters and his staff were exhausted trying to match his endless energy as he shuttled around the world.

Kissinger's personal brand of "shuttle diplomacy" produced results. He finally negotiated an end to the war in Vietnam. For that he and the North Vietnamese negotiator, Le Duc Tho, were given the Nobel Peace Prize in 1973. Le Duc Tho refused to accept the award until there was real peace in Vietnam. Kissinger also negotiated the way for opening United States relations with Communist China. He promoted détente with Soviet Russia. And he led the way toward peace between Egypt and Israel. When President Ford came to office, he kept Kissinger as Secretary of State, and so preserved the continuity of American foreign policy.

During the early 1970s some old problems were resolved. There was also a shift in the balance of world forces. Complicated new problems arose. The struggle between the "two Germanys"—a Communist east and a democratic west—had threatened European peace ever since the end of World War II. In 1972 East Germany and West Germany finally signed a treaty of mutual recognition. The following year both nations were admitted to the UN.

After the Yom Kippur War in the Middle East between the Arabs and Israel in 1973, the United States and Russia pushed a cease-fire resolution through the UN Security Council. United Nations troops were sent in to separate the opposing forces. Then Kissinger's shuttle diplomacy served a very practical purpose. Since the two sides would not speak to each other, Kissinger shuttled back and forth between them. He made it possible for them to communicate and so finally come to some sort of agreement. The result was a pullback of the troops of both sides. A buffer zone between Egypt and Israel and Israel and Syria was manned by UN forces.

By another exercise in shuttle diplomacy in 1975, Kissinger persuaded Egypt and Israel to renounce the use of force to settle their differences. They both agreed to move farther back and create a much larger buffer zone. The 1975 agreement was made possible because the United States agreed to station 200 American civilian technicians at two main passes on the Sinai peninsula. They would electronically monitor the cease-fire to give an early warning in case either side moved to attack.

The end in Vietnam. The long United States presence in the former lands of French Indochina came to an end in 1975. Even after the United States withdrew its armed forces there, the fighting had never stopped despite the signing of a cease-fire in 1974. As Communist troops in Cambodia and

South Vietnam advanced, President Ford asked Congress to increase military aid to the two non-Communist governments. But Congress had had enough. It failed to act.

The government of Cambodia had already been weakened when Nixon widened the war in Vietnam. On April 12, 1975, Phnom Penh, the capital of the country, fell to the Khmer Rouge—the Cambodian Communists. The new Communist government moved with ruthless speed to empty its cities and force the people back to the land, where uncounted thousands died. Phnom Penh became silent as a tomb.

The end in South Vietnam came with stunning swiftness. A tactical retreat ordered by President Thieu suddenly turned into a panicky rout as the South Vietnamese forces lost all order and fled south. North Vietnamese soldiers escorted by tanks entered Saigon on April 30. At the same time, United States helicopters evacuated 1000 Americans and more than 5000 Vietnamese to United States Navy ships waiting offshore. The last helicopter left the roof of the United States embassy in Saigon as the North Vietnamese closed in.

Laos, the country north of Cambodia and bordering North Vietnam, also had been weakened when South Vietnamese troops, aided by United States aircraft, invaded the country (p. 685). The pro-Communist Pathet Lao movement deposed the king in December 1975 and proclaimed a People's Democratic Republic. Now the last of the dominoes seemed to have fallen. But instead of putting up a united Communist front against the world, the new Communist governments soon started to fight each other. Communist North Vietnam invaded Communist Cambodia and installed a puppet government. Communist China then attacked North Vietnam to punish it for its Cambodian venture. Indochina still lacked peace.

From the debacle in Indochina the United States emerged chastened but wiser. There were some goals that industrial force could not achieve. In the jungle, guerrilla warfare could prevail against giant technology. Yet a great and powerful nation dared not withdraw from the world to lick its wounds. Warfare anywhere on the globe threatened every nation. The United States could not abdicate its historic role as the hope of free people everywhere.

New initiatives by Carter. With the election of Jimmy Carter, Kissinger stepped aside for the new administration. Abroad, both friends and foes

As the North Vietnamese swept toward Saigon, thousands of South Vietnamese fled in terror.

Mark Godfrey/Magnum

hoped that the election of a Democratic President with his party holding a majority in Congress would mean that Congress would agree to the President's policies in foreign affairs. Their hopes were short-lived. Congress, still remembering the disaster of Vietnam, was determined never again to allow a President to lead it into an undeclared war.

President Carter's first initiative in foreign affairs was to make a bold stand for human rights. He angered the Russians by praising their dissident citizens. He cut off military aid to Argentina, Brazil, and Ethiopia, all of which had been accused of political repression.

The image of the United States crusading for human rights worried both our allies and our enemies. They had been more at ease with Henry Kissinger's power diplomacy. Still, many victims of tyranny across the world admired the leadership of the United States in the cause of freedom.

Dealing with Russia.

Relations with the Russians worsened when Carter hastily proposed his plans for arms limitation. The Soviets quickly rejected the President's scheme. They objected that the proposals unfairly favored the United States. Détente seemed a lost cause.

In July 1977, President Carter made an effort to improve our relations with the Soviets. He admitted that there were reasons why the Russians might fear the arms developments he had ordered—such as the production of a low-flying cruise missile. He became less outspoken about Russian infringements of human rights. The Russians, too, became more conciliatory. Détente seemed back on the track.

This change in attitude by both sides made it possible for the Strategic Arms Limitation Treaty (SALT) talks to go forward. And in June 1979 Carter and Brezhnev met in Vienna to sign the SALT II agreement. This was intended to slow the arms race between the two nations. The Senate scheduled lengthy hearings. Under the Constitution, the treaty could not take effect without a two-thirds majority of the Senate members present voting for it.

The Panama Canal treaties.

President Carter inherited the problem of the Panama Canal. Many people in the Republic of Panama were angered by the existence within their nation of a canal zone. That zone was controlled "in perpetuity"—that is, forever—by the United States under the old treaty of 1903. In 1964 bloody riots there led President Johnson to begin talks about a new treaty.

When Carter took office, the talks were still continuing. Finally, in August 1977 two treaties emerged. In one treaty the United States agreed to hand over the canal to Panama at noon on December 31, 1999. Meanwhile, the canal would be run jointly by the United States and Panama. Panama would receive a larger share of the canal tolls than it had in the past. The second treaty made the canal a neutral waterway open to all shipping after 1999. The United States was given the permanent right to protect and defend that neutrality.

The Panama Canal treaties helped our relations with the Latin American nations. But many Americans were disturbed. Without looking too closely at how we had acquired the canal in the first place (p. 438), they simply said that the canal was ours. We had built it and paid for it. Why, they asked, should we give it away?

Carter had had little to do with negotiating the canal treaties. Still, he had to see the treaties through Congress. He feared that a defeat would seem a sign of weakness in the administration and make it difficult to pass other legislation. Carter and his aides did everything in their power to get the treaties approved. The Senate finally ratified the treaties in March and April 1978.

A changing world.

The world had become much more complicated since the days of Secretary Dulles's "pactomania" (p. 607). Back in the 1950s his alliances had aimed to line up the free nations against the others. Now the grand alliances of the free world were coming apart. SEATO (in Southeast Asia) dissolved in June 1977. In 1979 CENTO (earlier known as METO) began to close up shop. By then this Middle Eastern alliance was merely a shadow anyway, since both Pakistan and Iran had already withdrawn. It was plain, too, that many of these "free" nations were not so free after all.

Only NATO remained. After France withdrew its military support of NATO in 1966, the headquarters moved from Paris to Brussels. In 1974 Greece, too, withdrew its armed forces from NATO. Still, the United States was pressing efforts to strengthen the organization to meet a build-up of Soviet forces in Eastern Europe. Between the Communist Soviet Union and their allies and the capitalist United States and our allies, suspicion and fear prevailed.

But now there were more than just these two "worlds." There was also a "Third World." These were a varied group of nations in Europe, Latin America, Asia, and Africa. Many of them felt no strong attachment either to the Soviets or the United States. They wanted to be a third force in the world.

Then the world was also split between the developed nations which used so much of the earth's resources and the "underdeveloped" or "developing" nations. These poorer nations wanted aid from both the East and the West as they tried to feed their people and build better standards of living. On this one planet, how many different "worlds" could there be?

For all these reasons the relations between the United States and the Soviets were not so simple anymore. Sometimes the two countries competed, sometimes they worked together. With their SALT agreements they were actually cooperating to keep the planet at peace.

While some of the new elements were threatening or puzzling, others seemed promising. Communist China, now very much in the picture, feared and hated the Russians, and became a balance against them. Japan, which had become one of the world's great industrial powers, was going its own way. And the nations of Western Europe had founded a newly flourishing European Community with its own parliament.

The Middle East. The Middle East remained a tinderbox. A fire begun there might blaze into a world war. There were many causes—old and new—for conflict. There were religious problems—between Muslims, Christians, and Jews—over control of Jerusalem, which was sacred to them all. The state of Israel had been founded with United Nations support in 1948, but Arab countries had denied the right of Israel to exist. The PLO (Palestine Liberation Organization), by repeated acts of terrorism, tried to abolish Israel. Israel survived, but the problems of self-government for Palestinians, who had once lived in Israel and still considered it their land, remained. In November 1977 President Anwar el-Sadat of Egypt took a courageous initiative for peace. He was the first leader of an Arab country to visit the state of Israel.

After the signing of the peace treaty between Egypt and Israel, President Sadat (left) and Prime Minister Begin shake hands.

In Jerusalem he delivered a moving plea for peace, while the world watched on television.

Still, it would take time, goodwill, and ingenuity to bring together two countries that had been fighting for 25 years. President Carter made his own bold move. He invited Sadat and Israeli Prime Minister Menachem Begin to his mountain hideaway at Camp David to work out their differences. On September 17, 1978, after thirteen days of grueling negotiation, the three leaders finally produced a framework for peace between Israel and Egypt. Early in 1979 a peace treaty was signed.

Other Arab nations objected to Egypt's action. They said the two-way accord had done nothing to solve the problem of the Palestinians. In anger, these other Arab nations imposed an economic boycott on Egypt.

Iran and Nicaragua. The United States was plagued in 1979 by the fall of two friendly leaders on opposite sides of the globe. In Iran, early in the year, the Shah was overthrown. The Shah had used dictatorship, corruption, and torture to hasten the country into the industrial era. He had been helped to power by the United States (p. 607). His government had improved education and public health and given new opportunities to women. The dictator who replaced the Shah was Ayatollah Khomeini, a fanatical Muslim leader who tried to return the country to the Middle Ages. Khomeini and his fellow religious leaders (mullahs) disliked both the United States and Russia. This hurt the United States, for a friendly Iran was important to American defense. From bases there, American spy planes and listening posts could survey Soviet missile sites and see that SALT agreements were not violated.

Then, in July in Nicaragua, the largest country in Central America, dictator Anastasio Somoza was toppled by Marxist rebels supported by Costa Rica, Panama, and Cuba. Somoza's father had been helped to power in 1933 by United States Marines, and his family had run the country as if it were their private property. The United States quickly recognized the rebel government and worked to keep it from becoming another foothold for communism in Latin America.

Many Americans were distressed by the loss of these two friendly dictators. This was not because Americans loved dictators, but because both propped up American defense. And their successors might be worse for their own people as well as unfriendly to the United States. Still, in the post-Vietnam atmosphere, Congress would not go along with any attempt to intervene with American troops.

Even though the United States remained the most powerful nation in the world, Americans had come to realize that they could not change the world alone. The experience of Vietnam made clear how hard it was to influence the internal politics of other nations—and how costly and frustrating it might be to try. The United States instead pursued the slow policy of détente. It helped its friends when it could, and at the same time traded and cooperated with its enemies.

Americans could remember the hopes of the makers of the American Revolution and the framers of the Constitution. People all over the world could still be inspired, and their spirits lifted up, by the example of a great nation that remained strong and free. They would admire the unceasing American struggle to give every person a voice, everyone an opportunity, to be governed by freely elected representatives, to test the old and try the new. The meaning of America was not power, but example. This is what President Lincoln meant when he called our nation "the last best hope of earth."

SECTION REVIEW

1. Identify or explain: shuttle diplomacy, Khmer Rouge, Pathet Lao, SALT II, Third World, Anwar el-Sadat, Menachem Begin, Ayatollah Khomeini, Anastasio Somoza.

2. Give examples of Kissinger's diplomatic successes and failures.

3. What happened in Southeast Asia after United States forces withdrew from Vietnam?

4. How did Carter antagonize and then calm the Soviet leaders?

5. Why was our government willing to make new treaties on the Panama Canal? What did the treaties provide?

6. What contribution did Carter make to the peace treaty between Egypt and Israel?

7. How did government upheavals in Iran and Nicaragua affect the United States?

CHAPTER REVIEW

MEETING OUR EARLIER SELVES

1. For many years both major parties have allowed their presidential nominees to pick the candidates for Vice-President to be their running mates. Under the 25th Amendment the President also nominates a Vice-President when the office is vacant. Should the President or

the candidate for President have such a strong voice in the selection of the Vice-President? Why?

2. What arguments would you expect people to give for or against President Ford's clemency plan for Vietnam War deserters and draft evaders?

3. John F. Kennedy served as President for 34 months and Gerald Ford for 29 months. Compare their problems and their successes as President.

4. In the 1976 election campaign Jimmy Carter made many promises—far more than presidential candidates customarily had made. How did this strategy hurt him after he became President?

5. Like slavery in the 1850s, some of today's issues that concern special-interest groups do not lend themselves to compromise. What are some of these hard-to-compromise issues? Why do the major parties prefer to avoid them?

6. Support or attack the proposition that the advancement of "human rights" around the world should be a cornerstone of American foreign policy.

7. How had foreign policy become more complicated by the 1970s than it had been in the preceding twenty years?

QUESTIONS FOR TODAY

1. What success is the United States having (a) in energy conservation? (b) in increasing the output of our own energy resources?

2. Which of the above two approaches to the energy problem would an environmentalist favor? Why?

3. What government agencies now and in the next ten years might have personal information about you in their files? How could incorrect information harm you? How does the Privacy Act of 1974 protect you?

YOUR REGION IN HISTORY

1. How have antipollution laws and the regulations of the Environmental Protection Agency affected industries in your area? What have been the effects on your family or neighborhood?

2. What measures were taken by your state and local officials to deal with the energy crises of the 1970s?

3. Identify organizations in your community that engage in political action on a particular issue. What civic groups in your locality deal with broad issues of general concern?

SKILLS TO MAKE OUR PAST VIVID

1. Select a current topic that should appear in the next edition of this textbook. Write a 200–400 word account for a supplement to be used by next year's history class.

2. Select a table from the *Statistical Abstract* that shows recent trends in an area that interests you. Present the data in a line graph or bar graph.

3. Write five multiple-choice test questions dealing with material in this chapter.

Epilogue

The mysterious future

Georgia O'Keeffe suggests the mysterious promise of the land in her 1960 painting "It Was Blue and Green" inspired by her view from a high-flying airplane.

When we look back on the story of America, we feel very wise. In some ways we really are even wiser than William Bradford or Benjamin Franklin or George Washington or Abraham Lincoln.

We know what they did not know. What for us is history, for them would have been prophecy. For we know how it turned out. They had to guess.

We can see how right it was for the Pilgrims to risk the long voyage across the wild ocean. We see how lucky it was that the thirteen little colonies somehow united for independence. We can see how much better the American Revolution would have been fought with a stronger, more unified Continental Army.

We can see how futile were all the "compromises" on slavery before the Civil War. We can see, too, the Civil War toll in blood and hate. We can see that while the Civil War abolished slavery and saved the Union, it cost more than 600,000 lives and created new hates that would not quickly die.

From American history we can learn that the future is always full of surprising secrets. This New World has been such an exciting place because it has been so new. The great achievements of America are mostly things that never before seemed possible.

Which signers of the Declaration of Independence in 1776 could have imagined that their feeble little confederation, in two centuries, would be the world's greatest democracy—a continent-nation of more than 200 million people, the refuge of the world, the strongest nation on earth?

Of those 55 men in Philadelphia struggling in the hot summer of 1787 to agree on how to prevent the colonies from falling apart—how many would have believed that their work would become the longest-lived written constitution in history?

Who would have imagined that a nation of immigrants, the most miscellaneous people on earth, would someday be the most powerful? Or that men and women from the Western Hemisphere, from all over Europe, from Africa and Asia—of many races and religions and traditions—would adopt one language, and become loyal builders of one new nation?

Who would have guessed that out of the American wilderness (still only half explored in 1850) so soon would come men to explore the moon, and then to send marvelously complicated machines into space to photograph and study the planets of our solar system? Or that modern science, which brings us from the whole universe the boundless vistas of the radio-telescope, would discover strange new kinds of knowledge, and keep us ever faithful to the motto, "Toward the Unknown!"

These were some of the happy surprises. But there were others not quite so happy, and to the founders of our nation just as secret.

Who would have guessed that, within less than 200 years, a trackless, half-mapped continent could be crisscrossed by superhighways, defaced by billboards and tin cans? Who would have guessed that Americans would perfect horseless carriages to go a hundred miles an hour—and yet be stuck in traffic jams where they could not even move as fast as a walking horse? Or that ten times as many would be killed by these horseless carriages every year as were killed in all the battles of the American Revolution?

Who would have imagined that the fresh air of a New World would begin to be smoke-filled? Or that the sparkling waters of lakes and rivers would become so darkened and dirtied by factory sewage that even the fish found them unlivable and the birds no longer enjoyed their shores?

Who would have believed that the wonderful American silences—once broken by Indian chants or the songs of birds or the call of the coyote—would be shattered by the roar of speeding jets, lumbering trucks, and ear-jarring motorcycles? Who would have believed that a continent, once frightening by its emptiness, would now terrify people by crowding them together?

Who would have believed that a nation of nations, created by peoples of all races from everywhere, which had suffered through a bloody war for union and for freedom, would see new forms of racism?

Who would have believed that a nation designed to be a refuge for all people from the violence of the Old World could ever be plagued by reckless violence within?

Who would have foreseen that a nation rich in natural resources—in coal, oil, uranium, natural gas, and flowing water—would fear that it might be crippled by a lack of enough energy to run its cars and factories and to warm its houses?

But Americans have always faced hard problems. We, even more than other people, love the adventure of the unexpected. Ours has always been a story of dealing with the unknown, a story of movement and discovery—to America, within America, from America. The future is just as much a mystery story as it ever was.

Americans have been planters in this faraway land, builders of cities in the wilderness, Go-Getters. Americans—makers of something out of nothing—have delivered a new way of life to far corners of the world.

If the future is a mystery story, then, that does not frighten Americans. For we Americans have always lived in the world's greatest treasure house of the unexpected.

APPENDIX

North America
Physical

ARCTIC OCEAN

BERING SEA

Bering Strait

Point Barrow

BROOKS RANGE

Yukon

Mt. McKinley

YUKON

Mt. Logan

ROCKY

ALEXANDER ARCHIPELAGO

COAST RANGE

Mackenzie R.

Great Bear Lake

ARCTIC CIRCLE

Great Slave Lake

MOUNTAINS

C A N A D A

L A U R E N T I A N   U P L A N D

HUDSON BAY

UNGAVA PEN.

Ungava Bay

BAFFIN BAY

GREENLAND

ICELAND

GULF OF ST. LAWRENCE

St. Lawrence R.

UPLANDS

Hudson R.

Lake Manitoba

Lake Winnipeg

Great Lakes

PACIFIC OCEAN

SELKIRK MTS.

Columbia R.

CASCADE RANGE

GREAT BASIN

COAST RANGE

SIERRA NEVADA

Mt. Whitney

Great Salt Lake

Colorado R.

ROCKY

MOUNTAINS

G R E A T   P L A I N S

U N I T E D

Missouri R.

S T A T E S

Arkansas R.

OZARK PLATEAU

Red R.

Ohio R.

Mississippi R.

ALLEGHENY MOUNTAINS

APPALACHIAN

BLUE RIDGE

Chesapeake Bay

ATLANTIC

OCEAN

TROPIC OF CANCER

GULF OF CALIFORNIA

M E X I C O

SIERRA MADRE ORIENTAL

Rio Grande

SIERRA MADRE OCCIDENTAL

CENTRAL PLATEAU

Mt. Orizaba

BAY OF CAMPECHE

YUCATAN PEN.

GULF OF MEXICO

Straits of Florida

CARIBBEAN SEA

BEAUFORT SEA

0   1200 Miles

0   1200 Kilometers

744

USSR

ARCTIC OCEAN

ICELAND

70° N

60° N

180°

160° W

140° W

120° W

100° W

80° W

70° W

60° W

40° W

30° W

10° W

GREENLAND
(DENMARK)

Thule

NORTHWEST

ARCTIC CIRCLE

TERRITORIES

50° N

40° N

PACIFIC

OCEAN

30° N

Fairbanks

Anchorage
Seward

Dawson

YUKON
TERR.

Whitehorse

Skagway
Juneau

Ketchikan

BRITISH
COLUMBIA

Dawson
Creek

ALBERTA

Vancouver

Victoria

Edmonton

Calgary

Seattle

Spokane

Portland

Butte

Boise

Salt Lake City

San Francisco

Los Angeles
San Diego

Phoenix

SASKATCHEWAN

Regina

Yellowknife

HUDSON

BAY

Churchill

MANITOBA

CANADA

NEWFOUNDLAND

Goose
Bay

Gander

St. John's

Winnipeg

Bismarck

Minneapolis

Fort
Albany

ONTARIO

QUEBEC

Quebec

50° W

UNITED

Denver

STATES

Los
Alamos

MEXICO

San Antonio

Mexico City

Guadalupe-
Hidalgo

Kansas City

St. Louis

Chicago

Detroit

Toronto

Cleveland
Pittsburgh

Montreal

Ottawa

Fredericton

N.B.

P.E.I.

Charlottetown

N.S.

Halifax

Portland
Portsmouth

Boston

New York

Philadelphia

Baltimore

Washington, D.C.

Raleigh

Atlanta

ATLANTIC

Dallas

Houston

New Orleans

Tampa

Miami

BAHAMA IS.

OCEAN

TROPIC OF CANCER

20° N

GULF
OF
MEXICO

Havana

CUBA

HAITI

DOMINICAN
REPUBLIC

PUERTO
RICO
(U.S.)

VIRGIN IS.
(U.S.)

JAMAICA

CARIBBEAN SEA

North America
Political

10° N

BELIZE

GUATEMALA

HONDURAS

EL SALVADOR

NICARAGUA

0   1200 Miles

0   1200 Kilometers

COSTA
RICA

PANAMA

120° W

110° W

100° W

90° W

80° W

70° W

10°W   60°N

ORKNEY
ISLANDS

HEBRIDES

MERIDIAN OF GREENWICH

Bergen   N O R W A Y   Oslo   SW

55°N   • Gotteborg

N O R T H

SCOTLAND   S E A   D E N M A R K

• Edinburgh   Copenhagen   • Malm
Londonderry   Glasgow   Kiel
• Belfast   UNITED KINGDOM   HELIGOLAND   • Lübeck   DEMOCRATIC
REPUBLIC   Hamburg   Hamburg
OF   Liverpool • Leeds   Amsterdam   Bremen   Berlin
IRELAND   Dublin   • Manchester   The Hague   Hannover   Potsdam
• Sheffield   Rotterdam   REPUBLIC OF
50°N   WALES • Birmingham   NETHERLANDS   Essen   GERMANY
• Cork   Cardiff   London   Antwerp   Cologne   • Leipzig
Plymouth   Bristol   Greenwich   Dover   Ghent   FEDERAL   Weimar • Dresden
Portsmouth   Calais   BELGIUM   Brussels   Bonn   Frankfurt
Dunkirk   Lille   Bastogne
Cherbourg   Le Havre   LUX.   REPUBLIC OF   Nuremberg
Brest •   Rouen   Reims   Verdun   Danube R.
Seine R.   Paris   Strasbourg   GERMANY   Stuttgart
Versailles   Munich
Orléans   Bern   Zürich   AUST

Loire   Lausanne   SWITZERLAND
Nantes   R.   Geneva
F R A N C E
Lyon •   Milan   Venice   Trieste
Bordeaux •   Turin   Po   R.
BAY   Garonne R.   Genoa   Bologna
OF   Toulouse   Avignon   I T A L
BISCAY   Nice   MONACO   Florence
Marseille   Toulon   ITALY

Vigo •   Bilbao   ANDORRA   CORSICA   Ajaccio   Rome
Pôrto •   Ebro R.   Ajaccio   Anzio
40°N   Zaragoza   Ávila   N
Madrid   Barcelona
Lisbon   Tagus R.   S P A I N   MAJORCA   MINORCA   SARDINIA
• Valencia   BALEARIC ISLANDS   TYRRHENI
Córdoba   SEA
Seville •   Granada   Cagliari   Palermo
Cádiz •   Málaga
Strait of Gibraltar   Algeciras   M E D I T E R R A N E A N
Algiers
35°N   Tunis
MOROCCO   Oran   A L G E R I A   TUNISIA
5°W   0°   5°E   10°E

P O R T U G A L

A T L A N T I C   O C E A N

ENGLISH CHANNEL

Rhine R.
Rhone R.

FINLAND

Leningrad

35°E

Helsinki

Tallinn

Volga R.

GOTLAND

Riga

S O V I E T

BALTIC SEA

Memel

Smolensk

Tilsit

Neman R. Kaunas

Kaliningrad

Vilnius

Minsk

U N I O N

Gdansk

Dnepr R.

P O L A N D

Warsaw

Brest

Łódź

Kiev

Wrocław

Vistula R.

Kraków

L'vov

Dnestr R.

OSLOVAKIA

Bratislava

Odessa

Budapest

H U N G A R Y

R O M A N I A

Tisza R.

Zagreb

Sava R.

Bucharest

Y U G O S L A V I A

Belgrade

Danube R.

B L A C K   S E A

Sarajevo

Sofia

30°E

Dubrovnik

B U L G A R I A

Bosporus

Edirne

Istanbul

C   S E A

A L B A N I A

Tirana

Gallipoli

T U R K E Y

Foggia   Bari

Salonica
(Thessalonika)

Taranto

Dardanelles

Izmir

G R E E C E

A E G E A N   S E A

IONIAN
SEA

Athens

Catania

SEA

CRETE

20°E

25°E

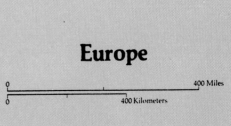

Europe

0   400 Miles

0   400 Kilometers

747

Eurasia

1600 Miles

1600 Kilometers

Africa

0 ————————————— 1200 Miles
0 ————————————— 1200 Kilometers

30°N

TROPIC OF CANCER

South America

W E S T
I N D I E S

Havana

CUBA

DOMINICAN
REPUBLIC

HAITI

Port-au-Prince   Santo Domingo

JAMAICA Kingston

PUERTO
RICO

LEEWARD IS.

0   1200 Miles

0   1200 Kilometers

Belmopan
BELIZE

EMALA

HONDURAS

Tegucigalpa

San
Salvador

nala

ALVADOR

NICARAGUA
Managua

San Jose

COSTA RICA

PANAMA

Panama City

Panama Canal

CARIBBEAN SEA

Barranquilla
Cartagena

Maracaibo

Lake
Maracaibo

Caracas

WINDWARD IS.

Port-of-Spain

TRINIDAD AND TOBAGO

VENEZUELA

Georgetown

Paramaribo

GUYANA

Cayenne

SURINAM

FR.
GUIANA

Medellín

Cauca R.

Magdalena R.

Bogotá

Orinoco R.

COLOMBIA

Rio   Negro

EQUATOR

GALÁPAGOS
ISLANDS

Quito

ECUADOR

Guayaquil

Amazon R.

Belém

Fortaleza

PACIFIC

Iquitos

Manaus

Amazon R.

Tocantins R.

Recife

Maceió

Cajamarca

PERU

Madeira R.

B R A Z I L

ANDES MOUNTAINS

Salvador

Lima

Cuzco

Machu Picchu

Lake
Titicaca

Cuiaba

Brasília

São Francisco R.

OCEAN

Arequipa

La Paz

BOLIVIA

Belo Horizonte

Arica

Sucre

Iquique

PARAGUAY

Rio de Janeiro

São Paulo

Asunción

Santos

20°S

Antofagasta

TROPIC OF CAPRICORN

Tucumán

A R G E N T I N A

Paraná R.

Pôrto Alegre

CHILE

Cordoba

ANDES MOUNTAINS

Mendoza

Rosario

URUGUAY

Montevideo

Valparaíso
Santiago

Buenos Aires

Río de la Plata

ATLANTIC OCEAN

30°S

Concepcion

Bahía Blanca

Puerto Montt

40°S

FALKLAND IS.
(Britain)

Strait of
Magellan

Punta Arenas   TIERRA DEL FUEGO

50°S

Cape Horn

80°W   70°W   60°W   50°W   40°W   30°W

130°   120°   50°   Calgary   C   110°   A   100°

PACIFIC   WASHINGTON
Seattle   Olympia   Tacoma   Spokane   Columbia   Regina
Columbia   Portland   Salem   MONTANA   NORTH DAK
OREGON   IDAHO   Missouri   Great Falls   R.   Bismarck
40°   Boise   Helena   Butte   Yellowstone   SOUTH DAK
Snake   R.   Pocatello   WYOMING   Pierre
OCEAN   Humboldt   R.   Great   Ogden   Casper   Missouri
Sacramento   Reno   NEVADA   Salt   Salt Lake   Cheyenne   NEBRASK
San Francisco   Carson City   Lake   City   Platte
Oakland   UTAH   Denver   COLORADO   KAN
Las Vegas   Colorado   Pueblo   Arkansas
Los Angeles   ARIZONA   Albuquerque   Santa Fe   Amarillo   OH
San Diego   Colorado   Phoenix   NEW MEXICO   Oklahom
120°   R.   Tucson   Rio   Pecos   El Paso   T   E   X
30°

PACIFIC   OCEAN

BERING SEA   170   180   170   Barrow   150   140   160   22 30   157 30
Cape Prince of Wales   Strait   SEWARD PEN.   70   KAUAI   San Antoni
Nome   Fairbanks   Klondike   NIIHAU   OAHU   Honolulu   Corp Chris
NUNIVAK ISLAND   Yukon R.   Pearl Harbor   MOLOKAI
PRIBILOF ISLANDS   Anchorage   PACIFIC   LANAI   MAUI   155
ALEUTIAN   KENAI PEN.   Seward   KAHOOLAWE
Dutch Harbor   ALASKA PEN.   Kodiak   GULF OF ALASKA   OCEAN   HAWAII   Hilo
ALASKA   ISLANDS   Juneau   Sitka   HAWAII
750 Miles   Ketchikan   Prince Rupert   0   100 Miles
750 Kilometers   PACIFIC OCEAN   QUEEN CHARLOTTE ISLANDS   0   100 Kilometers

CANADA

L. Superior

MINNESOTA
Duluth
Minneapolis
St. Paul

WISCONSIN
Green Bay
Madison
Milwaukee

MICHIGAN
L. Michigan
Grand Rapids
Flint
Lansing
Detroit

L. Huron

Sault Ste. Marie

Quebec

St. Lawrence R.

Montreal

Ottawa

MAINE
Augusta
Fredericton
St. John

Burlington
VT.
Montpelier
Concord
N.H.
Portland

Manchester
Boston
Worcester
Providence

MASS.
Hartford
CONN.
R.I.
New Haven

Albany

NEW YORK
Rochester
Syracuse
Buffalo

Toronto
Hamilton

L. Ontario
L. Erie

Erie
Cleveland

Scranton
PENNSYLVANIA
Pittsburgh
Harrisburg

Newark
New York
Trenton
NEW JERSEY
Philadelphia
Wilmington
DELAWARE
Dover

40°

Sioux City
IOWA
Des Moines

Chicago
Gary
Fort Wayne

INDIANA

ILLINOIS
Indianapolis
Springfield
Peoria

OHIO
Toledo
Akron
Columbus
Dayton
Cincinnati

Ohio R.

WEST VIRGINIA
Huntington
Charleston

MARYLAND
Washington
D.C.
Annapolis
Baltimore

Richmond

Norfolk

VIRGINIA

ATLANTIC OCEAN

as City
Kansas City
Jefferson City
St. Louis

MISSOURI

Evansville
Louisville
Frankfort

KENTUCKY

Nashville
Knoxville

TENNESSEE
Chattanooga

NORTH CAROLINA
Raleigh
Charlotte

Tulsa
MA
Fort Smith

ARKANSAS
Little Rock

Memphis

SOUTH CAROLINA
Columbia

Charleston

Mississippi R.

as
Shreveport

LOUISIANA

MISSISSIPPI
Meridian
Jackson

ALABAMA
Birmingham
Columbus
Montgomery

Atlanta

GEORGIA

Savannah

30°

Sabine R.

Beaumont
ston

New Orleans

Baton Rouge

Mobile

FLORIDA
Tallahassee

Jacksonville

GULF OF MEXICO

Tampa

Miami

Key West

Straits of Florida

BAHAMA ISLANDS

United States
Political

Havana

CUBA

80°

0   1000 Miles
0   1000 Kilometers

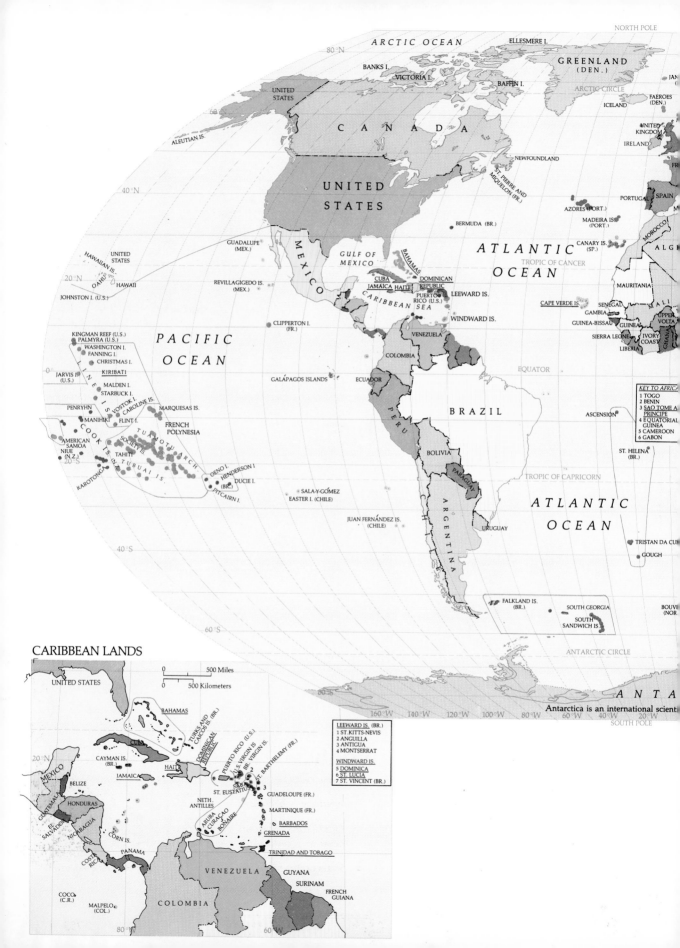

Political Map of the World

Natural Scale 1: 100,000,000   Wagner's Near-Equal-Area Projection

---- International boundaries.

⎯⎯ Line to show ownership groupings of islands;
ocean areas enclosed are mainly international waters.

▫ States or dependencies so small their actual shapes cannot be shown.

⎯⎯ Island Nations are underlined

0   3000 Miles

0   3000 Kilometers

755

The Declaration of Independence

We Americans are luckier than most other people because the Founders of our new nation left us a short, clear, and simple list of reasons for the founding. The Declaration of Independence is our nation's birth certificate. It tells us in a few words what were the parent-ideas and hopes out of which the nation was born.

In the following pages we print the Declaration of Independence. We explain why it happened to say what it did, and what it has come to mean to Americans and to people everywhere in the world. The Declaration of Independence, like the Constitution, is a sacred document for Americans. This is because it is a *living* document. Of course it was written by living men in 1776 to suit the needs of American patriots in the Revolution. But it proved to have a life much longer than that of the men who adopted it. It is still very much alive. To understand why and how it lives will help us understand our country, and where it has

been going in the centuries since 1776.

Why there had to be a Declaration of Independence, and how it fits into the story of the Revolution, is explained earlier in this book (pp. 68–81). In the following pages we provide in the center column the words of the Declaration precisely as Jefferson, helped by John Adams and Benjamin Franklin, wrote it. These very words were adopted by the Continental Congress in Independence Hall (which we can still visit) in Philadelphia on July 4, 1776. We have left their spelling, their punctuation, and their capitalization precisely as they wrote it. Even if this looks a little odd to us, it will help us remember that the Declaration was written two centuries ago. And this will not get in the way of our understanding.

In the left-hand column (*Origins*) we give some of the reasons why they wrote those words. In the right-hand column (*Afterlife*) we see what those words have come to mean in later years.

THE DECLARATION OF INDEPENDENCE

When in the Course of human events, it becomes necessary for one people to dissolve the political bands which have connected them with another, and to assume among the powers of the earth, the separate and equal station to which the Laws of Nature and of Nature's God entitle them, a decent respect to the opinions of mankind requires that they should declare the causes which impel them to the separation.

We hold these truths to be self-evident, that all men are created equal, that they are endowed by their Creator with certain unalienable Rights, that among these are Life, Liberty and the pursuit of Happiness. That to secure these rights, Governments are instituted among Men, deriving their just powers from the consent of the governed, That whenever any Form of Government becomes destructive of these ends it is the Right of the People to alter or to abolish it, and to institute new Government, laying its foundation on such principles and organizing its powers in such form, as to them shall seem most likely to effect their Safety and Happiness. Prudence, indeed, will dictate that Governments long established should not be changed for light and transient causes; and accordingly all experience has shewn, that mankind are more disposed to suffer, while evils are sufferable, than to right themselves by abolishing the forms to which they are accustomed. But when a long train of abuses and usurpations, pursuing invariably the same Object evinces a design to reduce them under absolute Despotism, it is their right, it is their duty, to throw off such Government, and to provide new Guards for their future security. Such has been the patient sufferance of these Colonies; and such is now the necessity which constrains them to alter their former Systems of Government. The history of the present King of Great Britain is a history of repeated injuries and usurpations, all having in direct object the establishment of an absolute Tyranny over these States. To prove this, let Facts be submitted to a candid world.

He has refused his Assent to Laws, the most wholesome and necessary for the public good.

He has forbidden his Governors to pass Laws of immediate and pressing importance, unless suspended in their operation till his Assent should be obtained; and when so suspended, he has utterly neglected to attend to them. He has refused to pass other Laws for the accommodation of large districts of people, unless those people would relinquish the right of Representation in the Legislature, a right inestimable to them and formidable to tyrants only.

He has called together legislative bodies at places unusual, uncomfortable, and distant from the depository of their public Records, for the sole purpose of fatiguing them into compliance with his measures.

He has dissolved Representative Houses repeatedly, for opposing with manly firmness his invasions on the rights of the people.

He has refused for a long time, after such dissolutions, to cause others to be elected; whereby the Legislative powers, incapable of Annihilation, have returned to the People at large for their exercise; the State remaining in the mean time exposed to all the dangers of invasion from without, and convulsions within.

He has endeavoured to prevent the population of these States; for that purpose obstructing the Laws for Naturalization of Foreigners; refusing to pass others to encourage their migrations hither, and raising the conditions of new Appropriations of Lands.

He has obstructed the Administration of Justice, by refusing his Assent to Laws for establishing Judiciary powers.

He has made Judges dependent on his Will alone, for the tenure of their offices, and the amount and payment of their salaries.

He has erected a multitude of New Offices, and sent hither swarms of Officers to harass our People, and eat out their substance.

He has kept among us, in times of peace, standing Armies without the Consent of our legislatures.

He has affected to render the Military independent of and superior to the Civil power.

He has combined with others to subject us to a jurisdiction foreign to our constitution, and unacknowledged by our laws; giving his Assent to their Acts of pretended Legislation:

For Quartering large bodies of armed troops among us:

For protecting them, by a mock Trial, from punishment for any Murders which they should commit on the Inhabitants of these States:

For cutting off our Trade with all parts of the world:

For imposing Taxes on us without our Consent:

For depriving us in many cases of the benefits of Trial by Jury:

For transporting us beyond Seas to be tried for pretended offences:

For abolishing the free System of English Laws in a neighbouring Province, establishing therein an Arbitrary government, and enlarging its Boundaries so as to render it at once an example and fit instrument for introducing the same absolute rule into these Colonies:

For taking away our Charters, abolishing our most valuable Laws, and altering fundamentally the Forms of our Governments:

For suspending our own Legislatures, and declaring themselves invested with power to legislate for us in all cases whatsoever.

He has abdicated Government here, by declaring us out of his Protection and waging War against us.

He has plundered our seas, ravaged our Coasts, burnt our towns, and destroyed the Lives of our people.

He is at this time transporting large Armies of foreign Mercenaries to compleat the works of death, desolation and tyranny, already begun with circumstances of Cruelty & perfidy scarcely paralleled in the most barbarous ages, and totally unworthy the Head of a civilized nation.

He has constrained our fellow Citizens taken Captive on the high Seas to bear Arms against their Country, to become the executioners of their friends and Brethren, or to fall themselves by their Hands.

He has excited domestic insurrections amongst us, and has endeavoured to bring on the inhabitants of our frontiers, the merciless Indian Savages, whose known rule of warfare, is an undistinguished destruction of all ages, sexes and conditions.

In every stage of these Oppressions We have Petitioned for Redress in the most humble terms: Our repeated Petitions have been answered only by repeated injury. A Prince, whose character is thus marked by every act which may define a Tyrant, is unfit to be the ruler of a free people.

Nor have We been wanting in attentions to our Brittish brethren. We have warned them from time to time of attempts by their legislature to extend an unwarrantable jurisdiction over us. We have reminded them of the circumstances of our emigration and settlement here. We have appealed to their native justice and magnanimity, and we have conjured them by the ties of our common kindred to disavow these usurpations, which, would inevitably interrupt our connections and correspondence. They too have been deaf to the voice of Justice and of consanguinity. We must, therefore, acquiesce in the necessity, which denounces our Separation, and hold them, as we hold the rest of mankind, Enemies in War, in Peace Friends.

We, therefore, the Representatives of the united States of America, in General Congress, Assembled, appealing to the Supreme Judge of the world for the rectitude of our intentions, do, in the Name, and by Authority of the good People of these Colonies, solemnly publish and declare, That these United Colonies are, and of Right ought to be Free and Independent States; that they are Absolved from all Allegiance to the British Crown, and that all political connection between them and the State of Great Britain, is and ought to be totally dissolved; and that as Free and Independent States, they have full Power to levy War, conclude Peace, contract Alliances, establish Commerce, and to do all other Acts and Things which Independent States may of right do. And for the support of this Declaration, with a firm reliance on the protection of divine Providence, we mutually pledge to each other our Lives, our Fortunes and our sacred Honor.

John Hancock

Button Gwinnett	James Wilson
Lyman Hall	Geo. Ross
Geo Walton.	Caesar Rodney
Wm. Hooper	Geo Read
Joseph Hewes,	Tho M:Kean
John Penn	Wm. Floyd
Edward Rutledge.	Phil. Livingston
Thos. Heyward Junr.	Frans. Lewis
Thomas Lynch Junr.	Lewis Morris
Arthur Middleton	Richd. Stockton
Samuel Chase	Jno Witherspoon
Wm. Paca	Fras. Hopkinson
Thos. Stone	John Hart
Charles Carroll of Carrollton	Abra Clark
George Wythe	Josiah Bartlett
Richard Henry Lee	Wm: Whipple
Th: Jefferson	Saml. Adams
Benja. Harrison	John Adams
Thos. Nelson jr.	Robt. Treat Paine
Francis Lightfoot Lee	Elbridge Gerry
Carter Braxton	Step. Hopkins
Robt. Morris	William Ellery
Benjamin Rush	Roger Sherman
Benja. Franklin	Saml. Huntington
John Morton	Wm. Williams
Geo Clymer	Oliver Wolcott
Jas. Smith.	Matthew Thornton
Geo. Taylor	

Note: This text of the Declaration of Independence is taken from the reprint in the Revised Statutes of the United States, corrected by comparison with the version printed in the journal of the Continental Congress. The original manuscript can be seen in the National Archives, Washington, D. C.

The Preamble. The Declaration of Independence was directed not just to a few insiders—American colonists who wanted their independence—but to the whole world. It had to be plain and simple. The first part therefore had to state the "common sense" of the subject. The opening words of the Declaration, like the opening words of the Constitution, gave the basis for the whole argument. They expressed not only what most Americans believed, but also what would seem "self-evident" (needing no proof) to Britons of goodwill, and to people in France and other countries from whom the Americans wanted help.

Since Jefferson was not aiming to devise a new theory, it is not surprising that he wrote his draft in short order. On June 28, 1776, only about two weeks after he received the assignment, the energetic 33-year-old lawyer from Virginia managed to have his Declaration approved by the Committee and submitted to the Continental Congress. If he had needed a lot of research and reflection, it would have taken him much longer. He did not even need a library. He explained that he had purposely not referred to any books or pamphlets for special arguments. He wrote the Declaration in Philadelphia on a desk in the second-floor parlor of the house of a young German immigrant bricklayer where he was staying. He wanted to be sure that what he was saying simply summed up what educated people already knew from their schoolbooks.

The basis for government described here is precisely what Englishmen had accepted in their Glorious Revolution of 1688. All good Whigs in England still believed those principles. The Englishman John Locke had been the philosopher of that Glorious Revolution. His sacred three purposes of government were life, liberty, and property. Jefferson preferred "Life, Liberty, and the pursuit of Happiness."

The List of Grievances. Thomas Jefferson was a lawyer. He had studied law at William and Mary College. He was admitted to the Virginia bar in 1767 and was a successful practicing lawyer until the cause of Independence focused his talents on public issues. One of the main reasons why Jefferson was chosen to write the Declaration was that in 1774 he had written a brilliant *Summary View of the Rights of British America.* This eloquent little pamphlet brought him wide notice both as a learned lawyer and a lively stylist. There he had

At the time, to the colonists, Jefferson's legalistic list of grievances seemed the heart of their case. These "facts submitted to a candid world" against the king of England justified the colonies' independence. The Preamble was only the "common sense" basis behind those grievances. In later years, after the United States had fought for and won independence, the facts of that day came to seem less interesting. To understand those facts required an understanding of history, of the sort we have tried to give in this book. Since they were in lawyers' language, they were easy to forget.

The Preamble, by contrast, stated the principles of free government. Jefferson's flowing language could not be forgotten. It is not surprising, then, that in the years since 1776 the Preamble has overshadowed all the rest of the document. Who can forget these words? "We hold these truths to be self-evident, that all men are created equal, that they are endowed by their Creator with certain unalienable Rights, that among these are Life, Liberty and the pursuit of Happiness. That to secure these rights, Governments are instituted among Men, deriving their just powers from the consent of the governed."

These words of the Preamble resound down the centuries. They have a wonderful ring, but Americans have not always agreed on what they meant.

Elizabeth Cady Stanton and her companions at the women's rights convention at Seneca Falls, New York, in 1848, issued their own "Declaration" modeled on Jefferson's work of 1776. They began "When, in the course of human events . . ." and went on to their own list of "self-evident" truths, and their grievances against man for oppressing woman.

The Civil War would have to be fought to secure agreement on what the Declaration meant when it said that "all men are created equal." When the southern states seceded they, too, declared that they were only following the principles of the Declaration of 1776.

Even today Americans disagree over precisely what a government should do to help Americans in the "pursuit of Happiness." But Jefferson's words in the Declaration of Independence still provide an American creed. We can all agree to this statement of principles. If the words had been more prosaic or more limited, they might not have lived.

proven that the Parliament had no authority at all over the colonies. He did concede that the colonists, of their own free will, had submitted to the king as their connecting link with the home country.

And Jefferson was a careful lawyer. This explains why Jefferson's Declaration of Independence makes no mention at all of the British Parliament. On one occasion he mentions that "the present King of Great Britain" (George III) "has combined with *others*" for his nefarious purposes. Those "others" were, of course, the Parliament. But the lawyerly Jefferson would not do them the honor of naming them by name! From a lawyer's point of view the king was to blame, and had to take all the blame for allowing those "others" to oppress the colonies.

The list that Jefferson provides is detailed and technical. The colonists' rights, he says, were the traditional rights of all British subjects. This, of course, prevented the Declaration from having a radical sound. According to Jefferson's Declaration the colonists were now declaring their independence simply to preserve the rights that Britons had fought for and won over the past centuries.

We can already see here the need for compromise among the States, which would appear so plainly in the Constitution. The list of grievances that finally was approved by the Continental Congress was not precisely that which Jefferson included in his draft. Some sentimental members of the Continental Congress removed a few of Jefferson's personal remarks about George III. Out of tenderness to some delegates from the slave states, they also removed Jefferson's bitter attack on slavery and the slave-trade, for which he held the British king responsible.

And we might have lacked the eloquent standard by which we can still judge ourselves.

The Declaration of Independence and the World. Jefferson's words have appealed to freedom-loving people everywhere. No other human document has been so inspiring to people with grievances against their government. The men and women who made the French Revolution of 1789 appealed to the Declaration. English reformers, and Irish rebels against English oppression, appealed to the Declaration. In the early 19th century, translated into Spanish, the Declaration inspired colonists in South America to become independent. It was translated into German and Italian to support liberal revolutions in the 1830s and 1840s. It was translated into scores of other languages, and everywhere has encouraged people fighting for freedom, helping them explain their cause to the world.

Jefferson himself knew that his Declaration was a voice for posterity and that it would have an Afterlife without end. He wrote his own epitaph. After a long life of countless achievements, he chose to have it written on his tombstone (along with his recognition as author of the Virginia statute for religious freedom and as father of the University of Virginia) that he was the author of the Declaration of Independence.

The Constitution of the United States

INTRODUCTION

These pages give us the text of the Constitution, and they will help us understand why it was written this way, and how it has changed. For Americans, the Constitution is a sacred document. The Constitution itself prescribes that before taking office, each American President must "solemnly swear (or affirm) that I will . . . to the best of my Ability, preserve, protect and defend the Constitution of the United States." (Article II, section 1) While the Constitution is our sacred national document, it is not a fossil. It can be changed and has changed. Most of this book could be considered a history of how the Constitution has worked.

We have arranged the following pages on the Constitution to show that the Constitution was a *living* document. In the Convention in Philadelphia in the hot summer of 1787 the Framers had reasons for everything that they said. We can understand these reasons by our study of history. It was written by living people for their living needs. It would be changed slowly over the centuries to meet the needs of other living people, including ourselves.

In the middle column (*The Text*) we print the Constitution as the Framers approved it on September 15 and signed it in Independence Hall in Philadelphia (a place we can still visit) on September 17, 1787. Their spelling, their punctuation, and their capitalizing of words may look a little odd to us. But we have left the document the way they wrote it, to remind us that it was written a long time ago. This, too, will remind us of the miracle of the survival of our Constitution as the frame of government of a great nation. None of the peculiarities will get in the way of our understanding.

In the left-hand column (*Origins*) we see some of the reasons that led men of the eighteenth century to write the words as they did. Here we have a glimpse of their arguments, disagreements, and compromises before they settled on the words we now read. All these are explained at greater length in the earlier pages of this book. The references to chapters and sections within chapters appear in brackets: [4:1] is Chapter 4, Section 1.

In the right-hand column (*Afterlife*) we see how the meaning of the document has changed to suit needs that the Framers never imagined. Some of their words were not clear, and the meanings of some words would change. These changes, too, are described in the earlier pages of this book.

The story of the Constitution itself is one of the most remarkable in all history. Like the life of a person, it is full of surprises—and disappointments. But the story as a whole must make Americans proud. We can still prosper under this Constitution written two centuries ago.

One of the best features of the document was that it was so short. It is shorter than the Constitution of any of the states. The Framers wanted to provide for the future, but they did not try to second-guess the future. They believed in change—otherwise they would not have dared to start a new nation and write a new constitution. They respected the wisdom of the future. They left plenty of room for future Americans to make this Constitution serve their needs.

The Constitution survives because it is a living document. The Framers intended this Constitution to *live*. We help it live by understanding what they intended, why and how they wanted it to endure, why and how it has been changed, and how it can still be changed. And by seeing its wonderful simplicity and wisdom.

THE CONSTITUTION OF THE UNITED STATES

We the People of the United States, in Order to form a more perfect Union, establish Justice, insure domestic Tranquillity, provide for the common defence, promote the general Welfare, and secure the Blessings of Liberty to ourselves and our Posterity, do ordain and establish this Constitution for the United States of America.

ORIGINS

The Preamble. This is not merely an introduction, but one of the most important passages in the Constitution. It describes both the *basis* of government and the *purposes* of government. The Framers chose their words carefully.

A new basis. The weak Articles of Confederation (1781; see p. 98) had been formed by "Delegates of the States." To make "a more perfect Union," the Constitution of the new nation was now ordained and established by "the People of the United States." To make a fresh start, the voters of the whole country (strictly limited at that time to certain white male property owners) delegated certain powers to the new national government, others to the states.

The purposes. The "in Order to" items were a list of the worries of Americans at the time. They wanted to "establish Justice" (which the British government had denied the colonies). They wanted to "insure domestic Tranquillity" (which Shays's Rebellion in Massachusetts, August 1786–February 1787 [5:3], and other riots had threatened). They wanted better to "provide for the common defence" (the weak Continental Congress had almost lost the Revolution) [4:3]. They wanted to "promote the general Welfare" (till then threatened by inflation and rivalries between the states). They wanted to "secure the Blessings of Liberty" not only to themselves but to their "Posterity" (that's us!), which required a firm and durable Constitution.

The Framers in the Federal Convention in Philadelphia in August–September 1787 worked over this language for the Preamble. The final form was given by Gouverneur Morris of Pennsylvania, who had signed the Articles of Confederation, had helped manage the troubled finances under the weak Articles, and had good reason to want a strong national government.

AFTERLIFE

The Preamble. While the Federalist Framers thought the meaning of this preamble was clear, it would not be so clear to all later generations. The Civil War would be fought partly over the precise meaning of the words. If the basis of government really was not "the People" of the whole United States but only the states—then what the states had made by coming together they could destroy by seceding. In 1819, Chief Justice John Marshall, drawing on the preamble, declared in *McCulloch* v. *Maryland* [8:2], "The government of the Union . . . is emphatically and truly a government of the people. In form and in substance it emanated from them, its powers are granted by them, and are to be exercised directly on them, and for their benefit." But in the years before the Civil War, John C. Calhoun and other Southern secessionists did not agree. The Civil War settled that issue.

The Constitution does not define *who* "the People" are. Like much else in the document the meaning of this phrase has changed. At first, "the People" were only white male property owners. Then all white males were included. Later black males were added by the 15th Amendment [14:3], then women by the 19th Amendment [22:1], and all citizens 18 years old or older by the 26th Amendment [33:3].

ARTICLE I

Section 1. All legislative Powers herein granted shall be vested in a Congress of the United States, which shall consist of a Senate and House of Representatives.

Section 2. The House of Representatives shall be composed of Members chosen every second Year by the People of the several States, and the Elec-

the ratio is one member for about every 500,000 persons.

• The House "impeaches" and the Senate (sec. 3, pars. 6–7) tries the impeachment [8:3, 14:3, 33:3].

Art. I

Section 3. The Senate of the United States shall be composed of two Sena- ■ tors from each State, chosen by the Legislature thereof, for six Years; and each Senator shall have one Vote.

Immediately after they shall be assembled in Consequence of the first Election, they shall be divided as equally as may be into three Classes. The Seats of the Senators of the first Class shall be vacated at the Expiration of the second Year, of the second Class at the Expiration of the fourth Year, and of the third Class at the Expiration of the sixth Year, so that one third may be chosen every second Year; and if vacancies happen by Resignation, or otherwise, during the Recess of the Legislature of any State, the Executive thereof may make temporary Appointments until the next Meeting of the Legislature, which shall then fill such Vacancies.

No Person shall be a Senator who shall not have attained to the Age of thirty Years, and been nine Years a Citizen of the United States, and who shall not, when elected, be an Inhabitant of that State for which he shall be chosen.

The Vice President of the United States shall be President of the Senate, but shall have no Vote, unless they be equally divided.

The Senate shall chuse their other Officers, and also a President pro ▲ tempore, in the Absence of the Vice President, or when he shall exercise the Office of President of the United States.

The Senate shall have the sole Power to try all Impeachments. When sitting for that Purpose, they shall be on Oath or Affirmation. When the President of the United States is tried the Chief Justice shall preside: And no Person shall be convicted without the Concurrence of two thirds of the Members present.

Judgment in Cases of Impeachment shall not extend further than to removal from Office, and disqualification to hold and enjoy any Office of honor, Trust or Profit under the United States: but the Party convicted shall nevertheless be liable and subject to Indictment, Trial, Judgment and Punishment, according to Law.

AFTERLIFE

■ The 17th Amendment (1913) provided for the election of senators directly by the people instead of by state legislatures [20:2].

▲ The 25th Amendment now provides for filling the Vice-Presidency when the office becomes vacant. Gerald Ford was the first person to be selected by this procedure [33:3].

Section 4. The Times, Places and Manner of holding Elections for Senators and Representatives, shall be prescribed in each State by the Legislature thereof; but the Congress may at any time by Law make or alter such Regulations, except as to the Places of chusing Senators.

The Congress shall assemble at least once in every Year, and such Meeting shall be on the first Monday in December, unless they shall by Law appoint a different Day. ■

AFTERLIFE

Under federal law all the states now hold elections for Congress on the first Tuesday after the first Monday in November in even-numbered years.

■ The meeting time of Congress was changed in the 20th Amendment, section 2 [24:1].

Section 5. Each House shall be the Judge of the Elections, Returns and Qualifications of its own Members, and a Majority of each shall constitute a Quorum to do Business; but a smaller Number may adjourn from day to day, and may be authorized to compel the Attendance of absent Members, in such Manner, and under such Penalties as each House may provide.

Each House may determine the Rules of its Proceedings, punish its Members for disorderly Behaviour, and, with the Concurrence of two thirds, expel a Member.

Each House shall keep a Journal of its Proceedings, and from time to time publish the same, excepting such Parts as may in their Judgment require Secrecy; and the Yeas and Nays of the Members of either House on any question shall, at the Desire of one fifth of those Present, be entered on the Journal.

Neither House, during the Session of Congress, shall, without the Consent of the other, adjourn for more than three days, nor to any other Place than that in which the two Houses shall be sitting.

AFTERLIFE

The right of each house to punish its own members has enabled them to discipline senators and representatives whose activities are judged to be improper. For example, under this clause Senator Joseph R. McCarthy was condemned in 1954, Representative Adam Clayton Powell was denied his seat in 1967 on the charge that he misused government funds, and Senator Herman Talmadge was "denounced" in 1979 for financial irregularities.

Section 6. The Senators and Representatives shall receive a Compensation for their Services, to be ascertained by Law, and paid out of the Treasury of the United States. They shall in all Cases, except Treason, Felony and Breach of the Peace, be privileged from Arrest during their attendance at the Session of their respective Houses, and in going to and returning from the same; and for any Speech or Debate in either House, they shall not be questioned in any other Place.

No Senator or Representative shall, during the Time for which he was elected, be appointed to any civil Office under the Authority of the United States, which shall have been created, or the Emoluments whereof shall have been encreased during such time; and no Person holding any Office under the United States, shall be a Member of either House during his Continuance in Office.

Section 7. All Bills for raising Revenue shall originate in the House of Representatives; but the Senate may propose or concur with amendments as on other Bills.

Every Bill which shall have passed the House of Representatives and the Senate, shall, before it become a Law, be presented to the President of the United States; If he approve he shall sign it, but if not he shall return it, with his Objections to that House in which it shall have originated, who shall enter the Objections at large on their Journal, and proceed to reconsider it. If after such Reconsideration two thirds of that House shall agree to pass the Bill, it shall be sent, together with the Objections, to the other House, by which it shall likewise be reconsidered, and if approved by two thirds of that House, it shall become a Law. But in all such Cases the Votes of both Houses shall be determined by yeas and Nays, and the Names of the Persons voting for and against the Bill shall be entered on the Journal of each House respectively. If any Bill shall not be returned by the President within ten Days (Sunday excepted) after it shall have been presented to him, the Same shall be a Law, in like Manner as if he had signed it, unless the Congress by their Adjournment prevent its Return, in which Case it shall not be a Law.

Every Order, Resolution, or Vote to which the Concurrence of the Senate and House of Representatives may be necessary (except on a question of Adjournment) shall be presented to the President of the United States; and before the Same shall take Effect, shall be approved by him, or being disapproved by him, shall be repassed by two thirds of the Senate and House of Representatives, according to the Rules and Limitations prescribed in the Case of a Bill.

AFTERLIFE

Although section 1 grants all legislative power to Congress, all bills must be submitted to the President. The President may then sign the bill and make it a law, or let it become a law without signing it. The President may also refuse to sign and return the bill with his reasons for doing so—that is, "veto" it. The bill can then become law only if each house passes it by a two-thirds majority. A bill sent to the President in the last ten days of a session of Congress does not become law if the President does not sign it. This is called a "pocket veto."

Andrew Jackson was the first president actively to use the veto power. He believed that the President had an equal right with the legislature and the courts to decide what was constitutional. He also thought that the President, as the only person elected by all the people, could veto measures passed by Congress if he disapproved of them even if they were clearly constitutional. Jackson vetoed more bills than all the Presidents who served before him put together. Among the other active Presidents, such as Lincoln, Theodore Roosevelt, and Wilson, none used the veto power more vigorously than Franklin D. Roosevelt. He vetoed more than 600 bills during his twelve years in office. Congress was able to override his veto only nine times.

Art. I

Section 8. The Congress shall have Power To lay and collect Taxes, Duties, Imposts and Excises, to pay the Debts and provide for the common Defence and general Welfare of the United States; but all Duties, Imposts and Excises shall be uniform throughout the United States;

To borrow Money on the credit of the United States;

To regulate Commerce with foreign Nations, and among the several States, and with the Indian Tribes;

To establish an uniform Rule of Naturalization, and uniform Laws on the subject of Bankruptcies throughout the United States;

To coin Money, regulate the Value thereof, and of foreign Coin, and fix the Standard of Weights and Measures;

To provide for the Punishment of counterfeiting the Securities and current Coin of the United States;

To establish Post Offices and post Roads;

To promote the Progress of Science and useful Arts, by securing for limited Times to Authors and Inventors the exclusive Right to their respective Writings and Discoveries;

To constitute Tribunals inferior to the supreme Court;

To define and punish Piracies and Felonies committed on the high Seas, and Offences against the Law of Nations;

- To declare War, grant Letters of Marque and Reprisal, and make Rules concerning Captures on Land and Water;

ORIGINS

- On letters of marque, see page 59.

AFTERLIFE

One of the most disputed of the enumerated powers has been the right of Congress "to regulate Commerce." Exactly what the Framers meant both by "regulate" and by "Commerce" was unclear. In the case of *Gibbons* v. *Ogden* (1824) the Supreme Court laid down rules about a state establishing a monopoly [8:2]. There Marshall also declared that Congress's power over commerce "may very well be restricted to that commerce which concerns more states than one"—that is, "interstate commerce." But Marshall also saw that commercial transactions taking place entirely within a state could influence commerce among the states. Since the late 1930s the Court has followed that line of reasoning to allow Congress a broad power to regulate commerce.

For example, the court has interpreted the "Commerce" clause in such a way that it not only allows the regulation of railroads, pipelines, and other clearly interstate activities, but also permits minimum wage regulation and prohibitions on child labor. In the case of *NLRB* v. *Jones and Laughlin Corp.* (1937), the Court declared that the Wagner Act [25:4], dealing with the rights of labor to organize and to bargain collectively, was constitutional. Justice Benjamin Cardozo stated that the power to regulate commerce was "as broad as the need that evokes it."

Art. I
Sec. 8

To raise and support Armies, but no Appropriation of Money to that Use shall be for a longer Term than two Years;

To provide and maintain a Navy;

To make Rules for the Government and Regulation of the land and naval Forces;

To provide for calling forth the Militia to execute the Laws of the Union, suppress Insurrections and repel Invasions;

To provide for organizing, arming, and disciplining, the Militia, and for governing such Part of them as may be employed in the Service of the United States, reserving to the States respectively, the Appointment of the Officers, and the Authority of training the Militia according to the discipline prescribed by Congress;

To exercise exclusive Legislation in all Cases whatsoever, over such District (not exceeding ten Miles square) as may, by Cession of Particular States, and the Acceptance of Congress, become the Seat of the Government of the United States, and to exercise like Authority over all Places purchased by the Consent of the Legislature of the State in which the Same shall be, for the Erection of Forts, Magazines, Arsenals, dock-Yards, and other needful Buildings;—And

To make all Laws which shall be necessary and proper for carrying into ■ Execution the foregoing Powers, and all other Powers vested by this Constitution in the Government of the United States, or in any Department or Officer thereof.

■ The meaning of this "necessary and proper" clause (or "elastic clause") was the dividing line between broad and strict constructionists. The first dispute occurred over Alexander Hamilton's proposal for a national bank [6:2]. The Supreme Court under John Marshall in *McCulloch* v. *Maryland* (1819) agreed with the broad constructionists [8:2]. Since the government was granted wide powers "on the due exercise of which the happiness and prosperity of the nation so vitally depends," Marshall ruled, it "must also be entrusted with ample means for their execution."

Art. I

▲ **Section 9.** The Migration or Importation of such Persons as any of the States now existing shall think proper to admit, shall not be prohibited by the Congress prior to the Year one thousand eight hundred and eight, but a Tax or duty may be imposed on such Importation, not exceeding ten dollars for each Person.

ORIGINS

Absolute prohibitions on Congress.
▲ This clause was inserted to prevent Congress from outlawing the foreign slave trade before 1808.

AFTERLIFE

In 1808 Congress did outlaw the foreign slave trade.

Art. I
Sec. 9

The Privilege of the Writ of Habeas Corpus shall not be suspended, unless when in Cases of Rebellion or Invasion the public Safety may require it.
■ No Bill of Attainder or ex post facto Law shall be passed.

ORIGINS

On the writ of *habeas corpus,* see pages 280–281.
■ A *bill of attainder* is a legislative act pronouncing an individual guilty of a crime, usually treason, without a trial. It had been used by kings and queens to get rid of personal or political enemies.

An *ex post facto* law is a law passed after the fact, and was a way of punishing people whom the ruling powers disliked, even though they had not violated any existing law.

AFTERLIFE

During the Civil War, Abraham Lincoln suspended the writ of habeas corpus in certain areas [13:1]. When he suspended it in Maryland, Chief Justice Taney ruled in the *Merryman* case (1861) that only Congress had the right to suspend the writ of habeas corpus. Lincoln did not agree and continued to follow his own interpretation of the Constitution.

Art. I
Sec. 9

No Capitation, or other direct, Tax shall be laid, unless in Proportion to the Census of Enumeration herein before directed to be taken.

AFTERLIFE

In *Pollock* v. *Farmers' Loan and Trust Co.* (1895), the Supreme Court ruled that a federal income tax was unconstitutional because it was a direct tax, but not laid in proportion to the census [18:5]. An income tax was made legal by the 16th Amendment (1913).

No Tax or Duty shall be laid on Articles exported from any State.

No Preference shall be given by any Regulation of Commerce or Revenue to the Ports of one State over those of another; nor shall Vessels bound to, or from, one State, be obliged to enter, clear or pay Duties in another.

No Money shall be drawn from the Treasury, but in Consequence of Appropriations made by Law; and a regular Statement and Account of the Receipts and Expenditures of all public Money shall be published from time to time.

No Title of Nobility shall be granted by the United States: And no Person holding any Office of Profit or Trust under them, shall, without the Consent of the Congress, accept of any present, Emolument, Office, or Title, of any kind whatever, from any King, Prince or foreign State.

Section 10. No State shall enter into any Treaty, Alliance, or Confederation; grant Letters of Marque and Reprisal; coin Money; emit Bills of Credit; make any Thing but gold and silver Coin a Tender in Payment of Debts; pass any Bill of Attainder, ex post facto Law, or Law impairing the Obligation of Contracts, or grant any Title of Nobility.

No State shall, without the Consent of the Congress, lay any Imposts or Duties on Imports or Exports, except what may be absolutely necessary for executing it's inspection Laws: and the net Produce of all Duties and Imposts, laid by any State on Imports or Exports, shall be for the Use of the Treasury of the United States; and all such Laws shall be subject to the Revision and Controul of the Congress.

No State shall, without the Consent of Congress, lay any Duty of Tonnage, keep Troops, or Ships of War in time of Peace, enter into any Agreement or Compact with another State, or with a foreign Power, or engage in War, unless actually invaded, or in such imminent Danger as will not admit of delay.

ARTICLE II

● **Section 1**. The executive Power shall be vested in a President of the United States of America. He shall hold his Office during the term of four Years, and, together with the Vice President, chosen for the same Term, be elected, as follows

ORIGINS

● *"The executive Power."* The Presidency was one of the boldest inventions of the Framers. By creating a strong President, they showed their faith in representative government. They believed that a strong Congress and a strong judiciary would protect the people from any President's misuse of powers. During the Constitutional Convention there was much heated discussion of the problem of the executive. Some, like Roger Sherman of Connecticut, feared a strong President. They

AFTERLIFE

While the President was given many powers in the Constitution, Article II does not say how the President is to use those powers. Whether the office is weak or strong depends on how the President interprets the Constitution and uses the powers it gives.

The powers of the office have grown, especially under such Presidents as Jackson, Lincoln, Theodore Roosevelt, Wilson, and Franklin D. Roosevelt. As Jefferson's purchase of Louisiana showed, even a wanted him to be nothing but a kind of super-policeman, who would see that the laws of Congress were enforced. But Gouverneur Morris wanted a President who would be "the guardian of the people, even of the lower classes, against Legislative tyranny," and many others agreed with him. His views finally prevailed.

During the Convention, the draft of this article was revised again and again. Some members, afraid that a single President might become a despot, argued for a three-man executive, one from each part of the country. Some wanted the President to be chosen by the Congress to be sure that he would enforce the will of Congress. The first draft they agreed on provided for a single executive, but had him chosen by the Congress. He was to be elected for a single term of seven years and could not be reelected.

Gradually in the Convention the movement for a strong, independent President made headway. The ingenious device of an Electoral College allowed him to be elected, indirectly, by "the People." Then the Convention agreed that the President should be elected for four years with no limit on the number of his terms. More and more powers were given to him, including the power to make treaties (with the advice and consent of the Senate). He was given the power to veto acts of Congress. But his veto could be overridden by a two-thirds vote of both houses. And there was insurance against a despot, for the President could be removed from office "on Impeachment for, and Conviction of, Treason, Bribery, or other high Crimes and Misdemeanors."

The Framers were influenced not only by the fearful example of British tyranny over the colonies, but also luckily by the inspiring example of the heroic leader of the Revolution. "Many of the members cast their eyes toward General Washington as President," Pierce Butler of South Carolina who was at the Convention noted, "and shaped their ideas of the Powers to be given a President, by their opinions of his Virtue."

President who considered himself a strict constructionist could act in such a way as to enlarge greatly the powers of the office [7:2].

Art. II
Sec. 1

Each State shall appoint, in such Manner as the Legislature thereof may direct, a number of Electors, equal to the whole Number of Senators and Representatives to which the State may be entitled in the Congress: but no

AMENDMENT [XIV.]

Section 1. All persons born or naturalized in the United States and subject to the jurisdiction thereof, are citizens of the United States and of the State wherein they reside. No State shall make or enforce any law which shall abridge the privileges or immunities of citizens of the United States; or shall any State deprive any person of life, liberty, or property, without due process of law; nor deny to any person within its jurisdiction the equal protection of the laws.

ORIGINS

In the *Dred Scott* case (1857), Chief Justice Taney had stated that blacks were not citizens when the Constitution was adopted and were not covered by its provisions [12:3]. By the 14th Amendment blacks were made citizens, and the privileges and immunities of citizens of the United States were extended to citizens of the states.

ORIGINS *(Section 2, below)*

The fear that southern states would keep blacks from voting prompted this provision. It provides that a state's representation in Congress may be cut if it denies the right to vote to any group of adult male citizens.

AFTERLIFE

The 14th Amendment is the most important amendment added to the Constitution since the Bill of Rights. The key part is Section 1 which contains the potent, but undefined phrases, "due process of law" and "equal protection of the laws."

Often in the 19th and early 20th centuries the Court used the amendment to protect corporations (which it defined as "persons") from state regulation, but in *Munn* v. *Illinois* (1877) and other later decisions the right of states and the federal government to regulate wage rates, hours, and other terms of employment was recognized [18:3].

Over time the amendment has been increasingly interpreted to extend the protection of the Bill of Rights to citizens from actions by the states as well as against the federal government. Although in *Plessy* v. *Ferguson* (1896) [29:3] the Court upheld the "separate but equal" doctrine which legalized racial segregation, that was completely overturned in the series of decisions that culminated in *Brown* v. *Board of Education* (1954) [29:3]. In such cases as *Gideon* v. *Wainwright* (1963), *Escobedo* v. *Illinois* (1964), and *Miranda* v. *Arizona* (1966) [33:7] the Court greatly enlarged the rights of accused persons in state courts.

[XIV] **Section 2.** Representatives shall be apportioned among the several States according to their respective numbers, counting the whole number of persons in each State, excluding Indians not taxed. But when the right to vote at any election for the choice of electors for President and Vice President of the United States, Representatives in Congress, the Executive and Judicial officers of a State, or the members of the Legislature thereof, is denied to any of the male inhabitants of such State, being twenty-one years of age, and citizens of the United States, or in any way abridged, except for participation in rebellion, or other crime, the basis of representation therein shall be reduced in the proportion which the number of such male citizens shall bear to the whole number of male citizens twenty-one years of age in such State.

[XIV]   **Section 3.** No person shall be a Senator or Representative in Congress, or elector of President and Vice President, or hold any office, civil or military, under the United States, or under any State, who, having previously taken an oath, as a member of Congress, or as an officer of the United States, or as a member of any State legislature, or as an executive or judicial officer of any State, to support the Constitution of the United States, shall have engaged in insurrection or rebellion against the same, or given aid or comfort to the enemies thereof. But Congress may by a vote of two-thirds of each House, remove such disability.

[XIV]   ● **Section 4.** The validity of the public debt of the United States, authorized by law, including debts incurred for payment of pensions and bounties for services in suppressing insurrection or rebellion, shall not be questioned. But neither the United States nor any State shall assume or pay any debt or obligation incurred in aid of insurrection or rebellion against the United States, or any claim for the loss or emancipation of any slave; but all such debts, obligations and claims shall be held illegal and void.

[XIV]   **Section 5.** The Congress shall have power to enforce, by appropriate legislation, the provisions of this article.

ORIGINS

This clause barred from federal office any former federal or state official who had served the Confederacy in the Civil War—unless Congress removed the ban by a two-thirds vote of each house.
● This section legalized the federal Civil War debt and voided all debts incurred by the Confederate states.

See p. 307 for further discussion of the origin of the 14th Amendment. Submitted to the states in 1866, ratified in 1868.

AMENDMENT [XV.]

Section 1. The right of citizens of the United States to vote shall not be denied or abridged by the United States or by any State on account of race, color, or previous condition of servitude.

Section 2. The Congress shall have power to enforce this article by appropriate legislation.

ORIGINS

The 15th Amendment attempted to insure that blacks would have the vote. Submitted to the states in 1869, ratified in 1870.

AFTERLIFE

The 15th Amendment did not, as it turned out, prevent blacks from being kept from the polls in the South. In the beginning, the Ku Klux Klan and other groups harassed and intimidated them [14:3]. Then a variety of legal tricks was used to deprive them of the vote [25:2]. It has needed strong federal activity to insure their right to vote (see [29:3, 31:4, 32:1] and especially [33:1] on the Voting Rights Act).

AMENDMENT [XVI.]

The Congress shall have power to lay and collect taxes on incomes, from whatever source derived, without apportionment among the several States, and without regard to any census or enumeration.

ORIGINS

In *Pollock* v. *Farmers' Loan and Trust Co.* (1895), the Supreme Court declared that an income tax was unconstitutional. As a result the 16th Amendment was passed [18:3]. Submitted to the states in 1909, ratified in 1913.

AMENDMENT [XVII.]

The Senate of the United States shall be composed of two Senators from each State, elected by the people thereof, for six years; and each Senator shall have one vote. The electors in each State shall have the qualifications requisite for electors of the most numerous branch of the State legislatures.

When vacancies happen in the representation of any State in the Senate, the executive authority of such State shall issue writs of election to fill such vacancies: *Provided*, That the legislature of any State may empower the executive thereof to make temporary appointments until the people fill the vacancies by election as the legislature may direct.

This amendment shall not be so construed as to affect the election or term of any Senator chosen before it becomes valid as part of the Constitution.

ORIGINS

The Framers of the Constitution distrusted "the people" in the mass and tried to restrict their role to electing only the representatives. The dominance of the electoral college by political parties soon gave the people control of presidential elections. But the Senate continued to be elected by the state legislatures, and since wealthy men were often able to use their cash to buy their elections, the Senate became a "rich man's club." This amendment gave the election of senators to the people [20:2]. Submitted to the states in 1912, ratified in 1913.

AMENDMENT [XVIII.]

Section 1. After one year from the ratification of this article the manufacture, sale, or transportation of intoxicating liquors within, the importation thereof into, or the exportation thereof from the United States and all territory subject to the jurisdiction thereof for beverage purposes is hereby prohibited.

[*XVIII*]   **Sec. 2.** The Congress and the several States shall have concurrent power to enforce this article by appropriate legislation.

Sec. 3. This article shall be inoperative unless it shall have been ratified as an amendment to the Constitution by the legislatures of the several States, as provided in the Constitution, within seven years from the date of the submission hereof to the States by the Congress.

ORIGINS

In the moral fervor of World War I, national prohibition was enacted [22:1]. Submitted to the states in 1917, ratified in 1919.

AFTERLIFE

The "noble experiment" of Prohibition turned out to be a disaster. Millions of Americans became lawbreakers, and criminals took over the liquor trade [22:1].

AMENDMENT [*XIX.*]

The right of citizens of the United States to vote shall not be denied or abridged by the United States or by any State on account of sex.

Congress shall have power to enforce this article by appropriate legislation.

ORIGINS

After World War I, during which the work of women in the war effort had been important and conspicuous, women's suffrage was enacted [22:1]. Submitted to the states in 1919, ratified in 1920.

AFTERLIFE

The suffragists, who worked for the right to vote, had hoped that when women could go to the polls they would improve their chances to be treated equally. But women often failed to vote and did not vote as a bloc [25:3].

AMENDMENT [*XX.*]

Section 1. The terms of the President and Vice President shall end at noon on the 20th day of January, and the terms of Senators and Representatives at noon on the 3d day of January, of the years in which such terms would have ended if this article had not been ratified; and the terms of their successors shall then begin.

Sec. 2. The Congress shall assemble at least once in every year, and such meeting shall begin at noon on the 3d day of January, unless they shall by law appoint a different day.

ORIGINS

The "Lame Duck" Amendment. A lame duck is an official who continues to serve to the end of his term even though he has not been reelected. Prior to this amendment a President leaving office was a "lame duck" for four months, since he left office on March 4. By pushing back the inauguration to January 20, the amendment shortened the time between when a President was elected (in early November) and when he took office. Submitted to the states in 1932, ratified in 1933.

Sec. 3. If, at the time fixed for the beginning of the term of the President, the President elect shall have died, the Vice President elect shall become President. If a President shall not have been chosen before the time fixed for the beginning of his term, or if the President elect shall have failed to qualify, then the Vice President elect shall act as President until a President shall have qualified; and the Congress may by law provide for the case wherein neither a President elect nor a Vice President elect shall have qualified, declaring who shall then act as President, or the manner in which one who is to act shall be selected, and such person shall act accordingly until a President or Vice President shall have qualified.

Sec. 4. The Congress may by law provide for the case of the death of any of the persons from whom the House of Representatives may choose a President whenever the right of choice shall have devolved upon them, and for the case of the death of any of the persons from whom the Senate may choose a Vice President whenever the right of choice shall have devolved upon them.

Sec. 5. Sections 1 and 2 shall take effect on the 15th day of October following the ratification of this article.

Sec. 6. This article shall be inoperative unless it shall have been ratified as an amendment to the Constitution by the legislatures of three-fourths of the several States within seven years from the date of its submission.

AMENDMENT [XXI.]

Section 1. The eighteenth article of amendment to the Constitution of the United States is hereby repealed.

Sec. 2. The transportation or importation into any State, Territory or possession of the United States for delivery or use therein of intoxicating liquors, in violation of the laws thereof, is hereby prohibited.

Sec. 3. This article shall be inoperative unless it shall have been ratified as an amendment to the Constitution by conventions in the several States, as provided in the Constitution, within seven years from the date of the submission hereof to the States by the Congress.

ORIGINS

Disappointment over Prohibition, disgust at the activities of gangsters, and fear that disrespect for this one law would breed disrespect for all laws brought about the repeal of Prohibition in 1933 [24:1]. Submitted to the states in 1933, ratified in 1933.

AMENDMENT [XXII.]

Section 1. No person shall be elected to the office of the President more than twice, and no person who has held the office of President, or acted as President, for more than two years of a term to which some other person was elected President shall be elected to the office of the President more than once. But this Article shall not apply to any person holding the office of President when this Article was proposed by the Congress, and shall not prevent any person who may be holding the office of President, or acting as President, during the term within which this Article becomes operative from holding the office of President or acting as President during the remainder of such term.

Sec. 2. This Article shall be inoperative unless it shall have been ratified as an amendment to the Constitution by the legislatures of three-fourths of the several States within seven years from the date of its submission to the States by the Congress.

ORIGINS

In 1947 for the first time in 14 years, the Republicans controlled both houses of Congress. Since President Washington there had been an unwritten tradition limiting a President to two terms. To strike at the Democrats and at Franklin D. Roosevelt, who had been elected four times, the Republicans proposed and supported this amendment making the tradition into law. [28:2]. Submitted to the states in 1947, ratified in 1951.

AMENDMENT [XXIII.]

Section 1. The District constituting the seat of Government of the United States shall appoint in such manner as the Congress may direct:

A number of electors of President and Vice President equal to the whole number of Senators and Representatives in Congress to which the District would be entitled if it were a State, but in no event more than the least populous State; they shall be in addition to those appointed by the States, but they shall be considered, for the purposes of the election of President and Vice President, to be electors appointed by a State; and they shall meet in the District and perform such duties as provided by the twelfth article of amendment.

Sec. 2. The Congress shall have power to enforce this article by appropriate legislation.

ORIGINS

Since the District of Columbia was not a state, its residents had no vote in presidential elections. This amendment gave them the right to vote. Submitted to the states in 1960, ratified in 1961.

AFTERLIFE

Numerous proposals have been made for an amendment to give the District of Columbia representation in the House and in the Senate, but none has been adopted.

AMENDMENT [XXIV.]

Section 1. The right of citizens of the United States to vote in any primary or other election for President or Vice President, for electors for President or

and a special collection of Grandma Moses paintings. The outdoor *Shelburne Museum* at Shelburne encompasses 18th- and 19th-C. houses as well as a 1903 side-wheel steamboat.

VIRGINIA *Arlington National Cemetery* contains the graves of many famous Americans as well as thousands of war veterans. *Arlington House,* preserved there, was the home of Robert E. Lee. Near Charlottesville is *Monticello,* the elegant and functional house designed by Thomas Jefferson himself. *Jamestown Colonial* ✪ marks the site of the original settlement. Nearby is *Jamestown Festival Park* containing a recreation of the town. At *Mount Vernon* stands the lovely home of George Washington. The *Valentine Museum* in Richmond exhibits the history of the city and the state. *Williamsburg* is the grand restoration of the colonial capital with over 100 historic buildings—showing the ways of governing, living, and worshiping, with craftsmen working as they did in colonial days.

WASHINGTON The *Museum of History and Industry,* Seattle, displays Indian artifacts and relics of Seattle's early history. *Point Defiance Park,* Tacoma, holds a replica of the first fort built by the Hudson's Bay Company on the Pacific Coast (1833), an old logging camp, and the 1865 Job Carr house. At Walla Walla are the *Whitman*

Mission Ⓝ, which contains the partially restored mission site, and *Fort Walla Walla Museum,* an 1856 army post.

WEST VIRGINIA *Fort New Salem,* Salem, reconstructs a settlement founded in 1792. *Harpers Ferry* ⒽΗ preserves much of the 19th-C. town where John Brown led his raid in 1859.

WISCONSIN *Stonefield,* at Cassfield, holds a 19th-C. frontier village, the home of a gentleman farmer, and a museum on early farming. In Greenbush, *Old Wade House* Ⓠ has a restored stagecoach inn as well as other buildings and a carriage museum.

WYOMING At Cody, the *Whitney Gallery of Western Art* has paintings and sculptures by Bierstadt, Catlin, Remington, and Russell, among others. The *Grand Encampment Museum,* Encampment, is a recreation of a pioneer mining town. On the old Oregon Trail are *Fort Bridger* Ⓢ, a restoration of the fort and trading post established by mountain man Jim Bridger in 1843, and *Fort Laramie* Ⓝ, where many of the original buildings show what life was like at a western army post.

PUERTO RICO *San Juan* Ⓝ contains the Spanish fortresses *Castillo El Morro* and *Castillo San Cristóbal, San Juan Gate,* a portion of the old city wall, as well as *La Fortaleza,* the governor's palace which was built in the 1530s as a fortress.

A Note on American Pictorial Art

The illustrations in this book not only show the American past. They are selected especially to introduce you to American art. In every chapter, the paintings, drawings, engravings, lithographs, photographs, and objects shown come from the very period described in that chapter. They are authentic witnesses of our art—and of our history. To help you understand and enjoy the pictures in this book and to encourage you to visit your neighboring art galleries, here is a thumbnail history of American art.

Most early settlers of our country had little time for the fine arts. Building villages and clearing the wilderness kept them busy enough. But as the 17th century advanced, some of these new Americans had the leisure to enjoy the arts, and the money to commission a portrait. Of course they could not be photographed, for that invention was still two centuries in the future!

Portraits were the main form of painting in the colonial era. Over the years, portrait painters became ever more skillful. Among the best in the 18th century were John Smibert, an English immigrant, Robert Feke, Joseph Badger, John Singleton Copley, Charles Willson Peale, Ralph Earl, Gilbert Stuart, and Benjamin West. Copley

and West left America and went to England, where they painted statesmen and wealthy aristocrats and won international reputations.

Benjamin West was one of the earliest American painters to focus on historical events, like the "Death of General Wolfe" (1771). Following his example, John Trumbull painted a whole series on the American Revolution. Citizens sometimes commissioned a view of their harbor or their city for proud display in the town hall.

In the 19th century, American artists became increasingly aware of the peculiar charms of America. Between 1829 and 1838, George Catlin, fascinated by the handsome Indians, recorded their colorful costumes and dances, and painted 600 Indian portraits. The skilled brushes of Karl Bodmer, Alfred Jacob Miller, and others depicted the Native Americans at home, on the hunt, and at war. John James Audubon's stunning 4-volume *Birds of America* (1827-1838, called "the elephant folio" because of its enormous size) still helps us identify our splendid American birds.

Meanwhile some artists were captivated by the romantic beauty of the American wilderness. Thomas Cole, Asher B. Durand, and other brilliant landscape painters came to be called "The Hudson River School." They were followed by Thomas Moran and Thomas Hill, both born in England, and Albert Bierstadt, a German—who traveled all over the West. Their gigantic canvases capture the wild continent which was everywhere then, but which now we must seek out in specially preserved wilderness areas.

After the Civil War, more American painters began to look to Europe, especially to the French Impressionists, for new ways of using color. Childe Hassam, Mary Cassatt, and others imported their techniques. Still Winslow Homer, Thomas Eakins, and Albert Pinkham Ryder resisted European influences and went their own American ways.

In the 20th century American painting has run the gamut from the photograph-like work of Andrew Wyeth and the pop art of Andy Warhol to the abstract expressionism of Willem de Kooning and Jackson Pollock, with just about every variation in between. These range from the seamy realism of Edward Hopper and the regionalism of Thomas Hart Benton or Grant Wood to the elegant abstractions of Georgia O'Keeffe.

We should not forget, in even the briefest survey, the so-called "primitives." These were the amateur artists who lacked formal training. For this very reason they gave their work a naive charm and offered a fresh insight into the American past. Most of their names remain unknown. Two whose names do survive are Horace Pickens and Grandma Moses.

Painting, of course, is only one kind of pictorial art. In the days before photography, the engraving and (beginning about 1800) the lithograph provided inexpensive copies of political cartoons, propaganda and advertising messages, romantic landscapes, battle scenes, and likenesses of George Washington for the home, the office, or the classroom. Nathaniel Currier and James M. Ives, for much of the 19th century, sold thousands of copies of colorful lithographs which recapture for us the pleasures of ice-skating, horse-racing, and steamboat-riding. Their works became less popular with the rise of photography.

The political cartoon has flourished ever since colonial days. German-born Thomas Nast and Austrian-born Joseph Keppler brought here their sharp eye for caricature. Their hard-hitting attacks made corrupt politicians miserable. Other cartoonists, over the years, have used a variety of styles to deliver a political or moral message—or just to poke fun at us. Among the more influential have been Daniel Fitzpatrick, especially in the 1930s and 1940s, Bill Mauldin (famous for his "G.I. Joe") beginning in World War II, and Herblock (Herbert Block), whose caricatures of Joseph McCarthy and Richard Nixon became classics.

Photography was introduced into the United States with an assist from the versatile painter-inventor Samuel F. B. Morse. In 1840 he reported from France on the daguerreotype process by which (in half an hour!) a photographic image could be captured on silver-plated copper. Mathew Brady, the great Civil War photographer, first worked with daguerreotypes, but then learned the more flexible (but terribly complicated) wet-plate process. Brady and his team, wandering about with their "what-is-it" buggy filled with chemicals, made the first photographic record of warfare. And they risked their lives, too, because mystified soldiers in the field thought the camera was a new kind of artillery.

Not until the 1880s with easy-to-use dry and flexible film invented by George Eastman, and his simple box camera, could photography go everywhere. The Danish-born journalist-reformer Jacob Riis took his camera into alleys and tenements and then shocked Americans by his pictures of big-city slums. In the 1930s the power of the camera worked again—now through the photographs of the impoverished and the unemployed taken by Ben Shahn, Walker Evans, Dorothea Lange, and others under the auspices of the Farm Security Administration. World War II was brought home to the people of the United States by daring photographers like Robert Capa and Margaret Bourke-White. Capa, the first American to be killed in Vietnam, lost his life to a land mine in 1954 while photographing the war.

Looking at pictures—paintings, drawings, photographs, even posters, advertisements and other commercial art—like reading or visiting museums and historic places, is a happy way of studying our past. We hope that the illustrations in this book and this brief note on American art will entice you to seek out and enjoy American artists, cartoonists, and photographers to open up vistas that you cannot find in words.

Presidents and Vice-Presidents of the United States

President	Years in office	Party	Born	Died	State Born / Home	Vice-President
1. George Washington	1789–1797		1732	1799	Virginia	John Adams
2 John Adams	1797–1801	Federalist	1735	1826	Massachusetts	Thomas Jefferson
3 Thomas Jefferson	1801–1809	Republican	1743	1826	Virginia	Aaron Burr George Clinton
4 James Madison	1809–1817	Republican	1751	1836	Virginia	George Clinton Elbridge Gerry
5 James Monroe	1817–1825	Republican	1758	1831	Virginia	Daniel D. Tompkins
6 John Quincy Adams	1825–1829	Nat. Rep.	1767	1848	Massachusetts	John C. Calhoun
7 Andrew Jackson	1829–1837	Democratic	1767	1845	S.C. / Tenn.	John C. Calhoun Martin Van Buren
8 Martin Van Buren	1837–1841	Democratic	1782	1862	New York	Richard M. Johnson
9 William Henry Harrison	Mar. 1841	Whig	1773	1841	Va. / Ohio	John Tyler
10 John Tyler	1841–1845	Whig	1790	1862	Virginia	
11 James K. Polk	1845–1849	Democratic	1795	1849	N.C. / Tenn.	George M. Dallas
12 Zachary Taylor	1849–1850	Whig	1784	1850	Va. / La.	Millard Fillmore
13 Millard Fillmore	1850–1853	Whig	1800	1874	New York	
14 Franklin Pierce	1853–1857	Democratic	1804	1869	New Hampshire	William R. D. King
15 James Buchanan	1857–1861	Democratic	1791	1868	Pennsylvania	John C. Breckinridge
16 Abraham Lincoln	1861–1865	Republican	1809	1865	Ky. / Ill.	Hannibal Hamlin Andrew Johnson
17 Andrew Johnson	1865–1869	Republican	1808	1875	N.C. / Tenn.	
18 Ulysses S. Grant	1869–1877	Republican	1822	1885	Ohio / Ill.	Schuyler Colfax Henry Wilson
19 Rutherford B. Hayes	1877–1881	Repubican	1822	1893	Ohio	William A. Wheeler
20 James A. Garfield	1881	Republican	1831	1881	Ohio	Chester A. Arthur
21 Chester A. Arthur	1881–1885	Republican	1830	1886	Vt. / N.Y.	
22 Grover Cleveland	1885–1889	Democratic	1837	1908	N.J. / N.Y.	Thomas A. Hendricks
23 Benjamin Harrison	1889–1893	Republican	1833	1901	Ohio / Ind.	Levi P. Morton
24 Grover Cleveland	1893–1897	Democratic	1837	1908	N.J. / N.Y.	Adlai E. Stevenson
25 William McKinley	1897–1901	Republican	1843	1901	Ohio	Garret A. Hobart Theodore Roosevelt
26 Theodore Roosevelt	1901–1909	Republican	1858	1919	New York	Charles W. Fairbanks
27 William Howard Taft	1909–1913	Republican	1857	1930	Ohio	James S. Sherman
28 Woodrow Wilson	1913–1921	Democratic	1856	1924	Va. / N.J.	Thomas R. Marshall
29 Warren G. Harding	1921–1923	Republican	1865	1923	Ohio	Calvin Coolidge
30 Calvin Coolidge	1923–1929	Republican	1872	1933	Vt. / Mass.	Charles G. Dawes
31 Herbert C. Hoover	1929–1933	Republican	1874	1964	Iowa / Cal.	Charles Curtis
32 Franklin D. Roosevelt	1933–1945	Democratic	1882	1945	New York	John N. Garner Henry A. Wallace Harry S. Truman
33 Harry S. Truman	1945–1953	Democratic	1884	1972	Missouri	Alben W. Barkley
34 Dwight D. Eisenhower	1953–1961	Republican	1890	1969	Tex. / N.Y., Pa.	Richard M. Nixon
35 John F. Kennedy	1961–1963	Democratic	1917	1963	Massachusetts	Lyndon B. Johnson
36 Lyndon B. Johnson	1963–1969	Democratic	1908	1973	Texas	Hubert H. Humphrey
37 Richard M. Nixon	1969–1974	Republican	1913		Ca. / N.Y., Cal.	Spiro T. Agnew Gerald R. Ford
38 Gerald R. Ford	1974–1977	Republican	1913		Neb. / Mich.	Nelson A. Rockefeller
39 Jimmy (James Earl) Carter	1977–1981	Democratic	1924		Georgia	Walter F. Mondale
40 Ronald Reagan	1981–	Republican	1911		Ill. / Cal.	George Bush

Some Facts about Our States

	State	Date of admission	Capital	Area (sq. mi.)	Land area	Population (1979 est.)	Density[1]	Cities 100,000+	Population in SMSAs[2]
1	Delaware	1787	Dover	2,057	1,982	582,000	293	—	69%
2	Pennsylvania	1787	Harrisburg	45,333	44,966	11,731,000	261	4	80
3	New Jersey	1787	Trenton	7,836	7,521	7,332,000	975	6	92
4	Georgia	1788	Atlanta	58,876	58,073	5,118,000	88	4	57
5	Connecticut	1788	Hartford	5,009	4,862	3,115,000	641	5	88
6	Massachusetts	1788	Boston	8,257	7,826	5,769,000	737	4	86
7	Maryland	1788	Annapolis	10,577	9,891	4,149,000	419	1	85
8	South Carolina	1788	Columbia	31,055	30,255	2,932,000	97	1	47
9	New Hampshire	1788	Concord	9,304	9,027	887,000	98	—	36
10	Virginia	1788	Richmond	40,817	39,780	5,197,000	131	7	65
11	New York	1788	Albany	49,576	47,831	17,649,000	369	6	88
12	North Carolina	1789	Raleigh	52,586	48,798	5,606,000	115	4	45
13	Rhode Island	1790	Providence	1,214	1,049	929,000	886	1	92
14	Vermont	1791	Montpelier	9,609	9,267	493,000	53	—	0
15	Kentucky	1792	Frankfort	40,395	39,650	3,527,000	89	2	45
16	Tennessee	1796	Nashville	42,244	41,328	4,380,000	106	4	63
17	Ohio	1803	Columbus	41,222	40,975	10,731,000	262	8	80
18	Louisiana	1812	Baton Rouge	48,523	44,930	4,026,000	90	3	64
19	Indiana	1816	Indianapolis	36,291	36,097	5,400,000	150	6	67
20	Mississippi	1817	Jackson	47,716	47,296	2,406,000	51	1	27
21	Illinois	1818	Springfield	56,400	55,748	11,230,000	201	3	81
22	Alabama	1819	Montgomery	51,609	50,708	3,769,000	74	4	62
23	Maine	1820	Augusta	33,215	30,920	1,097,000	35	—	23
24	Missouri	1821	Jefferson City	69,686	68,995	4,868,000	71	4	63
25	Arkansas	1836	Little Rock	53,104	51,945	2,180,000	42	1	39
26	Michigan	1837	Lansing	58,216	56,817	9,208,000	162	7	81
27	Florida	1845	Tallahassee	58,560	54,090	8,860,000	164	8	86
28	Texas	1845	Austin	267,338	262,134	13,385,000	51	10	80
29	Iowa	1846	Des Moines	56,290	55,941	2,903,000	52	2	38
30	Wisconsin	1848	Madison	56,154	54,464	4,720,000	87	2	60
31	California	1850	Sacramento	158,693	156,361	22,696,000	145	20	92
32	Minnesota	1858	St. Paul	84,068	79,289	4,060,000	51	2	64
33	Oregon	1859	Salem	96,981	96,184	2,527,000	26	1	59
34	Kansas	1861	Topeka	82,264	81,787	2,369,000	29	3	45
35	West Virginia	1863	Charleston	24,181	24,070	1,878,000	78	—	36
36	Nevada	1864	Carson City	110,540	109,889	702,000	6	1	81
37	Nebraska	1867	Lincoln	77,227	76,483	1,574,000	21	2	45
38	Colorado	1876	Denver	104,247	103,766	2,772,000	27	2	81
39	North Dakota	1889	Bismarck	70,665	69,273	657,000	9	—	23
40	South Dakota	1889	Pierre	77,047	75,955	689,000	9	—	15
41	Montana	1889	Helena	147,138	145,587	786,000	5	—	25
42	Washington	1889	Olympia	68,192	66,570	3,926,000	59	3	71
43	Idaho	1890	Boise	83,577	82,677	905,000	11	—	17
44	Wyoming	1890	Cheyenne	97,914	97,203	450,000	5	—	0
45	Utah	1896	Salt Lake City	84,916	82,096	1,367,000	17	1	78
46	Oklahoma	1907	Oklahoma City	69,919	68,782	2,892,000	42	2	56
47	New Mexico	1912	Santa Fe	121,666	121,412	1,241,000	10	1	34
48	Arizona	1912	Phoenix	113,909	113,417	2,450,000	22	2	75
49	Alaska	1959	Juneau	589,757	569,600	406,000	1	1	44
50	Hawaii	1959	Honolulu	6,450	6,425	915,000	142	1	80
	Dist. of Columbia		Washington	67	61	656,000	10,754	1	100
	Puerto Rico		San Juan	3,435	3,421	3,400,000	994		
	Guam		Agana		209	107,000	512		
	American Samoa		Fagotogo		76	32,000	421		
	Virgin Islands		Charlotte Amalie		132	100,000	758		

[1]Density: persons per square miles of land area

[2]Percent of population living in metropolitan areas (SMSAs)

Federal Election Campaign-funding Reform Act, 723
Federal Emergency Relief Act, (1933), 512, 527
Federal Farm Board, 492
Federal Farm Loan Act, 437
Federal Hall, *il.*, 119, 121
Federal Housing Administration (FHA), 510
Federal Reserve Act of 1913, 292, 435–436; Great Depression and, 492
Federal Reserve banks, 435–436, 492
Federal Reserve Board, 480, 508, 520
Federal Reserve notes, 435–436
Federal Trade Commission (FTC), 436, 480
Federal Writers' Project, 531
Federalist Papers, The, 111
Federalist party, 124, 126–127, 129–130, 133–134; protests Louisiana Purchase, 149–150; and "midnight judges," 151–152; and Hartford Convention, 167–168; death of, 168, 171
Federalists (supporters of Constitution), 109–111
Federation of Organized Trades and Labor Unions, 362
Feminine Mystique, The (Friedan), 707
Ferdinand, king of Spain, 16
Ferguson, Miriam A. ("Ma"), 479
Fermi, Enrico, 575
Ferrer, José, 713
Fetterman, W. J., 323
Field, Cyrus W., 212; song dedicated to, *il.*, 213
Fifteenth Amendment, 310, 312, 319, 528
Figuero, José, 713
Fiji Islands, 562, 563
Filibuster, 672; of electoral reform bill, 392; of civil rights bills, 590, 615, 662
Filipinos in America, 525, 711
Fillmore, Millard, 255, 256, 262–263; and expansion, 404
Financier, The (Dreiser), 427
Finland: immigrants from, 47, 54; and World War I debt, 476, 496; and Hitler-Stalin pact, 543; in World War II, 545
Finney, Charles Grandison, 229
Fireside chats, by F. D. Roosevelt, 519, 544
Firestone Rubber Company, 534
First Amendment, 635; 665; and religious exercises, 681
First Continental Congress, 76
Fishing, 23, 151; by colonial New Englanders, 52–54; and Treaty of Paris, 90
Fisk University, 306
Fitch, John, 116
Fitzgerald, F. Scott, 473
Five Power Treaty, 475
Flag, American, adopted, 178
"Flexible response," 648
Florence, Italy, 23
Florida, 127; explorations of, 19, 21; settlement of, 27; in Peace of Paris, 64; and War of 1812, 160, 161, 164; ceded by Spain, 172; Indian war in, 193; secession of, 268; Reconstruction government in, 311, 316, 317; Ku Klux Klan in, 312; in 1876 election, 315; offshore oil, 608; cities in, 627; Cubans in, 703
Flying Cloud (ship), 251
"Flying fortresses," 547, 565; *photo*, 566
Following the Color Line (Baker), 428
Food Administration, 459; *il.*, 459
Food stamps, 663
Foote, A. H., 284, 286
Foraker Act, 416
Forbes, Charles R., 476
Forbestown, California, *painting*, 330
"Force Bill," 196
Ford, Gerald R.: becomes Vice-President, 692; becomes President, 695; career, 720–

721; as President, 720–724, 731, 733–735; pardons Nixon, 722; in 1976 election, 724–726
Ford, Henry, 484, 525, 634; World War I and, 445; "Peace Ship," *photo*, 445; assembly line, *il.*, 484
Fordney-McCumber tariff, 475
Foreign affairs, *see* Presidents by name
Foreign aid: under Truman, 584–587, 592, 600; to France in Indochina, 606; Eisenhower Doctrine, 618; Alliance for Progress, 648–649; Peace Corps, 649
Forest Service, established, 424
Forests, national, 424, 432
Formosa, *see* Taiwan
Formosa Strait, 605, 619
Fort Jackson, Treaty of, 164
Fort Monmouth, New Jersey, 610
Fort Myers, Florida, 21
Fort Washington, New York, Battle of, 88
Fort Washington (Cincinnati), Ohio, settled, 103
Fort Wayne, Indiana, 125
Forts: Dearborn, 162; Donelson, 284–285; Duquesne, 62–63, 64; Frontenac, 64; Frye, 103; Harmar, 103; Henry, 284–285; Leavenworth, 249; McHenry, 164; Mandan, 149; at Mobile, 61; Moultrie, 193; at Natchez, 61; Pitt, 64, 68; Sumter, 269, 274, 304; Ticonderoga, 78, 79; western, 322
Forty-ninth parallel, in Rush-Bagot Agreement, 172
Foster, John, *woodcut*, 41
Four Freedoms, 550
Four Power Treaty, 475
Fourdrinier, Pierre, *engraving*, 45
Fourteen Points, 451, 461–463
Fourteenth Amendment, 307, 308, 312, 319; and wage laws, 517; segregation and, 612; women's rights and, 709
Fox Indians, 193
France: explorations and claims by, 22–24; North American settlements, 42, *map*, 63; French and Indian War, 61–64; and Peace of Paris, 64–65, *map*, 69; aids American Revolution, 79, 86, 88, 91, 118, 120; and Treaty of Paris, 90; western land claims and, 99; troubles with, in 1790s, 125–127, 131–133; Louisiana Purchase, 145–146; Napoleonic Europe, *map*, 155; Jefferson's embargo, 154–157, Nonintercourse Act, 159–160; immigrants from, 221; Texas independence and, 246; gold rush and, 253; Napoleon III and Mexico, 406–407; in Far East, 416, *map*, 417; Panama Canal and, 438–439; and Algeciras Conference, 440; and World War I, 444–445, 448, 451–454; *maps*, 444, 452, 455; Versailles Treaty and, 462–464, *map*, 462; troops to Russia, 469; war debts, 476; and naval treaties, 475, 496–497; and Kellogg-Briand Pact, 496; Munich Pact and, 542; in World War II, 543, 545, 546, 550, 552, 560, 564, 566–569, *maps*, 551, 571; in UN, 583; and Marshall Plan, 586, 587; as postwar ally, 591–592; war in Indochina, 605–606; in SEATO, 607; in Suez War, 615–616; Kennedy and, 652
Francis Ferdinand, Archduke, 444
Francis I of France, 22, 23
Franciscans, in California, 241
Franco, Francisco, 540
Frankenthaler, Helen, 636; *painting*, 636
Frankfurter, Felix, 507
Franklin, Benjamin, 57, 65; warns British, 63, 71–72; attempts colonial union, 62, 76; in American Revolution, 80, 90, 96, 131; at Constitutional Convention, 107; on postage stamp, 212; quoted, 131; *il.*, 81, 91
Franklin, William Temple, *il.*, 91

Freake family, *portrait*, 55
Fredericksburg, Virginia, 290; fighting at, *il.*, 276
Free enterprise system, World War I limits, 455. *See also* Business and industry; Capitalism
"Free silver" issue, 386, 392–393; and gold crisis 397; Populists and, 396; and 1896 election, 399–401; and 1900 election, 414
Free-Soil party, 253, 264; organized in Massachusetts, *il.*, 254; attacked in Kansas, *il.*, 261
Free Speech Movement, 671
Freedmen's Bureau, 306, 307
Freedom: protected by state constitutions, 95; Bill of Rights, 109–111; equality and, 698–700. *See also* Civil rights and liberties
Freedom of Information Act, 723
Freedom marchers and riders, 655, 656
Freedom train, *il.*, 237
Freeport, Illinois, 265
"Freeport Doctrine," 265
Frémont, John C., 249, 262–263, 281
French-Canadians, 162
French and Indian War, 47, 61–64
French Resistance in World War II, 567, 568
French Revolution, 139, 145, 221; *il.*, 125, 126
French West Indies, 68, 70
Friedan, Betty, 707, 708
Frolic (ship), 162
From Here to Eternity (Jones), 638
Frontier, 320–341; in 1775, *map*, 49; Indians on, 320–321; opportunity on, 320, 327–330; mining on, 327–330, *map*, 329; law on, 330; cattle raising, 330–335; farming on, 335–340; vanishing western, *map*, 339; urbanization on, 371
Frost, Robert, 644
Fuchs, Klaus, 596, 597
Fugitive Slave Act, 254–256, 260; rally opposing, *il.*, 257
Fulbright, J. William, 674
Fuller, Margaret, 231
Fulton, Robert, 207; and *Gibbons* v. *Ogden*, 173
Fulton, Missouri, 584
"Fundamental Orders" of Connecticut, 41
Future, mysterious, 741–742

G

Gaddis, John, *paintings*, 293
Gadsden, James, 258
Gadsden Purchase, 249, 258
"Gag rule," 244
Gagarin, Yuri, 650
Galena, Illinois, 284
Gallatin, Albert, 143, 153; quoted, 157
Gallipolis, Ohio, 103
Galloway, Joseph, 76
Gallup poll, 681
Galveston, Texas, 425
Gandhi, Mahatma, 231
Garden cities, 383
Garden Cities of Tomorrow (Howard), 383
Garfield, James A., 313, 388; campaign ribbon, *il.*, 388
Garner, John Nance, 499, 517; *photo*, 500
Garrison, William Lloyd, 236–237, 268, 289
Gates, Horatio, 87
Gauge, standard, of railroad track, 347–348
"Geese in Flight," *painting*, 202–203
Geiger counters, 575
General Accounting Office, 475
General Assembly, UN, 582, 599
General Electric Company, 634; and labor unions, 534
General Motors Corporation, 491, 634; and labor unions, 534; sit-down strike, *photo*, 535
Genêt, "Citizen" Edmond, 126–127

Turner, Frederick Jackson, 371
Turner, Nat, 194, 226, 528
Turnpikes, 204–206. *See also* Roads and highways
Tuskegee Institute, 377–378; *photo*, 377
Tutuila, Samoa, 407
Twain, Mark, 329, 330, 414
Tweed, William M., 311
Tweed Ring, 314–315; "Boss" Tweed, *cartoon*, 316
Twelfth Amendment, 134
Twentieth Amendment, 507
Twenty-fifth Amendment, 692, 721
Twenty-first Amendment, 509
Twenty-fourth Amendment, 654, 701
Twenty-second Amendment, 589
Twenty-sixth Amendment, 690
Two Years Before the Mast (Dana), 241
Tydings-McDuffie Act, 541, 574
Tyler, John B., 200, 245, 246; and China, 404
Typographical Union, 534

U-2 plane, 607–608, 620, 650
Ukraine, 568
"Ultra" decoder, 548, 560
Un-American Activities Committee, House (HUAC), 595, 682
Uncle Tom's Cabin (Stowe), 257–258, 325
Underdeveloped nations, 737; Peace Corps in, 649
Underground Railroad, 256; freedom train, *il.*, 237
Underwood, Oscar, 432, 434–435
Underwood-Simmons Bill, 435
Unemployment: Georgia colony and, 45; and Panic of 1873, 314; during 1930s, 493–495, 498, 520–521; and the New Deal, 511–513, 535; drops in World War II, 554; automation and, 633, 634; distressed area aid and, 654. *See also* Depression
Unemployment insurance, 516, 654
"Uniformity system," 218
Union Pacific Railroad, 332; and Crédit Mobilier scandal, 313
Union party: in 1864 election, 304; in 1936 election, 518–519
Union of Russian Workers, 470
Union shop, 589
Union of Soviet Socialist Republics, *see* Soviet Union
Unions, labor: rise of, 361–362; and Sherman Antitrust Act, 398; strikes by, 360–361, 385, 397, 398, 420–421, 469, 534, 588; AF of L founded, 362; in World War I, 460; after World War I, 469; New Deal and, 511–512, 515, 516–517, 533–535; Wagner Act and, 516–517; CIO founded, 534–535; Truman and, 588, 589; Taft-Hartley Act, 589; for farm workers, 710–711. *See also* Labor *and unions by name*
United Auto Workers, sit-down strike, *photo*, 535
United Farm Workers Organizing Committee, 711
United Mine Workers, 421, 533
United Nations: discussed at Yalta, 570; organization and functions, 583–584; and Korean armistice, 605; new African states in, 612; and Suez War, 616; missile crisis and, 651; equality in, 718
United Nations Relief and Rehabilitation Administration (UNRRA), 583
United States Housing Authority, 510
United States Steel Corporation, 350, 424–425, 654; and Taft, 431; labor strike against, 469; and stock market crash, 491; and labor unions, 534
Universities, *see* Colleges and universities

Unitarian church, 229
Unsafe at Any Speed (Nader), 666–667
Urban Development Act of 1965, 665
Urban renewal, 654, 665
Urbanization, 222, 365–384; in the West, 333–334; and suburbs, 382–384, 625, 627; city government reform, 425; urban riots in 1919, 469; black migration of 1940s, 556. *See also* Cities and towns
Up from Slavery (Washington), 377
Utah: and Mormons, 242–243, 249, 320, 339; and women's suffrage, 375, 706
Ute Indians, 239

V-1 flying bombs, 566
V-2 rockets, 566, 617
Vachon, John, *photo*, 521
Vagrancy law, in "Black Codes," 304–305
Vallard, Nicolas, map by, *il.*, 24
Valley Forge, Pennsylvania, 86, 88
Valparaiso, Chile, 407
Van Buren, Martin, 189, 245, 246, 253; Presidency of, 198–199; and 1840 election, 199–200; *il.*, 197, 199, 200
Vandalia, Illinois, 204
Vanguard rocket, 617
Vanzetti, Bartolomeo, 471; *il.*, 472
Vasco da Gama, 16
Vassar, Matthew, 377
Vassar College, 235, 377
Vaux, Calvert, 383
Vaux, France, in World War I, 454
V-E (Victory in Europe) Day, 572
Venezuela, 620; boundary dispute, 409–410; OPEC and, 724
Venice, Italy, 13; life in, *il.*, 12
Veracruz, Mexico, 441
Verdun, France, in World War I, *il.*, 454
Vergennes, quoted, 90
Vermont, 157, 162, 260
Verrazano, Giovanni da, 22–23; *il.*, 23
Versailles, Treaty of, 461–465, 474, 476; Hitler and, 538; *map*, 462
Vesey, Denmark, 191, 194, 528
Vespucci, Amerigo, 15; *il.*, 14
Veterans: pension vetoes by Cleveland, 390; and bonus bill, 476; women as, 555; G.I. Bill, 587; picket coal mine, *photo*, 588; education for, 635
Veto, in United Nations, 583, 584, 598
Vichy French, 560
Vicksburg, Mississippi, 286, 290, 294; school for freed slaves, *il.*, 307
Vienna, Austria, 1961 conference, 647
Viet Cong, 653, 673, 675. *See also* Vietnam War
Viet Minh, 606, 653
Vietnam: war with France, 606; SEATO and, 607; *map*, 672. *See also* Vietnam War
Vietnam War: Kennedy and, 653; *map*, 672; L. B. Johnson and, 672–677; reasons for U.S. in, 673; refugees, *photo*, 673; demonstrations against, *photo*, 675; and 1968 election, 679; Nixon and, 683, 685; ended, 686, 734–735; Pentagon Papers and, 688; clemency program, 722; fall of South Vietnam, *photo*, 735
Vikings, *see* Norsemen
Villa, Pancho, 441
Vincennes, Indiana, 87, 161; French fort at, 61
Vineyard Sound, 23
Virgin Islands, 105, 406
Virginia, 102; Indians in, 10; settlement of, 32–35, 37–38; colonial life, 48, 50–51, 56; and Proclamation Line of 1763, 69; and American Revolution, 76, 87–88, 96; western land claims, 99; and Annapolis meeting, 105; and Constitution, 106, 107,

110–111; national capital and, 121–122; Virginia Resolutions, 133; Virginia dynasty, 138, 167–168, 171; suffrage in, 185; slave rebellion in, 194; abolition debated in, 236; and John Brown, 266; in Civil War, 282, 286, 288, 295–296, 297–298; Reconstruction in, 311; school integration in, 613; aristocracy in, 700
Virginia (ship), 286
Virginia City, Nevada, 326, 327
Virginia Company, 34–35, 37
Virginia and Kentucky Resolutions, 133, 191–192
Virginia Plan, 107
Visscher, John, *engraving* by, 34
Visual pollution, 666
Vittoria (ship), 18
Volunteers in Service to America (VISTA), 662
Von Arnim, General, 564
Von Braun, Wernher, 617
Von Neumann, John, 633
Voting rights: denied Margret Brent in Maryland colony, 54; in colonial Virginia, 138; broadened, 184–185; for blacks, 185, 187, 304, 317, 528, 612, 615; and 14th and 15th amendments, 307; and Radical Republicans, 308; for women, 185, 187, 374–375, 427, 473, 531, 706, 709; and electoral reform bill, 392; and Civil Rights Act of 1964, 662; black revolt and, 668–669
Voting Rights Act of 1965, 668–669, 701
Voting turnout: of blacks, 627; in 1972 election, 690

W-abash River, 125
WACS (Women's Army Corps), 555
Wade-Davis bill, 302
Wage-price controls and guidelines, 558, 654, 667, 687, 729
Wages and salaries: increases in World War I, 460; as a cause of Great Depression, 491; World War II freeze, 558; minimum, 517, 521, 595, 610, 654, 729; for women, 707. *See also* Unions, labor
Wagner, Robert, 516; *photo*, 506
Wagner Act, 516, 520, 533
Wagner-Steagall Act, 510
Wagon trains, 241, 242; *il.*, 242
Wake Island, 562
Walden Pond, 231
Waldseemüller, Martin, 15; *map by il.*, 15
Wall Street, 448; and Panic of 1907, 424–425; and reforms under Wilson, 435; 1929 stock market boom and crash, 488–491. *See also* Stock market
Wall Street Journal, 620
Walla Walla, Washington, 239
Wallace, George C., 656, 668, 680, 681, 689
Wallace, Henry A., 507, 511, 521, 549, 586, 594
Wallace, Henry C., 474
Walls, Josiah T., *il.*, 311
Waltham, Massachusetts, 215–217
Wanghia, Treaty of, 404
War, Department of, 119
War bonds (war loans), 459, 558; *il.*, 458
War crimes trials, 591
War debts, European, after World War I, 476
War Hawks, 160
War Industries Board, 459–460, 511
War of 1812, 143, 159–167, 192, 204, 286; results of, 169; effect on industry, 215; and Oregon, 239; *map*, 165
War on Poverty, 662, 665; Kennedy and, 655
War referendum, 541
War resistance, during World War I, 461
Ward, Montgomery, 353–355; *il.*, 354

Ward, Robert DeCourcy, 371
Warfare: European and American compared, 82–83; changes during Civil War, 275–277; in World War I, 446–448, 451; in World War II, 545–546, 547–548
Warhol, Andy, 638
Warm Springs, Georgia, 572
Warren, Charles, 371
Warren, Earl, 593, 657, 680, 687
Warren, Mercy Otis, *needlepoint* by, 57
Warren Commission, 657
Warsaw, Poland, 568
Washington, Booker T., 377–378, 528
Washington, George, 54, 138, 295; in French and Indian War, 62, 116; in Revolution, 77, 79, 83–84, 86, 87–88, 89, 90, 91, 96; Constitution and, 107, 110, 111; Presidency of, 114, 118–129; and naval war with France, 132; Jefferson contrasted with, 140, 142; as national symbol, 178, 179; on postage stamp, 212; *portrait*, 118; Mt. Vernon, *il.*, 117
Washington, Martha, 288
Washington (state), 320, 340. *See also* Oregon
Washington, D.C.: site picked, 121–122; in 1801, 139–140; L'Enfant plan for, *il.*, 139; attacked by British in 1814, 164; in 1826, *il.*, 184–185; and the telegraph, 212; during Civil War, 280, 282; 1941 march on, 556; school integration, 612; 1963 march on, 656, *photo*, 657; rioting in, 677
Washington, Treaty of, 406
Washington Conference, 475
Washington Post, 404, 495, 691
Wasp (ship), 162; *cartoon*, 163
Waste disposal, 731
Waste Land, The (Eliot), 473
Water pollution, 666, 667
Water Quality Act of 1965, 667
Watergate Affair, 690–691, 692–694; Nixon pardon, 722; and electoral reform, 723; Senate committee, *photo*, 692; Nixon explains tapes, *photo*, 693
Waterloo, Battle of, 277
Watertown, Massachusetts, 39
Watkins, Carleton, *photo*, 423
Watson, Tom, quoted, 396
Watts (Los Angeles), 669
WAVES (Navy), 555
Wayne, Anthony, 127; *il.*, 129
We (Lindbergh), 483
Weaver, James B., 397
Weaver, Robert C., 655, 665
Weber, Brian, 705
Weber, Max, *painting*, 502–503
Webster, Daniel, 181, 191–192, 245; and 1836 election, 198; slavery and, 254–255; reply to Hayne, *il.*, 192
Webster, Noah, 179
Webster-Ashburton Treaty, 245, 249
Webster-Hayne debate, 191–192
Weed, Thurlow, quoted, 183
Weehawken, New Jersey, 150
Welch, Joseph, *photo*, 611
Weld, Theodore Dwight, 236, 257
Welfare programs: in post-Civil War South, 310–311; provided by Social Security Act, 516; Carter and, 728; inflation and, 729
Welles, Gideon, 286
Wellesley College, 377
Wellington, Duke of, 164
Wells-Barnett, Ida B., 375
Welty, Eudora, 638
Wesleyan College, 233
West, Benjamin, *painting*, 91
West Berlin, Germany, 619
West Florida, 145, 153
West Germany, 734; created, 591–592; and Marshall Plan, 587; in NATO, 593, 607

West Indies, 5–7, 21, 22, 54, 154; British, trade with U.S., 126; Danish, 406; French, 125–126; and slave trade, 54, 226, 404
West Virginia, 283, 290, 642
Western Hemisphere, 18; Waldseemüller *map*, *il.*, 15; Monroe Doctrine and, *map*, 177
Westminster College, 584
Westmoreland, William, 675, 676
"Wetbacks," 710
Wethersfield, Connecticut, 41
Weyler, Valeriano, 410
Whalers, 54; in Hawaii, 404–405
Wheat, 222; and the Embargo Act, 157; and economy of West, 215; and the depression, 492
Wheaton, Harriet Douglas, *photo*, 279
Wheeling, West Virginia, 204
Whigs, 198, 245, 246, 253, 260, 267; and 1840 election, 199–200; U.S. expansion and, 249; and 1852 election, 256; fall of party, 257, 262
Whiskey Rebellion, 128–129, 143
Whiskey Ring scandal of 1873, 314
White, Hugh L., 198
White, Walter, 529
White Brotherhood, North Carolina, 312
White Rose, Mississippi Society of the, 312
Whitman, Marcus, 239
Whitman, Narcissa Prentice, 239
Whitney, Eli, 117, 174, 217–218, 353
Whitney, Richard, 490
Why England Slept (Kennedy), 644
Wilderness Act of 1964, 663
Wilhelm, Kaiser, 446
Wilkinson, James, 150
Willard, Frances, 374–375
William of Orange, *see* William and Mary
William and Mary, English rulers, 58, 61, 80
William and Mary College, 56
Williams, John and Eunice, 62
Williams, Roger, 40
Willkie, Wendell L., 549–550, 569
Wilmington, Delaware, 43
Wilmot, David, 253
Wilmot Proviso, 253, 255
Wilson, Charles E., 605
Wilson, Edith, 464
Wilson, James, 104
Wilson, Woodrow, 398, 479; career of, 431, 434; and 1912 election, 432–433; administration of, 434–441, 473, 487, 530; and immigrants, 372; and Mexico, 440–441; and World War I, 445–448, 450, 459–461; and 1916 election, 448–449; Fourteen Points, 451; and Versailles Treaty, 461–464; and League of Nations, 463, 464–465; *photos*, 433, 435, 463
Wilson-Gorman tariff, 398
Windsor, Connecticut, 41
Winnemucca, Sarah, 326
Winsor, Joshua, house of, *il.*, 52
Winthrop, John, 39–40; *portrait*, 39
Wiretapping, 690, 722
Wisconsin: Indians in, 193; Union troops from, *il.*, 293; lumbering in, 338, *il.*, 337, 338; one-room school, *il.*, 376; governmental reform in, 426, 427
Wolcott, Oliver, 96
Wolfe, James, 64
Women: in Spanish colonies, 29; in British colonies, 54, 56; and American Revolution, 88–89; suffrage for, 185, 187, 235, 374–375, 427, 473, 706–707, *il.*, 375, 706, 707; employment of, 216–217, 233–234, 278–280, 360, 460, 557–558, 706–709; education and, 56, 232–233, 377, *il.*, 233; rights movement, 89, 233–235, 705–709, *il.*, 709; in Civil War, 278–280; on western frontier, 330–331, *il.*, 331; and social work,

373–375; wage laws for, 426; in World War I, 456, 460; in government and politics, 479, 507, 531–533; in World War II, 555, 557–558, *photo*, 558; longevity of, 628
Women, Commission on Status of, 707
Women's Air Forces Service, 555
Women's Christian Temperance Union, 374
Women's Rights Convention, 234
Women's suffrage, 185–187, 235, 374–375, 427, 473, 706–707; *poster*, 375; *photos*, 706, 707
Wood, Leonard, 416, 474
Woodward, Robert, 690–691
Worcester v. *Georgia* (1832), 194
Work relief, New Deal, 512–513
Workmen's Compensation Laws, 426
Works Progress Administration (WPA), 514, 520–521; *photo*, 512
World Court, 541, 583
World War I: outbreak, 443–445; and U.S. neutrality, 445–448; "Peace Ship," *photo*, 445; preparedness, 448–449; United States in, 450–454; homefront, 455–461; Versailles Treaty and League of Nations, 461–465; *maps*, 444, 452, 455, 462
World War II: events leading to, 537–543; early phases of, 543–552; mobilization for, 554–558; United States in, 553, 558–578; cost of, 576, 578; *maps*, 544, 551, 559, 562, 571, 578; postwar Europe, *map*, 590
Wouk, Herman, 638
Wounded Knee, South Dakota, 324, 715
Wright, Fielding, 593
Wyandot Indians, 127
Wyeth, Andrew, 638
Wyeth, Nathaniel J., 239
Wythe, George, 96
Wyoming: mining in, 326; and women's suffrage, 331, 375, 706; statehood for, 340; bridge building, *il.*, 346

X
Xerography, 630–633
XYZ Affair, 131

Y
Yale University, 56, 731
Yalta Conference, 569–570, 584; *photo*, 570
Yalu River, 600
Yamamoto, Admiral, 562, 563
Yellow fever, 146, 416, 438–439
"Yellow Press," 410–411
Yellowstone (steamboat), *il.*, 175
Yellowstone National Park, *painting*, 423
Yippies, 679
Yom Kippur War, 692, 723
York, Ontario (Toronto), 164
York River, 286
Yorktown, Battle of, 87–88
Yorktown (carrier), 512
Yoruba, and slave trade, 226
Yosemite Valley, *photo*, 423
Young, Brigham, 243
Youth: in colonies, 54–56; of 1960s, 670–671, 679
Youth International Party (Yippies), 679
Yugoslavia, 584, 652

Z
Zavala, Lorenzo de, 243–244
Zenger, John Peter, 57
Zimmerman, Arthur, 450
Zimmermann note, 450
Zuñi, 10, 21
Zwicker, Ralph, 610